'A HAPPY HOLIDAY':
ENGLISH CANADIANS AND TRANSA
1870–1930

One of the most revealing things about national character is the way that citizens react to and report on their travels abroad. Oftentimes a tourist's experience with a foreign place says as much about their country of origin as it does about their destination. '*A Happy Holiday*' examines the travels of English-speaking Canadian men and women to Britain and Europe during the late nineteenth and early twentieth centuries. It describes the experiences of tourists, detailing where they went and their reactions to tourist sites, and draws attention to the centrality of culture and the sensory dimensions of overseas tourism.

Among the specific topics explored are travellers' class relationships with people in the tourism industry, impressions of historic landscapes in Britain and Europe, descriptions of imperial spectacles and cultural sights, the use of public spaces, and encounters with fellow tourists and how such encounters either solidified or unsettled national subjectivities. Cecilia Morgan draws our attention to the important ambiguities between empire and nation, and how this relationship was dealt with by tourists in foreign lands. Based on personal letters, diaries, newspapers, and periodicals from across Canada, '*A Happy Holiday*' argues that overseas tourism offered people the chance to explore questions of identity during this period, a time in which issues such as gender, nation, and empire were the subject of much public debate and discussion.

CECILIA MORGAN is an associate professor in the Department of History at the Ontario Institute for Studies in Education, University of Toronto.

CECILIA MORGAN

'A Happy Holiday'

English Canadians and Transatlantic Tourism, 1870–1930

UNIVERSITY OF TORONTO PRESS
Toronto Buffalo London

© University of Toronto Press Incorporated 2008
Toronto Buffalo London
www.utppublishing.com
Printed in Canada

ISBN 978-0-8020-9758-3 (cloth)
ISBN 978-0-8020-9518-3 (paper)

Library and Archives Canada Cataloguing in Publication

Morgan, Cecilia Louise, 1958–
A happy holiday: English Canadians and transatlantic tourism, 1870–1930 /
Cecilia Morgan.

Includes bibliographical references and index.
ISBN 978-0-8020–9758-3 (bound)   ISBN 978-0-8020–9518-3 (pbk.)

1. Canadians, English-speaking – Travel – Great Britain – History.
2. Canadians, English-speaking – Travel – Europe – History.   I. Title.

G156.M67 2008   914.1'0089112   C2007-906001-3

University of Toronto Press acknowledges the financial assistance to its
publishing program of the Canada Council for the Arts and the Ontario
Arts Council.

University of Toronto Press acknowledges the financial support for its
publishing activities of the Government of Canada through the Book
Publishing Industry Development Program (BPIDP).

This book has been published with the help of a grant from the Canadian
Federation for the Humanities and Social Sciences, through the Aid to
Scholarly Publications Programme, using funds provided by the Social
Sciences and Humanities Research Council of Canada.

To Paul

Contents

viii Contents

Acknowledgments

It is hard to be brief, as this is a fairly long book (although it could well have been longer!), and I've accumulated many debts along the way.

I first must thank Queen's University, which in 1996 supported my initial research with a small-scale grant from its Advisory Research Committee. Nancy Wood, Office of Research Services, Queen's, provided critical advice and encouragement that was of great assistance in developing a larger funding proposal. The Social Sciences and Humanities Research Council provided me with a Standard Research Grant; the anonymous reviewers of my proposal also gave well-considered feedback and advice. The University of Toronto's Connaught Fund supported this work with a New Faculty Grant and a New Staff Matching Research Award. The financial support of all these institutions was vital in order to undertake the travel needed to write a book about transatlantic tourism. It also allowed me to hire a number of research assistants, whose dedication to and excitement about this project was truly gratifying: John Allison, Martha Donkor, Pamela Genn, Arlis Peer, Elizabeth Price, Joan Simalchik, and Nicole Woodman-Harvey.

Across Canada, a very wide circle of archivists and librarians, from Halifax to Victoria and in local, regional, provincial, and national institutions, generously offered their knowledge and made helpful suggestions for material, both published and unpublished. Pamela Miller of McGill University's Osler Library generously gave me the considerable benefit of her wealth of knowledge of English Canada's elite. I couldn't follow up on all of her wonderful suggestions but learned much from our discussion. Thanks are due to Dena Doroshenko of the Ontario Heritage Foundation for her generosity in granting me access to the Ashbridge Family Papers at the Foundation's Ashbridge House,

for sharing her knowledge of the family's history, and for suggesting
that I consult the Fulford Family Papers. My thanks to the following
for permission to reproduce visual material: the Archives of Ontario,
the D. B. Weldon Library at the University of Western Ontario, Library
and Archives Canada, and the McCord Museum, Montreal. I thank
Victoria University Library for granting me permission to quote from
the Kathleen Coburn papers.

My intellectual debts are very large and probably can't be repaid. A
number of historians of the British Empire introduced me to new bodies of historiography and gave me the benefit of their rich knowledge
of its history. It would be very hard to write imperial, transatlantic,
and transnational histories without such scholarly generosity. Sandra
den Otter read the initial grant proposal and offered very good advice
for its improvement. Stephen Heathorn and Paul Deslandes have not
only been good friends over the years but in 1997 also were kind
enough to invite me to participate in a panel on national identities
at the North American Conference on British Studies (NACBS) at
Asilomar, California. I am extremely grateful to them for introducing
me to NACBS: the Association's gatherings have been a wonderful
source of intellectual stimulation and that initial meeting introduced
me to Angela Woollacott. Her work on white Australian women travellers has been a great source of inspiration and her friendship and
support have been equally important. For their interest, enthusiasm,
and very insightful suggestions, I also would like to thank Anne
Clendinning and Matthew Hendley. Closer to 'home,' Karen Dubinsky's
enthusiasm for this project has been truly gratifying. In 1996 she had
the prescience to tell me that this would be my next book: not only
was she right but she also was generous enough to read the first draft
and to give me wonderful advice and suggestions for its improvement. Brian Young, whose work has shown us how to look at the
privileged with critical and perceptive eyes, was a constant source of
enthusiasm and support. I must also thank Elizabeth Kirkland for
so generously sharing her knowledge of Montreal's Clouston and
Roddick families. My thanks to audiences at the following conferences and seminars: the Canadian Historical Association; NACBS;
Cultural Approaches to the Study of Canadian Nationalism, Nipissing
University; Queen's University History Department's Faculty-Graduate
Seminar; and the Victorian Studies Association of Ontario. Special
thanks to Barbara Lorenzkowski and Steve High for inviting me to
participate in the Nipissing Conference, an experience that helped

refine my thoughts on English-Canadian nationalism. The anonymous readers of the manuscript provided wonderful suggestions and
comments; I have attempted to incorporate as much of their advice as
I could.

Lori May, Communications and Special Projects Coordinator, Department of Theory and Policy Studies, OISE/UT, gave me much-needed
help with the initial scanning of the images used in this book. I also
would like to thank the staff at Brock University Library's Office of
Reproduction Services for their generous and patient work in scanning
many of the images from the *Canadian Magazine*. At the University of
Toronto Press, it has been a great pleasure to work with Len Husband
as my editor: I thank him for his support, his good advice and humour,
and his enthusiasm for something this long and with so many illustrations. Thanks too to my copy-editors, Kate Baltais and Harold Otto, for
their expertise and patience, both of which made this book much more
pleasant to read. Frances Mundy shepherded this book through its
final stages with professionalism and care.

Eleanor Cardoza and Jeremy Morgan offered great hospitality in
Saskatoon and Suzanne Morton did the same in Montreal. Over the
years of working on this book I've been fortunate to have the friendship and support of Karen Dubinsky, Nancy M. Forestell, Franca
Iacovetta, Lynne Marks, and Katherine McPherson, even if we don't
get to see each other as often as we might like to. Suzanne Morton has
been a true friend, both about this project and many other things: it is
a great treat to acknowledge her wit and wisdom in matters academic, historical, and otherwise. Thanks, as always, to my family, for
their consistent support of and interest in my work. Saving the best
for last, Paul Jenkins has seen this project through to its completion
without flagging in his enthusiasm and loving encouragement. Here's
to many 'happy holidays.'

Prologue. 'It seems a long time since I have seen anything Canadian': Mary Leslie's Transatlantic Travel, 1867–1868

'The noise was fearful, the children screaming and vomiting and my fellow-sufferers groaning,' wrote Mary Leslie to her mother at the family's home in Guelph, Ontario. Leslie herself had been delirious and was unable to retain anything – food, water, or medicine – in her stomach; a visit from a young and, it seems, rather brusque doctor was successful only in sedating her. Her letter described not a hospital ward where all were stricken by some deadly disease but, rather, the cabin of a transatlantic ship bound for Liverpool, England, overbooked with passengers in the throes of violent seasickness. From the moment she set foot on board, the trip did not bode well for Leslie. She had been 'horrified' by the sight of her small and overcrowded cabin, with its cloying smell of new paint and lack of ventilation. The disagreeable behaviour of one of her cabin mates did not help, for Miss 'L' 'always dressed first in the morning, *took full an hour* and had the door shut *all* the time nearly suffocating us poor creatures in our beds.' Leslie's plight would have been wretched indeed had it not been for the kindness of her capable stewardess, a fifty-year-old with 'not a grey hair and rosy cheeks,' who had been twenty-two years at sea and had sailed to almost 'every port.' Her diet of beef tea and gruel managed to stay in Leslie's stomach, and she was able to receive a visit from one of the French Roman Catholic priests on board, the only passenger, she told her mother, who came to see her.[1] These men were initially 'shunned and treated with contempt by all the good Protestant passengers, but before the voyage was out they were very popular.'[2]

Once the ship reached the Irish coast and calmer waters Mary Leslie was able to remain on deck for most of the day, enjoying the 'coast that appeared to you so desolate and frowning ... the dark rocks were

clothed in the brightest and softest greenest moss I ever saw in my life.'
She attended a benefit concert for a 'poor widow' travelling in steerage, who was returning to Cornwall after her husband's death in a
Quebec mining accident. Various songs were sung, and Shakespeare
was recited 'very badly,' but the evening's efforts raised £7 for the
woman and her three children. Leslie also contributed to other charitable collections for steerage passengers (a sick woman, a elderly man),
explaining to her father that 'I had suffered so much myself and I had a
great many more comforts than these poor miserable creatures that I
felt it would be a sin not to give something.' On disembarking in Liverpool she gave her stewardess a half sovereign and the steward 5s, as
she felt that she had given them more trouble than anyone else on
board. Her voyage ended on a somewhat sour note with her efforts to
tip the doctor. 'I am paid by the shipowners,' he told Leslie but 'if you
like to give me a fee, I am a poor man and not above being paid like
any other "servant."' Forced to ask him the amount, Leslie was visibly
shaken when he quoted her two sovereigns. Seeing her distress, the
doctor relented and took only one. 'You are not so rich as I supposed,'
he told her, '"I know you think two too much for you changed colour,
you value your life at one sovereign – good bye take care of your body
– though women never do that," and so I took back the sovereign and
we parted.'[3]

The most gruelling part of her journey to England over, Leslie took
the train to London, where she spent the next four months with her
paternal uncle William and his family in Dulwich. An aspiring writer
who had travelled overseas to find a publisher, Mary Leslie spent her
time sightseeing, visiting relatives and family friends, and observing
the foibles of the English. In October she responded to a *Times* advertisement for an English governess in a German school in Amsterdam.
In return for two hours of English lessons and drawing instruction, she
was to receive board, lodging, washing, and instruction in German,
French, and music (*'but no salary,'* she emphasized to her parents, the
recipients of a number of requests for money). The reference for the
school was a good one, she reassured them, as it came from the chap-
lain of the British Consul in Amsterdam.[4] Once in the Netherlands,
Leslie continued to write home, describing and commenting on Dutch
manners and customs. Her letters to Guelph end 15 March 1868, with a
description of a Dutch wedding and a promise that she would bring
home 'green cheddar and chocolate' for her mother's birthday.[5]

Mary Leslie's account of her experiences across the Atlantic Ocean helps introduce many of the themes of this book's. Leslie was far from being a 'typical' English-Canadian traveller. She would go on to have a career as a writer of history, poetry for children, and fiction, and her ability to observe with a sceptical (one might say acerbic) writer's eye is apparent in her letters.[6] Nor can I argue that Leslie's experiences completely foreshadowed those reported by the English-Canadian travel writers and tourists whose accounts are examined in detail in this study; they did not entirely replicate Leslie's cultural and social experiences. Although there were many similarities between Leslie's story in Dulwich and Amsterdam and the sojourns of Canadians who came after her, there were also a number of differences. Leslie herself both resembled and was different from her fellow travelling Canadians. Both the similarities and the differences are worth exploring to understand the varied meanings of Canadians' transatlantic travel and tourism from the 1870s to the 1920s.

From the start of her stay in England, Leslie openly professed a profound ambivalence towards England and 'the English,' and the depth of this ambivalence sets her apart from many of the English-Canadians who visited Britain in the first five decades after Confederation. To be sure, like most every other tourist, she participated in viewing royalty. One of her first recorded experiences in London was the sight of Princess Alice ('at least I saw a little pale face that they said was the Princess Alice that I should not know again'), the Prince of Wales, and the Queen of Prussia.[7] Yet as her comment about the nondescript appearance of Princess Alice suggests, Leslie's report of seeing the royal family was perfunctory, recorded more as a duty, and quite different from the descriptions of the emotionally charged spectacles provided by later tourists. To some extent such contrast may be explained by the relative lack of pomp and display surrounding public appearances of English royalty around the time of Leslie's visit. Such was no longer the case by the 1880s and 1890s.[8] Leslie went on to tell her family that 'what was better I saw the Life guards blue and red with their gorgeous uniforms and beautiful horses, and I can't tell you how many coachmen and footmen in rich liveries.'[9] Horses clearly interested Leslie more than titled or fashionable personages. She enjoyed the 'pretty dresses and the liveries' of Rotten Row, but confessed that 'I would walk ten mile a day (if I had the strength) to see such beautiful horses as I saw this evening.'[10] Leslie had little patience with what she perceived as 'English' deference and unwarranted respect for the titled. One time she 'had a good look at Lady Palmerston driving along in an open carriage looking rather desolate I thought with her white hair and widow's cap.' Another time, as she and her friend Mrs Williamson were leaving Rotten Row, they stopped to watch the occupant of a carriage descend from it and enter his house. A 'gross gouty over-grown old man, like old Jones in the face, but coarser and more surly ... Mrs Williamson slightly pulled my sleeve and we stood back till the old fellow got up the steps and into his own house, with the assistance of a most gentlemanly looking man (who proved to be the butler) and just as I was honouring her in my heart for her deference to old age, she whispered *deferentially "that was Lord Lowborough."'*[11]

London would send many Canadian visitors into paroxysms of delight. Mary Leslie judged it far more critically and at times quite harshly. After she took a trip along the Thames to Greenwich on the smallest steamboat she had ever seen, she reported that the river 'exceeds my expectations for I had not imagination enough to conceive anything so filthy and abominable. The stench nearly made me sick, and entirely spoiled the pleasure of looking at the Traitor's Gate, Somerset House, and the London Docks.' Greenwich itself, though, was 'wonderful,' with its portrait and death mask of Nelson, relics of the Franklin Expedition, and Van Dyke's portrait of Prince Rupert's 'dark spirited face with a smiling satirical mask that would surely have said something saucy to me if I had stood there a minute longer.'[12] At the Adelphi Theatre she saw the final performance of Kate Terry, a 'pet actress' who was leaving the stage to marry a rich man, and found it enjoyable – at least to a degree. Terry, appearing in *Much Ado about Nothing*, 'played with great spirit and had a nice Irish voice.' The audience gave her a 'thundering cheer' on her first entrance and afterwards two curtain calls of her own. Leslie was 'supplied with a pair of opera goggles and stared through them the whole evening like a black beetle. The dresses of the performers were very rich, magnificent brocades and velvets and once they used the magnesium lights to represent noonday and it was wonderfully natural.' But the theatre was 'crowded to excess and the heat insufferable' and, apart from Terry, the 'only two good actors were a Mr Henry N (a scion of the aristocracy who has been cut by his family for becoming an actor) and Mr Clarke who acted Dogberry.'[13]

Leslie's critical evaluation of English society touched on a wide variety of topics. She told her mother that 'I have scarcely seen a pair of rosy cheeks since I came to England, scarcely a character who has a better complexion than myself' and that her uncle's tea was 'poor stuff' (although she admitted that another group of relatives 'know how to brew a cup of tea'). Much of her correspondence hints at pent-up frustration with her new surroundings. After telling her mother that the flowers in England were 'magnificent' and better than those in Canada, she tartly observed that 'the kitchen ranges are decidedly inferior to the Canadian stoves – miserable things to iron and bathe with and not a bit better for roasting than the stoves, and the people of England are a slow people and take twice as long to do things as the Canadians do.'[14] She did not like London's weather, or the polluted air. 'It is not a climate I admire at least near London – in the first place it is very damp and chilly and you are never sure of the rain and in the next it is always dull and smoky, you can never see any distance for the smoke even in Dulwich and one knows that is dirty coal smoke, and not the gentle haze of Indian summer.'[15]

Unhealthy complexions, mediocre household technology, and a bad climate were only some of England's shortcomings. Leslie's severest criticisms of her ancestral homeland stemmed from her view of the English attitude towards those weaker than themselves. Lifting her head from the letter she was writing, Leslie watched a team of plough horses for a few moments and was reminded that 'the people of England are a cruel people to animals the donkeys are dreadfully ill-used and so are the omnibus horses and all the conveyances public and private are too large and heavy for the animals that draw them.'[16] Although she experienced 'hospitality and kindness' in all the homes in which she was a guest, 'for all this I cannot help observing the *intense selfishness*, the utter indifference of nearly everybody I have seen to those outside their own family ... their callousness about the dreadful poverty and human misery that festers under the nose of everybody who lives in London and even of those merely passing through, the general suspicion, and repugnance and objection they have to everybody who is poor and in misery.' To illustrate her point Leslie told her father of an incident she had witnessed en route to the theatre with her cousins. Walking through

a dirty back street, a sort of arched back way not far from the Adelphi the-atre, *I daresay you know the place* and there was a number of blind men there standing against the wall with their hats held out before them mis-erable looking creatures most of them were, but one in particular who was tapping the pavement with his stick and feeling his way slowly along was the most wretched looking fellow creature I ever beheld. He was evidently sight-less, his face scarred almost out of the form of humanity, he was thin to emaciation and the rags he had on scarcely covered his nakedness. He carried a board on his waist with large printed letters on it appealing to the charity of his fellow creatures by telling them that he had lost his sight in a coal mine accident many years before. I was sorry but I had left my purse at home for fear of thieves and had not even a penny to give him and I said so. 'It is very sad my dear,' said cousin Anne drawing her skirts up round her plump person and stepping back a little as he passed us. Mr Green came up just then and he said with a look of repugnance to the beggars 'you chose a very unpleasant way to come Mamma,' and offered an arm to each of us. He never gave any of those poor old fellows a half-penny and I don't believe it ever occurred to him that he was of the same humanity as them, or that there was any connection between the wife who walked by his side, and the little daughter he had been petting at dinner-time, and a poor dirty woman and child whom we saw asleep on a door step. I think if Christ came back to the earth that these wealthy Britons would be as hard upon him as the rich Jews were of old, and consider him a 'pestilent fellow' for healing and comforting the poor – indeed I am sure of this point the way I have heard nearly every body speak of Lord Shaftesbury, Dr Marsh and his daughter who did so much good among the navvies.[17]

This lack of compassion and humanitarianism was not limited to Leslie's family. In English society

Charles Dickens is very much liked and everybody speaks well of him but in a tolerant half-patronizing sort of way. They tolerate him because he is amusing and gives them hard hits in a pleasant general way and his lectures are well attended *not* because they are *given for the benefit of the poor* but because the people who go are sure of spending a pleasant evening and getting their shilling's worth. Everybody whom I have heard speak of his lectures has gone from this motive and no other. They praise him for his genius and wit, and admire him for his wealth, and in consideration of those qualities forgive him for his philanthropy and his '*infatuation about the poor.*' (I am quoting a tradesman who has heard his lectures for many a long yr) and look upon him as a wealthy and eccentric old idiot and feel on the whole rather proud to have him as a countryman.[18]

Leslie went on to explain that, 'Lord Shaftesbury is universally disliked – he is accused of *taking up* the poor and putting absurd notions
into their heads instead of keeping them in their *"proper place."* Now
though I listen politely and never contradict (when I can help it) I
haven't a feeling in common with these over-fed Britons – I honour
Lord S and Miss Marsh and her father and I love Charles Dickens not
because he is a great genius but because he is a man no longer young,
and not strong who labors nobly for his fellow creatures.' She ended
angrily by telling her parents that 'there is even less charity here than
in Canada for those who have lost the respectability and strayed out of
the paths of virtue – if you fall in England it is like the fall of Lucifer
you can never rise again, unless you should happen to stray to the
door of such foolish men as Mr Dickens or Lord Shaftesbury; and they
would try to help you up and clean the mud from your garments – but
what are two men or half a dozen among millions?'[19]

Although Leslie's sympathies were generally with the English 'poor'
and, as we shall see, not with the middle class (particularly those newly
arrived in it), she was not reluctant to pass judgment on working-class
behaviour. The customers who patronized her uncle William's shop in
Dulwich 'are in general a very poor class of customers, who come in for
"a haporth of tea, a pinch of pickles."' Among their numbers were
'brickmakers' wives, who 'are always quarrelling with their husbands,'
their children, and the brickmakers themselves who come in Saturday
nights, after drinking 'more than is good for them,' to purchase pipes
and tobacco. Uncle William also sold groceries to the 'better families' in
the area (clerks in banks and lawyers' offices), who sent their servants
to the shop on their behalf. Often these servants gossiped freely about
their employers, who, Mary Leslie informed her parents, were *'without
exception* dissenters. Not 10 minutes ago I heard a young lady complain
that her mistress would make her go and hear Mr Spurgeon preach
whereas she had been brought up to the Established Church, "He ain't
so *vulgar* as he used to be," said she, "but he'll never be a gentlemen
and that I tell my mistress." "She's a *mean one*," the young lady went on
"she makes a bread pudding without eggs or milk and she will have
the bedroom scrubbed every week and keeps me a going from morning
to night."'[20]

Some of Leslie's encounters with London's working-class and poor
people were a great source of entertainment. On the way to the park
one Sunday morning with her relatives, Leslie came up to a 'great

crowd of dirty-looking, disreputable men and boys.' She stood aside in a doorway, shielded by a 'solemn policeman.' 'I felt a dirty little hand in my pocket' but fortunately the pocket was completely empty. 'I turned round quickly and said "you did not get much little boy."' This reaction, coupled with her lack of interest in chasing the child, appears to have endeared Leslie to the young pickpocket. He winked, crossed the road, and continued his work – with more success. Leslie continued to watch him 'having put on my spectacles for that purpose while the policeman who should have been minding his business' was talking to a colleague. At last he spotted the boy and 'held up his finger in a stern and warning way as only a policeman can do,' whereupon 'my young friend' performed a song and dance that mocked the policeman 'after which he cut off ... singing out "a pig for Isabeller and her gingham umbrella" ... but I took it as a compliment that he was not afraid of my giving him "in charge."' Her sympathies for what she clearly saw as picaresque did not prevent Leslie from informing her family that 'Miss Williamson had her pocket picked in the House of Lords not long since, the money extracted and the purse restored.'[21]

The materialism and philistinism of the middle-class women and men with whom Leslie was most intimate upset her the most. She was slightly scandalized by the 'enormous' amount of eating and drinking indulged in by the English and told her mother that 'if I drank as much as Mr and Mrs Green do I should be all under the table. I went to bed drunk every night I was there and I got drunk every day at dinnertime but it was always under strong persuasion and never without resistance. They thought me a North American savage never to have tasted claret, champagne or Chablis, and looked upon me with an eye of pity.'[22] In response to her father's request for information about the people she met, Leslie wrote that 'there is no fear of my being starved to death for all the families in which I have stayed ... think of nothing but eating and drinking from morning till night.'[23] While staying with her cousin Charlotte a month later, the two spent their suppertime getting 'as drunk as lords or fishers ... [It's] a great proof of our respectability that we never misbehaved ourselves in that state, and a great proof of my individual sagacity but I never speak upon subjects of which in my moments of sobriety I think it is better to be silent ... although I pass through all stages of intoxication from maudlin sentimentality and extreme gloom to a depth of wisdom so profound that even I myself cannot fathom it, I never mention my aspirations to authorship.'[24]

If Leslie's confessions of drunkenness shocked her family, there is no hint of such a reaction in their letters. Her parents did attempt to persuade her to remain with her uncle William and his family, but it was that group of people that, I suspect, either predisposed Leslie to see so many of England's shortcomings or, at the very least, contributed to her disenchantment. In response to her father's offer to pay her board at her uncle's home through the winter, Leslie replied that 'for many reasons I do not wish to stay [here] during the winter any more than I wish to trust myself to the tender mercies of Neptune ... this fall.' She admitted that her uncle, aunt, and cousins were very kind, but added 'I have every comfort but the comfort of privacy.' Leslie described how she shared a bedroom with her two female cousins, who were not 'well bred' and who talked constantly, which left her with no solitude in which to read her psalms, say her prayers, write, or copy her work for an editor. Moreover, their kindness extended to washing her clothes and that left her with the ironing; the household's inferior kitchen range meant that Leslie spent all her time, when not sightseeing or writing letters, ironing and not working on her writing. 'Now if Uncle William or his family had an idea that such was my object in visiting England they would think me fit for a lunatic asylum (for they are all matter of fact ... and as much opposed to novels as they are to religion).'[25]

The problem, it seems, was not confined to her relatives' disdain of culture and spirituality. Leslie felt she was treated as a 'colonial cousin,' a being who lacked the critical social refinements of London's middle class. Her remark about being seen as a 'North American savage' (itself suggestive of racially charged perceptions) for not being acquainted with particular wines and spirits suggests such social classifications, as do her comments about clothing. The trip to the Adelphi theatre had originally been planned as an outing to the opera but Leslie lacked a 'fall dress' and had no opera cloak, and so her friends 'kindly changed their plans.'[26] But her cousins were less charitable, being 'great snobs about dress ... and always want[ed] me to wear their clothes, assuring me many of the things I have "*Never are worn in good society.*" They made me quite uncomfortable when I went to the Greens so uncomfortable indeed that I had a horror of the visit and would rather have gone to Tyburn to have been hanged.' She found, though, that Mrs Green was more concerned about Leslie's dinner than her attire and admired her purple dress considerably. Nevertheless, Leslie smarted under her hosts' ignorance of Canada. Mrs Green was sure that clothes were very expensive there, '*judging from the price they were in the Southern States at the time of the war'* and told her that she must stock up on clothes before she left London: 'there is a beautiful brown satin in a shop in Regent Street only two sovereigns and a half which is very cheap for a material of a best quality ... Neither the Greens nor Cousin Charlotte have any idea of how we are circumstanced in Canada they speak as if we were all well off as they are or better – they seem to think any body who possessed land must be rich.'[27]

'On the whole,' she announced to her father, 'I feel proud of my country and like it much better than the old, and think it has greater natural advantages (except the extreme cold and heat) and hope it will be a finer country than England some day, and I never see a picturesque old church and parsonage without wishing I could transfer it to Meaford or some other Canadian village where it was needed.' As she made clear in describing an English couple who had emigrated to New Zealand *'and were the better for it,'* Leslie preferred such colonies and their residents to an 'old country' or its populace.[28] Leslie's intense dislike of perceived English condescension towards and ignorance of Canada was very similar to the feelings aroused in Australian women who travelled to Britain in the years shortly after Leslie's trip. In Leslie's case, however, given her identification with English literature, music, and art, her impatience with her relatives came at least partially from what she saw as their lack of appreciation for their own cultural 'heritage.' Being a 'white colonial,' as historian Angela Woollacott has shown, was not an uncomplicated identity.[29]

But if Leslie's distancing herself from contemporary English society was more pronounced than that of later English-speaking Canadian travellers, she eagerly recorded the social and cultural 'customs and traditions' of the Dutch. In many ways she thought more highly of Holland than of England, telling her family that 'Rotterdam is the most beautiful city I have ever seen ... the buildings are fine and picturesque and the streets are clean to a marvel.' En route to Amsterdam, Leslie saw 'peasant women with snow white caps and wooden shoes, little carts drawn by dogs,' as well as 'fine fat cattle,' goats, windmills, 'picturesque houses ... and canals canals everywhere.' Although she did not much like her Dutch and German male travelling companions' habit of smoking ('in my face for *twenty four* miles'),[30] and was disconcerted by the poor English spoken by her fellow teachers and students, Leslie found the area of Amsterdam in which she stayed quite charming and picturesque. Despite the fact that 'in Holland unmarried ladies are not allowed to walk *alone*,' she went for a stroll every morning after breakfast, figuring that 'the privilege is accorded to me as the ignorant foreigner who knows no better.'[31]

Although her letters were not as numerous as those from London, Leslie's correspondence from Holland was full of descriptions. Dutch food included lots of vinegar, arrowroot broth, stringy beef (but good German sausages), boiled chestnuts, hot drinks, and plum pudding. Regarding table manners, she reported that forks were held in the right hand. She commented on the Dutch language, which she was learning quickly: 'it is a very unmusical tongue, composed of snufflings, sneezings, and strange gurglings in the throat.'[32] In her last letter home, she described attending a Dutch wedding, where, she observed, 'she was a novelty,' although most of the forty-two guests preferred to flirt with each other than speak to her. The fashions were unremarkable (even the bride and groom were plainly dressed) except in the case of one woman.

> I know the meaning of *Dutch courage* now. One old lady had a cap literally covered with rubies and I don't know *which* but either diamonds or paste. They flashed and sparkled in a wonderful way whenever she moved her head. She was the wife of a *burgermeister* (whatever that is) and every one paid her great respect. I don't like to say she was treated with great *servility* but it was something very like it. She had no teeth and her hair was as white as snow. She looked a strange figure so gaily caparisoned, the cap was a *national* cap without a bit of border and fitted the head like a skull cap – having long tippets at the ears hanging down straight like rabbits-ears.[33]

An uncomfortable voyage across the ocean, seeing royalty, window shopping on Regent Street, going to the theatre and to see art exhibits, writing social commentary on class and gender relations, and noting 'national' clothing, food, and other types of customs in both Britain and Europe: these and other types of experiences and their assessments would be the stuff of many English-Canadian tourists' transatlantic expeditions from the 1870s to the 1920s. Let us turn now to these and other, related, themes.

'A HAPPY HOLIDAY':
ENGLISH CANADIANS AND TRANSATLANTIC TOURISM,
1870–1930

Introduction: Holidays, Happiness, and Transatlantic Tourism

This book began with a diary or, rather, a number of diaries.[1] Sequestered from the mugginess of the southern Ontario summer of 1995 in the University of Western Ontario's Archives, I was working my way through the papers of Harriett Priddis. As she had been an active member of the London and Middlesex Historical Society, I hoped that Priddis's writings would give me more insight into the writing of history by English-Canadian middle-class women in late-Victorian and Edwardian Canada.

In addition to providing information on Priddis's work as a historian, her papers held something else: a collection of three typescript diaries that documented her travels to the Philadelphia Exposition of 1876, to Britain and Europe in 1906, and to Britain in 1911. Although they had, ostensibly, little or nothing to do with the project that had taken me to London – the commemoration of Laura Secord – the diaries caught my eye for a number of reasons. For one, they were quite lengthy. Priddis's accounts of her overseas trips covered well over three hundred pages. Moreover, even a cursory flip through them made it clear that they were more than just lists of places visited and sights seen, for Priddis was indefatigable when it came to recording her impressions of her travels. Not only had she left very detailed descriptions of monuments, castles, and cathedrals, she also recorded her perceptions of the people she met, whether locals or other tourists, in the course of her travels. The diaries also let me see how the daily experiences of transatlantic tourism in this period – the scramble to get on the right train at the right time, to have the correct papers for 'foreign' customs inspectors, to find one's eyeglasses oneself when Thomas Cook's agency proved incompetent – could be both amusing and provoking, well organized and maddeningly confusing.

Harriett Priddis was a delightful diarist: observant, amusing, and often self-deprecating, able to laugh at her own foibles as a tourist as well as muse about the historical, national, and imperial dimensions of the tourist landscape. While it would be exaggerating, with the benefit of 20/20 hindsight, to claim that I experienced an epiphany on finding her diaries, nevertheless I believed that I had made a 'find' – that sought-after but all-too-rarely felt archival experience – although at that point I was not sure what I would do with it. (It also must be said that I had recently returned from a three-week trip to Scotland and England and a number of Priddis's observations about overseas travel had a familiar ring.) In examining other historical societies' records I had run across similar accounts, although they were not as lengthy or as all-encompassing as Priddis's. Yet talks given to these groups, such as Constance Boulton's 'A Canadian Bicycle in Europe' or Miss Peake's 'How a Toronto Girl Saw the Queen,' when placed alongside Priddis's diary, made me wonder if overseas travel and tourism was a subject worth considering.

As this book suggests, I believe that it is. Not only, as I discovered, was there a wealth of primary sources to explore – diaries, letters, newspaper articles and advertisements, periodical literature, and published travelogues – by the mid-1990s a large body of secondary literature had become available that examined the meanings and significance of travel and tourism for the nineteenth and early twentieth centuries. The latter included literary historian Eva-Marie Kröller's 1987 study, Canadians Abroad, which examined Canadians' transatlantic tourism from 1850 until 1900.[2] Kröller's work explored themes that I too was finding in the diaries and travelogues: issues of gender, questions of national and imperial identity, and the pursuit of culture in Britain and Europe. Where we differ most is in the periods we examine (I start and end later), the 'cast' of tourists (she included French Canadians and I did not – about which decision more later; I also tried to have a wider degree of regional coverage), and the scope of our sources (her work focused on unpublished material, whereas this book includes published sources). Finally, the question of the timing of our research is critical: her pioneering study came just as a wide range of international scholars were starting to explore travel and tourism. Thus I benefited from Kröller's study and the work of other scholars, as well as having a broader historiographical context within the field of Canadian history and, in particular, the 'new' imperial history in which to situate this book. My study of transatlantic tourism thus builds on Kröller's work while simultaneously deviating from it and, I believe, expanding the field of inquiry. It also responds to international scholarship on travel and tourism by literary scholars, sociologists, and historians.³ As well, 'A Happy Holiday' has been influenced by the work of historians of tourism in Canada who have examined, for example, trips to Niagara Falls, excursions down the St Lawrence River and into Ontario's central and northern regions, and the state of tourism and tourist promoters in Nova Scotia.⁴

Tourism and the English-Speaking Canadian Middle Class

Diaries entitled 'My Trip to Britain and Time on the Continent,' newspaper columns called 'Travel, Adventure, and National Customs,' and books with titles such as *Our Trip to Europe* suggest that, for middle- and upper-middle-class English Canadians, transatlantic tourism was desirable for its own sake, as well as offering multiple opportunities for reflection on, and perhaps for testing and questioning, social and cultural sensibilities. This is not to argue that a trip overseas became de rigueur for all those who thought of themselves, and were seen by others, as middle class (although for some it clearly was). Not all were able to or even wanted to visit London, Edinburgh, Brussels, Berne, or Rome – although this book will be about those who could and did. However, the press and periodical literature, texts that helped constitute the public spheres of the nineteenth-century middle classes, constantly and consistently invited those who might never venture further than Truro, Hamilton, Selkirk, or Victoria to imagine themselves as doing so, to acquire and share in the social and cultural tastes, knowledge, and customs of like-minded men and women.

Most of the people in this study went overseas primarily to see sights and to be informally educated, as well as to be entertained. I have included a few Canadians who were overseas for other reasons, such as professional, familial, political, or business, because they also used those opportunities to travel around Britain and Europe as tourists and left detailed and rich records of their experiences. However, particularly in the case of those who travelled to Britain and Europe for professional and artistic training, the range of material and questions to be asked would be so extensive as to warrant another, separate study. Nevertheless, culture plays an important role in this book, as I explore how a range of cultural genres including theatre, art, music, history, and literature featured in middle-class Canadians' overseas

travel. Furthermore, because so many wrote of their reactions to
Herbert Beerbohm Tree's Shakespearean productions or about the religious art of Italy, I also can examine their reception of culture, a
question that, although important, is often difficult for historians.[5]

Although the term 'middle class' obviously has utility and weight for
this period in Canadian history, it does not imply homogeneity. As a
group these tourists might be said to comprise an elite; they were middle
class, English-speaking, and (in general) Protestant. But I caution against
treating them belonging to a homogeneous group, for gender and gradations of wealth and privilege within that supposedly all-encompassing
category, middle class, might create rather different experiences of overseas tourism. Harriett Priddis was a single elderly woman at the time of
her transatlantic travels. Ever-conscious of the need to economize while
abroad, she did not enjoy the same privileges and luxuries in Britain and
Europe as did Montreal's Edward Greenshields, a member of that city's
wealthy anglophone elite. Where Priddis took advantage of Cook's
tours and third-class rail fares in Europe, and queued for cut-rate theatre
tickets in London, Greenshields hired a car and chauffeur to take himself
and his wife, Elvira, through southern Spain, France, and Britain. The
Greenshields were able to see a wide range of theatre, opera, dance,
and musical performances (not to mention private art showings)
throughout their travels.[6] If wealth divided travellers, so did their
social and cultural backgrounds. Thus, although a number of the diaries and letters left by Canadian travellers speak of sensibilities forged
in larger urban centres such as Halifax, Montreal, Toronto, Hamilton,
Ottawa, Winnipeg, Vancouver, and Victoria, residents of small-town
and rural Canada also travelled overseas. They did so either independently or, like their big-city counterparts, as members of group tours
organized by churches, schools and universities, educational leagues,
and sporting teams.

'A Happy Holiday' focuses on the tourists' discourses and practices,
less so on the British and European tourist industries as such. Nevertheless, this book has been enriched by the literature on transatlantic
travel for this period and on the structures and organization of tourism
in Britain and Europe.[7] Often the tourists themselves were well aware
that they were being confronted with carefully orchestrated phenomena (sometimes pleasing, sometimes not) and that various types of
tourist infrastructure surrounded and shaped their activities. Furthermore, they might freely assume the designation of 'tourist.' Occasionally, it is more difficult to know whether some particular experience – of

a landscape or local residents – was less obviously mediated and managed by the local or regional tourist industry. Travellers were quite selective about their experiences and made choices about what to see and how to report what they saw. These processes were, I argue, clearest in their understanding of Ireland. Chapter 4 will examine how different political and social sensibilities – those of Irish-Canadian writer Margaret Dixon McDougall and the Catholic priest Mortimer Shea – produced an Irish landscape at odds with that presented by other travel writers and diarists. Selectivity was demonstrably at work in these travellers' dealings with people who worked in the tourist industry. Canadian tourists were voluble in cataloguing the sights they saw, their likes and dislikes, and as was the case with British and Americain tourists, they employed a range of strategies when recording their thoughts and impressions of the porters, guides, waiters, and other workers whose labour was essential to their travels. At times workers in the tourist industry were simply rendered silent, their presence not deemed worthy of comment, while at other times a tourist could not stop going on about the porter who had demanded a (seemingly undeserved) tip or the guide who had given wrong – or too much – information.[8]

As chapter 1 will demonstrate there is plenty of evidence of such incidents; it is more difficult to determine why they became so ubiquitous in tourists' discourse, although I do suggest a few explanations. The record of these exchanges is weighted more heavily in favour of the tourists' voices and perspectives, a problem (by no means new to historians) that needs to be considered. To no small extent this is a problem of lack of sources. It is a problem related to relations of power, which, as social historians have told us, have shaped the sources we use, not least because these relations determined who had literacy skills and the leisure to exercise them. This is not to suggest that historians should abandon inquiries. It is possible, for example, to follow in the footsteps of social historians and try to read the travelogues, diaries, and letters against the grain; or as a cultural historian might put it, look for the fault lines in the tourists' discourse, be sensitive to those moments when contradictions became apparent, and (where possible) point to gaps, absences, and silences. At times I have attempted to do just that: for example, travellers' frequent discussions about guides and porters suggests to me a perhaps not always welcome degree of dependency and reliance that might have been motivated by a number of reasons, ones that chapter 1 explores.[9] Furthermore, as I argue in chapter 4, guides too may have been playing along in this act, creating and performing in character for reasons both tangible and less obvious. Yet none of this, I caution, should let us forget the relationships of class, ethnicity and race, nation and empire, and gender that framed and encoded transatlantic tourism, relationships that resulted in some people being able to represent themselves more fully for the benefit of themselves and (although they might not have intended to do so) for historians. For various reasons, others have not been able to do so.

Nation, Empire, Gender, and Religion in Transatlantic Tourism

Middle-class Canadian tourists were also imperial and national subjects. As Harmut Berghoff and Barbara Korte have argued, 'despite its transnational character tourism plays a prominent role in the formation of national identities and stereotypes.'[10] Tourists and travel literature participated in the construction of national and imperial communities at a time when Canadians were attempting to identify their own personal relationships to nation and empire. In choosing Britain as an important cultural destination for themselves, English-speaking Canadian travellers were choosing to participate in the 'British world.' Such a community, historians have argued, took shape between the 1880s and the 1950s, as British networks around the globe were forged by more efficient and frequent transoceanic travel and communications.[11] These networks were clearly depicted in newspapers, the periodical literature, travelogues, illustrated talks, and in the correspondence of friends and family members who had been on overseas trips before them; these were the cultural genres that educated men and women about the need to visit Britain.[12] These tourists, whose travels are the focus of this book, also would have been exposed to discussions of matters such as imperial federation, the meanings of 'Canada,' and Canada's relationship to the British Empire.[13] Furthermore, in Britain itself during these decades public manifestations of the far-reaching and complex relations of empire were to be found in myriad places.

Many of these tourists arrived in Britain carrying notions of themselves as 'Canadians,' as members of the British Empire, and of the historical and cultural landscapes through which they would be moving. Their sense of themselves as part of a nation that was enfolded into a larger entity, the empire, complicated their reactions to its staging: as chapters 3, 5, and 9 will show, 'neo-Britains' might occupy a complex and at times ambivalent relationship to the originals. For some Canadians, travel to Britain may have been a more self-conscious endeavour in which such complications could be sorted out, an attempt to come to terms with various identities and subjectivities – regional and provincial, national, and imperial. Others signed on for overseas tours without, it seems, giving much thought to their own personal position within nation and empire, yet the structures of their travels ensured that they were confronted with such issues and compelled to engage with these questions all the same. This is not to argue that travel did, or even could, bring such matters to an easy resolution, or that determining 'who one was' or was not vis-à-vis 'Canada' or 'the Empire' was a matter to be settled by visits to Westminster Abbey and the Lake District (or, for some, Versailles or the Coliseum in Rome). As a number of scholars have reminded us, constructing such meanings is a practice that involves constant repetition and reiteration, an open-ended procedure subject to revision and alteration.[14] Yet just as other travellers negotiated their national and imperial sense of themselves through travels that emanated from the imperial centre to the so-called 'colonial' margins, travel to the metropole for these colonial subjects frequently produced similar moments of self-consciousness and reflection. The result might be self-congratulation on being a member of a white, settler dominion and thus closest to the top of the imperial hierarchy; conversely, the process might involve moments of doubt and consternation about being a 'colonial cousin,' and thus only an indirect heir to the cultural, social, and political privileges of empire.[15]

Tours of Britain and Europe were not the only trips abroad taken by these Canadians. To date we do not have a study that focuses on English Canadians' travel in other countries during this period; however, some of the individuals examined here did so for both education and entertainment. Harriett Priddis visited Philadelphia for the 1876 Exhibition. George Pack, of Victoria, British Columbia, used his railroad trip to New York City's docks to stop and tour Chicago, Albany, and Boston.[16] Mary Bain went by train from Vancouver to visit Chicago and them spent a few days in New York, where she discovered that 'Central Park was so sunny and bright it seemed almost like southern California'; her papers, located in the Public Archives of British Columbia, include a diary of a nine-month trip to South America, taken just after she returned from her trip to Britain and Europe.[17] Others ventured even further afield. In 1896–97 Ellen Bilborough of Belleville, Ontario, visited Japan, China, Australia, New Zealand, Fiji, and Hawaii.[18] George Fulford left his Brockville home in 1902 and set out on a five-month 'world tour' that took him to London and Paris, as well as Egypt, India, Singapore, and Japan.[19] That being said, travel to Britain – and, to a certain extent, Europe – was understood to be the apogee of an education, formal and informal, in culture, history, and progress; many aspects of these overseas trips resembled the early modern Grand Tour undertaken by young male aristocrats who wished to further their education in the classics.[20] People who undertook such a trip could reassure themselves that they would be exposed to 'the very best' and that by taking such a trip they could claim membership in a community of cultured, enlightened, and modern men and women. Moreover, while travel within Canada was becoming increasingly popular and accessible during this period, the few individuals who left documents comparing Canada's tourist sites with those in Britain tended to reinforce this belief.[21] Natural wonders such as Niagara Falls or the Canadian Rockies were remarkable and should be seen; however, it was the Atlantic crossing that would bring those Canadians face to face with the pinnacle of history and culture.

The writings of the tourists who included Europe in their overseas trips help us understand the contingent and shifting nature of the lines of affiliation to empire and their links to the racialized discourses of civilization in late-Victorian and Edwardian anglophone Canada.[22] As chapters 6 and 8 will show, Europe was an important cultural destination, desired because of its rich store of art and architecture and scenes of immense natural beauty, such as the Alps and the Mediterranean coastline. Europe also was a place where quaint folk customs, particularly interesting types of peasant dress, might be observed and recorded. Europe also was in many ways the 'other' and experiencing Europe served to strengthen these English-Canadians' ties to Britain and their sense that they themselves were members of a civilized, progressive nation and empire. Europe housed the artefacts that they felt were part of their cultural heritage. Also in Europe, as it was plain to see, were societies that were socially backward, societies that, in the estimation of the Canadian tourists, were missing the most essential features of progress and British imperial greatness.

Nowhere was this more obvious than the organization of gender relations in European peasant societies. In the agricultural regions of countries such as Switzerland and Italy, what they saw of women's labour (and, conversely, men's apparent idleness) spoke to these Canadian tourists of societies that clung to primitive, not progressive, habits. At the very least, such observations suggested that European nations were not yet fully formed entities, that civilized habits and social structures had not yet taken full root across all sectors of society. In time, perhaps, with the good example set by the continent's improving middle class, such habits and structures would become widespread. But some Europeans might, though, have more in common with such 'racially backward' groups as Native peoples: they were not really members of nations at all. All of this appeared to some travellers to be very unlike the Dominion of Canada, where the middle-class, English-speaking, Protestant population was making a considerable effort to assimilate both Aboriginal peoples and European immigrants into modern, English-Canadian ways.[23] As a group of Manitoba school teachers, who toured Britain and Ireland in 1910 themselves put it, their work for the dominion and empire involved convincing both materialistic Americans and a plethora of European ethnicities of the formers' benefits; by bringing them into contact with the 'real thing,' overseas travel would strengthen their commitment to national and imperial projects.[24] Transatlantic tourism did not abolish the racial and ethnically charged hierarchies of power that structured Canadian society; rather, it might at times have confirmed the view that such hierarchies were necessary components of 'civilized' society, along with 'appropriate' gender roles, certain cultural genres, and particular norms of behaviour.

Such hierarchies of power included their belief that English, not French, Canada represented the nation, a belief expressed in ways more implicit than explicit. I chose to confine my focus to English-speaking and (mostly) Protestant Canadians and to omit French-speaking (mostly) Catholics – a choice shaped by considerations such as the sheer volume of sources and the intricacies of questions surrounding issues of religious, national, and imperial identities. But I should note that, although French Canada appears conspicuous by its absence from this study, this absence is not entirely because of my choices as a historian. The absence of French Canada and French-speaking Canadians is also a reflection of the very conspicuous absence of French Canada and French Canadians from the individual and, I would argue, collective consciousness of my research subjects. To be sure, a number of them used their departing or returning stops in Montreal or Quebec City as opportunities to tour those cities, and they might have observed Quebec's landscape as they sailed the St Lawrence.[25] Yet, once they reached the other side of the Atlantic, Quebec – or the notion that Canada included that province and its inhabitants – vanished from their sensibilities (or at least was eclipsed from the historian's eye by other considerations). There is not the slightest indication in these accounts that travels around France evoked comparisons, for better or worse, with Quebec's society and culture; the religiously inspired cultural tours of Italy's cathedrals and galleries did not elicit musings about the church's cultural influence on or in French-speaking, Catholic Canada. In reports of their travels in Ireland, where we might have expected to find various comparisons between Catholic peasantries on both sides of the ocean, Canadian tourists either were silent on such matters or considered it was more salient to discuss Ireland's relationship with England. Widespread absences and silences like these can be difficult for the historian, given our discipline's epistemological and methodological preference for that which is tangibly present and visible. Nevertheless, while outside the scope of this work, the general absence of French Canada from these men's and women's consciousness of nation and empire is a topic that warrants its own historian, for absences and exclusions do not occur naturally or inevitably: they are as a much a product of historical processes as are inclusions and presences.

If being a Canadian was predicated on an identification with Britain that actively excluded (or, at the very least, ignored) French Canada, these travellers' sensibilities concerning gender relations were often acute; moreover, their experiences of transatlantic tourism were shaped and structured by gender relations in a number of ways. As is the case with the other types of affiliations discussed in this book, gender roles and constructs were not static. The ways in which they thought about themselves as men and women were inflected by their other relationships and ways of imagining themselves: class, for one, and nation and empire, for another (and vice versa). Travel and tourism were structured by the discourses and practices associated with normative gender roles, although not always in predictable or straightforward ways. It would be claiming too much to argue that late-Victorian and Edwardian middle-class femininity and masculinity were fundamentally challenged or reshaped by the experiences of being abroad, if for no other reason than the sources and methodology I employ do not permit an extensive exploration of such a claim: my study ends as the passengers disembarked from the steamers at Halifax or Quebec. Nevertheless, these travellers' sense of being in different situations, as well as the genre of travel writing itself (which is explored in more depth later in this chapter), prompted them to record impressions in which their own understandings of gender were never far from the surface, whether in discussing their own movements or describing the gender relations and roles of those among whom they moved. At times their writings suggest more complicated and nuanced ways of conducting themselves as men and (especially) women than I had assumed, possibly because our understandings of these issues in the context of middle-class English-speaking Canadian society are not as extensive or as nuanced as they might be. Furthermore, their writings hint that at times these travellers also inhabited those liminal spaces discussed by sociologists of modern tourism, in which they suspended or at least stretched the boundaries of customary norms of gendered behaviour in order to indulge playful and permissive desires and whims – witness, for example, Mary Leslie's drinking or the delightful anonymity offered by London's streets enjoyed by Mabel Cameron, a young schoolteacher from Victoria – that probably would have been denied them at home.[26]

While class, nationalism and imperialism, race and ethnicity, and gender all helped constitute English-Canadian tourism, religious affiliations and beliefs also played a part in shaping these tourists' gazes. Much has been written over the past twenty-five years of the dynamic history of Canadian Protestantism during the period covered by this study: the complicated connections between earlier forms of evangelicalism and late-nineteenth-century liberal Protestantism; debates over secularism, social reform, and the place of the state; the complex relationship of white, middle-class women to organized religion, social reform, and the suffrage movement; the impact of overseas and domestic missionary movements; and the question of working-class English-speaking Canadians' attitudes towards organized religion (and vice versa).[27] It should not be surprising that these tourists were far from unanimous on these issues or that they showed varying degrees of interest in them. Emily Murphy, as chapter 6 will show, made it quite clear that she thoroughly disapproved of the appearance of anything associated with Roman Catholicism rearing its 'decadent head' in an Anglican service, and Edward Greenshields, a member of Montreal's St Paul's Presbyterian Church, shared her sentiments.[28] George Pack had a wide range of interests that included both the architecture of churches and the services held within them, but he seemed less interested in theological matters than Murphy or Greenshields.[29] Mary Bain, who judging from her searches for 'Scottish churches' in unfamiliar cities, was a Presbyterian, had little to say about the precise content of services unless she found them disagreeable, as in the case of the sermon preached on Christmas Day in 1910 at a 'poor little church' in Venice by a young missionary. 'I daresay the poor young fellow meant well,' Bain mused, 'but I did not care for his sermon. For one thing he said Christianity was a losing force, and I certainly don't agree with him about that, and then he did not seem to approve of Christmas, for he made no reference to it in his sermon, nor were any of the hymns of the Christmas order.'[30]

Murphy, Greenshields, and Bain were quite open about their denominational affiliations, although Pack was not so clear about his (he may have been a Methodist, judging from his liking of their chapels). I have not been able to discover the denomination of every traveller in this study, but their accounts make it clear that Christianity (and, for the vast majority, Protestantism) underpinned their trips abroad in myriad ways,[31] some of them obvious: tours were organized by ministers, such as Ontario's William H. Withrow or New Brunswick's Dr Borden, and certain prominent churches and cathedrals in Britain and Europe, Protestant and Catholic, were frequently visited attractions. These Canadians also toured and attended services in a number of smaller, more obscure churches and chapels; in all cases, they compared, weighed, and evaluated religious institutions and their clergy for their performances of piety. In religion, as in other aspects of their travels, these tourists were not passive recipients of the sights upon which they gazed. As Kröller has pointed out, not all Protestant Canadians displayed reactionary or bigoted attitudes when faced with the material manifestations of Roman Catholicism; their assessments of Catholicism as displayed in church architecture, art, and sculpture were complex and multilayered.[32] As well as visiting religious sites, these tourists constructed narratives meant to explain and order the landscapes through which they moved, ones in which the centrality of religion coexisted and, at times, was intertwined with secular accounts of nation and region.

Religious beliefs and religious practices were fundamental to the cultural and social framework that these tourists carried with them, although simultaneously for some these might be subjected to degrees of questioning and critical scrutiny. Judging from the frequency of their references to church attendance overseas, this weekly ritual could both diminish *and* reinforce the more unsettling dimensions of their travel, whether they managed to find the 'right' service, chose or were forced to sample another Protestant denomination, or attended Catholic masses. The modernity that, as I will explore later in this chapter,

was central to transatlantic tourism did not preclude them from dwelling on spiritual matters and their religious heritage. Rather, it perhaps
encouraged and fostered private reflections and public acts of veneration that helped buttress the hegemonic influence of religion that,
Marguerite Van Die has argued, became a central dimension of public
life within nineteenth-century Canada.[33]

Spaces and Senses: Performances of Tourism

As well as cathedrals and churches, the public spaces frequented by
these tourists included museums, shops and markets, restaurants, educational and social welfare institutions, trains and omnibuses, and of
course, the streets, plazas, and piazzas where they observed 'the locals'
and where, we must remember, they were observed (both by the locals
and by other tourists). Guidebooks, travelogues, and newspaper and
periodical articles about tourist sites helped shape these tourists' sense
of what could be entered, traversed, and known. Yet their accounts
make it clear that, although they had been educated to find and
explore spots such as the Tower of London or Le Bon Marché, they also
brought their own needs, fantasies, and desires to bear on the meanings that they attributed to such attractions. These were not uncomplicated processes. As feminist scholars have argued, such spaces and the
processes that forged them were not without their contradictions, nor
could all who circulated within them participate equally in their possibilities and pleasures.[34] Moreover, certain types of elite spaces – the
homes of the British and European upper middle class, aristocracy, and
royalty, or the classrooms of schools such as England's Eton – were, for
the vast majority of these Canadian tourists, open only on a very limited basis (tours of Windsor Castle, for example) or through particular
kinds of lenses – through the fiction of Canadian novelists such as Sara
Jeannette Duncan (Mrs Everard Cotes), Maria Amelia Fytche, and
Alice Jones, for example. Other areas – the homes of peasants, the
workplaces of souvenir makers, and the bedrooms and dining rooms
of orphanages, workhouses, and hospitals – were opened up for curious and ethnographically minded tourists, who could and did judge
and analyse their residents' living and working conditions.

Transatlantic tourism was not only about seeing places and recording
impressions. As sociologists of tourism have observed, travel was a performed art: it was stylized, it was self-conscious, and it involved a reper-
toire that was repeated and reiterated, albeit with various levels of

negotiation.[35] English-Canadian travel writing and tourists' own accounts suggest that tourists were always 'performing' to various degrees and in various ways, even when within the four walls of their hotel rooms or pensions. Communication studies scholar Della Pollock's observation about the subject/object split that performers encounter – they are simultaneously speaking and enacting subjects that are gazed upon and assessed by their audiences – seems germane for understanding the experiences and assessments of Canadians who moved through the transatlantic world of overseas tourism.[36] But performance is a concept not limited to tourists. Although it is not always possible to know what their audiences made of these visitors from the other side of the Atlantic, such enactments and transactions needed fellow actors and audiences. The discourses and practices of nineteenth-century tourism were dependent on local residents and workers in the tourist industry enacting particular categories and identities: the Cockney cabby, for example, or the Sicilian street beggar. As the domestic spaces and 'private lives' of peasants and working class people were laid open for tourists' scrutiny, they too became part of the theatre of tourism, one forged by the relations of capitalism, consumerism, and, in many cases, colonialism. Yet while scripts might be adhered to and cues picked up according to agreed-on conventions, at times both tourists and their fellow participants in a performance might deviate from the script or miss, possibly ignore, the conventions.

Performances of travel and tourism had sensory dimensions. Although not reducible to relationships of power, their meanings were inflected and shaped by gender, class, race and ethnicity, colonialism, and nationalism. This book details some of the minutiae of the daily practices of tourism, minutiae that might seem at first glance trivial but that, I would argue, play a critical part in facilitating insights into the larger subjectivities and relationships. The details of tourists' experiences and perceptions were central to the practices of tourism: it mattered whether the food was palatable, whether the streets were redolent of delightful aromas or reeking of sewage, whether the guides and porters were willing and obliging or rapacious and sullen, clearly understood or unintelligible, and whether the tour of the Louvre or Windsor Castle resulted in feet so sore that the sensory delights offered were lost on the visitor. Despite the many complaints about the negative aspects of travel, it bears emphasizing that the subjects of this book boarded transatlantic steamships expecting to be both educated *and* entertained, to have their senses stimulated in ways that were uplifting *and* enjoyable. This book describes describes the smells, sights, sounds, and, for some, textures that these women and men encountered, evaluated, and attempted to sort into various categories and typologies. No study of their experiences abroad would be complete without mention of the roar of London's traffic, the smells of Naples, the taste of Dutch food, the glitter of Italian jewelry, and the daring of French Impressionist pointillism. Tourism is a way to further our understanding of the role of sensation and pleasure within this group, one that has not been much noted for its ability to have fun.[37] Harriett Priddis, who spent a great deal of time in London attending meetings of various imperial associations and social reform groups, also had a wonderful time at Ascot until she spilled the whiskey from her flask.

Anglophone Canadian Tourism and Modernity

Hovering over all of this is the question of modernity, one that has been addressed only sparingly in Canadian historiography. While modernity often has been relegated to the twentieth century or explored as 'modernization' (as in, for example, transitions from agricultural to commercial economies or secularization), I argue that by examining transatlantic tourism for this period we can see the multifaceted ways and means in which modernity shaped the lives and identities of the subjects of this study. In many respects this aspect of late-Victorian and Edwardian tourism seems so obvious as not to warrant any special discussion. Various scholars have pointed out that nineteenth-century tourism was intricately and intimately tied to modernity. Technological and cultural forms of modernity took tourists to the steamship dock in the first place. Modernity brought them into contact with 'Others.' Shaped by technologies (the railroad, the steamship, the telegram) modernity encouraged ever-faster movement across geographical regions and time zones, and thus collapsed time and space, perhaps encouraging a sense of fragmented identity and uncertainty, and modernity was deeply implicated in commercial and industrial capitalism.[38] In his study of Toronto's Industrial Exhibition, historian Keith Walden has pointed to the many lessons in modernity that attending that event entailed – 'learning how to control fleeting moments and impressions, how to interpret delicate, shifting gradations of taste, how to interact with strangers in chance encounters, how to cope with ambiguity, how to sustain coherence and self-possession in the face of dizzying sensory overload'[39] – lessons that seem equally applicable to the experiences of overseas tourism. Scholars who have studied the complicated relationships between modernity and imperialism from the eighteenth century on have drawn our attention to the growth of nation states, an increased centralization of power, the development of global commerce and industrialization, and the expansion of intellectual and cultural networks through such media as the press.[40] Historian Kathleen Wilson has argued that, starting in the eighteenth century, modernity has involved an 'unfolding set of relationships' that have produced modern selves and subjectivities, with their expectations of 'perfection and progress.'[41]

All of these processes can be seen at work in anglophone Canadians' experiences of tourism, down to the expectation – not always fulfilled – that they would have the 'perfect' encounter with, say, the Scottish Highlands or Italian art. Transatlantic tourism drew men and women from across English Canada into wide-ranging global networks, especially those of British imperialism. For anglophone Canadian women in particular, travel in both Britain and Europe offered opportunities to experience movement through time and space and to reflect both privately (in their diaries) and publicly (as travel writers) on modernity's potential for individual fulfilment and the creation of liberal subjectivities. London was for most the epicentre of imperial modernity, a central staging ground for the performance of modern, gendered imperial identities constructed in relation both to their British 'family' and to other members of the empire.[42] Equally importantly, English-speaking Canadian tourists' own writings demonstrate that these travellers were engaged in modernity themselves before they even got on the ship and that their expectations of what they would see and how they would go about doing it were shaped by these processes. With the 1920s, the contours and public dimensions of modernity shifted somewhat, in response to new forms of technology and consumption, not to mention the growing political uncertainties of the interwar decades. And for some postwar tourists, the timbre of modernity was registered in a somewhat different key. Kathleen Coburn, of Toronto, for example, felt a greater sense of fragmentation and ambivalence, particularly concerning political developments, much more acutely than did many of her fellow tourists, who continued to express their optimism about progress in the more straightforward fashion of the tourists before them.

The role of modernity in transatlantic tourism is underscored by antimodern discourses, modernity's alter ego (which, interestingly, have received more attention from Canadian historians).[43] Antimodernism was not, however, always and automatically the dominant cultural mode used to give meaning to the tourist landscapes of Britain and Europe. Tourists' desire to find signs of imperial progress in Britain, and their pleasure when they did so – for example, looking at sites of social reform or participating in modern British culture – should caution us against labeling all tourists who were interested in history and historical sites as antimodern. Some travel writers luxuriated – one might say wallowed – in antimodernist judgments about quaint English cottages or charming Breton peasants, but theirs was in no way the perspective shared by all of the diarists and letter writers introduced here. And even the tourists who were of the opinion that their travels among peasant and rural societies overseas would unlock for them a lost world of innocence and purity did not necessarily or automatically draw from them lessons for rejuvenating and reinvigorating their own society and nation.[44]

Therefore, 'A Happy Holiday' takes a two-pronged approach. It examines overseas tourism in its own right, as an important activity surrounded by varying levels of a tourist industry that, over the course of the nineteenth century, grew in size and complexity. Simultaneously, it demonstrates that tourism can be useful in exploring a range of issues, the most central and recurring one being the role it played in forging and sharpening middle-class identities and perceptions. Using tourism as a way into questions of gender, national and imperial identity, class, racial and ethnic relations offers the possibility of understanding how, when, where, and (possibly) why these themes were interrelated and intertwined.

Chronology and Themes

Two factors led me to choose the decades between 1870 and 1930. Many fine works of cultural history have selected a small slice of time (and, on occasion, a small cast of characters) to investigate large questions and themes at a microscopic level.[45] For this study, I made a conscious and deliberate choice to widen my chronological canvas in order to determine both commonalities and differences of various kinds. Canadian historians have seen this period as having a particular kind of unity that makes the category of 'nation' – at least in English-speaking Canada – most relevant and important, reaching beyond the obvious political structures and processes such as increased industrialization, urbanization, immigration, the growing consolidation of the middle class, certain kinds of challenges to gender relations, and the expansion of the dominion government's power, particularly over Aboriginal peoples. While this book makes no claims to be a comprehensive 'national' history, it does attempt to look beyond one region of English-speaking Canada in an effort to gauge whether significant regional distinctions were apparent in transatlantic tourism.[46] My findings on that question, though, are not straightforward. Region undoubtedly played a role in determining the ease and affordability of transatlantic tourism. It was much easier and cheaper for anglophone Canadians in Ontario, Quebec, and the Maritimes to travel across the ocean, in comparison with the length of time and expense of the journey for British Columbians. Moreover, for much of this period, it is probably safe to say that western Canadian and British Columbian society possessed a much smaller middle class than did other regions of Canada. Nevertheless, British Columbians such as Mary Bain, George Pack, Mabel Cameron, and Sophie and Ada Pemberton did not appear to me to view their experiences through an especially regional lens or, indeed, to have experiences that varied much from those of tourists from other regions of the dominion – individual personalities, gender, age, and economic position made more of a difference.

The other factor, simply put, was the growth of overseas tourist traffic during this period and thus the richness of the sources: diaries, letters, travelogues, and newspaper coverage proliferated in the decades leading up to the First World War and continued after the war was over. Mary Leslie's diary and Kröller's study both attest that voyages back and forth across the Atlantic, and North American tourists' explorations of Britain and Europe, were not unknown prior to and just after Confederation; nevertheless, the decades that I examine here witnessed a steady growth of overseas travel from Canada. Tourism is a phenomenon difficult to quantify for this period, especially when spread over a large geographical canvas. It would not be possible, for example, to discern just how many Canadian tourists embarked for overseas from a number of ports such as Quebec, Montreal, Halifax, New York, and Boston or how many toured certain sights like the Tower of London, Versailles, the Alps, or the Vatican. Nor is it possible to argue that the types of cultural discourses and practices that I point to, such as a desire to see the landscapes of British history or visit the Sistine Chapel, were shared equally across the dominion's Protestant, English-speaking middle class. As Ian McKay has argued, there are no easy conceptual or methodological tools for historians 'to conclusively resolve the vexed question of how to assess the impact of a given cultural practice.'[47]

I would submit, however, that the fact that the sources for this book include just under fifty unpublished document collections from locations in Prince Edward Island to British Columbia, a large selection of newspaper and periodical coverage of overseas tourism, and lengthy lists published in the press of departures to and arrivals from overseas indicates that during the period under consideration transatlantic tourism was in no way atypical for middle-and upper-middle-class anglophone Canadians. Furthermore, the common experiences of both travel writers and tourists themselves, not to mention their commonly expressed view that such experiences were desirable (indeed, almost obligatory) to their sense of self, suggests a cultural significance and meaning that numbers alone cannot capture.

My choice to examine a period of sixty years raises the question of change over time, particularly change between the late 1870s and 1914. In general, I treat the decades before the First World War as one significant period and the 1920s as another, a chronological distinction that warrants some explanation. Although not as rich in tourists' diaries and letters as I might have wished, the 1870s yielded numerous articles about overseas tourism and 'foreign lands,' as well as lists of the people who travelled back and forth across the Atlantic. The production of tourist literature, published and unpublished, accelerated in the 1880s and continued to grow until 1914; however, the list of sites to be seen by travellers and the various stances they took on seeing them did not differ radically over these decades. To be sure, the contexts in which people visited Britain and Europe did not remain static. Over time, certain types of attractions were added to the Canadian tourist's itinerary, as imperial spectacles such as Queen Victoria's jubilees, royal funerals and coronations, and exhibitions grew in both number and scale. Later on, in the 1900s the British women's suffrage movement caught the attention a number of Canadian women.

Where I found 'difference,' it resided in the perspectives and attitudes held by the tourists themselves, difference more synchronic than chronological. Some writers and diarists were ambivalent about, and sometimes bored with, various aspects of 'high culture,' whether they were exposed to it in the 1870s or in the 1900s, yet, the Mediterranean coast was as dazzling in 1913 as it was in 1891. I made a very considered decision not to examine wartime discourses and practices. It would be possible to examine the experiences of Canadians stationed overseas within the framework of tourism (leaves and furloughs in Britain, for example, and soldiers' diaries describe their impressions of France and Belgium). The magnitude of such a project, however, not to mention the specificities of the war, places it outside the realm of this study's possibilities. I pick up the narrative in the 1920s. As chapter 9 will demonstrate, relative to the period before the war, transatlantic travel by anglophone Canadians in the 1920s embodied both continuities and changes, an observation that permits some (albeit more tentative) suggestions concerning the prevalent arguments concerning national and imperial identities in inter war Canada. Shifting forms of modernity, meant shifts in the timbre – if not the actual content – of tourists' experiences, and yet there remained important continuities with the late Victorian and Edwardian years. While tourists, such as Kathleen Coburn in 1930, made the case for experiencing Britain and Europe from a 'Canadian' perspective, the long-prevailing notion that Britain held significant cultural and historical meanings for English-Canadians persisted throughout the 1920s.

. In organizing this book, I have used both chronology and some recurring themes, such as history and imperial identity, landscape, public space, and culture, framed within the borders of nation and continent: Scotland, England, Ireland, and Europe. This schema should not be taken as somehow natural: these lines of demarcation were as much imagined and constructed as any of the other types of relationships examined in this book. There were many similarities in tourists' perceptions of people and practices in Britain and Europe: often peasants in Europe were viewed with the same cosmopolitan eye as agricultural workers and rural residents in parts of England and Ireland. Porters and guides in Ireland, Italy, and Switzerland tended to amuse, enchant, irritate, or annoy in very similar ways. Yet for quite obvious reasons – a basic but important one being linguistic distinctions – travel on the Continent was not the same experience, nor did it have quite the same meanings for anglophone Canadians, as did travel in Britain. Furthermore, not every Canadian tourist spent the same amount of time as every other Canadian tourist in each of these countries. Virtually all of these tourists went to see Britain, but a few of them, such as Toronto's Thomas Langton, preferred to spend most of their time in Italy, France, and Switzerland, while some others apparently did not care to cross the channel and spent all of their time in Britain.

Writing about 'Abroad': Sources and Authors

Given that so much of this book is based on two different groups of sources, published versus unpublished, it seems appropriate before taking the reader overseas to explore some of the distinctions between these sources and the individuals who generated them. From the 1870s on, the press in Halifax, Saint John, Ottawa, Montreal, Toronto, and Victoria ran numerous articles and columns about places beyond Canada's borders. Such items, often unsigned, discussed 'the state of things' – socioeconomic, cultural, and political – in a wide range of countries, not all of which anglophone Canadians visited. Direct accounts of their travels were contributed by people who had gone to London, Naples, or Berlin, and were eager to share their impressions and experiences and to inform future tourists of both the pitfalls and the pleasures. Although for some articles the writer's nationality was unclear, in many the authors were self-identified 'Canadians' who believed that their national identity gave them a particular perspective on matters abroad.

This literature should not be read as a straightforward or uncomplicated documentary reportage of 'other lands.' For one thing – and this should not be surprising – it helped construct and shape conceptions of 'nations' and their 'peoples' and to order men, women, and children, the spaces that they inhabited, and their social, cultural, and political beliefs and practices under the rubric of nation. The anglophone Canadian readership thus was invited to imagine the world as an arrangement of easily identified places demarcated both by the official means of the state – borders, currencies, and armies – and through other, less formal but no less important mechanisms, such as food, clothing, architecture, music, religion, and (especially) gender roles and relations. Such conceptions of nation were important, both as ways of thinking about the places so designated and because they helped middle-class anglophone Canadians to define their own sense of self within a larger context, even if this process, taking place within the gendered and racialized contexts of imperial modernity, was an ongoing, never-completed one.[48] More specifically, this literature addressed and helped shape 'the tourist' and the tourist's destination. Articles such as one entitled 'The Progress of Italy', published in 1878, informed readers (New Brunswickers at least) that Italy, despite the many obstacles placed in its way (French interference, internal strife, financial hardships brought about by war, and clerical opposition), was making progress. Tourists were reportedly 'flocking' to its north and central regions, to Turin, Milan, Genoa, Venice, and Florence, and the long-standing jealousies of these rival cities were now being super-seded by feelings of national unity. The 'country' was busy seculariz-ing, as the government took control of estates of the religious orders education, and the diffusion of 'knowledge to promote commercial progress.'[49] Not all of this literature fell under the rubric of travel writ-ing. Articles such as 'Education in France' or 'Turkey's Parliament' also appeared in the *Saint John Daily telegraph* in the 1870s. These were not written in the self-conscious voice of the observing (and observant) traveller, offering tips on 'what to see' and 'how to see it,' yet when considered together and viewed as a continuum, such articles offered a panoramic view of foreign lands, one that would educate readers who might never leave home and provide useful background knowledge for those who might.[50] Armed thereby with facts and informed opin-ions, English Canadians would be able to compete with American and British tourists, showing themselves on the international stage to be in possession of the social and cultural capital that marked them as deni-zens of a modern, liberal nation.

Would-be travellers and tourists might educate and enlighten them-selves about the places they planned to visit through other kinds of print media. Baedeker's and Ruskin's guidebooks were used by many anglophone Canadian travellers, although as we shall see, opinions varied as to their utility and suitability. Furthermore, with Confedera-tion the Dominion of Canada was established and from the 1870s on newspapers ran more and more columns that offered the 'Canadian' perspective on overseas travel, with features such as the *Montreal Daily Star*'s 'Letters from London' and the *Saint John Daily Telegraph*'s 'A New Brunswicker Abroad.'[51] The *Canadian Magazine*, founded in 1893 and catering predominately to upper-and middle-class anglophone Canadi-ans, ran a number of this sort of article, as well as reports on various attractions in Britain and Europe. Local newspapers and periodicals covered group tours of anglophone Canadians overseas for sporting competitions (lacrosse, shooting, and rowing), on institutionally spon-sored excursions (the Manitoba Department of Education's Teachers' Trip of 1910, the church or university-run tours led by the Methodist minister W.H. Withrow or Mount Allison's Dr Borden), or on tours sponsored by the newspapers themselves (Hamilton's 'Spectator Girls' and the *Toronto Daily Mail*'s 'Maple Blossom Girls'). Such articles gave detailed accounts of the places that had been visited and their histories and offered suggestions for further reading, in the form of either travel guides or histories. Many publications provided copious illustrations of both the people and places that should be seen; this book features a number of such photographs and sketches in an attempt to suggest how middle-class anglophone Canadians' visual sense might have been aroused by the prospect of transatlantic travel. The Canadian press played a significant role in shaping and promoting the desire to travel overseas and the national and imperial memberships that such travel facilitated.[52] Although it existed primarily for the benefit of Britons who might be interested in investing in or emigrating to Canada, the periodical *Canada: An Illustrated Journal*, founded by its editor Hugh Allan in 1906, regularly published the names of Canadians about to depart for overseas and from time to time ran articles about Britain, as well as advertisements for London hotels and services.

It could not be said that spontaneity was actively discouraged (and, as we shall see, the unexpected did occur). Nevertheless, this literature insisted that tourists should be well prepared in order to appreciate fully the landscape, monuments, architecture, and people they would see. Possibly because the time spent overseas by many middle-class English-Canadians was quite short the desire was so intense to arrive there with clear agendas and a clear understanding of what to expect.[53] Their desire to arrive well prepared also might be linked to middle-class eagerness for efficiency, made more urgent by a sense of the quickening pace of modernity, a sense exacerbated by technologies such as steamships and rail travel. Travellers without dependants or the demands of regular daily employment, such as young, single middle-class women or wealthy middle-class men, sometimes were away for as long as a year, but most middle-class tourists went for two or three months. A minority spent only a few weeks overseas.

Whatever the length of time spent, though, most travel writers would have been pleased by the *Canadian Magazine*'s tale of the four young women whose plans to make 'the grand tour' for the summer of 1904 had gone awry and had to be postponed. Instead of despairing, the young women decided that they would 'visit' London (a trip that included Stratford-on-Avon, Oxford, and Warwick), France, Germany, and Italy with the help of their friends' 'guide-books, collections of foreign photographs, and museum and art gallery catalogues.'[54] They also wrote to 'a well-known man of learning for a list of the best books to read in order to become thoroughly "acquainted" with the places which they have chosen for their "travels."' Having received a list that included *Shakespeare's England*, *Dickens's London*, Ruskin's *Stones of Venice*, and George Eliot's *Romola*, they then ordered from an American firm (one of many that offered such items) pictures of Italian sites and art. Their 'trips' having been set for the rest of the summer and into the winter, the young women felt glad to have waited: 'for we are beginning to realize how shockingly unprepared we were ... Just think how much more fully we shall appreciate and understand it all when at last we do go.' By the next summer, they would have 'a much more intelligent and comprehensive knowledge of the places we intend to study and of the treasures of history and art which they contain than hundreds of the people who are going abroad this year will have. At least, it will be our own fault if we don't.'[55]

Travel to Britain and Europe need not – indeed, should not – be undertaken by the uninformed and uneducated. It helped to have a well-travelled circle of friends, as well as the address of a 'well-known man of learning' disposed to dispense reading lists. But the pedagogy of travel did not stop with these four young women. Readers of the article also could pick up tips as what they themselves should read and see (and how much time they should spend in doing so) before setting sail. This education was performed in various ways and underpinned by patriarchal gender relations (the male academic tutoring of young female students), the mass-market commodification of 'travel' (the American firms who sold pictures of landscapes and art for a penny each), and the linking of travel to the world of 'high culture,' history, and art, not to mention the disdain for fellow travellers who set off unprepared and thus did not even realize the depth of their ignorance. It was no coincidence that a tour of Britain and Europe would bring the traveller into contact with the familiar and recognizable: travel writers sought to ensure that what was seen would be already known and anticipated so that the traveller's corporeal encounter with Westminster Abbey or the Sistine Chapel would be appreciated to the fullest intellectual and emotional extent.

Although the 'expert' was in this case male, women comprised a significant group among anglophone Canadian travel writers. To be sure, middle-class men led overseas tours; as chapter 3 will explore, the travels of some groups of women, such as the Manitoba teachers or Hamilton's 'Spectator Girls,' were organized displays of anglophone Canadian womanhood in which women's agency was a complicated question. English-speaking Canadian women also feature in this study in other ways. The fortunes of 'Canadians abroad' was a popular subject for many editors, and the *Canadian Magazine* often carried reports on the successful literary, musical, and artistic careers of anglophone Canadian women overseas and on English-Canadian women in imperial organizations or, perhaps less frequently, their marriages to British aristocrats.[56]

Middle-class women were the authors of their own experiences overseas, and they would entertain, inform, and advise readers about travel in Britain and Europe: Constance Boulton, in her accounts of her trips in 'A Canadian Bicycle in Europe'; writers such as Louisa Hayter Birchall, Jane Lavender, Mary Spencer Warren, Winnifred Wilton, Estelle Kerr, Emily P. Weaver, and E. Fannie Jones, in the *Canadian Magazine*; 'Penelope' in the *Montreal Daily Star*; as well as book authors such as Maria Elise Turner Lauder, Emily Murphy, Margaret Dixon McDougall, and Irene Simmonds.[57] A few of the published items considered here, such as Sara Jeannette Duncan's *Cousin Cinderella* (1908) and Maria Lauder's *Evergreen Leaves, Being Notes from My Travel Book by 'Toofie'* (1877), were written either as novels or quasi-fictional travelogues. Their authors couched their messages about life among the British aristocracy (Duncan) or travel around Britain (Lauder) in a genre one step removed from the direct reporting of columnists and the *Canadian Magazine*'s writers. Duncan's fiction was couched in a realist style, and Lauder had travelled extensively in Europe and was a well-known travel writer.[58] Their writings thus mediated their own impressions through the voices and personas of the characters they created, such as Duncan's Mary Trent, who describes her impressions of the British aristocracy's social rituals, or the family in *Evergreen Leaves* who muse on the Scottish landscape and its brutal history.

Middle-class English-Canadian women's published travel writing both resembled and differed from men's, and women travel writers adopted a variety of voices and styles that make a homogeneous characterization of their work impossible. As scholars who have studied middle-class women's production of travel texts within colonial and imperial contexts have pointed out, to treat these texts as simply reflective of their authors' subordinate status within gendered hierarchies and thus typifying a unified feminine 'voice' drastically oversimplifies matters.[59] For one, such an approach overlooks these women's racial and class privileges, privileges no less real for being complicated by gender. Furthermore, even women who came from similar socioeconomic backgrounds did not always choose to write about their experiences in the same manner, nor did they have identical experiences. Other than the fact that both authors visited some of the same tourist sites, and were written by women, there is little similarity between little Lauder's *Evergreen Leaves* and Murphy's *The Impressions of Janey Canuck Abroad* (1902). The former is a whimsical and light-hearted narrative (albeit one with heavy doses of British history) of a family's trip through Britain, while the latter is full of didactic anecdotes that illustrate the problematic and often degraded 'Old World,' including the ridiculous and 'effeminate' nature of High Anglicanism and the need for temperance in working-class London.[60] Boulton wrote about her bicycle through Europe in a humorous and self-deprecating voice, mocking her status as a tourist and her abilities as a cyclist; other women writers, for example, Louise Hayter Birchall, assumed a self-confident and competent persona, one very similar to that of their male colleagues.[61] Yet despite these differences, many of these women did adopt the posture and tone of the *flâneuse*, a style that, as chapter 5 will explore, was particularly popular in writing about London.[62] The unpublished diaries and letters of anglophone Canadian women are also full of such observations.

Travel writers' and journalists' impressions and analyses of the landscapes and societies of Britain and Europe enjoyed a complex relationship to the experiences and accounts of the travellers whose diaries and letters remained unpublished. Both groups agreed on the general lineaments and structures of their journeys. They visited mostly the same places and the recommended sites, but they did not always concur on the significance and meaning of what they had seen and experienced. Diarists did not participate in antimodernist ruminations to the degree that their published fellow tourists did; rather, they celebrated progress wherever they thought they saw it and, in turn, lamented its absence in places or peoples who seemed untouched by its benefits.[63] Travel writers at times assumed an air of professionalism and expertise, yet those who may have read their accounts before venturing overseas themselves did not acknowledge the former's superior knowledge as providing a template on which to map their own adventures, although they may well have done so. And, as we shall see, guidebooks, such as Baedeker's or Ruskin's, were just as likely to inspire complaints as they did praise.

Many of the diaries examined in this book exemplify the genre's growing tendency in the late nineteenth century to serve as a record of individual emotions and private opinions,[64] as their writers reflected on the subjective and emotional dimensions of their travels. These might range from lengthy meditations on the exalted or moving nature of historic sites, such as Canterbury Cathedral or the dungeons of Europe's castles, to bursts of vexation provoked by supposedly incompetent hotel workers and avaricious guides. In the diaries such experiences were described in a much more direct and at times ethnocentric idiom than that used in published accounts. Not surprisingly, the diaries and letters also highlight individual traits and tendencies, such as the writer's personality, desire to see some things and not others, experiences in coping with unexpected or emotionally charged experiences, and the writer's own particular understandings of class, gender, nation and empire, and religion. If there was one widely shared intention among the authors of these collections of private writings, I would argue that it was the need to keep an inventory or catalogue of one's travels in order to ensure that their memory – shaped as it might be by varying degrees of sensations of difference across time and place – could be recalled and preserved. The pages of diaries, collections of postcards, and, in some cases, sketches, photographs, and scrapbooks could help sort, classify, and organize those experiences that otherwise might well have been only vaguely recollected as a jumble of sights, sounds, and smells.[65] Moreover, while travel diarists were of course not alone in their desire to capture the immediate past, I would argue that, as a genre, these texts were particularly influenced by the modernity of late nineteenth-century tourism.

Yet as much as there might be some important distinctions between the two types of writing and writers, travel writers were as much tourists as were the travellers who did not publish accounts of their 'happy holidays,' a fact that the former sometimes acknowledged in their work. Furthermore, the two bodies of writing and writers – the diary and letter versus the advice column and book, the unknown tourist (George Pack) versus the more celebrated author (Emily Murphy) cannot and should not be separated into overly rigid categories. Travel writers also filled their pages with reflections on their emotional reactions to the sun rising over the Alps or the ambivalence they experienced when touring the Tower of London. In turn, diarists such as Harriett Priddis, Mabel Cameron, George Pack, and Edward Greenshields not only kept extremely detailed accounts but spent much time on stories and anecdotes that were not far removed from published accounts of travel in terms of their flair and how they capture 'local colour.' 'A Happy Holiday' thus explores the similarities that bound these individuals and groups together, while at the same time it draws our attention to the nuances of transatlantic tourism, ones in which contradictory or ambivalent attitudes might be manifested.[66.]

As chapter 1 will demonstrate, such contradictions and ambivalences were very much on display when middle-class anglophone Canadian tourists reflected on the practical aspects of transatlantic travel. Contradictions and ambivalences were particularly apparent when they came into contact with the people whose work made their exercises of immersion in history and culture possible.

1 Porters, Guides, and the Middle-Class Tourist: The Practices of Transatlantic Tourism

Fred Martin's 1881 Atlantic journey began on 21 May with his departure from his home in Woodstock, Ontario, for Toronto and then Montreal, where he took the time to admire the Church of Our Lady of Lourdes and Notre Dame Cathedral. He travelled on to Quebec, a city that impressed him as 'the most peculiar' he had ever seen. It had 'narrow streets more like lanes but well paved' but hills so steep that he could not imagine how heavy loads were transported up them (he was afraid of falling out of his carriage). Next it was on Montmorency Falls, which were 'indeed very grand.' To àdd to the area's interest, Martin was saluted by children along the way, 'a characteristic of the French people so our Hibernian driver tells us.'[1]

At the dock in Quebec 'the passengers were all on deck in the greatest glee. Young ladies with huge bouquets of flowers in their hands (among them a magnificent one sent by Mrs Chapleau presented to Lady Macdonald). Others with the latest novels. The matronly old woman annoying the stewards about her luggage and bandboxes and the men smoking and walking the decks as though they were practicing for a six days "go as you please" walking match. We have a "pair" of ladies of an uncertain age on board that would be a terror to a census taker but from the number of interrogations they put to everyone they meet would make excellent enumerators.' Then, promptly at 10 o'clock, the bell warning of the steamer's departure rang, the decks were cleared of the well-wishers, 'the hawser is thrown off and the *Parisian* gently and gracefully glides from the wharf into midstream and a gun from the Citadel announces our departure. Hundreds of handkerchiefs floating in the air. Steaming down the River we see the Falls of Montmorency in the distance and pass several sailing vessels.'

Almost on cue, Martin wrote, 'pencils came out' for those farewell letters that would be sent home at Rimouski. [2]

The Glasgow-built *Parisian* was a far cry from the pitching and tossing vessel that had taken Mary Leslie across the Atlantic in 1867. The steamer had accommodations for two hundred cabin passengers and more than a thousand in steerage. Martin was pleased to note that 'the material used on the construction [had been] subjected to the most rigourous [sic] tests by both Lloyds and [the] owners' own surveyors.' Not only was the *Parisian* very sturdy, she also had been outfitted with side keels to prevent a 'rolling motion' and 'any appliance that can increase the safety or enhance the comfort of the passengers both cabin and steerage and intermediate will be found in the *Parisian*.' Martin appreciated the punctuality and frequency with which meals were served and found that 'the servants are all attention and the head Steward in the salon does all he can for the comfort of his passengers and you have only to express a wish and it is filled.' Martin was not so impressed by the chief steward, a Mr Melville, noting only 'the less said of him the better as he is not as agreeable as he might be.'[3]

Once overseas, Martin continued to be struck by the demeanour of workers in the tourist industry, particularly in Europe. During his sojourn on a Rhine River boat, he found his guidebook indispensable, 'for if you ask any of the officers or men belonging to the boat they have not the slightest idea of the name of the place alluded to and pointed out although they pass it every day. They will however always tell you some name. Never say they don't know but if you hunt it up and locate the place on the map you will find they are invariably wrong. The officers have this in their favor – they are extremely kind and courteous and all attentive to the slightest wish of their passengers and this steamer is the finest running on the Rhine.' Not so accommodating were the 'sharks of guides' in Cologne, who tried to trick Martin into paying them for a tour of the cathedral. 'Talk about Niagara Falls sharks … the only way for the Traveller to get even with them is to break in on their story when describing anything as they have to begin over again when once interrupted for their stereotyped lingo they go over with every visitor.'[4]

It is impossible to know what Mr Melville, the *Parisian*'s chief steward, made of Mr Martin. Had the latter done something to offend him, for example? Nor do I know if the *Parisian*'s steerage offered the safety and comfort that Martin claimed (another traveller, as we shall see, would have disagreed vehemently). And it could well be that Martin had misunderstood the protocol for tourists to be taken on a guided tour of Cologne Cathedral, as diaries and letters home are full of such mix-ups and misapprehensions. Passages such as those quoted above, though, form an important part of the pages of transatlantic travel accounts. As historians of tourism have noted, the process of arriving at a destination may take up almost as much room in the tourist's account of the trip as experiencing the destination itself.[5] Comfortable cabins and dining rooms on board ship reassured these tourists of their class position and privilege, as they either delighted in them or accepted them as an expected component of their trip. Those who grumbled about their absence revealed that they fully expected to be surrounded by the comforts of home (or perhaps even better). More-over, the descriptions of the departure and ocean voyage testify to the centrality of modernity to transatlantic tourism. Witness, for example, Martin's description of the 'thoroughly modern cultural ritual of the dockside farewell' and the extensive photo taking that accompanied it, as well as the collapsing of distance and time represented by, among other things, the eagerly scribbled letters home that went onshore at Rimouski and the telegrams that, for some, might be received or sent during the voyage itself, communications that kept the tourist in touch with developments on both sides of the Atlantic (see figs. 1.1 and 1.2).[6]

People who worked in the tourist and service industry were treated by travel writers and diarists in a number of ways. They might be praised for their local knowledge and diligent assistance, be the target of grumbling for their refusal or inability to provide either, or, simply, become invisible. While such sketches are often amusing, these accounts of the encounters with guides, porters, and waiters are more than just entertaining anecdotes that allow the historian to chuckle at the tourist's expense. They also offer us glimpses of the relationships and structures of power in which tourists were embedded, most notably those of class but also of gender, ethnicity and race, and empire and nation.

Atlantic Crossing

If they set off across the ocean to be educated in history and culture, such thoughts were not uppermost in the mind of these men and women as their steamers pulled out of Quebec City, Halifax, or Manhattan.[7] The furnishings, the weather, and the degree of seasickness endured were the first subjects mentioned in of most letters, diaries,

1.1. The dockside farewell (Harriet Priddis's Diary, 1906, Harriett Priddis Fonds, B4272, J.J. Talman Regional Collection, University of Western Ontario Archives. Photograph reproduced courtesy of the UWO Archives)

CABIN PASSENGERS
PER
ALLAN ROYAL MAIL STEAMSHIP "PARISIAN"
JAMES WYLIE, COMMANDER.

From QUEBEC to LIVERPOOL, 21st May, 1881.

Miss Catherine Abbott
Miss Emma Abbott
Mr. Lewis J. Almon
Mrs. Almon
  and Two Children
Miss Auld
Miss S. C. Bailey
Miss Barnard
Mr. H. R. Beveridge
Mrs. Black
Mr. B. A. Boas
Miss A. Bowes
Miss G. Bowes
Mr. Gordon Brown
Mrs. Brydges
Miss Brydges
Mr. Allan Cameron
Mr. A. F. Cameron
Mr. James Carlyle
Mr. James E. Clark
Prof. J. B. Cherriman
Mrs. Cherriman
Mr. Wm. B. Cogswell
Mrs. Corbett
Mrs. Cotele
Miss Cotele
Mr. James Croil
Mr. M. E. David
Mrs. David
Mr. Rankin Dawson
Mr. Percy Dean
Mrs. Dean
Hon. A. Decosmos, M.P.
Rev. Dr. Dewart
Mrs. Dewart
Mr. Charles E. DeWolf
Mrs. DeWolf
Mr. Doherty
Mr. Jonathan Dorr
Mrs. Dorr
Master Dorr
Mr. A. T. Drummond
Mr. Wm. Eaves
Mrs. Eaves
Master William Eaves
Mr. Evans
Dr. O. F. Fassett
Mrs. Fassett
Miss Mary A. Foster

Miss Sarah H. Foster
Mr. M. H. Gault, M.P.
Mrs. Gault
Miss Florence Gault
Miss Louisa Gault
Miss Ida C. Gibb
Miss A. M. Gibb
Mr. Gibb's
  Infant and Nurse
Mrs. Glasco
Mr. T. P. Glidden
Mrs. Glidden
Mr. Jacques Grenier
Mr. G. W. Grant
Miss Hall
Miss Hartt
Mr. Roland Hazard
Mrs. Hazard
Mr. Holderness
Miss Holderness
Miss James
Mrs. Johnston
Miss Johnston
Mr. Richard Kidston
Mr. Thomas Kinnear
Miss Langlands
Miss Leigh
Mr. H. J. Levetus
Mr. Levy
Mrs. Levy
Mr. T. J. Little
Mrs. Little
Master Edward Little
Master Frank Little
Mr. Long
Miss R. P. Loring
Right Hon. Sir John
  A. Macdonald, K.C.B.
Lady Macdonald
Rev. A. D. McDonald
Mr. Mackay
Miss McAleenan
Dr. McMichael
Mr. W. R. McRae
Mr. A. W. Manning
Mr. Fred. C. Martin
Mrs. Martin
Mr. James Minnes
Mr. Robert Moat

Mrs. Moat
Miss Bella Moat
  and Nurse
Mr. D. Moore
Mrs. Moore
Miss Moore
Mr. Morgan
Mrs. Morgan
Miss Morgan
Mr. Mossop
Mr. J. W. Nelles
Miss Parter
Mr. J. X. Perrault
Mr. H. W. Powis
Mr. P. Price
Dr. R. A. Reeve
Mr. J. F. Robinson
Mr. Rooney
Mr. Brackley Shaw
Mrs. Shaw
Master Howard Shaw
Master Sutherland Shaw
Mrs. Simpson
Miss Simpson
Hon. J. Gregory Smith
Mrs. Smith
Mr. E. C. Smith
Miss Smith
Mr. Edward Smith, Jr.
Mr. Cyril Stanley
Mr. W. A. Sweet
Mr. Tait
Mrs. Tait
Mr. Wm. S. Taylor
Mr. Chas. Thompson
Mrs. Thompson
Master Arthur Thompson
Master Geo. Thompson
Master Bertie Thompson
Master Frank Thompson
Mr. T. M. Thomson
Miss Thomson
Mr. J. T. Vanneck
Dr. Wallace
Mrs. Wallace
Miss Wallace
Colonel C. M. White
Rev. W. A White
Miss Louise N. White

1.2. Cabin passenger list, S.S. *Parisian* (Fred C. Martin Diary, 1881, Fred C. Martin Fonds, 1848–1909, R7742-0-1-E, Library and Archives Canada) and published travelogues. Irene Simmonds, who sailed for Ireland in 1909 on the Cunard Line's *Saxonia*, was delighted to find herself and her husband installed in a fine stateroom, with a large closet, sofa, two big windows, and 'very nice beds.' The ship's dining room was 'elegant and spacious,' the weather was ideal, and the religious service was held on the main deck, itself 'beautifully' decorated with flags.[8] George Pack, a Victoria house decorator who in 1911 travelled to Britain on the Cunard Line's *Franconia* for the coronation of George V, enjoyed the comforts of a cabin fitted with mahogany, a 'splendid' bunk, and curtained portholes; the ship also had a three-hundred-seat dining room, a walnut smoking room, a white-paneled and rose-upholstered ladies' room, and running water in her 'ample' baths and toilets (see figs. 1.3 and 1.4).[9]

By the first decade of the twentieth century, travelling on a Canadian steamship line might be a source of national pride, proof that Canada could boast modes of modern transportation: Canadians were truly part of an international and technologically sophisticated community. In 1906 the *Canadian Magazine* helped its readers to recall that 'not more than five years ago ... a Canadian would almost unclass himself socially if he went to England by a Canadian steamer.' New York had been the preferred port of departure of those with 'social standing and a bank account. Only labouring people, ministers, students, artists and those with a "past"' left from Montreal or Quebec, declared the author of 'The Atlantic Passage,' a piece that appeared in the magazine's column 'Canada for the Canadians: A Department for Business Men.' Now, though, the Allan line's *Victorian* and *Virginian*, along with the Canadian Pacific's *Empress of Ireland* and *Empress of Britain*, had made departures from Quebec, Montreal, Saint John, and Halifax eminently desirable: these ships were 'larger and more commodious,' dredging and improved lighting of the St Lawrence Channel made it an easier passage, and trade with and travel to Europe was fast increasing. 'Canada,' the author was proud to assert, 'is getting big, and every time she adds an inch to her stature, she grows less dependent on the United States.'[10]

Not all travellers had either Simmonds's comforts or the assurance that their travels were part of nation building. James Hall, aboard the SS *Polynesian* in 1878 en route to Britain and the Paris Exposition, reported that the ship struck an iceberg near the Labrador coast and that the impact threw him out of his berth. The next day Hall suffered from seasickness. Although he recovered for the rest of the voyage, he did little but read, as the weather was 'misty and disagreeable.'[11] While

1.3. Catering to the leisured class on the Allan Line (*Canadian Magazine*, March 1907. Reproduction courtesy of the Archives of Ontario)

1.4. Sleeping in style (*Canadian Magazine*, March 1907. Reproduction courtesy of the Archives of Ontario)

a few Canadian tourists travelled first class, the majority went second class. In an attempt to save money, in 1907 George Disbrowe travelled steerage, an experience he found so unpleasant that he went home on a second-class ticket.[12] To be sure, his crossing the ocean in December was partially responsible for Disbrowe's travails: most tourists sailed between May and October.

The dire Atlantic storms that made Mary Leslie's trip so miserable were atypical, but seasickness was an all too common experience. Margaret Thomson of Winnipeg had a few 'touches' of it on her first transatlantic voyage in 1897, although on her subsequent trips in 1898, 1910, and 1914 she either had better luck or a more seasoned stomach.[13] Most letter and diary writers referred to their bouts of seasickness in a matter-of-fact, laconic manner; published travelogues, though, might run to the quasi-operatic. Emily Murphy described how she experienced the 'dolours of the sea':

> The steamer groans, sighs and grumbles in unison with me. I have nothing more to anticipate in this life. My utter lassitude, my complete collapse of body and soul indicated that the limits of human endurance have been reached. The 'large, airy stateroom' becomes a maddening cubicle and I strangle for air. I am in a floating hospital and there are dismal sounds of retching and wailing, of gasping and gurgling, notes of appalling mortal woe that are distressing in the extreme to hear. After awhile the 'contrary winds' abate and I get a sharp appetite, but the very superior stewardess insists on the discipline of renunciation. It saves her trouble; nevertheless it is a good axiom in travel to eat when you can. There is a fortune in store for the person who will write a practical book on 'How to Be Happy Through Travelling.'[14]

Murphy certainly was not a candidate to author such a publication: most of her travel account is decidedly dyspeptic in its tone and attitude.

Seasickness was a highly unpleasant experience, but some passengers endured – and succumbed to – more serious illnesses. Maria Lauder's quasi-fictional narrative of a trip to Britain opens with the death from consumption of Mary, a young Irishwoman who was returning home after finding out that her fiancé (who had previously emigrated to North America) had married during their time apart. Despite the nursing efforts of Aunt Jessie, who was granted permission to move the young woman from steerage to first class, Mary 'was doomed to sleep her last sleep at the bottom of the ocean.'[15] As her prediction of Mary's fate suggests, these 'Notes from My Travel Book' were replete with sentimental imagery, including Aunt Jessie's benevolent 'rescue' of Mary from steerage, the young niece's recitation of her pathetic search for her betrothed, her request that Aunt Jessie send an account of her last words to her mother, and the details of the end of Mary's sorry life. '"Poor mother!" and Mary wept long and bitterly – her last tears *forever!*'[16] Lauder proceeded to describe her consignment to the sea: 'How glorious the sea looked that morning, as the Irish maiden was lowered to rest among the billows and the seaweed! She had passed away in peace, among kind friends God had given her amid strangers, and strong and stern were the judgments against him who had caused Mary's broken heart and early death. It was a solemn, awe-inspiring hour, and all day only a subdued murmur of voices was heard.'[17]

Lauder's use of sentiment as a way of understanding and giving meaning to Mary's narrative helped obscure from her readers the historical developments that underpinned her life, such as the class and colonial relations that necessitated the emigration of young Irish women and men to North America.[18] The very fact that Lauder, and not Mary, was able to recount the latter's distressing tale for the reading public is indicative of the two women's very different positions in the ship's hierarchy, itself a microcosm of the transatlantic worlds of Britain and North America in which some women were confident travellers and others desperate emigrants. Lauder's narrative about Mary's short life and sad end was framed by the vantage point of a tourist who travelled not just across the ocean but also within the life of this young Irishwoman, a life shaped by different configurations of class, ethnic, and gender relations than her own. Yet at least Lauder's sentimental account gave Mary a name, a history, and a moving end. George Pack noted in his diary that on 2 June, he was given some cold cream by a fellow passenger, and 'we had I believe two funerals or so was the common rumour one a girl about twenty the other an infant both were buried at daylight from the third class.'[19]

The deaths of steerage passengers, whether recounted with emotion and detail or in a casual and remote fashion, were not the only moments when the class relations that structured tourists' voyages became apparent. Simmonds, Pack, and Martin travelled in luxurious surroundings, and thus were well aware that stewards and stewardesses could make the difference between a pleasant voyage and a disagreeable one. Yet it was far more common for diary and letter writers *not* to mention the daily presence and labour of the women and men who worked on board ship. Instead, these people featured mostly as special sights and spectacles to be gazed at and commented on, when, for example, passengers from the upper decks were taken on conducted tours of the engine room, a place normally off-limits for passengers. Both men and women participated in this tourism of the ship's depths, which resembled visits to the Paris morgue, explorations of that city's sewers, or journeys through Rome's Catacombs. Emily Murphy and her husband 'climbed down to where the stunning uproar and pulsing thuds of the ship's naked heart upset any preconceived ideas we had on descending. It was a submarine inferno.' She was impressed by the noise of the engines, the glare of the volcanic furnaces, and the stokers, those 'swarthy, half-naked men, with blood-shot eyes.' Earning twenty dollars a month, and working four hours at a stretch, the stokers, she reported, saw 'visitors as their lawful prey, and accordingly, one of them chalked the door-step and we had to pay our footing.' Upon receiving the money, the stoker 'with a lubricous [*sic*] air of grandissimo, made a profound bow and shouted a song for our entertainment. "Oh what care we when on the sea, for weather fair or fine? For toil we must, in smoke and dust, Below the water line."'[20]

Edith Chown, of Kingston, Ontario, travelled to England in 1910 with her suffragist aunt Alice Chown. She found her trip through the engine room 'by far the most interesting experience while on board.' She was as impressed as Murphy by the 'great big hole filled with machinery' that she stared into before descending the iron stairs, her hand protected by a piece of cloth given to her by her guide. In the stoke hold Edith was particularly interested in one of the 'innumerable' machines, a device that turned saltwater into fresh. But unlike Murphy, she saw no display of half-clothed working-class male bodies (if the stokers were shirtless, she did not mention their attire). Instead, she was given a tour of the stokers' living quarters and later confessed that 'your head ached for those poor stokers, standing in that burning heat for so many hours.' At the end of her tour Edith and her companions were allowed to throw some coals into the ship's furnace.[21]

Not all on board went to see their ship's steerage, although as Lauder's account suggests, there were moments when they became aware of its passengers. No one was more acutely conscious of them than George Disbrowe, who blamed the squalid conditions of steerage partly on the presence of 'Dagos and Hunkies,' whom he held responsible for the 'dirty dishes and awful tea and coffee' at breakfast.[22] Disbrowe, as the son of an Anglican canon, was also bothered by his

1.5. Galician steerage passengers, deck of S. S. *Numidian,* 1900 (Photograph by George R. Lighthall, Notman Photographic Archives, McCord Museum, Montreal, MP-1984.44.6.181. Photograph reproduced courtesy of the McCord Museum)

fellow passengers' Sunday card playing and drinking, although he admitted to having had a 'nice evening,' as he had persuaded a young man with a mandolin to play some hymns.[23] Facing a dinner on 22 December that 'was just as bad as breakfast,' Disbrowe fervently wished that he had sailed second class (see fig. 1.5).[24]

Disbrowe's sense of himself as a 'better' type of traveller was shaped by pejorative notions of his fellow-passengers' ethnicity. Canadians who sailed second and first class used perceived national and ethnic distinctions to observe, classify, and judge passengers with whom they shared decks and dining tables. Thomas Langton, of Toronto, endured what for him was a tedious Atlantic voyage in 1888, one with few women and with 'mostly German' men who 'converse in their gullets with one another.'[25] On her voyage Edith Chown noted the presence of Irishmen but also the English, who interested her because 'they all wish and expect to return to Canada.'[26] George Pack had a 'nice talk with a young Yankee lady who is going to Germany to study music also an English girl with whom I played dominoes.'[27] J.E. Wetherell, a school inspector from Strathroy, Ontario, suggested that 'there are travelers – and travelers.' As described in his book, *Over the Sea* (1892), the cast of characters on board the *Nevada* was plentiful: the Chicago merchant who had spent his life building his fortune and was now eagerly anticipating visiting places in Europe 'of which he knows as little as he does of the constellations in the heavens above him'; the 'chronic grumbler' from New England; and the 'jolly fat bachelor from Toronto whose genial countenance, affable manners, and delightful talk make him the most striking figure on board.'[28] As much as he appeared to enjoy pigeonholing his fellow passengers, Wetherell complained that they were the prime detraction from the 'romance of a sea-voyage.' It was necessary to retire to a secluded part of the deck, 'far from the engines, and far too from all distracting human influences' in order to be 'in touch with the spirits of wave and wind and sky.'[29]

Those who commented on other passengers were rarely prodded (or prodded themselves) to reflect on their own baggage of national identities or to consider that, just as they saw others as 'Yankees' and 'Germans,' they in turn might be seen as 'Canadians.' Yet, the 'score of English people' on board Emily Murphy's ship were quite willing to inform her about the meanings of 'Canadian.' While they did not call Canada that 'blawsted colony,' they appeared to accept its depiction by nineteenth-century writer Anna Jameson as a 'small community of fourth-rate, half-educated people, where local politics of the meanest kind engross the men, and petty gossip and household affairs the women.' Furthermore, Canadians were considered bad mannered and gruff, more like the Americans than the British. 'One gentleman pressed the matter rather ... when he said that we had the same nasal monotone and the tiresome habit of braggadocio. In the future he will have absolutely no doubts as to Canadian bluntness, for I told him that Miss Isabella Baird, his countrywoman, had given as the result of many years travel, the interesting decision that while the Americans were *nationally* assumptive, the English were *personally* so.'[30]

Murphy's blunt retort to imperial assumptions about Canada and Canadians *and* her perception that she was being seen through such lenses were exceptionally strong. As we shall see, such matters were no less complicated once these tourists arrived at their respective destinations. Yet while the Atlantic voyage offered opportunities to mark national distinctions and differences, various shipboard experiences brought these men and women together in ways that testify to their shared religion, class, and race. Such might be the case with church services, attended along with the majority of passengers on their deck, or the kinds of leisure activities commonly offered to second-and first-class passengers: lounging in deck chairs; playing deck quoits (in which Pack attempted to instruct the German tourists) and shuffle-board; or frequenting the smoking and music rooms. On his 1894 trip, Montreal banker Edward Greenshields read *Trilby* and listened to a concert one evening, which he judged to be 'usual average, but relieved by the pleasant manner and good style in which Dr de Segundo sang, and played his own accompaniments.'[31] Greenshields was in Europe again in 1906, and 1911, a trip that was perhaps a bit livelier, with a contest staged for the passengers that consisted of two blind-folded men who attempted to hit each other with a paper bat.[32] During his 1913 transatlantic voyage, Greenshields met a 'lady sculptor,' who sketched his portrait although, he confided to his diary, she was not well liked by the 'very agreeable' ladies who shared his table in the ship's dining salon.[33]

There were those who either witnessed or participated in another form of shipboard entertainment, the blackface minstrel show. In his 1878 travelogue, *Eastward Ho!*, writer J.T.P.K. described in some detail the Christy Minstrel performance held on the quarter-deck. It followed an afternoon 'passed in extensive preparation' of rehearsing, putting together costumes, and applying blackface makeup. 'The "end man" was our gallant Colonel in a stand up collar and spotless white shirt. The gentleman with the brown face and our Naval Officer are ladies of brunette complexion dressed in petticoats borrowed from lady passengers. The later prisoner and his counsel, with a good-natured colonist from Halifax City, complete the troop. The performance is patronized by the Bishop and all the passengers are present. Even the Captain is seen to enjoy the fun. Some of the songs were very old, and the conundrums far from being original, but there must be some good influence in the sea air, for everybody laughed heartily, and said that the performance was capital.'[34] On her 1897 trip, Margaret Thomson watched 'a very good minstrel performance last night [held] to celebrate the Queen's birthday.'[35] Travelling to England, in 1887, on the SS *Furnessia* as a member of the Toronto Cricket Club's tour of Britain, George Lindsey recorded that he and his teammates were made up for the 'negro minstrel show' by an actress on board. 'Considering the short time we had for preparation and the limited supply of appliances necessary for such a performance, these minstrels were a success. We took some little trouble with them, and with the valuable assistance of some Harvard and Yale students, capital fellows, managed to keep the audience in good humour for an hour. The stewards put on a show for us.'[36] While perhaps the transatlantic voyage might not offer as many opportunities for crafting white imperial identities as did the passage from Australia to England, the ocean travelled by these steamships nevertheless might be a 'blackface' Atlantic, a space in which white identity was reinforced through this manipulation of stereotypes of 'others' deemed racially and socially inferior.[37]

Leaving behind them, at least for the time being, seasickness and shuffleboard, not to mention inversions of gender and race, Canadian tourists disembarked at Liverpool in various states of mind. 'Land! Land! Land! The joyous cry of land!' wrote Aird Dundas Flavelle, a lumber manufacturer from British Columbia, as his ship entered the Mersey River in July 1900.[38] Not surprisingly, given the travails of his voyage, Disbrowe described his ships arrival with a similar degree of excitement. 'On solid land at last! ... We had dinner – the first clean meal since Montreal.'[39] The amount of bureaucracy and the lack of organization sometimes proved quite vexing. Fred Martin complained that the Liverpool railway porters were very slow in unloading the luggage: 'One of our Railway Porters with a good truck would handle more luggage in half-an-hour than all of them put together.' Furthermore, he found going through customs and getting his luggage onto the same train as himself tiresome, as three porters were involved and all expected tips: 'a little of our Railway Checking system would help this country considerable [*sic*].'[40] Emily Murphy and her family were brought to shore in a tender; much to her annoyance, they were 'transported with an ill-smelling crowd of steerage passengers,' and once the gangplank was lowered, they were 'crushed down by them.' To while away the (considerable) time it took to unload their luggage, they passengers watched a 'confused heap of towzle-headed uncared-for youngsters, balancing on an iron rail which edged the dock. They kept us in a considerable state of nervousness and trepidation, and then considering their acrobatic feats were worthy of monetary reward, extended grubby little digits for pennies and followed us with a fire of appeals.'[41] Not all tourists registered complaints and dissatisfaction. Edith Chown also was taken from her steamship to the docks in a tender, but upon stepping onto land, she was extremely excited and could not quite believe that she was really in England.[42]

Most Canadian tourists spent little time in Liverpool, preferring to head south to London as soon as they could. Gertrude Fleming, on her honeymoon tour of London and Europe in 1891, found her hotel in Liverpool comfortable, but she was 'dying' to get to London. 'I long for my sunny skies,' she confessed, 'and am prepared to take "below zero" in return for this penetrating enveloping dampness!' It did not help that her dinner companions were 'ten lonely and sad-looking people – eating in ... silence at different tables.'[43] Fred Martin stayed overnight in Liverpool at the Adelphi Hotel, a favourite spot with many English-speaking Canadians, and caught the next day's train to London, but not without more grumbling about the British system of handling baggage: 'the greatest difficulty one has in taking a train is not being able to check [one's] luggage. You have to get your porter and watch your luggage till it is put on the luggage rack and the Porter is more intent on watching for his "tip" than he is in looking after the trunks.'[44] Victoria's Ada Pemberton and her sister Sophie landed in Liverpool at 11:30 the morning of 7 May 1897, boarded an 8 o'clock train to Euston 8 May, and attended an Ibsen play that same afternoon.[45]

Porters and Guides

Martin's annoyance with the supposedly venal porter was not just a personal idiosyncrasy. In addition to tutoring anglophone tourists about appropriate cultural and historical sites, travel writers offered advice, both explicit and implicit, on the practicalities of movement through unfamiliar places. Newspapers ran pieces on the obstacles and hazards of overseas travel: instructions about packing, how to cope with seasickness, European customs inspection, and the inconvenience of British train-ticketing practices.[46] A few writers told their readers to be wary of unscrupulous practices, such as European hoteliers' habits of charging guests exorbitant prices for candles.[47] But if there was one topic that travel writers were certain that their audiences needed advice on, at the very least – and at the worst, dire warnings about – it was tipping. Narratives of travel throughout the Mediterranean world and the Middle East were full of descriptions of local residents' demands for 'baksheesh.' As well as alerting prospective visitors of the need to carry spare change, such discussions about tipping contributed to a portrait of countries where begging and importuning substituted for 'honest hard work.'[48] By the 1900s, though, travel writers were beginning to weigh in on the issue of tipping in Britain and Western Europe. Some defended tipping as a voluntary means of achieving good service, while others believed it had an unattractive coercive dimension. The latter camp conceded, however that the practice might assist underpaid waiters, as tips were a well-deserved form of recognition of a waiter's skills and could give them some protection against those confidence men and women who might leave without paying.[49] Some writers tried to sort out matters for women travellers, telling them that when staying in private homes they did not tip male servants, although tips should be offered to staff while travelling on boats and trains. Furthermore, Louise Hayter Birchall advised, English porters were very helpful but 'foreign' ones were far less so, and guides in European countries were likely to cheat the Canadian tourist.[50]

These bits of advice may not have done much to allay tourists' qualms about tipping, for the diaries and letters are full of complaints about rapacious waiters, guides, porters, and railway guards. Travel on the Continent, especially, could be marked by the sight of one outstretched hand after another, straining both wallets and the understanding that many services either were not commodities or had already been paid for in the price of their meal, rail ticket, or hotel room. Many travellers either noted, or complained, about the number of men, women, and children, particularly in Ireland and southern Europe, who wanted to sell them something. Peddling goods, however, was less objectionable: it might even result in the purchase of a quaint or memorable souvenir. Tipping – for those opposed to the practice – seemed to be an exchange in which tourists paid for something that they already were entitled to receive.

English-Canadian tourists occasionally commented on the people who gave them directions, took their luggage, and staffed tourist sites in England and Scotland. In Europe, however, these men, women, and children jostled their way into the tourists' collective and individual consciousness with much greater determination. Enacting the role of the tourist in Paris, Lausanne, or Rome inevitably meant, for better or worse, acknowledging the presence of and engaging with 'the porter,' 'the guide,' and 'the waiter.' These encounters began the moment the Channel steamer landed on the 'other' side of the English Channel. Edith Chown and her aunt Alice went ashore at Ostende, Belgium, where, she wrote in a letter home, 'we had the greatest lot of difficulty making the porter understand that we wanted to leave our luggage in the baggage room for the night. Then he wanted an outrageous price for carrying our valise but we stood firm. I thought he had us for we were foreigners.' Matters improved, though, once they reached their chosen hotel and successfully booked their room for the night.[51] The porter that James Hall engaged in Brussels proved more useful to him and his party. Although they attempted to walk from the train station to their hotel, 'it was fearfully hot and seemed to be such a long way' that, after about a mile's hike, they hired a porter who carried their bags with a strap around his forehead. Hall felt that, even if they were charged 'about three times what a cabman would have cost ... he earned his money.'[52]

Linguistic mix-ups might lie at the root of these complaints and confusion, since only a few anglophone Canadian tourists were fluent enough in French to negotiate with porters and customs officials in that language (and very few had more than rudimentary Italian, if even that). Edith Chown's example hints at the hubbub of landing and subsequent disorientation for the traveller, a state of affairs that was felt more acutely in Mediterranean ports. But if porters were either a hindrance or a help, the guide was even more central to a tourist's ability to be enlightened and entertained. Relationships with guides might be unpredictable and ambivalent, as far as those who hired them were concerned. Irene Simmonds was quite pleased with her guide in Rome: 'a gentleman in every way, knew the whole history of Rome, and explained everything to us, which made our sightseeing very interesting.'[53] Far more common were complaints about guides. Sometimes the problem lay in the sheer volume of information and how it was presented. 'Miss Dick,' who took Harriett Priddis's party around the Coliseum in Rome, in 1906, 'gives such an immense amount of information it is difficult to grasp it and my head is buzzing now.' Unable to take notes, Priddis gave up and tried to just listen and enjoy, 'and I am afraid I forgot.'[54] Mary Bain engaged a guide to show herself and her husband around Florence, but soon found that she regretted her attempt to be educated. After going to at least four churches, the Uffizi Gallery (where she saw 'numerous paintings by the old masters, but it would be impossible, even if I could remember them, to single them all out'), Dante's birthplace, and Michaelangelo's terrace in the space of one day, Bain found herself 'dead tired of our guide, so we paid him and told him we would not need his services any more.'[55] She found it a relief to wake up the next morning 'and know that we could get up when we please and do as we please all day, for we have got rather tired of being trotted around by a guide and lectured to about all sorts of churches and saints and things in which we were not a bit interested.'[56]

Edward Greenshields was most definitely interested in 'churches and saints and things' but not sure that his guide was worth the money. He could be useful, Greenshields wrote in 1906, in getting luggage off the train and securing seats, since 'you must be down at the station very early' in order to get the latter. 'Outside of this, and writing to the hotels securing rooms etc a courier is no use *in countries where you know a little of the language.*'[57] The person in question, Lehuard, was a man, sixty years old, and according to his employer a temperate, reliable, and trustworthy guide, who was 'very accurate about many matters.' Nevertheless, Lehuard was a 'bother and great expense,' and Greenshields did not want him in between train trips, even though he was 'not obtrusive … and although I know he did not like it, he never said anything to us about not being taken everywhere.' Lehuard did accompany Greenshields and his wife Eliza on tours of Naples and Rome, and around some of the Italian lakes, for Greenshields 'did not wish him not to enjoy himself.' Lehuard 'did his work very well, and we are satisfied but feel freer without this portion of our retinue.'[58] However, when the Greenshields returned to Europe five years later, Lehuard met them in Gibraltar and accompanied them through Spain and into France.[59]

As Fred Martin's description of the 'Niagara Falls sharks' in Cologne attests, guides might be not so much tedious as bothersome and grasping. John Mackinnon observed that the tourist who walked around the Alpine glacier of Grindelwald was 'continually waylaid by men and boys importuning to be taken as guides or porters. They seem to have no idea of doing the smallest service without a reward – for a word spoken or finger pointed, a fee is expected.'[60] Margaret Thomson reported that on their way to see the cathedral in Pisa, she and her family had to 'run the gauntlet of cab drivers and guides.'[61] Thomas Langton was never loath to criticize Europeans who provided (or wanted to provide) services to tourists, was determined not to pay them, and tried to avoid hiring guides in both his 1888 and 1906 overseas trips. Instead, he relied on his guidebooks. He discovered though, that guidebooks were not infallible; travelling in Italy was expensive, he confided to his diary, and Baedeker's prices were 'seldom accurate.'[62]

To be sure, this experience did not put Langton off using guidebooks entirely. On his first trip to Europe, he was tempted to bypass Rome. As he reasoned, he had a number of good guidebooks to choose from, a limited amount of time to study them, and he needed to read up on the city 'in order to enjoy it.'[63] He put guidebooks in a hierarchy, having considerable faith in Baedeker, the 'infallible and practical,' but less in John Ruskin, 'the tyrannical and truth tinged,' while both were superior to 'the inaccurate Hare.'[64] When Langton eschewed both guide and guidebook, however, the result was not always successful. Wandering about the streets of Naples, on their second visit, Langton and his wife decided not to hire a guide because they 'knew' the city (although they had been there only once, nineteen years before). On the way back to their hotel they became lost in the 'queerest narrowest dirtiest crowded things they called streets that you can imagine macaroni shops cook shops fruit stands barbers tobacconists. At last TL condescended to ask a policeman and found that he was going all right tho' progress slow – At last we emerged into a delightful street in fact the Via Nationale a block beyond where we wanted to go.'[65]

Friendly policemen might help out in a pinch, but of equal importance in tourists' narratives were the children who, particularly in Italy and other areas of southern Europe, congregated around tourists. In many ways they were the direct opposite of the orphans and foundlings who were the forcus of British philanthropic institutions (whose attractions will be discussed in chapter 6). Unlike such children in Britain, who were secluded and displayed to the public under carefully regulated conditions, European children of the urban working class appeared to have free range of spaces such as street corners and piazzas. Moreover, while British children in institutions symbolized the potential of liberal humanitarian reform to create order and structure, for English-speaking Canadian tourists European child workers disrupted order and appeared to live lives bereft of structure – not to mention soap and water. And, although the eventual fate of orphans and foundlings was to take up a useful trade and become productive members of the British (or transatlantic) working class, European children were already workers in the tourist industry (although, conversely, their greatest fault was their seeming lack of useful employment). One spring day as they were walking down a laneway in Rome, Osla Clouston and her party were accompanied by a 'dirty little Italian boy, who had greeted us at the top of the steps with a demand for money turning cartwheels before us. I may mention here that he got nothing but abuse from us.'[66] In Rome in 1888 Langton and his family found themselves 'greatly pestered with the number of little boys who were desirous of guiding us and we weren't in need of any of the services they could render but we engaged one of them more to keep the others away than for anything else.' Once they had finished with his services, 'we gave him a few coppers but my lord was not pleased and wanted something more.'[67]

Other Canadian tourists reported being more grateful for the services offered on an informal basis. Mary Bain and her husband became 'hopelessly lost' while trying to find La Ponti Rialto in Venice ('immortalized by Shakespeare in *The Merchant of Venice*'), 'so got a couple of little boys to guide us there. And such a maze of streets as we threaded, crossing innumerable small canals and winding about in and out.'[68] Child guides also might entertain and amuse the traveller. In Prague Grace Denison engaged a 'carriage and a very cute little boy for a quiet drive up and down the queer, quaint story-book looking streets.' She was fascinated with his explanation of the citizens' custom of pitching elected representatives who had fallen out of favour from the windows of the town hall: 'on my asking what good, pitching the mayor and aldermen out o windows did, he said he didn't know, but that it *had been done*.'[69]

Children usually offered their services on what appeared to be an informal or ad hoc basis. Religious orders often staffed monasteries and churches and showed tourists around, explaining relics and religious art and architecture; the majority of these guides were men. One such individual showed Langton's party around Rome's St Francis of Assisi Church. Appearing in Langton's account as a bit of a trickster, the 'old beggar of a sacristan was a knowing old boy and earned his francs.' He began by taking the party of Canadians for Italians and then 'tipped us the history' of St Francis's miracles, as they were represented in the church's frescoes, 'with a twinkle in his eye which seemed to say, "you're quite at liberty to believe all this if you like, in my opinion it is all poppycock."' The fellow was delighted, though, when he saw that Langton was preparing to take pictures of the frescoes. He seized Langton's daughter by both shoulders, 'and gave her a fatherly shake of joy exclaiming "Is he going to take it! Bravo!" and then vigorously assisted me to raise the camera to the required height by placing upon the altar (mark you) a footstool, a big service book, and a bible.' Earlier, at lunch, 'the girls did not dare look at him but I enjoyed him hugely. He snuffled, smacked his lips, gulped his soup and wine sonorously, ate with his mouth open, wiped his mouth two big prominent red eyes and his perspiring forehead and head with his napkin, all the while paying strict attention to his food and drawing in his breath with a snort every now and then under pressure of his exertions and generally looking and behaving as much like a pig as a man could do.'[70]

Monks and priests do not always appear as such Rabelaisian figures in these travellers' accounts. At the American monastery in Venice, Fred Martin found the monks to be 'very kind and received us very cordially conveying us all over the monastery.'[71] Harriett Priddis toured Rome's Catacombs guided by a 'nice old bearded Carthusian monk ... who speaks English with a decided accent.'[72] Priddis was a little less comfortable in her encounter with a young priest who gave her directions to the 'Jesuit Church' in Rome. She emerged from touring that church to find him waiting for her on the steps; while walking together, he told her that he was from Sicily and was attending the Roman College 'but was so particular in his inquiries as to where I was stopping, address, etc., that I began to think there was a little too much of the Jesuit about it, so said good-bye. I am rather sorry now, he would have been a good guide for the neighbourhood and was a nice looking musical voiced young fellow.'[73]

The majority of the guides, whether formally hired or picked up spontaneously, were men. Occasionally, however, Canadian tourists encountered European women in this capacity. The 'very bent but active old woman' who showed Langton and his wife around a church near Ferrara was a far cry from his winking and snuffling sacristan. When she found some of the locks difficult to turn and Langton suggested the problem was 'antico,' 'my humour met with an expected riposte, "no signor é modorno ... sous antica." I suggested she was juvenility itself when she with great emphasis and apparent pride informed us that she had ninety years, and barring her good wind for stairs and historical exposition she looked every year of it. She apologized for not showing us the dungeons by saying that it was not safe either for ninety years or for ladies dressed in white blouses.'[74]

As well as hiring guides in particular cities and sites, tourists engaged the services of Cook's, sometimes to forward luggage and mail and sometimes for their guided tours. Priddis used Thomas Cook's travel agency to help structure her tours of Europe. She did not, however, always stay with the group, instead leaving and rejoining it as it suited her. Sometimes she found them an acute source of annoyance when, for example, they kept her waiting at hotels and railway stations. 'Do not like waiting around anywhere and particularly dislike posing as Cook's advertisement,' she wrote of her stop at Brussels.[75] 'Though convenient, Cook's neither cheap nor interesting,' she wrote in Waterloo, where her group boarded a third-class railcar for Paris. Priddis said goodbye here to her tour conductor and apologized for being a 'great nuisance, with her erratic habits. He said, not at all, he had enjoyed my company very much, I was a variety and quite an inspiration to the party with my enthusiasm. He had seldom enjoyed a trip more, the party was not too large and all liberal and intelligent. They say he conducted the Duchess of Battenburg through Egypt. He is a Syrian and polite.'[76] Harriett Priddis's low regard for Cook's was not raised in Paris, where she visited its main office: 'an immense place. The American voice predominates. Too busy to be very attentive, I much prefer American Express.'[77] Like a number of her fellow Canadians, despite her use of Cook's, Priddis also displayed a degree of 'anti-tourist' snobbery towards the agency. While she was watching the weavers at the tapestry works in Gobelin, a party of over forty 'Cook's trippers' came in and stayed for less than ten minutes. In contrast, Priddis was at the factory for more than two hours and confessed that she left still not understanding the process.[78] Her scorn for Cook's intensified when her glasses, lost somewhere in mid-Europe, were sent on by the German hotel which she had contacted herself – Cook's, she wrote, was of no help.[79]

In addition to porters and guides, English-Canadian tourists encountered a wide range of men, women, and children who offered them other services and goods. Encounters with cab drivers were slightly less intimate than those with guides, nevertheless the cabbies might amuse (as in Grace Denison's account) but, more often, provoke. In Paris George Pack and his party searched for the 'Irish cab driver' previously hired by a friend but were unable to find him: 'we did make an exhibition of ourselves by trying to get another in French to understand us finally we got a couple of girls speaking in English to help us and we got away.'[80] James Hall and his party missed their steamer at Lake Lucerne, but 'after a few hearty abuses at our driver who took them with stolid German indifference we made the best of it by having something to eat.'[81] Neapolitan cab drivers caused Thomas Langton to be 'in a perpetual condition of boiling over in imperfect Italian at cab-men beggars hotel porters shopkeepers peddlers and all the other vari-eties aforesaid ... Twice recently having bundled the girls into the only possible cab, the hotel being two miles away, I have begun to bargain with the cabman and his terms (three times his fare) not being satisfac-tory I have descended both times and ordered them all out whereupon the cabman and I have generally compromised upon about double his proper fare.'[82] Langton did not specify what that was or how he calcu-lated it; the fare may have been suggested by his guidebooks.

Even when they were not concerned about being cheated or over-charged by drivers, English-Canadian tourists found their driving too aggressive and a touch foolhardy. Cab drivers in Florence perplexed Edward Greenshields: 'the use the drivers here, and elsewhere in Italy, make of their whips, cracking them when they turn corners into narrow streets, and using them as signals, and the way they use their brakes on the carriages is peculiar ... The street cars do not go at the rate they do with us. It is the cabs the pedestrians are afraid of.'[83] George Pack noted that cabbies in Florence had the same 'habit as at Marseilles, but not quite so bad. That is everlastingly cracking their whips.'[84] The cab driv-ers of France and Italy elicited far less concern and sympathy, however, than did their counterparts in London; after watching the drivers 'batter-ing' the horses' heads at their drinking fountain in Paris, Pack concluded that 'the men are generally cruel here.'[85]

This type of humanitarian concern about the suffering of animals, while undoubtedly sincere, was rarely extended to the people who made their living from tourism. Like the sellers of poteen and souve-nirs in Ireland (who will be discussed in chapter 4), Canadians did not exactly welcome individuals who offered them tourist goods in Europe. In addition to the men and boys clamouring for work as guides in the Alps, John Mackinnon told his readers that 'natives here are wonderfully keen for business – even in pouring rain girls were stationed along the track' trying to sell pictures, wood sculptures, ber-ries, and trinkets. Yet to make matters worse (and blurring the bound-aries between the various kinds of activities involved), 'beggars, lame, halt, and variously afflicted, sat from morn till night (rain or shine) at their dreary posts.'[86] In Capri's Blue Grotto, Thomas Langton noted that 'every little boy we meet is dying (or being killed) of hunger and wants a soldo "per accore de Dio." Some of the little beggars look as if they had just wiped their mouths after macaroni.'[87]

To be sure, not everyone was as hostile or exasperated by vendors of goods as was Langton. Emily Murphy reported that at German train stations 'fleshy, broad-faced women thronged the car-windows to sell us ripe mulberries, scones, cheese, hard-boiled eggs and cherries,' an observation that lacked her usual irritation with the tourist economy and the people who worked in it.[88] One could grow accustomed (or at least resigned) to being importuned to buy souvenirs. On her boat ride to Capri Irene Simmonds was surrounded by men selling coral beads and other jewelry, whom she admitted were 'experts at their trade, and made people buy, if only to get rid of them.'[89] On his trip to Monte Cristo Island George Pack wrote resignedly that 'we had the usual lot of peddlers selling cards spectacles field glasses and opera glasses,' as well as 'a couple of young chaps playing fiddles then they go around and take up a collection.'[90] Clara Bowslaugh, of Grimsby, Ontario, did not mind being approached by a man 'of the working type' who visited her party's carriage on the train for Pompeii. 'We soon found he was a peddler and provided ourselves with lead pencils and penholders carved in lava – with each a guide book of Pompeii ... our friend left us before we arrived in Pompeii to ply his trade on a train on another route.'[91]

In addition to the 'peddlers' and vendors, who gathered at sites where tourists congregated, these travellers encountered men (and a few women) who offered goods and services in what, to the former, was a more conventional manner. Despite being pressed for time, James Hall decided to have a shave between seeing Aix-la-Chapelle and catching the train to Brussels; after all, he wrote in his diary, it was Sunday and a 'likely man' presented himself and his services. 'I have never ceased to regret it,' he reflected, ' not because it hurt so much more than usual but it took up valuable time and a continental shave is as uncomfortable a thing as can be well imagined': clothed in his nightshirt and seated in a low-backed chair with no head support, the operator wielding a dull razor and stropping it on his boot or hand, and 'a small towel under your chin is all that is considered necessary and they don't even wipe off the lather after they are done.'[92] Pack had fewer complaints about his visit to a Roman barber, although he did observe that 'all barbers in this country use curling tongs for the moustache.'[93]

Most of these tourists' contact with such workers took place by the latter 'presenting themselves' on an ad hoc and for a short-term basis (they also might be arranged through their hotel). Travellers who took their children with them also might engage governesses and nurses from the local population.[94] Emily Murphy was less than pleased with the nursemaid she hired for her daughter. 'We call her Gretchen,' she told her readers, 'and she is the most sullen savage in Germany. My attempts at making her understand what I require of her are as ludicrous as they are useless.' Despite Murphy's efforts to communicate in German and through 'pantomime,' 'Gretchen' was unable (or, Murphy hinted, refused) to understand her employer's instructions, on one occasion eating up a restaurant dinner that Murphy had asked her to fetch back to their lodgings for her own consumption.[95]

Murphy's annoyance with Gretchen aside, other tourists depicted their dealings with workers in the service industry as comical – at least in their eyes – interludes that broke up the serious business of appreciating culture and history. When Margaret Thomson tried to have her clothes laundered in Paris, as she confused the terms for whitening and alteration and was unable 'to make the maid understand.'[96] (Thomson did not write that she herself was unable to find the right vocabulary). When they did not provide comic relief, such encounters generally were just irritating and frustrating. Thomson observed on her next trip that Venice's 'shopkeepers or rather the men they keep at the doors and on the streets and the guides are a dreadful nuisance.'[97] Yet guides and shopkeepers might become more than just a 'dreadful nuisance.' At her hotel in Naples, Mary Bain 'trotted across the street to have a peep at some stores which I could see from my bedroom window but was so besieged by cab-drivers and fairly pulled into one little dark store after filled with Italian men, that I became terrified, got out of the store as fast as I could and hied me home with the determination not to be caught out alone in an Italian city, unless they are different from this one.'[98]

Bain's terror at being surrounded by unfamiliar men, who spoke to her in a language she did not understand and who seemed intent on keeping her in their 'dark little stores,' was in all likelihood sincerely felt. However, her observation that the men were 'Italian' also suggests an animosity and suspicion based on their gender and ethnicity. (Her account of this incident, with its emphasis on foreign men physically besieging Canadian womanhood also suggests that Bain might well have been influenced by either white-slave or captivity narratives, or possibly both). Bain's is one of the very few accounts that relates such overt fear of 'foreign men' in the European context. Other Canadian tourists treated the guides and vendors as mere annoyances and threats only to their peaceful enjoyment of tourist sites, however, it is probably no accident that Bain experienced such emotions in Naples. Anglophone Canadian tourists often observed that Naples and the Neapolitans had more in common with northern African and Middle Eastern cities and people than with those of northern Italy or the rest of Europe. It was not just Thomas Langton who felt that Neapolitan cab drivers, guides, and vendors were ubiquitous, although he was by far the most exasperated by their presence. Entering the city after a trip to Capri to see its Blue Grotto, Clara Bowslaugh and her party 'were much amused at the way Reverend S. cleared the way when we were landing – we were besieged by large and small fry trying to force our luggage out of our hands but Brother S. had suffered from mal-de-mer and was in no very gentle mood – and rapidly scattered the *would-be* porters.'[99] Irene Simmonds, who generally enjoyed her encounters with local residents, observed on her way to Gibraltar that 'I am not very sorry to leave Naples. The scenery is just delightful, but the people are not very nice, their main object seems to be to fleece every stranger they see.'[100]

Canadian travellers' discomfort with the tourist economy in Naples could be attributed to the number of people perceived to be begging, an activity that (as we will see) met with their disapproval in Ireland. Souvenir selling and offering services might have been perceived as being only one step from begging. Based on middle-class notions of the importance of 'honest labour,' and bolstered by a Protestantism that had little room for the holy mendicant, anglophone Canadian tourists' disapproval was not just limited to Italy. However, the frequency of their comments about Italy and begging implies that they supposed that more of these, to their minds, economically unproductive and morally suspect activities went on in that country. 'Italy certainly takes first place for beggars,' Simmonds told her readers after describing her trip to Pompeii, an observation that many of her fellow tourists would have echoed.[101]

Canadian tourists' observations about cab drivers and guides were underpinned by assumptions concerning class and ethnicity, the superiority of their own versus the inferiority of the latter. There is another important dimension of their relationship: that of the tourist's reliance on these workers. I would caution that historians must be extremely careful to not overlook the unequal distribution of power that shaped these interactions. As Tina Loo has pointed out, in the context of wild-game hunting in western Canada during this same period, white, middle-class, urban men viewed the guides on whom they depended with a mixture of both envy and condescension, an attitude that was even more pronounced when the guide was Aboriginal. However, as Loo has argued, some rural and Aboriginal men were able to take advantage of this situation and make a living as guides by capitalizing on the 'authenticity that had been claimed for them.'[102] Similar dynamics, I believe, were at work here, although whether European and, as we shall see, Irish guides were seen as truly 'authentic' was at times doubtful. Moreover, the sources used here only hint of the workers' socioeconomic dependence on foreign tourists, let alone suggest anything of the ways in which their dependence might have figured in the vendors and shopkeepers' own subjectivities. Nevertheless, the frequency with which vendors and shopkeepers appear in these accounts, both published and unpublished, indicates that a number of these travellers needed the local knowledge and linguistic skills of their drivers and guides. A knowledgeable and amusing guide or driver might make a great deal of difference to the tourist's ability to 'know' and enjoy a landscape: no small matter given that these were the fundamental reasons for these Canadians' travel to Britain and Europe in the first place.

Another dimension of these tourists' power was their capacity to represent these men and women for either a reading audience or for themselves in their diaries, to create 'the Neapolitan cab driver' or 'the Roman guide' as characters in their travelogues. Such a capacity might have been important in the tourists' own sense of themselves as knowledgeable, cultured, 'travelling subjects': as men and women with special and sophisticated understanding of Europe because of their proven abilities to have their desires met and needs satisfied in their negotiations with workers in the tourist industry. At the very least, these writers could have the satisfaction of warning others about the difficulties that such individuals might present. Without the tourist workers, a crucial dimension of the tourist's own identity – whether as a cultured being or as someone with important lessons to impart back home – was missing.

Furthermore, most of these Canadian tourists would get no closer to the residents of the countries that they visited – especially in Europe – than guides, porters, waiters, and cab drivers. It is possible, then, to see the guide and his fellow-workers as a kind of synecdoche in tourists' writings, a sector of European societies that stood in for the whole. Some of the annoyance *and* fascination that the people in the tourist industry sparked, time and time again, thus might be representative of the tourists' attitudes towards those nations which, on the one hand, housed sites and artefacts that they had been told on good authority were the very basis of civilization, yet which at times also insisted on maintaining social habits and structures that appeared to the tourists to be the antithesis of civilized society. The people who conveyed them to and showed them around those all-important museums, cathedrals, and galleries may well have embodied the class- and race-based ambivalence that these English Canadians felt about Europe and Europeans: Could such societies be proper custodians of the cultural riches that drew Canadians to them?

Amusing and by turns exasperating workers in the tourist industry were not, however, what had prompted these departures from Quebec City or Halifax. English-Canadian tourists went to view historic sites and landscapes, to test the reality of castles and cathedrals against the representations they had so diligently studied at home. One of the first places in which they sought them out was Scotland, where landscape and history came together in ways both poignant and disturbing.

2 The Landscape of History and Empire, Part 1: Scotland

For young people, fresh from school or college, nothing will fix more firmly in their minds what they have studied than travel in the countries and cities of which they have heretofore only read. History, which to many is a tiresome subject, becomes full of vital interest when we visit the scenes of stirring creation in olden times. How great is the difference, for example, between reading an account in our History of some famous battle which decided, perhaps the fate of a nation, standing on the scene of that battle. In the first place, interest may be aroused, but of a vague, impersonal sort. In the second we can almost conjure up the scene – the opposing armies, the strife, the result.[1]

'The Advantages of Travel' (1910)

The anonymous author of 'The Advantages of Travel' would have been pleased with her fellow Canadians' understandings of the landscapes through which they travelled. While these travellers conceived of tourism in Britain and Europe as a multifaceted experience, one that ranged from the healthful properties of walking in the Swiss Alps to the no less beneficial effects of shopping in London, Paris, and Venice, perhaps their most commonly reiterated desire was to see the past made manifest in specific sites and landscapes. As chapter 7 will demonstrate, such landscapes were not confined to the British Isles: in Europe, city and countryside might be replete with political, social, and cultural history. Yet for this group of anglophone Canadians tourists, British cities, towns, villages, and rural areas evoked a history with particular and specific meanings, ones intertwined with questions of national identity and, for some, membership in an 'imperial' family. But familial membership was not without its complexities or moments of ambivalence, and the category of 'imperial' might have its own internal contradictions. This was especially the case with Scotland, a landscape that had witnessed romance and tragedy, progress and disaster, its cities and countryside haunted by the ghosts of those who enjoyed great achievements and those who suffered terrible catastrophes.

Seen as both an integral part of Britain and as a region with its own distinct historical landscape, Scotland offered moral lessons and cultural treats that might be found in Glasgow, Edinburgh, the Highlands, Sir Walter Scott's 'castle' at Abbotsford, and Robert Burns's cottage at Ayr. English-speaking Canadians were by no means the first tourists to seek out these sites; indeed, by the late nineteenth century they were well-established components of Scotland's tourist economy. As historian Alastair J. Durie argues, middle-class tourists had been arriving in Scotland in increasingly large numbers since the early nineteenth century: so much so that by this period the economies of areas such as the Highlands, the Trossachs, the Borders, and the Clyde were heavily dependent on the tourist trade.[2] Drawn first by Sir Walter Scott's reinventions of the landscape, then by Queen Victoria's love of the Highlands and Sir Edwin Landseer's paintings of Balmoral, by the mid-nineteenth century tourists could find their way around Scotland via a fairly extensive network of rail and lake steamers (a far cry from the area's rough patchwork of roads traversed by eighteenth-century visitors).[3] Landscape photography in illustrated journals, souvenir views, lantern slides, and stereoscopic photos helped to advertise Scottish scenery, as did the numerous official guides published by the railway lines and sold in England, especially in London.[4] By 1914 five major rail companies covered most of Scotland, and between 1840 and 1900, 190 hotels were built in the Highlands to accommodate visitors from the rest of Britain, Europe, and the United States.[5]

As he did elsewhere in Britain and Europe, Thomas Cook played his part in organizing the Scottish landscape for the tourist's appreciative gaze. Cook began to run trips to Scotland in 1846, and in 1873, his 'First Educational Tour of Britain and Europe' took 150 American schoolteachers and ministers through Glasgow, the Trossachs, Edinburgh, and Abbotsford, an event that helped inspire the overseas travels of a number of student groups from the United States to Scotland.[6] Anglophone Canadians thus inherited a social and physical infrastructure, cultural maps, and modes of seeing Scotland, although that did not mean that they merely, or only, followed these routes unquestioningly. While historians of Scottish tourism argue that by the late nineteenth century Scott and Burns were somewhat less popular as a means of imagining Scotland for British and European tourists, this was not the case, as we shall see, for English-speaking Canadians overseas.[7]

Few of these tourists participated in the favourite 'Scottish' pastimes of the late Victorian and Edwardian English aristocracy and upper-middle class: hunting, fishing, golf, and mountaineering. The reasons are not hard to imagine. For one, by the late nineteenth century such recreations were available much closer to home and thus probably much more affordable and accessible than they would have been in Scotland.[8] An exception was Edward Greenshields, who with his family, rented rooms in a waterfront lodging house at Dunoon. The view was lovely, but the family had to overcome a number of drawbacks: the beach was pebbly and offered little opportunity for comfortable bathing; moreover, 'Eliza [his wife] got a great shock last night after dinner to find that lodgers here bring all the provisions, and that the landlady provides nothing, and does not order anything wanted, but attends to the cooking ... We expected to have our meals arranged for us as in London lodgings, and just say what we liked each morning. This Scotch plan means regular housekeeping.'[9] Once they had bought provisions, however, and got over their first 'Scotch Sunday ... perhaps rather depressing,' the family adjusted nicely; they spent their time sailing, driving, and enjoying the views around the lochs.[10] The West Highland rail trip to Anvelar and Tarbet gave Greenshields a vantage point 'quite like a view of fairy land ... one beauty after another in a long panorama.'[11] When Greenshields returned to Scotland fifteen years later, he was chauffeured around the lochs by an intelligent, bespectacled young man, who 'looked like a schoolteacher.' Concerned mostly with the scenery and its history, Greenshields was less impressed with his fellow hotel guests. Although pleasant, they all were anglers: 'all about fish, fish, fish, big fish and little fish. Not another subject mentioned even,' he grumbled in his diary.[12]

Glasgow and Edinburgh: Modernity and History

Urban centres such as Glasgow and Edinburgh, with their industrial and commercial landscapes, piqued the curiosity of Canadian travellers. Those who disembarked at Glasgow described a variety of impressions that ranged from an appreciation of the surroundings and streetscape to horror at the pollution and poverty. W.C. Caldwell, a politician from the Ontario riding of Lanark North, enjoyed the scenery, as he sailed up the Clyde in July 1874. He observed that Glasgow's streets were 'wide and clean, a great deal of business is done and the shops look particularly well to a Canadian.' Nevertheless, he wondered at 'the great number of bare-footed, bare-headed women who poorly clad, throng the places and are in even fewer number on some of the principal streets.'[13] Returning to Glasgow a few weeks later, Caldwell watched the city's fire company extinguish a blaze in a house near his hotel and 'was not impressed by the way the firemen handled themselves. Went to the theatre in the evening. Poor affair.'[14]

William F. Munro, in Scotland in 1881 as an emigration agent for the Canada North West Land Company, was unable to see much of anything. Landing in January, Munro told his wife, Georgina, that 'the last three days have been densely foggy, they looked like days of doom, the dim gas light in every house, and the air so thick as to feel like smoke in the eyes.'[15] James Elgin Wetherell found Glasgow a city of 'smoke and turmoil, furnishing but few attractions to the tourist' but allowed that George Square, Scott's column, the monuments to David Livingstone, James Watt, and Robert Burns, and the cathedral were worth seeing. All in all, however,

> a visitor to Glasgow from across the sea whose advent occurs in Exhibition Week will see Old World life in some of its most sinister aspects. If he take a walk up Argyle Street at half-past nine in the evening – the twilight hour in July – he must be prepared to have his sensibilities continually shocked by horrible street brawls and harrowing scenes of poverty and sin. Throngs of drunken men, hundreds of half-clad women hurrying over the stones with bare and bleeding feet, scores of little children even at this late hour of the evening wandering aimlessly or crying in anxious quest – these are the pitiable creatures that our boasted civilization has failed to civilize, – and that too in a land where religion and education and philanthropy have reached [the] high-water mark. O these clamant social disorders of this nineteenth century! What beneficent angel from the merciful skies will bring the perfect panacea? Must patience have her perfect work in the slow evolution of better things, or is the great world soon to 'spin down the ringing grooves of change?'[16]

Wetherell was happy to flee from Glasgow's present troubles and future calamities to the Scottish countryside, where he fortified himself (and his readers) with the landscapes and stirring pasts of Robert Burns and Sir Walter Scott.

In contrast, Clara Bowslaugh, on a tour of Britain and Europe as a member of Methodist minister W.H. Withrow's party, described Glasgow as a city that combined a dignified and important past, marked by the presence of figures who had contributed to important political, scientific, and cultural developments. In her estimation, Glasgow was a 'beautiful' city, with its monuments to James Watt, Sir Walter Scott, and Sir Robert Peel; it had seen the birthplace of the steam engine and was home to a university, museum, Belgravia Ladies' College, and the Royal Exchange, not to mention important churches.[17] Irene Simmonds held similar opinions of Glasgow and was glad that a 'City Official' took her and her husband on a tour, believing that 'if we had been alone we would have missed a great deal.'[18] (She did think, however, that the city's stores did not measure up to London's). Possibly the comforts of the Station Hotel St Enoch shaped Simmonds's favourable assessment, as she found it to be a 'very swell place,' their room 'beautiful [with] elegant furniture upholstered in plush, beautiful mirrors and the softest carpets.'[19] And although Fred Martin reported that Glasgow as a city had 'little to interest a tourist' because it was a 'great shipbuilding and manufacturing city,' he undercut this evaluation with a list of all the sights that, as a tourist, he had explored and enjoyed: the historic cathedral, the museum, John Knox's monument, the university, fine shops, and the beautiful west end park.[20] Even as tourists adopted ironic attitudes of knowingness, they were not always aware of the contradictions between their critical examinations of the sites they visited and the practices in which they were embedded – and to which they contributed.

After a visit to Glasgow, tours of Scotland frequently proceeded to Edinburgh; that 'modern Athens' attracted Canadian visitors for various reasons.[21] Eleanor Garrard Watson, from Port Alberni, British Columbia, visited Edinburgh in 1892 en route to the Lake District. She stayed with friends in the city's southern Morningside district and toured the castle, the Law Courts, the National Gallery, the Scottish Parliament, and the university. Her brother Kenneth Garrard took her around Fettes' College, where he had been a student for six years. With Kenneth acting as guide Eleanor probably saw a somewhat different side of the university than did the tourists taken on official tours. She viewed the 'remnants of last night's "spree" … kettles cups and plates strawberry baskets etc strewn about,' looked out the windows where 'lovely visions of the Leith were obtained. We envied the boys this

beautiful field, swimming-bath and gymnasium, more than anything.'[22]
She was thrilled to watch 'Capping Day,' held in the university's Synod
Hall. The place was packed, and it was a 'very fine sight to see the fine-
looking professors and the students in their caps and gowns with their
various coloured hoods ... There were a good many black men and foreigners "capped" some as M.B.C.M. others taking law degrees etc.'[23]
Other tours promoted the city's reputation as the centre of the Scottish
Enlightenment: tourists wandered around the university, particularly
its medical school, saw the Law Courts, and visited the Parliament
Building.[24] Clara Bowslaugh reported that, among the many places she
had visited she had seen the Edinburgh Free Library (with its inscription 'let there be light'), Darwin's house, Charlotte Square (home to a
number of physicians), and the monument to the philanthropic
Catharine St Clair, 'the only one put up to a lady.'[25]

Edinburgh's history of progress continued in a modern, commercial
form. The city might not have held the broad range of attractions that
London did; nevertheless, Canadian visitors enjoyed strolling its
major streets and exploring its stores. Fred Martin judged the Princes
Street Gardens and promenade to be 'very fine,' so too, the shops. He
did observe, though, write that 'the Hotel Royal is without exception
the worst managed of any house I was put up at – great want of attendants and very poor meals wretchedly served – and it struck me the
fault was in trying to run it with very few servants.'[26] Margaret Thomson,
perhaps because she stayed with relatives and not at the badly run
Royal, paid many trips to the city and spent considerable time there
shopping, visiting art exhibits, attending the theatre, and seeing family and friends.[27] At an Edinburgh bicycle shop, in June 1897, she
'hired a wheel' and proceeded to tour the surrounding countryside.[28]
Although it was hard going up the many hills, and pushing was a last
resort ('anything but easy pushing a Scotch wheel'[29]) Thomson preferred the physical rigours of her bicycle trips to taking Edinburgh's
subway, a 'nasty smelling thing.'[30] Her poor opinion of it was confirmed when she took it to get home a few days later and 'heard a man
describe the subway as expeditious but odourous.'[31] Feminist historians have pointed to the freedom that the bicycle offered from
gender-based restrictions on middle-class women's movements (not
to mention the gendered fears and concerns it aroused in some quarters), but Thomson also seems to have embraced her 'wheel' because
of the freedom it offered her from proximity to people she perceived to
be social inferiors.[32]

Like Eleanor Watson, Margaret Thomson was reminded of the presence of the imperial links that tied Scotland to a wider world. Returning to Edinburgh with her friends after a drive to Abbotsford, she visited the 'manse' where they met a 'Miss N who had four little African children with her one of them a little princess, Alice.' According to Miss N, Alice had 'caused a tribal war' and been cast out of her tribe, lying out in the open for five days before being found by a 'Miss P.' 'The other three were older, one of a pair of twins. One of the twins is always thrown out.'[33] On her return visit to Edinburgh, Thomson attended a production of A Midsummer Night's Dream ('splendid in every way'), made a social call during which she met two young men from the Transvaal, and attended a missionary meeting at Broughton Place, where she listened to addresses from missionaries on leave from Africa and China and heard 'of the "Canadians."'[34] For her part, Clara Bowslaugh reported in her diary that at St Giles she had spotted the Lord Provost of Scotland, accompanied by two 'Indian princes.'[35]

Edinburgh was attractive for more than its imperial modernity. It offered tourists opportunities to reflect on aspects of Britain's past through the lens of Scottish history, a history that by turns could be amusing, inspiring, and sometimes deeply troubling. During a service at St Giles dedicated to soldiers, Watson thought it 'very funny to think we were in the very place where Jennie Geddes threw her stool at John Knox; what an excitement it must have caused!'[36] The repetition of this anecdote in a number of tourists' diaries and letters suggests that it featured prominently in the cathedral's folklore[37] but it also functioned as comic relief in the city's historical landscape that offered little else in the way of mirth. Viewing historic sites in Edinburgh and its environs was often a serious matter for these tourists, one that involved weighty cultural, religious, and political affairs. Knox's home and grave, Scott's monument, Roslyn Chapel, Edinburgh Castle – all evoked a distinctive identity for Scotland, just as Canterbury Cathedral, Shakespeare's home, and Westminster Abbey helped make up the meanings of 'England.'[38] For this group of Canadians ties to Scotland, its landscape, culture, and history, might be as integral a part of 'Britishness' as English identity was, although sorting out the tensions of England's colonial relationship to Scotland was a task very few attempted.[39]

The history evoked by these places was a moving and romantic narrative, one that stimulated passion and excitement. After touring a number of the historic sites of Edinburgh (as well as visiting Inverary Castle, Loch Lomond, Stirling Castle, Bannockburn, and the Wallace

Monument), Irene Simmonds attended a production of *Rob Roy* at one of the city's theatres.[40] It was 'simply grand,' she told her readers, with the actors in 'Highland' costume, a large orchestra, and a sword dance. 'It was splendid, and stirred up every drop of Scotch blood that was in me. Rob Roy was a great tall strong looking man, just what a chieftain should be, and Ellen was all that could be desired as a chieftain's wife.'[41] But not everyone was able to perform 'Scottishness' quite so successfully. George Lindsey's cricket team spent an evening of music and dancing with their Scottish rivals and the latter tried to teach the Canadians the Highland Fling. 'One might as well expect to master the Indian war-dance,' he observed ruefully, 'even Terpsichore, we'll wager, couldn't manage it; we tried but failed.'[42]

George Pack toured the castle, stopping to talk to a 'soldier caretaker.' He approached Scottish history in an even less reverential manner, as it appeared. The solider was cleaning a helmet in the castle's collection of military artefacts, 'and I asked his permission to put it on and on it was,' Pack gleefully recorded in his diary.[43] Pack was one of a minority of tourists who refused to obey strictures about the separation of past and present and questioned the authority of the officials in charge of museums and other historical sites. Such a group insisted on asking bothersome questions of tour guides, wanted to handle artefacts, and attempted to assert their contemporary mastery over the past (by, for example, sitting on thrones or in other ceremonial chairs).[44] Although appreciative of the Scottish energy and enterprise that he found displayed along the banks of the Clyde, and the lovely scenery of the Lochs and Trossachs while en route to Edinburgh, 'A New Brunswicker Abroad' mocked what appeared to be the prescribed nature of tourism at certain Edinburgh sites. 'Everyone is expected to go into ecstasies' at the panoramic sight at Arthur's Seat, he told his readers, and one is also expected to 'strike an attitude, draw a long breath and exhaust himself in meaningless platitudes' as he is escorted through Mary Stuart's apartments (her story being well known).[45]

Yet a stroll through Edinburgh's 'most compelling' area – the Canongate, High Street, and Castle Hill – left the 'New Brunswicker' in no doubt about the significance of the city's past to its present. Despite the 'fine residences and its beautifully laid out streets, and its evidence of wealth and culture; and all the flow and activity of its bustling life,' the writer was unable to shake the pervasive 'connections and associations' with the past. High buildings looked down at the 'active present' in 'solemn mockery' and 'over-shadowed by the traditions of the past, the active life of today, as it throbs and beats about the relics of bygone ages, renders life here more than usually impressive.' Even while 'A New Brunswicker' lamented the 'base purposes' that had 'degraded' those buildings that once housed 'nobility and wealth,' leaving them presenting scenes of 'filth and sqalour,' he could not completely erase the 'attractions of that gay life that ebbed and flowed through these narrow and winding streets.' Those same streets had been the setting in which the Pretender had been welcomed by the people of Edinburgh, and they had witnessed the 'anguish' that accompanied the news of his defeat at Culloden.[46]

The Scots' past was anything but a light-hearted affair. Leaving aside for the moment William Wallace, the Jacobite uprising in 1745, and the Highland Clearances, the history of Edinburgh was full of not just tragedies but also cruelty and brutality. Holyrood Castle was perhaps the most evocative of such narratives. Fred Martin found Mary Stuart's apartments 'the most interesting in the palace and [they] remain to some extent in the same state as when first occupied by the unhappy Princess.' He visited the exact spot where the 'conspirators' had found David Rizzio, the Queen's Italian secretary, and dragged him away to be stabbed to death.[47] J.E. Wetherell declared that 'Mary Queen of Scots must always be the central figure in all the descriptions of Holyrood.' He was moved to find that her apartments were in 'nearly the same condition' as when she had lived in them and noted the 'vestibule with dark stains supposedly of Rizzio's blood,' the audience chamber with its 'ancient and decaying tapestry,' and the old chairs 'adorned with rich embroidery.'[48] Montreal financier Edward Greenshields examined Darnley and Mary Stuart's small rooms and private staircase at Holyrood, declaring them 'insignificant as they are but full of history.'[49] Although Holyrood was not directly implicated in Mary Stuart's death, those who wrote about seeing Holyrood could not but have been well aware of her sorry fate.

Holyrood was not the only place in Edinburgh that evoked a past shaped by violence. On a walk through Canongate, Clara Bowslaugh saw Moray House, which, although a teachers' training college in 1897, had housed Oliver Cromwell in 1648. From its balcony the newlyweds Lord Lorne and Lady Mary Stuart had watched the Marquis of Montrose ride to his execution, but eleven years later Lorne 'perished himself at the cross.' Bowslaugh passed over the state prison in which he was kept before his execution.[50] In taking his readers through Canongate, Wetherell became emotive, collapsing linear time and bringing a wide cast of historical characters 'alive' synchronically. He described how the streets were peopled with the ghosts of royalty, nobles, and burgesses: Montrose was dragged on a hurdle, and Knox stood 'grim and stern' after his interview with Mary Stuart, 'unmelted by the tears of a queen'; then along rode the Pretender, dazzled by thoughts of a crown and trailed by pipers and adoring Jacobite women.[51] Tourists made pilgrimages to the Martyrs' Monument. Bowslaugh dutifully recorded that one hundred Scots were executed in Edinburgh from the time of the Stuart Restoration until the Glorious Revolution.[52] In this history of violence it was not just Protestants being persecuted by Catholics: Pack observed that one of the rooms in Knox's house had a Bible but also a scold's bridle, as well as the boards and wrist-cuffs that held down prisoners being taken to jail or for execution.[53]

Yet one visitor did not find that the past appeared to him in Edinburgh's streets and closes. Newton MacTavish, from 1906 to 1926 the editor of the *Canadian Magazine,* arrived in Edinburgh in 1910 for a sporting event, his head full of images of Scottish history and culture that he longed to find in the city's material landscape. He also arrived with an empty stomach, and an attempt to fill it with whiskey and haggis ended with MacTavish being led by two ragged youths into one of Edinburgh's 'rat holes,' where he was accosted by a crowd of children begging for (or in his account, demanding) coins. After throwing a shower of half-pennies into the crowd, MacTavish was able to listen to the conversations of the drunken and 'unkempt and haggard' men and women who passed by him on their way to the various taprooms, and he was disappointed to realize that their conversations were not about John Knox and Jenny Geddes, Robert Louis Stevenson, Tobias Smollett, or Sir Walter Scott – but of socialism. The majority of his fellow travel writers and diarists would make some comments on contemporary problems but then move quickly into the past. MacTavish's attempts to replace the flesh and blood human beings with whom he was surrounded by historical and literary figures were confounded, not just by the prevailing poverty but also by his awareness of it.[54]

The Romantic and Tragic Past

Outside of Glasgow and Edinburgh, the Highlands evoked wonder both for their natural beauty and their tragic, doomed history.[55] Wetherell, who had a flair for hyperbole, declared that 'nowhere in the world, surely, can be found scenery more picturesque and romantic.' As his steamer left Balloch pier a vision of majesty and loveliness was gradually unfolded that could not be exaggerated by painter or by poet. We threaded our way amongst innumerable islands crowned with verdure of matchless variety and beauty. As I heard 'the accents of the mountain tongue' in the speech of those about me, and saw those blooming northern faces, as I glanced to the ancient hills and mountains that cradled us in on every side, to the myriads of rills that leaped and gushed down grassy slopes and rugged steeps, to the exquisite contour of the coast as satisfying as the plump roundness of childish cheeks, to the limpid waters that rippled to the gentle breeze, to the wreaths of mist that would swoop down upon us as if by magic and then silently and suddenly steal away, as I viewed the gorgeous coloring of the scene around me, the blue of sky and water, the green of tree and plant, the white of mist and cloud, the purple heather, the gray cliff, the brown or shadowy gorge, the azure of the distant hills, and all these continually varying their hues with the very-changing light – I felt that I had drifted clean away from the common-place work-a-day world, and had entered an ideal realm haunted by [the] spirit of beauty and touched with the witchery of an immortal hand.[56]

Others writers agreed, with Wetherell, if in less flowery and effusive prose. Ethel Davies, from Prince Edward Island, was enamoured with the Queen's View (a place where Victoria had stopped for lunch in the valley of Glencoe): 'the air was so pure and strong and the scenery beautifully wild with every here and there a mountain torrent coming tumbling down on the side of the mountain pierced by a gloomy rugged cairn of some historic value.' Davies was captivated by the beauty of the heather and the golden bracken, and although walking with her older relatives was far from easy, the view rewarded them. 'It was indeed glorious! Away to the right stretched Loch Levan for seven or eight miles between the hills beneath us at our feet lay the valley of the "Coe" and on the breast of a small hill stood the house – down further by the shores of the lake like tiny white specks nestled the cottages with their low thatched roofs. Away to the left as far as the eye could see stretched the Glen wrapped in mists.'[57]

But Davis was also aware that two centuries earlier this 'mist-wrapped' vista had seen 'that terrible massacre ... when the clan of MacDonalds were slaughtered by the Campbells and here to this day a MacDonald never shakes hands with a Campbell.'[58] The Scottish landscape was scarred by a ferocious history, almost overwhelming in its violence. The western end of Loch Lomond, a 'bare and bleak and desolate' site, was for Wetherell 'a fit region this for the exploits of Rob

Roy and the MacGregors, for every fastness of these barren shores could tell its terrible tale of suffering and of bloodshed.'[59] Gazing at the field of Bannockburn, Irene Simmonds fancied 'I could see the troops marching mid the din of battle and brave men falling to rise no more, and I thought of the anxious wives and mothers waiting in far off homes for news of their dear ones.'[60] Like the musings of those who visited Holyrood and meditated on the life and loves of Mary Stuart, in this passage Simmonds created a Scottish historical landscape in which private and public, families and armies, were closely interlinked. In a similar vein, the 'wild beauty' around Jedburgh enthralled the *Montreal Daily Star*'s columnist 'Penelope,' where she visited the thatched cottage in which Mary Stuart had stayed after her return from France. Here the queen had tried to bring 'order and manners' to the Border nobles, including Bothwell, whom she nursed after he was wounded: 'yielding,' Penelope noted, to her 'woman's heart, as she was too apt to do.' She then became sick herself and very nearly died, which 'would have saved her reputation and her neck if she had.' On recovering, Mary Stuart made a number of bequests to those who had helped her through her illness and 'promptly ordered herself a new dress with true feminine attention to her appearance in public.'[61]

The commemorations were evocative not only of 'suffering and bloodshed.' After his failed attempts to learn the Highland fling, George Lindsey drove past Stirling, 'the historic battlefield where Scotland's independence was secured and the royal standard of the Bruces floated on the breeze.'[62] Although he devoted over fifty pages to a discussion of the tragedies of Scottish history (the deaths of Montrose and Mary Stuart and Charles II's cruel treatment of the Scottish Covenantors), John Mackinnon viewed Oban with an eye both appreciative and ironic, describing it as a 'handsome place' with its 'broad, clean streets, fine churches, palace hotels, and general appointments … Few surpass Oban in varied attractions, and recognizing this fact, natives mark their service and cheer at high figures … watermen are soliciting fares, and in no place did I find hotel drummers more aggressive, kind and fierce than in this pocket city.' Mackinnon's historic sympathies tended towards the Scots, as he told his readers that the Duke of Cumberland's butchery and brutal murder of the rank and file at Culloden was unwarranted. Moreover, while the 'great Scottish patriot,' Duncan Forbes, 'did much to save a throne for the Hanoverian blockheads,' as he prevented the MacLeod and MacDonald clans from rising, Forbes was not compensated by the English government for his services. 'The

Georges had enough money to spend on court festivities and lewd
women, but not a crown to pay what was many times a debt of honour.'
Nevertheless, Mackinnon judged that the result – the abolition of the
clans – was for the people's good, as the former had impeded Scottish
reform and progress. Far from rhapsodizing about doomed Jacobites,
he believed that 'Bonnie Prince Charlie' was a drunken, 'bloated profli-
gate' who had abused and beaten his 'princely young wife': no tragic
hero but an 'unworthy sot and debased libertine.'[63]
   If these tourists did not always conjure up identical histories from the
same landscape, they did agree that one Scot in particular – the 'bard of
Abbotsford,' had helped shape their conceptions of Scotland's history
and landscape. As literary scholar Elizabeth Waterston has argued,
Sir Walter Scott's narrative poems and his historical novels captured the
imagination of many Canadian readers during this period.[64] Wetherell,
for one, saw the 'narrow, rugged glen' of the Trossachs through the lens
of Scott's writing:

> No other spot in the wide world has been honoured with such a descrip-
> tion, and as long as the English language lives a never-ending procession
> of curious travelers will explore this 'dark and narrow dell.' The intrinsic
> attractions of the Pass are such as to oppress the beholder with a sense of
> awe and majesty, and the glamour of poetic glory that the 'magician of the
> north' has cast about it makes its charms more potent still. The powerful
> influence of [the] poet's song has caused a palatial hotel to rise at the east-
> ern limit of the Trossachs. It is a beautiful edifice, stately and turreted, not
> out of harmony with the sublime scenery within view of it.[65]

   Scott's writings created an imagined and material topography for
both tourists and tourist promoters alike (even the boat that took
George Pack around Loch Lomond was named *Sir Walter Scott*).[66] In
addition to the ruined castles, mysterious glens, and former battlefields, Scott's residence at Abbotsford formed part of the tour. By the
mid-nineteenth century Abbotsford had become an important historical and cultural landmark, visited by such cultural and social luminaries as Charles Dickens, Charlotte Brontë, and Harriet Martineau; in the
latter decades of the century, the house saw on average at least six
thousand visitors a year.[67] Margaret Thomson was not given to lengthy
descriptions of landscape. She enjoyed the scenery around Abbotsford
very much, however, and carefully made a note of the most significant
contents of Walter Scott's home: 'all the books are as he left them,' his

canes and pipes, the chair made from the wood of the home where
Wallace was captured, Rob Roy's purse, the hairs of Wellington and
Bonnie Prince Charlie.[68] She returned the next year, in 1897, and saw
'just the same things,' including Scott's grave, and recorded a tale of
Scott's ancestors that involved imprisonment and the threat of execution, both of which were thwarted by a romance that ended in marriage.[69] In her tour of Abbotsford, Mary Lauder observed that 'among
the armour are instruments of torture, and the mask worn by Wishart
at the stake! It seemed a holy spot, and one suggestive of a thousand
reflections.'[70]

Unlike their urban counterparts, the men, women, and children
who peopled the Scottish countryside did not tend to inspire letter
writers and diarists. Possibly Scottish history itself was responsible for
this. However, despite the depopulation of the Highlands and emigration (not least to colonies such as British North America), the very
active tourist trade of late nineteenth-century Scotland should caution
us against assuming that rural Scots were physically absent from
Canadian tourists' travels. Historians of Scottish tourism, for example,
make it abundantly clear that rural Scots were very much part of the
tourist infrastructure. A far more likely explanation is that their techniques of seeing the landscape, ones both metaphorical and literal, rendered these Canadian tourists mute about any individual rural Scots.
(For, as we have seen, the people who worked in the tourist industry
did not elicit description, comment, and analysis unless they were
deemed unusually picturesque or irritatingly incompetent – the two
qualities, of course, might be related.)

It is equally possible, however, that anglophone Canadian tourists'
omission of rural Scots in their writings resulted from the structure of
their travels through rural Scotland. Few travellers 'rambled' through
the Scottish countryside in quite the same way as they did in England
or even strolled through the streets of Scottish cities. Most tourists took
trains and steamers around Scotland, and thus they had fewer opportunities to speak directly to villagers and farmers than they did on
walking holidays south of the border. The author of 'From Inverness to
Glasgow via the Caledonian Canal' did not speak to any of the rural
tenants on whom he had trained his field glass from the steamer.
Below the panorama of Ben Nevis lay poor soil for farming: 'the ten-
antry live in wretchedly miserable hovels' that lacked chimneys, with
heather- and clay-clad roofs, and were so low that a man could barely
stand upright in them. In short, they were very close to pigsties and

cowsheds.' Oppressive landlords were seen to be the culprits, men who lived in elegant mansions or castles on the their estates for only a few months and then spent much of the income derived from their tenants in London. However, the preferred solution was not land reform and redistribution of agricultural profits: why, mused the writer, did these men put up with such conditions when New Brunswick or the Canadian northwest was presented to them?[71]

Other reporters were more enthusiastic, not to mention charitable, in their assessments of 'the' rural Scottish character. Emma Baker, a teacher at Mount Allison's Ladies' College, believed that the Scots 'fully reflect their rugged country' and that they '[are] a great link' to their land, more so, she felt, than the 'Oriental' in his 'gardens of barbaric splendour.' Here Baker's reaction to the Scottish landscape and its inhabitants reflects what Elizabeth Waterston has argued to be Scott's 'vision of the interface between individuals, nation, and race.'[72] With a 'tradition' that included values such as chivalry and individuals such as William Wallace, the Scots have become a 'dominating race ... born leaders of men.' The Scots' commitment to education, their habits of economy, and their special combination of 'force and tenderness' have placed a 'racial mark on Sandy and [have] help[ed] him upwards. Yet, no matter where he goes, Baker told her readers, 'Sandy' does not lose his 'love of Scotland.'[73]

Ada McLeod visited the Isle of Skye. Her account of life there was a more nuanced attempt to capture the complexities of rural society. The island, which first appeared 'austere and forbidding,' was to her a place of magic, folklore, and history, marked by the presence of the church, the sadness of the past, and its many exiles. The MacLeod clan chief gave her a tour of Skye's history that brought together past and present and featured the romance of Dunvegan Castle with its fairy flag and the graves of Flora Macdonald and Lady Grainge. The thatched cottages on the island, with their earth floors, had an 'organic' character, as did the island women's textile work. Yet McLeod was well aware that Skye was not an enclave of 'quaint' rural customs that could be easily subjected to an antimodernist, not to mention sentimental, gaze. Skye was located on of a well-worn tourist route and offered many comforts, such as the hotels in Portree. Skye textiles were in great demand among upper-class 'British ladies.' The thatched cottages housed not just looms but also many books, and in addition to textiles and peat-cutting, the island boasted industrial development, with coal mining, iron ore, and marble quarrying. Skye's history was not confined to the epic tale of Highland chieftains. Ada McLeod also visited the site of an 1881 crofter uprising where there had been a confrontation between elderly women and the police. For at least twenty years, students had not been punished for speaking Gaelic in school. Gaelic had become quite popular, and its widespread use had promoted closer links between lairds and tenants. McLeod believed that Skye's inhabitants had inherited a tradition of 'simple living and moral integrity.' Rather than there by being condemned to rural backwardness, such habits meant that the 'Skyeman is a force to be reckoned with' and someone 'so important' in shaping both the Empire and Canada.[74] Yet, writing about Skye two years later, in 1913, McLeod lamented to her readers that ceilidhs, peat fires, tales of Ossian and the occult (Kelpies, mermaids, witches, fairies, the second sight, and the evil eye), and the heavy, all-wool blankets, woven by Skye women and sheltering young bachelors in the Canadian west, were things of the past only. Stories had made way for the newspaper and bannock for bread: 'and in both cases the gains are doubtful.' She found that what Skye had gained in worldliness it had had lost in community and in its treasure trove of living memory.[75]

The countryside of Ayrshire and Robert Burns's home induced yet another set of memories and associations, although these were not as clearly fraught over the question of the benefits and shortfall of modernity. As Waterston has argued, 'reverence and respect' for the poetry of Robert Burns was widely felt across English-speaking Canada, and in this Canadians were not alone. By the mid-1850s Burns's home had become a 'tourist shrine.'[76] In his account, Wetherell fluctuated between providing the facts that tourists needed (the bridge that led up to the cottage was in 'perfect' condition, the entrance to the 'long low white building' cost 6d, and on Saturdays over one thousand tourists might visit) and reverence for the poet's legacy. What was it, he mused, that brought 'curious travelers from distant continents and the remotest isles of the sea' to the 'lowly cottage of Scotland's peasant bard!' For Wetherell, it was clearly a place of pilgrimage, one where 'noisy voices will be hushed to a whisper, and reverent heads will be uncovered, and careful hand will touch thy sacred contents, and beating hearts will feel thy subtle influence and soaring spirits will fly away beyond thy narrow bounds to commune with the spirit of him who has given us so many breathing thoughts and burning words ... The glory of thy ploughboy's genius has touched thy simplicity and turned it into splendor, has touched thy poverty and made it grandly rich.'[77] As he drove away from Ayr Wetherell speculated on the loss to literature that might have resulted, if 'poor Burns, oppressed with many cares,' had followed through on the voyage to Jamaica that he had once contemplated.[78]

Not all pilgrims had such a moving, not to mention transcendental, experience. Visiting Ayr twelve years later, Harriett Priddis confessed that she was 'disappointed in Burns' house cottage a museum and stall for selling post cards. Garden prim "keep off the grass" style. Monument in tea garden near by too ornate for a man of Burns' simple unaffected style.'[79] Priddis's disenchantment with the commemoration of the 'people's poet' should not obscure, however, the fact that she had gone to Ayr in hopes of having the kind of experience described by Wetherell and many others.[80]

Glasgow, Edinburgh, the Highlands, Abbotsford, and 'Burns' country' were not the only sites in Scotland in which history and memory, Scottish identity and culture, were lodged so firmly for Canadian visitors. Writing in the *Canadian Magazine* in 1908, Jean Blewett stated that Lanark must be remembered as 'the Cradle of Scottish Liberty,' both for the memory of William Wallace and for that of Robert Owen and his 'noble but doomed' efforts (see fig. 2.1).[81] Entering Scotland along the Borders, Maria Lauder's fictional 'Toofie' mused on the history of the hero Lochinvar and other figures of the medieval and early modern period. The dungeons of Liddesdale's Hermitage Castle conjured up memories of past torture, the 'groans of anguish and despair,' even as the castle itself was ringed with beautiful – not to mention 'sketchworthy' – bluebells. Lauder's character happily recited a poem that detailed the gruesome fate of Lord William Soulis, said to have been wrapped in lead sheets and then boiled alive. Yet despite her fascination with anecdotes about physical sufferings, Toofie quickly admitted that Soulis had in fact been convicted of treason, for which crime he was imprisoned in Dunbarton Castle.[82]

Lauder's characters, particularly the women, spent much time discussing and detailing cruelties of the past. Visitors to London and certain European centres had similar reactions to historical sites, particularly those that were testimonials to the power of the monarchy. It may well be that reflecting on 'history,' or at least certain facets of it, was one way in which middle-class women, both young and middle-aged, could openly contemplate physical violence, particularly that of the state. This subject supposedly was prohibited in 'respectable' women's conversation, yet travel writers and tourists insisted on addressing it. One of

2.1. Commemorating romance and tragedy: William Wallace's cave (*Canadian Magazine*, May 1908. Reproduction courtesy of the Archives of Ontario)

Lauder's female characters suggested, for example, that 'bonny Scotland' had enough 'material' 'for a persecution as bloody and cruel as in the days of the Romans.' Her book's only male character, brother Fred, then quickly insisted that such 'dark ages' had been left behind and that 'we want *light*'; moreover, 'the world has come to know her need and possesses the manhood that can enforce her claim.' A woman in the party supported his claim, as she believed that 'so long as Germany can boast another man such as Bismarck, moral light will intensify itself.'[83] Lauder tried to put the issue of society's lack of morality into frameworks that depended on strict divisions of past and present, with the latter occupying the higher moral ground and being associated with modern, middle-class masculinity. Yet in Lauder's and others' accounts, a ferocious national past continued to haunt the more pacific and civilized present. Even those traits of heroic masculinity that these anglophone Canadian tourists admired and were willing to 'see' manifested in the Scottish landscape – clan loyalty, the defence of honour, and the physical and moral ability to lead other men – might result in disaster for those unable to demonstrate them, namely, women and children.

As well as raising questions about the gendered nature of historical narratives, Canadian tourists' travels in Scotland remind us that, despite the monolithic qualities that have been ascribed to the category 'British,' there were times when it fractured and fissured along lines of region, ethnicity, and history. Much of the violence, tragedy, and romance that these tourists felt they witnessed occurred because of battles that sprang from England's claim to sovereignty over Scotland. While their enthusiasm for the region south of Carlisle did not lead many travellers to confront English imperialism and Scottish nationalism directly, such questions, like the ghosts of Mary Stuart and William Wallace, were not completely laid to rest. Indeed, they might be said to have haunted Canadians' travels through Scotland, returning as the 'uncanny,' something that could not be easily settled or assimilated into triumphalist narratives of progress.[84] Such narratives were told more easily as they headed south for the countryside and provincial cities of England.

3 The Landscape of History and Empire, Part 2: England

Any Canadian traveller visiting England should obtain from the Great Western Railway Company their illustrated book on the Historic Sites and Scenes of England. The descriptive matter is delightful, and the information is valuable. In fact, it is a model railway guide book which has been especially prepared for American visitors. It contains a good map and an adequate hotel list.[1]

'Historic England' (1905)

We go to Canada to get a realisation of the meaning of *space* and they come here to get a fuller content to the idea of *time*.[2]

Kate Stevens (1911)

If Scotland could inspire and evoke both awe and sadness, what associations and feelings were sparked in England? As chapter 5 will argue, while the landscape and historical sites of London moved these tourists to effusive outpourings of national and imperial sentiment, other areas in England held the key to national and imperial subjectivities, whether through historical sites, various 'natural' features of the landscape, or the people who lived there. As with Scotland, tourists' choice of places such as the southern and western countryside, cathedral towns like York and Canterbury, the Lake District and Stratford-on-Avon, Oxford and Cambridge, and ports like Bristol or Plymouth were not made in cultural vacuums: lessons in English history and literature, as well as exposure to travel writing, had inculcated these travellers' desires and inspired their fantasies of what should be visited, how it should be viewed, and why it was significant to a sense of membership in national and imperial communities.³ Through organized tours of Britain undertaken by groups such as the teachers from Manitoba, the 'Maple Blossoms' from Toronto, and the 'Spectator Girls' from Hamilton, Ontario, English-Canadian women could become living embodiments of imperial ties, intimating that the best aspects of England's past were manifested in them in the present. Yet the meanings of these landscapes and sites were not always hegemonic or received uncritically, particularly where the empire's relationship to the Dominion of Canada was concerned.

Landing in Liverpool

The first sight of England was, more often than not, Liverpool. George Disbrowe spent a December afternoon there, observing 'the buildings are massive and very black' and a number of small stores had 'nice window displays,' but that there were 'a tremendous number of drinking places, and they are open at all hours.' The 'many women going in, and coming out with their jugfuls – small children too' particularly offended him.⁴ Maria Lauder's travellers thought Liverpool a 'commercial capital' with its mercantile houses and its docks, but they also attended a flower show and drove out of the city through 'quintessential English countryside' to see the Earl of Derby's seat at Knowsley Park.⁵ In the 1890s the city appeared as 'not a showy place' to Prince Edward Islander John Mackinnon, but it did have many 'fine buildings,' such as St George's Hall, the Walker Art Gallery, the town hall, the railway station, and the YMCA and boasted a number of museums, parks, and monuments to the distinguished: Queen Victoria, Prince Albert, Wellington, and Nelson. Mackinnon was particularly impressed with the city's Blue Coat School that housed 300 pupils. In fact, he submitted, with its sailors' homes, seamen's orphanages, infirmary for the poor, and school for the death and dumb, Liverpool 'abounds with charitable and reform institutions.' 'Yet in common with large seaports,' he told his readers, Liverpool has 'swarms of unemployed and indigent people.'⁶

Emily Murphy, 'struck' by the city's 'solidity and finish,' enjoyed riding on top of omnibuses. She was awestruck by the size and bustle of the docks and disgusted at the state of Liverpool's poor and working-class residents: the women were prostitutes, the children rogues and beggars, and the men drunks. Although Murphy constructed a picture of degradation and immiseration for her middle-class, Canadian readers, she conceded that the city's environment bore much responsibility. 'With the lean wolf of hunger always crouching at the door; sleeping in squalid homes where cleanliness and decency are impossible, and living in foul streets with so many tempting facilities to vice, the deterioration of mankind, both spiritually and physically is inevitable.'[7] In contrast, the author of the *Canadian Magazine*'s article, entitled 'Liverpool Today,' made no mention of the city's poor or its social problems. Allowing that Liverpool now held almost nothing of 'historical and antiquarian interest,' since 'modern improvements' had 'swept' such sites away, the most interesting objects to visit were the 'magnificent docks,' which were interesting for their history, contemporary administration, and visual impact. With their 'forests of masts' and 'streets of towering warehouses,' the docks were an 'impressive, almost magical sight' that was not sufficiently appreciated by overseas tourists.[8]

Warnings of the city's dangers penned by the likes of Murphy were either unheard or unheeded. On her 1906 trip to Britain and Europe, Harriett Priddis decided to explore Liverpool on her own when her friends could not meet her boat. After checking into her room at the YWCA, which although 'high up' was near the bathroom and 'very comfy,' Priddis toured Christ Church Cathedral, then took a tram to Princess Park, with its 'pretty grounds with lake swans, bridges, fine walks, and beautiful flowers. I never thought of anything of the kind in Liverpool.' Having seen the city's gallery and museum, she then tried to find the Corn Exchange but became lost. On seeing a man standing in a doorway, Priddis asked him the way to the Exchange. Once he found out that she was not going to meet anyone there, and that she was a Canadian, the stranger offered to take her himself. 'You Canadians,' he told Priddis, 'may well take interest in our market, you make a lot of money out of us.' Off they went to the Exchange, which was 'not like the stock exchange in New York or Manchester, but a large building with offices or stall [s] with names no [*sic*] men rushing in and out and samples of grain in evidence.' Her anonymous guide also took her to the town hall and then, over Priddis's protests that she had already taken up two hours of his time, 'down Bold Street,' where he pointed out the lions. On leaving each other, she asked 'whom I was to thank for all this kindness and he said just a Liverpool man proud of his city.' They shook hands, he wished her a pleasant visit, and she took the first tram 'straight home.'[9]

Priddis had many such adventures in her travels around Britain and Europe, often because she was lost or had given her friends the wrong time to meet her. She had little compunction about starting conversations with strangers on public transit or on the street and rarely, if ever, expressed any concerns for her personal safety. Nevertheless, Priddis was not alone in finding Liverpool a pleasurable spot. Vancouver's Mary Bain, departing from Liverpool in February 1911, after a three-month tour that began in the Mediterranean and encompassed Italy, France, and England, was happily surprised by it. Its exteriors looked 'pretty much as I expected,' Bain wrote, 'big and grey and grimey-looking,' but the shops and the State Café on Dale Street, which had crowds of shoppers, good food, and music, were an unexpected treat. 'In fact the dainty and artistic appearance of [the café's] interior struck me as a direct and delightful contrast to anything else I had seen in Liverpool. Of course the Adelphi Hotel, at which we are staying, is exceedingly nice too.'[10] Bain observed that the Adelphi was the only hotel 'where we had fingerbowls [with] perfumed water.'[11]

England's 'Green and Pleasant Land'

As in Scotland, signs of England's industrial and commercial progress and prosperity were reassuring to the anglophone Canadian tourist and mitigated some of the more troubling aspects of urban life. Yet there was no denying the traveller's desire for the less-recent English past. At times tourist sites and landscapes in England had a 'history' attributed to them that was at best fuzzy about dates, events, and people: everything evoked an undifferentiated 'times past' comprised of symbols and signifiers that ranged from beneficent monarchs to thatched cottages. Not surprisingly, perhaps, such descriptions hinted at an antimodernist attitude and suggested that the English landscape might provide a refreshing antidote to modernity's frantic pace. In an article published in 1907, travel writer Jane Lavender promised that, from Edinburgh to London, the 'King's Highway' would provide a leisurely pace for the tourist's journey, one that would permit reflections on the 'glamour of romance, the great pageants of history, the trace of chivalry and the dignity of an age that are connected with this ancient and honourable institution.'[12] The Highway brought together many historical sites and delights, including the 'whitewashed, pink washed, thatch-roofed and tiled' country cottages that 'are still the typical spots along the country highways.'[13] It also allowed the tourist to encounter characters that could be grouped under the rubric of 'Old Country People,' such as 'the Fisherman of the Dee' and 'the Country Squire.'

No matter that 'you read that folk the world around now-a-days dress and look alike, a perennial interest remains, a something new for every new tourist in the actual meeting with residents of any other country whatever than his own.'[14]

We cannot know whether Mabel Cameron read Lavender's piece, yet a chauffeur-driven trip along the Highway from London to Winchester, in 1911, provoked a similar reaction in her. Although she recorded going much faster than at Lavender's recommended relaxed tempo, she and her aunt saw 'one quaint little village ... by way of Guildford and Farnham. All along the road were numerous inns, whose names rather took our fancy – The Seven Starts, The Dog and Duck, The Hop Poles, the Angel Family, the Mow and Meadow. Thatched cottages with ivy-covered walls peeped out from sheltering trees and the whole ride was a dear delight.'[15]

As these examples suggest, the southern and southwestern English countryside was fertile ground for a number of travel writers. Much has been written about the urban *flâneur* (and now *flâneuse*), but Canadian male writers and tourists often also adopted the persona of the 'rural rambler,' the traveller who eschewed the bustling cities and towns for the more pastoral pleasures of the countryside and village. The pieces written by these men about their 'country strolls' mixed nineteenth-century romanticism's appreciation of nature with the flâneur's knowingness and critical commentary on the landscape, its history and inhabitants, and the local customs and practices. The Reverend Frederick Hastings, of New Brunswick, published several articles in 1874 that detailed his 'rambles' and 'tramping' in western England. They started in Somersetshire, 'the country of Tory squires and ill-paid peasantry.'[16] Some of Hastings's pieces praised the pastoral beauty of the rural landscape, such as the 'most richly cultivated country' near the Bleadon hills with its green fields, 'glistening' white cottages, 'ruddy' farmhouses, and 'grey and grand mansions.'[17]

Rural England also was full of lessons about the past. Lintern Abbey, a 'magnificent ruinous pile,' inspired Hastings to imagine that he could hear the voice of an 'old, serge-clad, hooded monk reading to his fellows, while they feasted on the good things of the fruitful valley and the fine salmon of the Wye.' Lest his readers think that Hastings had fallen under the spell of Catholicism, though, he pointed out that it was even easier to imagine the past there as it became dark, 'to repeople the spot in imagination, as it will never again be repopulated with monks and abbots in reality.' These ghosts having been put firmly in their place and the sixteenth-century rupture with England's Catholic past supposedly secured, Hastings went on to tour the castle where the republican Henry Martyn was imprisoned 'by that most high and mighty, King Charles II, of detestable memory.'[18] Near Glastonbury he stayed at an inn that had been the abbot's guesthouse, yet another proof of a history that, although it might offer some romantic, possibly melancholic, pleasure, was decidedly and thankfully (at least for Hastings) over and done with.[19]

The countryside, however, was not just pleasant sights and 'times past.' Hastings also was concerned about the low wages of agricultural workers, and he lectured his readers about rural poverty and the labourers' movement.[20] His meeting with a farm worker led into a discussion of the latter's 'sorry life': his low wages, a family to support, and backbreaking work. 'I left them, telling them I hoped better times for them would come along.'[21] Hastings was by no means unique in his awareness of rural poverty. John Mackinnon stopped on the Duke of Westminster's land to speak to a 'hind' who was trimming the walks. Thinking that anyone in the duke's employ must have 'an easy billet for a man with a Niagara of gold must have a big heart within him' (Westminster was said to be one of the wealthiest men in the world), Mackinnon was quickly disabused of this notion. The worker told him that he only received sixteen shillings per week to support a wife and eight children, and out of that wage he owed the duke five pounds per year rent for his cottage, 'in default of which he was at liberty to hunt for new pastures. Hearing this mine ire kindled, my countenance fell and I hastily started.'[22]

Although this landscape was clearly not a bucolic paradise, like those who commented on rural Scotland, these writers were not about to prescribe significant social and political reorganization. James Rupert Elliott believed that

if the landlord has been nothing more, and has accomplished nothing else, he has placed sentiment, refinement, ideals, as something above material profits, and so preserved and nurtured the belongings of the estate, and we have now for our pleasure everywhere England's noble avenues, her beautiful shrubbery, her splendid winding roads, her charming little lanes, her history and tradition in country as is nowhere else to be found in the world. Consequently, would it not be a calamity to ruthlessly destroy the anchorage which has a safety for all this, and set the tide in the other direction by placing it within the power of another class who despise sentiment along this line, and also would think only of immediate material pride? I think so.[23]

As well as provoking social commentary and conflicting attitudes about class relations and modernity, the rural landscape offered the rambler various amenities. Hastings saw the villagers' homes as not just picturesque sights but also as part of the tourist infrastructure that supported his rambles. He and his companion stopped at a farmhouse for a drink of milk and, none being available from the farmer's wife, had to pay for water, an unusual situation brought about by that summer's drought.[24] On finding that the nearest public house in the village of Toxton was four miles away (a fact that pleased Hastings, a temperance advocate), the two tourists went into a grocery store and asked for food, reassuring the owner that they would pay. 'The good woman said she could make us some tea,' and, according to Hastings, quickly served them a 'most delicious meal' of cream, ham, eggs, and mushrooms, charging them only eighteen pence, which they insisted on topping up as 'of course' it was far too small an amount.[25] Hastings had few qualms about entering what middle-class culture deemed 'private' spaces in order to obtain food and drink, whether given freely or as part of a commercial transaction, an attitude that he shared with other tourists.

When they were not impoverished labourers or generous hosts, rural residents were judged and found wanting. They might lack aesthetic sensibility, as in the case of the countrywoman who gave them directions and 'thought we were mad to stay on our course when we could save a mile by keeping to [the] high road. She could not see the beauty we saw in the quaint cottages and farmhouses we passed in our detour.'[26] A woman they met while sheltering from a storm three miles from Porlock was unable to tell them the distance. 'I ha' lived here these seventeen years, but have never been as far as Porlock.' I looked at her with amazement. I could hardly have believed that such contentedness or indifference to the outside world could have been found. Here was a woman strong, able to walk, and with a face that was rather intelligent for a country woman, and who yet had not seen the nearest little market town during all these years.'[27] While complaining about what might seem to be different attitudes – indifference to historic beauty, on the one hand, and insularity and parochialism, on the other – Hastings's critiques of these rural women were not as contradictory as they might appear. As historians of tourism have pointed out, middle-class observers of colonized peoples, peasants, and the working classes saw these groups as lacking in schooling and unable either to appreciate or care for the treasures among which they lived;

their lack of formal education and their 'primitive' state also accounted for their supposed lack of curiosity in their surroundings.[28]

These writers' accounts were thus shot through with both notions of class superiority and the condescension of the urbane cosmopolite towards what they judged to be a backwards peasantry. Even notions of a shared ancestry might not transcend other lines of affiliation and identity. The rambler adopted a sensibility and subjectivity very similar to both that of the flâneur and the social investigator, qualified by his gender and class position to observe with detachment and to offer his readers the 'truth' about rural England. Furthermore, for once, the ability to assess with a 'colonial' eye was an asset, not a drawback or limitation. The white, middle-class male rambler from English-speaking Canada had been instructed in English history and culture, while simultaneously he was slightly removed from English society and thus considered himself to be a more objective observer of it. To be sure, not all writers were as quick to pass critical judgment on England's rural dwellers as Hastings. In 1914, writing about his walking tour through Cornwall, Devon, Cumberland, and Westmoreland, G.L.B. Mackenzie described how he was impressed by Cornwall's bicycle-riding well-built, 'handsome' Coast Guardsmen, who owing to their Celtic ancestry, were the 'sunniest,' best tempered, and best mannered of all the English, always 'genial' and eager to talk to tourists. Yet an antimodernist desire to find enclaves removed from the stress of modernity underlay Mackenzie's account. Cornwall, he told his readers, was not 'cursed' with 'large manufacturing towns' and most of her people 'in spite of the mines, [are] healthy rustics' who make their living from the sea and the land.[29] Similar notions were at work in H.M. Clark's assessments of his 1912 travels through the West Country, a place of 'haunting placidity' and 'immemorial civilization,' where the inhabitants were living in a 'past of strange beliefs, intolerant of a present which seeks to give [them] agricultural innovations and haste and things modern.'[30]

Goldwin Smith reported that rural life in England had greatly improved. In his 1891 travelogue, A Trip to England, he told his readers that in any other country the capital city was the centre of things, but that in England the countryside played that role. His vantage point a train carriage, Smith observed the 'charm' of country life, represented by the church spire and rectory, the squire's hall, the tenant farmer's homestead, and the labourer's cottage.[31] These signifiers of 'rural England' might have come straight out of an Anthony Trollope novel, but Smith did not shy away from rural society's difficulties of the past twenty years (the 1870s depression, the influx of cheap American and Indian grain, heavy mortgages and a subsequent drop in rents being paid, and the costs of primogeniture), not to mention the insularity of rural society, and the problem of absentee landlords. Nevertheless, he believed that there had been progress. 'Primitive implements and antiquated ways' had been replaced by machinery and new methods; 'improving and philanthropic' landlords had torn down clay cottages with thatched roofs and put up slate-roofed brick houses; and there were correspondingly visible improvements in 'Hodge's lot.' Those 'picturesque cottages' had often housed 'penury and misery,' 'grossest ignorance,' 'uncleanness, physical and moral, which is the consequence of overcrowding.'[32] All of this had made way for higher wages, improvements in 'home and habits,' compulsory education, an opening up of the labour market through rail transportation (instead of being 'bound like a serf'), and not least of all, enfranchisement.[33] Smith asserted that no man works as hard as 'Hodge.' Even if the latter went too much to the 'village ale-house,' at home he has 'been generally true and kind to "his old woman," as she has been to "her __old man."' Finally, there has been a 'touching dignity in his resignation to his hard lot and in the mournful complacency with which he has looked forward to "a decent burial." He has, for the most part, kept out of the workhouse when he could.'[34] As these passages suggest, Smith was capable of being no less condescending than the other writers. Moreover, according to Smith, changes in English rural society had been set in motion not because of demands made by 'Hodge' but by the actions of 'improving' landlords, buoyed (not surprisingly) by the greater prosperity brought about by free trade.

The countryside seen by the rural rambler (or, in Smith's case, rail passenger) was populated by figures who lived out stereotyped gendered roles. Its women included the helpful 'good wife,' who fed hungry travellers and who lived a life of quiet domesticity, loyal to her husband. Rural England also was home to the ignorant and close-minded woman who refused exposure to the modern world or was too uneducated to realize the cultural treasures around her. Rural masculinity was present predominantly as the humble figure of the oppressed male farm worker, a devoted husband and father of many children, who was almost doglike in his devotion, industriousness, and lack of ambition. In certain contexts, though, the rural male might be a 'fine figure' of a man capable of carrying out hard physical labour (unlike the rural rambler) or serving in the Cornish Coast Guard. As such, and also as the father of many children, there was just a hint of masculine sexuality, a suggestion that English rural life, (and those who lived it) might not be the haven of purity and innocence that some might wish it to be.[35]

Gender relations shaped this type of tourism as it was performed and then recorded. Many of the tourists who undertook these types of rural excursions were men. Women might cycle around the countryside with friends or family members or (as discussed later in this chapter) go hiking in the Lake District. Ethel Davies spent the winter of 1899–1900 staying with family in Bloxham, where she toured the surrounding north Oxfordshire countryside on her bicycle with 'L.' Like Hastings, she toured the ruins of a former Catholic institution, in this case the Black Friars' monastery. But for Davies England's Catholic past did not haunt these ruins. She thought them 'very picturesque, all grown over with ivy as is the fashion in England' but, unlike Hastings's Lintern Abbey, the remains of this monastery housed old people, sailors, soldiers, and servants ('and they seem very contented and happy'), one of whom, a 'quaint old pensioner,' took Davies and her companion on a tour of the building and grounds.[36] On one occasion while out driving with her friends Sir Charles and Lady Tupper, Amy Redpath Roddick, of Montreal became enchanted with the rural landscape outside of London. 'The gypsy fruit pickers with their encampments add to the picturesqueness [sic] of many of the views,' she wrote in her diary. While the cottages needed a lot of work, 'the orchards and the corn, fruit and potato fields are all so exquisitely tidy ... What a contrast to the wooden shanties and stony fields of Quebec!'[37]

Although middle-class women increasingly were moving about urban centres on their own, they did so using various forms of mechanized transportation – bicycles, streetcars, buses, underground rail, and taxis – as well as walking. Pastimes such as mountain climbing or hiking, although certainly not completely prohibited for women, were dominated by men.[38] Questions of personal safety in more isolated spots might well have played a role. Moreover, a 'respectable' middle-class man who found himself too far from a hotel or inn could spend a warm summer's night in a barn or farm outbuilding, an option that seems to have been unavailable to a female tourist. Canadian women certainly travelled about rural England, but they usually did so as part of a family group or with friends, either on horse-drawn conveyances or trains.

Trains, however, might offer their challenges, with connections to be made, luggage to be watched, and on at least one occasion, industrial disputes to navigate. Harriet Priddis had to cope with a rail strike while touring northern England, first outside a suburb of York where 'the streets were packed with a hooting crowd of men.' The guard reassured her that the men were simply 'showing their displeasure' with 'a scab who had filled the signal box' and that they were 'all respectable workmen fighting for their rights if it had not been for those d — scabs the Capitalists would have given way long ago.' Still not too sure about her safety, Priddis retreated to a sweet shop until the streets were quiet. She noted that the strikers 'really were a respectable looking lot of men clean washed and shaven and dressed in their Sunday clothes.'[39] The next day she found the train station 'in the hands of mounted police a regiment of soldiers stationed along the line,' Priddis felt sorry for the 'poor soldier boys lying around sleeping in corners.'[40] Overall, though, the strike proved more of an inconvenience than a danger; it might even be 'the time for funny sights.'[41] While sitting in her railway car waiting for the train to leave York, Priddis was quite entertained by the sight of a 'dandified fellow in knickers' with a pile of luggage ('golf kit, shawl strap and various bags') being forced to move it himself, a young woman in a 'navy blue traveling suit' wheeling her luggage cart 'with a bright smile and rather saucy nod … a general laugh and great cheers' as she passed, and a 'portly florid gentlemen' with his daughters who were forced to race for the train when they could not find assistance, the taller daughter's long tight skirt being pulled up above her knees and 'exposing a long straight length of black stockings and tights … we all laughed so heartily that the ice was broken.'[42]

Cathedrals and Colleges

England was not only rose-covered cottages, narrow hedge-bordered roads, hard-working 'Hodges,' and interesting adventures on its railways. The history of England encompassed prominent cathedrals in towns such as York, Canterbury, and Chester, buildings that were quite literally 'sacred sites.'[43] Their mere presence testified to England's veneration for the divine as a constant feature of its history, before and after the Reformation, their seeming permanence on the landscape as fundamental and telling a symbol as Smith's spires and parsonages. The cathedral – and the town that surrounded it – reinforced an understanding of

English history as fundamentally Protestant and – admiration for Catholic architecture and art and some unfortunate lapses notwithstanding – fundamentally moral. While travel writers, especially those published in the *Canadian Magazine*, might be nostalgic for the medieval period and its architectural beauties, they took pains to remind readers that many of these sites served an important contemporary purpose, tying past, present, and future together within their stone walls.

John Mackinnon pointed out that Chester had once been 'of some importance' as a result of its position as a Roman site. This significance, though, was quickly superseded in his account by the reigns of Mary I and Charles I, with their penchant for choosing the wrong religion and making life uncomfortable for Protestants. Nevertheless, the cathedral was a 'fine Gothic' building,[44] an evaluation with which the Methodist minister Hugh Johnston, touring England in 1892 as part of his trip to the Wesleyan Conference in Bradford, agreed (Johnston noted that the cathedral's site had been both a Druid grove and a temple to Apollo).[45] In her walk around Chester, Edith Chown observed the attempts of its residents to preserve older homes; she was impressed with the cathedral's stone mosaics and the fan-vaulting in its nave, as well as the 'quaint names' of the city's inns.[46]

Trips to York also presented an opportunity to look on and be impressed by medieval architecture and its preservation, both within the cathedral and on the city's walls. Mabel Cameron found that York Minster was 'a vast, impressive building' that simply could not be described adequately; instead, she recorded the conversation that she and aunt had with a group of choristers.[47] She recovered her descriptive abilities at Durham, though. Since a service was in progress during her visit to the cathedral Cameron spent the time gazing at her surroundings, noting the vast pillars, the tomb that held the remains of the Venerable Bede, and other architectural features which brought to mind various anecdotes from early medieval history. She found the site impressive and judged that her time had been 'well spent.' But as a supporter of women's enfranchisement, she also noticed the blue marble strip in the nave beyond which women were not allowed. 'The old verger said, "I hear they are anxious to have this taken up from here and put down in the House of Parliament, London." So he gave the suffragettes a nasty little hit. By the time we had seen all the points of interest (which were many) it was almost one o'clock. In thanking the verger for his lively, epigrammatic guidance he said "It's the visitor that makes the verger. If I took around sticks all the time I would soon be a stick myself."'[48]

Cameron's sceptical, almost iconoclastic attitude towards certain features of English history and social hierarchy was far from unique. Harriett Priddis neatly itemized the various aspects of York Minster, compared them with other cathedrals (Glasgow, Westminster, and Durham), and decided that York reminded her of Chicago: 'it has the second biggest of everything the very biggest of nothing.'[49] Yet when faced with centuries-old buildings that they saw as repositories of significant national memories, most of these tourists adopted tones and struck poses of serious reflection and reverence.[50] Like their reactions to certain landscapes and buildings in Scotland, these Canadians also registered the violence that ran throughout the history of English religion and that was etched in certain sites. Perhaps not surprisingly, given its famous association with the clash between the monarchy and the Church, Canterbury Cathedral was a favourite spot for reflecting on such matters. Marshall S. Snow published an article in 1900, entitled 'English History in Canterbury Cathedral.' It began with Chaucer's pilgrims, who in turn gave way to a modern descendant 'coming it may be from a land unknown to the wisest of Chaucer's company.'[51] In the cathedral the visitor was transported through time to the twelfth century and to the 'man and the event which gave to Canterbury its martyr and its shrine,' not to mention four hundred years of pilgrimages.[52] Snow went on to recount the story of Thomas à Becket, the Archbishop of Canterbury, and his dispute with King Henry II over the clergy's immunity from secular authority. The struggle ended with Becket's death in the cathedral at the hands of four of Henry's knights, the King's penitence, the dedication of Becket's shrine, and the great influence wielded by archbishops of Canterbury until Cromwell's Interregnum. Snow asserted to his readers that Canterbury and its history bring the visitor 'near the beginning of all English things that are good,' at the start of a list that included the 'constitution of Church and State in England by which now the British Empire is fastened together.'[53]

Snow was far from being the only Canadian visitor to note that Canterbury's significance was tied to Becket's death and the relationship between 'Church and State.' While Canterbury itself appeared to Edith Chown to be 'the quaintest little town ... [with] such old fashioned houses with projecting stories that one sees nowhere else,' it was at the cathedral, she pointed out, that 'history' was made manifest. Here was the place, she wrote in her diary, where Thomas à Becket was murdered, the staircase where 'he was urged to escape but he remained firm. We were shown the steps that the pilgrims went up and down to worship at the shrine of Becket. This is what Chaucer writes about in his *Canterbury Tales*.'[54] Priddis was struck by a number of the cathedral's features, including its beauty, tombs, and Becket's shrine, of which 'there is nothing to mark the spot now except the furrows in the stone floor worn by the feet and knees of the pilgrims which marks the limit of their approach' (it had been 'despoiled' by Henry VIII).[55] Priddis took copious notes on various aspects of the cathedral's architecture, yet over and over again her account returned to the details of Becket's martyrdom. She characterized her walk through the cathedral as a pilgrimage, and registered a (literally) blow-by-blow account of the archbishop's brutal demise: each spot represented Becket's last moments, and the cathedral's every stone was a monument to his protest against monarchical tyranny and for freedom of religion.[56] These venerations of Becket and Canterbury often elided – or ignored completely – that being 'near the beginning' of all that was 'good' in England also meant that the religious freedom that Becket embodied was that of Roman Catholicism, an institution usually seen by these Canadian tourists as one of the less fortunate aspects of British history. Opposing the autocratic power of the Crown could be heralded, it seems, so long as the religious principles at stake were left abstract and not tied to a specific denomination (see fig. 3.1).

Not all the places cherished by Canadian tourists for their link to English history and imperial greatness were associated with such tragedies (however inspirational). Oxford was a 'seat of learning, a view both ancient and renowned / where statesmen, scholars, poets, too, are graduate and gowned,' as Mount Allison Ladies' College student M.A. Black described her visit in her poem, 'Echoes from Our Trip, published in 1907.'[57] The college buildings and beautiful gardens quite overcame Chown and she was obliged to tell her family back home in Kingston, Ontario, that 'I saw so much that I can't tell you what I did see.'[58] Mackinnon had no such difficulty and offered his readers a detailed statistical appraisal of the number of students at Oxford, the histories of its colleges, the university's architectural appeal, and the treasures of the museum and the Bodleian Library.[59] Writing in the *Canadian Magazine* in 1912, Professor Archibald MacMechan of Dalhousie University focused less on the university's history, preferring to describe undergraduate life at Oxford, with its healthful and 'civilizing' effects on youth. MacMechan stayed at the university for twenty-four hours, thanks to a former student who was now a Rhodes Scholar there. Through a combination of a beautiful

3.1. Religious tourism: The Manitoba teachers at St Albans Cathedral, Hertfordshire (*Britishers in Britain*, 1911)

setting, hived off from the modern city, the 'paternal guidance' of the scouts, and the 'rigid, monastic routine' of rowing, together with the absence of luxuries, strict curfew, and early morning training, MacMechan explained, the youth of Oxford (a typical example being his former student) were able to work 'marvels' in improving themselves not just physically but also morally, spiritually, and intellectually.[60] Insofar as MacMechan mentions the presence of young women in Oxford, they appeared only, dressed in their 'gala attire,' in the magnificent Christ Church meadows, lying back as passengers in the comfort of the punt. But MacMechan assured his readers that Canadian 'girls' need not fear any comparison with these 'English cousins,' either in looks or in the 'fashion of their rainment.'[61]

Arnold Haultain wrote 'Oxford and the Oxford Man' in the Bodleian Library, a 'sacred and historic space,' but on looking up from his seat he saw 'flitting among these musty tomes, youthful women, good to look at, gentle, with fly-away hats and tight-fitting skirts.'[62] Peering out the window he saw 'bands of hatless youth,' evidence that adolescence in

Oxford was 'just as interesting as antiquity.' Unlike MacMechan, however, he thought that the 'Oxford man' was 'a bit too self-absorbed and self-important.' He might be cultivated and polite, but he could also become 'brusque and insouciant,' lacking in sweetness and catholicity of taste.[63] Men at Oxford were too easily caught up in internal controversies trivial to others, Haultain believed, the Tractarian movement having been one such example – and such defects were serious matters, since 'Oxford men' followed a narrow trajectory from the university to Whitehall.[64] In other universities across the empire, explained Haultain 'many of [their] sons spend the long vacation in penetrating with rod and gun, far into the worlds of nature, carrying their packs, and portaging their canoes, like the humblest habitants; or supplement a scanty income by signing on as rod-men or claim-men or ... donning jeans and overalls and learning the ABC as well as XYZ or exploring or surveying or mining or constructing. At the heart of somnolent England such things may be unknown, unnecessary ... but on the outskirts of Empire somebody must and will do them.' Haultain's list of Canadian paragons of such vigorous and practically minded masculinity included a commander of horse troops, a gold prospector in the subarctic, and a lawmaker in a new territory who was creating a legal code for a people fragmented by race, religion, and custom.[65] Haultain spoke from personal experience, as he told his readers, having come from the 'outskirts' but receiving his education in England. But, he wrote, England no longer meant just the United Kingdom, for now it encompassed 'an Empire vast and complex.' To that end he wanted to see the model of Oxford questioned and a royal or imperial commission established to investigate the education of the empire's youth and explore 'how they might best be tutored in the responsibilities which the governance of that Empire entails.'[66]

Goldwin Smith, less caught up in Haultain's romance of the frontier,[67] explained that both 'Oxford and Cambridge belong at once to the past and to the present.' Oxford's apogee had been in the thirteenth century, when it was 'in the van of progress political and religious as well as scientific'; however, the clerical hold over the university that began during the Middle Ages meant that the colleges became 'paralyzed ... after the Reformation and made them and the universities which they had absorbed little more than seminaries of the clerical profession. Oxford especially sank into an organ of the Jacobite clergy and their party.' A century and a half of 'literary and scientific torpor' ensued that was not to be lifted until nineteenth-century emancipation. Now the universities were back in the 'van of intellectual England,' but they never would 'be again what they were in the thirteenth century, when the only source of knowledge was the oral teaching of the professor.' Smith was of the opinion that a married professoriate had improved matters and that 'intellectuality, combined with the simplicity of living enforced by moderate incomes,' produced a very pleasant society. As for the student body, while conceding that the image might well be that of the 'fast' set of 'wealth and aristocracy,' Smith also had found 'hard study, high aspirations, [and] ardent friendships,' not to mention 'romance' and 'refined' cultural pursuits. But Oxford's and Cambridge's famed athleticism left Smith sceptical. He decided that it was too early to tell whether it would develop healthy, strong characters. Notwithstanding the 'philosophical justification' for such pursuits, he pointed out that the boat race and cricket were recent developments, and their public demonstration 'an ominous exhibition of levity and fatalism.' Smith advised the would-be tourist to visit Oxford in May or June, 'when the place is at once in its full beauty and thoroughly academical.'[68]

These passages suggest that their authors took it for granted that the students, professors, and the spaces they inhabited at Oxford were masculine. Although Haultain reported that he saw women in the library, they were notable solely for their physical appearance, not because they were denied equal access to the university: his critique of the 'Oxbridge' system rested on its inadequate preparation of men for imperial service and did not stretch to imperial womanhood's exclusion. We might expect that, given her support for woman's suffrage, Mabel Cameron would have had something to say on this subject; however, she too focused on the appearance and historical flavour of these sites, preferring Cambridge over Oxford for the colleges' domination over the town. This more favourable impression of Cambridge may have been influenced by her delight in the pageant that she attended of great women presented in the town's Guildhall. Its author, actress Cicely Hamilton, portrayed 'the important role of women,' the great actress Ellen Terry's daughter Miss Craig depicted the french painter Rosa Bonheur, and the proceeds went to the women's suffrage movement.[69]

Playwrights and Poets

A short train journey from Oxford, the town of Stratford-on-Avon had become a popular spot on the tourist itinerary. As Ian Ousby has pointed out, by 1900 Stratford had become extremely popular, and visitors were expected to worship in an 'exalted and sanctified' manner.[70] George

Pack toured the town's church, the graces of Shakespeare and Anne Hathaway, and looked at the register in which Shakespeare's birth and death are recorded. He then went to see Hathaway's cottage, noting her bedclothes and furniture, and then proceeded to what had been the home of popular novelist Marie Corelli, He concluded his explorations with a visit to the house where the mother of John Harvard, 'Harvard College's founder,' was born and which had been preserved by Americans and displayed the Stars and Stripes.[71] Pack tended to be matter of fact in his assessments, but other writers were more enthusiastic. Edith Chown visited Shakespeare's daughter's home, his place of death, the grammar school he attended, the family graves, Anne Hathaway's 'very picturesque' cottage, and Shakespeare's house. She told her family that none of the latter's furniture 'is claimed to be Shakespeare's but just of his time.' She found the walk through the graveyard, with its overarching trees, 'beautiful,' and a 'knowledgeable verger' took her through the parish church. After seeing the cottage, Chown 'wandered through the fields that Shakespeare used to tread as he went to see Anne Hathaway.'[72] Like Pack, Cameron visited not only memorials to Shakespeare and Hathaway but also looked over the exterior of Corelli's house; she was more moved by the experience, though, noting that 'by the time we had to leave to catch the train back to London we all felt we had greatly profited by our visit to the shrine.'[73]

Just as not everyone was overwhelmed with Oxford and Cambridge as repositories of English history and culture, not all tourists registered only feelings of awe at Stratford. The Manitoba teachers were one of the few groups or individuals to feel inspired by their trip to the birthplace of 'their Poet and the corner-stone of the great Literary Temple of the Anglo-Saxon race.'[74] Ada Pemberton saw almost all of the requisite 'sights' in Stratford, but was most interested in sketching Hathaway's cottage, finding 'the old well and the old woman most interesting studies.'[75] Irene Simmonds, normally an enthusiast in her travels, visited the church and Hathaway's cottage but of the latter felt, 'there was little to see.'[76] Mackinnon reported that the wall of Shakespeare's home was covered with visitors' names and that P.T. Barnum had wanted to buy the house and send it to New York, but his plans were thwarted when the town officials learned of the idea 'just in time.' Many of these Canadian tourists were suitably enthralled by performances of Shakespeare in London, particularly Beerbohm Tree's productions of the historical plays, but for some of them his birthplace was not quite as evocative as Abbotsford or Ayr.

The Lake District had become a popular tourist spot during Wordsworth's lifetime, with regular summer train service and guided coach tours around the lakes, it also featured a number of hotels and guesthouses.[77] Culturally it had multiple attractions. By the late nineteenth century the Lake District was firmly ensconced in travel guides, as a place whose natural beauty had become emblematic of 'Englishness.'[78] Various Canadian trip organizers recognized the area's appeal and significance. In announcing his 1907 'European Educational Tour,' Dr Borden of Mount Allison informed prospective travellers that they would dock in Liverpool on 15 June and go straight to Windermere for the day, then take the steamer to Ambleside, and after a day there, travel by coach to Keswick and then on to Carlisle via the train.[79] The 1910 Manitoba teachers' trip included a stop in the Lake District where, reported journalist Newton MacTavish, the group went sailing on Lake Windermere. One of the teachers remembered that 'Wordsworth had occupied a cottage in the vicinity and had gazed for inspiration upon the superb beauties of the scenery,' a memory that 'immediately lent human interest to the whole countryside.'

Associations of various kinds were recalled for our enlightenment, and we began to realise that the haunts of Coleridge and Arnold were not places of imagination, but actual earthly paradises. Quotations, favourite and otherwise, began to effervesce, with the result that our average ignorance of lyric poetry became appalling. What were we to do? Here we were in the very birthplace of many poetic moods, and yet we knew them not. But there was meaning in it for us, because we had now visualisation of the environment, and we realised, even with our scant knowledge, that these masters of the lyric muse who had visited and dwelt here in their day with the truth and beauty of nature as their inspiration and genuineness as their foundation.[80]

In reporting his own travels, MacTavish was even more explicit about the importance of the Romantic poets and the ways in which they had become synonymous with the Lake District, and vice versa. Driving about the area in a tourist coach, he thought that while Canadian scenery, such as that of Gaspereau, Matepedia, and the Laurentians, was equally 'enthralling,' 'enchanting,' and more 'sublime, if not stupendous,' the work of Wordsworth, Coleridge, Southey, and Arnold demonstrated that 'man's hand' had been taming the English landscape for thousands of years.[81] But travel writing was not all lofty sentiments and elevated thoughts. As he did in his account of the teachers' trip, Mac-Tavish also poked fun at his (and, by extension, other tourists') ignorance when he attributed Southey's 'After Blenheim' to Wordsworth, a mistake that drew the mockery of his fellow tourists.[82] A partial redemption was achieved at teatime, at an inn near Dove Cottage, when MacTavish correctly quoted some lines from Wordsworth. The cultural competition having finished, MacTavish's mind returned to more lofty matters. As he gazed down from Coniston onto a pastoral scene of a shining lake surrounded by evening mist, cows returning from the fields for milking, a cottage surrounded by a stone fence, and an 'old man, smoking beneath the thatch,' who 'contemplates us with a[n] air of admirable detachment,' MacTavish was reminded that he and his companions were merely 'part of that restless, never-ending procession that fares merrily down the shining way, down to where the harvest moon gules gravely over Coniston.'[83]

Mabel Cameron too was moved by her trip to the Lake District. As she sat on Friar's Crag near the Ruskin Memorial on the shores of Derwentwater, she confided to her diary that 'the reflection of the moonlight on the lake, the island silhouetted against the dark sky formed a picture it will ever be a pleasure to recall,' and she walked very slowly 'as the beauties of the night called enticingly to us.'[84] Her pilgrimage included Wordsworth's birthplace (although she was able only to 'peep' at it since the owner did not allow visitors) and Ruskin's grave. She also went to the museum where, for 1d, she saw Ruskin's manuscripts, his personal items, and the linen pall used at his funeral (but was disappointed that his house also was off-limits to tourists).[85] Cameron's respect for these cultural figures did not, though, prevent her from enjoying humorous vignettes. Some little boys playing near the river's edge close to Wordsworth's birthplace had 'very interesting ideas indeed' about the poet. While stopping to take a photograph of a 'pretty pastoral scene' of cattle drinking near Grange Bridge, she opined that 'the cows resented this intrusion and started to leave. The picture June *did* get was quite different to the one we had wished for – two cows with tails upraised leaving the stream hastily and three already high and dry.'[86]

For Eleanor Watson, a trip to the Lake District was an opportunity to visit Coleridge's and Wordsworth's tombs, Coniston Church, and Wordsworth's grammar school. It also allowed her to go hiking and sketching with a group of women friends, tour abandoned lead mines, see both a circus and the procession advertising it, and watch an (unsuccessful) otter hunt (Watson found the latter quite exciting and was disappointed when the next day's hunt was moved to an out-of-the-way location).[87] Her account of the Lake District depicted a number of aspects of its 'history,' one of them being Ambleside's rush-bearing festival with its dancing and wrestling. A newspaper clipping pasted into her diary described the festival – (said to be a 'relic' of the time when church floors were covered with rushes, which were changed in mid-summer) as an *Old English* custom [that] reminds us that we are English, with a noble line of ancestors to be proud of and imitate.'[88] Like the rural ramblers, Watson also represented 'the past' as residing in the people of the Lake District. She described a woman who sat spinning at her cottage door at Chapeldale, a 'pretty and pleasing sight'; 'Darby and Joan,' their host and hostess at Keswick with whom they spent an evening by the kitchen fire ('Darby' read some 'killing tales in the Cumberland dialect which is very peculiar'); and the seventy-five-year-old sexton at Crosthwaite Church, the site of Southey's grave.[89] The sexton had known Coleridge, Wordsworth, and Southey 'intimately' but preferred the latter, as Wordsworth always seemed 'rather close and not inclined to talk to people; but Southey would never pass anyone without a word.'[90]

Other tourists also reinforced the distance between Watson and her group and 'times past.' Marching, 'travel-stained and draggle-tailed,' into the sitting room of the village of Patterdale's Temperance Hotel, the 'most interesting objects that met our gaze were three antiquated fossils, in the shape of three strong-minded "women's rights" sort of ladies, all seeming much suspicious' of Watson's party. Although they attempted to behave themselves 'in the presence of three such ladies,' devouring books as they waited to devour their tea, 'when one of our party, more wicked than the rest, took up her volume to hurl at a hat coquettishly appearing above a high-backed chair, it proved too much for our gravity and we gladly welcomed the summons to tea.'[91] While her diary depicts Watson and her companions as modern, 'new,' women who sported straw bowlers, shirtwaists, and long walking sticks and who – with the exception of a few days' visit from her brother – were quite capable of travelling independently as a group of single women, this vignette suggests that their claim to modernity was linked to their indifference to 'women's rights,' quite possibly because as 'modern women' they felt they had no need for such things.[92]

Secular and Sacred Past

While these attractions drew in many anglophone Canadian tourists, other places also had scenic and historical associations that promised to explain the meanings of 'Englishness.' A few travellers reached beyond the nineteenth century to link national identity to specific sites and anchor them in a historical narrative. Goldwin Smith began his historical tour of England with ancient Britons' hut-circles on Exmoor, earthworks at Whitby and Marlborough, and Stonehenge (which he believed had great contemporary relevance because these monuments belonged 'to a race which still lives'), and outings to Devon, Cornwall, the Welsh mountains, the Scottish Highlands, and 'above all in Ireland.' 'The history of England,' he explained, 'from one point of view may be regarded as a long effort to impart the political sentiments and institutions of the Anglo-Saxon to the remnants of the Celtic population' (success had been achieved in Scotland and western England, less in Wales, and the jury was still deliberating the case of Ireland). As well, he pointed out, history could be learned from Roman ruins (the only thing Britain had retained of that phase of its past); from the Saxons' tombs, burial urns, and weapons; from Berkshire Downs' White Horse (representative of 'the triumph of Christianity over heathendom'); and from Hastings, which had seen the death of King Harold ('one of the greatest catastrophes' of English history, since his demise brought about 'the fatal connection of England and France' and the 'evil traces' of the Norman aristocracy). The next four centuries, following Smith's narrative, marked the triumph of Catholicism and its 'peculiar morality,' of which beautiful Gothic cathedrals (Salisbury, Durham, Winchester, York, Ely, Canterbury, and Wells) were left as reminders.[93]

Despite his antipathy towards French Canadians and his belief in the superiority of Anglo-Saxon institutions, Smith did not argue that Catholicism and feudalism had been completely deleterious. Instead, he pointed out that, while by the time of their destruction the monasteries had become havens of vice, self-indulgence, superstition, intolerance, and idleness, prior to the sixteenth century they had served as refuges 'during the iron times of feudalism and private war.' Even their ruins provided the visitor with 'religious calm and tranquility' from the modern bustle. Furthermore, he continued, the nunneries had done good work: they had provided charity and hospitality and had 'preserved their purity and usefulness better than the monastic houses ... some of them were still doing good service in the education of women.' Although feudalism had its 'dark side,' Smith informed that in rural areas it was the 'only possible instrument of social and political organization' through which 'rough justice' and national defence might be organized; the tie between a 'good' lord and 'his vassals, though repugnant to the ideas of modern democracy, was not necessarily hateful or degrading; it has supplied congenial food for poetry and romance.' Resistance to overly strong kings might come from the barons, the 'rude champions' and 'trustees of liberty' who stood between the people and the despot's mercenaries. Moreover, he submitted, in feudalism's social structures might be glimpsed the dawning of a modern, domestic order. 'Nor ought it to be forgotten that rude and coarse as life in these castles was, in them took place a very happy change in the relations between the sexes and the and character of domestic life. In the cities of antiquity the men lived together in public, while the women were shut up at home almost as in a harem. But in the castle the sexes lived constantly together, and the lord must have learned to find his daily happiness in the company of his lady.'[94]

Leapfrogging over the Wars of the Roses and the accession of Henry Tudor, Smith moved next to the 'age of Elizabeth' in his assessment of those 'great houses,' such as Burleigh and Hatfield, which in their beauty, 'amplitude, solidity, and comfort ... no one has thought of improving them out of existence.' He dismissed the Stuarts' as an age of 'conflict and destruction' (with the exception of St Paul's Cathedral), although the fact that James II's statue still stood at the gates of Oxford's University College 'bespeaks the comparative mildness of the Second Revolution.' The eighteenth century could be tackled by visiting Blenheim, a place that conjured up Alexander Pope, the Duke of Marlborough, and Isaac Newton. Little was left of the palace's art and soon, Smith believed, its historical objects may be gone; nevertheless, the 'immemorial oaks' of its park would serve as reminders of this past. This period, though, was sadly deficient in moral conduct, wrote Smith, since the historical objects that once had filled its great houses had fallen 'into spendthrift hands.' Smith felt that here was a lesson for late-Victorian Canadians. The reason that those 'who inherited such abodes' could not be moral and happy lay in the manner of their acquisition: 'there is no virtue without labour.'[95]

As we have seen, while medieval cathedrals brought to mind specific historical scenes that spoke of larger themes – church-state relations, the virtues of a now-dominant Protestantism, or at times a nostalgic wistfulness for a supposedly simpler society – rarely did tourists dwell on the

Glorious Revolution or the Augustan age (as chapter 2 has explored, trips through Scotland readily evoked various episodes in Stuart and Jacobite history). At times certain places were visited for their associations with either seventeenth- and eighteenth-century culture or social 'progress,' particularly the beginning of English capitalism. Harriett Priddis visited the Doulton factory at Burslam and went to its church to see Josiah Wedgewood's bust. She then travelled to Stoke-on-Trent where, after a Spode factory tour, she searched for Josiah Spode's grave but could not find it, despite having had the assistance of the church's curate, organist, and six small boys.[96] Following those pilgrimages Priddis visited Lichfield, where she paid homage to the busts of Samuel Johnson and David Garrick and toured Johnson's infant school and childhood home. 'Oh dear,' Priddis confided to her diary, 'it seems as if I have gone right back to my school days.'[97] Other cultural associations were with writers such as George Eliot. Making her way to the school in Nuneaton, where her aunt was to lecture, Mabel Cameron passed a group of small boys 'and heard one say "What wench was that?" We knew indeed we were in George Eliot's haunts. This was her birth-place and the scene of many incidents in her books.' Their feeling of a connection with the past and its literary representation was reinforced when they arrived at the school and met an education councillor whose mother had gone to school with Eliot.[98] Priddis had a similar experience while travelling through Nuneaton Junction on her way to Richmond; seeing the countryside 'makes George Eliot Adam Bede etc. very real.'[99]

But if the eighteenth century was not particularly fascinating to many Canadian tourists, the Tudors, particularly Elizabeth, captured their imaginations. As chapter 5 will explore, in London the Tower and other sites sparked a host of associations with history, from the sumptuous to the tragic. A number of these tourists stopped at Kenilworth Castle in Warwickshire, built by that sixteenth-century Earl of Leicester, whose 'dark ambition,' according to Goldwin Smith, 'entertained the woman whose throne he hoped to share.'[100] More of this 'dark ambition' was alluded to by M.A. Black, in 'Echoes from Our Trip,' who described the ruined castle 'which speaks of glory vanished now into the long ago; with tear-dimmed eyes and thoughtful brow we nurse on "Amy's woe."' ('Amy' was the Earl's wife, whose death – believed to be either suicide or murder – at Kenilworth was popularly believed to have been engineered by her husband in order to attempt marriage with Elizabeth I).[101] John Mackinnon, though, assessed the ruin with his customary sceptical and not particularly teary eye, telling his readers that until sixty years ago it had been a quarry from which dykes and stables might be mended but now tourists are let in at a shilling per head, and from his exact description, one would supposed the guide had helped 'lay each stone in position.' Nor was Amy's woe uppermost in his mind as Mackinnon was shown around the various rooms. 'Not a few of these [scenes] are imaginary; but as the visitor has bought a book and paid for attendance he may as well not be too skeptical and take the worth of his money ... the ruin is worth a visit and would be more enjoyable if one were allowed to cruise round by himself and not be harassed with help at every turn.'[102]

England's glorious past also resided in her ports. From Plymouth and Bristol a particularly masculine type of 'Englishness' had ventured forth, embodied by explorers, merchants and traders, and the navy. Perhaps not surprisingly, Priddis's trip to Plymouth conjured up the 'Virgin Queen,' Walter Raleigh, and the Armada, although the friend that accompanied her 'told us so much that I am all mixed up. Will have to read up the history when I get home.'[103] For Emily Murphy, a six-week stay in Plymouth reminded her of Cavaliers, Roundheads, and the *Mayflower*, although the area near a 1648 battleground had less savoury contemporary connotations. 'It might be called "Freedom Field" too,' she wrote, 'because it is open at night and is a trysting place of questionable or rather unquestionable character, for the soldiers, marines and girls of the lowest stratum of society'[104] In Bristol, Murphy reported, a tourist could spend much time ruminating on any number of historical events and personalities linked to the transatlantic world: John and Sebastian Cabot, Martin Frobisher, the privateer Captain Rogers, and Alexander Selkirk.[105] Yet its history – and its connection to North America – was not just one of brave, if sometimes audacious, deeds. Underpinning the port's commercial success was the transatlantic slave trade from which many large fortunes had been made, either through the slaves' direct importation from West Africa or from their sale in the Caribbean after Britain ended its participation in the trade.[106] According to Methodist minister Hugh Johnston, though, Bristol might be partly redeemed, since it also had seen the first open-air preaching of both George Whitfield and John Wesley himself: transatlantic traffic, as the presence of a Canadian Methodist minister in the port suggested, might involve the circulation of more than just goods and bodies.[107]

As Johnston's comments indicate, religion was part of the tourist's landscape of English history. In addition to his rural rambles, the Reverend Frederick Hastings also made a pilgrimage to Bedford, the scene of

John Bunyan's 'sufferings and labors.' He admitted that he did not go wearing rough clothing and bearing a staff, 'trudging' along the road-side, and begging along his journey; instead, he went 'easily and com-fortably down by express train on the Midland route, paying for my ticket and discharging all expenses like an ordinary and honest man.' Once at Bedford, though, Hastings was a bit disappointed to find that the jail where Bunyan had been incarcerated and where he had written *Pilgrim's Progress* had been destroyed, although he did manage (albeit with some difficulty) to see some of his 'relics' in the Independent Chapel. These sites, along with a trip to Bunyan's home in the nearby village of Elston, worked their 'magic' for Hastings, who had no diffi-culty imagining his hero at work and in restful contemplation.[108]

The clergymen who wrote columns in the *Christian Guardian* about their travels through Britain and Europe were keen to visit areas and sites that had witnessed the progress of Methodism. Writing about his 1890 tour of England, the Reverend H.F. Bland reported that Wesley's first chapel was in Bristol and that it still existed, although he was none too happy that it had not been 'retained by the connexion' and now belonged to the Welsh Calvinistic Methodists.[109] Twenty-two years later the Reverend William Wakinshaw conducted a Wesleyan tour of Bristol for his Canadian readers, taking them through the fourteenth-century church of the Knights Templar (with memories good and bad), a spot where John Wesley 'had one of his many hair-breadth escapes from death' (an accident involving a horse and cart), and the chapel of Broad-mead, the oldest Methodist chapel in the world and a 'Bristol shrine' with an 'incomparable charm for every Methodist pilgrim.' The last stop on Wakinshaw's route was the site of the schools at Kingswood founded by the Wesleys and Whitfield, one for colliers' children, the other for the offspring of preachers. He was happy to note that the roof and walls 'remain practically as they were when the trio of heaven-inspired evangelists began the mightiest revival of religion that has aroused England since the Reformation.'[110]

Thus, despite the comfortable railcar that took the 'pilgrim' quickly to the desired shrine, the decidedly secular activity of tourism could be dedicated to a sacred purpose. Such narratives also served a more pointed political purpose, as they insisted that the meanings of England's past and present could be found just as readily in the chapel as in the cathedral; both sites were part of England's Protestant history and contemporary identity. Moreover, either by visiting directly or being transported by the medium of the travel account, both the writer's the reader's faith would be strengthened and intensified by, first, this reminder that it had a 'history' and, second, by the almost other-worldly sensation of walking with Bunyan or Wesley, touching the items that they had used, and standing in the places where they had experienced such strong religious feelings. These travel accounts were not unlike conversion narratives; both genres were premised on the belief that their authors could transport, move, inspire, and educate their readers in ways both spiritual and secular. While tourists experienced the landscapes of England through a web of physical sensations, they also peopled their travels with history's ghosts, phantoms that might range from the benevolent to the malevolent. In the case of religious tourism, though, for the most part the spectres conjured up were not just benevolent: they were inspirational.

Into the West: Wales

Southern and western England received its fair share of English-speaking Canadian tourists, and some ventured further west into Wales. Edward Greenshields started in Llangollen, home of a 'fine abbey,' many local landmarks, and the 'Ladies of Llangollen,' the latter having been two Irishwomen who dressed in riding habits, tall beaver hats, white shirts, and 'looked very like men in "their" get up.' One lived to be ninety, the other to seventy-six, and both were rich and well educated, kind to the poor, and became celebrities who were visited by the likes of the Duke of York, the Duke of Wellington, and Sir Walter Scott. Greenshields thought the town very 'picturesque' and was pleased to view the monument put up to the Ladies and their servant, Mary Carrell.[111] After Llandudno he travelled to Llanberis, where he visited a waterfall said to be haunted by the spirit of Sir John Wynn, a knight who had so badly oppressed the people of the area that he was doomed to eternal punishment (to be purged, spat on, and purified in the waterfall).[112] Greenshields also made a point of touring Carnarvon Castle, which he mistakenly identified as purportedly the 'finest in England'; however, it sported octagonal towers that he judged to be not as 'romantic or beautiful' as those of nearby Conway Castle.[113]

Harriett Priddis went to Wales primarily to visit family members, although she appreciated the beauties of the gorge near Brecon.[114] At a relative's farm she was treated to the sound of twenty 'young colliers' singing in the orchard (accompanied by a piano they had moved from the farmhouse). They sang the Welsh national anthem for her, for which Priddis thanked them and told them her mother had been a 'true Welshwoman.' 'What a safeguard from rowdyism music is,' she thought as she drove away.[115] Welsh history also interested Priddis, probably because of her familial connections (she also visited her mother's birthplace). Her travels in Wales, though, did not produce the same kinds of linear narratives that journeys around England or even Scotland elicited, possibly because she had not been given the same education in Welsh history as in the former. Priddis wrote of the Welsh past in fragments, and her account ranged over a number of discrete topics: the Romans ('it is difficult for a Canadian to realize how old things are here'[116]), Uther Pendragon, Robert of Normandy (she saw the window in Cardiff Castle, where he 'looked out with longing for liberty before he lost his eyesight'[117]); and the history of Monmouth, joined by Henry VIII to England 'but even yet it is spoken of as Wales.'[118] She also was keenly interested in present-day Welsh society, visiting the Newport docks with their 'wonderful new transportation bridge machinery that puts me in mind of the ship railway in Amherst Nova Scotia only this is to work through to a commercial success.'[119] Some women waiting on the Monmouth rail platform interested Priddis, who thought they had 'better features than in the North.'[120]

Neither Greenshields nor Priddis ventured into the coalfields of Wales. Frank Yeigh, however, found time to visit this 'Dantesque realm' of chimneys, smoke, and dust, and to observe the miners celebrating the Bank Holiday, coming home from their crowded pubs in a boisterous and at times unsteady fashion. Drinking, though, was not the sum of all that could be known about 'the Welshman' or his country, for Yeigh found it all too easy 'to lose your heart' to Wales. Newport, Cardiff, and Swansea enjoyed active civic lives, its industries vigorous, its population growing, and its history interesting, if bloody (the ferocity of the Welsh people's struggle to defend their territory from the English could, Yeigh wrote, be understood once one appreciated the 'entrancing' beauty of its landscape). The Welsh were a musical lot, Yeigh believed, and was proven right when he was treated to a concert on a railway platform, performed by a choir of young men on their way home from an Eisteddfod.[121]

Yeigh considered Wales to be as much a part of 'modern Britain' as Manchester or Liverpool, yet he could not resist the lure of nostalgia and his desire to find the Welsh past residing side by side with its present. Delighted to see a wedding party make its way into an 'ivy-clad' church, he watched as the 'slow and pretty' procession of the bride and maids wound its way through a 'maze of crooked lanes.' The sight became even more pleasurable when Yeigh spotted 'an old Welsh dame, whose only tongue was her native Welsh,' leaning on a 'bit of slate, that chronicled the last resting-place of a forgotten citizen.' He momentarily abandoned his own party for 'the wrinkled, shrunken bit of humanity' who 'willingly' faced his camera, but regretted that he was unable to capture her curtsey as she wished him good day.[122] Yeigh's encounter with the woman was not an unusual one within the context of transatlantic and international tourism, as it repeated the trope of the educated and enlightened man who used the technologies of modernity (the newspaper report and camera) to introduce the eld-erly, non–English-speaking, female artefact of 'times past' to a modern readership (see fig. 3.2).

'Among Those Dark, Satanic Mills'?

Not all of England or Wales was delightful. Some areas were so dis-agreeable that tourists who ventured into them registered only their desire to leave as soon as possible (and not return), or they expressed their discomfort through caricaturing or stereotyping the residents. To be sure, industrial centres such as Glasgow, the cities of the Potteries District, Birmingham, and Nottingham drew the attention of a number of diarists and travel writers (particularly, although not exclusively, the men), who praised them as the home of the Industrial Revolution or as places where the continuing industrial production of certain crafts – Spode china, Wedgwood cameos, or Nottingham lace – could reassure the tourist that 'English' commercial culture still flourished.[123]

According to Goldwin Smith, however, there was little that was 'pic-turesque' or 'romantic' about the Midlands: 'From the praise of English scenery and of the outward aspect of English life must be emphatically excepted the manufacturing districts. Than these, perhaps, earth hardly holds anything less attractive … The heart of the hideousness is the Black Country of Staffordshire, round Wolverhampton, where not only is the scene by day 'black' in the highest degree and in every sense of the term, but the night flares with dismal fires, while the clank of the forges completes the resemblance to Pandemonium. The dark realm extends with varying shades of darkness over a great part of the North Midland counties.'[124] Smith harked back to the days of 'pleas-ant' and unpolluted dales' (whose streams initially attracted industry). Yet he also pointed out that there were also great 'marvels of the earth'

3.2. From 'The Welshman at Home.' In the photograph, the woman's face is blurred, her individual identity obscured. (*Canadian Magazine*, March 1914)

to be seen in the Black Country, such as 'machinery, mechanical skill, and industrial production. Pay the homage due to the mighty power of production and gratefully acknowledge the vast addition which it has made to human wealth and comfort.'[125]

John Mackinnon was far less reflective, noting that, as his train travelled from London to Liverpool, pastoral beauty and order were replaced with Wolverhampton coal and iron. 'For miles the railway passes through a continuation of mining towns and villages; the air is thick with smoke and great heaps of refuse are on every hand. Tall chimneys pour their inky offerings into the upper blue and great furnaces give out volcanic fires.'[126]

The northeast of England, except for Durham Cathedral, fared even worse under the pens of Mabel Cameron and Margaret Thomson. These two were among the very few women to venture near Newcastle's shipping and ironwork industries or the collieries of rural Northumberland and Durham. For the most part, these areas (with the exception of the city of Durham itself, particularly its cathedral) did not figure in Canadian tourists' notions of 'England.' Cameron travelled first to Horden, a mining town north of Hartlepool, for one of her aunt's lectures. Perhaps the audience's lack of enthusiasm coloured her dislike for Hartlepool. She observed in her diary that 'it is to be regretted that we do not rave over "healthful Hartlepool" which phrase is – according to our guide book – not merely an alliteration but the truth. Maybe, but please don't send me there if I am to be shipped anywhere for my health. It would be quite sufficient to hasten the end. One lady accosting another in the street says "How are you?" "Champion! How's yourself?"'[127] A visit to South Shields just over a month later was equally unappealing: 'South Shields did not offer many attractions so I stayed in all morning.'[128] While Thomson visited Seaton Belaval, northeast of Newcastle, to see friends, she also toured a coal mine and went down the shaft to the first level. She noted the pervasive dirt and coal dust but on the whole was 'very pleased' with their expedition. Her only feeling of sympathy was for the pit ponies; it was decidedly not for the miners or their families. Repeating a tale told to her by her friends, the Andersons, Thomson believed that all miners' homes had pianos 'and everything,' including new potatoes before the Andersons could 'dream of buying them. During the long strike a few years ago they came begging in lovely sealskin jackets. They gamble dreadfully and the average amount of laudanum taken by the women of Seaton Belaval colliery alone and given to their children is a "gallon a week."'[129]

Coming 'Home' in the Empire? English-Speaking Canadians and Imperial Relations

Class relations thus inflected travellers' perceptions of these land-scapes, whether as idyllic (if illusory) refuges from modern industrial and urban conflict, examples of the sorry state of English agriculture, or historical sites that testified to English progress and moral rectitude. Yet despite any current problems that they may have noticed in their tours of the English countryside and provincial centres, and despite the scepticism with which some of them viewed England's tourist sites, these men and women from Victoria to Halifax visited Oxford and Cambridge, Stratford-on-Avon, the cathedrals, and the country-side in the expectation that there they would find the basis for their own histories, their own meanings of 'Canada,' and their own mem-bership in the British Empire. By and large they were not disappointed. Their diaries, letters, and travelogues reveal varied and nuanced responses and reactions, but they do not reject or renounce such histo-ries or the notion that these narratives formed the basis of 'Canadian' histories, of 'Canadian' mores and values. Even Arnold Haultain, who believed that Canadian education and social practices were now supe-rior to those of Oxbridge, felt obliged to use the latter as an important standard against which Canadian performance should be measured. While there were a number of norms involved in these Canadians' per-formances abroad, an important one was that of membership in the British Empire, a membership claimed and legitimated through a shared history, a national and imperial memory which in turn bol-stered Canada's status as a white settler colony and dominion and an integral part of the 'British world.'

Such claims were made frequently by a group of teachers from Man-itoba: their belief that they forged a living chain between the 'new' world and the 'old' was reiterated constantly throughout their 1910 tour of England. To no small extent such claims may not be surprising, as they were made in the aftermath of the Boer War, the passage of the controversial 1909 Naval Service Bill, debates over imperial federation, and arguments that suggested Canadian support for British imperial-ism was a moral, as well as political and military, imperative. By this time the metaphor of Canada as Britain's dutiful and loyal daughter was not new; nevertheless, it was put to work over and over again as a means of explaining the teachers' tour, their reason for going to Britain, and the warmth of their British colleagues' welcome (see fig. 3.3).

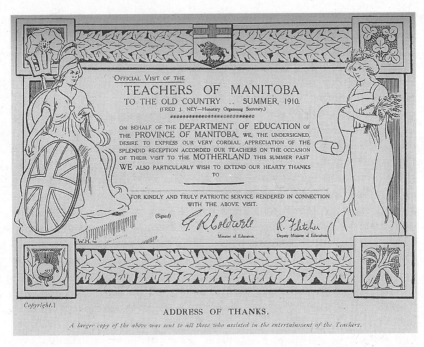

ADDRESS OF THANKS.

A larger copy of the above was sent to all those who assisted in the entertainment of the Teachers.

3.3. Family ties: the Manitoba teachers' tour, 1910 (*Britishers in Britain*, 1910)

'How,' asked tour organizer Frederick J. Ney, 'shall the daughter, separated by thousands of miles of sea, have that love of the Motherland if she know not the mother, or how shall the mother regard the daughter she has not seen?'[130] Ney found his answer in the trip, which was supported by Lord Strathcona, the Victoria League, and Lady Aberdeen, as well as G.R. Coldwell, the Manitoba minister of education. The teachers were, after all, 'of the young blood of the Great North-West, holding in their hands the destiny of the Mighty Dominion. Theirs is to make British the thousands of children of foreign birth (with their almost traditional dislike and jealousy of our race) who are peopling the Western prairies. Nobly and patriotically are they accomplishing their great National and Imperial task, and to them all praise is due.' And, just in case a British audience might not realize the challenges the teachers faced, Ney went on to list the many groups on the receiving end of this task: materialistic Americans; poverty-stricken Dukhobors and Galicians lacking any conception of 'nation'; Germans and French, whose problem was that their conception of nation referred only to their homelands; Italians and Greeks, whose longings for 'home' were tied to a desire for better weather; and Russians and Poles, who had just left bitter political conflict and were suspicious of any and all government.[131] Designed to 'further this great work of unification and nationalization, the one hundred and sixty five Manitobans came to the land of their forefathers' so that they 'could for themselves solve a great problem, that of deciding whether the British nation was still to be their ideal and their first love.'[132]

Their answer was a resounding and unequivocal yes. At every stop along their way the teachers reaffirmed their commitment to Britain and Canada's place in the empire.[133] This was made particularly evident when a small party who had decided to see France, Belgium, and Holland returned from Europe. Writing in the published account of their trip, Winnipeg's Margaret Dickie declared that their journey across the English Channel made them 'appreciate more fully England and its familiar customs and generous hospitality.' Despite having previously spent only two weeks in London, 'we felt we were returning home ... we rejoiced to see again the ancient landmarks of England and the monuments that mark the resting place of many of its famous men. We felt proud that we, too, were Britishers and that we also had a share in the great and glorious part of that country. Seeing other lands, had made our own dearer to us, and we thanked Providence that we lived under the dear old Union Jack.'[134]

Fellow Winnipeger Thomas Laidlaw echoed Dickie's reaffirmation of imperial identity. Although this was not his first trip overseas, Laidlaw was struck by the importance of the past to himself and his colleagues. Although they had known that the 'Old Land's' historical associations belonged to them and had always been 'proud of the traditions of our race,' the past took on a new, more forceful meaning when they 'stood by the tombs of the mighty dead, or gazed on buildings and scenes that were old and famous in history before Canada even had a name.'[135] However, unlike the characterizations of other nations' pasts found in imperial discourses, to them, Britain's 'glorious history' had nothing to do with decadence: 'our Empire is yet far from the zenith. In England and Scotland and Ireland, the past is all around you crying and urging you on; everywhere you see its lessons, its mistakes and its glorious achievements.'[136] The result was the return to Canada of a group with a much deeper and more sympathetic knowledge of 'their kin in the Motherland ... with a greater reverence for the Past and a higher hope of the Future ... they feel they will be better Canadians and better Britons because of this visit to the cradle of the race.'[137]

The Manitoba teachers were not the only advertisements for and public representations of the charms of white anglophone Canadian womanhood. Both the *Toronto World* and the *Hamilton Spectator* organized overseas tours in 1907 and 1908 intended to promote Canada, English-speaking Canadian women, and of course, the respective newspapers.[138] Following, it seems, on the heels of American papers' similar endeavours, the *World* organized a competition to send the eleven winners – or 'Maple Blossoms,' as the paper dubbed them – to London (the women canvassed for votes, sold subscriptions to the paper, and collected coupons in order to qualify). The competition combined elements of a horse race, election campaign, and marketing drive; the successful Maple Blossoms were touted as 'genetic Canadians,' most of them of the third generation.[139] The paper was particularly pleased to boast of the accomplishments of Lizzie Mcgregor, the first-place winner with over one and half million 'votes' who was of good 'Scottish' stock: a bright, able, and businesslike young woman who used her extensive network of personal and business contacts as a mantle-maker at Simpson's to garner support.[140] Other Maple Blossoms used contacts at Bell Telephone, the Freemasons, and Toronto's labour movement to win a place on the trip (see fig. 3.4).[141]

Although it is less clear how the *Hamilton Spectator* selected the thirty-two 'Spectator Girls' to travel through Britain and tour Paris (the trip was timed to coincide with the London Olympics), there were many similarities between their trip and that of the Maple Blossoms. Like the teachers' tour, in which Canadian nationalism and support for the imperial tie was a performance in which nationalism and imperialism were 'over the top,' heightened and exaggerated as a means of legitimating the enterprise and ensuring the continuation of such trips, nationalism and support for Britain linked these two tours. The young women were said to have been terribly excited at the prospect of seeing London and, in the case of the Spectator Girls, parts of Ireland, Scotland, and England as well. Both groups went to Paris, but neither was overly impressed; they found the city too expensive, the food unappetizing, and the Parisian way of life too 'fast.' As we shall see in chapter 8, though, other Canadian tourists were quite enthralled with Paris, particularly its outdoor life and culture. Indeed, so committed were the Spectator Girls to their home country and Britain that they insisted on cutting short their time in Paris in order to be back in London to see fellow-Hamiltonian Bobby Kerr receive his Olympic gold medal (see fig. 3.5).[142]

3.4. The 'Maple Blossoms' (*Toronto World*, 24 July 1907)

As Adele Perry and Katie Pickles have argued, nineteenth- and early twentieth-century colonial and imperial governments and voluntary organizations attempted to secure imperial ties through the importation and display of white British womanhood. The Manitoba teachers' and the newspaper-sponsored tours were similar exercises, albeit ones in which the transatlantic flow of women was reversed.[143] The teachers' and newspapers' tours advertised this version of Canadian womanhood for a number of purposes and audiences. For one, they reassured prospective British emigrants that, no matter its different landscape and climate, Canada would be familiar in many other ways. Such reassurance was necessary since the tours were full of hints that – as well as the satisfaction of seeing Buckingham Palace and Madame Tussaud's – romance and marriage might ensue. Ney, MacTavish, and the teachers themselves repeatedly reassured their audience (and, I suspect, themselves) that the women teachers were, on the one hand, professionals, 'new women' who were trained to uphold the empire in a disciplined manner, but on

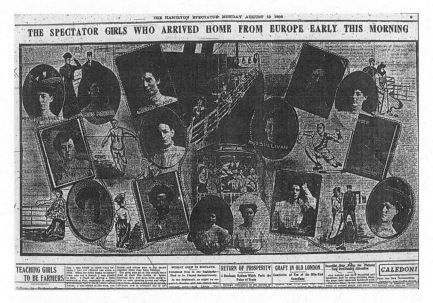

3.5. The 'Spectator Girls' (*Hamilton Spectator*, 24 July 1908)

the other hand, they also were proud specimens of Canadian femininity, ones whose looks and demeanour would send a message to their British siblings that life in Canada did not disrupt the norms of domesticity and heterosexuality held by its British parent. In his welcome address to the party, the Vicar of St Cuthbert's Church in Carlisle told the teachers that, while all were glad to see them, 'there was one section of the community who were more glad than all the rest. For a long time the bachelors of Carlisle had been looking forward with intense interest in the visit, and he only wanted to put in one word of warning – they must not forget in that connection that they were living not far from Gretna Green.'[144]

Dress and costume also featured in the staging of these women as suitably feminine representative of Canada. The *World* described the travelling costumes worn by the Maple Blossoms in careful detail, drawing special attention to their combination of practicality and feminine attractiveness, while the Hamilton newspaper was happy to report that the *Montreal Witness* thought the Spectator Girls to be fine examples of beguiling femininity.[145] The *Spectator* also reported the women's joking anecdotes of flirtations with the ship's crew, which came to a light-hearted end with the (expected) revelation in Liverpool that the

3.6. English-Canadian womanhood on display in the imperial capital (*Daily Express*, 14 Aug. 1907)

latter were all married men.[146] Such appeals for anglophone Canadians' acceptance as part of the imperial family thus were underpinned by the respectable, yet desirable, femininity of the tours' participants. It was no accident that the Spectator Girls supported and celebrated the rugged masculinity of Canadian men, expressed in one of its most physical manifestations in the theatre of international sports.

These presentations and performances of colonial belonging were acknowledged at the metropolitan level. London's *Daily Express* ran a large picture spread on the Maple Blossoms, having photographed them consulting guidebooks on the steps of the Tate Gallery, arriving at the British Museum, and posing with a very young Con Smythe, their 'pet.' This 'gay party of Canadian girls,' the *Express* noted, was trying to break the sightseeing record of Ohio's 'Buckeye Daisies' while in London (see fig. 3.6).[147] But as well as enacting these gendered roles for a metropolitan audience, these tours played various roles 'at home.' For one, there was the publicity generated for the sponsoring newspapers; accounts of how the Maple Blossoms, for example, won their places on the *Lake Manitoban* invariably mentioned the number of newspapers sold, not to say the role played by the paper in promoting Canadian interests. Although Manitoba's education department did not garner any immediate financial rewards from the teachers' tour, its organizers hoped to bolster the image of the public school teachers and the status of teaching as a cultured, educated, and knowledgeable profession, particularly in face of the increasing feminization of its workforce and growing concerns about the national, ethnic, and racial composition of the Canadian student body.[148] The tours were praised as a means whereby Canadians might learn more about Canada: the teachers were also exposed to the scenery and historical sites of Ontario and Quebec, while much was made of the Maple Blossoms' and the Spectator Girls' impressions of Montreal, which they toured before embarking on their overseas voyage.[149]

The presentation of these images and performances of gender and nation 'abroad' was aimed too at a home audience that had its own concerns and preoccupations about gender relations. Whether the image was of the competent yet still womanly schoolteachers or the businesslike yet attractive 'working girls' employed in southern Ontario's commercial and manufacturing sectors (who were also quite respectable, as comments about the 'Spectator Girls' adherence to temperance suggested), Canadian readers might receive much-needed reassurance of the modern, yet wholesome, nature of white anglophone Canadian womanhood. To audiences who had witnessed various challenges to gender roles, whether in the legislature, university lecture hall, or on the shop floor and picket line, the teachers, Maple Blossoms, and Spectator Girls may have been a comforting reminder that Canada remained stable and secure in both the private and public domains.

If English-speaking Canadian women were displayed *and* displayed themselves as desirable gendered representations of their country, demonstrations of British military technology, the spectacle of martial masculinity, and accounts of imperial warfare also caught the interest of diarists and travel writers. J. Rupert Elliott devoted an entire chapter in the account of his travels to the Great Naval Review at Spithead, where even the 'guns, anchors, chains and winches, so becomingly posed and arranged, are things of beauty today.' Elliott was excited to see the ships of other countries, the 'foreign men-of-war' of Russia,

Germany, Italy, France, Spain, the United States, China, and Japan (being particularly enthralled by the ships of the latter three countries).[150] The royal salute was thrilling, but Elliott took special pleasure in the knowledge that Nova Scotia's Samuel Cunard owned one of the three largest and fastest ships. 'No ship or company upon the Solent today makes a prettier appearance than the one carrying the colonial troops. Their varied uniforms are happily mixed, and the company seems very jolly as they pass us, waving their handkerchiefs. We all give them a cheer.'[151] Elliott was as delighted by the behaviour of the crowd as with the naval spectacle: 'the ill-sorted and rowdy element, which is usually enticed to such places, did not appear ... Each seemed to vie with the other in being the best behaved. I consider it at once a grand demonstration of what liberty may do to foster that magnanimity and nobility of nature which makes a people strong as well as great.' Having dealt with the present, Elliott then gave his readers a history of the Tudors' review of ships in the Solent.[152] Even John Mackinnon's iconoclasm was muted while he observed the military review at Aldershot, in which troops from India, Ireland, and the Highlands displayed trophies from overseas victories and received ovations from the cheering crowds. He watched from a hilltop the 'vast multitude melting away in all directions, troops and volunteers winding along the valley, each company headed by its band. To me the sight was particularly attractive.'[153]

Ethel Davies noted the progress of the Boer War throughout her stay in England. She felt its impact on both the imperial and domestic fronts, and its unfolding caused her worry, not delight at the prospect of military spectacle. In October 1899 Davies wrote that London's newspapers reported that the Boers were bearing the brunt of the damage: 'but I cannot bear to dwell on this war, it seems so barbarous and cruel in this age of civilization that no other method can obtain the desired result but bloody and fierce war.' Tis sad indeed to think of the many homes in England tonight mourning the loss of some brave father or son cut down perhaps in the prime of life.'[154] On a visit to Aldershot, where fourteen thousand soldiers were garrisoned, she observed Princess Beatrice Henry of Battenburg, who was looking very sad 'and troubled, too, thinking no doubt of her husband far away in Africa fighting England's battles.'[155] Her cousin was 'wild with enthusiasm and excitement' to be 'off to war ... but we all rather dread the thought of the battlefield.'[156] The coming of spring to the English countryside in early February, with its lambs, daffodils, and violets, was a jarring contrast with the news of

Spion Kop and Ladysmith: 'it all seems very dreadful while we are safe at home and our brave men dying and fighting for their lives out in Africa.'[157] The news improved later in the month, and by March Davies was thrilled to record the 'Glorious news! Ladysmith is relieved! ... the excitement and enthusiasm of everyone is unbounded. Bravo for our brave fellows.'[158] Returning to England after a side trip to Europe, Davies was thankful to record Mafeking's relief.[159]

War was not the only way that during their time in England English-speaking Canadians were reminded of their membership in a wide-ranging imagined community of the British Empire. At his cricket match in Brighton in 1887, George Lindsey observed that 'the last [Golden] Jubilee sightseers were taking their morning outing. Princes from the Indies and Chinese diplomats saluted English nobles, and goodness knew what.'[160] During his brief sojourn at Oxford, Archibald Mac-Mechan saw among the punters on the river 'two tall fellahin' who gave the impression of 'an undiscovered carving in the temple of Karnak ... [and] a well-dressed African negro who squired three white women.'[161] Oxford, he concluded approvingly, 'is cosmopolitan and hospitable.'[162] After her aunt's lecture near the New Forest (where the audience included two nieces of Joseph Chamberlain and Mrs Hargraves, Lewis Carroll's original 'Alice'), Mabel Cameron paid a visit to the nearby home of a 'Miss S,' which she was fascinated to note, was filled with Persian artefacts: tiles, carpets, pictures, and porcelain. Miss S and her brother, Major S, had lived in Persia 'long enough to understand this fascinating part of the world. Several books have come from the pens of these two Empire lovers. Miss S is just now keenly and vitally interested in Canada and is planning a comprehensive tour there in April.'[163]

As we shall see, such accounts flourished in the context of imperial London. Yet these tourists also experienced the ambivalence that, as Homi Bhabha has argued, resides within colonial encounters. Although in Bhabha's analysis such ambivalence is more frequently felt by the colonizer, when we explore the relationship of these white colonials to the imperial metropole it is clear that colonial ambivalence ran in many directions. While these Canadians frequently expressed and claimed kinship with England and the English (often because they might literally be kin),[164] when it came to British notions of Canada and Canadians, acting out one's role in the imperial family might be a complex performance. Despite its repeated assertion of membership in and devotion to the empire, the account of the Manitoba teachers' trip (and, in fact, the reason for the trip in the first place) made it clear that such feelings were not stable and could not be taken for granted. The party of English schoolteachers who welcomed the Canadians, their 'Over-Sea sisters and brothers,' in the Lake District first expected the group to be like the teachers from the United States who regularly visited the area, 'information-seeking, self-assertive, hurried globe trotters.'[165] To their great pleasure, they found that their guests' 'dress, appearance, and manners were not to be deprecated or sneered at'; in fact, in many ways the Canadians were seen to be 'the superiors' of those tourists who came to the Lake District in such large numbers.[166] Ney solicited the favourable opinions of other English 'hosts' who were happy to attest to the bonds that had developed between themselves and the Canadians.[167]

Yet imperial stereotypes and ignorance of Canada might linger and, at the very least, be a source of irritation. Staying near Hastings on a 1910 visit to Britain, Margaret Thomson went to hear a lecture, on Canada, given by a 'Professor McBride.' A graduate of Cambridge, McBride had taught at McGill University for twelve years but was not enthusiastic about Canada. 'Some of his statements,' Thomson noted, 'I think could well be challenged.'[168] Mabel Cameron was even more incensed – indeed, thoroughly disgusted – with a talk on Canada given that same year by Miss Ord Marshall, at London's Caxton Hall. She found Marshall's style to be both disorganized and flamboyant (she read her notes, mixed up the order of her slides, was dressed in a flowing opera cloak, and wielded a large handkerchief) and her content wanting. Marshall spoke of people who lived in woods and ate roots; her slides consisted of pictures of snow and ice. 'We thought she was never going to let up on these desolate views,' and from her 'weird descriptions no one would ever decide to go out to Canada in order to do better. It gives a totally wrong impression of our country.'[169]

Even when things went well, English-speaking Canadians' consciousness of being judged by the imperial centre was never far from the surface. Writing in the *Manitoba Free Press*, G.W. Bartlett was happy to report that the 'English hosts' had been very pleased with their guests. 'While none of the Manitobans wore blankets, scalp-locks, or feathers, there was an unconstrained frankness suggestive of the breezy West, a directness and a quickness of perception, which with the undeniable personal charms of our lady teachers made them the toast of the town.'[170] As with colonial ambivalence, colonial stereotypes might cut both ways. The teachers discovered that, despite the 'superficial differences,' 'the average Briton is neither a duke nor a flunkey. He does not speak patronizingly of "the Colonies," nor think that everything good is made in England.'"[171]

A number of tourists, however, found just the opposite and that more than one English person believed just that. Trains often were the staging ground in which these colonial encounters occurred, ones that might be even more difficult to manage than the representation of 'Canada' in imperial spectacles and exhibitions which (as we shall see) was important to English-speaking Canadian women. Here tourists were confronted directly with stereotypes about their society, ones that could not be dismissed as the work of a few misinformed individuals, such as Miss Ord Marshall, which did not resonate with the British population in general. Instead, they were forced to recognize that those men and women, whom they considered fellow members of their imperial family, saw English-speaking Canadians and their society as lacking in the social niceties and culture of Britain. Thus they were required to repeat the lessons that exhibition and pageant organizers had gone to such pains to inculcate, to (re)present themselves as representatives of a modern, 'civilized' people. Travelling back from her northern trip to York, Hartlepool, and Durham, Cameron was drawn into conversation with an Englishwoman who shared her train carriage. She asked Cameron many questions about British Columbia and then asked if people there spoke English. 'It set me thinking,' Cameron confessed to her diary, 'and I wondered what language I could have been using during our previous chat. "Does anyone die of pneumonia there?" "Oh, occasionally," I said. "Well, I suppose they have plenty of fever to make up for it." Law of compensation is evidently her motto.'"[172] Always eager to strike up discussions with fellow human beings, Harriett Priddis was en route from Liverpool to Stoke-on-Trent when she met a woman from India with her children and their governess, a 'bright Irish lady,' and a couple from Liverpool. The husband 'pitched into Americans and Canadians for being so cock sure they knew everything that no one bothered explaining the characteristics of older countries to them. I am sure he would change his mind if he had followed me around yesterday.'[173]

English-speaking Canadian women were more likely to record such instances of very personal and direct defences of their homeland in their diaries and letters home. However, their male counterparts also encountered similar moments, often when their own performances of Canadian manliness were misunderstood. After seeing the Indian and

Chinese princes at Brighton, Lindsey went over to the cricket ground, where he called out a greeting to a friend. His words 'dumbfounded a duchess-dowager spectator, who evidently thought that sort of thing was done by us by rubbing noses in Ojibway, for she ejaculated in blank astonishment and in an audible voice "why, I declare, they speak English!" This caused "the Baby," Fleury, to laugh so immoderately that the venerable lady formed a mental estimate that even if we had learned to speak English we had not yet learned to be polite, and relapsed into her seat, quite satisfied that she really knew all about the ways of the aborigines of the great North American Continent.'[174] Leaving Brighton for London another member of Lindsey's party was dressed in his cricketing gear, while a second player who went with him 'assures us that he was not taken for one of Buffalo Bill's Wild West men when he arrived in the metropolis, although he admits he excited a good deal of attention.'[175] Like the 'compliment' regarding the Manitoba schoolteachers' lack of feathers and blankets, these constructs of 'national' identity were enmeshed with notions of Aboriginality: some English observers of Canadians and Canada clearly conflated the two, and judging from Lindsey's account, English-speaking Canadian men might be willing to play such roles, albeit in a mocking fashion.

When faced with stereotypes and condescension to them as colonials, English-speaking Canadians drew on a number of strategies. As Lindsey's comments indicate, they either made fun of blatant ignorance or, as some of Cameron's diary entries suggests, challenged it directly. If circumstances or politeness did not permit either, there was always the tactic of biting one's tongue and then making sure that the transgressions of the 'imperial cousin' were duly recorded. Similarly, it did not hurt to display the (more positive) signs and signifiers of 'Canadianness' whenever possible. Cameron drew a large maple leaf for the local woman in charge of 'Canada' for a pageant of empire in the Lake District, while Edith Chown helped her aunt Alice construct the 'Canada' banner for the 1910 suffrage march through the streets of London to the Albert Hall (they also carried bundles of wheat, which fascinated spectators on the sidewalks).[176] Furthermore, these Canadians were not above indulging in certain stereotypes themselves. Witness the Manitoba teachers' and their organizers' desire to depict Manitobans as representative of a 'new country' in which directness, frankness, and a kind of breeziness compensated for a lack of historical landscapes, or Haultain's characterization of Canadian higher education as promoting a more corporeal and practical masculinity.[177]

To be sure, there were many powerful discursive and practical forces at work that shaped such self-characterization: the influence of popular culture and the media, both in Canada and abroad, which had already propagated such images, as well as the need to set oneself off from an imperial metropole that had already been imbued with 'history' and 'culture.' These could be almost impossible to resist, but like other stereotypes such markers of identity could be (and were, as some found out) used to create homogeneity, to sum up all that was known about Canada within narrow parameters. Moreover, not all found such markers and performances limiting. As Haultain's article suggests, English-speaking Canadian men could take on and perform the role of the white colonial masculine subject, one whose first-hand, experientially based knowledge of colonial projects, whether drawn from the command of horse troops or writing legal codes, was superior to that of his metropolitan counterparts. Similarly, after having been exposed to a hearty dose of British culture and history, anglophone Canadian women could impart the latters' lessons with a vigour and zeal that might be lacking in the 'mother country,' thus serving as the ideal of white, colonial womanhood. Thus English-speaking Canadians could go about the task of creating, in historian James Belich's words, 'better Britains.'[178]

This is not to argue that these tourists rejected England or Britain because of such encounters: national and imperial subjectivities were rarely forged, performed, and experienced in such unidirectional, linear fashions. It is merely to remind us that there were myriad ways for these English-speaking Canadians to be reminded of their connections to the imperial centre. On the one hand, both 'at home' and in the metropole they were assured that as representatives of a white, settler dominion with self-governing status they occupied a particular and privileged position in the imperial family. On the other, though, they might be confused with Americans. Moreover, even as white members of the imperial family, they were 'colonials' and as such were only indirect heirs to the historical landscape that surrounded them and about which they wrote so enthusiastically. As historian Angela Woollacott has argued, for Australian women in London during this period the status of 'colonials' was anything but desirable, as it was tied to notions of inferiority and dependency on the metropole for cultural, social, and political legitimacy.[179] While English-speaking Canadian tourists did not exhibit the degree of annoyance and sometimes anger as that of Australian women at being designated as 'colonial cousins,' they might feel compelled to mount demonstrations of nation and empire in which being from the 'other' side of the Atlantic was a source of pride and strength, not of isolation and parochialism.[180] But it also could be the source of tension and anxiety, fostering the need to constantly remind imperial audiences, and themselves, of their membership in nation and empire. The reiteration of that membership through national and imperial performances was ongoing and never complete, not least because these tourists were 'colonials' whose 'nation' was comprised not just of 'neo-Britains' but also of Aboriginal peoples, French-Canadians, and non-British immigrants.

Despite, however, their complicated status – elevated over some members of the empire because of skin colour, language, Protestant heritage, and a command of middle-class mores and manners, yet subordinated through assessments of geography, climate, and perceived cultural deficiencies – at the very least, these English-speaking Canadian tourists were not residents of Ireland. Although Ireland was not as popular a tourist spot as Scotland and England, a number of these travellers went there and wrote about their impressions and experiences. Their narratives illuminate further the intricacies and ambiguities of imperialist discourses and practices and their ability to both acknowledge and incorporate 'history,' while at the same time working diligently to deny and efface it.

4 'Paddy's Grief and Native Wit': Canadian Tourists and Ireland

Scotland and England held historical and cultural associations for English-speaking Canadian tourists and evoked reactions that ranged from pathos-tinged remembrances of the past to more celebratory affirmations of their contemporary membership in Empire. 'Ireland' – both the notion of the island itself and their encounters with its landscape and people – also induced manifold responses but these differed from those to other parts of the United Kingdom. The lenses through which travellers viewed Ireland and the categories they applied to sort out their reactions to it included history and the scenery, the contemporary political and socioeconomic situation there, and the 'character' of 'Paddy,' an entity often symbolized through the figure of the tourist guide. Some of their writings might seem predictable: tourists' variations on the stereotypes that circulated in North American and British nineteenth-century discourses about 'the Irish.'[1] Yet not all Canadians' reactions were predicated on notions of 'Paddy's grief and native wit.' Margaret Dixon McDougall's account of her 1882 trip demonstrated a greater understanding of colonialism's historical and ongoing presence and attempted to see the island's inhabitants in more complex and contextualized terms. But even the narratives that relied on stereotypes – whether of Irish history, society, or people – are worth exploring and interrogating. While they might not always tell us much about Ireland per se, nevertheless they enhance our understanding of how various kinds of discourses and ways of seeing shaped these anglophone Canadians' movements in the world of transatlantic tourism. Moreover, the history of tourism in Ireland has attracted less attention from scholars than is the case for Britain and many areas of Europe; thus these Canadians' travels can help contribute to an important but at present under-researched area of scholarship.[2]

Commerce, Industry, and the Colonial Past

'Ireland,' readers of the *Montreal Daily Star* were told in 1881, is a land
of impossibilities and contradictions. While intended to be a 'more
beautiful Holland' and to be inhabited by 'men half sailors and half
dairy maids,' instead it had been 'given' to those who were enamoured
of agricultural smallholdings, who 'multiply faster than their means,
and who have a special distaste or incapacity for the life of mariner,
fishermen, or seagoing traders.' And the one 'great race' who does not
'understand or like the Celtic genius' was bound by 'inexorable political geography to conciliate or govern Irishmen,' a group that was
essentially incapable of being governed.[3] Reprinted from the *London
Spectator*, this piece traded in some of the stock caricatures of the unre-
alistic and improvident, overly fertile, somewhat shiftless 'Irishman'
who, because of these characteristics, was fated to be ruled over by the
more successful and efficient (if less imaginative) 'great race.' Other
pieces reprinted from the international press also circulated related
types of images. Although an article entitled 'An Irish Fishing Village,'
originally published in *Harper's*, recognized that in fact fishing was
part of the island's economy, it gave the *Christian Guardian*'s readers an
even less flattering portrait of this community: isolated, prone to violence, poverty stricken, dirty, and smelly. What was worse, the village
women were idle gossips, who 'crouched ape-like' in front of their cabins in fruitless attempts to make the rags they wore provide modest
coverage. The only redeeming feature of the village was the welcome it
extended to its priest, the recipient of an extravagant hospitality that
was quite beyond the villagers' means. His response to their (mis-
guided) generosity was to scold them, like disobedient children, for
their faults and failings.[4]

   Anglophone Canadian tourists were not above replicating the image
of the feckless, happy-go-lucky, yet conversely priest-ridden Irish. Still
their own writings rarely produced images of such extreme immiseration and degradation or rendered the Irish so irrevocably to the status
of subhuman beings. Moreover, while rural Ireland promised a picturesque and romantic escape from late nineteenth-century society, Ireland's cities also appealed to Canadians. When not wandering through
rural England, in 1873 Fred Hastings found his strolls around Dublin's
main thoroughfares and sites – Grafton and Sackville Streets, Trinity
College, the Parliament Buildings, and Carlisle Bridge, as 'pleasant a
walk as will be found in any part of the British Metropolis.' Hastings
did, though, note the dirty condition of the Liffey, the city's smoke, and

its high mortality rates; he confessed that the city's physical environment was generally so unhealthy that he lodged outside its limits in
Kingstown. While unimpressed with some of its landmarks, particularly King William's and the Duke of Wellington's monuments, Hastings was quite taken with Dublin's police: 'a taller and more manly set
of men' could not be found, he told readers of the *Saint John Daily Telegraph*. And if the unhealthy conditions of Dublin became too oppressive, there was always the beauty of Phoenix Park. Not surprisingly,
Rev. Hastings was not pleased that St Patrick's Cathedral had been
restored with the financial assistance of the Guinness Brewery but he
allowed that Gratton Guinness had not only done 'much good' but
was a fine and able speaker to boot.[5]

Visiting two decades later, E. Dowsley, the author of a short series on
Ireland for the *Canadian Magazine*, agreed that Dublin had many attractions that should not be overlooked. It was not a commercial hub such
as London or Glasgow, did not boast the modern buildings of Paris or
Vienna, and did not have Edinburgh's blend of tradition and modernity, but there was much to see and enjoy in Dublin. The Ionic architecture of the Bank of Ireland, Trinity College, with its Elizabethan roots
and worldwide reputation (not to mention Canadian alumni), the
'wonderful structure' of the Custom House, the 'beautiful and interesting' St Patrick's Cathedral, the 'great Phoenix Park,' and the 'beautiful'
Glasnevin Cemetery, where one might see the remains of the 'great
Daniel O'Connell' – all these, explained Dowsley, could be viewed by
rambling through the city.[6] Father Mortimer Shea, a Catholic priest
from St Anthony's parish in Montreal, took great pleasure in his visit to
Dublin and had nothing but praise for that 'ancient city, so rich alike in
its historical, archaeological and architectural features.'[7] But it was not
just Dublin's history, important though it was, that enthralled and educated Shea. His tour, which included many of the same spots visited by
Hastings and Dowsley, proved Dublin to be a 'bright, cheerful city,
with every dignified attraction, and with thoroughfares constantly
filled with well-dressed and a business-like people' (see fig. 4.1).[8]

It is not surprising that Shea boosted not just Dublin but all of Ireland to his readers. Not only was he of Irish extraction, but he wrote
his book as a record of a trip subsidized by the archbishop of Montreal,
his fellow priests, and his parishioners. The travelogue was clearly
meant to impress on his readers that his journey had been morally beneficial and his experiences overwhelmingly positive.[9] But while Shea
was enthralled with Irish landscapes and sites that might be coded as

4.1. A modern Edwardian city for the Canadian tourist: Grafton Street, Dublin
(*Across Two Continents and through the Emerald Isle,* 1907)

'Catholic,' he did not stint in his praise of the island's northern cities
and their prosperity. From Derry's walls one could have a 'capital
view' of a 'modern and picturesque' city, one with 'edifices of
advanced architecture, monuments and cathedrals which redound to
its credit.'[10] With its 'wide and exceptionally clean' streets, Derry
boasted linen manufacturing, shipyards, iron foundries, distilleries,
and a large, year-round coastal trade.[11] Belfast, too, was one of the
most 'active and progressive cities' that Shea had seen. Clearly a
metropolis, Belfast had magnificent architecture, 'extensive and attractive shops,' 'ornate' warehouses, and the beautiful Botanic Gardens
Park: all supported by its long-established linen trade, booming shipbuilding industry, 'extensive' engineering trade, and the manufacture
of mineral waters.[12]

Shea was not alone in his appreciation of Belfast. In 1909 Irene
Simmonds found Belfast a 'large and beautiful city' and greatly
enjoyed her trip in a 'jaunting car' to the shipyards, where she
observed twenty steel steamships being built. 'Belfast must have great

wealth, to carry on so colossal a business (I wonder if we shall ever see steel shipbuilding in Halifax).'[13] As well as steel ships, though, Simmonds saw and purchased another Irish product, lace. 'I enjoyed going in the stores and seeing *real* Irish lace, made on the premises. We bought some beautiful lace handkerchiefs, and some fine linen ones. I bought some elegant towels. I wanted to buy heaps of them, they looked so nice.'[14] During their tour of Ireland, the Manitoba schoolteachers were treated to a commercial exhibition arranged by Lady Aberdeen, which featured carvings of bog oak, Connemara marble, and Irish poplin ties, linens, and laces: 'all representing Irish industry,' tour organizer Fred Ney reported.[15]

Cork, Drogheda, and Belfast's textile mills were on a number of itineraries, as were lace works in Youghall and Dublin.[16] Not everyone was as thrilled as Simmonds with her '*real*' Irish lace. Sophie Pemberton sniffed at the lace produced in Youghall, writing in her diary that, while the factory was 'most interesting,' the lace's 'design was mostly bad.'[17] Moreover, unlike other aspects of Ireland, and unlike the home-based production of textiles in areas such as Skye that (as we have seen), were linked to Scottish national character and its dissemination throughout the empire, even though the lace had to be 'real Irish' it and its producers were not held up as signifiers of 'Irishness,' as being somehow emblematic of ethnicity (although the poverty of the workers involved was, as will be discussed later, a matter of frequent comment). Instead, Belfast, with its large-scale industrial production, symbolized a particular type of 'Irish' spirit. In his 1911 article, Belfast: Ireland's Commercial Capital,' Alf S. Moore explained that the city's stimulating history of commercial growth – one of the most striking successes in Britain – could not be attributed to any geographical or climactic advantages; its boom and bustle were the result of the 'self-reliance, enterprise, and application' of its people. In Moore's estimation, the people of Belfast were a hybrid lot who combined 'the progressiveness of the Americans, the thrift of the Scotch and the pluck of the English, with a goodly flavour of the traditional hospitality of the native Hibernian race to leaven the lot' (see fig. 4.2).[18]

Although Moore heartily approved of the Belfast's economic success, he warned the would-be visitor that its architecture was, for the most part, 'utilitarian' and that the 'average Belfastman' 'is bluff to rudeness' and spends most of his time 'moneygrasping' and attending his 'Kirk where stern Calvinism is administered in more than homeopathic doses.' However, the 'philistine' nature of Belfast, which had

4.2. The Irish spirit on display: Belfast (*Canadian Magazine*, January 1911)

not been 'conducive' to literature, art, music, and drama, was being questioned and opposed; hope of even greater prominence might be found in its educational institutions, such as Queen's University.[19] In a similar vein, in 1909, Martin observed that Drogheda's linen factories, were the 'finest in the world' and employed a local population that was 'about two-thirds' Protestant. Drogheda itself 'has the thriftiest appearance of any city in Ireland.' it was clean, a 'good business place,' and in many ways resembled Manchester, without the smoke and dirt. At the York Street spinning works the workforce totalled three thousand and consisted mostly of girls and women 'barefooted and bareheaded. There is a fine cloak room erected to the memory of the late Prince Albert.'[20]

Industrial and civic accomplishments (the cleanliness of Drogheda's public thoroughfares, the impressiveness of Belfast's city hall), were in the context of Ireland synonymous with Protestantism. That these tourists saw them as one should not be overly surprising, given what we know about the linkage of public morality and prosperity to Protestantism in the Canadian context (and elsewhere).[21] But it is also worth noting that the 'Belfastman' was tantamount to the paragons of Protestant manliness said to have been responsible for the triumph of capitalism in cities such as Glasgow or Manchester and regions such as the Midlands. Such rhetoric obscured the presence of the minority Catholic population of Ireland's industrial north, both as a segment of society in general and as members of its workforce. It also suggested, Moore's recognition of 'Hibernian hospitality' notwithstanding, that if Ireland resembled Britain (or parts of Canada) it was the result of the spread of Protestant, 'British' institutions and values, a shared history of imperial progress.

As far as George Pack was concerned, Ireland's problems could be laid right at the church door. While viewing O'Connell's monument in Dublin – a 'fine shaft ... and which we might have gone up if we had paid a few coppers' – he struck up a conversation with the guide and asked him about the reasons for Daniel O'Connell's fame. When told that it was for trying to 'free' Ireland, 'I then and there asked him was not Ireland better off than France and Italy and what were they kicking out the nuns and priests for in those countries if they were so much better under Rome and the Pope than without them. He could not answer me.'[22] And the – by then – well-worn trope of the 'Catholic' landscape being dominated, literally and metaphorically, by the cathedral's spire made its appearance in travel writing. On approaching

4.3 The religious landscape of Ireland (*Across Two Continents and through the Emerald Isle*, 1907)

Queenstown in the southwest, Richard Duke informed readers of the *Christian Guardian*, in 1891, the most conspicuous sight from the harbour was the Catholic church. Although aware that its maintenance had swallowed up thousands of pounds, Duke felt that the building had been worth the expense.[23]

Father Shea's account of his travels in Ireland was, predictably, one of the few to praise the Church's presence there, to tie any signs of prosperity and improvement to its work, and to inform readers that Catholics were strong supporters of an institution represented by a very fine group of clergy (see fig. 4.3).[24] Yet, somewhat surprisingly, given the extent of anti-Catholicism in various parts of Canada during this period, most Canadians who wrote of their travels in Ireland had little to say about the Church itself as a factor for good or ill.[25] It was the infusion of religious doctrines and religious conflict into the secular arena of public politics that caused the most discussion in the pages of diaries and travelogues, particularly when their influence was visible in the streets of Dublin. The *Saint John Daily Telegraph*'s 'Occasional Correspondent' wrote that the 1875 commemoration of the hundredth anniversary of O'Connell's birth, 'which ... had never been equaled in the previous history of Ireland,' came very close to being a success. It attracted participants from all over Ireland, England, Scotland, France, America, and 'even Australia.' However, 'it failed, in being sectarian in its character, and in being almost devoid of members of the upper classes.' While many Protestants respected O'Connell's memory, they preferred to watch the ceremonies from their windows, having 'no desire to participate in what by some was considered a great Catholic demonstration presided over by Cardinal Cullen and a very bigoted Lord Mayor, while others looked upon it as a political affair and an intended defiance to the British government.' The ceremonies ended badly: Home Rulers in the crowd sparked a riot and prevented the mayor from reading an address on the 'Great Liberator's' life.[26]

Hastings noted the presence of placards in Dublin's streets that called for amnesty for political prisoners, but he did not approve of Home Rule 'agitation.'[27] While aware of the possibility of political violence, though, not everyone witnessed it or thought it was imminent during their travels. In Derry on 12 July 1887, George Lindsey wanted to see the day's celebrations of the Battle of the Boyne. Although Governor Walker's monument was decked out in orange, and many women in the town wore that colour (as well as sporting blue ribbons), 'the good-natured people did not look as if they would need the assistance of the Royal Irish Constabulary or of the local militia, which had been turned out for the occasion, to keep them from breaking the peace.'[28] Dowsley, eager to promote Ireland as a tourist destination, anticipated his read-ers' perception that the Irish lived in such a constant state of antago-nism towards the British soldiers in their midst that the two groups comprised separate classes, constantly at war with one another. Such was not the case, he assured his audience, and reported that he found that they enjoyed great friendships and shared public conviviality. Dowsley did feel compelled to address the Phoenix Park shootings of Lord Frederick Cavendish and Thomas Burke in 1882, but here again he cast the blame on a few cowardly individuals, men who did not repre-sent the Irish people in general and whose behaviour had unfairly tar-nished their countrymen's reputation. He was pleased to record many encounters with local residents who agreed with him.[29]

Mackinnon was a bit more sympathetic towards politically moti-vated violence. In Waterford he passed by a major hotel with a sentinel on guard who was not allowed to speak to him because a judge from Dublin was staying there. 'I thought this was going too far in a place seemingly quieter than Oxford; and I felt that were I a Waterford boy, I would try to set off a grenade under his honor's cassock.'[30] Mackinnon felt that Ireland was an unhappy island because of its landlords and its repressive laws, both of which kept it in a state 'similar to Turkey's'. Its laws did not suit the 'national disposition' of the 'fiery Celt,' and it was impossible for the Irish to live in a 'normal condition.' Instead, they had learned 'to agitate with fire, dynamite, and dagger.' But, like those who wrote about the sorry lot of agricultural workers in England, Mackinnon did not propose an end to 'landlordism' and colonial rule. 'In my opinion their great mistake is huddling together in that wretched country. No colonists get on better than the Irish in other lands – why therefore cling to where their lot is poverty and famine? One's country should be that in which he can live in the greatest comfort and ease.' The best way for them to take revenge on their 'oppressors' is to move and become 'in a sense independent.'[31]

Such commentary did not so much explicitly deny colonialism in Ireland as it elided various aspects of its history, avoided thorny questions of its relationship to capitalism, and downplayed the question of colonial appropriation of land and the distribution of power in Canada. It also relied on notions of essential and innate differences between 'Celts' and their British 'oppressors.'[32] To an even greater degree than in the case of Scotland and 1745, the question of England's 'conquest' of Ireland hovered over these discussions as something understood but not always clearly articulated. If the island was to no small extent a fundamental part of 'empire,' particularly as viewed from British North America, nevertheless its history could not be fashioned into the linear and successive narrative of imperial progress that England's landscape and sites elicited. Ireland could not be seen as a unified and politically independent entity and thus it was not a country, being tied to Britain politically and economically. It also, though, was not as central and basic to these Canadian tourists' understanding of 'British' and 'Britain' as were England, Scotland, and (for some) Wales.

Not all of these commentators were completely unaware of an Irish 'past' prior to the arrival of English rule. In his 1875 response to the letter of a P.J. Smyth, who had written to the *Saint John Daily Telegraph* on the subject of Ireland's 'ancient kingdom,' 'Mr. P' took issue with Smyth's conception of the island as a political unity. 'No doubt Ireland was at one time independent, and at another time united; but independence and unity were never severed at the same time. Her English invaders made her dependent; but after a time through much bloodshed and ruin gave her a political unity.' Waxing eloquent on the subject of political unification as a marker of 'the nation,' P went on to declare that 'when Ireland was conquered she was no more a "kingdom" than New Zealand at the time Englishmen first landed on her shores. Her provincial rulers could no more be called "Irish" in feeling or patriotism than the rulers of Burgundy, Lorraine, Brittany, and Normandy could be styled French in the days before their territories became part of what we now call France.'[33]

Even if Ireland may not have qualified for the status of 'kingdom,' Fred T. Hodgson had no qualms about discussing 'Erin' or 'the Irish' as an entity separate from England. His 'The Round Towers and Irish Art,' published in 1894, created a 'golden period of art and architecture,' 600–1000 AD, 'a time when Erin was the nursery of all the then known sciences, and she furnished the world with schoolmasters in the arts of building, music, literature and law.'[34] It was in Irish courts, Hodgson claimed, that 'the great Alfred first received the knowledge of law and military skill which gave to the Anglo-Saxon race trial by jury and the end of Danish predominance.'[35] He pointed out that this legacy of Irish greatness also could be seen in material form in those few towers left in Ireland (and that unfortunately hardly any of those erected in England, Italy, Spain, and Portugal had survived), in places such as Antrim, Meath, Kildare, Timahoe, Drogheda, Louth, and Kilkenny.[36] But this 'civilization' had not been meant to last. 'The Celt is epigrammatic and brilliant, and more daring than the Teuton, but he does not shed that lasting light the man of the more sober race does; and while he may dazzle and please and help materially to make life worth living, his efforts are not cemented to the foundations of time with certainty of their remaining there forever; though it cannot be denied that the world would have been a much worse place to live in, had it not been blessed with the presence of the brave, thoughtless, and artistic Celt.'[37]

Brilliance and bravery were all very well, then, but for sober, rational, and permanent contributions to 'civilization,' the visitor to Ireland would have to look to the more recent past. Those historic sites that were 'cemented to the foundations of time' were, with a few exceptions, places that were perceived as testaments to the English presence in Ireland, the spread of institutions to Ireland from England, and other markers of Irish encounters with English 'history.' Protestant churches were high on their lists of attractions, for they might provide such 'cement' and a reassurance that, despite Catholicism, true Christianity might be found in Ireland. Mackinnon spoke approvingly of Killarney's Episcopal church, and in that same town George Pack went walking and 'drifted into the place they use for a Methodist chapel a pretty tough place. A building set back behind some other buildings it is as old as Wesley's time and some of the old pioneers of Methodism had preached there and perhaps John Wesley himself.'[38] Visitors to Dublin were drawn equally to both Christ Church Cathedral and to St Patrick's Cathedral.[39] In writing about his trip to Cork, Duke noted the grandeur of the Anglican Cathedral of St Finbar's and related the tale of its bells, melted by Cromwell during the Civil War to punish the city for its loyalty to the Crown. But Shandon Cathedral also captured Duke's fancy: it was coterminous, he maintained, with Cork's 'ancient history' and deserved veneration from Catholic and Protestant alike.[40] Pack also toured this cathedral, although he seemed more impressed by St Finbar's, where not only had the 'ladies of Cork' raised $1,000 for a 'beautiful section' but also the 'only woman freemason' was buried there: 'the brass tablet is set into the floor and bears the following inscription: "Hon. Elizabeth Aldworth, 1695–1775, initiated into Freemasonry Doneraile Court, Co. Cork, 1712.'[41]

Ada Pemberton's list of attractions in Ireland was not lengthy but it did include the island's castles. In 1910 she made a 'successful pilgrimage' to Killachy Castle, the home of the Despard family, in County Kilkenny. 'We were very glad to see even these sad ruins as they conveyed more than any description. An idea of what a fine old castle the home of the Despards had been and indeed it was well that some members of the family should have visited it in time, for it will certainly not be long before the last vestige will have disappeared, before the greed of neighbouring builders' (Pemberton had, as we shall see, little time and even less empathy for the Irish who lived among her 'sacred sites').[42] On a previous trip, in 1897, Pemberton also had been very impressed with the Duke of Devonshire's 'beautiful' castle at Lismore and recorded a visit to Sir Walter Raleigh's home near Youghall, which was being restored by 'Lady Blake.'[43] As the accounts of Dublin tours reveal, the monuments to Wellington, Nelson, and O'Connell were popular with these Canadians, yet apart from describing the latter as 'great' few felt it necessary to explain their interest in him or reflect much on his role in Irish-English relations.[44]

If a history of colonial clashes and power struggles could be found explicitly spelled out in any of these Canadians' understandings of Ireland, it was in Shea's travelogue. As we have seen, Father Shea's travels took him in search of Catholic Ireland and in this search he turned,

from time to time, to a narrative of conflict and oppression. A trip to
the ruins of Muckross Abbey in Killarney, once the 'scene of the most
solemn ceremony of Holy Mass and the shrine of great devotion,' filled
Shea with 'profound feelings of sadness that so magnificent a temple
should in the height of its splendor and usefulness have been sup-
pressed and stripped of its sacred beauty by barbarous hands.'[45] But in
general Shea tempered his accounts. In Derry he noted that the city's
twelfth- and thirteenth-century churches had been 'unfortunately
demolished' in 1600 to provide materials for the city's fortification;
completed in 1618, the fortifications 'are to this very day kept in good
preservation and used as a promenade.'[46] At Drogheda, a 'good sized
town' with a 'history of interesting events,' Shea explained the Battle of
the Boyne by telling his readers that it was here that William of
Orange's troops 'engage[d] the sturdy Irish confederates under James
II.' 'James gave him battle, which lasted for hours and which resulted
in a bloody fight, with many killed and wounded on either side.'[47]

   While the narratives of Irish history that emerged from these travels
were selective and told piecemeal, it might well be argued that such is
a fundamental element of historical narrative, whether shaped and
expressed in the performance of travel and tourism or in other
genres.[48] Yet, as we have seen, those who framed their tours of
England with the past told – for the most part – a story that was progressive, teleological, and exemplary of empire's triumphant ascen-
dancy. Furthermore, notions of the superiority of British culture –
understood as both Scottish and English – led to pilgrimages to the
sites of cultural greatness. These Canadians' search for 'history' in Ireland differed from their trips to England and Scotland, in that they
were not predisposed to seek out the birthplaces, homes, and graves of
Irish cultural figures. If Richard Duke professed to be very impressed
with the 'artistic and literary' population of Cork, and others described
Dublin as the home of Sheridan, Swift, or Burke, those names and the
places associated with them were not imbued with the same aura of
the sacred or linked to the Irish landscape as were Wordsworth, Scott,
and Burns.[49] In general Ireland was not apprehended through the lens
of literary or other types of cultural expression. Moreover, in Europe
Canadian tourists made concerted efforts – to be sure, with the aid of
English language guidebooks – to seek out English writers, poets, and
other artists' European homes and gravesites. They searched diligently
in Venice, for example, for Elizabeth Barrett Browning's residence.[50]
Given what we know about the importance of various forms of culture

to notions of national identities (and vice versa) in the nineteenth century, the absence of such acts of cultural piety in Ireland seems significant.

Mountains, Glens, and Guides

Instead of a framework of individual and collective cultural efforts, Ireland was apprehended through the tourist lens of the picturesque and at times the sublime. Martin Ryle has argued that scenic tourism in Ireland began in the late eighteenth century and by the 1840s had become much more popular with English travellers, who sought in Ireland's west and northwest the landscapes that satisfied their romantic desires.[51] Yet by the latter half of the nineteenth century, Ryle pointed out, English visitors produced far fewer travelogues that focused on the delights of Irish scenery. Instead, their attitudes towards Ireland and the Irish were shaped by political events such as the Fenian uprisings and the Land War. Consequently, racial stereotypes and descriptions that emphasized squalor and poverty became the dominant themes in discussions of British tourists' travels in Ireland.[52] Dowsley may have had these travelogues in mind when he wrote his 'pleas': not for Home Rule but so that his fellow Canadians might appreciate Ireland's 'natural' beauties and advantages. Much was owed, he felt, to Lord and Lady Aberdeen for making the island's lovely – not to mention grand – scenery better known. The 'wild romantic grandeur' of Wicklow's 'sombre and gloomy' glen, the 'lovely valley' of Glendalough in its 'gloomy grandeur,' Bantry's 'wild and rugged grandeur,' and the 'peaceful, dreamlike quality of Killarney': all these places would be sources of inspiration for the pens of Canadian poets and scholars (see fig. 4.4). Perhaps, Dowsley ventured, the 'Irish Question' might be easier to solve if tourists came to Ireland and saw for themselves the island's attractions.[53]

The beauty of Killarney drew many visitors to Ireland in the first place, although (as we shall see) they did not often 'see' just what they expected.[54] When asked if Killarney's 'scenery and lakes' met his expectations, Father Shea replied that 'the scenery of the lakes like the music of the land is melodiously sweet, and of a beauty unspeakably tender.'[55] Shea found many other spots of great loveliness. The trip from Glendalough to the Vale of Avoca was memorable for both its beauty and the round towers and associations with St Kevin. A 'pleasing panorama' had spread out before him en route from Killarney to Kenmare. He found Glengariff to be a 'haven of absolute beauty,'

4.4. Glendalough's 'Gloomy Grandeur' (*Canadian Magazine*, January 1894)

while Bantry presented the 'striking' combination of 'glen, mountain and coast and the beautiful waters of the Atlantic.'[56] And although he did not find the views from Limerick to Galway, through County Clare's inland towns of Ennis, Lisdoonvarna, and Ballyvaughan to be as spectacular as those of the southern coast, Shea believed that Donegal's scenery equalled Calabria and Switzerland, both of which he had just seen.[57] For Duke, the best landscape in Ireland was that of the River Lee running west of Cork. There is 'not much in this round world to surpass it,' he told his *Christian Guardian* readers, as the river is wide, deep, and serpentine and includes a 'delighful promenade' along one bank, with a pleasant 'ornamental rest-house.'[58] The Giant's Causeway also attracted its share of admiration. Writing about his travels in the *Ottawa Daily Free Press*, J.H. Bell reported that the Causeway was curious and interesting but, except for its rock pools viewed from atop the cliff, not particularly sublime or grand. His opinion changed as the sun began to set, though: seen in darkness the Causeway became more mysterious and ghostlike, 'the wind as it whistles around the rocks about you, a sort of dirge exhorted by the sad remembrance of other years.'[59]

Although these tourists might describe themselves as being 'enchanted' by Irish scenery and landscape, only a minority saw Ireland as a land of folklore, a place where they might encounter 'wee folk,' hear of larger-than-life escapades of legendary giants and heroes, and possibly fall under mystical spells. During her trip around the west, Ada Pemberton spent a morning reading legends and then *Deirdre* in the afternoon, while at Dinish Island in Killarney Irene Simmonds was taken to see the place where 'the giant and his wife' had jumped across the lake.[60] Father Shea expressed his delight in such tales quite clearly and described Blarney as a 'fairy dell, a region of enchantment. Every inch of the grooves fairly bristles with legend, tradition, song, and story, and one could spend hours listening to the tales of the wonderful things done by supernatural or superhuman agencies.'[61] Dowsley noted that, while many 'tales and legends gather around the old ruin ... interest is generally centred upon the stone.' Since 'one of the first questions put to the newly returned traveller from Ireland is, "Did you kiss the Blarney Stone?"' Shea felt obliged to recount his experience: with the help of 'kind hands [that] have placed it in these modern days within tolerably easy reach,' he was able to do so without much trouble.[62] (His account does not suggest whether he was fundamentally transformed by the experience.) George Pack, who also joined the pilgrimage to Blarney Castle, wrote a matter-of-fact account of lying on his back with his ankles held by his guide, being lowered to the stone, and kissing it. He ended by telling his relatives that 'the present owner of the Castle ... lives in a fine mansion a snap shot of which I took from the top of Blarney.'[63]

Dowsley found his trip to Killarney via Bantry Bay to be an enchanting, spine-tingling event. The winding, twisting road, 'the only sign for miles around that civilization has broken in upon this solitude' transported him in more ways than one, as the sun began to set 'and shadows deepen around the path.' 'What thrilling sensations creep over one, while, in imagination, the old blunderbuss of stage coach days looks out at every turning, mingled with thoughts of spooks and pookas, and even childhood rhymes flash forth again, as yonder short and scrubby bushes appear like the beard, uncombed, of some ferocious giant, scouting for his "Jack, the Giant Killer."'[64] Dowsley's reverie was broken by the sudden appearance by the roadside of a group of young peasant men and women. Yet they too complemented the other-worldliness of the moment. 'Enjoying a song and a dance to the tune of a solitary violin or flute,' they greeted his coach with shouted good wishes and laughter, 'imparting to the scene such a spirit of life, of happiness and romance that I do not think it would be possible for any artist to portray it. One wonders, too, where these people come from, for no trace of house or dwelling appears from the roadside.'[65]

At other moments, however, these tourists did not so much wonder 'where these people come from' as wish that they would go away. Walking through Killarney's Gap of Dunloe, Dowsley described 'the manner in which travellers are pestered … by men and boys offering to rent their ponies, by women and girls selling potheen and goat's milk, by individuals firing volleys to awaken the echoes, and other like attractions, takes away something from the pleasure of this journey.'[66] Dowsley warned readers that, driving through the Kerry mountains into Killarney, he had encountered a few 'professional beggars for which Ireland at one time was noted' and that he had met crowds of children along the road who ran beside the carriage for miles proffering flowers for sale and performing acrobatic tricks (he noted that this phenomenon was not limited to Ireland but also occurred in Scotland, Switzerland, and other European countries where 'much driving is done'). Dowsley was not the only one to be struck by the presence of large groups of Irish men, women, and children who seemed to 'throng' around tourists. Embarking at the Queenstown docks, Richard Duke thought that there had been a great improvement in the appearance of 'jaunting cars' sent to meet passengers but was not so pleased in meeting an old Irishwoman who, part of the quayside crowd of vendors, literally thrust her shamrock on him.[67] J.H. Bell's appreciation of the Giant's Causeway was definitely for the scenery and not the people, whom he described in 1878, as 'beggars' and 'pestering land sharks' (an attentive reading of his description, though, suggests they were not begging but selling goods and offering their services as guides).[68]

Ada Pemberton saw the Irish as nothing other than an impediment to her enjoyment of the scenery. On her way to Killachy Castle, her chauffeur had to 'enquire his way at divers more or less disreputable pothouses.' A 'frowsy girl,' leaning over a stone wall, sent them to the site, 'telling us. that her father, an aged man could give us all needful information' but upon interrogating 'the old humbug [a local fisherman]' Pemberton's party found his 'memory proved of no assistance to us except in wholly irrelevant detail about a certain Miss C who was smothered by her drunken butler in an attempt to put out her hair which had caught fire from a candle by the light of which she was performing her evening toilet.' After seeing the castle, their ride back was 'enlivened by divers encounters with fractious horses and asses two legged and four legged.' She also 'interviewed the chief local authority on the castle but did not get very much information from him as he had never seen the edifice.'[69]

Pemberton generally was less than impressed with the infrastructure of Irish tourism, either the services offered formally in exchange for her cash or, as the above account suggests, the informal services that she solicited from 'locals' for nothing (in this practice she was not, of course, alone). During her 1897 trip, she observed that her accommodations in Galway were 'uncomfortable,' the railway hotel at Leenane was 'second rate,' that at Westport 'wretched,' and William Sheridan's Hotel at Achill was 'most Irish and unmethodical, long pauses between courses.'[70] Her tour in a jaunting car around Galway was marred by 'roads bad and high wind.' Pemberton did enjoy parts of her trip but not those in the south or west, preferring instead the 'most comfortable' Prince of Wales Hotel at Athlone, outings to Dublin's museums, cathedrals, and galleries, and a trip to the seaside south of Dublin: 'beautiful weather, warm summer day and beautiful scenery.'[71]

Ada Pemberton was the most vocal about the supposed deficiencies of 'the Irish.' Few others were as patronizing, expressed so clearly their belief that 'the locals' were there merely to expedite tourism, or were so vexed when they failed to do so. Indeed, Irish hotels and transportation might leave a very favourable impression. George Pack thought that Cork's Hotel Metropole was quite beautifully 'fitted up,' with its mahogany lift, electricity, marble-topped washstand in his bedroom, solid walnut furniture, and efficient staff.[72] And not all Canadian tourists were annoyed by the presence of vendors or unsympathetic to the need for infusions of cash into the local, poverty-stricken economies. At Dinish Island in Killarney, Irene Simmonds was happy to buy some 'pretty trinkets,' made mostly of bog oak, and postcards from an 'Irish lady in a cottage.'[73] Returning to town she observed women sitting by the roadside with 'baskets of lace and other stuff for sale. It seemed a very slow sale; an old ragged man came out of a hut holding out his hand for a penny. The guide said that he was more than one hundred years old. I could not help wondering what a dismal life it must be away up there in the mountain with no other habitation in sight.'[74] Father Shea encountered vendors in the Gap of Dunloe. He described them as 'very witty old ladies, who have many wares to dispose of. Usually the tourist is lured by the Mountain Dew and the winning smiles of the colleen, under whose pretty arm the Dew is generally

4.5. 'The winning smiles of the Colleen': the charms of tourism in Ireland.
(*Across Two Continents and through the Emerald Isle*, 1907)

kept. He then "acquiesces," pays his shilling and moves on and into other arms that welcome him to the Gap' (see fig. 4.5).[75] Far from being locustlike nuisances or objects of pity, these vendors seemed to Shea benign sirens, whose presence and wares merely added to the tourist's enjoyment and who should be acknowledged as performing not just a service but a role, part of the pleasant theatre of Irish tourism.

As well as the sellers of poteen, lace, postcards, and various knick-knacks, a recurring figure in these tourists' writings was 'Paddy' or 'Patsy,' the guide. This person was invariably male. In these accounts of Ireland, local women might 'speak' but only in the context of specific encounters that usually hinged around the hawking of goods, not because of their general knowledge of the landscape and history of the area (McDougall's descriptions of outspoken and active Irishwomen, which will be discussed later, were an exception). As scholarship of North American wilderness tourism or of attractions such as Niagara Falls attests, guiding as a masculine occupation was not a phenomenon confined to Ireland.[76] In some contexts, such as northern Ontario or western Canada, guides might be valued for their knowledge of local flora and fauna and depended on to protect as well as inform and instruct.[77] The Irish guides, though, inspired no such reverence, nor were Canadian tourists dependent on them for their personal safety as they might be in areas deemed 'remote' from white settlement. Canadians' dealings with 'Paddy' often hinged on this figure having a greater affinity with the stereotyped 'stage Irishman,' a humorous, at times less than reliable, but ultimately enjoyable and harmless type.[78] 'Paddy' personified a hybridity and liminality that could extend to the rest of his countrymen and women, being decidedly 'not English' but also being – albeit only just – English speaking. His words thus could be recorded more completely, his dialogue captured more fully, than was the case for French, German, and Italian guides; simultaneously, though, his differences – represented most fully by his 'brogue' and based on notions of class and ethnicity – made him a more entertaining figure than his English or even Scottish counterpart. English-speaking Canadian tourists' treatments of 'Paddy' presaged late twentieth-century travel literature about Ireland which, as Michael Cronin has argued, is 'less about post-modern spectacle and [has] more to do with a highly developed sense of theatricality,' a way of constructing 'the Irish' as 'garrulous, illogical, intuitive, [and] unreliable.'[79]

After being driven through Phoenix Park by 'Pat,' an 'anxious to please,' talkative, confidential, typical Irishman' (one most concerned that his fare knew of the importance of the Duke of Wellington), Dowsley hired 'Dennis Ryan' to take him through the valley of Glendalough.[80] 'A typical Irishman of that profession,' he appeared suddenly in Dowsley's narrative, interrupting a meditation on the sixth century, a time, Dowsley noted, when Irish influence on scholarship and religion was unparalleled in the 'western world.' Dowsley then created a great contrast between a glorious and vanished past and the rather more mundane present that the area's residents represented. Ryan was 'barefooted and of an honest face, producing his credentials in the way of a few cards from American visitors who have happened along that way, and "hired me and paid me well, yer 'oner."' There are many others besides Dennis, men and women, old and young, claiming for a like employment, and there would be no use in trying to go quietly about these parts without taking one of them along.'[81] Off they went, with Ryan informing his charge of such delights as the 'Baking Stone of Noah's Ark,' Finn Mac Cool's 'Razor and Strop' and 'Lathering Basin,' and other such sites. 'He points out so many places, all the time talking so rapidly, fairly bubbling over with Irish wit and blarney, that very little time is left to think.'[82]

Simmonds told her guides that the so-called giant's footprints in Lake Killarney looked as though they had been carved, 'but the men laughingly declared that they would lose their jobs if they told lies; but it seems to be part of their training to fib, if by so doing they amuse visitors.'[83] During their boat tour in Killarney the Manitoba schoolteachers were assured by their boatmen, who seemed to them to be 'accomplished beggars,' that the rain was just a 'gentle perspiration to lay the dust for us.' They were entertained throughout the ride by their guide, 'Patsy,' 'with stories and legends in his own inimitable way,' and as they drove around the shores of the lakes, 'the time was beguiled by numerous tales of adventure with ghosts, or of legends of the lakes told us by our witty Irish coachman.'[84] But while Dowsley also found the Killarney boatmen amusing, he could not help expressing a twinge of nostalgic sadness that their recounting of 'wonderful tales and legends' lacked their fathers' 'earnestness. The old superstitious belief attached to these stories no longer exists: they are told with only a laugh or a smile, and it is quite probably that in a few years more they will altogether depart from the memory, and Killarney will lose one of its many charms.'[85]

Whether or not Dowsley had been treated to a performance of earnestness by the older generation is impossible to know. However, his and others' descriptions of their guides' abilities as quick-witted raconteurs reveal the degree of performance that enveloped these encounters. While we cannot ignore the tourists' assumptions of their own class and ethnic superiority, more appears to have occurred than simply the replication of imperialist discourse about 'the natives.' For one, the readiness with which these tourists acknowledged the guides' knowingness and their own willingness to listen to 'tall tales' demonstrates both parties' complicity in this role playing. And without overlooking that only one side was able to leave their account of these exchanges, it is the guides' insistence on forcing their way into these narratives that is striking: they may well have been performing 'Paddy,' but they did so in ways that drew attention to the very staging of this role. It is their (admittedly circumscribed and limited) agency, their insistence on the smile and wink (and at times, perhaps, broadly exaggerated accent) that drew attention, not just the tourists' all too real condescension. Although only speculation is possible, in this instance the Irish guides to some degree resemble those Aboriginal male guides in twentieth-century western Canada who, Tina Loo has argued, used 'trickster tactics' in dealing with white urban hunters' condescension and incompetence: hidden smiles, their own Native languages, and passive resistance.[86]

It was not just the guides who spoke back to their supposedly worldly observers. 'Irish wit' could just as easily be turned on the ignorant and opinionated. Father Shea recounted the tale of 'John,' a young Irishman drawn into a conversation with an American woman tourist during a train trip from Bantry to Cork. Struck by 'all that lovely land going to waste,' she insisted on pursuing the topic of the 'lazy Irish' who refused to cultivate it. She was told that 'the ground has no surface – it is rock covered with a light moss ... They may cultivate it over in America, and if so, I'd be glad to cross the ocean with you to see it.' The tourist, however, would not listen to reason and still insisted 'that the Irish are lazy,' whereupon John replied that 'as the rivers have a right to run in Ireland, so have you a right to think as you please; but ... I don't think you are justified in accusing the Irish of being lazy, when neither you nor any other Yankee – woman or man – could do better in this given case.'[87] Dowsley's recollection of being 'pestered' in the Gap of Dunloe included an exchange with a 'bare-footed maiden,' who wanted him to buy the socks she had knitted so she might emigrate to America. 'Well,' I replied, 'perhaps they have enough of you there already.' 'Och thin, bedad! You might give me the two shillings to stay at home.'[88] The young woman's putdown of her interlocutor, using the stereotyped 'quick Irish wit,' suggests that performances of 'the local' versus 'the tourist' might get the better of the latter; they might be based on a script of which the latter was not the sole author and could not always control.[89]

The majority of the Canadians seemed to agree that Ireland's poverty was serious and widespread. Dowsley's articles were meant to correct the kinds of prejudice expressed by English and American travel writers: the latter in particular had 'eyes spectacled by such glasses' and thus saw only 'dirty cities,' 'filthy markets,' 'bedraggled women,' and 'drunken men, backed up by a good supply of imagination and exaggeration.'[90] Yet he admitted reluctantly that the 'beautiful and interesting' St Patrick's Cathedral was in one of the 'dirtiest' parts of Dublin 'and is approached by miserable streets, piled up with all sorts of second-hand goods, which probably only a Dickens could describe and frequented by as wretched a class of people as are to be found in the slums of London or New York.'[91] Although Pack found much of Ireland attractive and enjoyable, he observed, while on an evening stroll through the town of Killarney, 'quite a number of children around the streets a lot of them dirty little beggars. Men lounging around. Women sitting on the door steps with children in arms the young ragamuffins playing were as happy as could be and not in the least minding the dirt.'[92] (He also had reported that many of Cork's 'factory girls' had asked his party for money and that children had run alongside his carriage, begging for 'coppers.'[93]) The Manitoba teachers, who were so amused by their boatmen and guides, were initially surprised to find 'the much talked-of Killarney only a poverty-stricken village with several large summer hotels for tourists.'[94]

Not all impressions of Irish society or encounters with the Irish contributed to Dowsley's feared picture of impoverishment. Dowsley himself was eager to establish that that the Irish peasants, men and women, whom he passed on his way to Wicklow did not answer 'at all to the description we often hear of wretched people, miserable and ill clad.'[95] (Lindsey noted the greenery and neatness of the countryside between Derry and Dublin.[96]) While often shaped by notions of the 'amusing' or 'colourful' Irish, Pack's account also dealt with the fabric and texture of daily life. In Ireland (and elsewhere) Pack had an eye for a variety of scenes and experiences. His travel diary describes a visit to a 'real Irish cottage' with a peat fire and chickens in the kitchen ('the room seemed fairly clean the little girl looked rather nice'), a meeting at Bandon rail station (where a 'rather nice looking Irish girl about eighteen sang us a real Irish song,' and that 'nuns or some other nationalists' were now teaching their students 'Irish'.) On one occasion, while lying at the side of the road coming back from the Killarney lakes, 'two little chaps came along and we talked to them and they explained the differences between clover and shamrock.'[97] Pack went to see a trial at the Killarney courthouse and was impressed by the 'twelve or thirteen Royal Irish Constabulary fine looking fellows' in attendance. Before leaving Killarney he bought some cards: 'the girls in the store where I got the cards wanted me to take them out to Canada.'[98]

Pack continued his observations of local life in Dublin, where as he walked down Sackville Street, he saw 'boys singing on street for a copper ... women selling flowers and fruit we the men went into a saloon and it was just cram jam full we had to push our way through the crowd to get to the other end when we got there we just turned around and went back.'[99] The next day he watched a funeral procession make its way to Glasnevin and took note of the absence of pallbearers and that the cemetery officials allowed only the horses pulling the hearse into the grounds. Dublin, he observed, had many cyclists and early in the morning, while talking to some house painters about their trade and rates of pay, Pack was struck by the 'awful strings of bikes working people thousands of them all the buses were full taking what I supposed were working people.'[100] At Port-a-down, on his way to Belfast, Pack saw a 'young man he was starting for America he was crying quite a crowd down to see him off all the girls were singing him a farewell song quite a number of the girls were crying.' Then in Belfast he witnessed another kind of international travel. Out for an after-dinner walk, Pack and his friends saw some 'Malay or some other Southern Islanders … the poor beggars were followed by a crowd.' On seeing Pack and his friends, the Malaysians (who were probably sailors) offered them money 'some drunks or whiskey soaks tried to get the money from them and I then sent for a constable and as well as I could I explained the matter to him and advised him to take them to the docks and find their ship or someone who knew them. That's what he did.'[101]

A Colonial Witness: Margaret Dixon McDougall's Tour

Pack, Dowsley, Shea, Simmonds, Pemberton: they, and their peers, wrote about Ireland from the vantage points of men and women whose primary purpose in visiting the island was for leisure, however educational and uplifting some of their experiences might have been. In contrast, Margaret Dixon McDougall visited her birthplace for political and social reasons. While her account of her travels shares some of the features of other travelogues written for the tourist market, it also explores questions of poverty, land ownership, and 'Irish' character in greater depth and from a rather different perspective. It also suggests that tourists' records were not inevitably just descriptions of what they saw: other ways of viewing and of giving meaning to the landscape and people might be possible.

The daughter of an Irish Protestant family from Belfast, and a former schoolteacher and writer for the local press in her community of Pembroke, Ontario, McDougall travelled around Ireland in 1882 and published her observations as 'The Letters of "Norah"' in the Montreal paper the *Witness* (she also worked for the *New York Witness*).[102] Touring Ireland during the Land War of 1879–82, McDougall was determined to explore the conditions that had led to formation of the Land League, the league's operation, and the evictions of tenants. She made a point of covering those areas much affected by rising rents as well as those in which fewer evictions were under way, travelling throughout the north, west, south, and up the east coast of Ireland. While much of McDougall's time was spent in rural areas, she also wrote about her stays in Derry, Belfast, and Dublin.

McDougall was not the first to travel around Ireland as a social investigator. In 1869 the *Times* of London had sent a correspondent to report on the question of land reform.[103] Nor would she be the last: the eviction scenes that McDougall described in print would be captured in photographs and displayed as magic-lantern slide shows by Irish nationalists a few years later.[104] Although she might not have described herself as an Irish nationalist (she did not, for example, support Home Rule for Ireland), like the *Times* correspondent, McDougall believed that land reform was unavoidable.[105] Moreover, it was not just a matter of political expediency; she saw it as a moral issue and made it quite clear to her readers that, by and large, her sympathies were with the tenants. In many ways, McDougall's account owed more than a little to the conventions of humanitarian narratives of wrongs such as slavery, for her intention was not merely to report but also to convince her readers of past and present injustices and the need for fundamental change.

The photographs used for the nationalists' lantern slide shows were taken later after McDougall's trip. However, it is possible that McDougall saw and was influenced by similar photographs taken and circulated in the early 1880s. The resemblance between her writing and the photos of, for example, Dublin's William Lawrence are striking. These pictures depicted both the mechanics of evictions – the crowd that gathered to witness the reading of the order, the massed presence of police, the barricades erected by tenants, and the battering rams deployed to break through them – and the aftermath of the evictions: the elderly men and women, mothers and children, left in farmyards and on hillsides surrounded by their meagre possessions. [106] Just as the nationalists' exhibits of these photographs used a long-standing trope of 'mass unhoming' and domesticity under siege, so too did McDougall represent Irish domesticity as 'defined by broken walls and a disturbed hearth,'[107] a state of affairs that she attributed to the oppressive behaviour of landlords and not to any innate deficiency in the Irish.

McDougall's account emphasized the poverty of the tenant farmers, and explained that it was caused not by imprudence or alcohol but by the unreasonable rents extracted by greedy and abusive landlords. Near Milford she visited the estate of the murdered Lord Leitrim, who had left a 'woeful memory of himself' in the countryside. 'He must have had as many curses breathed against him as there are leaves on the trees, if what respectable people who dare speak of his doings say of him be true, which it undoubtedly is' (such people were, she pointed out, 'Godly' Scots of Covenanting and Presbyterian descent).[108] Leitrim's misdeeds included the abuse of a poor widow who had been hounded from her home and the eviction of the local minister and priest to make way for his preferred Episcopal church and clergy.[109] After going into the hills at Donegal, McDougall reported that she 'never, in Canada, saw pigs housed as I saw human beings here. Sickness, old age, childhood penned up on such places that one shuddered to go into them. Now, mark me! Every hovel paid rent, or was under eviction for failing to pay.' Landlords did not repair or upgrade their properties, she was told; instead, they set and collected rents, made rules at their own whim and often enforced them brutally, while the tenant was left without any voice. Their power was autocratic, exercised over people they saw and treated like serfs. When the latter could not pay, they were turned out onto the hillside to die, their deserted farms demolished to make way for the landlords' herds of cattle and flocks of sheep.[110] In Leitrim she saw 'some rich-looking fields, but most of the land has a poverty-stricken look and the large majority of the houses are simply abominable.'[111] McDougall heard 'one tale after another of harassment, misery and thoughtless oppression in Kiltyclogher till my heart was sick, and I felt one desire – to run away that I might hear no more.'[112]

Conditions were yet worst in Mayo, an area that was only (and barely) then recovering from the 1840s famine and its after-effects.[113] The labourers on a large country estate were not as well fed as the owner's beautiful, well-bred dogs, and at the gates McDougall saw 'with sad eyes the miserable cabins and barren fields ... People of the upper, middle and comfortable classes are so used to horrible cabins, thin labourers, old women, barefoot, toothless, ragged and wretched, begging by the wayside to keep out of the dreaded workhouse, that the sight makes not the slightest impression.'[114] McDougall's impression of the situation in the west was most vividly summed up in her picture of Lord Lucan's estate near Castlebar. The good land had been cleared of human habitation and the tenant homes became thicker as soon as barren, stony ground appeared. 'We passed a cabin of indescribable wretchedness; a woman who might have sat for a picture of famine stood at the door looking at us as we passed. She had a number of little children, of the raggedest they were, around her.'[115]

Throughout her reports, McDougall attempted to be fair to landlords. She constantly sought evidence that the tenants might be at fault, that not all landlords were greedy and heartless, and that there might be understandable reasons for their conduct. Gazing upon the beautiful, well-tended valley between Derry and Omagh, she vowed that 'whenever I come to careless husbandry, I will be sure to record it. I have seen nothing of the kind yet on mountainside or valley. I do not wish to fling a rose-covered veil over everything because it is Irish.'[116] Yet while she could cite two examples of landladies' kindness, in her eyes landlords and tenants were not equal. The latter had 'land hunger' simply that they might live, while the former hungered for land as a way of obtaining 'wealth, power, and position.[117] In Sligo, concerned that she had heard only one side of things, McDougall interviewed a few men who supported the landlords. They could not offer her any concrete suggestions, however, about the precise extent of reform, nor could they tell her why sweeping reforms were not desirable.[118] At Ballina she talked to a landlord who condemned the government's policy of supporting the evictions and emigration, admitted that rents were excessive and represented nothing more than premiums that tenants paid on their own labour, and even confessed to his own part, as both landlord and agent, in raising the rents. While McDougall was 'astonished' to hear such admissions, she was not convinced by his reassurances that he was busy making restitution to his tenants.[119] McDougall believed that the problem was not, overall, the landlords per se but rather an unfair system in which one class made the rules for another and then executed them through their control of the courts and police.[120]

Although her sympathies were clear, McDougall refused to condemn unequivocally the Royal Irish Constabulary for their role in this unfair system. At a village in Donegal, where they had been called in to enforce an eviction order, the police were met by a toddler who stretched out his arms to them; they, in return, petted and kissed him 'looking fatherly and human. I am sure the little kiss was sweet and welcome after the howls and hoots of the crowd and the sarcastic eloquence of Miss McConigle. I pity the police; they are under orders which they have to obey. I have never heard that they have delighted in doing their odious duty harshly and the bitter contempt of the people is, I am sure, hard to bear.'[121] She sought to impress upon readers the weightiness of the scenes of eviction and the tensions they involved. 'It is something awful to see a vast mass of human beings, packed as closely as there is standing room, swayed by some keen emotion, like the wind among the pines. It is wonderful, too, to see the effects of perfect discipline. The constabulary, a particularly fine body of men, with faces as stolid as if they were so many statues, bent on doing their duty faithfully and kindly. They formed a living wall across the road on each side of an open space on the bridge, backs to the space, faces to the crowd, vigilant, patient, unheeding of any uncomplimentary remarks.'[122]

By the time she got to Mayo, with its abject poverty and misery everywhere in evidence, McDougall's admiration might have slipped a little. Sharing a train compartment with a number of officers, she was struck by how quiet, trim, and clean they were. They could not possibly be proud of their duties, she mused, and observed that they looked 'well fed and comfortable,' a contrast with the hungry looking people from whom the bailiffs must be protected.[123] On the road in Mayo she watched the police march back to their barracks, looking hot and tired, lumbered with the arms they had to carry to protect the well-fed and healthy bailiff, agent, and sub-sherriff from a crowd of five hungry and peaceful men and three ragged women. 'The whole crowd might have been put to flight,' she wrote in disgust, 'by any one of the three with one hand tied behind him.'[124]

And if McDougall was concerned about the police force's reputation, she was far more interested in tracking down wrong opinions and rebutting stereotypes about the Irish peasantry. In this aspect, her writing and her performance of a concerned witness resembled other travel writers and tourists, such as Dowsley and Father Shea. She diligently reported on conversations about 'the Irish' held in the many public spaces to which her travels took her, remarking disapprovingly on opinions she thought wrong, and told readers of her attempts to argue and correct those so mistaken. In Moville McDougall interviewed the Presbyterian minister, who believed that, although great injustices had been committed, the law should be respected and Parnell was wrong to agitate against it. A member of this minister's congregation voiced his opinions about 'Paddy's laziness and carelessness ... I am very tired of these statements.' McDougall saw evidence of Irish industry all over the country, with every 'scrap' of land cultivated. Moreover, the opinionated man just quoted was inconsistent, telling her that while the peasants' poverty was caused by their laziness, he would not take the farms as a 'gift' when quizzed by McDougall on peasant ownership.[125] An English gentleman in her train car in Mayo posited that the area's problem was that of overpopulation. In reply McDougall looked out the window to a view in which there was no sign of human habitation, only 'utter desolation.' She turned to the man and said softly, 'Lift up thine eyes, sir stranger, and look northward and southward, eastward and westward. Is not the land desolate without inhabitant, where then is the over-population?' In response he stared fearfully at their fellow passengers, but McDougall shook her head, remarking that 'to doubt that this fair and desolate Mayo is over-populated is to show signs of lunacy or worse.'[126]

Men were not the only ones to express ill-informed and bigoted views. At a Presbyterian minister's manse at Clones, McDougall's discussion of land issues with a 'pleasant-faced, motherly-looking lady' ended with the latter throwing down her knitting and leaving the room. 'On the Land Question she had no ideas of either justice or mercy that could possibly extend beyond the privileged classes.' High rents were merely a matter of freedom of contract; landlords were not bound to respect historical agreements when they inherited new property; and the peasantry should accept that the workhouse was their fated destination – 'why did they not go at once without giving so much trouble[?]' Appealing to this woman's maternity was of no use: when asked if she would stave off the workhouse as long as possible, as it meant parting with one's children, 'the idea of mentioning her name in the same breath as these people precluded the possibility of answering.'[127] At this point the conversation ended abruptly.

McDougall's disapproval was particularly strong for tourists who refused to learn about the situation in Ireland and who viewed the Irish merely as an inconvenience (on that score she would have had little time for Pemberton). Some tourists, she reflected, 'are trying specimens of humanity.'[128] At a hotel in Cong in Connemara, where she was waited on by an eighty-year-old peasant woman who survived on the sale of her lace edgings for pillows to the 'lady tourists' (three pence per yard), McDougall met a party who told her of their annoyance and disgust in witnessing the departure of emigrants in Galway. The tourists were 'on pleasure bent' and could not see that this parting 'is as death' to many of the emigrants' elderly relatives. 'I could not help thinking how differently people are constituted. When I saw the streaming eyes, the faces swollen with weeping, and heard the agonized exclamations, the calls upon God for help to bear the parting, for a blessing on the departing, I had to weep with them' (and indeed she had wept upon seeing this scene). But the tourists were either 'indignant' or 'amused,' saw the elderly women as ill-bred, and mocked their grief and their clothes. 'Ah, well, these poor mountain peasants were not their neighbours, they were people to be looked at, laughed at, sneered at, and passed by on other side: but I – these people are my people and their sorrow moveth me.'[129]

It was not that McDougall did not participate in tourist activities, or that she could not identify with the needs and desires of tourists in Ireland. She noted that the hotels in Omagh were very expensive, while appreciating that they depended mostly on commercial travellers and tourists. 'Tourists are expected to be prepared to drop money as the child of the fairy tale dropped pearls and diamonds, on every possible occasion, and unless one is able to assert themselves they are liable to be let severely alone as far as comfort is concerned, or attendance; but when the *douceur* is expected plenty are on hand and smile serenely.'[130] She admitted, however, to reading the situation incorrectly in Omagh, when her offer to tip the young boy who carried her bag from the train station evoked not gratitude but instead tears of 'mortified anger,' as in his eyes he was only performing 'a good deed.'[131]

Far from being transported by the beauty of Killarney, like some of her other Canadian counterparts, McDougall observed the hordes of vendors who thronged the town and nearby areas, the 'relays of indefatigable women' who lay in wait for her boat and carriage, offering goats' milk, poteen, photos, socks, and bog oak knickknacks: 'everything is offered for sale and denial will not be taken.' The men of the area were willing to rouse the echoes with small cannon, bugles, and fiddles. All in all, McDougall found the vendors a 'persistent nuisance ... The tourists are to the inhabitants of Killarney what a wreck used to be to the coast people of Cornwall, a God-send.' Nevertheless, there was more to the situation than the disruption of her pleasure.

> One does feel inclined to lose all patience as they run the gauntlet here, and then one looks around at the miserable cabins built of loose stones, at those that are held on by ropes weighted by stones ... one sees that as there really is no industry in the place, of loom or factory, that want and encouragement have combined to make them come down like the wolf on

the fold to attack the tourists. It spoiled the view, it destroyed any pleasure the scenery might have afforded, and yet under the circumstances it
was natural enough on their part. 'We depend on the tourists, this is our
harvest,' the Carmen explained to us. From the hotelkeeper to the beggar
all depend on the tourist season.[132]

All in all, 'the wealth and the poverty, the unblushing begging, the
want of any remunerative industry, the idle listless people about the
corners, made Killarney a sad place to me.'[133] Matters were no better
during a trip to the island of Valentia, off the Kerry coast. The first
forty-five miles were through poverty-stricken countryside 'with such
cabins of mud and misery ... an amusement to the tourist and a pain
and a shame to the Irish lover of his country.'[134]

Not all Irish society and landscape were so demoralizing (and
demoralized) as the south and west. The manufacturing town of
Gilford was 'clean, pretty, and neat,' the young women who worked in
its mill 'trooping past looked clean, rosy, and cheerful,' and they were
'clad decently.'[135] Derry, with its textile industry, seemed a 'prosperous
old maid, proud of her past, proud of her present.' McDougall toured a
factory that employed twelve hundred, the 'most respectably dressed'
operatives that she saw in Ireland, with their bonnets and hats. She
confessed, though, that as worthy of admiration as Derry was, and as
hard as she tried to admire it, she still found it difficult to do so.[136]
Manufacturing seemed to do well by the Irish, as she mused while visiting a thread factory in Tandragee in Armagh. 'In whatever part of Ireland the tall factory chimney rises up into the air the people have not
the look of starvation that is stamped on the poor elsewhere' (although
in this town the workers were not paid as well as in others and had no
gardens, so 'cleanliness and tidy appearances of houses and workpeo-
ple are a credit to them').[137] In Galway, which she was 'disappointed'
to find was not looking as 'foreign' as she had hoped, McDougall saw
a very busy and thriving town, a 'nice change from the hopeless faces
and lounging gait of westerners.' The town's tall chimneys bring with
them, she thought, a population with a 'quick step and an all-alive
look.' Even the Claddagh area, which she had been warned was
unsafe, had no examples of 'extreme poverty.' Instead, she found
neatly whitewashed homes, a populace busy at work and comfortably
dressed, and many 'swarthy' beauties, young women with either blue-
black or extremely fair hair.[138]

   Unlike other Canadian tourists, McDougall was deeply interested in the island's public and social spaces, its hospitals, schools, and poor-houses (in this, as chapter 6 will explore, she resembled visitors to other parts of Britain). After touring the church at Knock she visited the local school, which had seventy-eight 'clean and decent' female students, one teacher, two monitors to assist her, and was kept in good order, with neat furniture, maps on the wall, and the children 'busy and interested.'[139] Schools in Ireland, McDougall reported to her Cana-dian readers, seemed to be run 'on the old plan.' Children learn at home as well as in school and repeat their lessons to their teachers; for their part, teachers are trained in 'obedience, respect for their superi-ors, and in order.'[140] But it was the Irish poorhouse that preoccupied McDougall. One of her first stops in Ireland was to Belfast's Poor House: 'a very noble building on well-kept grounds. Went on purpose to see a sick person and did not go all over it.' She was not very impressed with the Poor House itself, as there were many 'able-bodied looking young men and rosy-cheeked women' begging on the grounds, and the smell in parts of the building was 'dreadful.' Its hos-pital, though, was much better, with clean floors, and a very cheery head nurse, who showed McDougall 'all her curiosities, the little baby born into an overcrowded world on the street,' the latter providing a 'touching' sight, as 'beggar mothers' were feeding it as well as their own. Overall, though, 'a poor house is a helpless, hopeless mass of human misery.'[141] She was more cheered by the one in Ballymena, which was clean, 'sweet,' and well ordered. 'One is glad to think of the sick and suffering poor having such a refuge. What fine, patient, intel-ligent faces were among the sufferers in the infirmary. The children in the school-room looked rosy and well fed, and the babies were nursed by the old women.'[142] Although she did not consider the poorhouse to be a desirable solution to the problem of Irish poverty, she did observe that at least its inmates might re-establish those relationships of domesticity and family that had been so badly disrupted and damaged by the world outside their refuge.
   Things were very different at the Kiltyclogher poorhouse, though. McDougall was met and interrogated at the gate by its master about her political intentions. Each door was locked behind her as she moved from section to section, making it feel like a prison. She saw no nurses, not even the 'beggar nurses,' who had so touched her in Ballymena with their care for their fellow inmates, and there were many children

156 A Happy Holiday

who asked her for things 'with the air of little footpads. The women were little better.' This establishment was far below any other Irish poorhouse she visited, and McDougall did not wonder that people would prefer to starve outside, for 'entering it must be like the bitterness of death.'[143] McDougall believed that humanely run poorhouses might alleviate imminent suffering; however, ultimately she held the poorhouses and the Poor Law that established them responsible for the clear lack of sympathy for the poor that she found on her travels. The Poor Law, she wrote, 'educates people into hardness of heart.'[144]

While other travellers observed Irish people in the street or, in a few cases, in pubs, McDougall frequented a different type of public space: the political gathering. She attended a number of open-air meetings of the Ladies' Land League and witnessed a number of evictions that at times attracted large crowds. At a meeting in Omagh, held in a field outside the town, McDougall was invited to sit on the platform, as she had been mistaken for 'Miss (Anna) Parnell,' the head of the Ladies' Land League and Charles Parnell's sister (this happened to her on a number of occasions). The crowd gathered slowly, and most of the men wore corduroys 'of a great many varieties of colour and states of preservation or dilapidation.' Small boys crawled over and under the fence around the platform, squatting round her chair, and 'smiling up at me as if they expected a universal pat on the head.' At this gathering the speaker, while 'cold and clear and self-repressed,' was nevertheless persuasive and very audible (as well as being 'rather good looking, as black haired [and as] well made, lithe and nervous-looking' as an Indian').[145]

McDougall's descriptions of Irishmen were a far cry from the stereotypes found in the British press of this period, which depicted them as poorly clothed 'but sly and scheming peasant[s],' terrorists, or 'heavy-jowled Calibans.'[146] In her reports she paid attention to the Irishmen she saw in public places and refuted notions of their being violent or wild.[147] However, her narrative also differed from that of the British and Irish press in her treatment of the Ladies' Land League, an organization that was either ignored or derided by McDougall's contemporaries as being composed of female sans-culottes, 'shrieking and hysterical women degenerates.'[148] Far from overlooking these women, she was fascinated by their presence at rallies and evictions. At an eviction in Donegal, 'some of the women declared themselves willing to die for their country,' and at another, Mary McConigle delivered a speech full of 'fiery invective, withering sarcasm, and chaff for the police, who winced under it, poor fellows.'[149] On one occasion, while on her way back to her lodgings, McDougall passed a procession of the Ladies' Land League and was struck by the 'goodly number of bareheaded, sonsie lasses, wrapped in the inevitable shawl; rather good-looking, healthy and rosy-cheeked were they, with their hair smoothed back, and gathered into braids sleeking and shining ... These Land League maidens reminded me of other processions of ladies which I have seen marching in the temperance cause. They were half shame faced, half laughing, clinging to one another as if gathering their courage from numbers.'[150]

McDougall had an eye for the striking individuals who stood out in these groups of women. Aware of the power these women had to stir up the crowds (and at times she used the image of the French *citoyenne*), her descriptions hint at admiration for their courage and determination. At Manor Hamilton, where the police exerted such great discipline in keeping order over a crowd of thousands, she noted an 'elderly girl' who was the Land League's 'most active partisan ... the inventor and issuer of the most aggravating epithets that were put into circulation during the whole proceedings.' With her dark grey, defiant curls, 'the heat of her patriotism had worn off some of the hair, for she was getting a little bald through her curls – such an assertive, upturned little nose, such a firm mouth, such a determined protruding chin. This patriot had a short jacket of blue cloth, and could step as light and give a jump as if she had feathered heels. She reminded me of certain citizenesses in Dickens' *Tale of Two Cities*.'[151] In a Mayo village McDougall and her party witnessed an eviction at which a

slim, fair-haired woman, with her arms bare and her feet and legs in the same classic condition under her short dilapidated skirts, began to make some eloquent remarks. If there had been a thousand or two like her I do think the seventy police would have hard work to protect the bailiff. One of our company, a gentleman, remarked that she had a fine arm on her. 'Troth, sir,' said she, 'if I was as well fed as yourself it's finer it would be.' We agreed with this gentleman that if this woman was fed and clothed like other people she would certainly be a fine-looking person. She drew near to enquire if we were in any way connected with the police. Her enquiries were especially directed to myself. She was told that I was an American lady, and a few faces that scowled were smoothed into smiles immediately.[152]

And McDougall's departure from the village was marked by the cheers of small boys, who called out compliments to the 'noble lady' from America.[153]

It was not just at the land league's meetings or at evictions that McDougall took pride in Irishwomen's resistance and agency. In Mayo she applauded the actions of a local woman who had been sent to jail for reclaiming her cow, which had been taken from her 'in the dead of night.' As she often did with tales involving Irish women and children, McDougall wholeheartedly condemned this women's treatment. Her lawyer had argued that she did not know what she was doing, which McDougall thought was a 'mean, paltry defence.' The woman knew quite well that she wanted, and she needed to keep her cow. It was a 'monstrous law' that lets 'men of means' to strip 'poor wretches of everything that stands between them and their little children and starvation,' she wrote, and the only solution was to change it.[154] When not disfigured by poverty and oppression, Irishwomen's appearance and demeanour were interesting and appealing to McDougall's eye. The women she saw on market day in Skibbereen were with their stylish blue cloaks, 'shrouded as pretty black eyed, black haired, rosy-cheeked women as ever I saw,' wearing 'artistic' pleating around their shoulders and their wide-satin lined hoods: 'when worn around the face made the wearers look like fancy pictures.'[155]

Yet McDougall was deeply troubled by the potential for violence that she felt lurked under the surface of the peasants' dejection. Even though the people she met on the hillside farms of Leitrim were 'very civil, will tell you what they think will please you and are very reticent if they don't know your side,' she felt there were limits to their patience.[156] And the landlords had no idea of the 'amount of intensity of hidden feeling. I confess it frightens me.' Despite being impressed by the schools she saw, McDougall felt that too many Irishpeople were not well read and were apt to feel intensely about their troubles; moreover, reading material was too expensive and that which was circulated was one sided. 'The ignorance of one class, consequent upon their poverty, the insensibility of another class, are the two most dangerous elements I notice.'[157]

While she might not have used the term 'colonialism' to describe and diagnose affairs in Ireland, McDougall linked the problems facing the Irish peasantry to other kinds of exploitation. 'There is no possibility of understanding previous apathy from an American standpoint,' she lectured her readers, 'unless we think of the thoughtlessness with which the Indians have been treated.'[158] Some people would not even make that link. One (anonymous) 'noble and high-minded Irish gentleman, who feels strong sympathy with the Oka Indians' also thought that peasants who poached in Ireland were fair game for the warden's shotgun. Yet, McDougall reminded readers, the Irish had served the empire, having given their lives in England's wars from India to Crimea: their reward, though, was to contend with a caste system as strong as India's.[159] Perhaps, McDougall concluded, Scotland might serve as an example. Despite a history of suppression of its language and customs, the Scots were now in favour (after all, both Queen Victoria and members of her court had made homes there). What Ireland needed was its own Sir Walter Scott, to popularize and publicize the island and create a tradition and history for it. Such a writer 'would make Ireland's lakes and glens, mountain passes and battlemented rocks, ruined castles and mouldering abbeys, famous and fashionable as Scotland's brown heath and shaggy wood.'[160]

Margaret Dixon McDougall's accounts of her trip to Ireland were not written in an effort to persuade her fellow Canadians to visit there. Instead, she attempted to educate readers about the need for economic and political justice. Ireland, for her, was a place of sadness and tragedy, not quaint accents and comic encounters. To be sure, in Canadian tourists' accounts of travel overseas, Ireland was the only place they felt obliged to defend in promoting it to fellow Canadians. Father Shea ended the account of his trip, *Across Two Continents and through the Emerald Isle* (1907), by reminding his readers that tenants' rights had now been established in Ireland and that Irish society was improving, with the spread of higher education, better agricultural practices, and more incentives in manufacturing.[161] The vast majority of these Canadian tourist however, tended to see 'the Irish' refracted through configurations of class, religion, gender, and ethnicity that reduced them to comical children; furthermore, as in travel accounts of Europe, they fixated on appearance and behavioural characteristics as a means of knowing them and the society in which they lived. Moreover, there were those tourists who preferred not to know the Irish people at all and instead tried to focus on Ireland's landscape and scenery, although its residents persisted in jostling their way into their frame.

Unlike in their accounts of Scotland, these Canadian tourists did not become eloquent about the Irish contribution or relationship – for better or worse – to the empire's modernity. For most of these tourists, Ireland and the Irish existed not so much completely out of historical time but, rather, in their own particular and sometimes peculiar chronology, one that might bump up against the tempo of modernity at times but that was not fundamentally integrated into its rhythm. As these tourists saw them, the Irish could not be as easily written into a narrative of progress and development as the Scots and the English. Although the Belfast shipyards, Derry's textile mills, and Dublin's civic edifices testified to the island's modernity, they represented only select aspects of Irish society, not its entirety. And 'pestering' 'land sharks' and comical guides were seen not for what they were – evidence of an economy in which the modern tourist industry played a part – but as proof of a lack of progress that contradicted and undermined other indications of economic and social advancement. Their notions of Ireland's 'history' notwithstanding, by and large, these tourists did not think of Irish culture as providing the framework into which they might place Killarney's lakes and Dublin's streets; in fact, they were not sure that Ireland had a culture comparable to that of the rest of Britain.

Eager to find narratives of progress, desirous of modernity, culture, and imperialism, these anglophone Canadian tourists sought such things elsewhere. They would find them in the 'heart of the empire,' London.

5 'The Hot Life of London Is upon Us': Travel to the Imperial Capital

London, Mecca of our dreams!
Behind thee centuries stand;
The city great with commerce teems,
No peer in any land.
The Tower, Abbey, and St Paul so rich in relics rare,
With wealth and sculptured art withal,
What can with them compare!
We ride in hansom, bus, and brake,
Till we like Sheba's Queen, exclaim:
'My goodness gracious sake,
The half has not been seen!'[1]

M.A. Black, 'Echoes from Our Trip' (1907)

M.A. Black was not the only Canadian tourist to feel excited, stimulated, and a bit overwhelmed by a trip to the capital and heart of the empire. As they perused A.H. Morrison's 'Vignettes from St Pilgrim's Isle,' readers of the January 1894 issue of the *Canadian Magazine* were told that 'The hot life of London is upon us. Its maze of motion is in the air. The whirl of its wheels, the throb of its myriad hearts, the hum of its converse, the frenzy of its hurried day, the stealthy travel of its never-silent night is everywhere, permeating everything, actuating everything, filling everything. There is nothing else in the world, above the world, beneath the world, only London, London, London!'[2]

From the 1870s to well into the twentieth century, London was written about, visited, and 'produced' by a number of anglophone Canadians who saw it as the centrepiece of a transatlantic world. While other sites and landscapes in England and Scotland were important to them, London was at the core of their travels and integral to their having seen Britain. As scholars have pointed out, they were by no means alone. Over these decades London experienced an influx of transatlantic and transnational traffic from both colonies and dominions within the British Empire.[3] Like Australian tourists, Canadian white colonials also encountered questions of imperialism and nationalism in London's 'myriad haunts.' Previous chapters have suggested how particular conceptions of gender and the gendered relations of travel and tourism figured in their experiences. In London gendered hierarchies and shifting forms of gender relations intersected with these other relationships in critically important ways.[4] Not only did the imperial capital hold gendered, national, and imperial significance for these tourists, it also promised them countless other – albeit related – social and cultural encounters and experiences. London offered them opportunities to map out a panorama of a modern nation and empire in overlapping and converging moments, in ways both intellectual and sensory.

The Travel Writers' London

Canadians who disembarked at Liverpool and took the southbound train were, in all likelihood, no strangers to London, just as they were not strangers to other parts of Britain and Europe. Newspapers articles, travel books, periodical series, and public lectures that educated them about Britain's political, historical, and cultural significance were pedagogical texts in which London often took pride of place. The secular and religious press in Canada ran many articles that focused on London; writing about the capital appeared more frequently than on any other city, region, or country. Moreover, the various ways in which London was discussed helped shape a portrait of a multilayered and quite complex landscape. This 'city of dreams,' as writer Louise Hayter Birchall described it, was both a 'place in one thousand and one thousand places in one.'[5]

This sense of London's intricacies was also reflected in the various modes of presentation adopted by travel writers in the press and in book-length travelogues. Some treated London simply as a vast warehouse of goods and sites to be seen and consumed, and catalogued the city's attractions in a compendiumlike fashion (a style that was common in diary writing); others chose a variety of approaches and tropes. Some writers swept their reading audiences' eyes along a panorama, placing them on top of St Paul's, an omnibus, or the viewing roof of the Crystal Palace. For many tourists, their first impression of London was a sensory shock, as they struggled to cope with its visual and aural excess. Arriving in this 'Mecca of the English-speaking nation,' Father Mortimer Shea described a scene 'thronged with people' in which the tourist's ear encountered 'the shrill cry of the cabby, the rattling wheel, the murmur of the great crowd. On every side a living tide is in constant motion going to and fro, all hurrying as if preoccupied with serious errands.'[6] Metaphors of oceans and rivers were used to describe London: the city was 'awash' in 'tides of humanity' that 'streamed,' 'roaring like the ocean' from tubes, rail stations, and buildings, threatening to 'drown' the uninitiated tourist in its vast surge.[7] The 'most impressive' way to approach London, wrote Goldwin Smith, was via the Thames 'through the infinitude of docks, quays, and shipping.' Even seeing the city from a height, such as the roof of St Paul's Cathedral, would still not give the tourist 'anything like a view of the city as a whole ... It is indispensable, however, to make one or the other of those ascents when a clear day can be found, not so much because the view is fine, as because you will get a sensation of vastness and multitude not easily to be forgotten.'[8] Another stance taken by travel writers was one of irony toward the whole business of being a tourist, one that mocked the writer's self-professed ignorance of the city, her or his propensity to get lost in it, and the conceit of thinking that an entity like London could ever be 'known' by the casual visitor (see fig. 5.1).[9]

London might be exhilarating, promising an anonymity and freedom to experiment with various forms of recreation and leisure. As we shall see, many were eager to do just that. However, its very size and complexity also threatened to undermine a sense of self and might lead to soul-destroying alienation. Standing in the middle of Piccadilly Circus, a Canadian tourist might realize that everyone else was intent on going somewhere. 'Who are they? Where are they all going to? Everybody. Everywhere. And, yet, who are *you*? Nobody. And where are *you* going to? Nowhere.'[10] Unlike travellers from south Asia, who often felt quite conspicuous on the capital's streets, anglophone Canadian tourists were far more likely to blend into the crowd, an experience that could be both liberating and unsettling.[11] Canadian writers addressed the tourist's anonymity in London and warned potential visitors that the city was self-sufficient, a place that 'makes no effort to be friendly, has no desire to be known or to be admired.'[12] Tourists participated in its social life, Goldwin Smith warned, might well find that even its

5.1. The imperial centre displayed for English Canadians; Fleet Street, London (*Canadian Magazine*, November 1905)

brilliance could be overshadowed by the lack of intimacy engendered by the presence of so many people. Although fascinating, it had a 'hollowness' to it and an indifference to whether 'you were there or dead. Nothing is more dismal than the pomp of a funeral struggling with its mockery of woe to the Necropolis through the tide of business and pleasure in a London street.'[13] And even those who were not part of such circles should be on their guard in the city. A tourist's inexperience with the speed and volume of traffic in London might feel they threaten his or her physical well-being. 'The casual sight-seer, or the pedestrian on the streets,' Shea warned, 'must be constantly on the alert, otherwise he is likely to run into trouble or meet with an accident, which, of course, he did not anticipate.'[14]

   Not every Canadian who travelled to Britain, of course, went to London for very long, nor were all Canadian tourists as impressed by the city as the travel writers might have hoped. Out of the three months that George Disbrowe spent in England in 1907–8, only one day was passed in London. Disbrowe met an old friend, had glimpses of St Paul's, the Parliament Buildings, and the Bank of England, and then took the tube to Waterloo Station. 'The streets are narrow,' he confided to his diary, 'and I saw no electric cars, but lots of motors and buses.'[15] In 1883, William Munro spent about a week in the 'Great Babylon' but preferred his native Scotland. After leaving London for Kidderminster, where he toured a rug and carpet factory, Munro wrote to his wife, saying 'London was too much for me, when I begin to reflect at home I may tell you something.'[16] And while William Caldwell thought the fireworks at the Crystal Palace were 'magnificent, far ahead of anything of the kind that I have ever seen or conceived and in reality looked more like something from fairy land than the product of art,'[17] he declared that Paris 'from what I have seen I judge to be the finest place we have yet seen.'[18]

History at the Heart of the Empire

Anglophone Canadian tourists might escape the metropolitan hubbub temporarily by visiting the city's religious and historical sites. Westminster Abbey was mentioned in almost every Canadian's account of their time in London. It was both a place of worship and, as J. Rupert Elliott put it, a 'shrine of British history,' with its tombs of Edward the Confessor, Eleanor of Castile, Mary Stuart, John Milton, Chaucer, Ben Jonson, and William Wilberforce.[19] In December 1872, representing the Appleton Manufacturing Company of Hamilton, R.J. McLoughlin ended his business dealings and then took himself off to Westminster Abbey, the 'sepulchre of England's Kings and Queen's.' He found it difficult to 'describe a place each stone of which is a history in itself' and to 'portray the feelings of reverential awe which steal into the soul while admiring the vast wonders of this more than historical pile.'[20] It was hard for him to realize 'that I was in a church, such are the number of sculptured monuments erected to the memory of the departed dead.'[21] Ethel Davies loved the Abbey best, confiding to her diary that 'the dear old place will long remain a bright spot on memory's page. I shall never forget the music of those boys' voices echoing through the great arches and down the long aisles – and the beautiful statuary everywhere to add beauty to the grand old church.' Here she found the tombs of 'great ones, long dead,' whose numbers included kings and queens, 'soldiers who fought for England's glory, the great poets and painters that have told her story for her children yet to come.'[22] The Abbey, though, overwhelmed Margaret Thomson: it was first on her itinerary of 6 September 1898, but while she saw it 'thoroughly,' she found that she was unable 'to tell anything of it.'[23]

St Paul's Cathedral came a very close second to Westminster Abbey on the Canadian tourist's list of obligatory London sites. Davies observed that 'St Paul's is a magnificent cathedral of tremendous size and beautiful workmanship.'[24] Edith Chown told of the many tombs and monuments in St Paul's, a list that included Wellington, Nelson, Gordon, and Samuel Johnson; like Thomson in the Abbey, she found it 'hard' to describe the tombs or even the cathedral itself and merely noted that it was 'all wonderful and beautiful.'[25] These buildings were more than just their architecture or the bodies encased within them. The history of St Paul's would be incomplete without including the many important services (joyful and otherwise) that had been held there, wrote Elliott; his list included the 1872 thanksgiving service for the Prince of Wales's recovery and Nelson's funeral.[26] Mabel Cameron attended a memorial service at St Paul's for Florence Nightingale and was most impressed by the church itself, the Coldstream Guards' Band and the cathedral organist's rendition of the 'Dead March' from *Saul*, noting that it 'moved me as that solemn dirge has never done before.' She also was impressed by the seven hundred uniformed nurses who came 'to pay tribute to the wonderful founder of their profession.'[27] But while the abbey and St Paul's might move Canadian tourists, they did not abandon the critical faculties that they brought to tourist sites. Cameron, for example, walked out of a Christmas Day service at the abbey when she could not hear the sermon; she also disliked its wax effigies since they had been taken from death masks and 'consequently are not pleasing.'[28] In 1895, while Toronto's Isabella Montgomery found that the bust of 'Sir John A' in St Paul's was ' remarkably good,' the Communion Sunday service she and her sister Jess attended a few days later was 'unusually long.'[29]

Parliament was an important stop on the route Canadian tourists chose to pay homage to their political and cultural heritage. For many, Westminster was a museum filled with objects that would instruct the visitor in the important events of English political, military, and constitutional history: portraits of the monarchy, large paintings of the Battles of Trafalgar and Waterloo; and statues of English statesmen (Pitt the younger, Walpole, Chatham), not to mention the rooms and hallways that housed them.[30] A number of these tourists reflected on Westminster Hall, singled out by their guides and guidebooks as the location of both Charles I's trial and condemnation and the selection of Oliver Cromwell as Protector. Smith dubbed it 'sacred ground,' as the hall had seen preserved 'the great principles of justice, while over the rest of Europe prevailed arbitrary tribunals, secret procedure, imprisonment without legal warrant, and judicial torture.'[31] But while the art, sculpture, furnishings, and the rooms in which they were viewed were impressive and full of historical meaning, the parliamentary rituals and processes were the core of such visits. Westminster, Smith intoned, was the 'centre of politics' for not just London or Britain but the entire 'civilized world. All civilized nations both in Europe and America, as well as all the British Colonies, have now adopted the constitution which was here founded and developed.'[32] Thomson found the 1897 Speakers' Procession a 'most impressive performance,' with its leader who 'did not cut corners,' the mace-bearing sergeant-at-arms, and Speaker, his robe born by two attendants. Sitting in the Ladies' Gallery and listening to speeches on Gibraltar, she found it hard to 'imagine we were really in the House of Commons.'[33]

Not all Canadians were quite so awestruck by what they heard from the visitors' gallery in the Commons. James Hall and his companions, who had persuaded 'an old Scotchman' to get them in, listened to speeches 'of not much account' concerning a turnpike bill. As this seemed tedious, they decided to try their luck with the Lords and were fortunate to meet a clergyman who, knowing the doorkeepers, marched them in; they did not have the required passes and thus 'any of the policemen could have thought to have stopped us and it was a piece of luck that got us in.' Hall then heard the Irish Educational Bill being debated and was able to indulge in a bit of aristocratic 'celebrity' sighting, spotting the Dukes of Devonshire and Richmond, the Earls Granville and Spencer, Viscount Monck, and Lords Halifax, Cranworth, and Shaftesbury.[34] More than two decades later, travel writer Albert R. Carman observed that he was struck by the smallness of the Commons before he noticed its richness. With the exception of the Speaker's wig, the predominant attitude was one of informality: one member sat as though he were in a barber's chair (although as Carman left, he passed Cromwell's statue and was reminded of his work for parliamentary freedom).[35] Harriett Priddis listened to a debate on the Pension Bill but was more impressed by the tea served on the terrace, finding it 'quite up to my expectations' (Thomson also had tea overlooking the Thames, but there she was more struck by the 'very extraordinary females' she saw).[36] Those tourists who visited at the height of the militant suffrage campaign took note of women's exclusion from the gallery. Chown, who thought the Commons 'not nearly so grand as the House of Lords,' pointed out that it had been three years since women had been admitted, while George Pack (who listened to Winston Churchill speak about child labour and saw the gold Mace), reported that 'our Ladies had to stay outside because of the suffragettes they got tired of waiting and went home.'[37]

The Tower of London was another popular attraction. For one, it held the Crown jewels. After paying a shilling to an 'old Beef Eater,' who took charge of him and showed him around, Fred Martin was thrilled to see the 'magnificent' collection, which he catalogued in his diary, along with the history of each item. Emily Murphy let slip her customary caustic attitude towards England upon seeing the crown, with its 'seventeen hundred diamonds,' beautiful and 'inestimable' sapphire, and enormous ruby; she also noted 'diadems, scepters, swords, a wine fountain, coronation spurs, the Royal Baptismal Font' that made up a collection worth fifteen million dollars.[38] The tower, wrote Isabella Montgomery, was 'perfectly beautiful,' with the Beefeaters a 'novel' sight and the jewels 'elegant.'[39] However, although many agreed that the jewels were well worth seeing, not everyone was able to appreciate them so uncritically. Irene Simmonds complained that the guards moved her party along so quickly that she could not spend much time with them (and George Pack, in London for the coronation of George V, when admission was free, saw only a brass plate set in place of the jewels place).[40] John Mackinnon was not at all impressed by the jewels, suggesting that 'when one numbers the thousands of London who lack food, homes, or rainment, sleeping on bridges, around squares and wherever they find shelter, the thought naturally occurs – why not sell in job lots these cartloads of jewels and apply the proceeds towards raising those paupers to the ranks of decent people.'[41]

Sometimes the contrast between the luxurious display of the jewels before them and the tower's bleak past might be almost unbearable. In taking her fictional Canadian tourists around the tower, Maria Lauder saw a 'strange contrast' between the building's 'myriads of associations' and the English Regalia. 'This dazzling glitter of gold and costly stones seems a cutting sarcasm, a bitter irony, in the face of the grim Norman Keep, and the awful tragedies that have been enacted here on the stage of life!'[42] William Harrison told readers of the *Canadian Magazine* that the Crown jewels must be placed alongside the headsman's axe and mask, the thumb-screws, and chains.[43] The tower was a place where 'a veil of mystery hangs over many a tragic and dramatic episode of the gloomy past,' Murphy declared, and 'what diabolical knaveries, what cruel implacable things, what plots of treason have thickened to their

black finish within these drear precincts!'[44] Ghosts filled the building –
Thomas More, Thomas Cranmer, Walter Raleigh, Dudley, Anne Boleyn,
Lady Jane Grey, the Earl of Essex, to name but a few – and 'like dark
phantoms they seem to glide by us as we linger, and listen to the cries of
the boatmen, the tread of the soldier, the executioner with his axe.'[45]
According to Harrison, the tower was an example of the precariousness
of rank and hierarchy in England's past: its walls have seen both royalty's 'glittering processions' and 'throngs of illustrious prisoners' who
were marched to dungeons to suffer and endure a 'shameful, cruel
death; its rooms had rung with mirth, revelry, and shouts of pleasure,'
while its gloomy cells had resonated with the 'cries of deadliest pain
and muffled moans of broken, bleeding hearts.' Royalty had come
through its gates, exchanging honour, glory, and the brilliance of the
court for prison, torture, and the 'fatal block and axe.'[46]

Although they did not always rise to the impassioned heights of
prose scaled by travel journalists, women diarists and letter writers
made careful note of the women who had met a violent end at the
hands of the English state within the tower's walls. They walked themselves and, in the case of letter writers, their readers along the routes
these women had taken to their deaths. Traitor's Gate, wrote Clara
Bowslaugh, was the place where Anne Boleyn, Katherine Howard, and
Jane Grey had landed, and where all three were executed shortly after.
Standing on a spot on Tower Green, 'which marks the place of their executions,' Bowslaugh and her party 'plucked some maple leaves from a
tree overhanging it.' She then carefully listed the execution dates of a
number of women: Anne Boleyn, 1536; the Countess of Salisbury, 1541;
Katherine Howard, 1542; Viscountess Rochford, 1542; and Lady Jane
Grey, 1554 (Bowslaugh also threw in the Earl of Essex, 1601). 'Overlooking the "Green" is the window from which Lady Jane Grey saw her
husband go from Beauchamp Tower to the scaffold on Tower Hill, and
his headless body brought back for burial in chapel St Peters, where she
was also buried.'[47] Thomson, Bain, Chown, Simmonds, and Davies, too,
remarked on these deaths and paid a visit to the site of execution.[48]

Male visitors to the tower also reported that it was the place where,
as Pack put it, 'Queen Mary was beheaded and other notables.'[49]
Edwards Greenshields wrote in his diary that 'though historically one
of the most interesting places in England ... it is a sad place to visit,
with its gloomy passages and stairs, its old instruments of torture.'[50]
Women diarists and travel writers also dutifully listed the many men
who had died within the tower's walls. Nevertheless, it was women

who were particularly drawn to the history of noblewomen's deaths. Murphy was outraged by the execution of the Countess of Salisbury, the 'mother of Cardinal Pole,' who 'in spite of her age and grey hairs' was 'hacked to death with as little ceremony as an ox in a slaughter house' (she refused to lay her head on the block and, according to Murphy, was chased around it by the executioner).[51] She also was moved by the deaths of the princes: 'the Anglo-Saxon heart aches for the murdered boys who were hidden away under the awful stones.'[52] Murphy laid the blame for much of the tower's terrible and cruel history at the feet of Henry VIII, a 'merciless, malevolent despot, topful of unbridled lusts, his life is a filthy epistle showing the ultimate vileness, the black and dirty recesses of the human heart.'[53]

Murphy's was an explicitly gendered analysis of the abuse of monarchical and masculine power that Henry VIII represented to her. Harrison was more sanguine about the tower's history, contending that although it represented an era of 'fierce struggles,' 'ill-defined rights,' and the 'wildest passions,' this period had set the foundations for England's 'present prosperity, peace, and world-wide power.'[54] Now all the 'noise and tumult' heard within the tower's walls had died down, the scaffold had been replaced by a garden, and while the tumultuous days were long gone, nevertheless members of the British Empire should remember that 'the freedom which enriches your lives to-day has not been achieved without many a hard fought battle.'[55] But Davies was unable to take such a dispassionate view. She wondered, 'Could its old and crumpling walls speak, what horrors they would tell! These poor beings who have suffered and languished in its dreadful dungeons – justly perhaps yet my heart says *many* have suffered unjustly there.' Davies left, vowing 'enough of the Tower and its horrors! One thing I am thankful for, those bloody unchristian times have passed and that I live in a day when justice holds more sway and those who rule our nation rule not with selfish ends but for their peoples and their countries' goods.'[56]

Davies was not alone in refusing to see all of English history as an uncomplicated and celebratory narrative of progress, particularly for women. Simmonds would not have missed Madame Tussaud's Wax Museum 'for the world,' and she was delighted to see figures of the present-day royal family, the popes, various British statesmen, and Queen Victoria. But she was very disturbed by the tableau of Mary Stuart about to be beheaded. 'It all looked so real, I was glad to pass on,' she wrote. A display of the stocks, the pillory, and instruments of torture made her happy to live in the twentieth century, for she found it a 'mercy that these awful things are done away with!'[57] Davies had a similar reaction, declaring that while she and her cousin had had 'great fun' there with its 'wonderfully life like' figures, their trip to the Chamber of Horrors was quite short: 'ugh we took to our heels in a jiffy.'[58]

The evocation of the past cruelty was not always unsettling. Pack thought the Chamber of Horrors held a 'most remarkable collection of all classes of people kings princes queens then to murderers. So life like that many have been spoken to; the Queen of Spain, England, and other notables have on the latest dresses made by Worth of Paris.'[59] In August 1910, Mabel Cameron went to look at not just the wax figures but also at her fellow tourists. She 'took much pleasure and perhaps unkind delight in seeing the people ask for catalogues upon the wax figures seated at the entrance to the main room.'[60] Two months later, she noted that Harry Thaw had been added to a group of suffragettes, and she spent more time in the chamber on a trip the following March; however, although Napoleon's relics were very interesting, 'the rest is too grim to be thoroughly enjoyable.'[61] Like others, Martin was struck by the realism of the figures: the policeman at the front to whom visitors addressed questions, and the 'old Quaker man,' whose toes were constantly being trodden on and his pardon constantly begged, were both 'very amusing.' Martin was more fascinated than repelled by the Chamber of Horrors, with its Murderers' Room, desperadoes, guillotine, and block and axe. The assassinated Alexander II of Russia had just been added to the Hall of Kings, he observed. He summarized his trip to Tussaud's breathlessly: 'the gallery is very interesting and would take days to see it properly and I have only briefly described it and then had reference to the Guide Book which I find I am obliged to do as it is utterly impossible to remember when one sees so much but it will no doubt prove none the less interesting and will be more accurate.'[62]

The presentation in London of England's past was not exclusively an unrelenting litany of violence and state-sponsored cruelty. The Manitoba schoolteachers' tour included the Olde Curiosity Shop on its itinerary, as did Bowslaugh.[63] Pack toured Ben Johnson's tavern, where in its crypt he saw a 'small part of ancient London before the fire,' as well as some 'spider web covered bottle of wine, 1840.' The tavern's domestic scene was a far cry from the cells of the Tower, with the former displaying its 'old original kitchen bowls and other kitchen utensils.'[64] Yet these anglophone Canadian women's accounts of their encounters with English history, particularly as the latter was represented by the century that brought Protestantism, Elizabeth I, and the first English Empire, suggest that their usual understanding of their 'English' past – as a Whiggish narrative of progress and development – might be disrupted when the lives and fates of prominent women were brought to the centre of the story. If performances of Scotland's violent past allowed middle-class women to reflect on matters usually left unspoken, the production of similar histories in England, ones in which they might be particularly invested, deeply disturbed – to the point of repulsion – their female audiences.

'To See the Queen': Imperial Spectacle

Spectacles of imperialism and royalty in London promised a much better story so far as both gender relations and historical narratives in general were concerned. Unlike the mysterious and tragic histories of cruelty and violence hidden within the Tower's walls, celebrations of empire and the monarchy were open and easily accessible public events. They took place in the streets, concert halls, and cathedrals of London, and they were intended to draw out already-present sentiments of belonging to the imagined communities of nation and empire, as well as to create such emotions for those who might not already share them.[65] Anglophone Canadian tourists' reactions to these events reveal that they were not without their complications and complexities, particularly around questions of imperial hierarchies and gender relations. Nevertheless, the travelogues, diaries, and letters make it clear that, just as at home their authors might flock to such sights on the streets of Canada's cities and towns, in the British context they were willing spectators and performers in these theatres of nationalism and imperialism.[66]

Sighting royalty was one of the most commonly sought experiences when on a visit to London. Many Canadian women openly confessed their yearning to witness a public appearance by royalty and they were delighted when their longings were fulfilled. Miss Peake, the author of 'How a Toronto Girl Saw the Queen,' a paper delivered to the Toronto branch of the Women's Canadian Historical Society in 1901, framed her experience of seeing Queen Victoria as the fulfilment of a long-held aspiration: 'from my earliest childhood I always had a very strong desire to see the Queen.' Peake's narrative contained many of the elements common to such accounts. First, her success owed much to chance. The day after she arrived in London, 'a friend said, "Now if you wish to see the Queen to-day is your chance, as she is going to give a garden party at Buckingham Palace."' Next, she endured a long wait amid orderly crowds; her time, however, was not wasted. 'As we were early we had time to look at the beautiful park [Hyde], and handsome carriages which were constantly arriving. There were thousands of people all along the drive, and everything was orderly, no crowding or pushing.' (London crowds were almost always described as polite and well behaved.) Anticipation spread with word of the queen's imminent arrival, 'and presently along came the mounted police, then the Horse Guards, and then a carriage with its occupants – a little lady in a black bonnet with a white plume towards one side and a rather small quiet dignified face looking from under it.' (Like other accounts, this one contained the element of instant recognition of both Victoria and her family, a perceptiveness that may have been created through the commodification of British royalty's images in china, pottery, and through the press.[67]) 'Of course this was Her Majesty and on her left another lady who could not be mistaken for anyone but Princess Beatrice. On the seat in front was a young fair girl with a wide leghorn hat trimmed in daisies and black velvet, and having on a light blue silk dress. This was Princess Ena of Battenburg.' Once again, the crowd lived up to British standards for, as the royal party passed, 'the people cheered heartily, but even the cheers sounded dignified, not like the ordinary shouts one hears, but admiration, love, and respect, seemed to be embodied in the salute which the loyal subjects gave their Queen as she passed.'[68]

Yet this spectator was not satisfied and, once the procession had passed on, 'I began to realize that I had not seen nearly all I wanted to see.' So, assisted by friendly advice offered by a Londoner (another character who appears frequently in such accounts), they waited to see the queen return from the garden party.

It was after six o'clock now, the crowd was larger, but still not at all uncomfortable. Soon however carriages began to drive up and form a line, then another line on the other side of the road, and it began to look as if it might be possible that my view would be cut off; however it was suggested that we stand where we were till the party arrived, then step out into the road. This advice we followed, and as the guard passed we moved out and had another splendid view. This time I noticed several things I had not seen before. I saw what a soft creamy complexion the Queen had. So many of her portraits give the idea of a rather coarse wrinkled face. This was not my impression. She had a very thoughtful pleased look on her face, and when she bowed, which she did every little while, she did it so deferentially and kindly, as if she wanted to show the people that she really appreciated their love and good will. She did not look tired, but held herself erect in the carriage, and one would never imagine that she was under five feet in height.[69]

Their goal accomplished, the group started for home, 'quite persuaded that we had spent the most profitable afternoon of the holiday and satisfied that at last this long anticipation was a decided realization.' Yet, Peake added, 'I think it is a fact that some people at least are never satisfied. Having seen the Queen, I immediately determined that her sons and daughters must be interesting people too and I hoped I would be able to see them all before I left.' The next day her desires were met when she saw the Prince and Princess of Wales, knowing 'immediately that we were looking at [them] for they are very much like their pictures.'[70]

A newspaper notice alerted Ethel Davies that the queen 'was to go to her capital to see her peoples and be seen by them.' She too waited for three hours in the crowd (although 'there is much in a London crowd to amuse one and the time did not seem so long'). The queen's arrival was heralded by that of the luggage vans, Royal Carriage, and Horse Guards: 'such splendid men all over six feet and mounted on splendid black steeds prancing proudly along.' She was preceded by 'the advancing carriages with little Edward of York then the Indian Princes in their quaint costume and lastly her Majesty – with Princess Henry of Battenburg and Princess Victoria of Schleswig-Holstein. The crowd of people sent up cheer after cheer waving flags and singing the National Anthem. She bowed most graciously as she passed along in the splendid carriage with the postillion sitting on the horses and her grand Highlanders up behind.'[71] As Davies's description suggests, although such appearances were not as elaborately orchestrated as the jubilees, for those who viewed them they still had elements of a majestic spectacle. Murphy was uncharacteristically overwhelmed by the sounds that preceded the arrival of Queen Victoria. The 'clank' of bits and spurs, the 'clatter of steel-clad hoofs,' the 'rattle' of swords and bridle chains: all had 'a military ring that was entrancing' and induced a 'choke of emotion; a great heart-leap.'[72]

As did a number of her countrywomen, Davies mingled awe at seeing the queen with a domestication of the royal personage. In Davies's words, Victoria was a 'dear old lady' to her Canadian subjects, a reminder, perhaps even a reassurance, that imperial relationships were not just about trade conferences or negotiations of boundaries, the very matters that preoccupied Davies's father, Wilfrid Laurier's minister of marine and fisheries: they also came with a human and explicitly gendered connection to empire.[73] Although Murphy thought the queen's gown 'dowdy-looking,' she was so intent on watching the 'dear, faded, little mother, who has stamped her name and character on the world's golden age' that she could not tell whether the crowd cheered or not. 'God bless her!' she told her readers, 'As Queen of our hearts, she reigneth alone.'[74]

Even though Prince Albert's death was to be mourned, Victoria's was a far better story of marital happiness, domestic comfort, and national and imperial progress than the histories represented by the Tower of London. Victoria had a particular and intense appeal that, in all likelihood, her successors could not entirely match, but clearly the attraction of seeing royalty did not end with her death. In England some years later, Irene Simmonds quickly responded to a newspaper notice that King Edward VII, Queen Alexandra, and their daughter Victoria would be returning to Buckingham Palace. She and her husband waited patiently in the crowd and were rewarded by friendly guards, who helped them find a place close enough so that they could 'have a good look at their Majesties. We smiled at them as they drove slowly by, and the King raised his hat and the Queen bowed to us. I felt good all day after so much glory.' Alexandra, she thought, was very 'sweet looking' and looked as young as her daughter.[75]

It was not that men were uninterested in seeing and participating in royal spectacle. The first part of Elliott's travelogue was devoted to Queen Victoria's Diamond Jubilee in 1897. From the window of a friend's home in the Strand, he watched as 'Victoria turned her face towards us ... I was very pleased at this fortunate circumstance, for it gave me proof that none of her pictures flatter her. There was character and life in that look which she cast upon the people that no picture has yet shown.'[76] Yet none of the men's letters or diaries express the same deep desire and yearning to experience sighting the queen as do the women's. Men did not record hearing and following up rumours of her more 'spontaneous' appearances, and when they watched large-scale royal parades, they expressed somewhat different interests. Mackinnon, also in London for a Jubilee celebration, observed that the crowd cheered her continuously as her carriage passed by them, that 'Hats and linens fluttered like forest leaves in a tempest,' and that she bowed and smiled to all. But unlike Murphy, he was more concerned with the details of the event and its quantitative dimensions than in recording any strong emotions that might have stirred him: Queen Victoria, he calculated, must have to smile for sixty minutes at a stretch and nod every second. This, he decided, 'must have been irksome. It will thus be seen that royalty has its days of fagging toil like meaner people.'[77] In June 1911 Pack had too many problems in simply seeing George V and Queen Mary during their coronation procession (the coach was very low and the windows very small) to form much of an impression, domestic or otherwise. He did report, though, on the Royal Progress of the following day, that 'both were kept busy bowing the queen looked splendid. She is a good and sensible looking woman.'[78]

The royal residences, particularly Kensington and Buckingham Palaces and Windsor Castle, were examined and assessed in similar ways. Mary Spencer Warren provided those readers of the *Canadian Magazine* who could not attend 1897's Diamond Jubilee with a glowing account of 'The Queen's Horses and Carriages,' rounded off by 'twelve copyright photographs.' Describing in great detail the carriages, horses, and stable cats (many of them Purebred Persians) housed in the royal mews, Warren ended with a description of the skills of Mr Miller, the head coachman to the Queen. Miller could keep a team of six to eight horses calm in a royal procession, despite the noise of military bands, the ringing of bells, the waving of flags and handkerchiefs, and the shouting of the multitude. Not just a simple description of Miller's work, the article impressed on Canadians the excitement engendered when British royalty was on display (see fig. 5.2).[79]

Visitors to the palaces and to Windsor Castle certainly were thrilled by both their sumptuousness and the history on display. Elliott thought that all of Windsor, the building as well as its contents, represented English history. He was especially pleased with his trip because, although the royal apartments were closed to the public, he did get a glimpse of the queen being helped from her carriage by her Indian servants.[80] In her diary Thomson gave a very detailed description of the castle's furnishing and decor, including souvenirs of Waterloo, the flag that had flown over the British legation in Peking during the Boxer Rebellion, and a two-ton rug woven by convicts for the one of the Queen's Jubilees.[81] Lindsey saw many things 'upon which we dealt with reverence,' such as 'the gallant Chinese Gordon's' bible,' as well as items of curiosity (like Haydn's harpsichord) and marvel (like

5.2. Conveying Victoria to her loyal imperial subjects (*Canadian Magazine*, June 1897)

George IV's punch bowl). 'The presents from other monarchs were very numerous and beautiful, and made us feel how high our noble Queen stands in the estimation of the world.'[82]

But it was not just the queen's esteemed position on the international stage that impressed Lindsey. He also observed that the very spit in the kitchen, where oxen were roasted at Christmas for distribution to the poor, 'bore testimony to the fact that amidst all this wealth and grandeur of the Royal Palace the poor are not forgotten.' On entering Windsor Castle, Lindsey and his party 'felt it a great privilege to be allowed to wander at will among the drawing-rooms and salons, where our beloved Queen lives the domestic life of which her people are so proud.'[83] To these tourists the royal residences were public and national (and, as we shall see imperial) spaces, while simultaneously domestic interiors. In 'Victoria's English Palaces,' wrote travel writer and historian Emily Weaver in 1910, past and present mingled, for these buildings were a testimony to both the grandeur of the English state and to the history of a particularly English domesticity, exemplified by the monarch herself.[84] After paying an extra fee to one of the guides at Kensington Palace for the privilege of seeing rooms 'not generally open to the public,' Cameron inspected Queen Victoria's schoolroom; the boxes that held her wedding bonnet, wreath, and veil; the courtyard where she had played as a girl; and the window of the schoolroom from which she had first sighted her Albert.[85] Even Fred Martin, who did not go out of his way to look at royalty (preferring instead the ladies 'mounted on beautiful horses in Rotten Row') was impressed not just by the horses at Windsor's Royal Mews – 'such horses my pen cannot describe' – but also by the riding house where the royal children had been taught to ride as the queen looked on from its gallery.[86] Chown's tour of Kensington took her into the late queen's bedroom and nursery, where she saw her toys, wedding bonnet, and the dress she wore for her first opening of Parliament.[87]

Seeing and evaluating the monarchy in this manner was probably shaped by the structure of tours and the commentary of guides, for these tourists were not free to wander where they pleased at Windsor or in the palaces. Yet just as they could be critical of other sites or treat them with less than perfect reverence, so too did these colonial subjects yield various assessments of British tradition. Cameron, for one, was quite disappointed by the exteriors of Buckingham Palace and of St James's Palace.[88] Priddis was present at the unveiling of the Victoria Memorial and judged it to be 'more massive than graceful, more interesting than artistic.'[89] Cameron had little to say about the memorial itself but was quite interested in the unveiling ceremony, which was presided over in 1911 by both British and German royalty. The ceremony, she noted, 'went off very smoothly,' although the gun salutes agitated the nearby birds and the pelicans had been caged for fear they would fly off. Always a keen observer of the London crowds, Cameron recorded the presence of a number of venders selling 'badges, post cards, photos of Queen Victoria and the Kaiser, the programs printed on paper napkins and souvenirs of every description.'[90] She was far from overwhelmed by the Albert Memorial, though, judging it to be a 'useless expense – the money might have been expended to do more good and perpetuate Albert's memory in a more accessible way.'[91]

Chown, however, thought the Albert Memorial was 'a most wonderful structure,' with its representations of Asia, Europe, Africa, and America, not to mention the depictions of commerce, engineering, manufacture, agriculture, and culture carved into it.[92] Mackinnon found it looked much prettier close up, with its 'gems, gilt, tinsel, reliefs, [and] sculptures,' since from a distance it lacked the 'simple majesty of Scott's monument at Edinburgh, though costing over seven times as much dollars.'[93] Even when generally impressed, some commentators could not resist a hint of irreverence. Simmonds wanted to sit on the throne at Windsor, 'but a stern looking guard kept his eye on me, which made me afraid to try it.' Mackinnon grumbled that the town of Windsor's revenues 'consist mainly of court pickings and extortions from tourists. Summer visitors are frequent, and whatever favours they require are marked at fancy prices.'[94]

The royal residences, processions, and ceremonies not only affirmed these anglophone Canadians' links to British history and the British state. They also reminded Canadians that, through their ties to Britain, they were part of the larger imagined community of the British Empire. 'Britain' was not an enclosed or self-sufficient entity: imperial structures and relationships were apparent in many of these displays of London's public, national culture, and while other parts of Britain might remind Canadians of their membership in the empire, such opportunities abounded in London. Journalists and travel writers told readers that, as the 'heart of the empire,' London presented a narrative of its growth. Yet, unlike the combination of Britishness and domesticated femininity represented by Queen Victoria, the vision of imperial London that these writers forwarded often was a masculine one, based on images of those men who were important actors in international commerice, imperial politics, and the empire's military might. These writers pointed out that men from Japan, China, Australia, Africa, and America went to London to negotiate railroad deals with Britain's bankers, while the 'great rulers' of China, Persia, and Russia went there to see an even greater one. Hotels and pensions were 'filled with colonials and foreigners,' as were the shops of Holborn and Cheapside, of Oxford and Regent streets.[95] London was more likely to fulfil its promise of offering glimpses of 'exotic' people, particularly South Asians, through the latter's participation in imperial spectacles. Isabella Montgomery thought that the 1895 Indian Exhibition was both gorgeous and spectacular, and at the Jubilee which he attended Mackinnon noted that sixteen officers of the Indian cavalry preceded the state carriages and that 'not a few of the dusky warriors had testimonials of brave deeds on the field of battle.'[96] They were followed by the Indian princes, while at Westminster Abbey Mackinnon was especially taken with the 'eastern priests and shahs, their turbans ablaze with barbaric splendour.'[97]

Elliott saw many 'distinguished foreigners' in the Diamond Jubilee procession and thought that the sombre faces of Turkey's Munir Pasha and China's Chang Yew Jun 'were of special note.' He was very happy to see Sir Wilfrid Laurier in the Colonial Procession, which was led by Lord Roberts and 'met with an enthusiastic reception' (Laurier, in particular, with his 'polite bows' produced cheers all along the line), observing that 'the spectators evinced great pride and satisfaction with the stalwart Canadian troops in their serviceable and picturesque uniforms.'[98] But the most 'picturesque group were the coal black, strong, bearded troops of the Imperial Service, dressed in turbans and gorgeous Oriental uniforms. These men were led by Sir Pretab Singh.'[99] At George V's coronation fourteen years later the 'Indian princes' still retained their power to dazzle Canadians, for George Pack found them to be 'beyond description' in a 'most gorgeous turnout of horses and trappings.'[100]

Canadian tourists rarely came into direct contact with non-white members of the empire, but the social and cultural structures that imperial festivities created could bring about such encounters – and imperialism's commodification of cultural symbols might facilitate the introduction. At a garden party held after an imperial pageant in 1911, Harriett Priddis was helped to iced coffee by an 'Oriental,' who asked her if she was 'Anglo Indian, "I said oh no Anglo Canadian." Touching my necklet he said "but this is old Indian." "No I am sorry to say not Modern English about thirty years." "Indeed then it is a very good copy of one of our very best old Indian designs." He called a little lady in white Oriental costume near by and introduced his wife. She spoke English with a very sweet voice and accent. She said she learned it at school and from mixing with English friends at home. We talked of the general advance of women which has spread to the East and they laugh at the antics of the militant suffragettes as we do.'[101]

If Priddis (as we shall see) had mixed reactions to the 'antics of the militant suffragettes,' she – and, it seems, her new acquaintances – also appeared to subscribe to the belief that 'women's advancement' was a Western concept and phenomenon, to be learned along with English at school, and not something to which 'the East' might have made its own contributions.[102] This is not to suggest, though, that Priddis's copious travel diaries yield a wealth of Orientalist observations. Priddis was always open to new encounters with the people she met on her travels and thus met men and women: She talked to local residents in England, Scotland, and Wales; to 'foreigners' (Europeans and Americans), and to other 'colonials.' Furthermore, her writings are not sprinkled with the blatantly ethnocentric and pejorative assessments of 'foreigners' that some of her countrywomen like Emily Murphy, made – although Murphy saved her worst vitriol for the English.[103]

In recording their impressions of the 'Indian princes' in their letters or diaries, anglophone Canadian tourists rarely took the opportunity to congratulate themselves directly on occupying a supposedly superior position within the imperial hierarchy, that of a self-governing dominion with 'British' institutions and a predominantly white settler population. Nevertheless, it would be naive to assume that on some level such judgments and assessments were not there. Unlike the sensibly attired Canadians, the Indian troops might dazzle the spectator, but they were still 'dusky warriors.' The Indian troops and princes could be relegated to the realm of 'barbaric splendour,' one that existed outside of liberal progress, commercial and industrial capitalism, and modernity. These Canadian tourists valued representations of Canada that emphasized its contributions to precisely those entities and values, and they worried most acutely about Canada falling behind the United States – not India or Jamaica – in the eyes of the metropolis.[104] Even Priddis felt that she shared a special bond with people from the other dominions. In London, while waiting for theatre tickets, she was particularly pleased to meet a party of women from New Zealand and remarked approvingly on the number of fellow 'colonials' in the crowd.[105] Travelling around Europe, she once met a party of Australians, whom she liked 'very much, there is a freemasonry among colonists.'[106] In London various categories of 'exotic' races – some of whom were fellow members of the 'imperial family,' while others were not so fortunate – might be viewed within the context of 'representative government,' a setting that promised both titillation (that of being in London and of seeing 'curious foreigners') *and* security.[107] Non-white 'colonials and foreigners,' especially when juxtaposed against the Houses of Parliament, Westminster Abbey, or the British Museum, could reinforce among anglophone Canadian visitors an awareness of their deep-rooted ties to England and their supposedly 'higher' position – as members of a white dominion with 'English' institutions – within the imperial hierarchy.

Canada and Empire

Other displays of imperialism drew Canadian tourists and gave them ample opportunity to see representations of other parts of the empire and Canada. The Festival of Empire, wrote Randolph Carlyle in 1910, will be 'the most remarkable spectacle' of fifty years, with concerts, a costume ball, exhibits of both art and industry, and a pageant of twenty-four scenes and fifteen hundred performers (it was organized by Frank Lascelles, whose success the previous year at Quebec might well have inspired this event). Its promoters expected a hundred thousand visitors per day, and Carlyle was confident that this 1911 event would shore up the 'thin and atrophied' ties of empire; furthermore, it would prove that London's history 'is a history of the empire.' Anxious to impress on his readers that the pageant was not merely entertainment, Carlyle pointed out that the 'most eminent historians' would be providing research for it (but admitted that the 'Master of Pageantry' 'must have an eye for the theatrical').[108]

Not everyone shared Carlyle's optimism. Priddis recorded that 'it seems to me to be a big mistake to have the Coronation Exhibition and Festival of Empire the same season. They must interfere with each other financially and there is of course a great repetition.'[109] She was not pleased with the festival's parade, especially since it had been heavily advertised and she went into London with a friend just to see it. Standing in late summer heat at Hyde Park Corner for an event that was more than an hour behind schedule, Priddis deemed it 'a disappointment, not a grand procession at all, not a tenth of the characters seen on the ground ... Several large gilded cars like circus cars with characters of the tableaux principally representing the Colonies. Britannia in the first surrounded by guards. Miss Canada looked pretty in white with starry crown and her attendant maids scattering confetti like snow flakes. Queen Elizabeth and attendant courtiers on horseback. Some out west cowboys, a few of the settlers' carts, and this is what I had kept Mrs Penn waiting for. I felt rather ashamed of the adventure.'[110] Earlier in her diary Priddis had noted that, although 'Miss Merritt' had tried to persuade her to join in the Canadian pageant at the Crystal Palace, 'I have no fancy for dressing up and could not stand the rehearsals.'[111]

These imperial displays were not always disappointing, however. Mabel Cameron visited Imre Kiralfy's Coronation Exhibition at White City and found 'native workers busy amid scenes and surroundings of their homes. Men from India were engaged in the hammered brass work which they do with sharp chisels and little mallets. Others were carving wood and ivory, some were busy weaving rugs, women deftly did silk and gold thread embroidery, wax toys were being made, it was all very fascinating. In the West Indies sections negresses dressed in be-frilled and starched muslins were making baskets and weaving Panama hats.' She also enjoyed seeing the Chinese Garden, finding it 'most realistic and the real landscape blended well with the painted one.' In the Fine Arts Building, 'among the native workers one could not help but notice the great number of little children. Oftentimes these were occupying more attention than the handicrafts of their parents.' But 'Canada, with Niagara Falls as a great drawing-card, was crowded into a small building where a number of civilized-looking Indians were busy making snow-shoes, moccasins, and lacrosse sticks. I only trust the other buildings are truer representation of their respective countries than this is.'[112]

When the exhibits were opened at the Crystal Palace, Priddis seemed generally satisfied with the depiction of Canada: a panorama that displayed 'wheat fields, prosperous orchards and farms, herds of cattle, and the Parliament buildings. Niagara Falls is a great disappointment how could it be anything else, I am sorry for Minnie to have seen it.' (Her companion at the panorama, Minnie, accompanied her back to Canada where, presumably, she saw the genuine article.) Priddis did not share Cameron's disappointment with the Coronation Exhibition's execution of 'Canada.' Upon entering the palace she went straight to the Canada Building, where she saw the two-thirds scale model of Parliament and found

> comfy rest rooms, models of the life of the Indian at work, beavers at work, orchards with real apples in abundance, ranch farm grain fields, mining industry, pictures made of grain frames and all. I was indignant at first to see in the centre of the building a large snow covered building with Miss Canada on top garbed in toque and blanket coat with the ever present snow shoes and toboggan, with Kipling's abominable 'Lady of the Snows' in relief on every side. But when I got near I saw the joke: beneath the snow roof was a large collection of the most beautiful fruit grown in Canada, nothing equal to it on the ground even from the tropics. Adjoining it was a fine dairy exhibit.[113]

These anglophone Canadian women were particularly sensitive to representations of Canada, whether as displays of goods or enactments by individuals, that relied on symbols of endless winter and a barren landscape. Like their counterparts in imperial and national organizations in Britain and Canada, the formal exclusion of women from the franchise did not prevent them from crafting national and imperial subjectivities from which they might assess and criticize national and imperial images and performances.[114] Instead, these Canadian women wanted those at the imperial centre – and other tourists, other imperial subjects – to appreciate that Canada contributed to the domestic commodities displayed in imperial spectacles and performed in these theatres of imperialism as well as any other member of the empire.[115] Priddis was pleased to see her country portrayed at a garden party pageant in which 'London' received 'the young Queens from over the seas and show[ed] them some of her old time festivities. Canada I am glad to say in yellow dress and maple leaves not blanket coat and toque rather pertly said "they did not want to see her improvements they had plenty of that at home, but they had nothing old, that is what they came over the seas to enjoy."'[116] Mabel Cameron, too, was very conscious of British conceptions of her homeland and its position on the imperial map. She accompanied her aunt, as she gave lectures on Canada's charms, and gauged the audiences' reactions to the talks and slides. She was indignant at characterizations of Canada that did not accord with narratives of progress, prosperity, and settlement. Depictions of Native peoples were always a problem in this context, for while they could evoke an interest in the exotic other, much like the 'Indian princes,' if not carefully handled, their representations might also suggest wilderness and untamed savagery. These possibilities were not only unflattering to Canada, but they also might put off potential investors and emigrants: hence the industrious plying of Native crafts at the Coronation Exhibition.[117]

Exhibitions were not the only sites that elicited concerns about Canada's relationship with Britain. The ambivalence that (as chapter 3 has argued) permeated many of the Canadians' impressions of England was felt most acutely in London. More than one writer hinted at insecurities and voiced anxieties that in London Canadians were taken for granted or overlooked, particularly during the late Victorian and Edwardian years. When walking around London, an anonymous correspondent for the *Montreal Daily Star* wrote in 1882, one is 'often and painfully impressed with the entire absence of everything pertaining to the Dominion, in all matters which would come under the eyes of the *"flaneur."'* The presence of the United States, however, was everywhere: in consumer goods for sale, in the symbols displayed around the city, and in cultural artefacts, such as novels and plays. The Canadian government's offices in London were not in an 'attractive position,' and only two Canadian banks were to be found. There was hope, though, for this observer also noticed tinned fish from Prince Edward

Island and British Columbia, labelled 'Maple Leaf Brand,' on display in a shop window. 'I could not but be struck with the wisdom of that brand. It is just such things as that that captivates the popular fancy, and if there was a little more of the maple leaf in everything coming from Canada, it would, I think, bring the Dominion practically before the public.'[118] Edith Chown was happy to hear that an acquaintance from her hometown of Kingston maintained his own personal 'national brand,' writing home that 'the part I liked about him most that although he had been over here twelve or thirteen years he has not become at all Englishfied – is still a true Canadian.'[119]

Patriotic 'branding' was one strategy for reminding Londoners of the Dominion of Canada. So too was coverage of Canada by the London press. The *Canadian Magazine* was pleased to report in 1897 that the London newspaper, *National Review*, had started to run a column on colonial politics. 'Little Britain is beginning to realize that there is a greater Britain, that the people who live in the colonies are beings with souls, and sense, and intelligence, and culture, and feeling, and breeding and brains – just as other Britishers have.' Citing the *Review*, Canadians were presented with proof that at least some of those 'at home' believed in the common ties of empire: 'what our fellow-countrymen in Canada, Australia, and South Africa feel, is that in spite of our perpetual affirmations that "We are all Imperialists now" ... we, in the old country, do not take a very serious or intelligent interest in their affairs ... The Canadian visitor to London can hardly talk with any comfort about his political affairs, even with an educated Englishman, so grossly ignorant are they of Canadian questions"' (the same situation held true for Australians and Cape Colonists). 'This is perfectly correct,' the article in the *Canadian Magazine* stated, but it was 'refreshing to know' that 'at least one London periodical has undertaken to present colonial events in regular and readable form.' It was deemed that such a strengthening of the 'bonds of empire' would be in both Canada's and Britain's interest, for the latter 'has lost enough by secession; she cannot afford to have historical events repeated.'[120]

Canadian Women, Empire, and Spectacles of Suffrage

There were many imperial connections to be finessed and strengthened within London. While imperial conferences and transatlantic commerce drew Canadian politicians and businessmen to London, middle- and upper-middle-class Canadian women also came to the metropole for

Miss Harriett Priddis.

The High Commissioner for Canada
and Lady Strathcona
at Home
Monday. 2nd July. 1906
To celebrate Dominion Day.

The Imperial Institute.
South Kensington.
                                        10 o'clock.

(THE CANADIAN COURT AND EXHIBITS WILL BE OPEN FOR INSPECTION.)

5.3. A tourist's souvenir of nation and empire: Harriett Priddis celebrates Dominion Day in London, 1906. (Harriett Priddis Diary, 1906, Harriett Priddis Fonds B4272, J.J. Talman Regional Collection, University of Western Ontario Archives. Reproduced courtesy of UWO Archives)

international conferences on issues such as social welfare, promoting the empire, and promoting woman's rights (see fig. 5.3). The Ladies' Empire Club of London, a 'spacious' and welcoming townhouse on Grosvenor Street, was one place in which they might gather for meetings, lunches, teas, and dinners; it also offered reading, card, and smoking rooms (the latter having 'not a suggestion of the masculine smoking den,' but pale green chintz instead), as well as comfortable and attractive bedrooms. The club had three hundred 'colonial' members, among them one hundred and thirty Canadian women.[121] Apparently Mabel and Agnes Cameron were members. 'Dressed in our Sunday togs,' Mabel wrote, she and her aunt Agnes had dinner at the club, where they met two 'ladies from New Zealand.'[122] During her 1911 trip, Priddis spent a great deal of time visiting various mixed-sex and

5.4. Welcoming colonial women: The Ladies' Empire Club. Note the feminine, domestic decor of the smoking room. (*Canadian Magazine*, July 1904)

all-female imperial organizations, as well as social reform groups, including the Empire Club, the Imperial Institute, the Victoria League, the Dominion Club, and the YWCA (see fig. 5.4).[123]

Moreover, both women's own and the empire's potential were represented most clearly in the spectacles of women at public suffrage rallies and parades. Chown's sense of membership in a gendered community of nation and empire was intensified by her participation in the large 1910 suffrage procession to the Albert Hall. She and Alice had only intended to watch, but they were asked to walk in the parade, and so they 'got to work' and made a banner with 'Canada' and maple leaves emblazoned across it. 'It was very crude but rather effective.' Eight women (four English, 'Miss Cartwright' from Montreal, and one African) marched in their contingent, each carrying a bunch of wheat. 'The people were just crazy over the wheat and all wanted a piece as we passed. We could hear them say as we passed, "Oh Canada, that's the place, and other such expressions."' Although the Chowns did not finish the procession and took a cab the rest of the way, they felt it was a 'most wonderful sight to see Albert Hall filled with ten thousand people, mostly women.'[124]

Priddis decided during her 1911 trip not to watch the Women's Coronation Procession but instead went directly to the Albert Hall, where the procession ended in a large rally. She was very impressed with the leading committee: 'they are brilliantly organized.' En route to the hall she saw the 'actresses van all white with hooped canopy gaily decorated with artificial pink roses and green leaves.' Once inside, Priddis observed that Mrs Drummond, 'the leader still sat on her big horse looking very like Rosa Bonheur ... Joan of Arc in full armour stood beside her.' Although she had a good seat in the first row of the gallery, Priddis could not hear Emmeline Pankhurst, as her voice 'was not loud enough to fill the big hall.' She was able, though, to make out Annie Besant's speech on the 'pioneer days of the woman's movement. Her voice carries remarkably well and she is altogether a remarkable woman ... I do not know enough about all the movement to catch all that was said.' Priddis was impressed with the electric sign that kept a running total of donations: 'it was really very exciting and did not interfere with the speaking at all.' The meeting ended with the arrival on the platform of Christabel Pankhurst, who was 'received with loud clapping. A tall fine looking girl fashionably dressed in pale green with well shaped long arms which she used a great deal in gesticulating a clear full voice that filled the Hall ... She was quite dramatic when she stood perfectly still, looking young and strong and said in a peculiar voice our opponents say we have no staying qualities, no capacity for organization, then with a ringing voice throwing out both arms "Look around." There was no crowding or rushing in emptying the immense hall and we all walked off as quietly as from church.'[125]

Chown, Priddis, and the Camerons (who also attended a suffrage meeting at Queen's Hall and were enthralled by Christabel Pankhurst)[126] were in London at the height of the militant campaign that, as their writings suggest, became a tourist attraction as well as urban spectacle. Cameron wrote of hearing suffrage speeches at Wimbledon Common and in Parliament Square, the latter given by women who had recently been released from prison.[127] Chown wrote home that, after hearing Emmeline Pethwick-Lawrence, Christabel Pankhurst, and others speak, she 'thoroughly enjoyed the meeting – and am already a confirmed suffragist! It makes me mad to think every man is given a vote except that he be a lunatic or a criminal. To think of ranking woman with that class.'[128]

Margaret Thomson, who was fairly hostile to suffrage, was nevertheless fascinated by the movement. She remarked acerbically that at Speaker's Corner – where she heard, among others, representatives from the men's league for women's suffrage – 'the rubbish being proclaimed and the faces of the listeners were interesting for a little while.'[129] On holiday in a small town in Devon, Thomson and her husband, Joe, met a woman selling *Votes for Women*. 'The shop woman meekly produced a penny,' Thomson wrote, 'but when tackled Joe said "No I don't believe in it." "You would if you looked into it," said the girl. "Oh I'm ashamed of the women of England," said Joe. "Well I assure you they're not ashamed of themselves," retorted the Suffragette. She almost closed the door and then opened it again to exclaim, "Look what the men did to get a vote. Burned half Bristol in one night and even committed murder!" she looked really ready for a fight.'[130] Returning to England for a short trip in 1914, Thomson noted that her husband had found himself on 'top of a train with a lot of suffragettes coming to Bexhill for a demonstration. At first there was a second man then J braved it all alone. The "gettes" all carried white parasols painted round with remarks. Here they had a masked domino parade.'[131] From a London taxi, a month later, Thomson saw that 'the suffragettes had been "marching to Buckingham." It was over but crowds still hung round. There were said to be two thousand policemen and there were certainly a large number. Forty five arrests were made amid disgraceful scenes.'[132]

Suffrage rallies, processions, debates at Speaker's Corner, women selling *Votes for Women* on street corners, and suffragettes being released from jail were sights that Canadian women could not have seen at home, at least not on such a large scale.[133] As Thomson's remarks suggest, not all anglophone Canadian travellers supported the cause. Even Harriett Priddis recommended that 'votes for women' be demanded at appropriate moments, feeling that such a call was obtrusive when made unexpectedly.[134] Chown's insistence on displaying symbols of national identity suggests that anglophone Canadian women's membership within the suffrage movement might be both strengthened *and* complicated by imperial relationships.[135] Suffrage marches and rallies, carefully orchestrated in ways that linked British women to British history, offered English-speaking women tourists from Canada a link to political participation and national subjectivity (to return briefly to the Tower) not available through other spectacles of British history.[136]

The Sensory Capital: Galleries, Shops, and Theatres

Reinforcing imperial ties, royal ceremonies, imperial exhibitions, and women's suffrage demonstrations were sensory experiences, full of sound and sights: the jingle of horses' harnesses, the roar of crowds, Christabel Pankhurst's voice, the vivid colours of Indian princes' turbans, 'West Indian negresses' dresses at imperial exhibitions, or the mass of green, white, and purple dresses of the suffrage women carrying their various banners through the London streets. Writings about London often speak of the waves of sensation elicited by its streets and squares, of sensations awaiting the tourist around every corner, and in every nook and cranny of the city.

London's largest museums were full of visual and mental stimuli. Amy Redpath Roddick spent a 'delightful' afternoon at the South Kensington Museum, 'poring over letters and documents and manuscripts of celebrated men.' She also enjoyed the museum's collection of art by Caldicott and Cruikshank and Raphael's 'wonderful' cartoons.[137] Arthur Whitman was disappointed by his visit, in 1888, to the British Museum (he admitted that not all of it was open) but found the Natural History Museum 'much more interesting stuffed animals of all kinds fish flesh and fowl. The lovely birds of paradise some enormous skeletons of whales mastodons elephants giraffe.'[138] For Mackinnon, both institutions, with their collections of British, Egyptian, Japanese, and Indian 'histories,' were equally fascinating and instructive; he attempted to transmit their lessons to his readers with eight pages of statistics and lists.[139] Ethel Davies brought her customary enthusiasm to the British Museum and recorded in her diary a select list of the individuals whose letters and autographs she had seen there (Nelson, Wellington, Queen Victoria, General Gordon), as well as a few of the more memorable artefacts: Anne Boleyn's Bible and the Rosetta Stone, the latter intriguing since it 'allowed people to understand ancient languages ... giving us an insight into ancient history which otherwise might have remained a blank.'[140]

Not content with the historical and imperial insights gained from studying museum displays, these tourists furthered their cultural education with tours of London's galleries. Bond Street's art galleries, the National Gallery, the National Portrait Gallery, the Royal Academy, and the Tate: Canadian tourists flocked to these spots, gazed on the art displayed, and many of them meticulously recorded what they had seen and what they had made of it.[141] Travel writers were eager to offer tourists assistance in deciding what to see and how to see it. The *Montreal Daily Star's* 'Penelope,' author of the paper's woman's column, wrote in 'Our London Letter' of Bond Street's galleries, where she had admired the Hungarian artist Michael Munkaczy's *Christ Before Pilate* and the Royal Academy's annual exhibit, which had featured the unappealing pre-Raphaelites but also displayed more enjoyable paintings by 'ladies' such as Mrs Jepling and Mrs John Collier.[142] But few anglophone Canadian travellers had the money, time, and inclination for extensive visits to art galleries, public or private. An exception was Edward Greenshields, who had published a book of art criticism and thought of himself as a connoisseur. He made innumerable trips to galleries in London, Liverpool, and Edinburgh and wrote lengthy descriptions of the art works he saw, together with critiques of the artists' techniques and aesthetic effects.[143] At the National Gallery in 1895, Greenshields was pleased to find that, unlike during his previous visit when he had 'looked at the paintings merely with curiosity,' 'now they have so much more meaning.' His critical eye helped, and also the gallery had improved the arrangement of its paintings: 'I never realized before what a painter Sir Joshua Reynolds was – Gainsborough's Mrs Siddons certainly looks cold in colour before his.'[144] In general, though, Greenshields preferred European work, particularly Italian and Dutch paintings. After a visit to the Tate in 1906, where he found the art by Rosetti, Sergeant, Moore, Millais, Turner, Whistler, and Watts 'fine,' he mused that 'these pictures make a visit to this gallery a great pleasure, but the other pictures make one realize the inartistic character of the British nation. Rooms of stuff are there that is not worth looking at.'[145]

Greenshields' opinion that the British lacked artistic talent was not unanimous. Roddick's visit to the Tate left her delighted with 'the most beautiful collection' of modern British painters, 'the originals of so many pictures known through engravings.'[146] About to leave London for Liverpool, two weeks later, instead of spending her last afternoon shopping Roddick went to Westminster Abbey and the National Gallery, having concluded that 'shopping may be done at any time but it may be a long time before I have an opportunity of seeing these wonderful sights again.'[147] Although Thomson had visited the National Gallery many times on her previous trips to England, in 1910 she toured it with her friend Laura and found that she 'enjoyed the British school very much,' her favourite artists being Reynolds, Gainsborough, Romney, Landseer, and Rathburn.[148]

Despite Roddick's resolve to place history and art above 'shopping,' it is clear that to no small extent London's allure stemmed from its range of shops and stores, particularly those that catered to middle-class women. It was not that male tourists were impervious to such attractions; to Whitman, Pack, and Greenshields, London was a place to refurbish wardrobes and to buy treats for themselves and for family members at home.[149] Yet the most detailed accounts of London as a centre of consumption were from women tourists. As Erika Rappaport has shown, middle-class women's attraction to the shops of London's West End was no accident but a response carefully orchestrated by department store owners, mindful of the need to attract a 'respectable' female clientele.[150] And it was not just the efforts of department store owners and designers at work: Canadian women shoppers in London were encouraged to seek out West End stores by travel writers such as 'Penelope.' Before leaving London for a summer trip to Scotland, Penelope made one last visit to 'the emporium of all that is most tempting to women,' as she needed to 'tell country cousins what the latest fashions are.' 'Plunging' into the middle of the summer sales, she observed that 'everything that appertains to travelling is spread out to tempt the unwary fly into these spiders' webs of fashion.' Here she found 'delightful tailor-made costumes, pretty sailor hats ... and waterproof cloaks, hoods, and all manner of inventions to defy the weather.' On display were wide-brimmed straw hats in various colours, trimmed with ribbons, flowers, and fruits. For the heat there were fans – cheap, large, and useful ones, expensive ones trimmed with silk or mother-of-pearl, as well as fans made of scented white wood that had been autographed by London's celebrities such as Henry Irving, Madame Modjeska, Gladstone, and the artist Millais. The would-be shopper also would find caps and bonnets with silver, jewelled, or gilded pins (see figs. 5.5 and 5.6).[151]

Such writing not only helped to create 'London' for readers; it also shaped an image of the cultured and consuming middle-class female traveller and tourist. Such a woman could make discerning judgments about art and be knowledgeable about prominent political and cultural figures, but she also was open to the thrill of feminine accoutrements, both practical and fashionable. And she was no gullible dupe of advertising. Penelope's shopper was well aware that she, like the proverbial fly, was being tempted by the spider of consumption (after all, she might buy a cheap, large, and useful fan and a waterproof cloak, while all the time admiring the more expensive but less practical items).[152] Another 'London Letter' advised 'the ladies' of the 'ample amusement'

Fig. 5.5 – What to Wear and Where to Wear It (While in London). Source: *Canada, an Illustrated Journal*, 9 Jan. 1906.

that might be found by 'anyone who can walk well.' Touring Oxford, Regent, and Bond Streets, as well as Piccadilly, 'observing passing objects and the shop windows, slowly and quietly, not minding the risk of being put down as a country cousin – strange to the ways of London ... I ventured to do this the other day.' Passing a Piccadilly shop window filled with stuffed animals – crocodiles, giant frogs, fox and deer heads – as well as bones dug from deep in the London clay during excavations for a new bank at Charing Cross, Penelope was inspired to investigate further. 'I have a habit of reading up on and searching out any subject that interests me in the day's experience,' she told her readers, so over to the Linnean Society's library she went to research the city's 'prehistoric' past. 'But my peregrination did not

5.6. Consumption at the heart of the empire (*Canada, an Illustrated Journal,* 14 July 1906) cease with the lions of Charing Cross on the occasion when I assumed the role of a country cousin. Walking up Regent street, I delighted myself with a halt before the many bewitching bonnet shops in that locality.' Carrying on to Oxford Street, she discovered that jackets were out and dolmans were in. Penelope closed her letter with a detailed description of the clothing of a 'young lady' who had called on her, hoping to interest her in school board elections.[153]

Heeding Penelope's advice, Canadian tourists went to London to participate in its spectacular milieu of consumption.[154] 'I must say there are no shops like the London shops,' Ethel Davies mused (just after describing her sighting of the royal family at Paddington).[155] Only the 'wretched fog' in February prevented her from indulging one of her favourite pastimes, gazing 'at the windows for hours the colours are so beautiful.'[156] While full of other activities, Margaret Thomson's diary suggests a world of urban middle-class female consumption: looking at furs with her sister and mother, touring the army and navy stores, window-shopping along Tottenham Court Road, admiring the 'lovely jewellery shops' in High Holborn, and purchasing a dress in Harrod's, 'the nicest shop we have seen,' and another one in 'pale pink satin' at Peter Robinson's.'[157] But Thomson was not impressed with everything she saw, noting that the famous department store Whiteley's was a 'long way out,' lunch in the store was expensive, and she did not like the shop much.[158] Bain went shopping in Regent Street but did not have much success. 'Same old story every place we went – "bad time of year, stocks low and new ones not in yet." I didn't imagine stocks ever low in London.'[159] Despite her disappointment, her diary entry suggests that these women came to London with the expectation that London 'stocks' were ever plentiful and would fulfil their fantasies and imaginings. The *Toronto World's* 'Maple Blossoms,' who compared Regent Street's shops with Eaton's and found the former wanting (the displays were too small and the service slow), appear to have been in the minority.[160] While some of these women shopped in Europe – buying lace in Brussels, jewelry in Paris, Rome, and Venice, and dresses in Paris – they usually saw London as the arbiter of standards for fashionable dress, and purchased their coats, hats, dresses, and shoes there.[161] Although it is difficult to know at this point whether or not tourists' consumer desires and practices of consumption in London (and, as we shall see, in Europe as well) helped shape an emerging consumer culture in English Canada, nevertheless London's store windows were significant enticements for these English-Canadian tourists.[162]

Not all women, of course, had the desire or means to either window shop or purchase furs and jewelery in London. Neither Cameron nor Chown, for example, discussed shopping as extensively as some of their counterparts did. And London offered middle-class women more than sailor suits, straw hats, and silver pins. Penelope reflected on Darwin's scientific legacy during a visit to his grave and, after her trip to the emporium, she went to the Palace Theatre to hear the American lecturer Jennie Young speak on 'Woman and Her Work in the World.' At the meeting, chaired by Mrs Lucas, sister of Liberal politician John Bright, Penelope found Young's 'advocacy of the claim of woman to be allowed to earn independence for herself, to be free to follow any calling or profession for which she feels suited, and to take her place by the side of men in her life was almost thrilling.' But Penelope tempered her enthusiasm for Young's speech with some reflections on girls' education, both in London and in the countryside. In her opinion, it was more efficiently managed in the countryside, where subjects 'essential to a useful education' such as needlework, garment cutting, and simple cooking were taught. She had seen a very good practical exhibit in Bolton that featured not 'cram, or book learning' but instead displayed the 'neatest and most suitable costume for a working woman to wear at work' – unfortunately, Penelope did not describe this costume, leaving the occupation of the 'working woman' open to speculation.[163]

For those in need of respite from or uninterested in the stores, London's stages beckoned. Night after night Canadian tourists bought tickets to the comedies, dramas, and light operas of West End theatres, the opera at Covent Garden, the ballet at the Alhambra, the variety shows at the Hippodrome, and pantomimes.[164] By the late nineteenth century, they also went to see photography exhibits and films, technology that, as Lynda Nead has argued, helped give the 'metropolis a visual form and presence [and] actively constructed the image of the modern imperial city and mediated its meaning for viewers and audiences.'[165] Representations of both daily life and spectacular events attracted these tourists, and were particularly of interest if they had been present at them personally). Greenshields was very impressed to see the 'wonderful' 'kinetiscope moving pictures' at the Empire Theatre, where he watched films of a train's arrival, cavalry charging, and troops marching. 'It was all so "life like,"' he wrote, 'every person and movement being shown.'[166] After attending the unveiling of the Victoria Memorial, Cameron went to the La Scala Theatre to see the 'wonderful Kinemacolour Pictures ... taken from life and at the same time the natural colours and tints are recorded. No re-touching is done afterwards. It is a wonderful process and produces beautiful results. The opening flowers were charming. The unveiling of the Victoria Memorial was shown in all its splendour.'[167] Pack too was thrilled to see the 'New Kinneamator' pictures at La Scala; he watched the Coronation Procession, the Royal Progress, and the investiture of the Prince of Wales at Carnarvon. 'All in their natural colours and all well carried out,' he told his diary, accompanied by an orchestra, choir, and speakers who explained the pictures. 'Horses trotting auto horns blowing then guns firing ... the Prince of Wales was here last night to see himself as others see him.'[168]

Yet it was live performances in their various forms that drew in most of these tourists. The diaries of Whitman, Pack, and Martin, and Hall attest to their sampling of London's wide range of theatrical treats, from the Hippodrome's performing dogs playing football to Drury Lane's pantomimes and the Lyceum's Shakespearean productions, featuring luminaries such as Irving and Ellen Terry.[169] Here too, though, they were outdone by Greenshields, who was as assiduous a theatre-goer on his many lengthy trips as he was a gallery visitor. Greenshields also had catholic tastes when it came to London's performing arts: his diary includes descriptions of plays by Oscar Wilde and George Bernard Shaw, Beerbohm Tree's *Trilby*, as well as light comedy, historical dramas, variety shows, comic opera and operetta, and a number of performances by Anna Pavlova, which particularly impressed him.[170]

As with its shops, though, the West End's theatres offered a social space that had been designed to appeal to middle-class women who, in turn, appeared to have felt comfortable and welcome.[171] Women tourists' diaries and letters include much lengthier descriptions of experiences at theatres, many of which were in the West End, than do those of the vast majority of their male counterparts. Women's accounts also suggest that they attended more live performances than, with the exception of Greenshields, men did. And like the stores, the sights and – in this case – sounds of the London stage were powerful attractions. With her new husband, Gertrude Fleming went to a performance of *The Dancing Girl* and thought its female lead, Juli Dickson, 'quite the most beautiful heroine I'd ever seen and *that alluring*! As for Tree, he is *real* – not an actor at all in this play. Of course it was magnificently staged and the company to the bull dog perfect ... Tree has the most interesting face in the world, though he isn't good-looking he has much grace and much personality – and is best of all a real artist to his finger-tips.'[172] *The Beautiful Girl* at the Savoy was 'delightfully staged and most picturesque. The dance of the nautch girls and the oriental scenery perfectly carried out.' But while the Orientalist dimension of the play pleased Fleming, other aspects of it did not. 'My eyes were satisfied – but my ears were not so pleased – the libretto was poor, the plot strained and the music except in spots didn't mean anything. The dancing odalisque style was entrancing.'[173]

Fleming was enthusiastic about the London stage but not uncritical. An operatic comedy at the Prince of Wales Theatre was 'poor in every way to the last degree – poor music and acting – an impossibly ugly play. Haydn Coffin is very handsome and a good voice, Miss D. Moore pretty with no chance to show what she can/could do.' However, she also thought the curtain raiser, a parody of *The Dancing Girl*, entitled *The Prancing Girl*, 'clever.'[174] A few days later Fleming described an exciting a triple bill at the Royal Court Theatre that had ended with a Panto Rehearsal: 'nice men acting all so clever especially Weedon Grossmith and Brandon Thomas. The women were all well dressed and danced very prettily but the less said about their acting the better – except one a Miss Gertrude Kingston she was really clever in a little play by W.G. called A Commissioner.'[175]

While Fleming enjoyed a more privileged, upper-middle-class background (she had just married Sanford Fleming's son), she was by no means alone in her appreciation for theatre and in her knowing, critical stance towards the many productions that she and her counterparts saw. Montgomery went to see the popular *The Shop Girl* in 1895, but was disappointed: 'it was a miserable failure' (she also bought tickets to *Charley's Aunt* but did not record her impressions of it).[176] Vancouver's Sophie Pemberton thought Terry was 'perfect' but was greatly disappointed in Irving in *Napoleon and Josephine*; he made it up to her, though, in another, unnamed production (probably *Hamlet*) in which his face 'in the firelight and in the court scene [was] wonderful.'[177] She found the famous Sarah Bernhardt, appearing in *Magda* at the Adelphi, 'very powerful but disagreeable.'[178] Although Pemberton saw a great deal of theatre while in London, her tastes did not run towards Ibsen's social realist drama. *The Wild Duck*, running at the Globe, to her seemed 'morbid and unhealthy. His mission in life. Very Long.'[179]

Cameron did not share Pemberton's reaction to the New Drama. To her, Gertrude Kingston's Little Theatre was 'more like a dainty house than a theatre,' with its lounge and reading room decorated in pale mauve and white and hung with watercolours. Here she saw four short plays, including '*The Dragon of Wrath*, presented by Mme Chung and her company of Chinese Actors and Actresses. The stage setting was beautiful especially the filmy scarf dance. Mme Chung managed to get round the stage in rapid time considering the size of her feet.'[180] Along with a number of fellow English-speaking Canadians, Cameron also went to see an example of French idealist theatre, Maurice Maeterlinck's *Blue Bird*, at the Haymarket. 'This was a treat indeed. The stage effects and beautiful thoughts in the play will be long in the memory. While we were being most classical in our entertainment the rest of the family attended *Charlie's Aunt* at the Savoy.'[181] Seven months (and many other productions) later, Cameron took in George Bernard Shaw's *Fanny's First Play*, also at the Little Theatre. She found it 'quite out of the usual style' but 'replete with wholesome humour. The atmosphere of the "Little Theatre" is always so friendly and this I think means much for both players and audience.'[182] Like Greenshields, Cameron's taste in theatre was wide-ranging. She was 'delighted' to see the 'Irish Players' (the members of Dublin's Abbey Theatre) but was also thrilled to attend a Boxing Day pantomime at Drury Lane, telling her diary that 'suffice it to say that the performances started at 7.30 and we were all kept in shrieks of laughter until 12.40. The audience itself was a source of wonder and delight. Our seats gave us a view of the whole house – probably 8000 people.'[183] Chown also went to see 'an Irish theatre company' that 'had set out to awaken the Irish drama.' She saw W.B. Yeats's *Kathleen ni Houlihan*, (the 'spirit of Ireland') and J.M. Synge's *Playboy of the Western World* (a 'queer little play in three acts').[184]

Synge, Shaw, and Yeats were not to everyone's taste. More visitors were attracted to Tree's popular Shakespearean and historical productions, which relied on both literal realism and well-known actors in leading roles. Tree's historical productions were both shaped by and helped contribute to a heightened sense of nationalism and imperialism in late Victorian and Edwardian Britain, especially in coronation years.[185] Davies thought that *King John* was a 'splendid play and grandly acted.' Tree, as the lead, 'was strong and grand. Lewis Walker as Phillip Falconbridge acted splendidly and Julia Neilson made us thrill with the passion of her part as Caroline the mother of poor little Arthur. She is a wonderous woman.'[186] Bain was enthralled by *Henry VIII*, another Tree production. 'It was a magnificent production and I enjoyed it thoroughly. Herbert Tree as Cardinal Wolsey was splendid. Arthur was good as Henry VIII and Violet Vanbrugh excellent as the poor deposed Queen

Catherine. Laura C took the part of Anne Boleyn but does not figure very conspicuously!'[187] Priddis saw *Richard III* in Tree's Shakespearean festival, commenting that 'I should like to hear Herbert Tree in *Henry VIII* everyone is talking about it.' Even so, she was 'glad to have seen [*Richard IIII*] as my first memory of Shakespeare is hearing father reading it aloud mother talking of Macready in the character.'[188]

Theatre-going, like all other aspects of tourism, was shaped by class relationships. The diaries and letters are almost uniformly silent on these tourists' interactions with store clerks and ticket sellers: these women wrote out from their accounts people who were an integral part of their commercial and cultural transactions.[189] Yet such silences such should not obscure the fact that, as shoppers and audience members in the West End, these Canadians – particularly women – participated in the ongoing creation of privileged spaces in which culture and consumption were intertwined. As the world of West End 'fashion' permeated these theatres' costumes and scenery, London's upper-middle class, seated in the more costly section of the orchestra or boxes, saw facets of their lives reflected back to them through acts of elite consumption onstage.[190] Bain, for one, was well aware of this process. She noted that after seeing a production of *The Waltz Dream* at Daly's Theatre that 'the girls in the London shows are all so pretty and fresh-looking and such pretty, simple but stunning frocks.'[191] *The Quaker Girl* 'was the cutest thing ... I never saw such a lot of exquisite frocks together before.'[192] Their attendance at these productions was of course dependent on their financial status: Fleming and Bain expressed no interest over the cost of theatre tickets, while Priddis was always concerned about getting 'a bargain.' A warm July evening in 1911 saw her lining up for cheap tickets to see *Kismet* at the Garrick Theatre, where she struck up a conversation with two young women from New Zealand, who remarked that at home 'we would not be paid to stand in the street in a crowd.' They agreed that 'no one knows us here, another thing there are so many good things to see, we could not afford high prices.'[193]

This plethora of 'so many good things' evoked a range of reactions. The London stage engaged these tourists' visual and auditory senses, as well as providing them with additional instruction (historical and moral), thus combining entertainment and education. As these diary excerpts suggest theatre-going was not a passive experience. Far from simply being overwhelmed by the plethora of theatrical entertainments that London offered, these women actively assessed and critiqued the sights and sounds of London's stages. And far from being untutored or naive audience members, they brought with them definite tastes and assumptions about acting, writing, and production values and did not hesitate to denounce or praise performances according to already formed standards. But as well as their self-imposed role as cultural critics, accounts of Canadian tourists' time spent in London suggest how nationalism and imperialism might be closely entwined with modernity, consumption, and culture. While it might be tempting, seemingly more clear-cut, for the historian to hive off a trip to the Pantomime from seeing Queen Victoria in person, buying a dress at Harrod's from waiting for George V's Coronation Procession, the multiple ways in which these diverse experiences were woven into the fabric of these women's and men's passages around the city, suggest otherwise. Being a 'Canadian,' who was part of the British Empire, could mean inheriting 'British' democratic 'traditions,' ones reaffirmed by seeing the Magna Carta in the British Museum, but it also could mean playing a role in contemporary British society and culture.[194]

London was much more than just a city. In its historic buildings, public spectacles of empire and nation, cultural venues, and displays of consumption, it offered English-speaking Canadians tourists numerous opportunities to explore and articulate the interlinked meanings of gender, modernity, nation, and empire. But London – and other parts of Britain – also offered them the chance to reflect on on class relations and the varied social spaces in which these relations might be manifested. As they travelled throughout Britain, anglophone Canadian tourists recorded their impressions of those other dimensions of the empire's public sphere.

6 The Street, the Regatta, and the Orphanage: The Public and Social Spaces of Tourism in Britain

The wee boys and girls in their small uniforms were at service. We were rather amused at the flutter of the white aprons just before the prayer when every girlie covered her face with her apron during prayers. The uniforms of the children were the prettiest we had seen for any institution. The girls were dressed exactly as those in the picture of 'The Foundling Girls.'[1]

Mabel Cameron, Travel Diary (1910)

The vendors of iced drinks, fruit, fried fish, cakes and other refreshments, have reached up this way, but they keep well by the towing-path. There are thousands here to-day that care not a jot for the races, but they come with their bags and their baskets and their paper parcels, and here, at the top of the field, away from the sports, they open their bags and uncork their bottles and smoke their pipes and chatter, and lie upon the grass and dream away the time.[2]

James Rupert Elliott, *Rambles in Merrie, Merrie England* (1897)

Mabel Cameron recorded her impressions of the 'wee boys and girls' that she saw while on a visit to London's Foundling Hospital's chapel for its morning service, while James Rupert Elliott's description is of the scene at the Henley Regatta. Although they would appear to be very different phenomena – the benefits of philanthropic institutions versus a major sporting event – happy orphans, ice-drink vendors, and contented holidaymakers were part of the wide spectrum of public and social spaces for late-Victorian and Edwardian tourists. These locations included sporting events, religious services, courtrooms and prisons, and military encampments. And for some tourists, the drawing rooms, dining rooms, and other places in which Britain's upper class displayed themselves were forms of social space that, although not strictly 'public,' were made so by the pens of Canadian travel writers and novelists. For English-speaking Canadians all these public and social spaces played as important a role in both education and entertainment as historical landscapes and cultural sites, as they explored such spaces with an eye to their ethnographic dimensions, analysing and assessing British society. As the above passages make clear, examining orphanages and regattas also illuminates the ways in which class relations shaped tourists' impressions. Finally, examining the social spaces of tourism helps enrich our understanding of gender relations and their place in tourism, particularly where middle-class women's navigation of tourist sites was concerned.

Tourists and the Urban Streetscape

One of the most frequently discussed public sites of tourism was the street and those who frequented it. As we have seen in previous chapters, Canadian tourists were often fascinated with the streetscapes of manufacturing towns and other cities. If tourists usually judged such locales in Ireland approvingly, as chapter 3 has shown, they were more ambivalent regarding cities such as Liverpool, Glasgow, and Edinburgh – places in which evidence of both the progress and the problems of urbanization and capitalism were clearly on display. For many tourists and travel writers, though, the streets of London's East End were particularly appropriate places on which to gaze on such manifestations and consider such issues, not least because they were interwoven with the question of the city's moral character – or lack of it. In this these Canadians were not original. By the 1890s guidebooks such as Baedeker's supplied tourists with maps of the Eastend, highlighting its philanthropic institutions.[3] Writing in the *Saint John Daily Telegraph*, the Reverend Frederick Hastings deplored London's lack of Sabbath observance and the 10,300 pubs that were open on Sunday in places such as Rag Fair, Brick Lane, New Cut, and Goldsmiths' Row. 'The scenes one witnesses have a very depressing effect on the spirits. In Rag Fair mostly Jews congregate. Many English are doubtless there also.' Hastings's division of London's inhabitants into 'Jews' and 'English' was by no means unique to travel writing, although he was particularly strident in his insistence that at the fair he had witnessed many scenes of pickpocketing and double dealing. In New Cut, he observed navvies and labourers gathered to find work, buy food and clothes and less benign items such as 'immoral cards' and the wares of 'quacks,' and take in 'peep shows.' But the worst was Brick Lane, with its narrow streets, atmosphere 'most pestiferous and choked with the greasy steam from the rank fish pans of the frying shops.' All kinds of birds, rats, and dogs were for sale, and the observer could read men's enjoyment of 'cruel sports' on their faces. The clergyman was particularly upset at the sight of crowds of women walking under the Great Eastern Railway arch, carrying home meat and vegetables for their families' dinners. 'How,' he asked readers, 'to stem the torrent of sin and Sabbath desecration ... how were these poor people to be elevated to better habits and tastes?' One answer, he proposed, was that London's working men must be given their wages early enough on Saturday afternoon for their wives to go shopping before the stores closed.[4]

Such commentaries were more likely to come from the pens of evangelical Protestants, both women and men. Twenty years after Brick Lane had so upset Hastings, Emily Murphy took her readers through 'Petticoat Lane [which] ... presents a novel prospect of squalor and dinginess. It is a terra incognita to us, and so we pressed through the bidding, jostling throngs with all the zest of discoverers.' Here Murphy found 'miles of "toggery" ranging from "sober livery" and livery of bright sulphur yellow' to gay kerchiefs, bedraggled skirts ... in greatest contrasts of colour.' She also observed 'Jews and Gentiles' bargaining over 'second-handed ulsterettes.'[5]

Murphy proceeded to tour the 'East-end Ghetto' with the help of a policeman (London police appear in many accounts, published and manuscript), where she observed kosher-butchers' stalls, pawnshops, and a synagogue. Tailors' shops with 'sweated labour' illustrated for Murphy the worst part of 'Darkest England': 'some people quickly kill their decrepit and starveling poor, but these English torture them in a slow and more refined method.' Matters became worse, though, as Murphy and her guide left the 'Jew quarters, through streets of untraceable crookedness.' Gazing at the scenes of the Ripper murders, she 'shudder[ed] past the hulking ruffians who "lurk privily" in dark alleyways,' yet she reassured her readers that 'the fear is almost groundless, for the police are Argus-eyed, and crime no longer runs riot. Whitechapel thugs prefer to ply their iniquities in ... gin-palaces, where ugly vice is shrouded by a tawdry glitter. It is a land that flows with blood and beer.'[6] While did confess to finding some interesting and lively scenes, Murphy deemed working-class gender relations pathological, particularly as manifested in women's bodies: battered women were prevalent on the streets; young girls were debauched with alcohol, then sexually abused and prostituted by their mothers before they turned fifteen.[7] The Salvation Army, Murphy admitted, was doing much good work, with their practical methods and unselfish spirit. But the root cause of this 'sin-cursed region,' the 'garbage-heap of the wealthiest city in the world,' was alcohol: 'the intemperate class have congested in Whitechapel. The result can only be untold depravity and unalloyed misery.'[8]

Murphy's fulminations and her anti-Semitism might well have made a vivid impression on some readers, who may have been convinced that the sights and sounds of London added up to an unending parade of viciousness and racial and class degeneration. Yet Murphy's and Hastings's depictions of London were not echoed by the majority, for many of the writings examined here presented a more complex picture of the city's streetscapes. Goldwin Smith was all too ready to depict the 'bad quarters' of London as a 'sad sight' – 'sources of social and political danger ... the English Faubourg St Antoine' – yet he admitted that the 'pictures of London misery have been sought out and presented in the most glaring colours for the purposes of literary sensation,' pointing out that a city of five million inhabitants was bound to have its share of poverty, disease, and crime, and that despite the destitution of some of them, nevertheless it was the case that those who dispensed charity to them 'pass safely on their missions even through the worst of streets.'[9] 'Is London Immoral?' asked a writer in British Columbia's *Victoria Daily Times*. Written as a rejoinder to the 'jeremiads of noisy journalists who dread obscurity,' this article answered the question with a qualified no. London might house a number of professional criminals but, again, that was only to be expected, given its size. All things considered, the city was a 'marvel of virtuous dullness,' a place of 'domestic innocence' where home life was 'cultivated,' charities abounded, and English hospitality predominated.[10] At the other end of Canada, readers in Saint John were informed that within 'the sound of Bow Bells are streets and alleys, the haunts of thieves and gamblers, where a well-dressed person is not safe by night or day'; however, London was in no danger of emulating Babylon or Rome, for it was certain that social inequalities would decline, poverty would be alleviated, and 'crime made to slink back abashed from quarters where it now holds high carnival.'[11] Journalist

Norman Patterson told readers that, even when vice and crime might lurk in Piccadilly Circus (with its 'throngs of fallen women and licentious men') and in the East End (home to both 'workmen and idlers'), in general, London offered clean, safe streets, beneficent and efficient police, parks and embankments, and restored and preserved historic buildings. Lacking both the graft of American municipal politics and the inefficiencies of Canadian urban affairs, the city combined liberty with the law to a state of perfection, he concluded.[12]

And there were those individual tourists who did not let such menaces, whether highlighted or hinted at, prevent them from setting off to 'explore' working-class and poor areas. No intimation of danger interfered with George Pack's Sunday enjoyment of seeing business conducted in Whitechapel's Jewish section ('they sell nearly everything cats coins old cloth'). A few days later, he went back on the underground and found that, as well as the great range of vendors, he could also watch the 'great line of men women boys girls' waiting to get into a moving picture show, guided by three or four policemen (he did observe that the customers at the open beer counters and saloons included hundreds of women and girls).[13] John Mackinnon, always on the alert for a 'type' to amuse his readers, described an elderly woman seen selling leeks in Covent Garden. Fast asleep 'among the rush and din of trading,' this street vendor wore a curious headdress, an odd shrewd expression on her red bloated features ... This sleeping beauty reposed serenely as in a curtained alcove by a crook of the Nile.'[14]

Touring the East End's streets seemed to be mostly, although not exclusively, a masculine endeavour. Only a small minority of the women tourists followed Emily Murphy's example, but those that did wrote about the experience in some detail. Margaret Thomson's 1898 trip included an omnibus ride to Whitechapel and Mile End Road, where she walked through part of Whitechapel and then ventured onto a side street. She toured a 'kind of market – all sorts of things – fruit! meat!! and fish and all kinds of wearing apparel. Here were all numbers of Jews. The policemen were all two and two. The odor was anything but pleasant.'[15] Thomson's identification of 'Jews' with a variety of consumer goods, potential criminal activities, and bad smells was, as we have seen, not that different from Murphy's, although she lacked Murphy's hyperbolic language and did not discuss the evil effects of alcohol on the area's residents. Nor, interestingly, did her account rely explicitly on the spectre of Jack the Ripper; as in Murphy's description, the stalwart British policemen, 'two and two,' may have banished that threat.

Mabel Cameron was far less, if at all, concerned about such matters, and she visited the East End almost fifteen years after the Ripper murders. Possessed of boundless curiosity, she happily set off on expeditions to various working-class areas, with their markets and fairs. A 'Rag Fair' held on Smithfield's grounds astounded her: 'I have seen second-hand stores, auction rooms, etc, not a few, which contained what I thought a representative stock of junk but this Rag-Fair!!!! Here we saw the queerest collection of queer things. Everything one could think of and parts of everything one would never dream of.' Cameron's list of items ranged from clothing and books to household wares. It also included 'old gals bringing in their treasure in prams surmounted with a pair of moose horns, people declaring they could buy clothes cheaper in Montreal and being told to go to Montreal, the bus fare won't cost you no more than tuppence ... Over the noise of this medley of wares and people in a shrill squeaky voice a singer was heard giving through the medium of a gramophone, "My Rosary."' 'A motley collection of people and things and a sight never to be forgotten.'[16] The next day Cameron and her aunt visited Billingsgate, where they saw much fish but did not hear any of the famous 'Billingsgate' language. 'The floor was rather slippery and slimy but we paddled through. An impression that struck us all was that the men and boys here were of a much finer physique than those we had seen elsewhere in London. They seemed of a happier nature, as well. The jovial looking man accosted Auntie with "I've a lovely cod, can you do with it madame?" Much to his disappointment Auntie could not. He tried me next but I was not out for the purpose of buying cod.'[17]

Cameron's observations on the 'fine physique' of the Billingsgate fishmongers hint at a sexualization and an ethnographic surveying of these working-class men. Her aunt's emigration work often predisposed Cameron towards assessments of English working-class potential for physical labour. For the young schoolteacher from Victoria, the entire city offered a cornucopia of sensory delight and stimulation: it was not divided into areas of enjoyment and those of menace. Many of the goods for sale in Petticoat Lane were 'said' to have been 'pilfered during the week,' 'many rough characters are supposed to do business here,' and pickpockets were believed to have been rife. But Cameron treated these dangers in a cavalier manner, describing such scenes as if they were in a picaresque novel (and to some extent very much like Mary Leslie's encounters with London street life, recorded more than forty years earlier). She did not see any 'very tempting bargains altho' tweed caps were being sold for 6d. Who would be without a cap?'[18]

The following week Mabel Cameron and her brother went out in pursuit of a snapshot of the 'mokes' (donkeys) who pulled barrows for London's street vendors. Unsuccessful at Covent Garden, Tottenham Court Road, and Euston Road, they finally found their quarry outside a pub in Whitechapel. A tanner 'induced' the owner to move the barrow into the sun, and 'after taking the picture he said to me "Will it be in the Dily Mile?"'[19] Cameron attempted to use the 'London bus' to spend New Year's Eve in the East End; she and her companions were very 'annoyed' with the bus driver who refused to take them there (until they realized that they would not be able to return that night). They settled for St Paul's, where a 'great crowd had gathered – but such an orderly New Year's Eve gathering we had never seen. It was so disappointing to them. 'Beyond a few feeble cheers and a murmur of Auld Lang Syne there were no signs of gaiety. At twelve the great mass dispersed quietly and we started to walk home. Coming upon four girls dancing in the street our hopes revived but two "peelers" quickly put an end to their fun. Thus in a most decorous manner was 1911 ushered in.'[20] When it came to the sights and sounds of the city, Cameron's London held few of the terrors and dangers that had been outlined by Hastings and Murphy.

The fact that, as Mackinnon pointed out, 'London streets are never empty' may have accounted for many of these tourists' lack of concern over their physical safety.[21] Furthermore, as we have seen in other contexts, they brought across the Atlantic a sense of imperial and middle-class entitlement to all that the capital – and Britain in general – might offer. London crowds were not the mysterious, possibly threatening, denizens of northern African or southern Italian cities, collectivities that some anglophone Canadian tourists found quite troubling.[22] Despite its history of demonstrations and riots (including that which occurred when London's imperial volunteers returned from the Boer War),[23] these tourist men and women decided that contemporary London crowds were well behaved and, for the most part, welcoming. Elliott had been warned that a London crowd would be a thieving mass of people who would cheat him, crush him, and not allow him to see a bit of the Diamond Jubilee Procession in 1897, but he experienced nothing of the sort. 'A better behaved great collection of people I have never seen ... than in the streets of London this past week' (unlike those he had seen in New York and Boston).[24] Although the streets and rail stations were congested, there was no 'inconvenience' in getting to his viewing stand: 'every one got to his place as courteously as would become a drawing room' and several million people gathered so calmly and in such an orderly manner that Britons' hearts should be filled with 'commendable pride.'[25] Elliott concluded that 'if for no other reason, my trip to England this year has been to me invaluable in the proof that I have seen displayed that England's methods are the correct ones for the higher civilization, where social problems will have their only and proper solution all along the way' (the 'methods' included English history, law, constitution, public amenities, and art).[26]

Others might not wax quite so enthusiastic as Elliott. Still their accounts are full of the helpful nature of working-class Britons and the skill of the London police. Edith Chown, set out early one morning to see Edward VII's funeral and found herself completely blocked by the heads and shoulders of those standing on boxes and chairs. 'I shouldn't have seen a thing if a working man hadn't kindly let me put one foot on his box. He had very ingeniously wrapped his little box up on newspaper for there was an order that no boxes or chairs were to be carried.' She enjoyed, though, watching the London police break up such devices, reporting (as did so many others) that 'it was wonderful to see the way they handle a London crowd.'[27] Mabel Cameron observed the 'restraint' and 'dignity' of those gathered on the streets to witness royalty's passage, although she was less complimentary than others when she confessed that 'I rather prefer sudden out-bursts to this even tenor, but then I'm only a barbarian from the outer world!'[28]

It was not just trips to the East End or the crowds that thronged to see jubilee or coronation processions that inspired advice and reflections on how to navigate urban spaces. English-speaking Canadian travel writers spent considerable time educating their readers about the best ways to get around the central districts of London, Glasgow, and Edinburgh. A number of such pieces were written from the perspective of the *flâneur*, the detached (and, at least to a degree, knowing) male urban stroller who takes in and assesses all that he sees, hears, and (at times) smells but who is protected from detection by the anonymity of the crowd.[29] Some women travel writers adopted aspects of the flâneur's style while simultaneously admitting that London in particular might be daunting. Writing in the *Canadian Magazine*, Louise Hayter Birchall described the 'nightmare' of first encountering London's transportation system, and of how she went into a 'complete panic' on the Fulham Road while trying to return to her lodgings and had to ask a policeman for directions. Such scenarios might easily be taken to be particularly gendered performances, in which the disoriented and frightened female tourist, unable to cope in an unfamiliar public space, is dependent on local male authority to restore her equilibrium. Yet once Birchall understood the system it became quite simple, her panic subsided, and she set out to enjoy the city wholeheartedly.

For Birchall, the main distinction separating those visiting London was not so obviously gender as length of stay. She distinguished the short-term tourist – who would leave in 'confusion and delight' after racing through monuments, parks, 'Clubland,' theatres, and galleries – from the 'instinctive traveller, the cosmopolite.' This latter figure could stroll into the Savoy, the Ritz, or the Café Royal and be amused at the sight of the 'elegantly turned-out, brilliantly-jewelled, so-called smart women and their juvenile escorts' (the latter often young enough to be their sons, she added). The cosmopolite also could watch lurid trials, such as that of the wife-murderer Dr Crippen, or from the top of an omnibus take in the bustling, scurrying crowds. Birchall's 'cosmopolite' sounds distinctly like the masculine flâneur, with her constant reminders of her six-month sojourn in London, her discovery of its 'many-sidedness,' and her identification with the amused onlooker at the 'Café Royal.'[30]

Like their male counterparts, anglophone Canadian women tourists travelled around London and other cities on the tops of buses, on the underground, in cabs, on bicycles, and on foot. Their diaries and letters reflect various kinds of optical perspectives, particularly on London, that spanned the panoramic view afforded by the omnibus to the close-range, detailed observation of street life available to the urban stroller.[31] By the 1880s it was not unusual or shocking, of course, for middle-class women to be seen in such public settings. But historians also have pointed to the kinds of surveillance and sexual harassment from 'respectable gentlemen' that women using London's streets for shopping, philanthropic activity, and work experienced.[32] Even Australian women travellers, despite their confident negotiation of London, were well aware of the city's sexual and physical dangers.[33]

These Canadian women, though, seldom expressed much overt concern about their vulnerability in England's public places. They appear to have travelled in pairs, frequently with other female friends or relatives, or in a family grouping, and their diaries and letters discuss these movements in a matter-of-fact way. London appears in their writings as a city, not of danger, but of delight, or at least of great interest. Gertrude Fleming, in London as part of her 1891 honeymoon tour, wrote that 'no woman goes out alone walking I believe in London after

3 o'clock,' but few others offered any awareness of such restrictions.[34] In fact, it is often difficult to determine whether or not these women were accompanied in their travels. Frequently, they might mention that they were not alone only as an aside, after lengthy discussions and descriptions of Westminster Abbey, a play, or the excitement of seeing royalty. Mary Bain, for example, recorded in her diary that she had walked up the Strand on her own, bought theatre tickets, and then gone window-shopping in Piccadilly and along Regent Street. After having lunch she proceeded to the Mall, where 'we were joined by an impecunious gentleman who on hearing us wondering what certain buildings were, volunteered that information, and deftly attaching himself to us, soon became our self-appointed guide.'[35] As we have seen, when Harriett Priddis missed meeting those husbands and brothers of her friends who had been sent to pick her up from a train station or hotel, she simply struck up a conversation with fellow travellers and found her own way to her destination.

Friends and family, male and female, might accompany these women. But in their writings their travel is performed as if by autonomous and self-sufficient beings, who capable of independent movement, plot their own courses around the city's streets and on public transit. After a few days in London Priddis went 'back to Waterloo by tube and Metropolitan and home, I feel quite proud of finding myself so comfortably around London.'[36] While Priddis's were certainly the most adventuresome travels – few other women recorded initiating encounters with unfamiliar men on train platforms or even on the street (see chapter 3)[37] – her buoyancy and ability to cope with strange streets, trains, and men, either on her own or with other women companions, was not unique. Losing their luggage in transit caused women more concern than did the dangers of meeting up with 'white slavers.'

For those women who could spend more time in London, becoming acquainted with the city was a great pleasure. After less than a month in England, Ethel Davies thought London 'a grand old city. I am feeling quite at home here now in the centre of all its noise and the hurry of many feet.'[38] When their own feet grew sore, there was also the thrill of riding around on the tops of the city's omnibuses. 'I just love the top of these buses,' Priddis wrote, 'I quite understand Ethel Gibson's warwhoop of freedom when she mounted one and went flying through the streets of London.'[39] Comfortable as she was with London, Davies felt that after being in 'perfect bewilderment all the time as we dash along in the underground then emerge from the mass of human beings on the crowded railway platforms outside the rushing mass of humanity in the streets ... there is no better place to study human nature than from the top of a London bus.'[40] After six weeks there, Cameron felt quite 'London-ish' when she was able to give directions to fellow tourists in St Paul's.[41]

'Beside the Seaside': Viewing the English Working Class at Play

The city streets were not the only places in which the behaviour and appearance of Britain's working class might be viewed. Emily Murphy spent a Bank Holiday in Southend-on-Sea, which attracted 150,000 of London's 'labouring class,' personified by "Arry' and "Arriet.' Decked out in a large, 'pretentious' hat decorated with 'velveteen, feathers, and flowers' (and usually rented), "Arriet' was not good-looking but, rather, 'vulgar and coarse,' an aficionado of 'high-kicking and dancing,' when not 'heavily enceinte.' 'Drunk before dinner,' she fetched a considerably lower price than rubies, according to Murphy, and was 'considerably lower than the angels.'[42] Her companion 'grins like a dog and runs about the city,' sings loudly and tunelessly, dances with "Arriet' 'to the strains of the detestable accordion,' and 'bashfully attitudinises before the camera on the beach.'[43] It was possible to see 'respectable mechanics and their families,' many of whom had friends and relatives who had gone to Canada (but who had been deterred themselves by talk of wolves, buffaloes, and revolver fights).[44] However, the overall atmosphere was not much better than than in Whitechapel, with the stalls filled with cheap toys and trinkets and entertainments that ranged from gypsy fortune telling, 'burnt-cork comedians,' and burlesque dancing (of the kind to which a young woman would hesitate to take her mother).[45] Despite the good work of the local Salvation Army, a day filled with drinking turned into a 'mad whirling night with its garish glitter and boisterous conviviality [which] took on the nature of a Saturnalia. It was a lively demonstration of "midnight shout and revelry, tipsy dance and jollity," and all else that goes to make an English holiday.'[46] In contrast, Murphy spent her seaside holiday in respectable middle-class domestic pursuits, watching her children build sandcastles and loafing on the beach.[47]

Murphy invariably cast herself in the role of the sceptical and often disapproving Canadian onlooker in a way that heightened the moral superiority of her persona. But other tourists were less than enamoured with the displays of working-class culture that were in evidence

6.1. The Manitoba teachers go to the seaside. (*Britishers in Britain*, 1910)

at 'the seaside.' Harriett Priddis went to Southend, with her relatives and their small children and confessed that she enjoyed seeing different coastal spots, 'every one has its own characteristics.' Still, although Southend was undoubtedly convenient for Londoners, 'it is of the common tripper type,' with its 'donkey-riding, jumping dogs, a Punch and Judy show, drinks and sweets for sale and the usual uncouth drinking.'[48] But such scenes might also be quite enjoyable. Leonore Gordon, a member of the Manitoba teachers' group on tour, had very fond memories of her day at Margate. She was delighted with the promenade's elaborate decorations, the fresh air (after London's 'damp oppressiveness'), the tasty meals served at the pavilion, and the 'throngs of happy idlers on the beautiful sands' (see fig. 6.1). [49] And although it had different class connotations than Southend, Brighton appealed to Edward Greenshields, as he walked along the Parade, sat on the West Pier, lunched at the Metropole Hotel, and gazed happily at the sun, blue sky, water, and the crowds. He described Brighton as having 'the advantage over Atlantic City of ... a very fine carriage drive as well as the walk, all along the sea front.'[50]

Watching 'the English'

Public parks, and zoological, botanical, and pleasure gardens, in both London and other British cities, were social spaces in which tourists enjoyed flora and fauna of various kinds.[51] The gardens at Kew were a favourite destination, with their 'delicious retirement' of well-kept lawns, fine trees, palm-filled conservatories, and 'lovely ferns.' Maria Lauder thought they surpassed even the Botanic Gardens and the Zoo; Margaret Thomson grumbled, though, that Kew offered 'very poor refreshment'.[52] After a visit to Hampton Court ('it is Versailles over again'), Isabella Montgomery took the bus to Richmond and then the train to Kew: 'the day was a red letter one,' she told her diary.[53] Although she and her children were much entertained by the lemurs at the London Zoo, Emily Murphy noted that one was dying of consumption and that she longed to liberate the eagles from their cages, as they were 'mean and ugly' tied to earth. Like many other visitors to the zoo, Murphy and members of her family rode both the camel and the elephant; she found the first 'scrawny' and knock-kneed' and the ride offered by the second painful and unpleasant, 'not unlike a storm at sea.'[54]

Human beings, though, were equally interesting to observe, particularly when they could be categorized and classified according to national type. At Richmond, James Rupert Elliott watched the groups of young men and women, 'some fine specimens of early manhood and womanhood, some ordinary, though all interesting to look upon or study as they appear in the group.' A 'spirited' party, they 'move, chatter, and laugh ... Englishmen, I think, do not appear so very much superior to Americans, though they certainly have finer physiques. Englishwomen, on the whole, are very beautiful and delightful in their manners, and apparently very good.'[55] Harriett Priddis did not agree. Although generally not as judgmental as Murphy, she was not pleased with what she saw while boating on the Thames. During a stop at the hotel on Eel Pie Island, she went in for a glass of ginger wine and was astonished when she 'saw two girls in harem skirts smoking cigarettes. They were tighter and not as modest as the costumes I saw at Briglands. It was an experience, but I should not care to repeat it. The way nice lady-looking girls loll and are embraced in the boats is a shocker.'[56] Women's dress seems to have been one of the few things that could pique her displeasure. At a public concert in Vanity Fair, she noted that 'I don't see how it can be considered good taste to be out of doors in public places, in what are virtually low neck short sleeved dresses, the coverings are such sheer net.'[57]

In London's Rotten Row another 'type' was on display: the British upper class and aristocracy. James Hall found Rotten Row quite crowded and thought that 'although the carriages and horses were magnificent the girls driving were as a rule almost ugly. Some of those riding however looked better.' He was gratified to spot the Prince of Wales ('getting quite gray'), Prince Leopold, the Duke of Connaught, and the Princess of Wales who 'is certainly very pretty and we had a first rate view.'[58] (This young Canadian flâneur also assessed the women on display at the Covent Garden Opera, finding that the ladies' dresses were striking and the number of stout girls observable.'[59]) Fred Martin seemed quite pleased to observe the riders, although it is difficult to tell from his diary entry whether or not it was the 'hundreds of ladies' or the 'beautiful horses' that drew him to Rotten Row.[60]

Watching the 'hundreds of ladies' mounted on expensive horseflesh was not just a masculine pastime. Murphy was not as scathing about this English custom, for she noted 'some smart turnouts' on 'the Lady's Mile' and enjoyed the 'carefully toileted men, the acme of elegance.' She could not resist a poke at the 'effeminate' English, though, finding that the younger men were not as 'robust and manly as their seniors,' had figures like Harper's Bazaar models, and a general air of pallor and languor: 'it would do them good to loosen out in a street fight.'[61] Their female counterpart also suffered from an overly cultivated appearance, with ruffles that hid a painfully tight-laced corset and, although her skin was delicate, eyes 'like violets,' and her head and throat had a 'queenly set,' 'alas! [she has] a loose jointed walk.'[62] Edith Chown also paid a visit to Rotten Row; unfortunately, with London's aristocracy in mourning for Edward VII, the few nobility who were there were not particularly 'gay.'[63] Although she displayed little inclination to assess the physique of the female riders, Mabel Cameron noted in her diary the stir created by Anna Held and her daughter riding astride in the Row.[64] Priddis simply noted of her trip to Rotten Row that 'every lady I commented upon as being stylish or handsome is an actress.'[65]

Sporting events such as the Henley Regatta, the Oxford and Cambridge boat race, Ascot, and the Derby could be enjoyed for their display of athletic prowess. They also were perfect sites for watching 'the English.' 'Henley,' George W. Orton wrote for the *Canadian Magazine* in 1900, evoked memories of countless English victories over 'foreign' (usually American) competitors but it also took place in a beautiful setting, a 'verdant' valley that typified English rural beauty. The town itself became a tourist attraction, decorated with bunting, flags, and flowers:

6.2. Watching the English 'at play' (*Canadian Magazine*, January 1900)

'a scene of lightness and gaiety.' And once the viewer reached the river, 'he' would be astonished by both the 'myriads of boats' and the 'sea of color' of the 'ladies' dresses, hats, and parasols and the men's 'boating-costumes' and blazers. Furthermore, 'this is no boorish mob' but, rather, the 'elite of fashion and culture of England.' Like the tourist standing in the London crowd, Orton was struck by the 'good-breeding, courtesy, [and] decorousness' of the Henley spectators; after all, 'this sporting event is also a great society function.'[66] Elliott was equally thrilled and delighted with the regatta, although he took his readers through the crowd of vendors (whose wares included everything from programs to fortunes) before he reached the boats, their portholes allowing him to glimpse the 'charming ladies' who, in white dresses and coloured sashes, were greeting friends, chatting, or just 'reclining upon rich chairs and sofas dreaming to the sound of the perpetual music. What a picture! These boats are costly luxuries.'[67] Of course, as Elliott's earlier description suggests, there were many people on the banks that 'care not a jot for the race' but were there simply to relax' (see fig. 6.2).[68]

Mabel Cameron was not quite so enthralled with the Oxford and Cambridge boat race, reporting that there was 'considerable difficulty' in 'handling' the large crowd at the end. She was far more excited by the appearance of four aeroplanes (two Bleriots and two biplanes): 'it was a pretty sight to watch these huge birds of the air, circling, wheeling and dipping and gliding in the clear air above us.'[69] She also went, with her parents, to the Crystal Palace to watch the 1911 Football Association Cup Final between Bradford City and Newcastle. Although 100,000 spectators had congregated, 'at no time was any great excitement worked up,' since neither side scored any goals. 'The Bradford defence was impregnable and was continually pressed by the opposing team.'[70] She had a much gayer time at the Derby a month later, setting off with ginger ale, lunch basket, 'Kodaks,' glasses, 'and very high spirits,' the latter being kept up by the throngs of people, many in rigs pulled by 'little mokes plodding on with gay costers and their girls – all jolly and gaily dressed.' The carriage ahead of Cameron's party was full of 'ladies, babies, and dogs,' as well as three 'foreigners, Persian lambs we called them. They needed refreshment whenever we stopped, which was quite frequent.' Cameron placed a small bet but lost it when the bookie absconded with her money (she observed that this happened to a number of others). She did not seem very upset by her loss. Still the trip home was not quite as amusing, since it poured rain and hailed (upsetting the 'Persian lambs') and, after the horses balked, their harness broke and they ran off. Once the horses were rounded up, so many vehicles were coming at them that they were unable to move. After a twenty-minute delay they were off again, only to have to change vehicles. 'We will not forget our first Derby,' Cameron vowed.[71]

Although Harriett Priddis took her binoculars to Ascot and was able to see the 'Royals' quite clearly in their box, she also relished her seat in the stand with the 'plebs. I do think the best of most things are kept for the English poor.' She was able to see 'such funny things' and hear much better. While watching the royal box, 'a nice little woman of the lodging house class' called the royal family by their first names while her husband, who worked on the railway, kept running off to bet. But then Priddis moved her chair to get a better view of the starting line, and spilled her whiskey and water all over her bag.[72]

Other sights and accents might, then, crowd into the tourists' sightlines, superseding those of the upper crust. If the vast majority of these tourists did not mingle in England's higher social circles, the more private spaces of elite drawing, dining, and ballrooms were not entirely hidden from view. Edward Greenshields, for one, had both business and personal contacts that gave him an entrée to such networks. His diaries are full of references to lunches and dinners with upper-middle class and, in some cases, aristocratic companions. Although he and his wife, Eliza, often visited friends in their homes, they also frequented elegant hotels, restaurants, and clubs, all of which Greenshields may have preferred during his winter stays in Britain. Despite being from Montreal, he found the home of the former mayor of Liverpool 'very cold, although [in the drawing room] there was a pale fire. All the houses are cold, especially in the halls and passages, and the people take cold easily and wear heavy clothing. They would be a great deal more comfortable with small furnaces in the houses. It is easy usually to keep warm outside but not in the houses. I much prefer Canadian custom of light clothing and warm houses.'[73]

For the benefit of those who might not have had Greenshields's social connections, journalists, travel writers, and novelists were happy to provide glimpses of British privilege and wealth. In her novel, *Cousin Cinderella*, which examines the adventures of two Canadians in Edwardian London's well-off social circles, Sara Jeannette Duncan sketches a portrait of the workings of high society. Her two protagonists, siblings Graham and Mary Trent, navigate their way through the maze of social customs and mores, particularly those surrounding marriages between the British aristocracy and their transatlantic 'cousins,' American and Canadian (see fig. 6.3).[74] And for writer Margaret Eadie Henderson there was no reason why real-life Canadian women should not emulate Duncan's Mary Trent. Writing in the *Canadian Magazine*, Henderson used the Marchioness of Donegal, Halifax-born Violet Twining, as an example of an English-Canadian woman who had married into the British aristocracy, part of 'another link in the chain of Empire.' Twining was one of a 'number of Canadian girls who – although not a large group – was bound to find the attractions of a castle and title irresistible.' While the 'chief' whose 'scalp' the Canadian woman might add to her belt could range in rank from a duke to a 'plain British-born man of affairs, a diplomat or a soldier,' nevertheless 'he will find the Canadian woman the equal of any in dignity and initiative.'[75] Henderson did not stop at the use of tropes of Aboriginality to demarcate 'Canadian' women from their British counterparts, for she also played on the theme of their superior physical prowess, telling her readers that, if they were anything like

6.3. Sara Jeannette Duncan's 'Transatlantic Cousins' (*Cousin Cinderella*, 1908)

Twining, these 'links of Empire' would stay true to their 'Canadian' background, maintaining a 'love of skating' and outdoor activities.[76]

To make such a conquest, however, it helped to have introductions to the correct set: 'coming out' in English society was one way of gaining an entrée. Canadian novelist Joanna E. Wood told the *Canadian Magazine*'s readers how such matters were done. She began with the criteria for eligibility and then took them through the invitation, the expected dress for a débutante, the arrival at court, the detailed procedure for being 'presented,' and capping it all off with the débutante's photograph and celebratory tea.[77] Wood's discussion of the débutante's appearance was extremely detailed and comprehensive; gown, train, hair and headdress, shoes, gloves, stockings, and bouquet were described in minute detail. Wood also included a full-length portrait of a court debutante.[78] But, like Priddis at Ascot, while she wanted her readers to appreciate the importance of having been presented to Queen Victoria ('the best queen of modern times, a woman who was the typification of what is best in her sex – the beauty of gentle maidenhood, wifehood, and motherhood'), she also entertained her readers with a description of the 'natural jesters,' those cockney cabdrivers whose wit kept the debutante amused while waiting in the line-up to enter the palace.[79]

Thus the classes deemed both above and below them fascinated anglophone Canadian tourists. As we shall see in chapter 8, they also made a point of describing and assessing European workers and peasants. Wood's readers may well have aspired to wear the white dress and long train and have used Wood's column as a guide and manual. Few tourists, though, for all they enjoyed visiting the East End, expressed a desire to dress as a cabdriver or as Murphy's 'Arriet.'[80] And while from time to time they also commented on the domestic habits of their middle-class counterparts, the British bourgeoisie, in general they did not see themselves as very different from that group and thus were not as fascinated with their clothing, manners, and customs.[81]

Inspecting Institutions

City streets, public gardens, elite drawing rooms, and sporting events were not the sole public and social spaces in which English-speaking Canadian tourists watched and judged members of their imperial family. They also put philanthropic and educational institutions on their lists of places to see.[82] Although schools and orphanages might be somewhat less obviously entertaining than the Henley Regatta or market day in Whitechapel, they were nevertheless important to many a tourist's sense of having seen the full range of British society, of having peered at and inspected all of its institutions and structures. For those who were directly involved in similar Canadian endeavours, an exploration of these sites in Britain allowed them to participate in transatlantic and transnational communities of philanthropy and social welfare.

Although only a minority subscribed to the notion of England's social degeneracy, nevertheless its care of the less fortunate fascinated many. Their concerns might start with the plight of those who took them to view the residents of the Foundlings' Hospital or Barnardo's Home. Goldwin Smith asked his readers not to forget the 'cabbie' for 'his lot is a still a hard one': out sitting on his box in all weathers, 'drenched to the skin,' 'racked with rheumatism,' and forced to live in 'miserable quarters' near the stables. Although 'the cabbie' was hardworking, honest (as witnessed by the large number of items turned over by drivers to Scotland Yard), respectable, and brought up his children to emulate his behaviour, the fact that he depended primarily on tips meant that 'his end is too often the workhouse.'[83] Murphy too noted the long hours and great stress endured by London cabbies, their sixteen-hour days and the 'great alertness of movement, keenness of eye and steadiness of nerve' that the job required. She believed that 'such an arbitrary, cruel strain must mitigate against the interest of the employees.'[84]

Not everyone was quite so solemn about the cabbie's lot. Like those who wrote about Irish guides, some preferred instead to focus on the cabbie's quick wit and his performance of the amusing 'cockney.' Eavesdropping on a discussion between two who drove horse-drawn cabs, the subject of which was 'their rival the Taxi-cabby who is attired in a navy blue suit and clean new white cap,' Cameron recorded their judgment: 'Oh! 'es a Commodore 'e is!'[85] Brian Bellasis's column, 'The Green Lawn Club,' in the *Canadian Magazine* took readers to a London cab shelter in which 'Cockney' cabdrivers mingled with the city's poor, artists, actors, and a few 'toffs,' the driver's tales and anecdotes a commentary on social and cultural matters around the city. Definitely not a source of sentiment or pity, these cabdrivers provided knowing and trenchant observations on the affairs of their so-called betters.[86]

Cab-drivers were far from being the only group whose welfare concerned Canadian tourists. Cameron was not alone in her interest in the Foundlings' Hospital, with its 'wee boys and girls' in their uniforms (and, as the quotation that opens this chapter demonstrates, she came prepared for such a delight because of a previously viewed painting). Thomson also paid this hospital a visit, while a church service was in progress. She was impressed by the sight of three hundred children, seated on either side of the organ, the boys dressed in brown suits with brass-buttoned red waistcoats and the girls in white aprons, kerchiefs, and caps. After hearing some good singing (she noted that six professionals helped the children), Thomson toured their dormitories (the girls' bedcovers in white and the boys' in blue and white), watched the children eat dinner (cold roast beef and baked potatoes), and inspected their schoolrooms and the picture gallery. 'None of these children know who their parents are,' she confided to her diary, 'and until they are four years old they are kept in the country.'[87] One of Montgomery's first stops in London was a service at the Foundlings' Church. 'The children looked cunning in white caps and aprons,' she wrote, 'how cute they looked and when they prayed devoutly with their aprons up to their faces. One or two looked mischievously around the corners' (she followed up the service with a less spiritual, although no less satisfying, tour of their dining hall, where she and her party watched the children have their roast beef dinner).[88]

Although she was upset by the violence of the Boer War, Ethel Davies thoroughly enjoyed her trip to the Gordon Boys' Home in Bayswater. She was shown their workshops, schoolrooms, gymnasium, and 230 boys, 'all as happy and jolly as can be.' As well as watching them work, she heard them perform in their 'splendid band ... most of the band boys go into the army when they leave the home as drummers or buglers. Indeed about one half the boys enter the army as soldiers. All the useful trades are taught and the little chaps look very happy at their work in the boot shop or the engineers' shop. On Sunday they all marched into chapel after parade, a dear little chapel in memory of the Duke of Clarence by the nation.'[89] Moreover, orphans and foundlings would be put to empire's use in English-Canadian communities and homes. In 1910 Chown visited Dr Barnardo's Home, stopping first at the boys' residence where three hundred boys, 'many of them deformed' and all of them homeless, were taught shoe-making, baking, tinsmithing, and tailoring. The Girls' Home housed fifteen hundred in cottages, each run by a 'mother' from whom they learnt housekeeping. Chown told her family, at home in Kingston, that Barnardo sent out three lots of children per year to Canada and, justifying her interest in this work, reminded them of the pictures shown them by 'that girl (Alice Roland I think) that we used to have when we were little.'[90]

Children, especially orphans, were especially interesting to these tourists when they could be seen at work, eating, or staging musical performances. The majority of those who observed children in these institutions both applauded the beneficence of their founders and the efforts of those who put into practice the founder's wishes; they also sketched portraits of their residents that were tinged with more than a hint of sentiment. While they emphasized the order in these displays of singing and playing and stressed the children's neatness, cleanliness, and prosperity – unlike the undisciplined, unclean, and poverty-stricken children of Europe's streets and alleys – they also called attention to their displays of humanity as they demonstrated their happiness and pleasure in performing. Women tourists devoted more time to visiting such sites and writing about them in their diaries; their male counterparts adopted a more formal and distanced voice when they wrote about such places, if they went to them in the first place. Mackinnon, for example, provided his readers with a list of the many public institutions of London, including the Jewish community's many charitable homes, relief societies, and schools, but he did not take his readers into a philanthropic institution. Smith ended his discussion of England with a 'tribute to philanthropic London,' its many hospitals and charitable institutions, that should prove a lesson to the New World, faced as it was with the start of the Old World's social problems.[91] Murphy, though, while noting that 'these little morsels of humanity are well-cared for,' told her readers that they 'are as happy as children could be, who are bundled up in barracks.'[92] Her visit to a home for disabled children at Westcliff was not at all optimistic for their futures: 'These children are brought up in wholesale fashion, very much like a litter of puppies. Their features indicate their birth and station to be of a low origin. England is not an Elysium for children. There are too many, and they are often shamefully neglected.'[93]

Yet Murphy was one of the few to express such scepticism – one that bordered on outright cynicism – about these institutions. Most of the other Canadian tourists were enthralled with the children's institutions they visited. Of course, displays of childhood being organized, ordered, and shaped through both institutional regimes and pleasurable pastimes were not unique to Britain, either through orphanage tours or in photographs of rescued and reformed children.[94] But as well as being spectacles of the efficacy of late Victorian and Edwardian philanthropy, these institutions and the children in them also functioned as tourist sites. Not only did the tourists see them through the gaze of the social reformer (and at times school inspector), their writings make it clear that they also saw them as pleasurable and entertaining scenes, as enjoyable as Kew Gardens or Regent Street's store windows.

Moreover, while orphanages brought particular pleasure to Canadian tourists, the sight of disciplined, industrious, and happy children in other settings interested them, too. Not surprisingly, the Manitoba teachers' itinerary was full of schools of varying levels and types: the London County Council's Central School of Arts and Crafts (where they viewed an exhibit of the students' work entered in the Council's Art Scholarship competition), the city's regular schools (in which displays of drill, manual work, and singing were performed for them, although they were unable to see much regular teaching because of the summer holidays), and Mrs Humphrey Ward's Vacation School.[95] Held on the outskirts of London's 'slums,' the Vacation School admitted one hundred pupils, boys and girls from five to thirteen, who otherwise would be left at home because their parents were working hard 'to keep together.' Like the children seen at the Foundlings' Hospital, these 'poorly clad' but happy children all seemed to enjoy performing their 'light and recreative tasks.' They were taught singing and vocal exercises 'with a view to modifying the harsh voice and accent.' The older girls learned to cook in the school's basement, where they chopped and kneaded in the preparation of 'the most nourishing and inexpensive dishes,' while lessons in basketball, musical drill, clay modelling, basket-work, drawing, and plain sewing were held outdoors, under the 'shade of lofty trees growing in and around the well-kept garden.

All were working hard and seemed very contented. Many of the pupils appeared to be most clever in their work. We talked to some and found them very bright and happy. The smaller children were enjoying the delights of fish-pond, draughts, and ludo, or were eagerly scanning the picture-books laid out for them on the tables. Such splendid work as is here being done is worthy of the highest praise. The members of the party who were fortunate enough to visit the school, came away with the deepest admiration and respect for Mrs Humphrey Ward, who is so admirably carrying out the behest of the Great Teacher: Inasmuch as ye have done it unto the least of them.[96]

Cameron probably saw more schools and institutions for children than any other Canadian tourist because of her aunt's lectures. Farringdon Street's Newsboy's Club in London, where the young street vendors could buy cheap coffee and buns, offered nightly activities and weekend concerts. 'The boys do enjoy them,' she wrote, and 'eventually these people are hoping to be able to send numbers of these boys to Canada and Australia. It is a great work.'[97] She was even more taken by the concert given by the Royal Normal College for the Blind. 'I came away with a grand wave of admiration sweeping over me as I thought of those brave persevering skillful boys and girls and considered myself a hopeless bungler. To listen to their sweet singing, recitations, and instrumental solos was indeed an inspiration.' Equally impressive were their demonstrations of typing, geometry, and geography; the latter featured 'little girls ... pointing out places on their relief maps, with great skill.' Cameron then accompanied her aunt to a lecture at the Newsboys' Club, delivered to 'sixty little urchins who seemed to enjoy it immensely' and may, she thought, be induced to emigrate.'[98] Her aunt's lecture at the Ladies' Horticultural College at Swanely exposed Cameron to vocational training for girls and young women: 'the busy students in their short skirts, leather gaiters (in some cases straw-tied-on hats) at work in various parts,' pruning, planting flowers and hedges, digging, and tying up vines,' as well as the more customary domestic training in cooking (a cod dinner and a jelly roll cake).[99]

Winchester's 'undergraduates' 'keenly enjoyed' Aunt Alice's talk and received the 'fruit pictures' 'with great gusto.'[100] While they were not thrilled with the 'whale picture,' a lack of enthusiasm that Cameron could not understand, she was happy to record that the boys at Oxley Farm School did, 'the first English audience' to do so. 'Their cheers at the end of the talk were very rousing.'[101] And a particular highlight of Cameron's tour of schools and institutions was the training ship *Essex*, where around eight hundred boys, ages eight to sixteen, were given marine instruction for careers in the British navy and merchant marine. All of them had been taken from the Poor Law Guardians' 'surveillance' and were being given 'a splendid chance.' As well as their nautical instruction, they were schooled in regular academic subjects, had a library with the daily papers, and, for the talented and proficient, could obtain musical training in the school's band. The boys listened to the aunt's talk 'with keen attention and at the end gave some rousing cheers and sang "God Save Our Gracious King" in quick march time.' After dinner Cameron and her aunt peeped into their bedrooms to see the boys 'fast asleep in their hammocks. If they are found talking after eight o'clock they are made to carry their hammocks round for half an hour.'[102]

Perhaps not surprisingly, here again Murphy's was a dissenting voice. The rector at Wolverhampton, with whom Murphy and her family were staying, took her to see its parish school. Her reactions were similar to those she felt at the Westliffe Orphanage. While the children rose en masse and saluted her, she felt that 'they have not the clever, wide-awake look possessed by Canadian children of the same class.' The children were made to display their learning for Murphy, 'and one pudgy little girl whose consonants were curiously mixed up recited Wordsworth's "Lucy Grey." I was not impressed with the standard of the school. It seemed greatly behind hand in appliances and methods, and the rooms were dark and small.' Explaining the English national and board schools to her readers, Murphy summed them up dismissively: 'No person who pretends to belong to the classes, ever dreams of sending his children to either Board or National Schools. They are only for the children of the masses.'[103]

While it might seem 'natural' for those interested and involved in formal education to observe its workings in Britain, class relations shaped decisions about which institutions and students would be put under the tourist microscope.[104] Although Cameron and her aunt toured Winchester's buildings, they do not appear to have sat in on a class, and they were initially refused entry to a chapel service on the grounds that it was 'private' (a more 'kindly' guide allowed them in; Cameron thought the students 'wiry' and 'quite unusual-looking').[105] At Harrow the next week, they toured the buildings and only saw the students processing to church, looking 'quite quaint with their bright blue flannel coats, tight gray trousers and wide-brimmed sailor hats.'[106] And, although during their trip to Windsor they saw the buildings of Eton College, the Manitoba teachers were not treated to a tour of its interior (to be sure, the students may not have been in residence during their visit).[107] Montreal's Osla Clouston was one of the very few who was admitted to the school's interior, since a family friend's son, Hugh Porter, was attending Eton at the time of her 1895 trip overseas. 'Afterwards he had five fags to wait up on him we saw the school room which was very old we also saw the switching block where you get the switch when you are naughty the old chapel was lovely we saw Gladstone's name carved on the schoolroom door you pay two shilling to have it done the walls are the mass of names.'[108]

If children, orphaned or not, were popular sights in this tourism of state regulation and philanthropy, what of the adults? Few replicated Margaret McDougall's extensive tour of Irish workhouses, possibly because the latter – English or Irish – were a less pleasant sight (as well, they might not have had the personal contacts to enter such institutions). Although the fog and smoke prevented William Munro from seeing much of Glasgow during his 1881 trip, he was taken by the governor, Joseph Black, to see first the Poor House and then the Asylum; they also went to a concert and ball held weekly for the patients.[109] Emily Murphy was linked to a number of charitable and philanthropic networks, partly through her own work in social reform and partly because of her husband's vocation. They were shown the Colchester Union Workhouse by an inmate, an 'old Canadian' who had become impoverished while trying to claim an English inheritance. She admitted that 'the rooms were clean and cozy' and that the inmates were given both tobacco and reading matter, but she saw those material benefits as counting for little when put beside the cost to human dignity that the workhouse exacted: children 'of the gutter-snipe species' who will soon 'slop over into Canada,' where their presence will be deplored; old men who had become 'lachrymose,' 'doleful,' and malcontented; and elderly women who were 'squat hags,' 'coarse-minded,' and obscene, from whose 'moral vileness' Murphy's party fled. While her account dealt with her customary themes of England as degraded and decaying, Murphy admitted that not all the residents were responsible for being in the workhouse. Some were the 'virtuous poor', brought to its doors by illness, financial mishap, and bad luck and to them, the 'Union is an "intermediate purgatory before the grave."'[110]

Earlier in her travels Murphy had gone 'slum-visiting' with the Anglican curate in Plymouth, an experience that she found harrowing and dispiriting. Here, Murphy claimed, were conditions worse than in Whitechapel: 'a heterogeneous horde, living from hand to mouth in the midst of revolting filth, of both the quick and the dead varieties.'[111] With its 'plague spots' of vermin-ridden and garbage-laden houses, whose top floors were reached by dark staircases and ropes for banisters, 'whole families' lived 'in promiscuity,' 'loud-voiced, bold-looking jades' lounged in doorways, a drunken woman, 'loathsome with disease and unmentionable filth,' lay prostrate and unconscious on the ground:[112] 'Outside, the slum-babies, "Satan's Godchildren," were dancing to the strains of a grind-organ and seemed the only happy things in the district. True! The little girls are bound in slavery to the ever-recurring infant of the household, but they seem to accept this as inevitable. In appearance they reminded me of Phil Robinson's description of the low-caste Indian children: "Images of God, cast in mud and never baked."'[113]

Although Murphy's disgust for both the community and its residents was framed in an imperial language which conflated race and class, her most vehement opprobrium was for the Anglican Church's ineffectual means of performing charitable work. At the bedside of a dying elderly woman, Murphy felt that 'our slumming suddenly became an impertinent intrusion, an ugly curiosity. We were looking at these people as we would fossilized toads in a museum.'[114] She despaired of the church's handling of the slums 'with dainty finger tips' and of her being 'content to touch the mere fringes of the work,' with the consequence that the church had lost touch and all influence with the very poor. The social and political consequences of this rift would be dire, Murphy warned. 'The working brutes in England's back-yard are growling, and it would not be strange if one day they broke their chains. It is a pressing and depressing question. The whole matter is not of today only: it casts a lurid darkness over the future.'[115]

Murphy's apocalyptic vision was far from being that of the majority. As well as finding 'much good' in the orphanages and schools, the Canadian tourists noted initiatives such as company housing schemes. Goldwin Smith urged his readers to visit Saltaire, the late Sir Titus Salt's model manufacturing community near Bradford. Salt had hoped to make factory life 'brighter, healthier, cleaner, and to place within the reach of his people the means of culture and enjoyment.' Happily for his workforce (and Smith's audience) his 'benevolence' 'which created and sustains it seems to be rewarded,' although, as in similar communities, 'there are difficulties to contend with in the somewhat stiff-necked independence of the people, by which the patience of philanthropy is apt to be sorely tried.'[116] Edith Chown found the Sunlight Soap's employees' village 'very neat and clean' but was not quite so enthusiastic about such communities as was Smith. 'The uniformity of everything grew tiresome,' she told her family, for 'there was no individuality about it.'[117]

In addition to inspecting the poor, as previously noted, these Canadian tourists might be active participants in social welfare and reform organizations, themselves part of a transatlantic and, in some cases, global network. In London, Ada Pemberton attended a meeting 'in aid of the Women's Institute,' while Murphy went to a meeting of the Church Missionary Society.[118] No tourist, though, appears to have attended as many of these gatherings as did Harriett Priddis. She was an indefatigable participant at the various imperial clubs' gatherings in London during the coronation year. She attended meetings of the Imperial Institute, the Dominion Club (where she met Princess Louise), and the Victoria League.[119] Priddis also was interested in social reform organizations such as the Young Women's Christian Association. At a tea at the London 'Y,' Priddis bought a book that described its work to take to the 'girls' at home (presumably her nieces). However, the woman who packed it included so many pamphlets that Priddis was unable to carry it. 'Though I paid her eight shillings for it she did not want at all to send it home though I told her anytime within the week would do ... I do wish Church and Charity workers could cultivate the courteous manner of society women.'[120]

When social welfare and philanthropy were not successful in solving the problems of the poor, however, the police and the courtroom might catch the tourist's attention. Mabel Cameron watched a crowd gather to see two policemen taking a young man to prison for stealing a bicycle;[121] seven months later she went with her father to see the proceedings at the Bow Street Police Court. Here she witnessed a number of young women being charged with street solicitation and fined around ten shillings; a young man brought in for causing a public obstruction by holding a meeting on the Tottenham Court Road but, there being no agreement about the size of crowd gathered, he was released with a promise not to do it again; and another young man, charged with fraud and put on remand for having promised a number of boarding-house owners that he would bring them business for the coronation but had failed to deliver after collecting the fees from them.[122] Cameron did not register any moral indignation about anything that she saw in the courts; these scenes were recorded in a lighthearted and quizzical tone concerning British life and society. Murphy's experience of witnessing 'British justice' was rather different, as she went to hear trials at the Courts of Justice and watched some of the proceedings in the Court of Queen's Bench, the Court of

Appeal, and the Admiralty Court (its 'chief decoration' a 'large gilt anchor entwined with a rope').[123] She was not terribly impressed with the ceremony and theatre of the court, writing that the judge's wig covered both his ears 'and so prevents his hearing either side of the case.'[124] Murphy also watched both bankruptcy and divorce proceedings, deciding that the latter was the 'usual story' of 'disillusionment, incompatibility, unabridgeable [sic] differences, blighted affections, osculatory indiscretions, and other post-nuptial unpleasantness.'[125]

A great deal more 'unpleasantness,' though, was on display when tourists decided to venture into the prisons that awaited some of those whose trials they watched. Some prisons had their own museums, as also did Scotland Yard, where Cameron inspected a 'grim collection of gruesome articles' that included Dr Crippen's relics, ropes from executions, evidence gathered from a number of murder cases (including Dr Cream's poison case), and the Ripper letters.[126] At Newgate Prison George Lindsey was entertained with 'a number of objects of interest,' including the gallows used to execute the last thirty years' worth of condemned criminals. 'Hard by was the bag of sand which had been used to test the rope by which Lipski had been hanged, and the good-natured warden who was shewing us about, "swung it into eternity," just to let us see "how it was done."'[127] Murphy was also taken on a tour of Newgate which, in her case, included the axe used for decapitating hanged prisoners before their bodies were consigned to quick-lime and a grave under a stone passage. However, she was sobered, not entertained, by her trip. In this 'grotesque gehenna,' 'strength and durability are written on every line of its thickly-massed masonry,' even though the building had been condemned and was scheduled for demolition.[128] Although many (in)famous prisoners had been confined to Newgate Prison (William Penn, Daniel Defoe, and Lord George Gordon), 'the prisoners are of a different stamp today. One may read "a dead soul's epitaph on every face." They are men without even hope. Some go insane ... A pall of sin and misery hangs over the whole place ... Newgate stands for "the abomination of desolation."'[129]

The sight of the British Army and the Royal Navy, though, tended to cheer up most Canadians. As we have seen in chapters 3 and 5, they enjoyed and made careful note of coronation or jubilee displays of Britain's imperial role manifested through the spectacle of masculinity in uniform, whether marching or on horseback. At the St Martin's-in-the-Field service that marked the hundred and fifth anniversary of

Trafalgar Day, Cameron was pleased to see the London Frontiersmen who 'attended in a body. They were all men of fine physique, whose uniform was much like that of the boy scouts.'[130] As well as seeing troops at such services, military camps and navy dockyards were on the itineraries of a number of tourists. Smith told his readers that, in addition to the professional manoeuvres that might be observed, the volunteer corps' training was uplifting. The recruitment of volunteers was 'the most wholesome movement' in England and, 'more than anything else on the social or political horizon, it gives reason for hope that the destinies of this country will be determined in the last resort by the spirit which has made it great.'[131] Although she was decidedly ambivalent about the armed power of the British state (telling her audience of her tour of the Harwich docks that 'when you examine a man-of-war every inch of it seems to be an implement of death planned with devilish ingenuity'), Murphy found the sailors' quarters at Plymouth well organized and clean, and their food properly prepared and nourishing.[132] She also found the sight of soldiers departing for South Africa a moving one and noted both the enthusiasm of the crowd and the impassive demeanour of the officers' mothers, wives, and sweethearts, who said goodbye 'with dry eyes, but pale, drawn faces. These women are of the best stock in the world and would consider any display of feeling as bad form. Their stoicism, if less admirable, is quite equal to that of the Red Indians.'[133]

Ties of Faith, Ties of Empire: Religion and English-Canadian Tourists

Philanthropic and imperial organizations, criminal justice, and the military: these institutions not only provided lessons about British society but they also might reassure most tourists that they had much in common with Britain (of course, a minority thought that in such matters Britain might do well to learn from Canada). Yet another point of commonality was organized religion for, as we have seen in discussions of historical landscapes, the conviction of Britain's fundamentally 'Protestant' nature was deeply engrained in their conceptions of its 'national' character and the implications for Canada. Furthermore, attending church services of one's own denomination was yet another way of feeling linked to a larger, transnational community. Unlike reflections on certain periods of British history, such services also were a less troublesome way of experiencing these ties. As well as touring historic cathedrals and village churches, English-speaking Canadian tourists were eager to include religious services on their itineraries (as we shall see, that included European ones) and compared the sermons and singing they heard, subjecting theology, style of preaching, and music to the same kind of critical appraisal with which they listened to concerts and theatre. On his 1874 trip, William Caldwell heard the revivalists Moody and Sankey in Scotland, 'who though certainly uneducated, yet delivered a most touching practical address.' He followed this up with a trip to a Free Church prayer meeting 'but thought there was rather too much of the exhortive revival feeling, mandated by the speakers.'[134] In London Caldwell was 'very well pleased' to hear Dr Spungeon at the Methodist Tabernacle, for his sermon was a 'plain, practical, and right one and one that could not help but to do good.'[135] However, he could not hear the sermon at St Paul's and found the one preached at the Congregational Temple to be 'middling ... not very clever.'[136] (As chapter 5 has shown a number of tourists complained about inaudibility at St Paul's and Westminster).[137] An English service might afford the opportunity to preview clerics bound for Canada: Greenshields went to London's St John's Presbyterian to hear the Reverend Bruce Taylor, who was soon to arrive at Montreal's St Paul's Church. Taylor, thought Greenshields, 'seems to be an interesting preacher, does not read his sermon very closely, is eloquent at times and affecting, but his chief quality seemed to be a thorough belief in what he was saying and intense earnestness.'[138]

The Canadian visitors they were fairly catholic in the range of churches they patronized and did not attend only those of their own denomination. As well as going to services at Westminster Abbey and St Paul's, tourists might participate in both a High Church of England service at London's St Alban's and another service at a Baptist Chapel.[139] A few ventured into less-frequented venues: Chown visited the London Friends' Meeting House, while Munro went to hear Annie Besant lecture in Glasgow, writing to his wife that 'she is a very clever woman, but too masculine.'[140] Munro went to a service in the church where his parents were married and where he was baptized and, while he felt that 'I see very little enjoyment ahead from Scotch theology ... I think I shall have plenty of friends.'[141]

Although they might have been critical of the singing and the style of preaching and have listened to sermons thoughtfully, these tourists tended to be quite tolerant of differences between their own denomination and the other Protestant churches that they visited. The only church service that seemed alien and, for some, distasteful, was that at St Albans, with its more elaborately staging, panoply of religious accoutrements, and overtones of Roman Catholicism. Margaret Thomson thought it to be 'quite a show,' with the priest's 'grand robes' and two small attendants in white and red. 'The singers took two steps forward two sideways – bowed to the altar then to each other. They burnt incense until we were nearly choked.'[142] Cameron thought it 'very high church, resembling the ritualistic Roman Catholic services.' The service began with a processional hymn sung by the clergy and the choirboys and led by an incense-bearer and banners (to which most of the congregation bowed). 'During the service the vestments of the priests were constantly changed, incense burned, and candles flickered. Personally, I like a simple service far better than one of this type. The City Temple is much more to my liking. The Reverend R.J. Campbell preached a sincere appealing service here tonight.'[143] It was not that Cameron was unappreciative of theatrical performances; as we have seen she was an enthusiastic and very frequent audience member at a wide variety of London productions. However, as well as the multiple blurring of lines between religion and performance at St Alban's, she may well have resented the sexes' separation: it was one of the first things she noticed in the church.[144]

Murphy, though, a staunch Low Church supporter, was infuriated at such displays of ritual. Visiting England during a period of intense debate within the Anglican Church between 'high' and 'low' factions, she sided with the latter and became quite upset at any displays of the former's style. In Liverpool she heard and commented favourably on the sermons and styles of Dr James Watson (also known as Ian Maclaren) and Dr Ryle, the bishop of Liverpool. Watson was a 'great divine,' his 'rhetoric copious and elegant,' 'versatile, passionate, sympathetic, and intellectually, a giant.' The bishop, despite his age and physical frailty, had an 'erect and stately carriage,' a 'handsome and scholarly face,' and spoke in a 'direct, terse, and pungent' manner that 'hit straight out, and hard' at the threat of High Church 'innovations' that would pull the Church of England back to Rome.[145] She then proceeded to describe a 'Ritualistic Church' service that she attended in that city in which the sexes were separated; altars had been erected to the Virgin Mary; the clergy dressed in elaborately trimmed gowns and cassocks that made them 'person[s] of ambiguous sex' who did not perform physical tasks such as turning the pages of their own prayerbooks.[146]

234 A Happy Holiday

I could not understand the tricks of scenic devotion or the minutiae of ritual, for the service throughout was a succession of tableaux and burlesques; it was playing at religion. Still I could not but admire the skill of muscular movement involved in the sinuous and sensuous manoeuvres of their strange and intricate quadrille. The priests would bow their heads almost to the floor, till I got alarmed lest their blood vessels burst. Absolute prostrations on the stone pavement of the chancel were followed by numerous posturings and gesticulatory embellishments. It was highly theatric, and without the clouds of incense, had been entirely trivial and vulgar.[147]

Dressing up so as to blur the boundaries between the sexes, dancing about the altar in a sexualized (but not masculine) fashion, and indulging in overly elaborate and 'vulgar' displays: all of this was the antithesis of the Evangelical service. While the Evangelical ministers of whom she approved also performed in particular ways (and had a long history of doing so), to Murphy's way of thinking theirs was a solid, manly, intellectually based, and rational form of worship. Murphy had theological reasons for objecting to the High Church faction, but she expressed most of her distaste by focusing on the ritualistic and more heightened sense of performance in their services and on the gendered dimensions and implications of such displays.[148] After attending a large Protestant demonstration at the Royal Albert Hall, held to protest the 'Romish practices now in vogue in thousands of churches,' Murphy noted approvingly that the Evangelicals had placed their hopes on Prebendary Peploe: 'His master-mind dominates the whole movement. He thoroughly understands the subject, is a quick and accurate disputant, and his words have a manly ring.'[149]

Unlike the exclusiveness of other types of tourism for this period, ones that might delineate the tourist space such as that of the elite, upper-middle-class hotel removed from commercial and metropolitan urban spaces, English-speaking Canadians cheerfully appropriated a wide range of urban public spaces and their inhabitants for their education and entertainment.[150] The markets of London's East End, the altars of the Church of England, or the banks of the Henley River were not always to be feared or disapproved of for, like the sight of the children, dressed in their uniforms and viewed en masse, they could well be sights of pleasure and signs of prosperity, not just harbingers of a threatened social (and imperial) order. Like the London shops, suffrage demonstrations, and theatrical performances, such sights and their locations were staging grounds of the imperial and commercial modernity of transatlantic tourism. These demonstrations and displays, with their appeals to sight, sound, and smell, also featured even more prominently in anglophone Canadian tourists' understanding of Europe. There, however, they were transposed into different national, ethnic, and, at times, racial keys.

7 'This Sight-Seeing Is a Strenuous Business': European Sojourns, Part I

Voiced as she prepared to leave Rome for Florence, Mary Bain's complaint about the 'strenuous business' of sightseeing' would have resonated with many of her fellow tourists.[1] Touring Britain might require bustle and enterprise, but sightseeing in Europe was an even busier undertaking as these anglophone Canadians navigated their way across multiple borders, frequently changing their modes of transportation along with the languages they heard, the landscapes they saw, and the local customs they observed. Gertrude Fleming's vow that 'with a fairly cheerful heart I realize my proud position as a tourist and intend to see everything,' also would have resonated with her fellow travellers (a vow made easier for Fleming to keep once the Roman sun came out and dissipated the gloom in which her first few days in the city were enveloped).[2]

Anglophone Canadian tourists were not, of course, the first to arrive in Europe, eager to see 'the Continent's' various sites and landscapes. Their travels through France, the Netherlands, Belgium, Germany, Switzerland, and Italy were shaped and mediated by an extensive infrastructure developed over the course of the nineteenth century in response to the desires and needs of tourists from Britain and the United States.[3] The Canadian press ran a wide variety of articles that discussed the cultural, historical, and scenic attractions to be found in Europe and that should be incorporated into a 'cultured' person's stock of knowledge.[4] Just as Britain was made possible and desirable through a variety of media, so too was Europe constructed for these travellers as an important destination, to be sought out for various reasons. Europe was desired for its history, religion, and culture, all of which promised intellectual, sensory, and moral stimulation as well as pleasure for the Canadian tourist.

The Cruel and Tragic Past: Historical Tourism in Europe

Europe could be approached in a number of ways. Those who began their transatlantic tours in Britain would cross the English Channel from either Dover or Newhaven, landing in Calais or Dieppe. They would then board trains for Paris, Brussels, The Hague, Amsterdam or Rotterdam. Having toured these urban centres and the surrounding countryside, they went on to Germany, where they visited Cologne Cathedral, took boat trips down the Rhine, and were fascinated by the duelling scars of Heidelberg's male students. After Germany they went to Switzerland, where they usually stayed in hotels in the lakeside cities of Lausanne and Geneva and invariably toured the Alps. Those with sufficient time and money travelled further south to Italy and the south of France, where their itineraries included Milan, Florence, Venice, Genoa, Rome, Naples, Nice, and Monte Carlo. While a few ventured further east and stopped in Vienna en route to Hungary, the majority of the Canadian tourists studied here seldom travelled east across the German or Austrian borders and only a few went north to see the Scandinavian countries.[5] And even though periodicals such as the *Canadian Magazine* told of the past glories of Granada and the romance of the Alhambra, not many of them went to Spain.[6] Some tourists' started their transatlantic trips in the Mediterranean, with their first port of call Madeira or the Azores, followed by stops at Algiers and Tunisia. These tourists first encountered 'Europe' in the Bay of Naples, where they disembarked and made their way north, replicating in reverse order the itineraries described above.

Just as Canadians saw the cities, towns, villages, and countryside of England and Scotland as offering important lessons about history, religion and culture, so too did they see Europe as a repository of such information. France, Belgium, the Netherlands, Germany, Switzerland, and Italy: all held possibilities for Canadian tourists to round off an overseas education that, for most, either had begun or would culminate across the Channel. Impressions of any particular place were not uniform among the tourists and travel writers; nevertheless their extensive lists of historical sites did not vary much, whether one compares unpublished accounts with each other or with the travelogues and magazine and newspaper articles. Paris was notable for some of its sites dating back to medieval times, attractions such as Notre Dame Cathedral and the Latin Quarter (although the latter was equally likely to of interest when seeking contemporary entertainment).[7] There often seemed little time to dwell on that early period, though Clara Bowslaugh's entry

'Henry IV murdered, died in the Louvre, many paintings' is a typical description.[8] Others looked for the city's more immediate past, the 1870–1 Franco-Prussian War and the siege of Paris, noting that at the Place de la Concorde there were black-draped statues of Alsace and Lorraine, serving as an *aide-memoire* of France's recent losses.[9] The Paris Commune of 1871 came in for its fair share of approbation: J.S. Gordon's disapproval of the 'vandal nature of the Paris mob' in its attempts to burn down Notre Dame was a standard reaction.[10] Several diarists recorded that they saw the *Panorama of Paris during the Siege*: Fred Martin described it as 'well worth a visit as it is really too natural to be pleasant.'[11]

Yet English-speaking Canadian travel writers were not uniformly royalists. John Mackinnon was unsympathetic to the Bonaparte regime, believing that its fate should be taken as a clear example of reaping what had been sown. He found the Tuileries to be 'an eldorado of pimps and parasites, panders and wantons,' in which perjury, violence, fraud, mendacity, and espionage reigned. Moreover, in his opinion, a breakdown in the gendered order of things was at the centre of the events of the late 1860s. 'Beneath his [Napoleon III] blighting rule French women sought to surpass each other in reckless extravagance and Frenchmen lost the courage which half redeemed their frivolity' (Mackinnon also characterized Paris as a 'dandy with beaver, cane, and kid gloves,' although this was meant as a compliment).[12] However, although he could see that one might conclude that the Communards did their country a favour, Mackinnon disapproved of their behaviour. At Notre Dame des Victoires, he thought about their blasphemous conduct towards the altar but 'they had their fun at the beginning, for next morning they found themselves prisoners, [and] were taken outside and shot.'[13] The Canadian tourists may well have been influenced by the narratives told about the Commune by monarchists, conservatives, and the Catholic church, ones that depicted the Communards as blasphemous maniacs who threatened private property, religion, and the very fundamentals of civilization itself.[14]

Versailles left these tourists with happier, gayer memories, as for many of them it was seen a wonderful and lavish collection of historical artefacts and art attributed to the 'Sun King's' vision and ambition, not to mention fundraising abilities. 'The palace cost 1000 million francs, Louis XIV,' Clara Bowslaugh recorded.[15] Ethel Davies wrote that Versailles 'was one of surpassing beauty of its special kind … One can have no idea before visiting Versailles of the grandeur and luxury surrounding the court of *le Grand Monarch*.'[16] Not everyone, though, was moved by the palace's historic significance and visual grandeur. While the fountains were 'very fine,' James Hall was 'rather disappointed' with them. 'In fact Versailles disappointed us all and the wind and the fact that the museum was closed were the only charming features about the place' (Hall tired quickly of museums and galleries).[17]

Paris and nearby Versailles brought to mind, of course, the French Revolution and Napoleon. Indeed, for tourists, Paris and the revolution were synonymous; reading their diaries and travelogues one would not know that it happened anywhere else in France. The Tuileries, the Place de la Concorde, Versailles, the Pantheon, and the Hôtel des Invalides: their significance as historical landmarks usually hinged on the connections that could be made between them and political upheaval, violent death, and war. Many of these writers mentioned Marie Antoinette's attempted flight from Versailles and reflected on her tragic, if perhaps inevitable end; however, few put it as succinctly as Harriett Priddis. She saw a place 'that has not altered as I remembered it all these years: the little old piano, group of pretty mothers and children, the Marie Antoinette furniture. Though I have seen so many homes of queens and martyrs the past few months the pathos of the story of this poor woman who did not know and could not understand still stands pre-eminent.'[18] John Mackinnon readily (one might say almost gleefully) listed the executions of prominent French subjects under the Terror, while Irene Simmonds told her readers of seeing 'the large courtyard [where] King Louis XVI and Marie Antoinette and about three thousand others were guillotined, Charlotte Corday among them, victims of the revolution of 1793' (Bowslaugh put the number at twenty-eight hundred).[19] Margaret Thomson did not go into such detail, but in 1897 she visited the Place de la Concorde twice and mentioned in entries for both dates that it was there that 'the guillotining was done.'[20]

After 'the guillotining' came Napoleon Bonaparte. Hugh Johnston included him on his list of 'demonic creatures' (Bonaparte shared that honour with Catherine de Medici), asserting that Napoleon's memory blighted the delights of Paris. Other English-speaking Canadians were not so quick to condemn him.[21] Bowslaugh's Methodism may have led her to record the story of Napoleon's coronation without registering outrage or indignation: 'Napoleon wrote to Pope Pius VII asking him to come and crown him adding a p.s. "If you don't come I'll come and fetch you." Pius came but Napoleon took the crown from him and crowned himself.'[22] Priddis was rather more fanciful, musing while at

Napoleon's statue at the Place Vendôme, 'I don't know why, but Napoleon does not seem at home in Paris, he seemed very much more a real person in London, Canada, than he does here.'[23] During her visit to Napoleon's tomb at Hôtel des Invalides Priddis saw the many sarcophagi of the Bonaparte family, and Napoleon's generals, and she overheard a guide tell his party that they were looking at the statue of Joseph Bonaparte, King of Spain and Napoleon's eldest brother – '"a great family ladies and gentlemen." And I thought of that batch of Corsican boys and girls who dared play with the lives of millions of men and topple over the thrones of Europe like a house of cards to end in this cold marble, which no one loves. I went down to the crypt below, and here somehow Napoleon seemed more human, guarded by his warm friends Bertrand and Duroc with the inscription over the locked door, "I desire that my ashes shall repose on the banks of the Seine in the midst of the people I so love."'[24] Edward Greenshields was less moved by pathos. The tomb was a 'beautiful sight' and far grander than those of the French kings, and for him, Napoleon 'was the greatest man since Louis XIV, and even if he was far from perfect, he was a genius in war, and in constructive work in the Empire.'[25]

English Canadians made a point of visiting Waterloo and touring the battlefield. They resisted what might have been an urge to gloat and noted in a matter-of-fact manner that they had seen the monument to Britain's victory, the different positions taken up by the opposing forces, Napoleon's resting place the night before the battle, and the museum with its exhibits of officers' autographs and London's newspaper coverage.[26] Mackinnon thought it was 'folly to attempt describing the battle myself,' before proceeding to do just that. He punctured any overly patriotic or romantic feelings that his readers might be harbouring by describing the 'guides [who] persistently offer help to the tourist – they describe situations and evolutions with as much cheek as if they had seen all in action. Their English may be bad, but they give good measure – they are not particular to facts so long as they can secure the money.' Nevertheless, he reminded readers that, 'most of us put the largest berry on top and strain the truth when so doing leads to money advantage.'[27]

The rest of Belgium, particularly Brussels, had a number of attractions, but with one exception its history was not of central interest. Most of the discussions of Belgium's past are reminiscent of these tourists' view of England's eighteenth century: peaceful, secure, and perhaps a little dull. During his 1878 visit to Brussels Hall made a point of seeing the Hôtel de

Ville where the Duchess of Richmond held her ball in 1815 'and which the "opening cannons' roar" rather spoiled and didn't give the boys half a chance at the supper.'[28] He enjoyed seeing the Houses of Parliament, particularly the Upper House with its 'splendid paintings of the old Kings around the walls.' Hall, though, was equally as (if not more) interested in the 'fittings and furnishings' of the Belgian Parliament as he was in its representation of the political history of Belgium. Somewhat disappointed that a thick 'turkey carpet' and not Brussels had been laid in the Upper Chamber, he concluded that 'the inside of the building is fitted up with more taste I think than any building of the kind I have seen.'[29] Canadian travel writer Estelle Kerr visited Belgium in 1914, with her friend Dorothy Stevens. Kerr was reminded of Charles II's stay in 'Bruges' during his European exile, where he was broke but very well liked. Kerr also saw Ghent, which she found to be a city where the medieval period coexisted with the modern.[30]

Belgium did attract attention for other reasons: the art and architecture of Brussels' cathedral, Belgian lace, and the relationships between its men and women. There were, however, aspects of Dutch and Belgian history that provoked musings on a 'history' of violence and tyranny, a past at odds with their supposed contemporary pacific nature. The explanation for this dichotomy was not hard to find: violence and cruelty had been eradicated with the Netherlands' liberation from Spanish rule, the securing of Protestantism as the state religion, and the subsequent end to religiously based persecution. En route to Antwerp Bowslaugh's train passed through Michelin, 'famous for its lace and the martyrdom of Tyndale.' In Antwerp she toured the 'old fortress' (presumably the Steen Museum) with its many instruments of torture 'employed during the Inquisition. We in its dungeons, Thirty Years' War and Spanish fury.'[31] In the Hague, Margaret Thomson saw the 'old furnishings' of the Houses of Parliament, but she also was taken to a prison where she and her family looked at the 'old instruments of torture,' the long spikes used to capture a famous Dutch hero, and a room where other prisoners were made to sit and watch the executions.[32] Travelling on to Antwerp, like Bowslaugh, Thomson too toured the Steen, given, she noted, by Charles V to city burghers and once the site of the Inquisition; the articles in it include 'old instruments of torture.'[33] Irene Simmonds's description of her tour of the 'old jail where the Spanish used to torture prisoners' at the Hague was perhaps the most graphic. There were the cells and the pillory, stocks, and gallows, the rack and branding irons. There was a bench used for decapitation and a room in which were kept those who were being starved to death (next to the kitchen, she noted with disgust). In another room a young priest, who had converted to Lutheranism and had been tortured and then strangled when he refused to recant, had dug a one-inch hole in the prison wall and written on the cell walls with his blood.[34]

History became a slightly, if not entirely, happier matter after the travellers crossed the Dutch-German border. The city of Frankfurt not only was home to monuments to Gutenberg, Schiller, and Goethe but it also offered the Jewish quarter, with 'Rothschild's "old homestead"' ('and a rum looking old house it is too,' thought Martin).[35] Ada Pemberton found Rothenberg 'most delightful picturesque and quaint' and a welcome contrast to the castle at Nuremberg – with its dungeons, torture chambers, underground rooms, stocks, and pillory. 'I was very glad to come to the upper air,' she confided to her diary.[36] In addition to their cultural and religious attractions, Heidelberg, Mainz, Weisbaden, Coblenz, and Cologne all had a degree of historical significance for these tourists. As might befit a tour led by a Protestant minister, Bowslaugh's expedition was taken through Worms, where she saw the cathedral in which Charles V signed his condemnation of Luther.[37] In Cologne, like many of her fellow Canadians, Priddis mused about Coleridge's famous poem on the city. But she was unable to find the '"rags and hags and hideous wenches" nor count two and seventy stenches ... I should think the Cologne fathers would appoint as a day of public mourning the anniversary of the day the fêted son of Devon chanced their way. Whether I am not gifted with acute senses or have been too busy with my eyes to notice them, except in a few of the narrow back streets in southern Italy, I have not noticed the many "stinks" so much condemned by tourists.' Priddis did feel, though, that 'after being surfeited with ruined castles and medieval legends we seem to be coming back to the history of today with monuments of the Kaiser and Augusta and the heroes of the Franco-Prussian war.'[38]

Boat trips on the Rhine, taken by many Canadian tourists, mingled leisure, amusing stories, and some tragic – but morally improving – history lessons in a manner not often replicated elsewhere in their travels. Sitting out on deck, meeting and chatting with other passengers, and sometimes having a glass of Rhine wine, while simultaneously gazing at the landscape they often found enchanting. Bowslaugh's description was typical where she wrote, 'We enjoyed so much our sail down the "storied Rhine," beautiful as a dream.'[39] Yet not all of the Rhine's stories were cheerful ones. There was the tale of Archbishop Hatto of Mainz, who denied his people grain and ended up devoured by rats in his own granary. The story, though, was not exactly a sad one, as it was often recounted to the tourists with a certain relish in the archbishop's getting his just deserts. And tourists might be sceptical of most of what they were told about the Rhine's castles. Martin gave the tale 'for what it is worth there are any number of legends of the Rhine but they are so absurd I refrain from giving them.'[40] Bowslaugh, though, may have been a little more inclined towards the romantic, as when she told the story of Roland's ruined castle. Hearing the (false) news of his death at the battles of Roncesvalles, his fiancée became a nun, 'and when he returned she was in the convent lost to him forever.' Roland then built a castle, Bowslaugh explained, where he could catch glimpses of her at her devotions or see the light of her taper in the window; upon hearing the bell toll and seeing her funeral procession, he did not speak again and was found dead at one that very morning, his eyes still and fixed on the convent chapel. 'This romantic story made a deep impression on three or four of our party – who watched the crumbling arch as far as they could see it,' Bowslaugh reported, although she did not admit whether she was one of the three or four.[41]

Not all of our travellers were so concerned with history, romantic, made-up, or otherwise. After passing by the Lorelei rock, Harriett Priddis observed that one might believe in the 'legend and story if you like. An immense rock rising straight out of the water. Puts me in mind of something else I have seen on a grander scale; but I can't think what.' Finding it too windy to read her guidebook, Priddis took shelter behind the gangway 'and am just going to look at castles and towns without knowing what they are and watch folks.'[42] Hall could not determine why Germany had 'so many barons semi-barbarous or otherwise and how they got money to build these very expensive houses are mysteries to me, but I suspect a large portion of the finest of them belonged to church dignitaries. Most of these castles are now ruinous and in such bad repair as to be uncomfortable as habitations even without the ghosts that certainly must luxuriate there.'[43] Hall was a little more interested, though, in the tale of Schomberg Castle, inhabited in the tenth century by 'seven beautiful damsels who would now-a-days be called flirts who after the manner of their sex deceived the unfortunate barons of the neighbourhood until Lurley the Queen of the Rhine either taking pity on the love-struck swains or wishing to have a monopoly of that business herself turned them into seven rocks which are still to be seen as a warning to ladies inclined to that pleasure if indeed there are any now' (the story, he insisted, was true as he had seen those same rocks). Hall enjoyed tales of perfidious women and romantic betrayals, noting the Gorge of the Lorelei, 'where that estimable female the siren Lurley bewitched to their destruction by her songs ... the amourous beer drinking Herr Schneiders of her acquaintance.' On seeing the castles at Liebenstein and Sterrenberg Hall told the legend of the two brothers, 'who as is so often the case at least in books fell in love with the same light haired blue eyed big waisted flat nosed fraulein,' who naturally fell for the less worthy one, who rewarded her affections by taking himself off to the Crusades and returning with a Greek wife 'and probably several children.' 'Taken aback' at this, the 'little fraulein,' Hall maintained, had 'retired to a convent' 'while the elder brother challenged the younger and sliced him up with a large sword, and probably married the widow. Shortly afterwards though the Guide books don't say so.'[44]

As far as Switzerland was concerned, English-speaking Canadians were more interested in 'Swiss life and scenery' than in its history.[45] Yet trips through the Alps and to lakeside towns might evoke Switzerland's histories of the Reformation and the Enlightenment, not to mention the very creation of that country.[46] In Geneva, Martin and Thomson noted the lives of Calvin and Voltaire; Martin also passed Germaine de Staël's house and the monument to Rousseau.[47] The Castle of Chillon at Montreux held a rather grisly fascination for both Bowslaugh (who at times relished recounting the gruesome statistics of the past) and Martin. Over its door, reported Bowslaugh, was the inscription, 'God bless all who go in and out here,' and her account of its former prisoners implied that they certainly had been in need of divine protection. Here was the dungeon in which the Duke of Savoy confined Francis Bonward and the seven galleries that Byron had written about in his 'Prisoner of Chillon' (Bonvard spent six years of his life in their gloom, four of them chained to a pillar). Further on was the room where prisoners had slept the night before their execution, from which they were taken to the gibbet, their 'bodies dragged across the hall and thrown in to Lac Lemau three hundred feet below.'[48] Martin reported that 'the pillars and arches and the other reminiscences of the time of the Duke of Savoy are interesting.' There was also a well with three steps down to it and then a 'pitchy darkness: prisoners were told that if they went down these steps they'd escape but instead at [the] third step they fell onto swords and went into the lake below.' The names on the pillars included Byron's and Victor Hugo's and, Martin noted, the castle had at times been both a state prison and a military arsenal: 'it is a horrid looking place,' where he did, however, purchase a cigarette holder and a card case, the former painted with a view of the castle.[49] Thomson, who was often taken by the less-salubrious details of British and European history, did not visit Montreux, on both her 1897 and 1898 trips to Europe, however, she made a point of seeing the 'Lion of Lucerne,' that city's monument to the Swiss guard who died defending the Tuilieries.[50] She also made mention of more recent violent events. She went to see the place in Geneva where the Halesburg Empress had been assassinated recently and noted in her diary that a large crowd lined up outside the Palace of Justice to hear the assassin's trial.[51]

European countries were perceived to be rich repositories of history, culture, and religion that combined to heighten their intellectual and sensory appeal. Nowhere was this more apparently the case than with Italy, though, whose sites combined all three of these elements along with (as we have seen), pestering guides, irritating souvenir sellers, and troubling beggars. 'History,' for these tourists, meant the Renaissance and imperial Rome. A few of the writers, to be sure, were interested in the more recent past of Italian unification, or at least they noted seeing the monuments to Victor Emmanuel and Garibaldi.[52] Some maintained that Italy was clearly an example of progress and improvement. C.R.W. Biggar, of Toronto, was most impressed by the changes he encountered in Rome. He visited Italy in 1875 and on his return trip twenty years later (also having had the advantage in the meantime of reading Mark Twain's *Innocents Abroad*) was pleasantly shocked to find 'New Rome ... one of the most progressive, cosmopolitan, clean, well-governed and beyond all doubt or comparison, the most interesting amongst the capitals of Europe.'[53]

Generally, though, these Canadian visitors were most concerned with the histories of Italy that had produced the genres of art that they classified as significant. Few diarists paused to consider the changes to Rome's urban landscape that had occurred after 1870, with the city's incorporation into the Italian state.[54] While there was much to see and wonder at in Venice, a central attraction was the Doges' Palace, with its architecture, paintings, and various references to the republic's history. Venice also had seen much state-sponsored cruelty, with its dungeons in which political prisoners were incarcerated, torture chambers, the spot where prisoners were guillotined, and, a favourite sight, the Bridge of Sighs through which prisoners entered the dungeons (political prisoners in one passage, criminals in another).[55] 'A horrible, damp place,' thought Martin. Priddis, who became separated from her Cook's party, saw even more of the dungeons with their histories of torture and execution. 'Our guide, not very interesting, told us the Bridge of Sighs was not used now; it has been condemned and is not open to passengers.'[56] Mary Bain, whose interest in history (and particularly its more grotesque elements) was not as fervid as Priddis's, was a little more lighthearted about what she saw in Venice. Although she toured 'the cells where the poor prisoners were then taken to the guillotine to have their heads chopped off ... the place where the guillotine used to be, and where the blood ran down and out through a hole in the floor ... upstairs the chamber where the sentences were pronounced ... we had such an amusing man take us through the prison, that the trip was not by any means as gruesome as it sounds.'[57] Visits to other Italian cities might equally produce a shiver up the tourist's back. Florence's Uffizi Gallery was a much desired destination, but as Bowslaugh pointed out, the city also housed the place where the monk Savonarola had been burned at the stake.[58] Of Pisa, the 'only thing' that remained in Gertrude Fleming's memory was the '"Tower of Hunger" where some wicked archbishop caused some rebellious count and his whole family to be starved to death – I wonder what he did.'[59]

   Not every site in Italy was a memorial to broken and decapitated bodies. The monument of Christopher Columbus drew some to the city of Genoa. Bowslaugh also remembered Genoa for its 'ducal palaces,' and Priddis thought it seemed 'so antique and so far away' (see fig. 7.1).[60] Dante's house and tomb in Florence were on Priddis's and Bain's lists of sights (as were that city's shops).[61] Once in Rome, though, there was no escaping death. 'Rome is of course full of interest,' Ethel Davies noted in her diary, but one of the most interesting places was the Coliseum. 'The saddest thought of all gazing on that huge arena is of the hundreds of martyrs of the Cross who have perished there. Trajan alone slaughtered two hundred and seventy by arrows. Others were torn by wild beasts or suffered other cruel and dreadful deaths and the solemn awe of this old ruin impressed me more than anything in my travels.'[62] Irene Simmonds too was moved: 'walking around the arena, I shuddered to think of the awful deeds done there, of the many martyrs torn to pieces by savage beasts, but not more savage than the people who gathered there.'[63] In addition to those 'martyrs of the Cross,' others pointed out that captive Jews had built the Forum and that the Forum had life after the imperial period as a fortress, hospital, and cotton manufactory (furthermore, Pope Benedict XIV had consecrated it to the memory of the Christian martyrs).[64] Pack's account of Rome's history

7.1. Transatlantic links: Genoa (*Canadian Magazine*, February 1905)

focused on the gladiators' fate, 'the cells where they would run to when wounded and where they would be killed three of four of the cells yet left in good condition.'[65]

The Catacombs – 'most interesting but the cobblestones most tiring,' as Ada Pemberton remarked[66] – reminded visitors of the events held in the Coliseum. Davies, for one, found the tour through the Catacombs to be 'of great interest, black as night and damp are these innumerable underground passages ... About 17,000 Christians are supposed to be buried there, it was during the persecution that they assembled in cata- combs to worship.'[67] In contrast to Pack's reaction – 'all damp a musty smell lots of old bones'[68] – Bowslaugh's registered a sense of the maca- bre, as she toured the Cataombs, along with a tourist's desire to gain knowledge and a small souvenir.

> We passed down a narrow stone stair, damp, dark and cold, with a draft causing our tapers to flicker at an alarming rate. We followed closely and had need to keep within touching distance of each other. The light of the taper is so feeble and there are so many turns – calling would be of little avail – we could not locate the voice – and oh to be lost here!!! *Gruesome*!!! The passages are narrow, a winding labyrinth, with open graves on each side. Fleshless skeletons on their stony beds – I picked a small stone from here as a memento of our visit; catacombs are excavated in volcanic rock, consist of corridors and chambers, rock can easily be cut with a knife.[69]

Priddis did not report the same spine-tingling reaction. Republican and imperial Rome's histories appeared most vividly to her in her three-hour morning drive around the city. 'I seem to have stepped bodily into Goldsmith's history,' she told her diary, 'the far, far away names are right here. Coliseum, Forum, Pantheon, Tiber. The bright new Palace of Justice with the new Pontes Victor Emmanuel and Umberto seem like interlopers who have no business here.'[70] Bowslaugh was reminded not just of history but also of historians. She noted that, in 1764, while seeing the Church of Ara Coli, the 'official church of medieval Rome,' Gibbon 'musing around the ruins of the Capitol and hearing the barefooted monks [at the church] chanting vespers got the idea of writing *The Decline and Fall of the Roman Empire*).'[71] Priddis was impressed with St Cecilia's grave, above which stood a copy of Stefano Modern's statue of the saint, although her body had been removed to her Trasteverian church.[72] At the Forum (which, Priddis reminded her- self, had been used as a quarry by 'degenerate Romans of the middle ages,' covered by the Tiber's overflow, and, forgotten for its historic meanings, was a cow pasture until the Italian government took it over in 1870), she saw the platform, from which Cicero spoke to the 'old Romans ... the tirade that brought on his assassination,' as well as the 'beautiful remains' of the temple of Castor and Pollux.[73] Bowslaugh wrote about seeing Temple Vesta, which had housed the sacred fire and the Vestal Virgins, who were charged with keeping the fire alight and if they neglected that duty they were 'severely punished and if they violated their vows they were *buried alive.*'[74] It was not just the early Christians who had suffered.

'The violence that was Rome,' could be easily attributed to the human 'savagery' of an imperial government that had not felt Christianity's civilizing influence (and in fact in these anglophone Canadians' eyes had worked quite ardently to not see it).[75] It was the savagery of nature that made Pompeii a tourist site that, in these tourists' writings, was both a morgue and museum. During her cycling tour of Europe, Constance Boulton, of Toronto, stopped at Pompeii, where her manner was equally suited to paying respects to a deceased relative as to viewing a tourist destination. This 'solemn, beautiful silent city of the dead,' she told readers of the *Canadian Magazine*, was desolate, and yet she and Peg (her cycling companion) felt it necessary to whisper solemnly to each other as they felt that the 'spirits of the departed life were hovering near.' Boulton was reluctant to discuss Pompeii in any detail, as she said the city filled the visitor 'with a sacred, thoughtful feeling and I cannot touch the subject lightly' (see fig. 7.2).[76] As Miss Graham wrote in the *Allisonia*, Pompeii was full of ghosts.[77]

Not everyone was so reluctant to describe the bodies, furnishings, and architecture left by the fatal explosion of the Vesuvius. Ethel Davies marvelled at the walls still standing and was fascinated by the excavations under way in Pompeii. Ada Pemberton made a lengthy list of all that she had seen there.[78] Clara Bowslaugh, armed with her lead pencil, penholder, and guidebook (purchased on the train), stepped onto the station's platform and found herself both 'besieged with chair men who wished to carry us through the ruins' and enchanted with the perfume of the thickly blooming oleander trees. She visited the museum where she saw 'carbonized limbs, skeletons of men and animals, bread, onions, bronzes, glasses, etc.,' the Temple of Apollo, and the Forum which, she pointed out, 'enclosed the tribunals where the Roman magistrates harangued the people.'[79] And despite herself, Mary Bain found Pompeii a 'wonderful and unique sight and one to

7.2. Constance Boulton's sacred site: Pompeii (*Canadian Magazine*, July 1896)

send thrills down to your very toes,' as she toured the house that had been preserved, including its 'beautiful paintings,' the theatres, and public baths (including, she noted, the Women's Bath), and the building for grinding grain.[80] Pompeii's sad past did not register with all tourists. Irene Simmonds had more to say about the supposedly shady practices of the litter-bearers who carried her to the top of Mount Vesuvius, while Harriett Priddis reported that, during her tour of the excavations, her guide offered to show her party 'some rooms not open to the general public from the obscenity of their decorations; but, we were not curious.'[81]

Pompeii was a site where social history might be experienced through artefacts and architecture, where the past was at least somewhat removed from the ferocity of the state and church. Such opportunities did not often present themselves. In Sicily Thomas Langton mused on the manifestations of the past and its all too-real location in the present. Sicilian agricultural methods, he wrote, 'go back to Gracci,' and he did not mean this as a compliment. The cities of Girgenti and Syracuse 'give one an idea of what a different country Sicily must have been in ancient times'; temples, he reported, seemed to dominate the landscape. 'Everybody must have lived inside the walls going out in fear and trembling with his hoe on his shoulder to attend to his agricultural duties.'[82] On seeing the fort at Syracuse, he felt compelled to say, 'I have never felt so in rapport with the ancients and my reading of Thucydides just before leaving was a capital preparation.'[83]

'The David Magnificent': Europe's Cultural Treasures

Yet there came a time when English-speaking Canadian tourists became, in Langton's words, 'tired of history' or at least preferred to have their European history wrapped in the colours and shapes of Europe's art, both performed and visual.[84] Gazing at paintings, sculptures, decorative arts, and artefacts (including jewelry, textiles, and furniture), opera, and ballet was not a foolproof method for leaving behind the misery and torments of the past, if only because their subject matter might represent tragic scenes. It might help, though, since the spectator could concentrate on technique and method of presentation. Furthermore, the emotional and sensory experience might transport the tourist and, at least temporarily, provide a respite from other concerns.

Anglophone Canadian tourists did not frequent French, German, or Italian theatre with the same zeal as they did London's. Nevertheless, European opera, ballet, and symphony concerts drew in some Canadians. Osla Clouston was among the few tourists who attended the French theatre (in all likelihood not many of them possessed a good enough command of French to do so). In Paris, during the winter of 1899, she saw Constant-Benoit Coquelin perform the role of Cyrano de Bergerac at the Porte-St-Martin; Coquelin (for whom Edmond Rostand had written the role) was 'splendid.'[85] But Clouston was even more enthralled with Sarah Bernhardt in *La Dame aux Camellias*. 'Oh! How fine she was and how I enjoyed it,' she told her diary (it also helped that the New Opéra Comique had 'one of the most beautiful ceilings I have ever seen' and many good paintings hung on its staircase).[86] However, just before leaving Paris Clouston saw Bernhardt in *Dalila*, but was 'rather disappointed. Sarah B was all that we could wish but we did not see enough of her.' Although the program had stated that six tableaux would be displayed, there were only five. Clouston thought that 'it was really rather funny to see how reluctantly the people left their seats, and what a time it took them to understand that there was no more to be' (see fig. 7.3).[87]

For those with the money and the inclination, opera in Europe played a role similar to that of the theatre in England. Some Canadian visitors were bemused by what they saw. In Milan, Mary Bain attended La Scala's production of *Siegfried*. In her opinion it was 'the queerest opera I ever hope to see. Only seven people in the whole cast – one solitary woman. One man did most of the singing. He was dressed in a coat of goatskins. The scenery was as lovely as I have ever

7.3. Osla Clouston sees the 'Divine Sarah.' (Osla Clouston Travel Diary, 1898–9, 18 March 1899, P007-A/4.6/1, McCord Museum. Reproduced Courtesy of the McCord Museum)

seen, and the orchestral music was grand at times, but the whole effect was distinctly queer.[88] Bain was less surprised but not terribly pleased by the Teatro della Pergola's production of *Tosca*. 'Nice voices, especially the sopranos, but a tragic unpleasant opera.'[89] Clouston and Greenshields were perhaps the most dedicated opera-goers of this group of Canadian tourists, probably because they had the appropriate money, time, and cultural education. Clouston spent two months in Dresden in 1898, during which time she saw a number of operas, including *Tannhaüser* with Therese Mallin as Elisabeth. This singer, Clouston reported, had celebreated twenty-five years with the Dresden Opera Company. She looked 'splendid,' and her admirers gave her a gold crown set with diamonds, as well as twenty encores, and numerous wreaths, which during the curtain calls were 'arranged artistically on stage' However, 'the evening did not end so well for Mallin in her excitement forgot the curtain, got right under it, and a heavy iron bar struck her full in the face, she could not appear again. I believe she is ill.'[90] Just before leaving the city Clouston went to see Mallin one last time. The singer took thirty curtain calls for her performance in *Fidelio*. 'I would give a great deal to know her, if I could *only* pluck up courage to go and see her, but I am afraid I can't, it will still have to remain one of [my] unrealized dreams.'[91] Earlier that week, after attending yet another opera with a 'splendid' female lead, Clouston mourned her own imminent departure from Dresden. To her, it meant the loss of her singing teacher whom, she was sure, could not be replaced by anyone in Paris, 'and I am quite sure there is not one half so sweet as Pamino in the opera there ... So what am I going to do! Oh!!! dear I shall be heart broken too. Our last *week* here it will be terrible leaving I really believe I like this place almost as much as Montreal' (see fig. 7.4).[92]

Edward Greenshields also enjoyed Dresden's opera. He saw *Rigoletto* and liked the tenor, baritone, and soprano, and thought that the singer cast in the lead role had a 'fine' voice, a 'beautiful method,' and was a 'great actor.'[93] On opera Greenshields had views. In Paris, eleven years later, he had mixed reactions to a production of *Lakome*. Saint-Saens's prelude was 'pretty' and 'nicely sung and acted,' and the female lead in *Lakome* (Madame Vauchelet) was a 'graceful actress' with a 'fine pure soprano voice,' but he did not think that the tenor was up to his part; Greenshields was mollified somewhat by the pretty staging and scenery, particularly the 'quiet but very pretty ballet of whirling girls in white, with a girl in red and blue at the centre.'[94] The opera *Don Giovanni* would be much improved, according to Greenshields, if two or three scenes were cut from it.[95] In Florence he saw Mascagni's *Iris* and predicted that, although the opera received a great ovation from a full house, it would not enjoy the success of that composer's *Cavalleria Rusticana*.[96] Greenfield was often quite happy to hear excerpts from favourite opera scores and symphonies played by the orchestras in the hotels in which he stayed. But the concert of Beethoven's music that he attended in Paris left him very dissatisfied. The musicians had no 'feeling or refinement' and were too 'elemental', the tenor soloist had a 'tremendously strong rough voice and shouted loudly,' the chorus shouted but could not be heard over the orchestra, and all in all, 'it was a very unfortunate introduction to the Ninth Symphony.' The audience consisted mostly of local men and women, 'artists, etc., the men with all sorts of queer hats – they looked as if they

7.4. The 'splendid' Therese Mallin (Osla Clouston Travel Diary, 1898–9, 20 June 1899, P007-A/4.5/1, McCord Museum. Reproduced Courtesy of the McCord Museum)

had come out of *Trilby*.' While he did enjoy the beer, chocolate, and little dishes of preserved cherries that were handed out for free, Greenshields complained that 'two men selected the Adagio of the Ninth Symphony as the time to collect the tickets.' Greenshields and his party left before the Oratorio – it was late, the seats were uncomfortable, and 'we had had enough.'[97]

Five days later, Edward Greenshields saw Isadora Duncan dance at the Trocadero, and was thrilled. She was accompanied by the Colonne Orchestra, which played Gluck's *Orpheus* in the first half and music by Brahms, Beethoven, and Schubert in the second. Duncan's dancing, reported Greenshields, 'was quite novel, going back to the simplicity of the Greeks, in the poses and movements. She holds that the emotions of humanity can be expressed by the movements of the body. She was certainly very fine in expressing the joy and sorrows of Eurydice, and she was really the poetry of motion.' Although pleased by the dancing of the young women who appeared with Duncan in the second half, he could see that they lacked Duncan's 'power and compelling attitude.' Back at his hotel Greenshields solicited more information about Duncan's history from the manager and compared her work with that of 'Miss Boni,' a ballet dancer who had appeared in an opera that Greenshields had seen recently. Both, he thought, were lovely examples of two very different styles: 'there is more artificiality in the tiptoe old-fashioned dances, yet Miss Boni's was beautiful and charming dancing. The other is grander and nobler and finer, but both were delightful.'[98]

Gertrude Fleming found Giacomo Meyerbeer's ballet, which she saw while in Nice, 'shocking from *every* point of view – we left after the *naked* ballet at the end of the fourth act. W was there after 12 o'clock and there was another act to follow. The smell of "Chypre" in the theatre made me faint.'[99] Hattiett Priddis was quite sanguine about her trip to La Scala 'to see the finest ballet in the world. The hotel porter told us. He evidently never saw the Hippodrome in New York.' She was much more interested in recording her party's attempt to get better seats for gallery tickets by sitting in a box. Finally, when the managers objected, her party paid a few more francs and was seated in a more comfortable place. She observed that the second half was a 'scientific burlesque'.[100]

Although Greenshields showed the most interest in the type of modernist art that Isadora Duncan represented, both he and a number of other English-speaking Canadian tourists were interested in variety shows and entertainments deemed 'popular.' Articles in the Canadian press at the time made it clear that Paris offered a wide range of cultural experiences and virtually insisted that the Canadian tourist visit both the Tuileries and the Latin Quarter. J.S. Gordon went to see the Latin Quarter with 'Smith,' a Toronto gentleman new to Paris and, it seems, its cosmopolitanism. Advised to come in 'bohemian' dress, Smith turned up dressed for the opera and insisted on going to the Café d'Harcourt, where he gaped at 'long-haired savants,' an elderly flower-seller 'who made a pathetic attempt at dancing,' and two 'rival beauties' who were engaged in a 'hair-pulling and bonnet-annihilating' contest over a 'Latin Quarter Adonis.' Women quickly surrounded Smith and asked him for food, beer, and cigarettes; still others showed 'an affectionate leaning' towards him. 'But I must draw a veil over the proceedings at this point,' Gordon wrote teasingly, 'as I am not anxious to raise any doubts or fears in the minds of those whose friends have traveled in France unaccompanied by a chaperon.' After putting the hapless Smith in a cab for his hotel, Gordon wandered the Quarter by himself until he came to Montmartre's Moulin Rouge, which has 'lapsed into a show place where the Anglo-Saxon visitor is regaled with an entertainment at once blasé and coarse.' Kept open primarily by English and American tourists, the club also attracted plenty of 'ladies,' 'especially American girls, whose desire to be mildly shocked is abundantly gratified.'[101]

Gordon submitted that Parisian entertainments were entertaining and perhaps slightly risqué but, to the sophisticated male tourist, not particularly troubling. His position was shared by American tourists who, as Harvey Levenstein has pointed out, were known to enjoy Montmartre. 'Much of its success,' Levenstein argued, 'rested on being accessible to respectable people who could patronize places frequented by low-lifes in a titillating yet entirely safe fashion.' In Paris, in 1878,[102] James Hall spent his days touring the exhibition and the Louvre and his evenings at the Folies Bergère, watching a 'sort of variety performance which was very good' (he particularly liked the tightrope, juggling, 'and the shooting of a man from a mortar up fully thirty feet').[103] One night he and his friends went to the Gaiety Theatre to see 'Puss in Boots with Ballet, Butterfly Dance, etc.' While a good performance, it was not 'in any way equal to the Alhambra in London.' After that they went to the Jardin de Butture 'and saw the Can Can in all its glory.' The room was very crowded but Hall 'was much disappointed with theperformance. The girls were not pretty and the dancing was miserable.'[104] On his trip to Paris more than three decades later, Edward Greenshields found the production at the Café Marign less 'daring'. It was a well-managed variety show, he thought, with 'any number of very beauti- fully dressed girls. The last two scenes were a little strongly Parisian, but there was very little objectionable and the different scenes followed each other very rapidly.' He was moved by the last scene, set in a grotto with water pouring down mid-stage and nymphs 'constantly sliding down in it was very pretty.'[105] But Greenshields's ability to take in things 'Parisian' was shaken a little on his visit to the Moulin Rouge: 'a number of hard specimens of women were there. It was a variety show, and very vulgar in a good many parts and nothing like as entertaining as the show at Marigny's last night.'[106]

Production standards might have changed in the time between Hall's and Bain's trips. When Bain and her husband visited the Folies Bergère, in 1911, she was thrilled and a bit titillated. 'Certainly my first experience of a Paris Theatre was not disappointing,' she confided to her diary. 'The show was immense equal to a whole season of Vancou- ver's musical comedies rolled into one. The costumes were magnifi- cent, but most distinctly daring. In fact, they would be awful anywhere but in Paris.'[107] But Fleming was shocked by what she saw of the ballet at the Folies – 'Paris is no place for me!!!', she exclaimed.[108] It is possi- ble that, even in the private forum of their diaries, 'respectable' women such as Gertrude Fleming felt obliged to profess some feelings of scan- dal on the subject of the can-can.

No matter how much some individuals appreciated various genres of the performing arts, most of all it was the Continent's displays of visual culture that drew anglophone Canadian tourists to Europe.[109] Their assessments of painting and sculpture varied, of course, being shaped by their particular backgrounds, degrees of cultural education, and finances available to support extensive gallery-going, and by the preferences of the parties with whom they were travelling. Some wrote at length about the specific paintings, sculptures, and other objects they saw, analysing technique and the artist's sensibilities quite criti- cally. Others merely wrote lists of the names and/or titles that they remembered from their visits to galleries, museums, and religious institutions. Few could match the tenacity of interest and attention to minute displayed by Edward Greenshields, not to mention the money and time that he had and took to see art both in public institutions and the collections of private dealers. Greenshields was a connoisseur and collector who published his own book of art criticism.[110] But even those tourists whose diary entries and letters home were far more perfunctory when speaking about their encounters with Rubens, Botticelli, and Giotto found it necessary and often delightful to see as much as they were able to.

The most popular place to look at paintings in Paris was the Louvre, followed a close second by the Luxembourg Palace. The Louvre, wrote Margaret Thomson in 1897, had 'splendid pictures' by artists such as da Vinci and Raphael, so much so that she made a second trip to it two days later.[111] And her return trip the next year she saw the *Venus de Milo* first and then the paintings by Rembrandt, Raphael, Rubens, and Van Dyck: 'simply got an idea of the vastness of the place were able only to see a few of the pictures.'[112] Like the British Museum, the Louvre was daunting in its size and scope. Fred Martin devoted a whole day to the Louvre, 'and I walked thro' it and saw pictures till I was completely exhausted and felt as tho' I didn't care if I never saw another painting – The gallery is magnificent really wants weeks to see it properly.' Martin attributed its magnificence to Napoleon's ransacking of other countries' art, although he was not prepared to take moral offence to activities that provided him the chance to see the works of Rubens, Rembrandt, Raphael, Van Dyck, Titian, Paolo Veronese, and da Vinci.[113] Gertrude Fleming was moved to tears by the collection's beauty (although she was often moved to tears, usually by grey weather, low spirits, and fatigue).[114] Harriett Priddis, more circumspect about her reaction to the art, mentioned seeing the *Venus de Milo* and the *Mona Lisa*. Of the latter she wrote that only the eyes, mouth, and hands could be seen, as the rest of the painting had faded. She was pleased, though, to get very close to it and to the artist who was copying the painting.[115] James Hall was one of the few to who reported being less than overwhelmed or pleased by the Louvre. He enjoyed the Egyptian and Assyrian 'curiosities,' the grand gallery's gilding and ornamentation, and the swords and crowns of various French royalty but as the Rubens, Raphaels, Murillos, Van Dycks, Corregios 'etc ... generally represent Saints, Madonnas, Crucifixions etc. didn't care for them.'[116]

Nor did he care much for the Luxembourg Palace's picture galleries.[117] But Hall was in a minority. On her first visit to Paris, Margaret Thomson thought the gallery 'splendid'. On her return visit the next year she 'liked some of the modern paintings very much. They were a relief after the Madonnas. Do not particularly admire the Impressionist school.'[118] When art became tiresome, the palace grounds offered a panoramic view of various aspects of Parisian society. Newton MacTavish thought it a 'lovely playground' that contrasted greatly, and favourably, 'from the garish gaiety' that defined Paris. It was an underappreciated place: hundreds of 'pilgrims' passed by, but unlike the more discerning author and his reader did not realize what they were missing. From its terrace it offered all kinds of sights and sounds. One could see the Punch and Judy shows, hear the band, the many birds, and the chattering 'bonne femmes,' or watch the young couples in love. As well, the asses pulling carts, the 'black-robed clerics,' and the 'gaily-clad ladies' might distract the tourist from realizing that he was standing in front of Marie de Medici's palace, the seat of the Directory, and the place where Louis Napoleon's trial was held. MacTavish admitted that the Luxembourg did not offer the lakes, riding paths, deer brakes, and ponds of the parks of London, New York, and Toronto (nor could two or three cars be driven there abreast of each other), although the grounds still contained quiet, open stretches of parkland, great trees, and interesting examples of landscape gardening and architecture. Moreover, at the Luxembourg one could see an incomparable 'disarrangement of the human tide that ebbs and flows all about you,' such as the nurse with her novel, the old woman with her knitting, and the painter with his sketchbox. And in the Luxembourg the tourist might transcend the barriers of language. While he was watching the Punch and Judy show, itself an example of 'timelessness,' at the moment when Punch knocks Judy over and sits on her, MacTavish turned to the 'anarchist' seated next to him and they shared their mutual appreciation of the scene by exchanging smiles, slight nods, and an elbow in the ribs.[119]

Priddis wrote little about the galleries or the Punch and Judy show. She did, though, go to the Luxembourg's garden to meet a friend, who was an aspiring artist and who took Priddis to the studio apartment she shared with another art student.[120] While most of these Canadian tourists were content to write about the art they saw or to confine their sketching to their private notebooks, a few of them took art lessons. Osla Clouston discovered that Paris 'studio life is a splendid life, despite the hard work involved'. She was so taken with her art instruction that she felt guilty for neglecting her French lessons and vowed to discontinue her trips to the studio.[121] Ada Pemberton's sister Sophie trained at a Paris atelier, around the turn of the century and some of the letters that discuss her adventures have survived in the family correspondence. 'With my real propensity for bohemian types I picked up

an old model Bibi ... such a character and wonderfully ragged clothes,'
she wrote to Ada in Victoria. Sophie asked 'Bibi' to visit the studio,
where 'Madame' had him sit for an evening sketching class. Sophie
planned to paint her model 'upstairs and I shall try to get the Voltaire
grin only Mme J. won't let me be in the room alone with him.'[122] After
his sitting, Bibi went around to her flat. He had with him a 'little image
blessed for me of St Genevieve and had said some masses for my
speedy recovery he looked at my photo and I gave him a glass of wine
we talked a while, then I suggested his taking my letters to the concierge to post. So he kissed my hand and departed – and I opened the
window a bit.'[123] As it turned out, 'Madame's' concern for Sophie Pemberton's safety (and possibly both their reputations) turned out to be
unnecessary.

Of course, Paris and its environs offered other museums and galleries too. James Hall was impressed with the 'magnificent vases and
china sets' at Sèvres which appeared to have greater visual appeal for
him than all the galleries,' 'Madonnas and Crucifixions.'[124] Martin
described the Cluny Museum as 'a most interesting old place contain-
ing a most exclusive and valuable collection of medieval objects of art
and products of industry of all kinds.' There one might see '10,350
objects of art to look at among them the *girdle* of *Francis I for his wife*
carved ivory with iron band and lock and key.'[125] And, even if they
might not compete with the Louvre, en route to Italy other cities' galleries and museums offered a range of visual treats. The art museum in
Brussels had only a few paintings, Martin confided to his diary, 'but all
excellent and so large.'[126] Thomson's list of them included paintings
those by Rubens, Rembrandt, Van Dyck, Champaigne, and Veronell. In
Antwerp, the following year, she noted that in addition to its instruments of torture she saw Rubens's biblical paintings (which she preferred to his allegorical ones), Brueghel's depiction of a Flemish church
feast ('most extraodinary'), and Beaufaux's painting of Salomé watching the beheading of John the Baptist.[127] Thomson and her family visited the gallery in Cologne and was reportedly pleased that it was
Wednesday afternoon, for she 'found something in Cologne for which
we were not charged.'[128]

But for these visitors most of all it was Italy that promised – and, in
general, delivered – 'art.' Venice, Florence, Milan, and, of course, Rome
are all featured in both the diaries and published travel accounts as cities rich with galleries, museums, churches, and cathedrals laden with
painting and sculpture, so much so that there the common complaint

about the Louvre and the British Museum also held true.[129] 'Such a
feast of pictures!,' wrote Bowslaugh about Florence's Uffizi Gallery,
'but oh so little time!'[130] Bain 'saw numerous paintings by old masters,
but it would be impossible, even if I could remember them, to single
them all out.' Nevertheless, she made a valiant effort and went on to
list Raphael, Michelangelo, da Vinci, Titian, Rembrandt, Rubens, and
Velazquez as artists who should be 'singled out.'[131] Believing herself to
be short of time, Priddis expressed her regret that she would not be
able to see Michelangelo's *David* while in Florence; however, before
leaving she found herself at the train station with an hour to spare, so
'drove quickly to the Academy and was quite paid for my trouble. The
David magnificent, beautifully placed.'[132] As well as looking at the art
in churches and the cathedral, Pack paid a visit to the Peruzzi stone-
works, where he watched the mosaic workers colouring, shaping, and
polishing the stone. 'It is hardly possible to believe,' he told his diary,
'that stone could be worked into such magnificent work little things
such as a man's wrinkle in his forehead eyebrows butterflies all made
from different coloured marble slate and other stones roses all the
shades of the leaves.'[133] In Venice and Milan Canadian tourists went to
see the paintings of Tintoretto, Veronese, Titian, Bellini, Vecchio, as well
as da Vinci's *Last Supper* and Canova's sculpture.[134]

Much of this art was viewed in institutions both secular and sacred.
The links between culture and religion were clearest, however, in
Rome. Greenshields thought that the Sistine Chapel was 'grand ...
nothing consoling or sweet about it, it is awe inspiring ... the whole
effect of the Sistine Chapel was fine beyond my expectation' (see
fig. 7.5). He then proceeded to stroll along the Appian Way, believing
that 'there is no doubt that St Paul walked along this Appian Road,
coming to Rome, and looked on the same scenery that we did' (unlike
many, though, he admitted that 'the city of Rome itself was very different').[135] The beauty of St Peters, Bain wrote, was 'beyond description
and one should have days to spend within its walls, to begin to grasp
its beauties.' She tried to put her impressions down in words but found
her talents inadequate and had to abandon the task.[136] While the Sistine Chapel's *Transfiguration* was different from what Langton had
expected and thus a bit disappointing, *The Last Communion of St Jerome*
'far exceeded any idea I had had of it.'[137] With her customary practical
attitude, Priddis found her opera glasses to be quite useful at the Sistine Chapel but wished that she had had hours for each picture. 'This
"doing" the galleries is terrible but instructive,' she wrote.[138]

7.5. Religion and culture: Michelangelo's decorative figures, Sistine Chapel (*Canadian Magazine*, April 1905)

Of course, viewing art in Italy was not purely an emotionally uplifting experience. Although Thomas Langton was deeply moved by much of the art he saw in Italy, he did not exempt Italian culture from an irreverent gaze. There were statues at Rome's Capitol, he reported, with sexual graffiti scribbled on them. In commeting on Perugia's frescoes, it was his opinion that while 'the guidebooks and writers talk to me in vain of the tranquility and sentiment and devotional mind of Perugia discernible through the features of those of these parties (Socrates, Scipio, and Horatio) being a Philistine I might discern prudence in a handsome gentle contemplative longbearded old gentleman but not Socrates.'[139] Langton was determined to distinguish his tastes from those of others, detesting Guido's painting of Beatrice Cenci 'as cordially as most people have admired it' and judging a painting in Venice acclaimed by Ruskin to be the third most beautiful in the world as 'the third ugliest.'[140] The thrill of seeing religious art in Venice was not shared by John Mackinnon, who thought that the 'pictures of Christ are nearly all disappointing – most of them looking either vicious or silly. The Virgin is often portrayed with extreme sweetness;

but I never saw a picture of Christ that entirely pleased me. In most instances instead of according to the artist a premium of fame and fortune, I would have him banished if not beheaded.' Mackinnon also disliked the nationalist impulse that he felt lay behind these depictions of Christ, one that led artists to take considerable licence and paint Christ as if he were their countryman.[141]

'How Do They Get the Bones Clean?' Religion in European Tourism

Mackinnon was distinctive in his unease about the blurring of religious representation by secular identities. However, most anglophone Canadian tourists likely would have agreed with Albert R. Carman that the best place to view religious art, the place it was most likely to 'come alive,' was in a church, not a museum (his list of such artists included Michelangelo, Raphael, Reni, and Botticelli).[142] Cathedrals and churches did not only house works of art but were works of art in their own right, and their form and decoration were to be viewed for both the aesthetic and the spiritual lessons they offered. Such was the case with Notre Dame in Paris, St Mark's in Venice, St Peter's in Rome, as well as the cathedrals of Milan, Florence, Pisa, and Siena; and the same could be said with regard to a host of smaller churches in France and Italy.[143] Thomson and Langton were particularly fond of the cathedral in Pisa. Langton believed it was the city's saving grace, as the rest of Pisa was a 'beastly hole.'[144] The catherdrals of Brussels, Cologne, and Antwerp also came in for their share of critical evaluation. Visitors were impressed by their architecture and ornamentation. Thomson's description of Cologne's cathedral as 'grand inside and out' was typical.[145] Yet these buildings might not entirely satisfy when compared with the cathedrals in Italy. Priddis did not think that Cologne's cathedral measured up to Milan's (and in turn she found that Florence's cathedral 'made me homesick for Rome').[146] In Cologne, though, the fault was not entirely that of the architecture: 'Cook's parties travel too rapidly to enjoy cathedrals; one cannot take in grandeur, only notice what is peculiar or fantastic.'[147]

Some English-speaking Canadians were made queasy by the preservation and display of relics in Catholic churches. Simmonds was disturbed by Cologne's Church of St Ursula's exhibition of the bones of both the saint and the 'eleven thousand virgins' who were martyred with her. To her, all the bones looked alike 'and very disgusting at that. I wonder if those priests who show visitors those horrid relics, believe themselves what they tell them. But it pays them well to tell extravagant stories, from the fees they collect. I thought it would have been much better to have buried the poor bones. Another thing seems queer: how do they get the bones clean?'[148] Obviously Simmonds was not overly fond of such displays, as she had a similar reaction to Rome's Capuchin church with the bones of its monks. 'A gruesome sight! How much better it would be to bury those poor bones, but of course everyone who goes to look at them pays a fee, and so a lot of idle men live off the dead. I could not help wondering how they cleaned all those bones before they decorated the rooms.'[149] Such questions did not disturb Emily Murphy, for she dubbed the church a 'vast charnel house' and noted, somewhat sceptically, that it was 'decorated' with the virgins' skulls, some 'partly covered with velvet.'[150] Pack called it 'some of the strangest sights we ever saw' and was fascinated by the story of the monk who dug up his predecessors and used their skeletons to decorate the rooms under the monastery. 'It certainly was a big job,' he thought, 'but it is well done.'[151] Priddis thought it 'rather uncanny, but not so repulsive as I expected,' while Bowslaugh judged it to be 'artistically decorated' and was fascinated with the details of the process of exhumation and display.[152] She did not enjoy what she found at Turin's Church of La Consolata, though: a 'miracle-working statue' of the Virgin and corridors hung with pictures of the 'wonderful cures' she had wrought, pictures that Bowslaugh thought were 'most grotesque caricatures.'[153]

Apart from bones and 'caricatures,' these tourists saw the paintings, sculpture, architecture, and other forms of decorative arts that had been generated and sponsored by Roman Catholicism to be of high cultural value. They respected, rather than criticized, the Catholic Church for having played a role as a patron of the arts, particularly insofar as the office of the pope was concerned. A few were eager and able to have an audience with the pontiff. Priddis arrayed herself in silk gloves and a veil made of three yards of Brussels' lace, and went with eight others from her party to be presented to Pope Pius X. 'His Holiness, a large stout Italian of the bourgeois class, face quite colorless, not healthy looking white serge costume very unbecoming, no ornaments but jeweled cross on breast. Kissed the ring on third finger of his right hand in groups of ten or fifteen kneeling.' Priddis described the various requests made of the pope that included the blessing of rosaries and the salvation of the poor in France. After a Latin benediction 'for which all knelt,' he left with his attendant (see fig. 7.6).

7.6. Pope Pius X: 'A large stout Italian of the bourgeois class' (Harriett Priddis) or a 'Man of God ... a fascinating figure, best loved of the chief pastors' (Mortimer O'Shea) (*Across Two Continents and through the Emerald Isle*, 1907)

Although Priddis might not have found the pope physically prepossessing, the ceremony inspired her to visit St Peter's again ('I never get enough of that'), inspect the Stuart Monument, watch a woman at St John Lateran Church say the rosary on her knees, and stop to hear vespers sung at St Lucia's.[154] Bowslaugh did not have a papal audience. Her tour of the Vatican involved a sight of the Pope's page, dressed in a cardinal-red satin coat, knee breeches, silk stockings, and grey curled hair tied with a cardinal-red ribbon. Passing the private entrances she smelled the appetizing odour of the papal lunch on the stove, and in the gardens stroked the pope's cat, 'rather hurriedly for we did not know what might be the penalty for touching the animal.'[155]

Not everyone had the chance to pet the pope's cat but many took the opportunity to watch Catholic baptisms, weddings, and funerals. At Notre Dame de Fourerière in Lyons, Pack had no compunction about observing people worshipping. He also found a Roman firefigher's funeral most interesting and took pictures of the soldiers who marched beside the flower-covered hearse.[156] Thomson quite enjoyed the chanting at a funeral service she witnessed in Antwerp. She also recorded her impressions of a service at the cathedral in Mainz during which the priest kept his back to the people and 'went through various performances.'[157] At Notre Dame Cathedral in Brussels, Simmonds was pleased to watch the marriage ceremony of a 'rich banker' to a baroness. The bride was in a long white dress with a train and an ankle-length veil and, when Simmonds smiled at her, she graciously returned the greeting with a smile and bow.[158]

Watching religious services might be merely a sign of interest, possibly even respect. It could also be a more voyeuristic act, as Pack's account of his photography at the funeral suggests, for it is unlikely that he would have taken photos of such processions in his home city of Victoria. Furthermore, despite their interest in Catholic services and respect for Catholic art works, these Protestant English-speaking Canadians were not free of anti-Catholicism. Their appreciation of religious themes in art and the absence of negative comments from them about the Pope may well have been linked to a class-based respect for both 'high culture' and religious hierarchy.[159] English-speaking Canadians tourists' diaries and letters do not suggest that their authors rivalled in rudeness their British counterparts who, as historian John Pemble has demonstrated, would talk, drink, push, and shove during Easter and Christmas services in Rome, as well as refuse to kneel or (if male) uncover their heads for the Pope (and who afterwords would write 'long angry screeds' about the services).[160] Nevertheless, these Canadians were dubious about the 'ordinary' priests and monks and the rituals they presided over churches and cathedrals, particularly in Italy. As well as Langton's trickster sacristan, Simmonds's idle, parasitic monks, and Priddis's insinuating novice with his 'touch of the Jesuit,' there were other examples of aspects of Italian Catholic culture that the Canadians saw as less than sincere. The objects in St Peter's were beautiful, Simmonds wrote. Yet she found it strange to have such wealth locked up in church; after all, she explained, Rome had more beggars and cripples than she had seen anywhere else.[161] Just as Murphy had criticized the High Anglicans for 'performing' piety, so too did Thomson characterize a 'performance of a christening' that she saw at a church in Battistero. At this christening, she reported, the priest put salt on certain parts of the baby, and turned it upside down and poured water over it, after which the attendant powdered its head, and the congregation, for its part, bought long candles wrapped in tissue paper.[162] The strongest critic of Italian Catholicism, though, was Langton. At Vespers in Siena's duomo the bishop 'exemplified the apparent absence of interest in the service taken by the ministers as well as those ministered to,' as he 'whined' his responses, chatted with his attendants and scolded his acolytes, took snuff and 'blew his episcopal nose with a coarse blue and white cotton pocket handkerchief'; and at a baptism in Florence the 'two priests shambled their way through the service,' muttered to themselves, and rubbed the baby's head with water as though 'polishing up the handle of the big front door.'[163]

History, culture, and religion were important categories of interest and the tools with which these tourists fashioned meanings out of the European landscape. They also were categories that were closely intertwined. Indeed, it is a somewhat artificial, if necessary, academic exercise to consider them as discretely as this chapter has done. Moreover, the letters, diaries, and published travel accounts examined for this study show no sign of the turn away from cultural tourism in favour only of leisure pursuits (such as staying in luxury hotels on the Riviera) that, for example, dominated American middle-class travels in France by the turn of the century.[164] Yet although these Canadians continued to prize their visits to Europe's galleries and museums, they also preferred to complete their cultural education with other sights and sensations. The Continent's 'natural' scenery and streetscapes, public institutions, and displays of 'national' cultures and social mores – all were described *and* constructed in the travelogues, diaries, and letters home. And, like history, culture, and religion, these other sites of tourism appealed both to these tourists' desires to analyse and classify Europeans and to their desire for sensory and emotional stimulation.

8 Natural Wonders and National Cultures: European Sojourns, Part 2

'I don't care at present if I ever see another altarpiece,' Thomas Langton confessed to his diary while taking a rest from Florence's churches, museums, and art galleries.[1] Not all tourists were quite so frank about their exhaustion and their occasional boredom with the wonders of European culture. Moreover, Langton recovered from his surfeit of altarpieces and proceeded to follow Baedeker's and Ruskin's cultural directives around Italy and Switzerland. Yet as much as the products of human history and artistic endeavour entranced them, these tourists also consumed Europe's 'natural' scenery, its streetscapes, public institutions and entertainments, and displays of 'national' cultures and social mores, not to mention the food and drink. While the writings of these Canadien visitors Europe bear witness to the ongoing process of fashioning and reinforcing various kinds of subjectivities – including those of gender, class, and nation – their travelogues, diaries, and letters also testify to the centrality of sensory dimensions to the tourist.

'Such a Sight I Have Never Beheld': Mountains and Coastlines

To state that the natural sights of these countries came as a surprise to Anglophone Canadian tourists would be naïve for, just as they had been educated in European art and history through a variety of media and genres, they arrived in the Alps or at the Bay of Naples prepared for a great deal of visual pleasure. One such genre was, of course, art. Although it appears that much of the European art that they admired was religious and not landscape painting, judging from the illustrations in periodicals such as the *Canadian Magazine* they were also exposed to paintings, sketches, and photographs of scenes like Mont Blanc or the canals of Venice. The texts that accompanied such illustrations or non-illustrated pieces about such places attempted to set out just what visitors would see and how they would feel as they did so. Not surprisingly, when they did arrive at places such as Switzerland, their impressions were mediated by concepts of the romantic and the sublime.[2] Moreover, on the basis of Marguerite Shaffer's examination of American tourists' appreciation of scenery such as Yosemite and the Grand Canyon in this period, we can see how it is likely that such descriptions allowed readers – and potential travellers – to see themselves as possessing the 'education and refined sensibility ... needed to fully appreciate natural scenes.'[3] E. Fannie Jones, writing in 1898 of 'Swiss Life and Scenery' for the *Canadian Magazine*, described the 'magnificent panorama' and the 'grandeur and beauty' that her readers would encounter on seeing the Alps.[4] Such stunning vistas had even more significant consequences than pleasing the tourist's eye. The 'rugged grandeur, and beauteous sublimities,' of Switzerland's mountains, Hedley P. Somner told the periodical's readers, 'have brought forth a race of hardy men, strong, independent, reliant upon themselves and their own resources.' These paragons of Swiss manliness included William Tell, the founders of the 'solemn league' against Hapsburg tyranny, and Swiss painters and poets, men of 'poetic genius' who had shown the rest of the world the inspiration to be found in the Alps.[5]

Even before Jones and Somner published their impressions of Switzerland, tourists had made a point of stopping in the Swiss and Italian Alps, and praised them for their beauty and ability to move them. James Hall's 1878 ascent of Mont Blanc exposed him to 'magnificent scenery' as well as the 'dark somber rocks and the roar of Griege Falls' (which made him think 'a water sprite might appear at any time'). The falls were 'magnificent and the rocks sublime.'[6] The next day Hall and his friends walked to Leukerbad and Kanderstag, during which trip they found themselves looking down into the valley of the River Arne: 'very picturesque and is on three sides surrounded by immense mountains and is the grandest and most imposing sight we have yet seen.'[7] Isabella Montgomery thought that the scenery at Interlaken in 1895 was 'indescribable' and, unlike many of her contemporaries, left matters at that.[8] Montgomery, it seems, drew on the (by then) 'well-worn tropes of the sublime,' ones that held that such vistas were best seen in person if one were to have a truly 'aesthetic and spiritual experience.'[9]

Clara Bowslaugh's powers of description did not fail her, however. At Rigi she and the rest of the Reverend William H. Withrow's party were woken up at four in the morning to see the sun rise over the Alps. They climbed to the top of Mount Rigi and stood on a small viewing stand. 'We soon noticed a pink flush the snow clad mountain opposite where we had been told the sun would appear. Then we saw a bit of the rim of sun. In a very little while the sun was shining and what a transformation!!! The ice tipped peaks were painted pink and pearl and gold – 130 peaks are visible – such a sight I have never beheld – It was well worth all the long journey to see that sun rise.' Bowslaugh described all the different mountains she could see and ended by exclaiming, 'Such a panorama of beauty.' The sun having risen, she then picked wildflowers before breakfast.[10] At Lausanne, Edward Greenshields was fortunate enough to behold 'a vision. Against the clear blue sky rose an immense shell, of pure white snow, curving up into the heaven, its edges showing clear against the blue. I have never seen anything so lovely in a mountain before, and it well deserves its name. The afternoon sun was shining on it, and it looked an emblem of purity towering up into the skies.'[11]

Appreciation of such beauty might come at a price. The switchback roads going through the Alps from Italy to Switzerland were 'delight-ful and exhilarating,' but the descent into Switzerland was quite dangerous, wrote S.H., another member of one of Withrow's European tours groups.[12] 'Climbing the Chamonix Aiguilles,' a description of the (at least in this article) masculine pursuit of mountaineering focused less on the beauty and more on the physical challenges encountered in scaling the Alps. Despite the author's assurance that mountaineering 'no longer involves an imputation of insanity ... the mountaineer is an ordinary healthy-minded mortal and scarcely lacking in intelligence,' the photographs that accompanied the article were of razor-sharp peaks and sheer rock faces (see fig. 8.1).[13]

The diaries and letters suggest that tourists took note of such warnings, explicit and implicit. The Alps were among the few places where they felt at least twinges, and sometimes more, of physical danger. Near Interlaken Irene Simmonds noted the stuffed St Bernard that was said to have saved a hundred and fifty lives. Such an achievement was not inconsequential for, as she explained, three climbers had been smothered in an avalanche that very day (although she thought that if the dog 'had done such good deeds in England he would have had a costly monument erected to his memory').[14] John Mackinnon told his readers that 'danger is ever present' in the mountains: 'precipice ... falling rocks, landslides, avalanches, and perishing in snowstorms.'[15]

8.1. 'The upper reaches of the Aiguille Charmoz ... where avalanches and other dangers await the lingering climber.' (*Canadian Magazine*, July 1906)

Greenshields, who often delighted in taking switchback roads and treacherous-looking passages, was sobered by the thought that the Jungfrau could be quite a dangerous peak to climb without a guide; 'there have been fatalities,' he noted.[16] And danger might be felt much more immediately. Hall's party followed another group and their guide over the Manvais Pas 'which goes along the edge of a precipice and which must have been extremely dangerous before the iron railing was put there and is still.' Hall was not averse to taking risks, though, for at the Griege Falls he and his friend removed a board from the fence that blocked their way to the rickety bridge above the water. He confessed, however, that 'if it wasn't for the vibration of the old bridge caused by the fall we would have enjoyed it wonderfully but we drew a relieved breath when we felt terra firm under our feet again.'[17]

Yet the delights and perils of the mountain passes were not untouched by other humans or by the travellers' more mundane concerns. The structural features of nineteenth-century tourism – resorts and their staff, guides, porters, and vendors of souvenirs – also shaped many of the areas of natural beauty that were to be found on the tourist's map. Canadian visitors were well aware that they were surrounded by elements of the tourist trade, and they wove these into their accounts of the wonders of the landscape. Always eager to evaluate and assess his lodgings, Greenshields reported that his hotel at Lausanne was comfortable and the staff attentive. 'I wonder,' he wrote, 'how all the hotels we have been at manage to get such excellent headwaiters and concierges. All clever capable smart men, thoroughly up in their business, and agreeable men with very good manners. It is quite delightful to be looked after by them' (the only disturbance that he noticed was the early morning sound of cowbells).[18] As Aird Dundas Flavelle travelled from Berne (where he had been greatly amused by the begging bears) to Interlaken, he observed that 'the country got more wild as we approached ... Interlaken is a most fashionable resort for Americans. We had our first chance to put on style here.'[19] After the experience of being moved by an Alpine sunrise, Bowslaugh spent the next day walking about Interlaken. Her party was met by forty-three busmen ('such an array we had not seen elsewhere') and was then driven to the Grand Hotel Victoria, from which she set off to see the town. She inspected 'three little one-roomed cottages, the homes of poor people and then returned to her hotel, where she saw some of 'the elite' who frequented the Victoria and noted that 'the gowns were very fine indeed.'[20]

Letter writers and diary keepers devoted large amounts of time and paper to their visual impressions of the countryside, motivated partly by cultural norms of what was pleasing – often orderly fields that displayed agrarian bounty – and, to no small extent, by the technology of rail transportation. In contrast with London's omnibuses and their 'bird's eye' view of its streetscapes, rail promoted a panoramic view of the landscape (although these tourists may have experienced panoramas initially as urban commercial phenomena). Belgium's countryside impressed Hall, who admired it from his train carriage window. With its 'magnificent' long avenues of walnut trees that stretched for miles, the entire country seemed to him to be one 'enormous' wheat field, 'broken only by these lines of trees.'[21] Travelling from Paris to Lyon on the train, Pack described the scenery as it unfurled in front of him: 'we passed some fine vine yards acres of them fine patches of wheat – and other stuffs on the farms, some very pretty looking country, hills and streams and cultivated country-side.'[22] From her railway carriage window as she went from Rotterdam to the Hague, Margaret Thomson had a 'nice view of the country. They seem to have ditches instead of fences and innumerable canals. It looks odd to see a sail apparently going across the fields. At one time, I counted sixteen windmills.' Her view also included pastureland, trees in long straight lines or arranged neatly in squares, and clipped willows.[23] Edward Greenshields filled many pages of his 1911 travel diary with descriptions of the scenery he saw while motoring from the Spanish border to Paris, although travel by car meant that the scenery unfolded at a somewhat slower pace than when seen from a train (particularly when tire punctures led to frequent stops).[24]

The Mediterranean coast, whether viewed from train or car window, moved a number of Canadian tourists to effusive outpourings of description of the scenery and of the emotions it invoked. Although they might not have been as enthusiastic about the people who lived along the coast as were British tourists, these anglophone Canadians shared with their British counterparts an aesthetic appreciation of the Mediterranean.[25] Mary Bain was perhaps the most self-contained, describing the scenery from Nice to Grasse as 'grand and I would not have missed it for the world.'[26] As she travelled from the Italian Alps towards Monte Carlo, Ethel Davies was struck by the vivid blue of the sea and decided that 'these southern places are so different from any others I have ever seen. The houses are mostly white so are the roads and rocks. Over the walls surrounding the gardens hang most beautiful flowers and creepers, of every colour – exquisite roses intertwined with vines of heliotrope, Oh the perfume was delicious! We passed many orchards of lemons, orange and olive trees and everywhere grew the palm in great abundance. Such a profusion of gay flowers I have never before seen.'[27] Gertrude Fleming, who seemingly had few qualms about expressing the depth of her emotions to her diary, found herself 'in a trance' at her railcar window as she gazed at the Mediterranean Sea en route to Nice, reporting that 'by the time we got to our hotel I was breathless with the joy of simply being alive!'[28] She spent the next day walking 'in the sun ... I can't get enough of it – And yet nothing seems strange or unfamiliar – I have been here before! And its O the blue sea – and O the blue sky the roses! The violets – the orange groves. The cypress ... the aloe trees, the geranium hedges and best of all the olive!'[29]

Greenshields concluded that the Amalfi coast and the Bay of Salerno 'all made one of the loveliest scenes I have ever beheld. The vivid impression it left can surely not fade away!'[30] Greenshields had, it is true, an artistic eye and literary flair, and he revelled in descriptions of scenery as much as he did of art. Driving along the Italian coast from Sestri, Greenshields was struck by the beautiful bloom of the white heather and its delicious smell and the splendid, fully blooming red rhododendrons.[31] The scenery of Provence, while somewhat wilder than the lush vistas of the Riviera, was also pleasing to him: 'very prominent red crags, steep, and remarkable,' the contrast with the 'sparkling blue sea and the red rocks is very fine.'[32] The drive from Hyères to Aix was 'grand,' Greenshields wrote, with its 'rugged barren and towering rocks' and high tableland that provided a 'splendid wide views and many fertile valleys surrounded by mountains' and one last view of the Mediterranean Sea.[33]

Like the Alps, the volcanoes Vesuvius and Etna combined the promise of thrilling sights with a frisson that a terrible natural disaster could occur at any time. Sailing into the Bay of Naples in 1906, Harriett Priddis was at first disappointed in the view, for it was 'so cloudy.' Fortunately, the sky soon cleared and she 'got a good view of Vesuvius constantly changing, sometimes a pillar of smoke branching out at the top, then again a cloud capped peak.'[34] Amy Redpath Roddick was carried up to the top of the volcano in a chair and, with her husband Reginald, went to the very brim of the crater, 'a truly awful sight,' she shuddered.[35] Langton was able to see Mount Etna 'long before we could believe it was Etna' but despite being close to Vesuvius he did not take the trip up.[36] This may have been because of his (regularly voiced) irritation with workers in the tourist sector, since some of those who did make the trip were less awe- and terror-struck than they were annoyed and frustrated.[37]

As well as pastoral scenes, coastal shorelines, and the Alps, Venice featured in travelogues and tourist writings for its considerable attractions. Those visitors who declared themselves in to be love with Venice listed its churches, galleries, architecture, hotels, and shops as the primary objects of their affection – all sites that had been shaped by human efforts. For some, though, Venice was an impressive mix of natural elements and human artistry. Although at first Priddis was distracted from her initial view of the city by the sight of 'two quite big boys in the water naked,' her attention was quickly drawn back to the larger view: 'everything just perfect; moon rising; sun setting in a perfect glow, Venus rising out of the sea the colouring ideal Venetian.'[38] Certain aspects of Venice were far less impressive when encountered at close quarters. Roddick confided to her diary that it had a 'weather beaten appearance which I did not expect,' and travel writer Erie Waters reported that the canal water was dirty and the houses on the smaller canals 'dingy.' Even Priddis was rather 'disappointed with the Grand Canal' and thought the palaces 'ought to be seen by gaslight or moonlight ... the water is slimy carrying off a lot of rubbish.'[39] Langton, never one to stint with his critcism, was of the opinion, in 1907, that Venice 'as a whole, and also as a detail, is twenty years older and more dishelved and disrepaired,' with its Grand Canal 'going to rack and ruin,' its palaces 'empty and boarded up' and waiting for renters, and its other buildings 'weather-stained,' their plaster unpainted 'so that everything looks twenty years dirtier than it was in my recollection.'[40]

Being in a gondola could make up for some of the city's less attractive features. Fred Martin, lying back in his with its two gondoliers, canopy, cushioned seats and backs, felt 'like the little boy that didn't care "whether school kept or not."'[41] Although her initial impression was disappointing, on their first night in Venice Roddick and her husband 'drifted about' in a gondola under the light of a full moon, entertained by music, the glow of Chinese lanterns, and the colours of the gondoliers' and musicians' clothes.[42] After a few overcoast days in Venice she beheld an 'entrancing sight,' when a ray of sun broke through the clouds over St Mark's Square and lit it up 'with a glory scarcely earthly' enhanced by the rainbow hanging behind it. 'Reg,' she confessed, 'is as much entranced with Venice as I.'[43] Waters, who admitted to great disappointment with Venice's canals and architecture, nevertheless found the

8.2. 'A typical gondolier': Gondoliers were once 'greatly respected' but had become a 'very inferior people' wrote Erie Waters in 'The Home of the Gondolier.' (*Canadian Magazine*, September 1906)

'grace and ease' of its gondoliers' motions 'delightful' (see fig. 8.2). [44] And even Langton left the city acknowledging that he had 'seen the last of Venice for this existence. It kept growing on me and I kept finding more and more places I wanted to see in particular lights of places I wanted to sit at for a long time waiting for foreground.' [45]

From the Café to the Marketplace: Street Life

But just as tourism in Britain combined both the beauties of landscape with the fascination of urban life, seeing Europe also involved its streetscapes and urban life. In their writings Canadian tourists dedicated much space and time to descriptions, analyses, and assessments of public life in European urban spaces. Partly it was cheap entertainment: something to while away the time when one's feet were sore and one's head stuffed with dates, names, and images. For travel writers and those diarists with literary inclinations, there also was the attraction of trying to capture scene and character, particularly if deemed amusing or unusual. Attempts to construct Europe's urban streetscapes were also a way of assessing national character, of judging local morality and decorum, and of marking and noting class, gender, and ethnicity.

These anglophone tourists were particularly impressed by the cafés of Paris and Italy and the beer gardens of Germany, partly because they might seldom (if ever) have encountered their equivalent at home and partly because these were ideal vantage points for absorbing city and town life.[46] From her table at Paris's Café de la Paix, Grace Denison could watch the streets, 'which were always an interesting study to me.' On one occasion, she was 'attracted by an awful looking figure, in a ragged surtout, with unkempt hair and glittering eyes, and as evil a look as one fancies one of Victor Hugo's terrible story people might wear.' A travel companion told her that the man was

> 'a sewer rat' and I watched him with great interest as he crept along in the gutter, his frowsy head covered with the tattered remains of a black fur cap, and in his claw-like fingers a long stick, with a little hook on the end. He paused near me, and his practiced eye saw something shining under a little table near us. He came creeping nearer, and with his stick sent the wee coin flying into the street, where he picked it up and put it directly into his cavernous mouth. Ugh! A horrible, horrible sight, this more than half savage creature, who had no home, and no friend but the Death that would some day end his hideous existence.[47]

Denison recovered fairly quickly from this display of human misery and her party proceeded on to a 'music hall, proper enough, but a noisy place.'[48] That Denison was consciously writing for an audience might well have influenced her description and led her to concentrate on the most disturbing details of the man's appearance in order to add a thrilling hint of (contained) danger to her experience of the Paris streets. There also is more than a touch of the *flâneuse* in this passage, as Denison styles herself as a culturally knowledgeable (the reference to Hugo, for example) onlooker who, although disturbed by the sight of the scavenger, observes and is not accosted by him. Denison did not always take a stance of anonymity, though, for she was not above reprimanding people she met for their behaviour. On seeing that a young working-class woman had been stealing from her bread basket in a Vienna café – where she had gone to hear the Lady Vienna Orchestra – Denison 'pointedly handed it over to the woman and her companions, telling them all 'sternly, "If you are hungry, eat … but let not the maiden steal."'[49]

As well as offering them a chance to see the city's poor, cafés could allow tourists a look at the demi-monde close up. While sitting in a Parisian café with her artist friend, Priddis observed women acting in ways that probably would not be on display in her hometown of London, Ontario. 'One of the fastest looking women I ever saw sat smoking at a table near us. Carrie says she is a very fine artist an English girl there is nothing the matter with her but bad taste in dress, she thinks it is artistic. She says most of the loud looking young women we see here are English. Adele Voorhees passed us by with a young man. Carrie says she comes here nearly every day with a different escort. She leaves for home tomorrow which is fortunate, she does not realize what is all right in New York is very dangerous in Paris.'[50] (Priddis did not specify precisely what she meant by 'very dangerous,' whether Voorhees was courting physical danger or social ostracism – or possibly both – by her public behaviour[51]). Some tourists found Parisian open-air café life simply delightful. John Mackinnon reported that a number of people in these cafés were drinking but there was 'no loud talk and not the least sign' of drunkenness: life 'is a daily picnic, the air always bright and surroundings pleasant' in Paris.[52]

Mackinnon's was a fairly typical attitude, one that viewed the open-air dining and drinking of the café and beer garden as exhilarating and stimulating, bringing men and women together in shared sociability. This sociability also extended to tourists, as when Priddis visited Heidelberg's concert gardens and 'took a stein of beer with the men instead of tea with the ladies for the sake of the song.'[53] Germany's beer gardens were attractive spots in the eyes of these tourists and rarely elicited much criticism for their very open sale of alcohol. To some extent this tolerance is surprising, since we have seen that these diarists and travel writers were not slow to condemn public drunkenness. The beer gardens had an aura of middle-class respectability and security, however, not least because they also offered (along with food and non-alcoholic refreshments) brass bands, orchestral music, and singing. Although not all English-Canadian tourists were devotees of European concert halls and opera, it seems that they thoroughly enjoyed hearing music in beer gardens and in public parks. In Brussels, the 'grand concert' held in the park, illuminated and bound by the Houses of Parliament and King's Palace, was part of the 'Contest of Musicians' that Hall described in his diary. 'It was altogether instrumental and was an opera performed by a very large number of first class musicians and was simply magnificent. The grounds were literally crammed full of people and those who could sat at tables and drank and those who could not get seated walked about.'[54]

Roadside vendors at tourist sites might annoy and pester, but like London's 'Rag Fair,' Europe's open-air markets were a tourist attraction in themselves. Unlike crowds of vendors in rural settings, who disturbed the supposedly pristine landscape and tourists' communion with nature, market sellers were an expected and usually enjoyable part of the topography of European cities. That they might not always live up to their reputation was something discovered by Hall in his visit to the Halles Centrales in Paris, where he and his friends had expected 'to see something of French peasant life but were disappointed. However, we went through meat, fish, fruit, poultry, and butter markets.'[55] For Bain, the Cannes market was a 'distinct contrast to the crowds of fashionably dressed people we have been used to seeing day after day in Nice. Here were huddled together men and women and children of all ages, dressed none too warmly, and doing their best to display their wares to the best advantage. And here were displayed every variety of vegetable, fruit, and flower almost that you could think of. Occasionally you would see one of the poor creatures snatching time to eat a bite. The marketplace is quite in the open with the exception of a bit of roof over the very centre and in the early hours of the morning it was none too warm, but they did not seem to mind, but jabbered away quite cheerfully.'[56] Osła Clouston enjoyed Rome's Rag Market 'very much. Not that it was different to any other fair I have seen on this side. We were jostled about, roared at to buy old pots and pans, buttons, lace, etc.' And she was very pleased that her bargaining with a vender of charcoal stoves resulted in her purchase being reduced by twelve lire.[57] As in London's East End, Europe's streetscapes also offered Jewish areas with markets and street vendors. Driving around Frankfurt, Martin went past the synagogues and then to the 'Jewish quarter which is now a pretty tough looking street filled with junk and second-hand "Old Clo" dealers.'[58] Denison was even less complementary about Prague's 'Jew Quarter, which is just what one could fancy it would be, from the name, a busy dingy odoriferous labyrinth of shops and narrow streets.'[59]

As these comments imply, the cleanliness of streets was a concern.[60] Although they had much more to say about the sanitation of Tunisia and the bazaars of Algiers, these tourists were bothered by the lack of

hygiene in Europe's boulevards and marketplaces.[61] Out for a walk
with a male friend in Rome, Pack caught sight of 'the most primitive
urinal we ever saw anywhere, just a [triangle shape, inverted without
horizontal bar at bottom] in a corner on one of the main streets. Everyone passing. No one seems to think of it. I heard of a man who while
standing making water saw a lady acquaintance coming along he just
turned his head and tipped his hat – these things are all through the
cities on the continent.'[62] Pack appears to have been the only male
tourist to have noticed these public toilets: he was the only one, at
least, to mention them in his diary. It is possible that women tourists
caught glimpses of them too, if they were indeed as frequent and as
prominent as Pack claimed, but they did not discuss them in their diaries, nor were they mentioned in travelogues. Washrooms in other
forms of public space, though, were of great importance to Edward
Greenshields, who pointed out that those on the train from Naples to
Palermo 'were as usual very bad. When Annie asked the conductor
which one was the ladies' room, he said, "Oh! Wherever you like!"'[63]
In Palermo, he was struck by how Italian hotels placed men's and
women's washrooms, 'always together. At Taomina they were right on
the hall, two doors close together. There, near the dining room there is
a large entrance of foyer, which "Messieurs and Dames" may enter
together, and continue on a few feet to their separate apartments.' He
did concede that 'this is not as bad however as on the Pullman car.'[64]
    But the lack of public 'facilities' was even worse than their being
highly visible. In Naples Bowslaugh's customary unruffled attitude
slipped when the beggars and people living on the streets disturbed
the usual calm with which she recorded her impressions. Few of them
could read, she reported, and 'many here have only one room to live
in. Such extreme poverty we saw nowhere else as in Naples and so
sunny and beautiful it is by nature. Yet spoiled utterly by its inhabitants, day and night we saw scores of them lying sleeping on the sidewalks. Some live in houses hewn out of the rock of the hillside. They
have no idea of sanitary arrangements and it is no wonder the mortality rate is so great. Our hotel is large and comfortable with French windows opening on a little balcony.'[65] Pack observed the many fountains
in Rome adding 'but if the people would use them for washing they
would be better off.'[66] That the poverty of southern Italians might be
linked to larger economic issues – one of them being, just possibly, the
tourist trade – did not occur to travellers such as Bowslaugh, who considered the Neapolitan poor to be impediments to her enjoyment of the

Mediterranean, much as the English tourists that Margaret Dixon McDougall had encountered who saw the distress of Irish emigrants merely as spoiling their pleasures.

Smells and Sounds in Urban Europe

Dirt and, in particular, smells were recurring themes in anglophone Canadian tourists' recorded impressions and evaluations, both of which they linked to public health and hygiene. To be sure, their concerns were not merely the product of class-based finickiness, since outbreaks of contagious diseases (or the threat of their imminence) did curtail some tourists' time in European cities or prevent them from crossing borders.[67] But even when cholera and plague did not loom, they were apprehensive about 'muck and stink.' Although most English-speaking Canadian tourists were struck by the cleanliness of Dutch streets, the author of 'Dutch Impressions' warned that, despite 'some show villages always being scrubbed,' Holland 'did not strike me as particularly clean.' For one thing, the ubiquity of its water led to an equally ubiquitous amount of mud and dust; even when it remained in its liquid state, the water of the canals, rivers, and ditches did not look or smell clean, especially because it sat atop several feet of soft black mud.[68] In Rotterdam Margaret Thomson followed a ditch of stagnant water, although 'Father had declared that this talk of sanitation is nonsense the people look so healthy.'[69] Strolls through Italian cities and towns brought forth the most frequent complaints of smells and dirt. Walking through the 'narrow streets' of Naples Greenshields mused that 'narrow and broad are always very smelly in places. I wonder how it is that the Italians do not seem to mind them! Then the drainage in all the crowded streets seems very imperfect.'[70] During his 1907 trip, Langton reported that his hotel in Genoa 'smells like a man but that is because the Germans smoke in it. The Hotel Smith is in the unpromising situation. There is not a dirty and smelly and ragged-rascal-infested a place in Toronto as the arcade into which the front door opens.'[71] By the time Langton and his wife reached Florence, however, he was convinced that 'a change seems to have come over Italy. They are taking to hygiene and when the authorities direct hygienic things to be done they have to be done down to the smallest detail – This town is certainly in its exterior much cleaner than Toronto.' The streets were being swept, washed, and cleansed of garbage; moreover, 'Edith reports there is scarcely a flea left in Italy. "Viva la hygiene!"'[72]

It was not just dirt and smells that made an impact: the landscaping and other spatial features of Europe's city streets were fascinating. Thomson enjoyed the trees that lined the street of Paris, 'what a change from London,' she wrote.[73] Mackinnon, who thought Paris was far superior to the imperial centre, was impressed by the wide boulevards, houses of six or seven stories, and the fact that the government, not individuals or corporations, was responsible for civic beautification. He also was please to nod that in Paris the 'streets are not infested with bootblacks, vendors of papers, matches, laces, etc., as in British cities'; instead, women sold newspapers in 'gay little kiosks' along the boulevards.[74] Martin enjoyed the layout of Parisian streets, with their shaded arcades and the cool breezes that circulated through them and thought that the shops, with their jewelry and fancy goods, were 'very attractive'.[75]

As well as the smells and spaces, Canadian tourists tended to be sensitive to the sounds of Europe's cities, not all of them welcome. The cracking of cab drivers' whips, for example, in parts of France and Italy meant danger to pedestrians and brutality to horses. Most of the complaints about noise (with the exception of the Swiss cowbell and horn) were voiced, like those about smells, with regard to Italy. 'Heat, mosquitoes, and noise,' surrounded Bain as she tried to get to sleep in her Venetian hotel,[76] while Langton, after being woken at four in the morning by 'five tenors, singing under his window, accompanied by a guitar player, fumed, 'These Italians! They conduct affairs in the tenor clef always! They are natural tenors! The performance (prejudice aside) was despicable.'[77] As well as being put off by the housing and lack of sanitation in Naples, Bowslaugh found that city's street noises aggravating. 'Oh the braying of the Neapolitan donkey is indescribable noise such noise morning noon and night, also midnight crying out papers – as did one voice in Rome regularly at four a.m. – just in front of our hotel – much to our disgust and annoyance.'[78] Certainly, donkeys braying and tenors singing were not noises that the Canadiens were accustomed to hearing early in the morning in front of their Vancouver or Toronto homes: complaints about noise in Italy also could be irritation at being kept awake by strange and unfamiliar sounds. Nevertheless, noise in London was heard as the 'roar and bustle' of a modern imperial centre; noise in Italian cities (especially in the south) was heard as the braying and shouting of a society that seem to be semi-rural, and only partially, and unevenly, modern.

'Capturing' Europeans in Photos and Prose

The life of European cities could offer more, though, than offensive smells and obnoxious noises. As well as the attractions of cafés and beer gardens, the street itself offered plenty of entertainment, whether in the form of people simply walking by or driving around, religious and national processions and parades, and parties. Fleming was quite impressed with the 'hundreds' of 'smart carriages' in the Bois de Boulogne, 'and the women frightfully pretty and well-dressed and as artificial as you please – but will you believe it this artificiality has a distinct charm of its own – it occurred to me that in Paris to be natural is to be gauche! And all this little air of I don't know what which I have noticed in the women seems to fit in exactly with the whole atmosphere.'[79] Langton spent a great deal of time during both his trips to Europe 'prowling,' as he described it, the streets of its cities hunting for subjects and locations to photograph and sketch. Many of his subjects were women. In Arles the 'narrow streeted town and its pretty women interesting tho' the women were not my style of beauty not petite or fair enough and a trifle large jowled' (he was happy to take a photograph of one young woman in a public garden, however, judging her 'fair and a capital specimen of the dignified Arles' beauty').[80] His most striking exercise of the male tourist's power was in Florence, where he enjoyed 'poking about the streets at a slow loaf camera in hand stalking genre. I stalked one nun inconspicuously till I believe I frightened her and she dodged into a courtyard to escape me.'[81] While Langton was not always successful in his attempts to represent those European 'others' that so captivated him, nevertheless this and similar diary entries suggest how tourists' gazes might affect the objects of their attention.[82]

Some tourists remained content to leave their impressions to the written word. The streets and public squares of Heidelberg held many amusements for Margaret Thompson. On her first visit there, she watched a singing society on its way home from a concert tour accompanied by a band, banners, green ribbons, and small and 'grown up' girls dressed in white with green sashes and carrying flowers. A few days later she and her family went to a local fair, which was very '"interessant"' and featured rows of stalls with brushes and clothing for sale, boat swings with 'various mottoes,' and a merry-go-round, 'another dreadful looking thing – going up and the carriages going round quite fast.'[83] Tourits in Paris on Bastille Day were thrilled by the sight of street dances, fireworks over the Seine, and illuminations of the Eiffel Tower. 'Festoons of gas banners with globes hung from gas post to gas post for miles and then the coloured lights' and other decorations hung in the Tuileries, wrote Martin, and 'altho' any amount of wine drank I did not see a drunken person.'[84] (The all-night singing and playing that followed did not, it seems, bother Martin.) As with the services discussed in chapter 7, religious processions often fascinated these Canadians, although whether they approved of them was another matter. In Naples Langton watched the residents mark Good Friday by carrying five or six groups of images, including one of the Virgin that was 'attended by girls in white,' who were followed by a group of black-garbed women; the procession also included three gentlemen in evening dress, the 'Bishop or Archbishop' under a canopy and 'clothed from head to toe in a big purple garment,' and thirteen life-size statues that represented the Last Supper. Those who carried the statues did not leave a very favourable impression on Langton. He noted that when they set them down they gesticulated to each other and the crowd. 'Their appearance in dirty linen overalls ... and the way they joked, talked, and laughed with themselves and the crowd took away any appearance of solemnity.'[85]

Members of the European military, who also made up part of the spectacle of urban life, were not seen to be anything but solemn and purposeful. Although tourists were struck by rural European women's appearance and deportment, the martial masculinity displayed in squares and piazzas also had their attention, initially attracted by the sights and sounds of military bands playing in town centres.[86] At the fair in Heidelberg, Thomson's eye was caught by an inspection of German troops. 'They looked awfully well and drilled splendidly only they march most peculiarly,' she reported, and she did not care for some of the dozen different kinds of uniforms on display. Nevertheless, the inspection impressed her: 'from the specimens we have seen of the armies, I wouldn't advise France to try for Strasbourg for a while yet,' she wrote.[87] Fleming spent one entire December morning watching 'the little French soldiers who are drilling all over the place. They are so *real* in their workaday clothes – dusty and dirty and not a bit quick and clean like the British but they really look as if war to them might mean something. I was glad to see it as one rather despised them before. They come in from the country and start their drill.' After eating their lunch under a tree, 'off they go again hard at it with much dash and swing – it is delightful.' Fleming was far less impressed with the officers, dubbing them 'horrid little men ... they are the most impossible creatures all curled hair oiled to a dazzling radiance and moustaches fierce ink and wax. His eyes bulging at women and stinking of scent! I can actually smell him as I write!'[88] She found that in Rome the sight of 'all sorts of beautiful soldier men with sort of winged helmets' that, she estimated, made them appear about nine feet tall, far more dazzling.[89]

Bain shared Fleming's fascination with the appearance of Italian soldiers and noted, in 1910, that 'the military element is very prominent everywhere in Italy and these soldiers with their varied uniforms and capes, and in some cases with wonderful helmets of gold with black or white horsehair hanging away down the back, lend a very picturesque element to the scene.'[90] European police, though, rarely appear in these Canadian tourists' accounts, perhaps because varying degrees of competence in French, Italian, German, and Dutch meant that these tourists had fewer direct encounters with them than they did with London's 'bobbies.' But their uniforms also attracted far less attention than those of the military. Pack, as he watched the King of Italy ceremoniously opening a building, observed that 'some of the policemen here wear an ugly gray hat with a peak and a very loose strap about three quarters of an inch wide all gray suits as well.'[91]

The sight of Europe's royalty was worth a mention in diaries and letters home. Greenshields's visit to the Alhambra was marked by the arrival of the Spanish queen, who came dressed in black and accompanied by many soldiers and cavalry. That evening she appeared at a concert in his hotel, having changed into pale blue and a 'white, fur-trimmed wrap' but still with a hefty military entourage. 'It was a fine show,' he decided.[92] A few days later the King of Spain was on the same train as Greenshields, bound for Madrid. Lots of people turned up to wave the monarch off; overall, thought Greenshields, 'he seems a very pleasant and agreeable young man.'[93] While staying in Dresden, Osla Clouston had to get up 'right away this morning to see the German Kaiser arrive he is such a good looking chappie.'[94] Few, though, recorded seeking out Europe's royals as assiduously as they did their British counterparts. While the crowned heads of European countries were interesting figures and certainly worth a look, they were not desired and personalized as were Queen Victoria and her descendants (despite the fact that some of the European monarchs they saw were, like the 'good-looking chappie,' related to the Windsors).

If very few Canadians were able to enter the social circles of Britain's elite, the salons and parlours of France, Germany, Belgium, the Netherlands, and Italy were even less accessible to them. Only a very small minority of the Canadian tourists considered here had the types of connections that would allow them to move in such circles (although they might participate vicariously by reading novels such as Maria Amelia Fytche's *Kerchiefs to Hunt Souls* or Alice Jones's *A Privateer's Fortune*).[95] The Cloustons were among their ranks. One of her excursions into 'high society' was an evening outing to the British Embassy in Rome with her mother and sister (but even then she only met mostly other 'foreigners'). The entrance hall was lined with 'a good number of flunkies in pinkish white livery and powdered heads.' Above them towered a 'long and imposing' staircase with women who 'looked so well in evening dress coming down it.' Lord Currie, the ambassador, brought Monsignor Stonor to meet them: 'such a swell in a long red silk cloak small red cap, gold chain with an emerald cross hanging from it and one of those rings with a large stone in it … a very nice old man with a round pink face and said he would do his bit to get us permission to see the Pope.' After introductions to other guests, the Cloustons settled down to watch the people since, after all, the 'French paper says "La mieux fleure de la société étrangère" was there'. If the gowns on display were not quite as interesting as Osla might have hoped, nonetheless their wearers – Russians, French, Italians, Germans, Japanese, and English – were. 'I think I liked the Japs best as they knew about as few people as we did. A little Jap lady dressed in white satin and pearls was quite swell.' Their evening ended at midnight, with Osla having seen 'Princess Victoria Colonna, the beauty of Rome … [and] the Duke of Cambridge looked fat and fatherly.'[96]

Entertainment and Display: Casinos and Exhibitions

If only a small number were afforded the chance to see the 'beauty of Rome' close up or meet the Roman Catholic hierarchy, European glamour and luxury were not entirely hidden from the tourist's gaze. Casinos fascinated a number of these Canadian tourists, particularly Monte Carlo.[97] Few went to gamble, as well as by only Bain and Fleming appeared to have wagered and won. Rather, the attraction was the spectacle of organized, large-scale, and socially sanctioned gambling, as well as by many other entertainments, conducted in a beautiful setting and patronized by Europe' elite. At the casino's music hall, Mary

Bain saw a performance 'of the variety order and considerably superior to what we see at the Orpheum.' She was especially taken by the
balance artist, who with one hand picked up a women sitting on a
chair placed on a table, while in the other, he held another seated
woman.[98] Bain also observed, on another visit, that there were so many
palms in the casino that it 'almost gives the effect of a garden. All this,
with the throngs of fashionably-dressed people continually moving
about, makes a very fascinating and animated scene.'[99] George Pack
was held up at the main door until he produced a travellers' cheque,
and yet he found Monte Carlo's 'interior in keeping with the outside.
Magnificent. Marble pillars. Giant paintings. Grand elevator. Chande-
liers four of them hanging from the corners of the paneled ceilings.'[100]

Paeans to Monte Carlo's glamour were accompanied, however, by
disapproval of the casino's main purpose. Fleming enjoyed a 'delightful' dinner in her nearby hotel, accompanied by lots of champagne
('which irritates me as it *will not* do anything to me') and watched as
'lovely women dressed not in evening dresses but with lace gauzes
and hats' were escorted by smart-looking men. But the casino itself
'seemed so sordid and didn't look like fun at all.' She also disliked the
casino's dim lighting and its silence, 'the only voice being the horrid
nasal voice of the croupier.'[101] Still, she was pleased to have won seven
pounds at *rouge et noir* and went back the next night 'but it was hateful'
– a man had shot himself 'and this news upset me so that I had to be
almost carried back to the hotel by B!'[102] Thomas Langton observed
that there were 'a great many women – or ladies – quite alone both at
dinner and at the Casino and most of them were rather dignified people' and that he had 'enjoyed the experience very much,' nevertheless
'[we] do not care to repeat it.'[103] In 1895, even Edward Greenshields,
who was very interested *in rouge et noir* and observed that the casino
was so orderly that 'ladies young and old' walked about unattended
and apparently unafraid of robbery, thought it 'saddest to see the very
young and the very old of both sexes playing. The whole place leaves a
very unpleasant impression, and must do a great deal of harm. It
should be closed up.'[104]

Despite their condemnation of Monte Carlo, it is possible that they
were more ambivalent. At Cannes, in 1913, Greenshields and his wife
dined at the casino in a 'beautiful and artistic looking room, all fine
white walls cornice and ceiling, with red carpets and red covered
chairs, and the electric lights looked well in the white ceiling.'
Although he did not find that the cooking measured up to that offered

by the Carlton Hotel, nevertheless, it was 'very good.' After dinner he watched 'all the finely dressed women' enter the Baccarat room and then the citizens of Cannes arriving for a ball hosted by the casino, 'all dressed in their best, but quite a different show to the gowns that went into the Baccarat room!'[105] George Pack observed that Monte Carlo tried to make its visitors 'forget your sorrows and yet [it is] a place that brings sorrow and death.' He himself soon forgot the latter and instead wrote of the glamourous interior and the fact that he saw 'Mrs Rothschild' gambling. 'She won very little while I was looking but I was told she cleaned up quite a bit before she left.'[106] Even children might be taken to casinos; during her stay at St Malo, in 1894, Clouston recorded a number of trips to the nearby casino to hear the band, see variety performances, and attend children's dances.[107] The disapproval voiced of the casino may well have been sincerely felt. It does seem, however, that these tourists succumbed (at least for a moment) to the casino's class-based allure, and then felt it necessary to quash such feelings by reminding themselves of its 'immoral' nature.[108]

Casinos were public spaces in that they were, technically, open to a wide range of tourists (Pack observed in of Monte Carlo that no locals were allowed into the casino[109]), but they were private in that they limited access only to those who could pay for a ticket or an entrance pass. Like their counterparts in Britain, Europe's commercial, industrial, and imperial exhibitions occupied a similar, albeit not identical, position. They charged admission fees but such attractions generally admitted a much wider range of 'the public' than did casinos. Historian E.A. Heaman has argued that only a small percentage of anglophone Canadians passed through the gates of displays such as the 1873 Vienna Exhibition and the Paris Exhibitions of 1878 and 1900. Even so the Canadian press ensured that its readers were kept informed of these events and of the impressions of Canadians who attended them.[110] Halifax's *Morning Chronicle* warned that 'great undertakings, such as is the Vienna Exhibition, are not set going without trouble' and that Vienna was no exception: it had not been ready in time, the weather had been bad, and hotel and lodging-house keepers had charged 'extortionate' prices. Happily, matters had taken a turn for the better, with exhibits almost ready, the weather had 'settled down into the loveliness of an Austrian summer,' and the 'caravanserai-brigands have been reduced to honesty by the prompt action of the government.'[111] The press also mused on other aspects of international exhibitions, such as the absence of representation for New Brunswick in Paris in 1878 and the contrast between that display and the Philadelphia Exhibition of 1876.[112] Although not impressed with the exterior of the Canadian pavilion at the Paris Exposition of 1900, W.R. Stewart, in an article in the *Canadian Magazine*, admitted that inside all was well arranged, with displays of natural history, agriculture, education, objects from private collections, and its reading and drawing rooms with Canadian papers and portraits by Canadian artists.[113]

Some of these Canadians clearly enjoyed continental exhibitions more than the art galleries and museums that they felt a cultural duty to visit. Hall, who was not fond of the religious themes of the painting in the Louvre, was much more interested in the art on show at the Paris Exhibition. 'The most noticeable feature in the French paintings is the number of entirely naked subjects,' he noted and on his second trip, he 'finished the Art Galleries, French, Italian and English of which the English is by far the best, the Italian not being worth looking at' (although he reported that the Italians had the best statuary).[114] As well as art, English cut glass and French jewelry caught James Hall's eye but, overall, he and his friends judged that the exhibition in Paris '*tout ensemble* was not equal to the Philadelphia one and the inside is certainly not so well arranged for serving.'[115] The Canadian Trophy, though, pleased Hall, as it was 'one of the most prominent features of the exhibition,' and the area in which it was displayed was crowded during his visit.[116] Arranging the world's nations according to their showing was a favourite pastime at both British and European fairs; Hall, for example, thought Spain was 'very poor, Russia, good, Austria, fair.'[117]

Exhibitions could intrigue and delight the visitor, but they also exhausted a weary tourist's senses (not to mention feet). Despite the smaller scale of an Italian 'centennial' display in Milan, Martin wrote that 'it made me "*tired*" the very moment I saw it, as it brought back very vividly the days spent at Philadelphia in 1876,' with its displays of silk spinning, velvets and satins, women's snake-skin boots. Moreover, 'the women working in the silk spinning department had such a queer local dress looked like silver spoons with the handles stuck in the hair.'[118] And even a display such as the 1900 Paris Exposition might not be enough to change a disillusioned tourist's mind. Flavelle visited numerous exhibits, including the Canadian pavilion, but he remained unimpressed by his 'poor' and 'very crowded' hotel and was 'sick of the place. Nothing I can drink. Food not extra scorching hot.'[119] On leaving Paris and its cultural attractions after a week's stay, Flavelle was 'never ... so glad to get out of a place.'[120]

Yet not everyone was so jaded. Grace Denison, who like Lauder, Boulton, and other women travel writers created an inquisitive and humorous persona, decided to hire a 'chairman' to take her about the sights, as she was determined to be rested '"for the *real* Paris, which is to be seen only by gaslight."' Thus she was taken down the street of 'The History of Habitation,' where she saw homes that ranged from the 'first three unhewn stones' of the earliest age to 'luxurious mansions of the Eastern Monarch,' a 'spotless Hindu house,' the 'flat-roofed Jewish home' mentioned in the Bible, 'the giddy Chinese pagoda and the curtained Persian or Moorish building, in which odalisques, with sequin chains in their hair, sold perfumery and carved knick-knacks.' But her attention was caught by

> the raised dwelling of the tree people (in which sat grotesque creatures), reached by a slat ladder of interlaced, tough vines, and the mud villa of the aborigines, the wigwam and the tent, the thatched cottage and the tiled mansions, all in proper sequence, formed a vista of surpassing interest, bringing really before one's eyes things read of and imagined. It was worth going to the Exposition only to see this one street; one brought away a queer, uncanny memory of gaunt creatures in the 'stone age,' huddled under a faded canopy of leaves and upright slabs of stone, almost naked, in their wrappings of leather and hair, with unshaven beards and unkempt locks. If they *were* Parisians gotten up for the occasion, it was a splendid disguise, for they only looked half human (but some Parisians are not even *that!*).[121]

Other anglophone Canadian tourists accepted that exhibitions would be organized around national typologies, but Denison's account commented most explicitly on the racial and ethnic categories that shaped her observations of the displays. As her description about the possibility of Parisians being 'gotten up' in stone-age drag suggests, Denison was aware of the staged nature of what she saw. She already had encountered such a performance, a 'funny little happening,' at a small exhibit in Berlin, in which a labyrinth had been constructed to end in a 'Turkish Harem, the curtains over which were drawn aside by an immense Nubian slave.' As Denison left, she remarked (in English, thinking she would not be understood), '"well, really, you look more like a plantation nigger than a *Nubian!*"' To her 'startled horror, the fixed black eyes rolled and twinkled, the black face expanded in a grin as wide as it was good-natured, and the "Nubian" replied, "God bless

you, Missie, so I is! a real South Carline nigger." In the midst of a laugh
at my expense, the Nubian deserted his post, and told me a long story
of his misfortunes alluding with shame-faced disgust to his masquer-
ading costume.' Denison was unable to describe his outfit to her readers, as it 'consisted of next to nothing at all,' but she noticed that his
necklets, armlets, and anklets 'were very handsome imitations of Eastern jewellery.' Denison, who was with a party of friends that included
a toddler, observed how good 'the Nubian' (who remained nameless)
was to the child, 'leading him safely through the labyrinth before he
raced back to what he had, I am sorry to say, described as "all dis d – d
foolishness."'[122]

The Poor, the Worker, and the Peasant

Thus even the exhibition, with its avowed intent of educating North
American and Western European publics with presentations of 'truth,'
might be a masquerade, using a type of blackface to represent Aborigines and people from the East. However, other kinds of public institutions in Europe were presented, and generally accepted, as sincere and
honest depictions of social organization and national character. Schools
and universities in Germany were particularly interesting to anglophone Canadian tourists. 'Life in a Typical German Boarding School,'
reported Eleanor B. Moss in the *Allisonia*, provided its female students
with 'conscientious training' for very useful occupations: housework
and the education of one's own – or other's – children. The regimenta-
tion, though, did not allow time for the 'development of the heart' and
for students to get to know one another. Upon graduation, however
they were not just 'blue stockings' in their store of general knowledge,
for they also possessed tact, sympathy, and broad-mindedness.[123] At
Rudesheim, 'a clean prosperous place with four thousand people,' John
Mackinnon watched as teachers and children went off to school at seven
each morning. 'All were clean, looked healthy and were dressed alike.
The teachers marched ahead, followed by the boys in military fashion,
the girls came next, equally trim and well dressed.'[124] Clara Bowslaugh
had a similar impression of educational facilities in Switzerland, where
she noticed a 'public school building better than any in Canada.'[125]

Fewer English-speaking Canadians went to tour Europe's philanthropic and social welfare institutions than they did in Britain; they
may not have had the same kinds of contacts that allowed them to enter
such places on the Continent. Denison, though, went off on her own to

see the Cologne hospital, doing so, it seems, on a whim, the thought coming to her after dinner one afternoon. After dodging 'squads' of German soldiers, with their 'handsome "tin hats" and long boots,' she boarded a tram that took her to the hospital. Her visit was not entirely successful: she managed to see a ward full of small boys, 'unwholesome looking' who covered up 'their pale little faces with the corners of unpleasant looking sheets.' The only official Denison could find was a friendly and pretty 'Sister,' who spoke English, German, and French simultaneously in an 'indescribable confusion that fairly bewildered me.' Although she took Denison on a quick tour of the women's and children's wards, she begged out of the men's wards, telling Denison that they were an uninteresting lot. Denison considered pressing her case but decided that she had had enough of the 'peculiar stuffy odor of this melancholy looking place … Yes, there are seven distinct bad smells in Cologne, and the smell in this hospital is one of the worst. It is a horrid place, and I don't like to think about it.'[126] She had a better impression of Paris's Hôtel Dieu. Although Denison had to find someone to vouch for her credentials to gain admission as a visitor (and that person, according to her, wildly exaggerated them, calling her a 'famous nurse from America'), she saw the entire institution and left with 'a vision of sisters of charity, jolly patients, ghastly wounds, and emaciated men and women and children, and suddenly appearing now and then the grandest bath on wheels, with a hose for hot and cold water and a thermometer and a douche, and altogether the completest and most convenient thing, which I don't think we have in our hospitals in Canada – at least I've never seen one.'[127]

The bodies of the sick and injured did not faze Denison; those of the dead were another matter. Without warning, her guide took her party through the door of the famous Paris morgue, where she immediately came 'face to face with – a corpse! The poor man was perched behind a glass refrigerator door, in a sitting posture, his hands folded on his lap, and his poor white head propped back against a rest.' She was equally horrified to see the body of a younger man, 'with a cruel wound over his temple, his little felt hat sat rakishly on his clustering curls, and a sad sort of smile on his white face.' Denison was grateful that these were the only corpses on display, and she and her party 'hurried past the row of glazed compartments with shrinking horror, and emerged to find our carriage with white cheeks and faint hearts.' Her guide was disappointed, though, that only two male bodies were on show: 'yesterday there was h'eight, five h'of 'em females."'[128] Mackinnon's visit left him far less moved; he noted only that people who had drowned ('by accident or design') were 'exposed three days for recognition. Every time I passed there were four cadavers on the slab, all of the poorer class.'[129]

Poor and working-class people could be observed in other ways and in other places, not just in hospital beds and on the slabs of a morgue. As in London, European tourism included shopping: Canadians bought shoes, hats, and dresses in Paris, glassware in Venice, jewelry in Florence, Geneva, Paris, and Venice, lace in Brussels, perfume and toilet water in Grasse and Cologne, and trolled the aisles of Paris's Bon Marché for a variety of goods.[130] But shopping also might involve inspecting the people who were making the lace, glass, perfume, and china taken back to Canada as souvenirs. Judging from the frequency of accounts of touring lace factories, lace making had particular appeal. Langton toured a Venetian establishment in which children were taught to make lace: 'when they pay their workers anything it is six pence a day and they sell their day's worth for ten pence, so that if a shawl costs one hundred francs it means that some girl has been at work at it for one hundred days and received two pounds and ten pence for the damage to her eyesight, or less than four dollars a month.' Black lace, he judged, was even harder on the eyes, so it was made by prisoners in their 'dungeon cells, which are of course so much lighter than daylight in the open air.'[131] Bain spent over an hour watching 'the girls' in a Venice factory making lace and bought a number of pieces, 'at what was supposed to be a great bargain, but probably was far too much for it. When you come across a smart Italian salesman or saleswoman, they are pretty slick.'[132] In Brussels Martin thought that lace making 'must be very trying to the eyes and they work so fast,' and the rates of pay were quite low. He secured a 'very *fair sample.*'[133] Denison, although she had entered the lace factory 'fully determined to damage one of my hundred franc notes' and found lovely pieces, was too upset by the thoughts of the damage done to the workers' eyesight to buy anything. 'My heart turned from them with a great cry of pity for my sister women, who barter God's precious gift of sight for twenty cents a day. I never can look at the fairy, delicate leaves and flowers of a bit of Brussels lace without feeling again the sharp, needle-like pain, and seeing the red-stained eyes of those poor lace-makers.'[134]

Few were as concerned as Denison – and, perhaps, Langton – about workers' health. Most tourists who visited factories were primarily interested in various aspects of the production of items and in feeling they had received some kind of bargain for purchasing goods there. Bain found her visit to Grasse's perfumery 'not particularly interesting as there were no fresh flowers being utilized at this season.' Her next stop was a candy factory where she watched candied violets being made; after that she toured a pottery factory.[135] Langton was delighted (and more impressed) with his serendipitous sighting of macaroni being made. His party was invited off the street to step into the hotel kitchen and watch the process: 'they were delighted to perform for us and showed us the pasta being kneaded with a big wheel turned by two men.' Langton admitted that 'the room looked what Baedeker calls "the Italian standard of cleanliness" but for all that when you consider that a fire is necessary for some part of the process and the only outlet for smoke is the door and that the room is not much higher than a man's head and the macaroni hung at about 5'8" and there were a good many people in the room and that they had something else to do than keep out of the way of the macaroni ... the macaroni was exquisitely clean.'[136]

These accounts of trips to lace and perfume factories and Langton's description of the macaroni makers reminds us of the power of the tourist trade's infrastructure to shape what was seen most directly and what remained either hidden or was only partially revealed. Although these tourists may well have glimpsed heavy industry in their European travels, they do not appear to have been invited to inspect its processes or comment on its workers. Travel to industrial areas to look at factories or assess working-class residential districts did not feature prominently in their European itinerary, although as we have seen they visited such sites in England, Scotland, and Ireland. Moreover, as historians of other tourist landscapes, such as nineteenth-century New England or early-twentieth-century British Columbia, have pointed out, industrial enterprise (or an area's potential for it) might attract tourists, drawn by the promise of seeing industrial capitalism's potential fulfilled.[137] Thus, for example, even though by the 1900s some tourists were well aware of Germany's industrial production of armaments, in their accounts 'work' in the European context was artisanal and directed towards the production of consumer goods, not towards the apparatus of modern industrial, not to mention imperial, societies.

Similar processes shaped anglophone Canadians observations of agricultural labourers, a group with whom they were fascinated. Travel writers suggested that agricultural work was particularly interesting and should be noted while in Europe. Alfred Andrews told the

Christian Guardian's readers that in Switzerland's Aarve Valley, 'the Swiss women, as usual, are at work in the fields – digging, pulling flax, binding or carrying home huge bundles of wheat from the fields,' while their menfolk ploughed and cut grain.[138] And from their train windows and carriage seats Canadian tourists also paid heed to Andrews's advice: numerous diarists, male and female, commented on the gendered organization of farm work in Europe. As he travelled from Bellario to Bologna, Langton 'thought that driving is the way to see the manner and customs. One kept seeing the odd things done as one drove through the streets of villages or between fields. Women hoeing the crops with a mighty hoe … Women are very industrious and do all kinds of work even what is generally supposed to be men's work. We saw them of course harvesting but also mending the roads, building walls, or carrying the stone and mortar for the work, and in one instance I saw a woman doing the Irish hod carrier up a ladder to a scaffolding … Men smoke and play bowls or rest and eat dinner which women bring them.' His landlady at Asciano had told him that such was the case; he had seen men carrying all other kinds of goods, such as 'baggage, wine casks, bags that seem to be presently remunerative.' Nevertheless, 'I do not remember ever seeing a man carry a load of … grass or hay or stone – the women have monopolized the carrying trade.' Unlike other observers of this division of labour, though, Langton did not automatically assume that Italian peasant and working-class women were downtrodden 'beasts of burden.' His impression of their return from the fields after a day's work was of 'such handsome tall and sturdy women with plenty of gay kerchiefs and looped up gay coloured dresses and singing and tramping a way with a vigour that told nothing of a twelve hour day's work.'[139] Ellen Bilborough, though, was far more judgmental, writing in her diary beside a photograph of Italian women knitting that their 'men folk' were quite lazy and lived on their wives' labour.[140]

It was not just Italian society that permitted such inversions of gender roles among the peasant class. In the Swiss village of Biasco, near the Italian border, Mackinnon reported seeing fourteen women (and only three men) carrying heavy loads of wood, grass, and ferns; some using creels and others with their burdens tied up only in ropes. 'I mention this trifling incident to show the terrible hard times women have in this country. Not only valleys but mountain sides are dotted with wretched-looking hamlets, seemingly abodes of stalwart misery.'[141] In Valais Canton, women carry 'manure in creels and are at other kinds of slavish work – mostly carrying a load of something. Their yellow, withered appearance indicates want and hard usage. Goitre and cretinis, which seem to result from poor lodgings and living, are frequent in this section.'[142] Mackinnon was disturbed by women's outdoor and labour-intensive work. He counted twenty-four women washing clothes in the river on his way to Turin ('no labour-saving appliances here,' he sniffed)[143] and in another part of the Alps he observe the 'disagreeable feature' of a number of women at work mowing, scything, carrying grain, and in one case, breaking stones (he did, though, admire their industry).[144] As he watched more women than men working in Germany's fields, Martin wondered 'who did the housework and got the meals.'[145]

A number of these Canadians were surprised to see Italian women who worked as train guards and flag attendants along the line in northern Italy; they did not, though, use this as evidence of women's degradation.[146] Although Mackinnon might have typified the scenes he saw as 'trifling incidents,' depictions of peasant, working-class, and colonized women performing heavy labour deemed by middle-class Western observers to be the province of men had a long history and a meaning of more than 'trifling' significance. Near Alassio, in 1907, Langton took a picture of an elderly couple with a donkey – the man riding, the woman walking – and commented that 'this old country is going on as it did twenty years and for the matter of that I daresay two hundred years ago.'[147] Such scenes represented societies that had not progressed sufficiently along the evolutionary scale, societies in which women were not only performing heavy work but were doing so within full view of the public's – and in this case, the foreigner's – gaze, not unlike the living exhibits of 'primitive' labour displayed in exhibitions and world's fairs. Moreover, the Canadians tourists who commented on such scenes of primitive, backward 'otherness' might also reassure themselves that they – and the nation they represented – were members of a more progressive, enlightened, and civilized society.[148]

Tourists and National Ethnographies

As well as their interest in gendered divisions of labour, anglophone Canadian tourists took pains to describe various forms of food, dress, habits, and manners, and thus created ethnographic portraits of the Europeans they observed. Like with their observations of gender and labour, the vast majority of these representations were of – or at least

8.3. Posing for the 'tourist gaze?' (*Canadian Magazine*, August 1909)

were construed as being of – European peasants. Published travel-ogues used these dimensions of European societies as signs of the essential and unchanging: Dutch women's headdresses on the island of Marken, for example, signified to the observer that here in the fishing village was an enclave of pre-industrial society untainted by modernity – despite the frequency with which Marken turned up on tourist itineraries and the infrastructure that brought tourists to observe that area (see fig. 8.3).[149] But as we shall see, antimodernist yearning was not the sole theme in diarists' and letter writers' descriptions of Europeans. Distinct types of dress and ornamentation were fascinating, but they also could represent societies that might well benefit from encounters with modernity.

Much the same might be said of European food, even though few of these Canadians wrote about 'peasant' or working-class fare: their observations on the subject of food generally were limited to what was put in front of them in hotels, restaurants, and cafés. So far as the diarists and letter writers were concerned, there was no consensus on what constituted national cuisine in each of the countries they visited, other than the realization that it tended to be very different from what they had consumed across the English Channel (not to mention across the Atlantic). Not everyone shared Flavelle's low opinion of the French food and drink that made him so glad to quit Paris. Hall was quite pleased with the good – not to mention, at least in his estimation, cheap – breakfasts he enjoyed in France and Switzerland (although he found the wine on the Rhine steamer rather expensive).[150] Fleming's Christmas dinner in Nice took her mind off her 'wail for home and mother,' as she dined 'very grandly with lots of wonderful champagne with some special vintage burgundy as a grand *pièce de résistance!*'[151] Meals in luxurious hotels may well have had a better chance of pleasing Canadian palates, since Bain's Christmas dinner in Venice, 'while not quite of the regulation order ... was very nice indeed.' Instead of turkey and cranberry sauce, she and her husband had pheasant, 'and the platter was decorated with the head and tail of the bird arranged in such a way that it looked as if the whole pheasant was there. The only real English thing about the dinner was a blazing plum-pudding.'[152]

Bain also was unimpressed by her first meal in Italy, as the soup served in her Genoese hotel 'was some awful mixture which looked for all the world like curdled milk and sea-weed and tasted not much better.'[153] Other tourists were at times confronted with food and drink that they saw as either a bit strange (the good-looking cake from an Antwerp bakery that disappointed Thomson[154]) – or revolting. The sherry and custard that Thomson was offered in Lugano was 'disgusting,' while Pack, who normally had nothing to say about his meals in either Britain or Europe, noted that the 'queer lunch' served by his hotel in Milan consisted of 'roosters' combs, curried rice beans and 'a lot of other stuff all mixed together we had to fill up on it or nothing some of the people could not eat it.'[155] Langton, who was not one to shy away from commentary on his surroundings, wondered how the proprietors of his hotel in Solva kept up 'the supply of chickens and wizened apples'[156] and noted, too, that he had eaten chestnut pancakes in Florence. 'I am glad,' he mused, 'that I can eat things that do not look like anything I ever ate before.'[157] The cauliflower soup in his hotel in Siena was not appetizing ('if I were not informed that it is made of good stuff I should not know it from grateful and comforting warm cauliflower water'), but he and his wife appreciated the cook's other dishes, such as cauliflower with custard cream, spinach soufflé, kidneys, and artichokes.[158]

Clothing, though, bore the burden of symbolizing national distinctions or, at the very least, attracted the intense gaze of curious tourists. As a number of cultural historians have argued, nineteenth-century bourgeois nationalisms often fixated on dress – frequently that of the peasantry – as an expression of the authentic 'national spirit' that they themselves might no longer possess (or have only in attenuated forms).[159] It might take, though, expert knowledge to seek out and inspect such embodiments of nationalism. Frank George Carpenter, writing in 1886 in the *Ottawa Daily Free Press* as a special correspondent from the Netherlands, told readers that 'the typical Dutchman of fiction and the past' could 'no longer be found in the streets of Rotterdam and Amsterdam.' Those searching for his 'long pipe, his knickerbockers, and his baggy form' would have to travel to the country's villages on a Sunday. In urban centres Holland's 'richer element, such as you see in the great hotels or at The Hague ... are no different in dress or manners from the ladies or gentlemen of the Paris salons or the London drawing rooms.' Notwithstanding Carpenter's belief that railroads and telegraphs 'are cosmopolitanizing the nations of the world,' change was rapidly occurring and that, by 1896, 'all Europe would probably be dressed in the same clothes,' it was still possible to find 'Holland families, and the laborers who hold to the customs of their fathers, and some of their dresses are quaint.' Such picturesque sights, observed by him on his train ride from Rotterdam to Leyden, in 1886, might consist of women's short black silk skirts, pink bodices, coral necklaces, and starched and lace-trimmed white caps, the latter adorned with gold balls and plates. Carpenter did not leave men out, observing that they were 'quite as queer in their dress as the women,' with their bowl-cut hairstyles, collarless shirts with 'gay neckerchiefs' fastened with large gold brooches, wide and short black velvet trousers held up with wide belts, and 'rings of gold in their ears.'[160]

Travel writer Emily Weaver made a similar point in 1911, in an article in the *Canadian Magazine*. She reminded readers that both American and European women were 'in thrall' to fashion but that fashion was constantly changing shape and undergoing metamorphoses, thus threatening to envelope the wearer's humanity. However, Weaver admitted that Western society loves beauty in all its aspects and that beauty included dress. To see an attractive type of dress that represented a more healthy continuity, she suggested her readers go to Brittany, where they might see women's clothing that had been handed down over generations. 'For the tourist, however,' Weaver admitted, 'those very fashions have the charm of novelty, of change, depending not on time but on place.' Some variation might be found from village to village, but peasant women (and only peasant women, Weaver made clear) wore wooden shoes, very wide skirts, and their aprons and caps outdoors. In keeping with the drab weather of the Côte du Nord, the women wore no ornaments and their dress was dreary and sombre (young girls, though, who like their Canadian counterparts were influenced by Parisian fashion, were 'bent on novelty at all costs of grace and convenience'). Lest her description sound too bleak, Weaver reassured readers that the massed effect of the white coifs at weddings and in the marketplace was quite picturesque and that in southern Brittany women wore gay, almost tropical-coloured clothing at weddings (see fig. 8.4). But this attention to dress did not mean that Breton women were selfish and narcissistic. Weaver ended her article with the story of a shipwreck in which a number of women drowned and those 'pitiful Breton maids' dressed these women in their own *coutumes de fête*, giving up their most 'prized possessions for strangers.'[161]

Swiss peasants attracted their fair share of commentary. E. Fannie Jones, whose 1898 articles 'Swiss Life and Scenery' were full of contradictory assessments of the impact of 'civilization' on rural Swiss society, was taken with the locals. Their 'physique is far above the average,' she wrote, and their faces were intelligent, particularly those of the women. The latter boasted 'bright dark eyes, good features, great masses of hair, and their dignified manner free from all shyness and awkwardness give unquestionable evidence of unusual natural refinement.' While in many ways Jones saw these peasant women as inhabiting a premodern world, one that the modern traveller could enter in order to be 'soothed and refreshed in body and soul,' she also saw a strong resemblance between Swiss peasant women and the 'New Woman': the former wore trousers to work in the fields and could only be distinguished from the men by their red handkerchiefs (on Sundays, though, they delighted Jones with their black dresses and red Tuscan hats trimmed with ribbons). The uniformity of Swiss women's dress had an important social function, Jones believed, as it headed off rivalry and jealousy between women over matters of dress (see fig. 8.5).[162]

Breton and Swiss peasant women's clothing served as an index of a community's moral probity, linked to its ability to steer clear of forces that would corrupt its simplicity and organic unity (unlike the clothing of the 'New Woman' that Jones and Weaver themselves, as travellers and journalists, personified, clothing that often drew opprobrium for its unsettling of unity and tradition – a contradiction that Jones did not dwell on). Another perspective argued that peasant dress could be an interesting sight, but it also might be a sign of backwardness that was

8.4. Dress as an index of community morality (*Canadian Magazine*, February 1911)

not to be admired, let alone emulated. As Kristen Hoganson has pointed out, American travel writers might see folk costumes as attractive but they also were 'suspect, for they connoted poverty, hard labor, ignorance, and backwardness to the observers who eyed them from the perspective of the fashionable world. And in contrast to fashion, which implied a transnational community of consumption, folk costume implied provincial sensibilities and tightly constricted communities.'[163] Osla Clouston, a very eager participant in the transnational world of fashion, voiced such thoughts. On a tour of Norway in 1895 Clouston and her family visited a Lapp village; her estimation of Laplanders was certainly not shaped by a wistful longing to be rejuvenated by their company. 'They are such queer dirty people and their dress is principally long loose fur gowns with belts round the waist and the men wear long painted caps the women square ones.'[164]

Clouston enjoyed herself more at Marken Island, where her father attempted to photograph a 'peasant woman' and her baby: 'but she

8.5. Note that the illustration for E. Fannie Jones's 'Swiss Life and Scenery' depicted healthier, more robust women workers than John Mackinnon's picture of wretched drudgery. (*Canadian Magazine*, August 1898)

would not let him but covered the child up and scowled. The women wear two long curls hanging down each side of their faces and have a most picturesque and pretty costume. They hate to be photoed [sic] but Ned by giving some money managed to take a group. The men wear large trousers almost like Turkish ones.'[165] The Marken women's clothing fascinated Simmonds, although she thought their dress was 'odd-looking.' Like Clouston, though, Irene Simmonds admitted that 'they all seemed beautifully clean, both their clothes and their homes.'[166] Just as Mary Leslie had paid special attention to Dutch women's head-dresses, so too did Margaret Thomson, who called them 'very funny,' with the tight-fitting 'white thing' that went over the head, shoulder cape, and brass ornaments on either side of the face. 'Some people put

their hat or bonnet on top of that and just make themselves look ridiculous. We have not seen so many wooden shoes but we have seen a
great many plush slippers.'[167] On getting ready to leave Europe to
return to England, Thomson realized that she had not been keeping
careful enough notes as to 'the costumes' and wrote in her diary of the
various ones she had seen, including Italian women with their lace
headscarves, the 'low necked dresses and elbow sleeves' of Switzerland's female citizens, and the 'huge' bows that German women tied to
their heads.[168]

It was not just peasant women's clothes that attracted Thomson's
attention, though. She noted that Venetian women wore their scarves
over their heads, 'and their slippers have no straps round their heel'; in
Lugano, she wrote, the townspeople were wearing a 'peculiar kind of
sandal thing' with stockings and a thick wooden sole, held on by a
leather strap.[169] She was in the habit of jotting down remarks about
fashions that she found noteworthy, such as the 'lower middle class'
Parisian women who went about hatless and the women cyclists in
bloomers: 'some of them look neat and some do not,' she decided.[170]
Some fashion choices were not just noteworthy but were tasteless, as in
the Alps near Lucerne where Thomson was struck by the way 'the people dress or rather hike up their dresses utterly disregarding appearances. I saw quite a few with their dresses hiked up round their waists
with a piece of string' (she did not link the two directly but went on to
note that there also were a number of honeymooners in the hotel).[171]
James Hall was a bit taken aback by Parisian women's display of their
ankles and reported that 'the women here and to some extent in London don't care a darn about showing their ankles but pull their dresses
up in some cases to their knees any way.'[172] This is not to say that Hall
disapproved of feminine attractiveness, as he found Belgian women to
be 'the prettiest as a general rule that we have seen since leaving home,
far ahead of either the English or French ladies, are with better figures
and have prettier faces.'[173] Edward Greenshields was always happy to
comment on feminine countenances that he found appealing, and the
sight of many beautiful women in Rome's Corso brought great pleasure to Gertrude Fleming.[174]

Whether these Canadian tourists experienced feelings of delight or
distaste about European men and women in 'peasant' clothing, they
could and did not ignore the fact that such scenes were not entirely
innocent of the tourist trade. At Mount Etna in 1910, Estelle Kerr
attempted to ignore her fellow tourists by trying to conjure up Greek

8.6. For Estelle Kerr, this 'ancient milkman' ostensibly 'truly belonged' to her ancient – and imagined – past. (*Canadian Magazine*, December 1910)

and Roman warriors, as well as Sicilian peasants, who would not 'strike the jarring note.' She immediately stumbled into what she initially thought was the 'authentic past' but found instead to be a group of people posed for a film. Despite robbing the scene of 'its poetry,' though, this knowledge did not 'entirely destroy its beauty' for Kerr, and she was grateful that even for commercial purposes 'the place could for a short time be peopled with types to which it truly belonged'[175](see fig. 8.6). (During her visit to Switzerland Jones praised the 'simple-minded' peasants who 'have not yet been rendered self-conscious by the presence of the modernizing tourist,' but she also was quite offended by those tourists who took photographs of them during church services. Where, Jones wondered, is our 'nineteenth-century civilization' heading?[176]) Langton was more cheerful (if also cynical) about staging the appearance and behaviour of locals for tourism. After watching a company of Swiss volunteers and their 'sweethearts' at Interlaken, the men in brown homespun and the women in Swiss bodices and starched white sleeves, he mused that

> these parties did a little but not much towards dispelling my notion that the Swiss nation is a thing of the past and that the present Swiss nation is one of hotelkeepers, woodcarvers, washerwomen, and curiosity mongers.

They all seem given up to entertaining the visitors more even than in
Italy. All the big houses in a town are hotels and the middle sized ones are
pensions ... They make a pretense of keeping up the women's costumes,
alpen horns, yodeling, wood-carving ... as national institutions but they
are principally used for the visitors. Most of the population carve wood
into bears and chalets all winter to sell in the summer and they sell better
through the medicine of a young woman dressed in the dear delightful
Swiss costume.[177]

Although tourists in other contexts attempted to link specific sexual
practices to notions of 'national' character, there is less evidence to suggest that these Canadians travellers saw Europeans in these ways.[178]
Direct discussions of sexuality were not as common as discussions
about dress or various kinds of social habits; however, from time to
time tourists and travel writers did comment on sexual mores and
practices that they linked to particular national boundaries. Not surprisingly, given English-speaking Canadians' history of associating
'the French' with libidinous sexuality, France was one of the few countries that evoked such discourse: a number of travel writers, for example, warned their readers that prostitution was sanctioned and
regulated in Paris (see fig. 8.7).[179] Their warnings were borne out for
George Pack, who after returning from a day of touring Versailles, was
walking down a side street with his male friend when they were
stopped by a 'girl smoking a cigarette ... she asked both Mr McBride Sr
and myself inside.' But, Pack assured readers, he and his friend did,
'not go there.'[180] In Lyons Pack was a bit non-plussed to see couples
openly and without any self-consciousness kissing in public: 'Seems
not to be anything out of the ordinary.'[181] After observing that mixed-
sex bathing occurred on the beach near Marseilles, Pack left the barber-
shop with his friend 'and had a good laugh. While we were looking at
some postcards on a stand a fine looking chap came up and talked
with us asking us if we would care to see some girls dancing the can
can. A dozen of very pretty girls. But as we knew what he was we did
not have anything to do with him he also wished to sell us some pictures of girls partly nude but we were buying only the other kind.'[182]
   Greenshields, not one averse to 'to the nude, or anything witty,' found
that a 'Humourists' Exhibit' in the Palais de Glace on the Champs
Elysées was simply too 'coarse' for his taste, with its cartoons that joked
about the female anatomy and masturbation. They were amusing, he
admitted, 'but there is so much of merely the lower animal side of man

8.7. As the female figure in the foreground suggests, the Moulin Rouge might be much more than a 'dance hall.' (*Canadian Magazine*, March 1893)

constantly shown, and with no context for it, simply the fact, bare and unpleasant, that to other nations who cannot see this peculiar humour, they are merely indecent.'[183] To be sure, Greenshields could not be described as prudish for his time. The frank announcements of two Dutch acquaintances of their wives' pregnancies at first took him by surprise, 'but there was nothing coarse in their way of talking – they simply took the arrival in a perfectly natural and unaffected way, with no attempt at concealment.'[184] Hall was impressed with Belgium's pretty women but thought far less of the country's well-known Pisse-Mannikin Fountain, judging that 'the less said about it the better.'[185]

Few women tourists had much to say about the sexual practices of European men (as we have seen, Mary Bain's anecdote about the Neapolitan store hinted at sexual danger). An exception was Emily Murphy, who informed her female readers – on no uncertain terms – to be on their guard when dealing with men in Hamburg. Do not look them directly in the eye, 'no matter how venerable' they might appear, she advised. A Hamburg man 'is sure to give [a woman] a knowing glance, and perhaps follow it up by some ingratiatory remarks, thereby hoping to lead up to his evil and unmentionable purpose.' However, in keeping with her mistrust of almost everything English, Murphy also hastened to add that 'some of these men, I am told, are loose-moraled Englishmen who come abroad for adventures,' even though they might have come from respectable families.[186]

In general, though, unpleasant 'foreign men' were more likely to have bad manners than to be sexual predators. Railway carriages were particularly apt to expose women tourists to the former, as it might be difficult to move to another carriage, and middle-class norms of feminine propriety often stopped these Canadians from asking the offending party to leave. 'There really should be a law,' thought Margaret Thomson, 'preventing people from eating garlic before traveling or at all event compelling them to travel third class. Poor Annie suffered agonies and we all got out the smelling salts. As we neared Turin the officer took off his white gloves and got his moustache in shape.'[187] Denison had less compunction about demanding that her fellow travellers refrain from annoying behaviour. On the train to Salzburg she rebuked an elderly Tyrolese man for smoking in a non-smoking car and a few days later, while en route to Munich, she reprimanded a pair of university students for smoking. The students proceeded to tease Denison and, in particular, the other young woman in the car; they stared at them and made speculative comments about their nationality.[188] Yet it was not just men that might irritate: Denison disliked many of the German women she encountered too, 'elderly *frau*[en]' who scowled at her and deferred too much to their husbands.[189]

There were other ways of judging and evaluating nationalities. Hall commented on the untidiness of the farms in France, which did not measure up to England's standards.[190] Langton seemed pleased that he had picked up the 'Italian' habit of bowing to company whenever he entered or left a room; he also prided himself on not being overwhelmed by Italy's art or history and recorded in Siena that 'we have been poking about so far looking at the ways of the people rather then at those of their ancestors.'[191] Notions of German and Swiss punctiliousness and mannerly conduct were expressed by Canadian tourists, often approvingly. But such approval was not without reservations. Langton noted of Switzerland that it was not 'a free country. Everybody is superior there.' He found few class distinctions, and 'there is a distinctiveness about the Swiss which has its points.' Nevertheless, 'one does not like to be asked for "tickets" in the tone of a drill sergeant,' an experience that he contrasted with being on an Italian train where conductors always asked very politely for his ticket.[192] Furthermore, as Denison's account of the German students on her train suggests, stereotypes of national conduct were not always borne out in actual encounters.

Sound, too, served as a marker of national difference, both in the level of noise that anglophone Canadian tourists assigned to various countries (with, as we have seen, Italy judged as one of the loudest) and in the sounds of 'foreign' languages. German and Dutch were often deemed unpleasant to the English-speaking ear, because of their 'guttural' intonations. Italian and French, however, were not always melodious, either. Although, as we have seen, some English-Canadian tourists spoke French and had a smattering of Italian, they described the sounds of both when spoken by working-class people or by large groups in public places as 'jabbering,' a description that characterized the French and Italians as apelike. Thomson, for example, thought that the Parisian women at a Bon Marché sale were like 'monkeys in the zoo'; they pulled 'the things about,' she wrote, 'and snatched whatever they fancied.'[193] Such objectification was much more common *and* much clearer in places such as Gibraltar and north Africa; nevertheless, it also was similar to the constant complaints about throngs of beggars, adults and children, who pressed themselves on tourists and disturbed – if only temporarily – their ability to watch and record.

Those 'Other' Tourists

But as much as they recorded beautiful landscapes, entertaining street life, souvenir vendors, or women hauling stones, anglophone Canadian tourists evaluated and judged other nations also by observing and assessing the other tourists that they met during their travels. That they brought already-formed conceptions of 'an American,' 'an English,' or 'a German' tourist to their encounters with men and women from other countries is not, of course, surprising. However, as well as shedding light on their ideas of national behaviour and characteristics, these also were some of the few times when they recorded impressions of middle-class – in their words – 'foreigners.' Furthermore, a consideration of considering how they looked on others leads us to the equally important, and related, question of how they saw themselves as both English-speaking Canadians and as tourists in Europe.

As we might expect, other tourists were encountered in public sites: hotels and pensions, trains, and tourist attractions. Few Canadien tourists spent much time in the homes of middle-class Europeans, although they might run into friends and acquaintances in the course of their travels.[194] Their encounters with other tourists ranged from observing and recording their impressions of their behaviour to more intimate mutual exchanges in which the Canadians shared their impressions of their travels and swapped details of their backgrounds and lives.

Americans, the English, and Germans were the most commonly noticed other tourists in these encounters.[195] To be sure, some Canadians dubbed themselves Americans; the majority, though, also wanted to establish that American tourists were clearly from another country and had distinct norms and values when it came to culture and social mores. Cleveland's 'Mamie in Venice,' according to travel writer Albert Carman, on a break from her job as a 'typewriter' for a Milan firm, was unable to transcend her brash, materialistic, and overly practical disposition. She had no sense of romance and history and incurred the rebuke of a poet she met for insisting on speaking of Venice as a modern American city.[196] In Denison's account, American tourists tended to be uncouth and frequently lacking in the cultural and linguistic sophistication that would allow them to truly appreciate Europe. They often, for example, were unilingual and frequently needed her assistance as a worldly (not to mention polyglot) traveller to explain their surroundings, help them order meals, and deal with service staff. However, as compensation for their ignorance, American tourists tended to be honest, open, friendly, and extremely grateful for her assistance.[197] Exceptions did exist, such as the party of young American women who spoiled Denison's contemplation of the Matterhorn with their 'unconscious vulgarity, their hideous candy gnawing and gum chewing, their insane chatter and their profane mention of the Matterhorn and Jung-frau and Pilatus as "dear old daisies," or "cunning old things."'[198] Moreover, although Denison believed that American women were much more emancipated than their decidedly non-liberated European counterparts, she also thought they had taken their freedoms too far and had become bossy and domineering.[199] (She was, though, extremely impressed on the boat home by the calm courtesy of that 'much-maligned Lady who once was nominated for the office of chief magistrate in the neighboring republic.'[200]) In their Paris-bound train carriage Edith Chown and her aunt Alice ran into two Americans who were 'so delighted to see some English speaking people that they quite forgot themselves. They were that kind that are so noted over here and give the Americans such a name' (it did not help matters that they lit their small stove on the train, scaring the French passengers who thought it was a bomb).[201]

Edward Greenshields, who so prided himself on his knowledge and appreciation of European culture, made fun of one of his fellow hotel guests in Venice, an 'apparition ... in the shape of a young lady from Boston, who had a New England conscience.' Her father had given her money for a European tour in exchange for his permission to marry a baker, but 'she said "St Mark's church was beastly, and the Doge's Palace horrid," and as for the Grand Canal, she had been once up it and nothing would induce her ever to go near the dirty, nasty place again. All she wanted was to be done with lover [the baker], and back in her dear old Boston again.'[202] In Switzerland Harriett Priddis met an American woman who did nothing but complain about the country's slow pace; she was more impressed with a 'very nice United States' lady she met in Germany. 'Americans *can* dress to travel that is sure. Why I do not think them lady-like I cannot make out, this one is particularly quiet and intelligent, but somehow she lacks the hall mark.'[203] (She might have unconsciously answered her own question when observing her friend's prospective sister-in-law, an Englishwoman whom Priddis found 'unattractive' and 'big-boned.' Wondering why American men did not marry their own 'dashing countrywomen' and instead opted for British women, she decided 'it must be the softer voice that wins them.'[204])

There well may have been more to their critiques than simply a straightforward nationalist distaste for one's southern neighbours. Upper-middle-class Americans were themselves engaged in put-downs of middle-class tourists, particularly women, who were openly mocked in American publications as being poorly educated and uni-lingual boors, incapable of properly appreciating the cultural riches of Europe. It is possible, for example, that English-speaking Canadians might have read satires such as Charles Loomis's 'Seeing France with Uncle John,' in which ill-informed middle-class American tourists race through Paris, ignorant of what little they see ('doing' the Louvre in twenty minutes, for example, and merely driving by the façades of other great cultural institutions.)[205] As Levenstein has pointed out, 'with so much written about American ignoramuses, cultured tourists were not surprised to encounter them,'[206] and Canadians may well have been conditioned to expect such encounters. Moreover, the fact that so many anglophone Canadian tourists singled out middle-class American women as being particularly irritating may not have been simply the result of animosity towards middle-class American women per se. By the late 1880s a significant proportion of Americans abroad *were* middle-class women, whose custom was courted by the French tourist industry but whose overseas presence was vehemently attacked by upper-class male writers in the United States.[207] Carman's 'Mamie in Venice' was not an isolated or unique figure in the world of transatlantic tourism.

If American tourists were unsophisticated and a bit déclassé, English tourists had their own failings. Europe shifted English-speaking Cana-dian tourists' vantage points on Englishness (although, as we shall see, the trip across the Channel to England could alter their perspectives). Some were quite glad to encounter other English-speaking travellers. Fred Martin enjoyed his first-class carriage ride to Bonn, which he shared with an English gentleman and a Belgian countess, her daugh-ter, and governess, since all spoke English fluently and 'were very talk-ative.'[208] However, moments of tension (at the very least, ambivalence) often punctuated these exchanges. Margarett Thomson made friends with a mother and daughter from London as they shared a carriage from Dieppe to Paris, while in Pisa Gertrude Fleming and her husband befriended a young English clergyman and his wife who were staying in their hotel.[209] 'They were frightfully interested in one being Canadi-ans [sic],' she wrote, 'and I know were secretly surprised to find us exactly like everyone else!' Fleming found herself surprised to learn

that they were 'truly British except that they are friendly but I supposed *that* is in account of his *cloth*!'[210]

A conviction that the middle-class English people that one met
abroad were often unfriendly and snobbish emerges in a number of
accounts. Writing of his fellow guests in his Cannes pension, Carman
described the English people as needing to take 'two or three trips
abroad before they become companionable to strangers whose heredi-
tary burying-places they do not know.'[211] They also, said some, refused
to learn other languages.[212] 'Nothing,' Langton wrote, 'can look more
stupid than an Englishman addressed in French and understanding
not – I have looked it and I have seen it and I have even acted as an
interpreter for a tongue-tied Englishman and have seen the Frenchman's face light up with joy at finding himself understood.' Never
afraid of mocking himself, though, Langton added that 'I have had a
voluble French sentence fired at me in consequence and have seen the
Frenchman's face resume its pained expression.'[213] On his 1888 trip to
Europe, Langton recorded that the American 'ladies' he met 'constantly struck us as being more wide awake than the English people
we have met' (although he noted that this extended to the ladies' belief
that they could talk about their fellow diners in their 'ordinary tones
[far reaching ones] ... without any danger').[214]

While in Europe again in 1907, Langton felt himself followed by the
'ever present traveling Englishwoman,' who could be identified easily
by her bringing of guidebooks to the dinner table. In his sketch of one
such character with jacket, sketchbook, wide-brimmed hat, and skirt
with a back pleat for easy hiking, he noted that they have a 'manly
tramp for the most part ... [and a] simplicity of costume which I am
sure must be the most comfortable.'[215] Langton's descriptions of
English women tourists feature bodies in constant motion and activity,
ones well placed to enjoy vigorous activities, who also appear quite
masculine in their appearance and abilities. Langton vowed that he
would not change his wife for the 'longest-legged reddest-elbowed
armswinging ... handiest bicycle-riding golf-playing mountain-climb-
ing Englishwoman in or out of England,' but he admitted that she, his
wife, was not much good at walking.[216] Not only were these women
too masculine, not surprisingly – at least as far as Langton was concerned – they were single. In Siena Langton and his wife went to visit a
church with a 'fear [of] old maids. The Italians are rapidly getting the
impression that the English are a nation of old maids. They trooped
flapping into church prayer books in one hand and Zed Baedeker in

the other.'[217] Perhaps Langton's customary confidence in his masculinity was a little rattled by the independence and physical vigour of these 'manly' Englishwomen.

Some Canadians did identify with 'the English' but simply did not want to see them on the Continent. Ned Clouston complained to his daughter Marjorie, while staying at Aix-le-Bains in 1904, that 'the place is full of stuffy English people – not a foreigner to be seen anywhere. I haven't any special desire to see my own race when I am abroad.'[218] Not all, however, shared his perspective. Mary Bain met an Englishwoman 'much-travelled ... with beautiful hands and a fearfully deaf husband,' who had a 'desperate prejudice against Americans and Germans.'[219] Although such beliefs were not held universally or even consistently, 'Mrs Smallman,' the Englishwoman, was not alone in her dislike of German tourists. As we have seen, Grace Denison was not impressed with the Germans that she encountered in her travels, and Langton quickly grew exasperated by the behaviour of German tourists in Capri's Blue Grotto. They sang and 'take their pleasure [in] shouting ... It goes without saying that they are always talking' whenever they meet; at the dinner table in his hotel the German party put an end to 'polite conversation' for the 'clatter is diabolical.' Langton described a German doctor he encountered in Syracuse. 'He talked with people eight or nine away ... eating all the time, shoveling in only the faster the more he talked. His eye dilated ... pointing the argument with the knife or fork, or both' (this behaviour was in contrast to 'the Italian' who, no matter how agitated he became, was always graceful).[220] On another trip to Europe, almost two decades later, in addition to the omnipresent English spinster, Langton reported that his path 'has so far been beset with Germans.'[221] However, the next month, on meeting a German baron who was married to a Russian woman, Langton was relieved to think that, although the former supposedly did not understand English, 'our strictures on foreigners happened to be confined to Italians.'[222]

Americans, the British, and Germans were not the only nationalities that Canadian tourists encountered in Europe. Even though she was annoyed with Cook's travel agency for keeping her waiting in her Frankfurt hotel, Priddis was delighted to meet two 'nice looking Finnish ladies one speaks English very well.' These Finns had seen a lot more of the city than had Priddis and her party, since they spoke German; furthermore, Priddis felt, they probably knew what they wanted to see.[223] Denison, who seemed to have Priddis's knack for striking up conversations with strangers, met a very charming Venetian woman who was married to a Russian officer and had a most interesting discussion with her as they shared a train carriage between Prague and Vienna. Her enjoyment of the Venitian woman's company, though, did not extend to that of her young son, in whom she saw all the hallmarks of masculine 'Tartar' dominance.[224]

Not only were they acutely aware of the presence of other tourists, most of these English-speaking Canadians were also conscious of their own identity as tourists. To be sure, they were capable of adopting an anti-tourist stance as an attempt to elevate themselves and their motivations for being abroad above the 'common horde' of their fellow tourists. Bain, for example, noted somewhat disdainfully that there were more tourists in the Place de la Concorde's tea shop than Parisians.[225] Italy, in 1888, appeared to Thomas Langton to be ridiculously 'visitor-ridden ... Some places seem to exist for the visitor only – of these Venice is chief.'[226] He also thought that Interlaken was a 'nice place though horribly given over to the visitors.'[227] Despite these comments, there is little doubt that the vast majority of these Canadians saw themselves as occupying Gertrude Fleming's 'proud position of a tourist.' Langton articulated this identity consistently throughout his diaries; he was more than aware of his desire to photograph, sketch, and write down every impression he formed of the landscape and, especially, the people. On the train from Alassio to Genoa he travelled third class but was unable to sit back, relax, and stare out of the window for fear of getting dirty: 'therefore unless for short distances I fancy that our study of the natives at short range has come to an end.'[228] In another Italian town he lamented that Sunday was not a good day for tourists, since the streets were full of local residents 'in their best (and their best are not as picturesque as their second best) who also have nothing to do and the tourist is not as free to poke about and look at things under the battery of eyes.'[229]

English-speaking Canadians in Europe either asserted or were reminded of their own national identity. Sophie Pemberton quarrelled with another woman in her pension in Paris, whereupon the latter 'goes around telling people after all I am a little colonial girl *mal élève*.'[230] On telling a German man at their hotel dining table in Rome that she and her party were Canadians, Fleming reported that he was delighted, as these were the first Canadians that he had met and besides he was 'secretly astonished at one being white!'[231] At times other tourists mistook them for Americans, and gaffes were committed by those who might be expected to know better. Margarett Thomson 'felt very badly' for herself and her companions when an American party in Cologne mistook their accents for American and insisted that they did not 'talk like Canadians.'[232] Thomas Langton, though, reacted with his typical aplomb when he responded to a Virginia woman's comment that '"I thought you were not an American and yet I thought you could not be English." Thus are we placed. A kind of hobbledehoy nation!'[233]

Anglophone Canadians had mixed reactions when they took their leave of Europe. Most probably would have agreed with Margarett Thomson that they had 'enjoyed the continent so much.'[234] Judging by the number of them who returned for a second (and, for some, third or fourth) trip, Canadians in Europe apparently did have a 'happy holiday.' This did not mean that their feelings towards European cities and country-side were uncomplicated. In Europe, history and culture were to be found alongside peasant communities that appeared to be structured by atavistic and primitive gender roles and relations (not to mention antiquated technology). Such scenes threatened to undercut the world-liness and sophistication symbolized by the treasures of high culture and arrays of consumer goods displayed in Europe's art galleries, museums, cathedrals, and shops, items that testified to their residents' status as citizens of modern, cultured, and cosmopolitan nations. How could English-speaking Canadian tourists, who thought of themselves as possessing modern, Protestant, bourgeois, urban sensibilities (no matter that they might live in small-town anglophone Canada), recon-cile such accomplishments with rural European women's drudgery in the fields and their male counterpart's (supposed) absence of manly, bourgeois initiative and work ethic? These sights might undermine the claims of European nationalists: possessing an agrarian, 'folk' culture might not be the key to the nation's vigour and purity but, rather, to its uneven and only partially achieved modernity (as was the case in Ireland). Furthermore, how did English-speaking Canadians tourists' acknowledgment of the glories of the Louvre, Uffizi, and Sistine Chapel accord with the disdain and contempt faced by many European immi-grants – not to mention French Canadians – in English Canada during this period?

Confidence in their own superior class position played a role in all of this, intertwined with particular notions of history and progress, con-ceptions of ethnicity, and the condescension of 'city folk' towards rural ones, notions that could be displayed towards European immigrants and agricultural communities within Canada.[235] And hovering over their assessments of Europe was the imagined community of Britain. Despite its foibles and failings, the vast majority of these Canadian tourists understood Britain to be the epitome of a 'real' nation and, in contrast they found countries such as France, Germany, and Italy – no matter how pleasing many of their aspects – lacking. Many of them would have agreed with Fred Martin that, on crossing the Channel, they were 'glad to be back in old England where everyone speaks English and under our own flag once more. It really seemed like coming home.'[236]

9 'A big Old Country Car, Speeding around a Winding Road': Transatlantic Tourism in the 1920s

It might be logical to think that Canadians' travel across the Atlantic underwent a fundamental shift in quantity and quality of after the first World War. The 1920s have been characterized by a number of Canadian historians as witnessing the start of a new 'Canadian' identity, a period when English-speaking Canadians in particular began to fashion their own cultural references into a nationalism that was increasingly less attached to Britain and empire.[1] Canadians' experiences in the First World War and changes in international relations in the interwar period also meant that Canada became an increasingly independent player in diplomatic affairs, a factor that, it has been argued, led to an English-Canadian nationalism separate from British identity.[2] Might we expect, then, to see anglophone-Canadian tourism in Britain, in particular, affected by these developments in ways quantitative and qualitative, perhaps decreasing in number and experienced by tourists whose sense of nation was increasingly distant, and distinct from, that of the 'mother country'?

It is difficult, probably impossible, to state unequivocally that the numbers of tourists who visited Britain and Europe in the 1920s and early 1930s decreased, increased, or remained the same. The number of travel diaries in the national, provincial, and local archives does not rival that of the 1890s and 1900s, although there may be many reasons to account for this phenomenon. Nevertheless, samples of passenger lists taken from *Canada: An Illustrated Journal*, as well as travel writing from the *Canadian Magazine* and *Christian Guardian*, suggest that men and women from across English-speaking Canada still saw going abroad as a significant aspect of being both a 'Canadian' and, equally importantly, an educated member of the middle class. And, while some tourists argued more strenuously for a distinct 'Canadian' perspective on what they saw, smelled, heard, and ate, they also demonstrated the complicated and ambiguous attitudes towards Britain that had marked the prewar travel writings produced by Canadians. Moreover, Europe still held much of the same cultural and social fascination it had before the war, although other ways of seeing the Continent and other considerations also came into play. Transatlantic tourism in the 1920s was marked by both change *and* continuity.

The Great War and Its Aftermath

To suggest that the war introduced only temporary changes – the cessation of recreational travel being the primary one – to overseas tourism would be naive. If nothing else, the growth of 'battlefield tourism' in the immediate postwar years and the arrival of tourists whose perceptions of the places they saw were overlaid with the more recent experiences of 1914–18 were critical changes.[3] Furthermore, periodicals such as *Canada: An Illustrated Journal* and the *Canadian Magazine* continued their presentations of Europe and Britain during the war years, although their coverage was less about the delights of London's shops or Venice's canals than the experiences of Canada's troops stationed overseas and the damage done to the European landscape.[4] The *Journal* ran articles entitled 'Canadians at the Front' with lists of the dead and wounded, and its 1915 article, 'Back from Germany,' told of the treatment of Canadian prisoners of war, including a report of bad food in the prison camps.[5] 'Note of the Week: Canada's Wards' applauded the 'strong support' for the war demonstrated by Canadian Native people, to the extent that eight battalions composed of Native soldiers could be formed. 'Nothing,' the writer believed 'has better justified the existence and the policy of the British Empire than the fervour with which the subject races have supported our cause against the Hun,' for all over the world 'chiefs and tribesmen' had sent money, goods, and men (not to mention public prayer). While 'the number of Indians in Canada today is small,' and there was no 'call' for them to go overseas and fight, nevertheless they supplied a 'substantial quota of their manhood. This is clear proof that in the treatment of her wards Canada has been just and kindly.'[6]

Native veterans such as Frederick Loft might not have agreed, nor would the Cayuga activist Deskeheh, whose trip to first Britain and then the League of Nations in 1922 to argue the case for Six Nations' sovereignty does not appear to have been covered by the *Illustrated Journal.*[7] But the war's many other effects were reflected in that periodical's pages. Its February 1919 list of 'Canadians in London' included many army, navy, and air force officers. Over the following months, the British government announced free fares for British women who wanted to join their Canadian husbands (also a way of promoting closer ties of emigration and trade between the two countries). The Repatriation Committee advertised its work in bringing Canadian soldiers' British-born dependants to Canada, and a special supplement on the Canadian YMCA featured its war work in England, France, and Siberia.[8] And on 4 July 1925 G. Howard Ferguson, the premier of Ontario, left London for Lille, from where he and his party toured the nearby battlefields before resuming other official tour in Britain.[9]

Anglophone Canadians with sufficient money and time also had other places to visit. While advertisements for cruises and trips to warmer, sunnier climates can be found in the pages of the press prior to 1914, they seem more prevalent in the 1920s. The White Star Dominion and Red Star Lines offered 'Winter Cruises' for either Egypt and the Mediterranean or the West Indies that would last either forty-six days or a month.[10] (Another advertisement featured the Dome of the Rock in Jerusalem and Martinique's rugged, not to mention volcanic, beauty[11]). 'Golf and Summer Bathing in Winter,' suggested the CNR, were available in the 'alluring resorts of the West and south [which] invite you to continue Summer's popular pastimes under warm, sunny skies' in British Columbia, California, Florida, and other southern states, and the West Indies, Bermuda, Cuba, South America, and the Mediterranean.

Yet, as it did before the war, publication in *Canada: An Illustrated Journal* monthly lists of Canadians staying in London hotels (many of them with West End addresses), personal columns, and announcements of steamers arriving from or departing for Canada suggests that a constant stream of English-speaking Canadians continued to go to Britain and Europe. In October 1927, for example, Mr and Mrs J.E. Baillie and Miss Baillie of Toronto were in London, staying at 33 Inveress Terrace, while fellow Montrealers might be able to look up Mr and Mrs Baldwin at the Waldorf, in response perhaps to an advertisement in the *Canadian Magazine*; J.H. Campbell of Montreal had chosen the Hotel Cecil (see fig. 9.1).[12] A week later Mrs Mercer J. Adams and Mary Adams, we learn, sailed back across the Atlantic, having spent the winter and early spring in Italy and the French Riviera and the summer 'motoring'

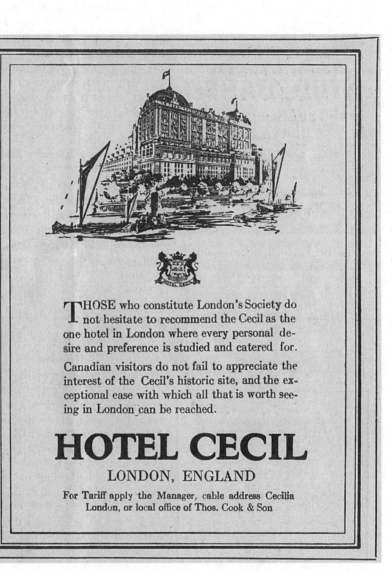

THOSE who constitute London's Society do not hesitate to recommend the Cecil as the one hotel in London where every personal desire and preference is studied and catered for.

Canadian visitors do not fail to appreciate the interest of the Cecil's historic site, and the exceptional ease with which all that is worth seeing in London can be reached.

HOTEL CECIL
LONDON, ENGLAND
For Tariff apply the Manager, cable address Cecilia London, or local office of Thos. Cook & Son

9.1. History and refinement for the Canadian tourist (*Canadian Magazine*, January 1925. Reproduction courtesy of the Archives of Ontario)

CANADIAN DEBUTANTES AT COURT.
Presentations Last Week at Buckingham Palace—Description of Dresses.

9.2 Mrs A.G.L. McNaughton, Miss Edith N. Baldwin, and Mrs J. Reid Hyde at Buckingham Palace (*Canada, an Illustrated Journal*, 1 July 1927)

through Britain.[13] And although many of the home addresses given are from Halifax, Montreal, Ottawa, and Toronto, the *Illustrated Journal* also testifies to the travels of men and women from cities in the Prairie Provinces and British Columbia (Winnipeg, Saskatoon, Regina, Edmonton, and Vancouver), as well as smaller places from across the country (Ste-Anne-de-Bellevue, North Bay, Guelph, Kitchener, Virden, New Westminster, and Salmon Arm).[14]

Judging by the coverage in *Canada: An Illustrated Journal*, upper-middle-class English-speaking Canadian women followed in Joanna Wood's prewar footsteps. Decked out in sequinned and embroidered georgette, taffeta, mousseline, chiffon, and satin, with bouquets and perhaps ostrich-feathered millinery, they might pose for a Bond Street photography studio, before they were presented at the court of George V's (see fig. 9.2).[15] While most of the travel considered here was for culturally instructive pleasure trips (or, as in the case of Oxford-bound Kathleen Coburn, was combined with the more specific pleasures of university education), postwar efforts to foster international peace, cooperation, and understanding also took Canadians across the Atlantic Ocean. Once again, Canadian teachers joined organized overseas tours that were designed to promote international goodwill and to expand their participants' cultural horizons.[16] Canadian musicians, writers, and performers went abroad on tour and, in some cases, to continue their training.[17]

Canadian travel writers and diarists followed much the same itineraries as their compatriots who had transatlantic trips before the war. They visited England, Scotland, Wales, Ireland, France, the Netherlands, Belgium, Germany, Switzerland, Italy: these countries continued to attract English-speaking Canadian tourists in the 1920s and for much the same reasons as they in the 1880s. Although journalist Frank Yeigh, who published many travel pieces in the 1920s and 1930s, promised readers that the automobile would make it possible for them to visit Scandinavia, Greece, and even war-torn Macedonia, not many took Yeigh up on it. These destinations were not on the itineraries of travellers such as Halifax schoolteacher Sophia Wilson, who in 1930 went to England and Europe with the Overseas Educational League's teachers' tour. Nor did they even appear to hold much interest for the four members of Toronto's Ashbridge family, who had their own car shipped from Canada for three months of driving around Britain. Parents Wellington and Mabel, and their daughters Betty and Dorothy, then toured Holland, France, and Switzerland by rail. Most Canadians' touring involved transportation far less luxurious than the Ashbridge's personal vehicle. Frank Duggan, son of Montreal sports' promoter Tom Duggan, went 'around the world' (across the Atlantic, through the Mediterranean, the Suez Canal, the Indian and Pacific Oceans, and the Panama Canal) working in the ship's laundry rooms; some of his stops were Cairo, Singapore, San Francisco, and Havana.[18] Torontonian W.G. Bligh, who 'for no ostensible reason was lured into three years of exile in the bush of New Zealand and Australia, incurring all sorts of hardship and even destitution,' answered a government advertisement for men to serve on a horse transport to England, survived to write about his experiences with the seven hundred horses and seventy '"horsemen."'[19]

Tourists and the Automobile

Travel writers hailed the automobile and wrote convincingly that it offered postwar tourists their most intense experience of modernity.[20] Cars, according to Frank Yeigh, exposed toursits to 'Old World' history more dramatically and revealed to them more detail than even rail travel. In the article entitled 'Scotland Once Again,' published in the *Presbyterian Witness*, readers were told about the 'rare privilege' of a trip to that country, with its 'own atmosphere and individuality,' its '"brown heath and shaggy wood," of moor and mountains; of loch and burn, of concentrated history as revealed in storied castle and ivy-clad ruin.' From his car Yeigh was able to hear the local accent at Berwick, watch and listen to a Girl Guide troop playing 'Scots airs' one of them using a mouth-organ, drive around Edinburgh (the '"British Athens"'). He paused to play golf, and then proceeded to tour the Highlands, 'passing rich in history, redolent or romance, saturated in tragedy.'[21] Yeigh continued his motor trip on the Continent. Never one to shrink from nostalgic musings, he saw the Brittany countryside as running 'centuries behind times,' although this only 'adds piquancy to the passing scenes; the peasants wear costumes of pre-historic tailoring, a long remove from the styles of Paris, while their chubby children are miniatures of their parents, with skirts down to their toes, stiff little collarettes and starched headgear – the quaintest mites of humanity imaginable. Further afield, the mileposts draw near the great sea – that mysterious world water peopled so wondrously in the minds of the simple, superstitious folk.'[22] St Malo was, he suggested, little changed since Jacques Cartier's day; the city was 'but a step from the twentieth century into the middle centuries, from today into a relatively remote yesterday.'[23]

Yet, while driving (literally) straight through the heart of such simple, atavistic scenes, Yeigh was also introducing his readers to 'modern' transportation. He did point out that he had had many exciting and hair-raising experiences of driving in Chicago, New York, Detroit, and Toronto – but 'for a blood-quickener, mind-accelerator, and nerve-stimulator, give me a big Old Country car, speeding around a winding road, negotiating invisible right-angle turns, taking a crooked hill at a gallop and heading lickety-split for a narrow old stone bridge.' English history rushed past and was 'recalled at every turn on such a run': Windsor Castle, Stoke Poges, the 'quaint hamlets' of North Wales, Stratford, Kenilworth, and the Druids of Cornwall.[24] In Yeigh's estimation, 'the motor car has long since invaded all the many British Isles ... It also long since conquered Europe.' The prewar leisurely rides or strolls through the streets of Paris, he warned, were replaced by the excitement of a cab ride at the maximum speed allowed, dodging in and out of heavy traffic, taking corners sharp and fast, and disregarding pedestrians, cyclists, and dogs. Moreover, 'if you yearn for a real shake-down, motor over the cobble stones of Belgrade or Budapest ... or Salonika or Athens ... or Naples. The tire or car that can stand up for any length of time under their types of pavement should be universally advertised as non-bustable! Of all the body-racking, liver-shaking, heart-dislocating experiences one of these gasoline journeys excels.'[25]

Yeigh mused on the meaning of such rapid journeys through the heart of the distant past. He concluded his piece on Brittany with the observation that while an auto driver was covering leagues 'in a twentieth-century conveyance, the surroundings suggest the fifteenth or sixteenth. The peasant folk fit in the frame of scenery and the old towns and time-mellowed hamlets make a speeding car almost a sacrilege.'[26] Yeigh's account thus assumed not just a modern but also a masculine driver, one unafraid to take the risks of driving fast and hard through unfamiliar cities and countryside; moreover, the car facilitated exploration of those unknown areas that were off the tourists' beaten paths. In writing on the joys of motoring, Yeigh reclothed the persona of the intrepid Victorian male explorer in twentieth-century digs, giving him the state of the art technology that allowed him to chart, at some degree of personal risk, routes that few had or would follow. Like explorers' narratives, Yeigh's articles suggested that he was on his own, however misleading (in both the past and present) this fact was. Like the explorer in the time of Queen Victoria, through his (supposedly) solitary, and masculine perceptions Yeigh introduced readers to the lands and peoples of places to which they had never been and probably would never go.

Mercy E. McCulloch wrote travel columns about Britain for the *Christian Guardian*. She too was entranced by the automobile, although she wrote not about taking her 'Henrietta' over the 'liver-shaking' roads of Greece or of mad dashes through the streets of Paris but, rather, about the conveniences that a car allowed her to enjoy. Even though while driving through the Lake District with its very steep grade she and her party had to get out and push, in general McCulloch seemed to glide about Britain in delightful comfort.[27] Preferring 'Henrietta' to the 'clumsy, swaying bus' or the swift but noisy 'Tube,' which she had taken earlier in the day to visit London's East End and West Kensington, she drove out in the evening to Kensington and Hyde Park, where she saw the Albert Memorial, Rotten Row, and the Marble Arch. McCulloch did admit that 'motoring on the streets of London in the daytime is not especially enjoyable,' for while the city had very few privately-owned cars, the ban on trams in the city's centre meant that traffic consisted of a 'constant procession of buses and taxi-cabs added to the stream of lorries, trucks, and other business vehicles.' The best time and place for a car was in the 'long evenings.'

But McCulloch and her party had to work at determining street names: 'the Englishman likes to build roads on the meandering plan of the Magnetawan River' and the names changed from one borough to the next. Although this meant that a tourist must always travel with a map, McCulloch did suggest that, 'after all, a winding road has its charms. It is more picturesque and adds to the interest of life, of who knows what exciting thing may lie just around the bend.'[28]

Just in case an unwelcome 'who knows what' was waiting around that bend, however, McCulloch's readers were reassured that help was close by. Unlike Yeigh, she was far from being alone on the road, left solely to her own ingenuity. On the drive to Brighton, passing through beautiful country lanes with rhododendrons, roses, holly trees, and beeches, McCulloch observed the pervasive presence of the Automobile Association, with its maps, signposts in villages, and sentry boxes in which could be found khaki-clad and saluting 'A.A. men,' noted for their useful and helpful nature.[29] She drove part of the way to Felixstowe guided through the narrow streets of Ipswich by a small boy who stood on the car's running boards. McCulloch might not have adopted Yeigh's attitude of masculine bravado, nor yet the stance of female independence favoured by upper middle-class women who took up auto touring in the United States.[30] McCulloch enjoyed the extension of her domestic comforts. She also viewed other tourists with a degree of snobbishness. Passing through Stratford, Ilford, and Chelmsford, McCulloch 'was amused by the signs on some of the inns – "No catering for buses or bean-fests!" "Positively no char-a-banc passengers!" – but having seen some of the public conveyances with their exuberant occupants our sympathies were entirely with the inn-keepers.'[31] If participation in Cook's tours might be the sign of a 'common tripper' in the late Victorian and Edwardian years, the bus tour, it seemed, served the same function in the postwar period.

The cars could bring a greater degree of privacy and comfort, and the freedom to travel unhindered by train and bus schedules. Tourists could venture down country lanes that they might not have had time to explore on foot and, with some planning, could enjoy picnics in farmers' fields or at the roadside.[32] Cars permitted the tourist to adopt a vantage point that invoked elements of the nineteenth-century's flâneur, free to gaze at the crowd and landscape spread out in a panorama beyond the car's windows (a vantage point available especially to those wealthy enough to hire a chauffeur and thus not have to be preoccupied with road conditions). Yet as Edward Greenshields's accounts of motor travel through Spain, France, and Britain before the Great War attest, automobiles did not free tourists from all concerns and worries. Although McCulloch's description of the masculine reassurance provided by the Automobile Association – its representatives the antithesis of Yeigh's reckless and solitary male driver – might have been intended to calm the fears of middle-class women readers, problems could arise. For one thing, those who toured with their own cars had to arrange for their shipping, both there and back, and had to wait in the port of arrival until the car was unloaded.[33] While coping with driving on the left in Britain (something the Ashbridges seemed to adapt to very quickly) Canadian motorists also might encounter an extra level of officialdom over and beyond that of the usual customs and passport inspectors. Making their way through Britain the Ashbridges were occasionally warned of and stopped at speed traps, although after showing their driving licences they were allowed to proceed. They arrived late one evening at Falmouth, and having problems finding a hotel, worried that they would 'get into trouble' with the police because the car lights were not set to English standards.[34] The Ashbridges did not experience the Greenshields's problems with frequent breakdowns and flat tires, possibly because British roads in 1927 were in better condition than they had been two decades earlier.[35] But motoring was not without its pitfalls for the Ashbridges. Driving from Chester to Liverpool Dorothy managed to change gears smoothly most of the way, but at one point she 'nearly put [them] out of joint,' while near Shrewsbury they almost ran out of gas and 'had a hard job to find anyone to give us some.'[36] And there was at least one reminder that Yeigh's style of intrepid motoring might well come at a high price. In Paris Dorothy and Betty saw a car accident; the car was badly smashed, its floor covered with blood, and the driver was taken to hospital with cuts to her face and neck.[37] For people who could travel by motorcar, the vehicle was in itself as much of a presence – often welcome, sometimes burdensome – in their travels as were the sights to which it took them.

'The Cutest Woman on the Throne': The English Past

The one area in which continuity with prewar tourism was evident was the desire of English-speaking Canadians to experience history in the places they visited and, in turn, to visit those places deemed 'historical.' In 'England's Medieval City, World-Famous and Sleepy Old

Chester,' N. Tourneur told readers of the *Christian Guardian* that this walled city, visited by thousands from overseas, had been an 'incomparable' centre of export and import fourteen centuries before Columbus's voyages. Its landscape conjured up 'the wild Welsh,' the Romans, Saxons, Danes, Normans, Richard II, and Charles I. A tourist might 'form a clear picture' of a medieval town simply by walking around the 'ancient walls and quaint streets' of Chester, seeing its 'picturesque houses, underground passages and crypts, and cathedral.' While the overall effect was not without charm, there was also the prison and the bridge that 'the doomed, before their execution, were marched across' to attend their last service.[38]

McCulloch's tourist map was full of historical sites. Bath's history began with the Saxons and then could be traced through the personas and periods of Edward I, the Elizabethan and Georgian eras, and Dickens's Little Nell. Sharing the prewar tourists' fascination with histories of cruelty and torture, she found Lancaster Castle noteworthy for its Court of Assize, dungeons, cat o' nine tails, scold's bridle, branding device, and Hanging Corner – although McCulloch was glad to have seen the castle, she also was relieved to leave it.[39] In London she visited the monument to the Great Fire and then the Tower. She went over the White Tower with its display of arms and armour and then saw the Beauchamp Tower with its prisoners' carvings, ending with the 'Bloody' Tower where the Beefeaters explained its history to her (the only spot in the Tower, she noted, where this happened), a narrative that included prominent male prisoners such as Cranmer, Ridley, Latimer, and Raleigh.[40] McCulloch made a 'pilgrimage to Canterbury,' a trip made even more delightful by a roadside picnic in a sheltered spot. In Canterbury she found the cathedral's 'graceful simplicity' most appealing and meditated on the fate of Thomas à Becket and Henry VIII's 'demonization' of him.[41] Her visit to Winchester Cathedral conjured up a history that included Mary Tudor, Henry Beaufort, and Charles II; she also noted in Winchester a Norman font, King Alfred's statue, and the Plague Monument.[42]

McCulloch's letters sketch a history in which male political and religious figures predominate; however, she was not unaware of women as historical actors. At the crypt at Warwick's Beauchamp Chapel's she and her husband viewed a ducking stool for scolding wives. Tied to a wheelbarrow, it was 'very convenient for trundling a belligerent female off to the pond where her excitement might be cooled by a sudden plunge.' McCulloch pointed out that the Beauchamp family line had passed a few times to the women of the family: 'the verger remarked that "the little habit of getting beheaded that they had was very hard on the male succession."'[43] McCulloch was concerned with historical representations of Englishwomen and thought they should be portrayed as more than victims of their conduct or circumstances. In London she observed that the only monuments of women were those of Queen Victoria, Sarah Siddons, Florence Nightingale, and Edith Cavell. Although women by no means made up the majority of Madame Tussaud's figures, the wax museum included Victoria, Cavell, Nightingale, Anne Boleyn, Lady Astor, and Madame Tussaud herself.[44] In York Cathedral Betty Ashbridge was impressed with the memorial to the nurses from the British Empire who had died in the First World War, and especially because 'in the tablets to their memory we saw many Canadian names.'[45]

Other anglophone Canadian women wrote about their impressions of women in British history, although they often did so not to commemorate heroines but to mourn the sadness of women's lives in the past. On visiting the castles in Wales London, Ontario, of Ada Turville was struck by both their antiquity and their isolation. Medieval queens in that area, she told readers of her hometown's *Free Press*, who lacked proper domestic quarters must have been very bored and lonely, a condition that she contrasted with the life of Queen Mary, with her busy round of philanthropic and social functions. 'The very forbidding aspect of the place [Conway Castle] suggests the crudeness of domestic life in the feudal era, and it is difficult to realize that people did actually live amid such comfortless surroundings.'[46] Saskatchewan journalist Effie Laurie Storer, like so many anglophone Canadian tourists, visited the Bloody Tower, and although she thought the Crown Jewels 'marvelous,' the dungeons and Bloody Arch, with their damp, worn stone steps, made her shudder. 'I'm afraid,' she told her friend, Winnipeger Beth Henderson, that 'our ancestors had a cruel streak which they might have called "justice" for their opponents,' and she noted that she had seen the spot where 'Lady Hamilton was it (Gray?) was beheaded ... I was glad to get away from the gloom it outbalanced the nice things to be seen.'[47] Her tour of Westminster Abbey made Susie Almon, who was from Halifax, feel quite sorry for Queen Anne, 'with her eighteen babies dying' (Almon appears to have avoided the sorrows and tragedies of the Tower).[48]

Tragedy was not uppermost in Dorothy Hutchinson's mind as she recorded her impressions of Kenilworth's ruins, or at least not the relatively well-known tragedy of 'poor Amy' that so many other tourists commented on. 'We met a caretaker who reinhabited [sic] it from Norman times and told us all the history of Elizabeth's visit there.' His account included the amount the Queen's stay had cost Leicester (£1,000 per day), the fact that both the earl and the queen shared birthdays and dates of incarceration in the Tower of London, and that 'he helped her to the throne and she wrote to him as my dearest Robin, but she found he had sent his wife to her death and didn't want the same to happen to her. She was the cutest woman on the throne.'[49]

The looming or lingering past in Britain was certainly not always gendered female. Margaret Bell wrote about 'The Old Inns of London' for the *Canadian Magazine*, establishments that for her evoked masculine symbols of urbanity and conviviality such as Beau Brummel and Falstaff.[50] 'The Home of General Wolfe' was, as one might suspect from an article with this title, about manly military service for the empire.[51] Writing about the past might be shaped by antimodernist attitudes of nostalgia and a desire to inhabit 'simpler times.' Bell, lamented the contemporary obsession with profits and the 'bolsheviking,' so different from the times evoked by the store-front signs to be seen along Mile Lane, Gresham Street, Euston Road, and Oxford Street.[52] Grace Hunter's 1924 trip to Canterbury, 'still a Mecca for pilgrims,' left her impressed with both the cathedral and its environs, full of 'charm and quaintness.' She mused about the histories of Becket, the 'tragedy of his assassination,' and of Henry VIII, a master in the 'sacrilegious' art of seizure and demolition of Church property. But Hunter was pleased to see that most of the town's buildings were at least two hundred years old and some dated to the fourteenth century, as their age ensured for her that the cathedral would be maintained in keeping with its surroundings. In Canterbury, Hunter proclaimed, the 'impious American habit of tearing down has never been the fashion. Only the ubiquitous 6d store, with its familiar staring red front, jerks one back to modern utility and ugliness.' The city's citizens were judged to have too much pride in their heritage to allow the 'undue encroachment of modern commercial enterprise.'[53]

As is the case with many writings imbued with nostalgia, even Hunter's clear disdain for the '6d store' and commercial modernity was not uncomplicated. She began her trip with a 'tiresome run of sixty miles or so' from London on an 'old compartment train which must have been young abut the same date as Victoria.' It seemed to her that 'ambling on a palfrey in the Kentish lanes would have been preferable to the antiquated railway carriage, with its lack of air and plethora of passengers.' But however slow and uncomfortable such nineteenth-century conveyances, they still were to be preferred to cantering, as the latter would bring result in 'meeting in some narrow turning a char-a-banc loaded with tourists,' one of those 'juggernauts which "thunder along."'[54] Perhaps nothing would have satisfied Hunter, caught between a yearning for the past and an obvious desire for modern conveniences without, though, the intrusions of modernity's increasing democratization of travel, a process of which Hunter was a beneficiary.

For Lester Pearson, writing on 'Oxford: Ancient and Modern' for the *Christian Guardian*, the issue in understanding Oxford was not the division between the past and present; he thought both coexisted quite happily in the university city. Rather, the more salient division was that between tourists (especially those from places like' Idaho and Saskatchewan') and the local residents (especially the students of Pearson's St John's College). No tourist visited England without a trip to Oxford, Pearson thought. They might arrive in groups of two or three, or alone, or in large parties 'but always with a loquacious guide.' Certainly Oxford was 'well worth visiting,' but to appreciate it properly it was necessary to live there and that was precisely what the 'average tourist' could not do. Coming 'up' on the 10:45 a.m. from Paddington and having dashed from college to college, the visitor would settle back in his compartment on the 4:40 p.m. (caught in order to give London the same treatment on the following day), 'muttering ... "Well, Mary, those old ivy walls are very pretty, but say, not one of their buildings can compare with our new technical school."' As for Pearson, 'we who are privileged to live and work here for a few happy years have a different viewpoint,' particularly when it came to Oxford's 'unique and nonmaterial' method of education with its emphasis on the classics, history, philosophy, and political science.[55]

Antimodernism was not a new departure for, as we have seen, travel writers in the Edwardian years, particularly those who wrote for the *Canadian Magazine*, expressed similar attitudes. But Frank Yeigh constructed himself (and his imagined reader) as a modern tourist, part of history and an active agent in it. This tourist would be refreshed and soothed by the simple, uncomplicated, and unknowing peasant, who Yeigh presented as being as much a feature of the landscape as buildings, rocks, and trees (his notions of 'the past' as a pure and noble time also can be found in his writings on the historical landscape of the

Niagara Peninsula).[56] Yet, instead of shrinking from or despising modernity, Yeigh celebrated its symbols: the liberated tourist happily ensconced in his motor car, ideally suited to inspect the historical landscapes and peoples of England and Europe. Tourists could find themselves surrounded by a surfeit of history, however. Dorothy Ashbridge was 'delighted' to visit Stonehenge, thinking that 'the stones left standing are not in the least disappointing, only making you wonder afresh how men ever got them into place,' while she found that in Winchester 'the history of this place would make you dippy.'[57] A few days later she went with her family to tour the House of Commons and wrote that 'of course the place is full of historical reminders, too many to mention.'[58] At Ely Cathedral, where the Ashbridges were taken around by a verger, she thought that it all was very 'interesting but of course I can't remember all the dates and facts now'[59] For Dorothy Ashbridge England had just a bit too much history.

Scotland and Ireland

English-speaking Canadian tourists continued to be drawn to Scotland's Highlands and Trossachs, in ways tinged with nostalgia and romanticism but also complicated by a sense of tragedy and a mourning of the past's brutality. Historians of Scottish tourism have argued that by the 1920s Scott and Burns had become less important in the construction of an imagined Scotland. But the diaries and letters of Canadians such as Susie Almon and the Ashbridges indicate that such a decline in popularity was not universal.[60] Canadian tourists and travel writers continued to visit the places made memorable by Scott.[61] The Ashbridges saw Melrose Abbey (which at first seemed less attractive than Jedburgh but then revealed itself to be 'larger and more elaborate') and then Abbotsford (which Mabel 'very much admired' with its wonderful collections and rooms).[62] 'Abbotsford afforded me much joy,' Susie Almon wrote in a letter home, with its display of Rob Roy's gun, Prince Charlie's hunting case, Mary Stuart's crucifix and, above all, Scott's study. 'It was so easy to picture him among them all,' she thought.[63] Ada Turville went for a tour around the shores of the Lochs in a 'coach and four,' an experience marked by her 'anxiety' as to 'how I was to remain in it' (her seat was quite narrow, the floor well below her feet, and the road so bumpy that she was afraid of being thrown out). She soon became used to the motion, however, and 'increasingly alert to the beauty of the surroundings.' Once, as they came over a hill, she saw 'the skirl of the bagpipes and just at a picturesque turn stood the piper, a boy in full Highland costume, thus completing the Scottish atmosphere. The hour's ride was, in spite of all anxieties, one never to be forgotten, and surely much more appreciated than a trip through the same region by a plutocrat in his luxurious Rolls-Royce.'[64]

Although privileged, the Ashbridges were by no means plutocrats (and the make of their car is not clear from the diaries or travel photos). But cars could make a difference to the tourist's sense of self and position in the landscape. In Stirling Mabel Ashbridge was struck by the large number of pedestrians on the street who 'always walk on the road. There is never much motor traffic and we feel like we had no business there.'[65] The car allowed them to drive north into landscape that impressed them with its melancholy and mournful nature. At Glamis, where the road was 'so narrow that we had to throw our grips in the back drive off to a wider place, as the trains can't pass if a car stops,' they saw Macbeth's castle and the place where Malcolm II was murdered.[66] The next day they toured the ruined cathedral at Elgin, saw the battlefield of Culloden ('the poor Highlanders,' Mabel mused), watched sheep being sheared, and near Inverness saw scenery that 'was the wildest yet, high on the mountain great masses of broom in full bloom and we passed the "blasted moor" Shakespeare speaks of where the three witches met Macbeth.'[67] At John O'Groats the Ashbridges looked out at the North Sea and the Orkneys. 'A wonderful drive over its heath,' wrote Mabel, 'a country much like the prairies except more bleak, no trees, and a desolate look to it. A poor looking stone house with thatched roof here and there and quite a few of the people digging and hauling peat which is piled outside to dry.' After a lunch at Thurso, where Mabel took photographs of fisherwomen, the Ashbridges drove back to Inverness, where 'for miles we saw no living thing,' including, Mabel observed, no other cars.[68] Effie Storer toured the Highlands and saw Marie Corelli's former home, 'Rob Roy country,' and 'wonderful Highlanders in their kilts at Inverness.' She was accompanied by a woman guide and, while listening to her, thought 'of all the mothers and widows who were left amid those lovely, lonely hills – I have fully realized that ours is not a new task but just [one] women have been living through. Rearing sons and enduring losses throughout the centuries.'[69]

Storer's sombre observation should not be surprising, given her recent widowhood. And while not all of Scotland was incorporated into these pictures of bleak, romantic wildness, sorrowful history, and notions of its cruel and tragic past, such narratives and images continued to shape tourists' understanding of Scotland. Edinburgh's attractions included the site of executions at Marketcross, the prison, the castle, John Knox's house, Greyfriars Cemetery, St Giles Church, and Holyrood.[70] Edinburgh was also 'one of the most romantically beautiful cities in Europe,' as William Morse told his readers, with its 'Art Gallery' with Holbein, Corot, Rembrandt, Reynolds, and Van Dyke.[71] Dorothy Hutchinson described Edinburgh as a 'very lovely place, wide streets and statues air of generosity and cleanliness – fine shops and good quality merchandise' (and after shopping, Hutchinson and her husband took in a movie).[72]

Edinburgh University for Ada Turville. was as much an attraction as Oxford or Cambridge. She toured its library, which had 'more than 200,000 volumes' and was an 'interesting ... juxtaposition' of old and modern with its 'American-style' stainless-steel shelves in a building that dated from 1796. Turville noted that the student body numbered four thousand and included both 1,250 women and students from all over the world, 'conspicuous among them being the dark-skinned Parsees from India.' She told her readers in London, Ontario, about the large bronze tablet erected to the memory of the university's alumni killed in the 'Great War.'[73] Her tour of the university included attending a lecture given by Ramsay Muir, 'man of letters, member of Parliament, and professor of history at Manchester.' Muir spoke on trade unions and their 'rapid' growth in membership and power since the 1880s. While Muir, reported Turville, would '"like to see strikes abolished,"' an opinion 'heartily seconded' by members of his audience, nevertheless he felt that they were still an important 'weapon' in negotiations. Turville concluded that general discontent since 1919 had mounted, culminating in the previous year's general strike, 'having probably its source in the instinctive sympathy of all for the suffering classes.'[74]

Glasgow continued to interest anglophone Canadian tourists. Morse enjoyed its gallery, docks, and shipyards, while Chamberlin thought that it had both its own merits and the appeal of West Coast and Hebridean steamers waiting at its quaysides.[75] Storer had quite a bit to say about the living conditions and women in Glasgow (in general she was interested in women's roles and appearances). Writing to her friend in Winnipeg, Storer reported that 'we meet the women of the slums all over the city. They wear shawls and no hat. Some are none too clean. Others appear to take a pride in their children they look well kept. But fancy living up a flight of stairs on a busy street and only one window. It is shrouded with curtains, dirty or otherwise, and usually

just a sickly plant or two stands on the window-ledge.' She attached a
'P.S.' that noted just how 'different' 'everything' was in Scotland. 'People work early and late. It gets me to see white women from the slums
standing around the street corners just as the half-breed women do at
home.'[76] A few days later Storer wrote again and summed up her
impressions of Glasgow: 'there are beautiful homes and wretched
slums. But on the whole the women look healthy. I do not think the
Scotch girls are pretty.' Storer's description illustrates how the gendered and racial discourses of a white settler colony might be put to
work in the metropolitan context – and not to the latter's advantage.
She did concede, however, that Glasgow had many attractions and
interesting spots, including its monuments, good tramcar service,
lovely commons, crowds of people, gas works, and coal mines.[77]

These Canadians made a number of observations about tourism in
Scotland and about the Scots in general. The Ashbridges may have been
unlucky in the timing of their visit, as Scotland seems to have had a
chilly and wet summer in 1927. Mabel felt the cold, inside and out: 1 July
in Edinburgh felt more like November to her. 'The people in this country
can't stand heat, for they open doors and windows wide and have no
heat on at all and we nearly freeze. Glad I bought a water bottle.'[78] At
the Station Hotel in Wick, where they were forced to stop because of
heavy fog, Mabel was much comforted by being able to sit 'in front of a
grate fire listening to the radio.' Matters improved once they reached
southern Scotland and the Trossachs, where Mabel confessed that she
'was forced to take off my coat for the first time since I left home
June 12.'[79] And although Dorothy Hutchinson found her room at Edinburgh's Old Waverley Hotel quite comfortable, Dorothy Ashbridge was
not impressed by the lack of running water in her hotel room in that city
(her room in Belfast's Grand Central Hotel offered running water, the
first place to do so, she noted, since she left Liverpool).[80] Stereotypes
about Scots' parsimony were provoked by the doling out of three
matches for the three candles in the Ashbridges' hotel rooms in Buc-
cleuch. 'It is a certainly a Scotch hotel for when we asked for matches to
light our candles with, they gave us just three!' Mabel exclaimed, while
Wellington observed, 'Surely we have reached Scotland.'[81]

William Morse peppered his travelogue with comments about the
Scots, thrift, and other stereotypes. Arriving at the Scottish border, he
remarked upon the inspiring view: 'behind us lay the land so full of history and before us the abode of the canny Scot, the country where no
Jews are able to survive the financial strains, and as report has it at

present time only one remains, and he can't get out because he isn't able to raise the money.'[82] (As we shall see, Morse's writing had its share of anti-Semitic comments.) In Edinburgh Morse observed more examples of what he deemed Scots' 'cheapness' and the difficulty that the 'wandering Jew' would encounter in trying to leave the country; he also wrote that 'red noses are prevalent in Edinburgh.'[83] His ethnic caricatures notwithstanding, Morse's travelogue shapes a portrait of Britain in which a 'British' identity was by no means agreed on. At his hotel in Durham, 'a little fun with the maid ... provoked some slight mirth. Traveller – "Are you English?" Maid – "No, thank God, I'm Scotch!"'[84] At the restaurant in the North British Station Hotel in Edinburgh, Morse's inquiry of his waiter if he was 'Scotch' was met with the vehement reply, '"God help us, no!"'[85] As he left Scotland Morse concluded that 'in the land of the Scot ... every native "takes pride in being bilingual," sees double and "refuses to merge his individuality with the Englishmen" – although first and last a citizen of the Empire.'[86]

The Ashbridges had little doubt that, although the Scots might share imperial citizenship with them, they clearly were in a different country from either Canada or England. Not only did they confront a paucity of matches, these Canadians did not always understand what was being said to them. Once, while walking in Edinburgh with an open guidebook to spot historical sites, Mabel and her family 'were quite amused at two little boys who stepped out and started to act as guides, pointing out places of interest and talking so Scotch we couldn't understand only a word here and there.'[87] Just outside Dundee, Dorothy wrote, 'a Scotch boy tried to warn us about a speed trap but was so Scotch we couldn't understand him.'[88] They appeared to have fared better with 'local accents' in Ireland, where they toured Belfast and Dublin. The Ashbridges were taken around Dublin's St Kevin's Church 'by a very Irish young man. He was worth the trip just to hear his accent, while he told us all the things he knew.' On leaving the church they walked about with a 'nice young Irish policeman, whom he talked with and asked questions of. He gave me the most wonderful salute,' wrote Mabel, 'when I said goodbye.'[89]

The next day they went about Dublin, where they saw the Bank of Ireland, Parliament, Glasnevin ('where Ireland's illustrious dead are buried'), St Patrick's, the Botanic Gardens, the library, and the cattle market, led by a guide who was 'a real Irishman with a wonderful brogue. He showed us where all the fighting was in 1916 to 1922 when they were given what they wanted and became a free state.'[90] The family's Dublin stay coincided with the funeral of the assassinated Cabinet Minister, Kevin O'Higgins, 'he being shot down by men for party reasons,' Mabel thought. 'The whole town and country mourns and all flags at half mast and businesses closed during procession.' They saw eight trucks laden with flowers, marching soldiers, a band, and 'such a lot of old men with silk hats, black ties and gloves. I rather wished we had been going to stay and see the funeral.'[91] Her daughters also noted the funeral, as it meant some government buildings were closed to the public, although Dorothy believed that, despite all the 'excitement,' 'I am sure it [Dublin] is as safe as Chicago.'[92] However, the Ashbridges were by no means supporters of Irish nationalism, for before arriving in Dublin they spent 12 July in Belfast, where they enjoyed watching the Orange parade. Dorothy thought that 'it seems quite the proper thing to see an Orange parade in Belfast, but we had hardly thought of it before.' She and her mother were impressed by the 'wonderful' banners and drummers; while there were no white horses as in Toronto's parade, 'the bands are much better.'[93]

London in the 1920s

British roads and railways took Canadian tourists to London as they had done before the war. And, like some of the English-speaking travellers before the war, not all postwar tourists were pleased with what they found. W.G. Worcester, a professor at the University of Saskatchewan, was thankful to leave London for Europe. 'Glad to leave London, don't like the place,' he confided to his diary.[94] English-speaking Canadians in the 1920s, as earlier, went warned of the dangers (or at least unpleasantness) of parts of the city. Norman Tucker, writing in 1922, painted an East End 'where the streets are narrow, the house congested, and innumerable families crowd together like rabbits in a warren. It is here that the public houses abound.' His report abounds with numerous examples of male drunkenness, brutality, and violence, but he told his readers, working-class women embodied the most pernicious effects of alcohol. Drunken women were everywhere: 'bare-headed' and 'slipping round the corner' carrying squat jugs. They collected outside the pubs, where they resembled 'Hags! Viragos! Unkempt, bedraggled, with bonnets awry; bleary eyes, bloated of countenances, with voices husky with alcohol, their coarse mouths full of raucous remarks.' Even children, including one 'radiant child' spotted by Tucker who was so dainty she resembled a fairy, drank but what, he asked, could you expect when 'mothers takes babies into bars and give them sips.' Canadians could expect to see only 'drink, depravity, distress, deformity, degradation, [and] despair' – at least in the East End, for while Tucker recognized that people in the West End drank, 'one gets drunk very aristocratically there, in evening dress!'[95]

Like the warnings that Frederick Hastings and Emily Murphy issued in the 1870s and '1890s, Tucker's appear to have gone largely unheeded. Although William Morse met 'some sort of a Sinn Feiner,' who appeared to be on 'mysterious business' and was 'prowling around the hotel' at breakfast, he was quickly forgotten in Morse's pursuit of the much more obvious and transparent pleasures of tourism.[96] An Anglican clergyman, Morse was interested in sampling a number of Sunday services and attended the Westminster Congregational Church, St Paul's afternoon service, and the sermon given by Dean Inge of St Martin's-in-the-Field's.[97] Sacred attractions were not for him the only reasons to be in London, however, as he enjoyed watching the 'flappers' making their way to work each morning through Trafalgar Square, had a good time shopping for shoes, and found the city's bookstores 'enchanting.'[98] The Ashbridges saw several wedding parties as they emerged from London's churches while they walked back to their hotel near the Strand from St Paul's. They toured the Tate and National Galleries, lunched at Harrod's, and took a bus ride to Shepherd's Bush and back.[99] Mabel was 'just so mad at ourselves for not having our cameras' as they watched the changing of the guard at Buckingham Palace; she also reported that they had seen the place where 'little Elizabeth, the Duchess of York's baby was born.'[100] On their return trip to London, and while watching the guards again, 'a miserable-looking man came up and wanted to sell us a tip on the races. Wellie said no to the tip but gave him a couple of pennies and at that minute up stepped an officer and hustled that man off so fast. He told us that he should have arrested him. He said people don't want to be annoyed by appeals and when you paid for "privacy" you wanted it, etc., etc.'[101]

As always, London's shops were a big attraction (see fig. 9.3). Although her tour of Big Ben, Westminster Abbey, No. 10 Downing Street, and the Cenotaph left Dorothy Hutchinson thinking that 'nothing seemed big enough,' she found the display at Liberty's 'remarkable for oak beams carved – the way goods all displayed and the beauty of the merchandise. Very expensive.'[102] The Ashbridge family shopped for hats, gloves, and shoes, shoes being a particular problem for Mabel who had difficulty with her narrow feet (a pair bought at Selfridge's

9.3. Consuming London in the 1920s (*Canada, an Illustrated Journal*, 1 July 1927)

had to be given to the chambermaid in her hotel).[103] They left their car and took the 'Tube' which, Betty wrote, was 'lots of fun. Mother says they are much nicer than the New York tubes.'[104] Tourists visited the large West End stores and also the Caledonia Market which Dorothy Hutchinson described as the 'Junk Shop of England – Thieves Market its [sic] called, silver brasses, copper and *junk* annoying types there – strange place.'[105] As Mercy McCulloch explained to her readers, a cattle and sheep market was held on the premises most of the week but on Friday it became a pedlars' market, with 'such a heterogen[e]ous collection of rusty nails, broken furniture, worn-out elastic, old china, clothing, food, soaps, and perfume, silverware, rugs, phonographs and every other imaginable kind of junk I never met before.' She admitted, however, that the market offered some 'good and expensive' items.[106]

Theatre occupied the postwar anglophone tourist's time in London, as it had in earlier decades, and here, too, English-speaking Canadians attended a range of performances and left with a range of reactions to what they saw. Sophia Wilson found the Gaiety production of *Love's Race* 'not 'high class, amusing for a certain time then monotonous.'[107] 'Theatres always attract the moths,' thought William Morse, who saw four 'popular' shows, including *The League of Nations, The Wrong Number, Bull-dog Drummond*, and another, unnamed production. They were 'at least interesting and liable to keep you awake,' but he did not think much of their 'patter.'[108] Other tourists were more enthusiastic about what they saw and heard on London's stages. For Dorothy Hutchinson, *Careless Rapture* at Drury Lane was a spectacle, with its 'singing and scenery fairly good.'[109] Mabel Ashbridge and her family went to *The Desert Song* at Drury Lane, 'which we enjoyed immensely. Lovely music and dancing and excellent acting.'[110]

'Of course,' McCulloch wrote, 'we went to see *Chu Chin Chow*, that marvellous Oriental spectacle,' in its sixth year of production and noted for its 'catchy music and colourful pageantry.' It was 'hung on,' she told her Canadian audience, the story of Ali Baba and the forty thieves and included the comedy of Ali Baba's love affair with his sister-in-law. 'The eternal triangle does not offend in the Oriental dress, for what else can be expected of the Oriental mind of long-past centuries, but the prevalence of the triangle's situation in books, stories, movies, plays, and newspapers, and real life is a bit thick in Merry England in the twentieth century.'

McCulloch was, after all, writing for the *Christian Guardian* and thus it is no surprise that she did not approve of the presence of the 'eternal triangle' in modern English culture (nor, perhaps, should we be surprised by her acceptance of Orientalist imagery on the London stage). Pursuing her theme of contemporary society's penchant for immorality, she became sidetracked from the theatre in order to indict a media that did not inform Londoners of the fate of a young woman hit by a car at Hyde Park Corner but that ran all the 'unsavory' details of divorce and murder trials. She came back to the topic of London theatre, though, by concluding that a 'brilliant political play, *The Grain of Mustardseed*, left a bad taste in one's mouth.'[111]

Susie Almon went to see *The Beggar's Opera* and enjoyed it 'thoroughly.' She wrote home to 'my dear Bruce' that 'some of the lines may have been a little coarse for twentieth century ears for only hummed parts of it and of course if you take it seriously its very? but its too nonsensical for words and the costumes were so pretty and MacHeath such an attractive rascal and Polly Peachum so dainty and engaging it was very delightful.'[112] There may have been levels of meaning in John

Gay's work that passed Almon by; however, her delight in theatrical
performances also extended to Shakespeare. She attended a production of *Twelfth Night* at the Old Vic and told 'Rollie' that 'anyone who
says Shakespeare is dry or dull or highbrow should see that acted
there. For a second I felt as if Shakespeare was there' (she planned to
return, as it was only 2/ for both performance and program).[113]

The Old Vic was a favourite spot for Kathleen Coburn, who went to
see a production of *Antony and Cleopatra* in 1930s during her first
Christmas break, 'and I'm sure,' she told her diary, 'the actors themselves rank it with the "big four" whatever armchair scholarship may
say. It was well-nigh perfect. And the Old Vic, of course, is just itself
and like nothing else.'[114] Later that winter Coburn saw a 'splendid
pair,' Dorothy Green and John Gielgud, in *Much Ado about Nothing*,
although she was 'astonished' to see the audience clap when the police
pounced on the villains, 'and a good lady next to me wept during the
wedding scene! Reactions just as to a modern play or picture by a
Canadian audience. Would that it were Shakespeare for them too. He is
of the very blood and marrow of these people, now, as three hundred
and thirty years ago. And they understand him, love his peculiar excel-
lence, he raises them to a point at which they are capable of perceptions finer than any they exercise in regard to real life, I warrant.'
Coburn went on to recount that 'contrary to all this, dear lady beside
me screwed up good courage to climb over her English reserve to ask
me "if this play is in printed form anywhere!" Actually! And then
"would it be a very dear book?"' She recovered from her shock about
the 'dear lady's' lack of cultural knowledge to discuss Lilian Baylis and
the wages of the 'girls' who worked in the theatre (15/ per week).[115]

Coburn was also interested in other playwrights. She went with a
group of friends to Eugene O'Neill's *Desire Under the Elms*, which had
been banned by the Lord Chamberlain's office and could be seen only
in private theatres. 'Agreed with J.B. as to never having seen so many
light women (and their consequent trail of tough men) all together in
one place at one time before. A most interesting audience, if horrid. A
powerful play – and if one believes in censorship, properly banned.'[116]
Ten months later she saw *Henry V* at Sadler's Wells, Noel Coward's
Cavalcade, and Ibsen's *The Master Builder* at the Duchess Theatre. After
the play by Ibsen she heard the 'Directress,' Nancy Price, speak of her
company's efforts to be a 'national theatre, and no rubbish – asked for
support ... I understand she smokes a pipe and has other peculiarities.'
(Precisely what those 'peculiarities' were, Coburn did not elaborate.)

She also went to hear the great American actor, singer, and activist Paul Robeson and was very glad she did so: he gave three encores and afterwards spoke to the audience. Coburn finished that evening with dinner in a 'Piccadilly Chinese restaurant.'[117]

Visiting historical sites, going shopping, and attending the theatre thus repeated late Victorian and Edwardian tourists' experiences of spectacles, consumption, and performance. But as well as these conti-nuities, London also offered postwar Canadian tourists a heightened exposure to various forms of modernity intensified in the interwar years by new forms of technology and performance. As historian Christopher Breward has pointed out, the entertainment industry of interwar London saw during this period 'unprecedented expansion, relative safety and carefree hedonism': the West End streets were lit up by electricity; new, elegant cinemas were built; and cafés, confection-ers, and fish and chip shops underwent extensive (and hygienic) remodelling in order to attract the growing number of window-shoppers and cinema-goers out after dark.[118] Anglophone Canadian tourists took advantage of these changes, confiding to their diaries and in their letters home that they also had spent time going to 'the movies' and noting carefully not just the title of the film itself but the entire experience. Effie Storer spent three hours at London's Stoll's picture house, where she saw some 'splendid' films, including *The Cradle's Lure*. She and her party sat on the main floor but were annoyed by men wearing their hats and by the smoking of both sexes, and so they ended up moving to the reserved seats 'which were only ordinary at that.' 'The ushers dress almost the same as Canadians,' she told her friend, with strawberry cambric, white muslin collars, bow ties, black belts, and velvet tams.[119] After a day working on the Coleridge papers at the British Museum, Kathleen Coburn was greatly impressed by Charlie Chaplin's *City Lights*. 'What a sadly sentimental little man he must be,' she mused, thinking the picture had 'clever acting ... and more artistry about its conception than most of them, with its superfi-cial exterior encasing a deep stream of forcefulness and darkness.[120] One day, while walking back to Hyde Park Corner Mercy McCulloch thought she might see King George and Queen Mary; instead, the crowds were gathered to 'catch a chance glimpse of Queen Mary Pick-ford and King Douglas Fairbanks whose arrival in England turned the heads of the people and the newspapers.' These members of 'movie royalty' were welcomed by airplanes, cameras, and 'throngs,' a recep-tion not given, McCulloch believed, to the majority of the large number of visitors from her hometown: 'there were other Toronto folk in the city but for some strange reason no such commotion was made on their account!'[121]

McCulloch, it seems, was not all that impressed by this new form of celebrity, a poor substitute for the experience of seeing 'real' royalty. Movies could be seen in Canadian cities, but other aspects of urban life were new to these tourists. For example, while on her way to Hammersmith and to see *The Beggar's Opera*, Susie Almon encountered her first moving stairway. 'I suppose I looked my horror,' she wrote to Rollie, 'for a nice looking young man who had got on first turned and asked me if I was nervous so I told him I was frightened to death ... I very nearly turned back to see that great crawling thing stretching for miles ahead of you – however with my reassuring friend just ahead of me and telling [me] to get off first with left foot – the only thing I didn't need to be told for I do read directions and it was plainly writ – I got off without mishap.'[122]

Effie Storer's time in London gave her lots of opportunity to think about her life as a widow and her purpose in society. The women at her hotel, the Balmoral, had many aristocratic ladies '"on pension," sitting around like comfortable cats with nothing to do. They get up, eat, walk, nap, play cards and go to bed by routine. They have lovely clothes and perfect taste, also beautiful jewelry.'[123] Five days later, having observed these women more closely, Storer declared, 'I have made up my mind to work until the last ditch is crossed. So many women sit here laden with jewels waiting for the end. Their forms are trembly and they have such a do-nothing air. With my health and energy I would not change places with any of them.' The same day she bade farewell to the city, telling Henderson, 'I am not sorry. I did not lose any wrinkles here although it has been a pleasant experience.'[124] Susie Almon had the sense that 'there must be an anti-climax soon. I can't go on enjoying each day more than the last like this.' Dorothy Ashbridge simply stated that 'it does seem rather wonderful to be in London.'[125]

Europe, 'Ancient' and Modern

'The Romance of the word "Europe" is based on a civilization much older than ours in America,' wrote William Inglis Morse in 1922.[126] However, Morse's account of his time in France – with visits to Cherbourg, Bayeux, Rouen, Caen, Deauville, Paris, and Chartres – revealed as much about his experiences with drivers and waiters as of his impressions of French history, culture, and landscape. Like that of earlier tourists such as Thomas Langton, Morse's tone was one of cheery scepticism and satire – often bordering on but thinly veiled contempt for those who worked in the tourist industry and the culture they represented. Sometimes French culture was the source of amusement for him. When Morse saw the Bayeux tapestry, he thought it notable for its 'scarcity of women' which, he believed, 'indicates the modesty of Norman ladies and retiring nature. We are evidently living in a different age.'[127] Versailles 'reeks with historical associations,' he decided, and suggested that the Louvre could use a bicycle tour. In general, 'scarcity of soap in Paris was noticeable. The water was hard. The dirt refused to come off. We refused Evian water and Vichy for inside purposes plus a little Sauterne.' The cooking, in his opinion, was excellent but expensive and 'the flies were in full assemblage – all married and grandfathers many times.'[128] Making it quite clear just who his audience was, Morse provided the title page of his chapter on Paris with a sketch of a stick man, with the caption 'You' and an arrow pointing towards it, ogling the legs of a woman wearing a short skirt, muff, fancy hat, and walking a poodle.[129]

Morse was full of advice about travel in France, for example, the need to make friends with the concierge while staying in 'foreign hotels:' 'He's a mine of information. A good tip is well spent on him if you plan to stay in his vicinity for many days. You can joke him, pull his whiskers, get him to translate English into French for you and loads of other tricks.'[130] Alas not even a friendly concierge could help Morse and his party when their car struck another in the Bois de Boulogne. Their 'side-gear' was knocked off, as was a front tire, and the 'hairs in the driver's mustachio stood up like quills. Excitement followed, talk, shaking of hands and vituperative remarks.'[131] Cynicism was not the prevailing tone for discussions about the Parisian tourist industry, though. Violet McNaughton, during her 1929 trip observed that tourists were 'well looked after' in Paris, with reasonable rates for hotels and taxis available and a healthy proliferation of sightseeing companies, so that 'one cannot fail to spend both time and money profitably without effort.' But she laboured under no delusions about the nature of tourism: 'looking after tourists is a business,' McNaughton pointed out, 'and to some extent prevents one from getting impressions of the French and their general life. Also some sights are to a degree stage managed.' Despite the staged quality of tourism, however, McNaughton was convinced that the 'buildings, works of art, and other historic spots are worth all one wishes them to be from a point of interest.'[132]

344 À Happy Holiday

Unlike William Morse in his book *Seeing Europe Backwards*, Ada Turville's travelogues did not offer readers amusing caricatures of the people who worked in the tourist industry. Her columns had little to say about them. Paris represented continuity, not change for Turville, with its boulevards, bridges, Notre Dame, the Luxembourg, Arc de Triomphe, Tuileries, district markets, and classical theatre. Turville was at the five-hundredth anniversary celebrations of the University of Louvain, an honorary degree was presented to Belgium's Queen Elizabeth. In Belgium she also attended the opening of a technical school and a women's psychiatric hospital, visited the monument to student war heroes and attended the university banquet – where she and the queen were the only women among the five hundred guests.[133] The Swiss Alps caused Turville to muse about the landscape and what it was like before tourists started to go there: the modern railway and the noise made by it struck her as almost sacrilegious but, she admitted, the journey was charming and picturesque.[134]

Ada Turville liked Italy. Venice was 'charming' and 'romantic' and Rome a 'wonderful mixture of the ancient' (the Tarpeian rock) and 'the modern' (the jazz bands that played in its cafés). Unlike tourists who complained about southern Italy's summer heat, she found the sea breezes made summer there preferable to summer in Canada (coming from southern Ontario, it appears that Turville thought of her home country as landlocked).[135] Florence held many attraction for her. She visited the straw hat market, had a look at the jewelry on the Ponte Vecchio, and toured the Royal University which, with its cosmopolitan summer student body made her think of it as a kind of 'League of Nations.'[136] The streets, coliseum, and churches of Fiesole took Turville into the vividly rendered past of one of 'the most ancient towns in Italy.'[137] In Assisi she observed the pilgrims who had come for the anniversary of the Special Indulgence. They were 'mostly peasant women, dressed in heavy, voluminous, long cloth skirts and white blouses surprisingly clean, on their heads cashmere shawls, on their feet either nothing but dust or a binding of cotton with sandals, or heavy leather boots which looked and sounded as hard as iron. Poverty, illiteracy, and hopelessness were written all [over] their faces, and the thought of the hardships and toil with which their daily course must be run brought the deepest sadness to our hearts.'[138] Turville produced a much happier depiction of southern Italians, if one framed by the same tourist lens that captured either downtrodden 'native' women or what remained of a romantic – and sanitary – past. At the

Palio festival in Siena, she was entertained by a pageant full of music, banners, and performers in 'picturesque' medieval and Renaissance costumes, with their velvet, feathers, puffed sleeves, and brilliant colours (she also enjoyed the knights' armour). She was impressed to see that the huge crowds in the square, policed by officers on horseback, included balloon and caramel sellers but not peanut vendors, so that the 'surprisingly clean' square remained so.[139]

Leaving their car in a London garage, the Ashbridges' European tour began in Holland where in Amsterdam, they were greeted by 'the funniest' Cook's man, who escorted them to their hotel and then took them around the city. 'A very clean place with all houses, built out to the street,' Mabel thought, and with 'canals all up and down and across the city one right in front of our hotel. The water is said to be changed every morning between four and six and well it might be for it smells none too sweet in spots. This morning as we came into the hotel we met two maids going out the front door with pails of dirty scrub water and they walked across the car tracks and threw it in the canal.' Although not overly impressed by the canal being used as a public drain, Mabel had never seen 'so much scrubbing in my life. This hotel has been scrubbed all day by about six girls and all along its streets we saw women and girls *scrubbing* steps and sidewalks and even front walls of its houses. Some wore wooden boots to do it in.'[140] Their tour of Amsterdam included the Queen's Palace, the 'Art Gallery' ('Rembrandt, Franz Hals, Vermeer'), a diamond-cutting factory, and window-shopping. They also visited a cheese factory, which resembled a 'private house' and was 'so scrubbed and clean, we could hardly believe it possible that any animal had ever been in.'

The Dutch communities of Volendorn and Marken continued to attract tourists, as they had before the Great War. As the steam yacht they were on pulled into Volendorn, Mabel Ashbridge noticed that 'great crowds from other boats kept landing and going away. This was a delight for all the people were dressed in their native dress all of them so anxious to have their pictures taken for money.' At Marken Mabel and her daughter Dorothy were caught by the people's 'costumes,' particularly the women's caps, which Mabel found so interesting and 'different' that she bought a young girl's (having already bought one in Volendorn). The Ashbridges toured a private home, which had curtained bunks built into its walls: 'I'd die in one I think,' wrote Mabel. Before leaving Marken they were quite 'pleased to see a gold cap on an old lady on Sat. night. It had a white cap with wide frill sticking out behind and for street wear a black bonnet was worn over it. These gold caps are heirlooms and only the older women wear them now.'[141] Mabel's daughter Betty observed from their train window that people in the Dutch countryside 'wore their everyday working clothes, not their dress-up Sunday ones,' and were thus very much like 'our own' (with the exception of the navy-blue peaked men's caps that she had seen in pictures). Still, the Ashbridges appear to have had better luck in seeing 'picuturesque' Dutch costumes than did Dorothy Hutchinson, who recorded somewhat wistfully, 'few windmills and no pantaloons as far as we saw. Men and boys in sabots not *plentiful*.'[142]

After a tour of Rotterdam, the next stop on the Ashbridge's itinerary was Paris, where they went to the Louvre, Arc de Triomphe, Hôtel des Invalides, Eiffel Tower, Pantheon, Notre Dame, and Père Lachaise, as well as Versailles and Fountainbleau. (The Ashbridges' tour of well-known and predictable stops stemmed partly from their use of a Cook's taxi tour for part of their trip). Some of Paris was entrancing. The Louvre was 'the best [gallery] in the world,' the Pantheon was 'beautiful,' and the Petit Trianon, Malmaison, and Fountainbleau all gave Mabel and the others great pleasure.[143] However, Mabel confessed to being disappointed in Notre Dame and found the crowds, heat, and her sore and blistered feet more than a little taxing.[144] She enjoyed the Comédie Française, though, where the family saw *Le Gendre de M. Poirer*, a play that Dorothy and Betty had just studied in school and which 'Wellie' had read to her last spring.[145] Mabel's more vivid impressions of Paris, though, were often of the shops and their employees. At the Louvre a non-English-speaking French clerk and a 'bewhiskered man in a frock coat' sold Mabel a pair of shoes that only temporarily solved her problems with walking. On the Avenue de la Père a 'lovely-looking store' beckoned, with English-speaking staff, 'and we were wafted from one upstairs to the dresses. As soon as we had seen the rooms, we decided we had made a mistake,' so they made their 'excuses and escaped' (the rooms were quite 'grand' with marble fireplaces and elaborately painted ceilings).[146] While her husband and daughters went up Notre Dame's tower, Mabel decided to buy envelopes in a nearby shop, where she was served 'by a girl who had her eyelids and under her eyes blackened. She was a fierce-looking saleslady.'[147] On various occasions Mabel and her daughters wrote of their confusion in trying to buy clothing in Paris, a confusion that stemmed mostly from their inability to speak much French. 'The French salespeople are funny, they never hurry and all talk at once and wave their hands so. We find them talking very loudly at us, as though we were deaf.'[148]

The Ashbridges did not venture into Italy. Their European travels took them only as far as Lucerne and (on a Cook's tour) the Rhone glacier. On their way to the glacier they saw women working in the fields and women selling fruit and flowers at the market stalls in Lucerne, and women in 'native dress' embroidering handkerchiefs outside in front of the city's shops.[149] In Switzerland the Ashbridges also took a Cook's tour to Eschenbach. They saw two 'fine' Catholic churches there and a nunnery with, Mabel noted, two orders of nuns, one that consisted of working sisters and the other of 'high born women from other countries who of course bring all their money to give in to the church. These are not allowed outside the walls nor to mix with "civil" persons.'[150] The Ashbridges enjoyed Switzerland, as they toured the 'old part' of Lucerne, went window-shopping, feasted their eyes on beautiful views of the lakes and mountains, and admired the chapel, birthplace, and monument of William Tell. Their drive to the glacier was 'the most wonderful' one that Mabel had had, 'for while the B.C. mountains are just as fine, we were up higher than we have ever been before and could see more.'[151] But what made the biggest impression on them were the 'lovely Swiss costumes.' Women wore long velvet skirts, silk waists, 'fancy colours,' ornamentation and beading, and silver-buckled black shoes, while the men were in 'short green trousers, green vest and black velvet coat, low black fedora with feather in the side.' Mabel reported seeing 'an elderly lady with high headdress of black material made wing shape with long fringe hanging down.'[152] Classifying 'foreign' cultures and nations by their dress, particularly women's, continued to be part of anglophone Canadian tourists' toolkit for marking identities, those of 'others' and their own.

Like Morse and Turville, the Ashbridges had a 'happy holiday' indeed in Europe. This could not be said of Effie Storer's trip through France. Her tour was arranged through Cook's, and like for many people who went to France in the 1920s, Storer's main purpose in visiting that country was to tour the battlefields of the Great War and visit loved ones' graves.[153] Her thoughts and sensations before she reached the battlefields were of the war years. At Calais the crowds reminded her of a 'troop-train crush,' and she met there a Scottish woman and her son, who were on their way to visit a gravesite near Ypres.[154] Effie Storer searched for the graves of her friend Beth Henderson's sons but was unable to find them, remarking that she could have had 'all sorts of trophies of German bayonets and other things but they have no lure.' Despite the sad nature of her trip, Storer was cheered by the beauty of the cemeteries and in her letter to her friend Beth Henderson wrote that 'foliage has done much to erase the horrors by covering them over.' The English cemeteries seemed to her 'so green and restful,' while the French had 'gay flowers but awful weeds.' The grave of Effie Storer's husband was in a 'lovely spot' and the prettiest that she saw. With its singing birds and general air of peace, she was reminded of parts of Battleford that held happy memories for their married life. While the experience left her feeling 'shakey,' nevertheless for Storer the cemeteries were lovely, 'truly God's acres,' and 'we can proudly say Canadians own a spot in France.'[155]

Storer's sadness was assuaged by the kindness she witnessed in France. She noticed a number of women who, accompanied by their young sons were looking for their older sons' graves, and the French people appeared to go out of their way to be helpful to them. 'Sometimes, though,' she wrote, 'you might as well ask a tree as some men. They seem to lack even ordinary intelligence but the women are alert.'[156] Always attentive to the roles and position of women in the countries that she visited, Storer noted the healthy-looking elderly women who presided over the *estaminets*; moreover, while widows, swathed in black with skirt-length veils, wore their weeds 'gracefully ... it would drive me melancholy' to be dressed in such a fashion.[157]

Sophia Wilson toured many of the same places in Paris as Storer and the Ashbridges did, but she had far less praise for its inhabitants and contemporary Parisian life. The drivers there were 'lawless,' and as far as she was concerned, pedestrians injured in road accidents were more likely to be arrested by the police than helped by them. Moreover, 'their sanitation laws are no more rigid than the traffic ones, case of suit yourself.' Anglophone Canadian tourists who had visited Paris before the war, unlike Wilson found its cafés and boulevard life less than enchanting. The cafés 'corral' the entire pavement, and people 'are served so called light wines all day and night. Most of them belong to the labouring people, one can easily understand their poverty, also why the expulsion of the Acadians was necessary.'[158] While the statues on the Champs de l'Elysée were wonderful, although it and the Louvre were in need of a good clean: Wilson could not find a place to sit in the Louvre's statuary section 'and the walls were too dirty to lean upon.' Moreover, while she thought that the miniatures of the *Mona Lisa* that were sold in the Louvre were very good, 'I never thought much of Mona,' she confessed to her brothers, 'her expression is crafty more so than in the original than in the copies.' Things improved with a trip to the opera to see *Samson and Delilah*, for the orchestra and lighting impressed Wilson, and she found that Delilah was a 'grand' and 'majestic' singer.[159] On Bastille Day, however, the Parisian crowds spent their time 'drinking, drinking, drinking ... I doubt whether many of them knew why the day is kept.'[160] The lighting at the Folies Bergère was the only thing worth seeing there. Sophia Wilson could not find any dresses she liked in Paris, and the women who served her hard brioche in the morning not only were hatless but their 'appearance is far from appealing.'[161] She was far from sorry to leave. 'We bade goodbye to Paris, noisy and much overrated Paris, demanding the prestige of its royal origin, the freedom and license of a republic, of gratuity without service, it screams, 'look what we suffered in the war,' but makes no effort to restore the damage, its men are content to sit for hours in drinking places tippling themselves more stupid than before, they smoke, they wear hats during theatre performances showing that after all they have not risen beyond the *sans collot* [*sic*].'[162] The past was to be preferred to the present: 'the glory of the place, the dignity of its buildings is another story and speaks of a truer, more courageous period.'[163]

Switzerland appealed far more to Wilson, who found its scenery, people, institutions, and even food far more congenial to her tastes than those of France. 'Why,' she wrote in a letter to her brothers, 'waste a week in Paris, dodging traffic, being cursed by taxi men, trying to enjoy hard crust rolls when such a pretty country invites us?'[164] In Switzerland she could enjoy Mont Blanc, and nearby the lovely scenery around Innsbruck, Austria. This city also won her approval for its preservation of historical buildings, unlike the situation in Halifax whose residents, she explained, suffered 'from the present day mania to destroy beautiful facades and stick up flat brick fronts that resemble nothing at all.'[165] In Geneva, Wilson visited the League of Nations and the International Labour Association, and was quite pleased to point out that Canada had donated the doors of the ILA's building.[166] Her party then moved on to Germany, where they stayed at Oberammergau and saw the Passion Play. Wilson, who had read about the production before leaving Canada, told her brothers about the theatre, the actors, the various twists and turns of the 'plot' (including Jesus' betrayal by the High Priests, rabbis, Caiphas, Annan, and Judas), and the effects that all of this had on the spectators: 'the hush, the quiet of the audience shows how deeply they are touched. There are Red Cross huts about on the grounds, their officers stand about in the theatre, now and again, as they watch the audience, someone is given a helping hand, returning in a short while to watch again. At the close of the Play that vast audience walks quietly away as from some solemn service. It is finished.'[167]

With her group Sophia Wilson toured Munich, Augsburg, Nordingen, Dresden, and Berlin, where their itinerary included museums, galleries, and historical sites. In keeping with the Overseas Educational League's desire to promote international understanding, though, they also were welcomed by Munich's mayor at a reception, treated to an exhibit of folk-dancing, taken to Bayreuth, addressed by Germany's ambassador to Austria, and shown around a Children's Village (a home for German war orphans), schools, settlements, and department stores.[168]

Like the Ashbridges and other Anglophone Canadians before her, however, Sophia Wilson was happy to leave Europe, telling her brothers that while had had interesting and grand experiences and hoped to return, 'We are English people, their ways are not our ways.'[169]

Nation and Empire in 1920s Tourism

As these commentaries suggest, ethnic and national characterizations – both of themselves and of others, whether tourists or residents – continued to shape transatlantic tourism after the First World War. Effie Storer, for example, found that 'the kindness of the French is so refreshing after the aloofness of England,' although she noted that the 'shopgirls' in the souvenir store at Arras, who so kindly went out of their way to talk to her, nevertheless increased the price of her purchases, 'as I was a tourist, so I left them there.'[170] To Storer, the French also seemed to be as indefatigable 'scrubbers' as the Dutch for Mabel Ashbridge: 'the people are clean and seem to be always looking for a place to scrub. Each woman scrubs the piece of sidewalk before her home.' However, 'evidently they never heard of microbes as the bread is carried in their hands, unwrapped, along the street. Children wishing to play set it on the sidewalk.'[171] But, as we have seen, Sophia Wilson had little good to say about the French; in addition to their dangerous driving, drinking, and lack of sanitation, their diets affected more than the tourists' palate. According to her, a woman fainted in the line-up at Malmaison as a result of standing too long, in close air, and the 'garlic laden breath which surrounded her.'[172] She ranked Germany and the Germans quite highly for their cleanliness and orderliness, although she thought that bus drivers in that country 'bungled' and caused long delays 'to annoy, otherwise they are stupider than the average labouring man' (if Wilson did not trade in national or ethnic stereotypes quite as much as some, she made up for it in class-based typecasting).[173]

Comments about the French liking to drink and the Germans enjoying order were not, of course, new, nor were they made only by English-speaking Canadians. Identifying and classifying Jews preoccupied more than one diarist and travel writer. William Morse's account of his European trip is full of such comments, which start during his journey across the ocean. 'Fifty per cent of the travelers are of semitic origin, well dressed and smart,' he told his readers. 'The hopes for the resettlement of these people in Palestine are not bright, because the sons of Abraham prefer the busy centres of the world or this ship, which has been dubbed the "Palestine Express."'[174] Morse's estimation of the qualities and character of a number of places in Britain included the qualities that he thought 'Jews' might find either appealing or a detriment and these descriptions traded quite explicitly in anti-Semitism: a large, enclosed yard for broken-down automobiles in Slough made Morse comment, 'What a chance for some Jew or dealer in such second-hand commodities.'[175] Kathleen Coburn noticed 'Jews' in ways both casual and pointed. Describing the ice-skating at Hammersmith, she wrote, 'tiny little handkerchief of ice, clientele largely Jewish, but they have one good thing to offer – speed skating for ladies only!'[176] After seeing *The Two Companions* at London's His Majesty's Theatre, Coburn and a friend went for a snack, and 'the view of the Jewish clientele was so overwhelming that Miss T had to be moved around the corner so as not to look right at them!'[177] During Effie Storer's visit to London, she found that 'everything interests me from the corpulent Jew strutting by to the vendors on the streets' (it is not stretching credibility to assume that she believed the latter were Jewish).[178]

It would, however, be reading too much into these examples, to claim that Morse's and Coburn's comments represent an intensification of anti-Semitism amongst middle-class English-speaking Canadian tourists. As we have seen, in the 1880s Canadian travel writers Emily Murphy and Grace Denison designated – and rarely with benign intent – certain neighbourhoods in Britain and Europe as 'Jewish.' Furthermore, attendance at Oberammergau, whether pre- or postwar, did not elicit or provoke anti-Semitic invective or outbursts on the part of travel writers (what happened outside of their readers' earshot might well be another matter). Nevertheless, such comments – whether explicitly denigrating and reliant on stereotypes of the money-grubbing and cosmopolitan Jewish man or simply denoting a supposed presence – suggest that notions of Jews as 'others' continued to function as part of these tourists' world-view, shaped their perceptions of urban landscapes, and in Britain contributed to their definitions of who was (and was not) an imperial subject.

Americans continued to come in for a fair share of comments. 'If I did not love the Yankees before I have less use for the class of tourists every day,' Storer wrote to Beth Henderson. 'They are so prodigal of money and bow so much. If they would even cut out affected nasal twangs I might forgive them some of their foolishness. They make me think of the proverb "a loud tongue and an empty head."'[179] Coburn was even less flattering about American tourists and American influence in general. When she was in Germany she recounted in her diary anecdotes that she had heard about American tourists' inability to speak anything but English. She described breakfasting with a group of American tourists who told her that they had eaten nothing but pork for five days, as they could not read German menus, and who also advised her to see Madame Tussaud's while in London, 'a city which they definitely did not like!'[180] Coburn also objected to the images she saw in American popular culture: a film at a Devon movie theatre exemplified 'the 'impossible dregs of American movie production ... no wonder the Americans are despised here.'[181] 'American films,' she believed after a discussion in her college, 'are to blame for a heap of dashed queer ideas about Canada and universities.'[182]

But it was not just Americans who were castigated. In Paris Effie Storer expressed the hope that 'French people do not judge our average young lady by the giddy [English] school teachers who tour and air their poor knowledge of French in a foolish way at the table.' Violet McNaughton was appalled by the behaviour of some of the English tourists she saw in Paris.

> Parisians on the street do not want to be pestered by foreigners and many refuse to even shake their heads to indicate they do not understand your request. You cannot blame them as some English-speaking people are abominably provoking. I heard one man creating quite a disturbance at the hotel because no one knew the French for "sherry" so he could not find out if any was to be had. He called the porters, the waiters and everyone in sight to find one who might know and seemed inconsolable at his lack of success even though there were 99 other varieties to choose from. Another man at Montmartre in a loud tone complained at the variety of ways the French dressed their food – Old London was good enough for him and he couldn't get there too soon. Another lady explained the lengths they went to ensure an English breakfast. I'll admit the breakfast is a shock at first – just French rolls and coffee and served very informally.

But the other 2 meals more than compensate and I enjoyed every one in spite of garnishes and strange flavourings. Shall never forget their cooking and serving of vegetables and compotes.'[183]

English-speaking Canadians tourists might go so far as to despise and mock what they considered to be English pretentiousness. Frank Duggan spent his time in London taking pictures of Westminster and Big Ben, visiting restaurants, nightclubs, and theatre, and strolling around Leicester Square and Piccadilly Circus, until he tired of 'stalling off prostitutes.' He found English service poor. 'They sure are slow here,' he complained about a wait to purchase a bus ticket, while at Simpsons' he and his friends 'had a great time razzing those dumb Englishmen: they seem to be all in a fog. They say the service here is good but so far we haven't seen any of it.'[184] Duggan was more than just irritated about the pace of English waiters, though. His walk through Leicester Square provoked the following outburst: 'these folks are very proud and "upstage." They are very polite and carry themselves as if it hurted [sic] them to move. Silk hats and full dress are very common. Even the poor wear spats, gloves, and carry a cane. They are so far behind America that they'll never catch up. I hate the lousy race of Englishmen!'[185] Unlike the vast majority of his fellow tourists, Duggan appeared uninterested in the riches of English culture and history, choosing instead to pursue a tourism of leisure and entertainment.

Duggan's diary suggests an enactment of a physically aggressive, and – at least as far as he was concerned – populist North American masculinity. He spent a great deal of time during his Atlantic crossings lifting weights, rowing, swimming, playing golf, watching boxing matches and hearing racing broadcasts, and eyeing certain women while simultaneously fending off others.[186] Although Duggan did not attribute his perceptions of the English to a particular Canadian set of perceptions, other tourists brought with them a sense of being 'Canadian.' Like their prewar predecessors, they were quick to note any ignorance and confusion about or denigration of their homeland. 'It was certainly good to hear from home after having no word for almost six weeks,' thought Betty Ashbridge, after picking up the family's mail in London. 'The papers tell practically nothing about Canada.'[187] Dorothy, after touring St Nicholas Cathedral in York, realized the next day that 'I forgot to mention one thing I disliked very much … and that was in one of the windows the U.S.A. was called America, as though Canada was someplace else.'[188]

Some publicly corrected their imperial relatives' misperceptions. Kathleen Coburn, who was keenly aware of being a 'colonial' at Oxford, and who often introduced new acquaintances in her diary by both name and country of origin, appears to have been adamant in correcting misconceptions. She left London for Oxford after setting 'a hairdresser right about the difference between Canadians and Americans.' On her arrival at St Hilda's College, the college porter took Coburn for a Scot.[189] Five months later she was still at it, having fought with a clerk in a London shoe store, who thought that Americans and Canadians were all the same.[190] Coburn's didacticism vis-à-vis her national identity appears to have been directed mostly at those in the service or retail industry. When meeting with Lord Coleridge, a 'firm and interesting person,' who was opposed to women at Oxford, English democracy, Canadians and Americans, prohibition, and the clergy, she does not appear to have debated with him his lumping Canada and the United States together.[191] To be sure, she attempted to disabuse the gentleman of his 'English dreams about Indians,' of which he 'refused to be disillusioned. Discussed every nationality going which, being all "foreigners" have some loathsome characteristics to an Englishmen.'[192] Thus, in most of her dealings with England and the English, Coburn usually felt herself quite clearly to be a Canadian (albeit an Irish Canadian) and saw Canada as a place of youthful vigour and energy.[193] Yet she also felt tied to Britain and, in particular, England. On leaving the Coleridges, Coburn felt that Lady Coleridge came very close to kissing her; however, 'both being very British, she didn't.'[194] And on returning to England after three months in Germany, Coburn told her diary that 'I'll be jiggered if I wasn't almost as thrilled to see the lights of Harwich as I should be to see the shores of the good old St Lawrence.'[195]

International Affairs

Their diaries and travelogues suggest that in the 1920s shifting forms of modernity – and modernism – played a role in shaping Anglophone Canadian tourists' expectations and experiences. But their sense of being in a world that had seen profound changes – despite the continuities in their travel experiences with the experiences of Canadian tourists in the decades before the war – was shaped not just by the presence (or absence) of cars, airplanes, moving sidewalks, and the amenities of hotel rooms. Their awareness of changing currents in the world around them also was shaped by the trajectories of international political

developments. Such perceptions were not forged overnight, as products of the war and the Treaty of Versailles. These tourists did not
replace the earlier Canadian tourists' sense of being imperial and
national subjects with the subjectivity of the international citizen. The
majority of them continued to see Britain as an imperial centre that
wielded enormous historical and cultural influence and that for them
was, in a variety of ways and contexts, 'home.' To no small extent organizations established before the war, such as the International Council
of Women and the Imperial Leagues, facilitated and made logical the
kinds of international ties, and travel, that characterized the interwar
decades. In 1920s London, for example, Canadian women might have
a range of voluntary societies and clubs available to them. A friend
took Effie Storer to the Cowdray Club, 'a very exceptional, beautiful
club for professional women.' A gift from Lady Cowdray, the club had
been one of the Asquith family's homes and now the addition of a
nurses' college was being planned for it. Over lunch at the club, Storer
and her friend 'did not mention immigration. I know now I do not
want a job in London ... Tell Anna that Miss Billington has added a
moustache to her billy-goat goatee. But her hair and dress were very
becoming and the tea was good.'[196]

It would be equally disingenuous, however, to overlook the influence
on postwar travel of a sense of international responsibility shaped by
the events of 1914–18.[197] A number of those listed in *Canada: An Illustrated Journal* as departing to or returning from overseas were women,
members of various voluntary social and political organizations that
had widespread international links. Dr Maude Abbott of McGill University was in London in April 1929 before she embarked on a three-
month tour of Italy and other parts of the Continent; she also, though,
was overseas to represent Canada at the International Women's Federation.[198] Two years earlier Mrs J.A. Wilson, Canadian president of the
National Council of Women, travelled to Geneva for the International
Council's June meeting. Mercy McCulloch attended the 1921 International Conference of the Federation of University Women of Great
Britain, where she met delegates from Japan, India, France, Spain,
Czechoslovakia, Belgium, and Italy, and also a woman 'from Vic' (University of Toronto's Victoria College) who also was going to attend an
international YWCA conference.[199] Violet McNaughton travelled overseas in 1929 to represent Saskatchewan at the International Congress of
the Women's International League for Peace and Freedom in Prague
and to attend its summer school in Hungary.[200]

Many of these women's discussions of international relations centred on the 'problem' of Germany and German reconstruction. Sophia
Wilson might not have appreciated the irony that she sailed to Europe
on the *Empress of Australia*, originally built for the Kaiser, but she was
well aware that the Overseas Educational League wanted to educate
its members about international affairs and promote better understanding between nations. As the league's convoy of buses drove
through the German countryside in 1930, 'we wave a friendly hand –
in the interest of World Peace – it is not uncommon, as one looks back,
to see the grownups double that waving hand and shake a fist after us,
or their children to pull faces and run out tongues – in the interest of
World Peace. Policy keeps them polite in the shops and hotels. Who
began the row anyway?'[201]

Wilson was sceptical of Germans' protestations of their desire to be
'good neighbours' on the international stage. She described to her
brothers a trip to Seulis, the site of the signing of the Armistice, where
(she believed) the Germans had 'such faith and confidence in the Allies'
that on hearing the declaration of peace they used all the women and
old men from the French village as 'human shields,' declaring that 'if
the Allies wanted to shoot, the French could shoot their own people'
(Wilson also was offended by the wartime use of the village church as a
stable).[202] The former German ambassador to Austria, who addressed
Wilson's party, did not impress her: 'of course he talked peace and good
will. His speech seemed weak and insincere. I may be wrong.'[203] On
leaving Germany Wilson reflected again on what she thought of as German 'fulsomeness' and insincerity about the war. 'Only this morning
the Senator at Hamburg referred to the war, to Germany's great desire
for peace with all. Blah! Blah! Who began it? Much better taste not to
allude to it at all, just treat us as casual visitors. No need either to blame
their rulers, they were all interested and would have boasted long and
loudly had they come out ahead. As it is they want to flood our markets
with their goods to the exclusion of our own.'[204]

Kathleen Coburn was more sympathetic to Germany and its citizens.
In Germany she stayed with the von Ruperti family, where she was
exposed to numerous discussions of the 'great War' and Germany's role
as aggressor and victim, international economics, and unemploy-
ment.[205] 'War guilt' was a subject much-discussed at lunches and dinners. Her German hosts told her of the fabrication of atrocity stories, the
starvation of German citizens near the end of the war, and the relief
work of the Quakers, who saved hundreds of women's and children's

lives with their food parcels. The 'present fear of German militarism continuing is absurd,' they informed Coburn.[206] She heard about the position of students in German universities who, she was told, were very politically minded. They feel they have to study politics, both domestic and international, her hosts explained, because 'Germany stands practically alone, a line drawn round her by the other great powers chiefly at the instigation of France.'[207] She was assured that the students desired to emulate England in creating the same kind of knowledge of political situations and constitutional history that they felt English students possessed.[208] Coburn did not sense in Germans the same 'chill and shudder' that the English experienced at the mention of war, but she did observe a deep concern for social conditions in Germany as the effects of the Depression began to be felt in East Prussia.[209]

To no small extent, Coburn was aware of such issues because of the involvement of her hostess in local social welfare initiatives. Frau von Ruperti took her guest to see the 'home for stray and delinquent girls' at Marthheim, which to Coburn appeared 'very casual and informal and unprison-like – perhaps rather unsupervised? ... Girls seemed rather happy but of course resentful of visitors.'[210] The next day she and Ruperti visited the matron in charge of social work for girls in Allenstein, who told them of an increase in young women seeking the help of social services, an increase that she attributed to harsher economic conditions and a greater presence of soldiers in the area.[211]

Coburn was most impressed, however, by the institute that offered training to 'girls from lower-class farm families' in 'Cultur': the young women (and some men) were given an education that combined practical instruction (outdoor farmwork, housekeeping, and handicrafts) with exposure to folk music and culture, all of this underpinned by discussions of German politics and the development of a 'national' culture. The institute's graduation ceremonies deeply moved Coburn; she saw a skit whose motif was the 'love of homeland and the necessity of faithfulness to her whether at home or abroad.' The institute's director gave a farewell speech to the girls that left them in tears. He spoke of the 'sturdiness' of character that was needed for Germany's future and the contributions that an individual could make to the nation's life. 'It is an attempt to raise the peasant class into human beings so that here, in this boundary province, they will not be mere nonentities or political pawns, but will have a background of German culture which improves their general standard of living and makes them more steadfast citizens. There was not one word of antagonism to any other culture.'

(Coburn also noted the presence of two Romanians and one Hungarian, all of whom spoke German.) This 'attempt' at nation building greatly moved Coburn: 'how I longed to talk to these people. The intensity of their devotion to a land where the difficulties of living and living as Germans is so great – and their determination to deal with those difficulties in a fundamental way appealed to me very much.' East Prussians, she thought, loved their land like a 'mother a crippled child,' and she could see that love 'clearly and deeply' in 'these simple people.'[212]

Coburn, it seemed, did not question such efforts at creating a German nation using the methods and imagery of 'the folk.'[213] Nor did she consider other developments in German politics and society, ones that might have caused her to doubt her hosts' continual assurances of Germany's lack of a militaristic ethos.[214] Yet despite her enthusiasm for the folk institute's work, she worried about the problems that Germany faced, particularly in East Prussia. After spending the morning before her departure for Köningsberg, she talked to Frau von Ruperti about her work as president of the local Frauenverein, a branch of the Red Cross, which was trying to form a confederation for the coming winter's hardships. Ruperti told Coburn that they work together 'harmoniously' but introducing men to the group also introduced Protestant-Catholic and other political conflicts. A case in point was the fate of Ruperti's initiative to distribute clothing to poor households in the region regardless of denominational membership. Initially received with great enthusiasm, the plan was upset once male political leaders became involved. Ruperti and her friends were very concerned about the coming winter and the maintenance of law and order; she was afraid of Communist riots and hoped that cooperative welfare efforts would keep the peace. Coburn was left contemplating her own good fortune, musing that 'Canada seems in a bad way this winter but surely not as bad as this. I can't picture such a state of affairs.'[215]

The records of English-speaking Canadian tourists' jaunts around Britain and Europe in the 1920s indicate how modernity might be made and remade, just as other relationships and subjectivities – gender, class, nationalism, and imperialism – with which it intersected and entwined also were subject to both instabilities *and* stabilities, fluctuations *and* endurances. A number of the shifts that occurred within interwar tourism would endure: the use of cars to shape the tourist's landscape being an obvious one. Travel as a form of international diplomacy appears to have been more pronounced in the 1920s than in the decades before the Great War. Yet many features of late Victorian and Edwardian Anglophone Canadians' travels prevailed: notions of 'nation' shaped through observations of local residents and of other tourists, a fascination with history, evaluations of nations and societies that were based on gendered assumptions, and the sensory dimensions of tourism that were experienced through art, theatre, music, consumption, and landscape.

The writings of the Canadian men and women tourists examined in this study reveal how transatlantic tourism helped hone and shape the subjectivity and understanding of middle-class, English-speaking Canadians and the role that travel played in prompting them to examine how the relationships of gender, class, nation, and empire structured their worlds, with all the attendant ambiguities and contradictions that this involved. Such perceptions and reflections on their experiences while away travelled back with them across the Atlantic, along with dresses from Harrods's, postcards of the Tower, West End theatre programs, Belgian lace, and perhaps photographs of the Mediterranean coast. What happened when all this baggage disembarked at Montreal, Toronto, Winnipeg, and Victoria is another story.

Epilogue

'As everyone is familiar with the luxury of a long pull on the Grand
Trunk I shall bring this journal to a close,' Fred Martin wrote as his
Toronto-bound train pulled out of the railway station at Quebec City.
He was not sorry to do so, admitting that 'I have had no end of trouble
in trying to keep it up, getting way behind lots of times and having to
make up from memory so goodbye old journal "what a pest" you have
been to take care of for the last four months and if ever I go again I certainly shall not take you or any of your family.' Nevertheless, Martin
ended with the observation that he had had a delightful trip: 'never
missed but one train – was not sea sick … and had excellent health.'[1]

Whether Martin changed his mind regarding his 'pest' on future
journeys is, unfortunately, impossible to know. His comment that
'everyone' was 'familiar' with a lengthy, luxurious train trip should
give the reader pause: his 'everyone' was, of course, far from an inclu-
sive or all-encompassing category and did not capture all the experiences of even this group of middle-class tourists. But his delight in his
travels as they approached their conclusion was shared by many of his
fellow Canadian tourists. 'There ended a very pleasant holiday, which
has left many agreeable impressions of places and persons and works
of art to recall and think about,' mused Edward Greenshields as he
made his way home to Montreal in 1906.[2] Despite Ethel Davies's
excitement about going home, she was very sorry to bid her English
relatives and friends goodbye (she was sobered once she arrived back
in Charlottetown by the news of a fire on an ocean liner in Manhattan
Harbour, in which the men in the holds had died)[3] Many Canadian
travelers shared Davies's pleasure at the prospect of being home again.
Near the end of her 'wonderful and delightful trip, ' Mary Bain could

not contain herself in her 'hooray for home.' Mabel Ashbridge thought she had 'a holiday to remember but it is nice to get home too. We traveled 3400 miles by our car in England, Scotland, and Wales and stayed in eight-six hotels altogether.'[4] A few tourists were simply exhausted and fed up. As he neared Corinth, Ontario, George Disbrowe was aware that he tired of travelling and that he had a bad headache, although he was soon relieved to find that all was well at home. And perhaps William Caldwell's grumbling about the duty he had to pay on returning to Canada was exacerbated by the cold he had caught while on board ship.[5]

What did all the time, expense, and energy that went into transatlantic tourism amount to for this particular group of Canadians once they landed back in Charlottetown, Corinth, Toronto, Vancouver, and Woodstock? Some left only their travel diary in the archive, and so while it is possible to catch glimpses of how their preconceptions of Britain and Europe might (or might not) have been changed by their travels, it is impossible to know how their time abroad shaped their identities and perceptions once they returned to Canada.[6] Even those tourists whose travel diaries and letters form part of a larger personal or family archive did not tend to provide much direct evidence of their reflections on their overseas experiences once they had returned home, unpacked, and resumed their daily lives. As I have argued earlier, the impact of cultural attitudes, values, and perceptions is not easy for the historian to measure. For example, I would hesitate to draw any straightforward or uncomplicated line between these tourists' assessments of the spectacles of British imperialism that they surveyed and support within anglophone Canada for imperial federation (although for some the former might have helped make up their minds on the latter – for better or worse). Unlike the people who wrote enthusiastically in the press and periodicals about the pedagogical values of travel, historians (including this one) have tended to be sceptical of claims that travel and tourism are necessarily or automatically educational, if we understand travel as leading to more tolerant and less judgmental shifts in perceptions and attitudes. As I have argued throughout this book, overseas tourism might well exacerbate existing prejudices and previously formed opinions; such could be said to be the case regarding both Naples *and* London. Not everything could be predicted and managed smoothly: historical and natural landscapes and sites might evoke unexpected depths and qualities of emotion, taking a wrong turn or missing a railway connection might result in a pleasant or at least instructive encounter with 'locals' or fellow tourists.

At the very least, '*A Happy Holiday*' demonstrates that an examination of overseas tourism can provide a number of insights into the subjectivities of some middle-class, English-speaking Canadian men and women in the first six decades after Confederation. Their time in Britain and on the Continent was about cultural instruction and pleasure as a means of considering, consolidating, and performing notions of gender, class, nation and empire, culture, and history. Their writings allow us a glimpse of the impact of various aspects of modernity, as these men and women struggled to cope with what at times seemed to be an excess of sights, sounds, smells, and feelings. As Keith Walden has written about the people who attended Toronto's Industrial Exhibition in the years from 1879 to 1903, an event that a number of these transatlantic tourists might well have attended: 'being modern' meant more than 'grasping grand theological and scientific schemes or master narratives propagated by popular media' (here I would add that one of those 'master narratives' was the desirability of transatlantic travel).[7] Being a 'modern tourist' in this transatlantic context might mean being overwhelmed by evidence of the cruelties and tragedies of the past; feelings of antimodernist nostalgia for a supposedly simpler and more innocent time evoked by seeing peasant communities or medieval buildings; constantly making assessments of the goods and sensations offered by the shops and on stages; and coping with guides and porters who seemed at the same time to represent primitive and/or rural societies and be well attuned to the capitalist and consumerist nexus of late-Victorian and early-twentieth-century tourism. The modern tourist might suspend, albeit temporarily, the conventions of customary daily behaviour to indulge in unfamiliar pleasures such as lying in gondolas, observing or even participating gambling at Monte Carlo, or just wandering alone through the streets of London or Paris. The modern tourist would likely experience a heightened awareness of being a traveller who has crossed national borders and boundaries and at the same time be mindful of a sense of belonging in national and imperial communities, ones constituted through political, social, and cultural networks and affiliations.

For this group of historical actors, travel to Britain and Europe was a hallmark of a discerning, cultured, liberal subjectivity, one deeply embedded in 'modern' ways of thinking and being. The historical, cultural, and social attractions these tourists visited were perceived to be 'the best,' the epitome of culture and civilization: direct knowledge of them, both intellectual and sensory, was crucial to their sense of themselves as enlightened and educated individuals.[8] Viewing, analysing, and assessing the landscapes and institutions of British and European tourism, and classifying and categorizing the people of the countries through which they moved (not to mention the other tourists encountered along the way) were practices heavily shaped and inflected by the notion of progress, both their own personal progress and, for many of them, that of the British Empire. As a plethora of scholarship has shown, in this period progress and civilization were in no way concepts innocent of relationships of power, particularly those of race and empire.[9] Few English-speaking Canadian tourists referred to themselves explicitly as 'white,' and in their travels around Britain and Europe they did not designate the Irish, Jews, or European peasants strictly speaking as *racial* others. Nevertheless, for them being Canadian and a member of the 'British world' was underpinned by a sense of belonging to a community of what they expressly considered to be civilized and superior men and women. Canada might be, in Thomas Langton's words, a 'hobble-de-hoy' arrangement, and its relationship to empire and the imperial centre might be a source of ambivalence and anxieties; nevertheless, in the jugement of these tourists, Canada had advanced beyond much of Europe (and certainly Ireland), and, they firmly believed, this was to no small extent because of Canada's ability to appreciate the cultural and political legacies that it had inherited from Britain and the lessons that Canadians had learned from British history.

If English-speaking Canadians needed further confirmation of their own civilized state and its merits, they needed only look out the window of their train carriage in Switzerland or Italy and see what happened to gender relations and roles when a society retained remnants of its medieval (or primitive) past: women were debased and degraded, their labouring bodies exposed to the curious tourist's public gaze; men wallowed in private selfishness and indolence, their decidedly non-labouring bodies engaged in pastimes that could lead to widespread public vice (excessive drinking and, possibly, gambling). Both sexes thus represented the antithesis of that moral and productive bourgeois femininity and masculinity on which nations and empires depended. It was no wonder to these Canadian tourists that so many European cultural treasures were produced by lost or vanished civilizations and that the European men, women, and children who ended up in Canada's cities and on its farms were in need of the lessons of culture and civilization, lessons to be imported by the likes of the Manitoba schoolteachers. Transatlantic tourism provided ample opportunity and space for

English-speaking Canadians to contemplate how they apportioned membership in the hierarchy of civilized nations and to reflect on the importance of culture and gender relations to these designations.

Postcards from Vimy: The 1936 pilgrimage

This book began with Mary Leslie's overseas travels in 1867, a trip structured by the relationships – literal and metaphoric – of the imperial family. It also was a pilgrimage of sorts; despite Leslie's disappointment with English society, we should not forget that for an aspiring anglophone Canadian writer, London was a cultural capital of overwhelming significance, its publishing houses and editors representative of the highest literary standards (notwithstanding the city's materialistic, uncultured, and greedy population, bad air, and poorly equipped kitchens).

In 1936 John Risser and Frank Fergusson made a much more self-conscious pilgrimage. With the other 'Vimy pilgrims,' Risser and Fergusson travelled back to France to witness the unveiling of Walter Allward's Vimy Memorial.[10] Risser, who was a commercial salesman from Riverport, Nova Scotia, published an account of his trip in a series of articles for a local newspaper, while Fergusson (whose occupation is unknown) left a typewritten diary that has come to rest in the Dalhousie University archives, in Halifax. While their time in France was significant and, for Fergusson in particular, their experience of the memorial's unveiling a sacred one,[11] equally important to both Risser and Fergusson was the chance to be a tourist, to wander the streets of London and Paris (and, in Risser's case, Manchester), visit historical sites, enjoy the English countryside, and make the acquaintance of strangers, whether fellow Canadian pilgrims or tourists from other countries.

Seeing the British monarchy was part of the Vimy trip, both at the memorial's unveiling and at a Buckingham Palace garden party hosted by the king. The emotional timbre of Fergusson's description of Edward VIII was not unlike that to be found in the works of anglophone Canadians writings about his great-grandmother, although in Fergusson's case it was Edward's populist appeal as a 'man of the people,' and not his domesticity, that was so compelling.

> Listening to the speech he made that day – if one could call such a simple and friendly talk by such a signified name – one can readily understand just why it is he has such a hold on the affections of his people ... it never

occurred to me that a King could be so very democratic, until in his talk to us his remark about the weather, 'which even I have no control over.' ... After hearing the many Englishmen and many more Canadians speak in the most glowing terms of their Ruler, it's a safe bet that it will be many long years before the Dictator will be in a position to do much dictating in the land of John Bull, or any of those mad fellows with wiry, black whiskers take the liberty of throwing a sputtering bomb in the direction of that blond haired lad who reigns so completely in the hearts of all his subjects.[12]

Risser was less impressed by the king and preferred instead to tell his readers about the Duchess of Gloucester's outfit, a dove grey dress with ostrich-feather trimming and matching hat in which she looked the 'perfect picture' (her husband at her side also appeared 'the picture of health').[13] Risser may have been influenced by reports of Edward's personal life: as he left the YMCA building, where he was staying, one evening he reported encountering 'some Mrs Simpson' who asked him to take her for a drink and who was surprised to hear that he was '"too busy."'[14]

But while Fergusson merely imagined the damage that both fascism and anarchism might wreck on England, Risser, taking a Thames boat trip, had the chance to meet and talk to two young German men, crew on a Hamburg–London steamer. 'They were non-committal about conditions in Germany and did not like it when we questioned them about Hitler, only to say "he was a good man." They highly resented the opinions we had of Hitler.'[15] The next day Risser visited the *Daily Express* building, which he thought was quite 'modern' with its black glass windows, and where he noted that the paper's displays featured the Spanish war, with maps of Spain set up and pins used to mark the different battles. Later that day he wandered around the various speakers in Trafalgar Square and stopped to hear the man who 'boosted' Mussolini's energy and vitality with the claim that this was the result of being a teetotal, non-smoking, vegetarian sportsman who steeped himself in Roman history. 'This speaker,' Risser wrote, 'at different times in his address gave the Fascist salute so as to "drive home" some of his remarks, and I noticed this salute was followed by a few sympathizers in the party who stood in the square beside him.'[16]

It is not, perhaps, surprising that international politics interested both men, given the reasons for their overseas trip and the relatively recent memory of their wartime service. Yet they were equally struck by the opportunities for entertainment and culture on offer in London.

Risser reported that on arriving in the city many of his compatriots enjoyed their first 'moving pictures' and then went on to the Hippodrome, where they saw a musical comedy with a cast of thirty-five, an orchestra of twenty musicians, and an auditorium packed and 'blue with smoke.'[17] A few weeks later he mingled with the crowds at the Olympia who had come to watch a display of televisions set up by Everready, Marconi, Westinghouse, and Phillips. Risser enjoyed watching the broadcast, which came from the Alexandra Palace, twelve miles away, and thought that 'the speaking also was good, considering that this is only in its infancy, and it all reminded me of sound pictures at a movie house.'[18] (Once Fergusson and his wife had attended the Buckingham Palace garden party, they too made a trip to the 'movie theatre' to watch the unveiling of the Vimy monument.[19]) Struck by the Strand Theatre's marquee which, outlined in electric lights, advertised the play *Aren't Men Beasts*, Risser considered going inside to remonstrate with the manager but decided against it, as he feared getting caught in a 'mixup' which would prolong his stay. The play had been running for some time to full houses that numbered in the thousands, 'no doubt wanting to know "why men were beasts,"' knowledge that would be denied Risser, as it had been sold out weeks in advance.[20] Lyon's Corner House, with its grocery and delicatessen, dining room, orchestra, and uniformed staff, also intrigued Risser, and he was pleased that it and similar establishments ensured English musicians plentiful opportunities for work. However, while he found the acrobats and the scantily clad dancer in the Tottenham Court Road Lyons 'in perfect decency and well conducted ... accomplished acrobats,' he did not find their performances particularly original or unusual, having seen very similar displays in circuses and other theatres.[21] Fergusson also had lunch at the Regent Street Lyons but was mostly concerned about his wife's time in Selfridge's. 'One lap around the ground floor with my wife and I called it a day, but I soon found out that she was just about to get her second wind, and was going to give the store a run for her money,' he confided to his diary. After lunch with a friend and a trip to Madame Tussaud's, Fergusson got lost walking back to his hotel, 'but by the faking of a cockney accent I made myself understood to the citizenry' and arrived 'home' only to find 'my wife is still in that dam [sic] store.'[22]

Fergusson tended to label as 'cockney' those British people whom he felt condescended towards him, such as the deck steward on the CPR's Le Havre–bound *Duchess of Bedford*, who ordered Fergusson and his friends off the upper deck. While well disposed towards the British with whom he had served, Fergusson had little time for anyone except his fellow pilgrims (in this he embodied the exclusivity that, Jonathan Vance has argued, was characteristic of Canadian veterans in the inter-war years).[23] He made many jabs at the 'enterprising French,' who displayed 'utter callousness' towards the veterans; moreover, rural French households had not changed much 'except, perhaps, that the filth in the farmers' yard smells a bit stronger. Boy, how those birds go in for pernicious effluvia in their domestic settings.'[24] Fergusson also shared in some of his predecessors' anti-Semitism: on boarding the ship home at Tilbury, he fumed at having to wait 'until those of more purple blood – including a few hook nosed birds whose very noses identified them as being of Semitic extraction – could be ushered to their cabins without the embarrassment of having to rub elbows with "the common herd."'[25] His anger grew when he and his wife were shown to their cabin 'far down in the bowels of the ship,' for 'what it lacked in size and appointments it sure made up in odour. It seems that when there is a shortage of Bohunks coming over from the cold steppes of Siberia to reap the golden harvests of Alberta, the big hearted CPR could not see the waste of carrying so much non-paying space, so had utilized such rooms for carrying cargo' (either, he thought, goats or guano).[26] Matters deteriorated even further for the Fergusson party when the boat stopped in France to pick up 'POLACKS. Yes, sir, from Warsaw and Czechoslovakia they came, arrayed as though for a trip to the North Pole, carrying bundles that would have made an artillery mule green with envy, and smelling like a herd of billy goats.' Before sailing Fergusson decided to go into town to 'get drunk, so that even Polacks wouldn't mean anything.' However, their first night at sea brought rough weather and the Polish and Czechoslovakian passengers were quite ill, with the result that the Canadian passengers formed a committee and forced the captain to move them up a deck to tourist class. The English businessmen on that deck, 'whose ancestry could have easily traced back as far as Moses,' then insisted on being moved to first class.[27]

Fergusson's account of his trip home was not very different from the steerage journey described by George Disbrowe of his trip to Britain in 1907; both men objected to the presence of Eastern Europeans on the grounds of the latter's ethnicity and class (note the collapsing of Poles and Czechs into the racially charged category of 'Polack'). Fergusson, though, was angriest with the CPR for its venality in taking advantage of the 'Vimy pilgrims,' wrapping up his account with the observations that 'the Pilgrimage is over, all hands had a wonderful time, the Legion is to be congratulated, Cooks [sic] made some money, even though the crowd was a bit too large for them. And the CPR, may they live long, and *never* prosper.'[28] Risser, in contrast, appeared to have had a very different trip there and back, apparently experiencing none of the class discrimination that Fergusson found endemic – and highly objection-able – on the ship (the fact that his account was for public consumption may, of course, have influenced its tone). He too noted that on the homeward voyage he was surprised to share his cabin with three com-panions from Poland and Austria, all of whom had been home to visit and were now returning to Canada. Risser commented that one of the men stored various meats and chicken under his berth for snacks, but the seasickness that Risser felt gave the room a 'ripe odour.' Unlike Fergusson, however, he chatted to his cabin mates and found that one was returning to his fruit and tea stand in downtown Toronto, while the other two men were returning to their mining jobs in northern Ontario. And, also unlike Fergusson, Risser was entertained by Marx Brothers and Joan Crawford movies on the way home, which may have made him more kindly disposed towards his companions.[29]

But if their racially inflected assessments of Europeans varied, Risser and Fergusson shared attitudes towards women that were at best con-descending and, at worst, clearly misogynist. Risser described the scene on board ship once the bar had opened: 'it's a common sight to see "Ladies" sipping beer and smoking at the same time, while later in life, some wonder why they need treatment in a sanitorium. Years ago they were spoken of as the "weaker sex."'[30] The smooth voyage was a boon for the men with artificial limbs 'and also very pleasant agreeable for the women – now nearly three score and ten years, tall and corpu-lent (would like to express myself in other ways) who have to hold on with both hands when about to negotiate stairways so you can imagine their predicament in adverse weather conditions.'[31] Fergusson con-trasted the solemnity of the Vimy pilgrims during the monument's dedication with the 'dizzy dame who, while the National Anthem of Britain was being played, and that mass of soldiers and civilians stood at stiff attention, passed along in front of the French soldiers now at "present arms," with a smoking cigarette in her rouged fingers, calling to her current boyfriend to join her.' Not that her flouting of propriety went unnoticed: 'I will leave to the imagination of my readers just what were the choice and opprobrious appellations hurled in her direction as she tripped lightly across the grass, while even the King himself remained standing "at attention." In most of their minds the incongruity of the occasion could only be equaled by playing a game of poker on the steps of St Paul's while service was going on.'[32] As we have seen, Fergusson also acted out the (much-stereotyped) role of the husband left to the mercy of his wife's consumerist desires: not only was he abandoned for the pleasures of Selfridge's, when it came time to pack, he had to cope with the results of her shopping spree. 'It was only then did I realize what a great mistake had been made when I left my wife alone in Selfridges,' he groused. 'The stuff one woman can kid herself into believing she needs when left to her own resources in one of those stores is really astonishing.'[33] And his displeasure at having to share his quarters home with Eastern European passengers was directed partly towards the women in that party, as his cabin was next to the women's washroom: 'the sounds emanating therefore were many and varied ... I must say there is absolutely no reason for any male going thru this sordid world ignorant of what the female form looks like unadorned, or otherwise, as long as he has the price of a one way passage on a boat carrying Polacks. Of course I mean that variety of Polack given to sea-sickness.'[34]

Overseas tourism thus continued to offer the possibility of seeing oneself and one's nation in the context of others, of exposing and confirming pre-existing prejudices and ethnocentric assumptions, and – perhaps – of challenging such beliefs. It would, of course, continue to do so after the Second World War, albeit in a different timbre, as travel to Britain and Europe increasingly became a mass-market phenomenon and as definitions of 'Europe' expanded (think of the migration of anglophone Canadian writers and artists to Greece, for example, as well as to Paris's Left Bank and to London). But that most definitely is another historian's story.

Notes

Abbreviations

AHM	Ashbridge House Museum, Toronto
AO	Archives of Ontario
DU-SC	Dalhousie University, Special Collections
FHM	Fulford House Museum, Brockville
HPL-LC	Hamilton Public Library, Local Collection
LAC	Library and Archives of Canada
MM	McCord Museum
MTRL-BR	Metropolitan Toronto Reference Library, Baldwin Room
MU-RBR	McGill University, Rare Books Room
PABC	Public Archives of British Columbia
PANS	Public Archives of Nova Scotia
PAS	Public Archives of Saskatchewan
QUA	Queen's University Archives
UG-ASC	University of Guelph, Archives and Special Collections
UWOA	University of Western Ontario Archives
VU-SC	Victoria University, Special Collections

Prologue

1 Mary Leslie to Elizabeth Leslie, 22 June 1867, AO, Box 5, Mary Leslie Papers, F 675.
2 Mary Leslie to John Leslie, 25 June, ibid.
3 Ibid.
4 Ibid., 7 Oct.
5 Mary Leslie to Elizabeth Leslie, 15 Mar. 1868, ibid.

6 For information on Mary Leslie (1842–1920), see Canada's Early Women Writers' database, www.lib.sfu.ca. Leslie's books included: *The Cromaboo Mail Carrier* (1878), *Rhymes of the Kings and Queens of England* (1896), and *Historical Sketches of Scotland, with an Account of Forty-eight of the Highlands Clans* (1905).

7 Mary Leslie to John Leslie, 2 July 1867, AO.

8 For accounts of that change, see David Cannadine, 'The Context, Performance and Meaning of Ritual'; Tori Smith, 'Almost Pathetic ... but Also Very Glorious.'

9 Mary Leslie to John Leslie, 2 July 1867, AO.

10 Ibid.

11 Ibid.

12 Ibid.

13 Mary Leslie to Elizabeth Leslie, 2 Aug. 1867, AO.

14 Ibid., 20 July 1867.

15 Mary Leslie to John Leslie, 6 Aug. 1867, AO.

16 Mary Leslie to Elizabeth Leslie, 2 Aug. 1867, AO.

17 Mary Leslie to John Leslie, 17 Aug. 1867, AO.

18 Ibid.

19 Ibid.

20 Ibid., 11 Aug. 1867, AO.

21 Ibid.

22 Mary Leslie to Elizabeth Leslie, 2 Aug. 1867, AO.

23 Mary Leslie to John Leslie, 6 Aug. 1867, AO.

24 Ibid., 17 Sept. 1867, AO.

25 Ibid., 6 Aug. 1867, AO.

26 Mary Leslie to Elizabeth Leslie, 2 Aug. 1867, AO.

27 Mary Leslie to?, n.d., AO.

28 Mary Leslie to John Leslie, 17 Aug. 1867, AO.

29 Angela Woollacott, *To Try Her Fortune in London*, 151–9.

30 Mary Leslie to John Leslie, 24 Oct. 1867, AO.

31 Ibid.

32 Mary Leslie to Mrs Geddes, 29 Dec. 1867, AO.

33 Mary Leslie to Elizabeth Leslie, 15 Mar. 1868.

Introduction

1 For discussions of the 'discovery of a diary' by historians, see H.V. Nelles, *The Art of Nation-Building*.

2 Eva-Marie Kröller, *Canadian Travellers in Europe, 1851–1900*.

3 For work on tourism and travel in Britain and Europe during this period, see Antoinette Burton, *At the Heart of the Empire*; Woollacott, *To Try Her Fortune in London*; Inderpal Grewal, *Home and Harem*; Neil Parsons, *King Khama, Emperor Joe, and the Great White Queen*; Cecilia Morgan, 'A Wigwam to Westminster'; William W. Stowe, *Going Abroad*; Marjorie Morgan, *National Identities and Travel in Victorian Britain*; Kröller, *Canadian Travellers in Europe*; John Sears, *Sacred Places*; Christopher Mulvey, *Anglo-American Landscapes*; Christopher Endy, 'Travel and World Power: Americans in Europe, 1890–1917'; and James Buzard, *The Beaten Track*.

4 Patricia Jasen, *Wild Things*; Karen Dubinsky, *The Second Greatest Disappointment*; Ian McKay, *The Quest of the Folk*. See also Michael Dawson, *Selling British Columbia*.

5 For English-speaking Canadians' engagement with so-called high culture for this period, see Maria Tippett, *Making Culture: English-Canadian Institutions and the Arts before the Massey Commission* (Toronto: University of Toronto Press, 1991).

6 See Harriett Priddis, Journals and Travel Diaries, 1876–1911, UWOA, J.J. Talman Regional Collection; Edward B. Greenshields, Travel Diaries, MM, Greenshields Family Papers, 1890–1913.

Very few tourists kept detailed accounts of the costs of their trip: based on the sources used for this research, it is difficult, if not impossible, to know what an 'average' tourist might spend. However, in this (as in other things) Greenshields was an exception, as he kept detailed records of his expenses. His 1894–5 trip, which lasted eight months, cost him over one thousand pounds; the following year he estimated to have spent roughly half that for about four months abroad (Travel Diaries 1894–6). In 1906 he calculated that a four-month trip that took in both parts of Europe and Britain ran to over $4,000 dollars – this covered tickets overseas for himself, his wife, and her maid; his European courier's fee; rail tickets in Europe; and $338 worth of purchases (Travel Diary 1906, File 469). However, the Greenshields party travelled first class, stayed in more luxurious hotels, ate in better restaurants, and shopped for fine goods; his costs would be considerably higher than those of other tourists. Contrast this with Saskatchewan resident Daniel Brown's 1906 trip to England, which lasted just over three months and included Manchester, Macclesfield, London, and Sheffield. Brown spent $620 to travel from Regina to Liverpool and back and (if his diary entries are accurate) less than twenty pounds while in England, as he stayed with family members and friends. His expenses in Toronto and Quebec City cost him under $4 dollars. (See Daniel Brown, Travel Diary 1906, PAS, Brown Family Papers, File IV, R-13300.2.

7 See John R. Walton, 'British Tourism between Industrialization and Globalization'; see also Walton's *The English Seaside Resort*; Alastair J. Durie, *Scotland for the Holidays*; John R. Gold and Margaret M. Gold, *Imagining Scotland*;
   John Beckerson, 'Marketing British Tourism.'
8 For a discussion of tourists' attitudes towards workers in the industry at
   Niagara Falls, see Dubinsky, *Second Greatest Disappointment*, 74–83.
9 See, e.g., Walton, 'British Tourism,' 123, on the agency of those upon whom
   tourists' gazes fell: 'The objects of this gaze have agency of their own, of
   course, and are capable of manipulating and making capital out of such
   perceptions, engaging in a dialogue of desire which results in tourist provi-
   sion that reflects the visitors' desire for some kind of authenticity or distinctive place-identity, however negotiated and refracted through a commercial
   prism this might be.'
10 Harmut Berghoff and Barbara Korte, Introduction, in Berghoff et al., *The
   Making of Modern Tourism*, 8.
11 Carl Bridge and Kent Federowich, 'Mapping the British World,' 3.
12 The pages of the *Canadian Magazine* from the 1890s until at least the 1920s
   are full of such articles. See also, e.g., the following travelogues written
   by Canadians: J.T.P.K., *Eastward Ho!*; Grace E. Denison, *A Happy Holiday*;
   J. Rupert Elliott, *Rambles in Merrie, Merrie England*; Emily Murphy, *The
   Impressions of Janey Canuck Abroad*; Irene Simmonds, *Our Trip to Europe*.
13 For discussions of imperialism's impact on English-Canadians, see Carl
   Berger, *The Sense of Power*; Mark Moss, *Manliness and Militarism*; Nancy M.
   Sheehan, 'Philosophy, Pedagogy, and Practice'; Katie Pickles, *Female Imperialism and National Identity*. The essays in Colin M. Coates, ed., *Imperial Canada, 1867–1917* point to, as Coates argues, the 'diversity of experience' of
   imperial ties during this period (at vii).
14 My thinking here is indebted to Benedict Anderson, *Imagined Communities*
   as well as the essays in Antoinette Burton, ed., *After the Imperial Turn*.
15 See Angela Woollacott, 'Metropolis as Crucible: Constructing Colonial,
   Imperial, and National Identities,' in *To Try Her Fortune in London*, for a
   particularly insightful discussion of how 'white colonials' coped with their
   relationship to empire in London. I would argue that, for Canadians, the
   question of racial identity and performance was one not always clearly
   spelled out (as it might be for South Asian travellers, for example) but that
   it manifested itself when, for example, the British conflated 'Canada' with
   'Aboriginality' – something that Canadians themselves both resisted and
   embraced. In *Imperial Dreams and Colonial Realities*, R.G. Moyles and
   Douglas Owram discuss British conceptions of 'Canadianess' that often
   relied heavily on images of Native people.

16 Harriett Priddis, 'Reminiscences of the Centennial 1876,' UWOA, J.J. Talman Regional Collection; George Pack, Travel Diary and Scrapbook 1911, 26, 28, 29 May, PABC, MS 0729.

17 Mary Bain, Travel Diary 1910, Nov., PABC, MS 2080 (her entries for the first month of her trip are not dated).

18 Ellen Bilborough, 'Diary of a Demi-Globe Trotter' (hereafter Travel Diary) 1896, LAC, MG 20/C106, Vol. I.

19 George Fulford to Mary Fulford, FHM, Fulford Family Papers, Senator George Fulford, Letters 1902–3. Date not always available for individual letters.

20 For the Grand Tour, see Chloe Chard, 'From the Sublime to the Ridiculous: The Anxieties of Sightseeing,' in Berghoff et al., *The Making of Modern Tourism*; see also Jeremy Black, *The British Abroad*, 47–68.

21 See, e.g., Newton MacTavish, 'Windermere to Coniston,' *Canadian Magazine* (Nov. 1912): 3–9, 3; also Mabel Ashbridge, Travel Diary 1927, 16 Aug., AHM, Ashbridge Family Papers.

22 Discussions of race and the development of race as an analytical category in English-Canadian society during this period include Mariana Valverde, *The Age of Light, Soap, and Water*; Peter Ward, *White Canada Forever: Popular Attitudes and Public Policy toward Orientals in British Columbia*, 2nd ed. (Montreal and Kingston: McGill-Queen's University Press, 1990); Kay J. Anderson, *Vancouver's Chinatown: Racial Discourse in Canada, 1875–1980*, 2nd ed. (Montreal and Kingston: McGill-Queen's University Press, 1991); Constance Backhouse, *Colour-Coded: A Legal History of Racism in Canada, 1900–1950* (Toronto: University of Toronto Press, 1999). For international work that deals with the racialization of the concept of civilization, see Gail Bederman, *Manliness and Civilization*.

23 Native people, however, were not as sequestered from modern society as some of these tourists might have believed; this period also saw the transatlantic movement of a number of Native men and women from Canada to Britain and Europe. While I had initially hoped to explore the overseas travels of a number of Native men and women to Britain and Europe at the same time as these non-Native Canadians, the amount and complexity of material for both groups convinced me that the former would be best served by their own, separate study, which will follow this one. In this project I will be exploring the transatlantic travels of Native peoples from British North America and Canada who went overseas as political petitioners, missionaries, performers, and students, 1780s–1920s (see Morgan, 'A Wigwam to Westminster').

24 Fred J. Ney, ed., *Britishers in Britain: Being the Record of the Official Visit of Teachers from Manitoba to the Old Country, Summer, 1910* (London: Times Book Club, 1911), 5.

25 See, e.g., my discussion in chapter 3 of the 'Spectator Girls' and 'Maple Blossoms' trips.

26 See John Urry, *The Tourist Gaze*, 2nd ed. (London: Sage, 2002), 10–13.

27 See, e.g., Ramsay Cook, *The Regenerators: Social Criticism in Late Victorian Canada* (Toronto: University of Toronto Press, 1985); John Webster Grant, *A Profusion of Spires: Religion in Nineteenth- Century Ontario* (Toronto: University of Toronto Press, 1988); David B. Marshall, *Secularizing the Faith: Canadian Protestant Clergy and the Crisis of Belief, 1850–1940* (Toronto: University of Toronto Press, 1992): Michael Gauvreau, *The Evangelical Century: College and Creed in English Canada from the Great Revival to the Great Depression* (Montreal: McGill-Queen's University Press, 1991); Mark A. Noll, David W. Bebbington, and George A. Rawlyk, eds., *Evangelicalism: Comparative Studies of Popular Protestantism in North America, the British Isles, and Beyond, 1700–1990* (New York: Oxford University Press, 1994); Lynne Marks, *Revivals and Roller Rinks: Religion, Leisure, and Identity in Late-Nineteenth-Century Small-Town Ontario* (Toronto: University of Toronto Press, 1992); Ruth Compton Brouwer, *New Women for God: Canadian Presbyterian Women and India Missions, 1876–1914* (Toronto: University of Toronto Press, 1990); Myra Rutherdale, *Women and the White Man's God: Gender and Race in the Canadian Mission Field* (Vancouver: UBC Press, 2002); Marguerite Van Die, ed., *Religion and Public Life in Canada: Historical and Comparative Perspectives* (Toronto: University of Toronto Press, 2001).

28 Greenshields, Travel Diaries: 1913, 21 May; 1895, 20 Jan., 28 May.

29 Pack, Travel Diary 1911, 25 June.

30 Ibid., Travel Diary 1910, 25 Dec.

31 Although I cannot state that all those who published travel accounts were Protestant, out of the diarists and travel writers only two, Osla Clouston and Mortimer Shea, were obviously Roman Catholics.

32 For a discussion of religion, see Kröller, *Canadians in Europe*.

33 Van Die, *Religion and Public Life in Canada*, 6.

34 The literature on this area is quite large, but see Woollacott, 'Inhabiting the Metropolis: Gendered Space and Colonialism,' in *To Try Her Fortune in London*; Judith Walkowitz, *City of Dreadful Delight*, 47–72; and her, 'Going Public'; Deborah Epstein Nord, *Walking the Victorian Streets*; Erika Diane Rappaport, *Shopping for Pleasure*; Dina Copelman, 'The Gendered Metropolis.'

35 Judith Adler, 'Travel as Performed Art'; Tim Edensor, 'Staging Tourism.' My thoughts on performance as a theoretical and analytical concept also have been influenced by Judith Butler, *Gender Trouble: Feminism and the Subversion of Identity* (London: Routledge, 1990); see also Butler, *Bodies that*

Matter: On the Discursive Limits of 'Sex' (London: Routledge, 1993); and Della Pollock, 'Making History Go.'

36 Pollock, 'Making History Go,' 6.

37 Historians of English Canada have focused on the role of moral reform as a central preoccupation of the middle class in this period and thus, perhaps unwittingly, have downplayed its desire for amusement and entertainment. But see Keith Walden, *Becoming Modern in Toronto*; also Nelles, *The Art of Nation-Building*.

38 For a exploration of this question in late nineteenth-century Canada, see Walden, *Becoming Modern*. For a discussion of modernity's centrality to late nineteenth- and early twentieth-century travel, see Woollacott, *To Try Her Fortune in London*, especially chapter 1, 'Australian Women's Voyages "Home": White Colonialism, Privilege, and Modernity,' 20–46.

39 Walden, *Becoming Modern*, 338.

40 C.A. Bayly, *The Birth of the Modern World, 1780–1914*, 11; Kathleen Wilson, *The Island Race*; Antoinette Burton, ed., *Gender, Sexuality and Colonial Modernities*.

41 Wilson, *Island Race*, 30.

42 London as a modern imperial centre is discussed in Woollacott, *To Try Her Fortune in London*; Burton, *At the Heart of the Empire*; and Jonathan Schneer, *London 1900*.

43 McKay, *Quest of the Folk*; also Donald A. Wright, 'W.D. Lighthall and David Ross McCord.'

44 This was unlike the type of antimodernism promoted by, for example, Nova Scotia's Helen Creighton in her cultural work. See McKay, *Quest of the Folk*, particularly chapter 2, 'Helen Creighton and the Rise of Folklore.'

45 See, e.g., Burton, *At the Heart of the Empire*, which focuses primarily on three imperial travellers; also Walden, *Becoming Modern*, and Nelles, *Art of Nation-Building*, which focus on a single institution or event.

46 As Suzanne Morton has argued, in *At Odds: Gambling and Canadians 1919–1969* (Toronto: University of Toronto Press, 2003), at 19, 'national studies' can be 'an opportunity to highlight diversity and address commonality rather than providing 'one big picture.' While region plays a much smaller role in this study – at least so far as English-speaking Canada is concerned – than in Morton's, nevertheless I agree with her insights into the need to cast a wide net while simultaneously *not* reverting to older national (and nationalist) frameworks.

47 McKay, *Quest of the Folk*, 215.

48 See Antoinette Burton, 'Introduction: The Unfinished Business of Colonial Modernities,' in Burton, ed., *Gender, Sexuality and Colonial Modernities*, 1–16.

49 N.a., 'The Progress of Italy,' *Saint John Daily Telegraph*, 9 Oct. 1878.

50 See, e.g., n.a., 'Education in France,' ibid., 9 Dec. 1874; n.a., 'Turkey's Parlia-
    ment,' ibid., 8 Jan. 1878.
51 N.a., 'A New Brunswicker Abroad,' ibid., 30 Oct. 1878; Penelope, 'For the
    Ladies: Our London Letter [1],' *Montreal Daily Star*, 17 June 1882.
52 For further discussion on the role of the press within late-Victorian and
    Edwardian imperialism, see Julie Codell, ed., *Imperial Co-histories*.
53 The rise of feminized, and well educated, American tourism in France is
    discussed by Harvey Levenstein, *Seductive Journey*, esp. chapter 9, 'The
    Feminization of American Tourism.'
54 N.t., *Canadian Magazine* (Aug. 1904): 372–3, 372.
55 Ibid., 273. See also, n.a., 'The Advantages of Travel,' *Allisonia*, (10 Mar.
    1910): 69.
56 See, e.g., the following articles in the *Canadian Magazine*: Joanna E. Wood,
    'Presentation at Court' (Oct. 1901): 306–10; Lally Bernard, 'The Ladies'
    Empire Club of London' (July 1904): 195–9; Margaret Eadie Henderson,
    'The Marchioness of Donegal' (Feb. 1905): 308–11; n.a., 'About New Books:
    Our Women Writers' (Oct. 1905): 584–5; W.T. Allison, 'A New Canadian
    Poet [Helena Coleman]' (Feb. 1907): 404–08; Newton McTavish, 'Laura
    Munz and Her Art' (Sept. 1911): 419–26; Florence E. Deacon, 'The Art of
    Mary Riter Hamilton' (Oct. 1912): 557–64.
57 Biographical information on some of these writers is available in Carl F.
    Klinck, ed., *A Literary History of Canada*; Norah Story, ed., *The Oxford Com-
    panion to Canadian History and Literature*; and the database 'Canada's Early
    Women Writers,' www.sfu.ca.
58 For a discussion of Duncan, see Misao Dean, *A Different Point of View: Sara
    Jeannette Duncan* (Kingston and Montreal: McGill-Queen's University Press,
    1991). For information on Maria Elise Turner Toof Lauder, see 'Canada's
    Early Women Writers,' in Henry Morgan, *Canadian Men and Women of the
    Time* (Toronto, 1898).
59 For discussions of these questions, see, e.g., Billie Melman, *Women's Orients*;
    Sara Mills, *Discourses of Difference*; Reina Lewis, *Gendering Orientalism*.
60 Maria Elise Turner Lauder, *Evergreen Leaves, Being Notes from My Travel
    Book by 'Toofie'* (Toronto: Belford Bros., 1877); Murphy, *Impressions of
    Janey Canuck*.
61 Constance Boulton, 'A Canadian Bicycle through Europe, Chapter IV,'
    Canadian Magazine (July 1896): 216–26 (this was one of the many instal-
    ments Boulton submitted to the periodical that chronicled her tour through
    Europe). In her *Impressions of Janey Canuck*, Murphy adopted an authorial
    voice decidedly different from Boulton's. See also Louise Hayter Birchall,
    'A City of Dreams,' *Canadian Magazine* 37, 4 (Aug. 1911): 316–20.

62 Angela Woollacott, 'The Colonial *Flaneuse*: Australian Women Negotiating Turn-of-the-Century London,' *Signs* 25, 3 (Spring 2000): 761–87. For a Canadian example of the *flaneuse*, see Birchall, 'City of Dreams.'

63 While it is beyond the scope of this study, this distinction between the two bodies of writing leads me to wonder if antimodernism was a cultural and social stance more commonly expressed and cultivated by English-Canadian intellectuals and cultural commentators than among the less-known middle class.

64 Bonnie Huskins and Michael Boudreau, 'Daily Allowances': Literary Conventions and Daily Life in the Diaries of Ida Louise Martin (nee Friars), Saint John, New Brunswick, 1945–1992,' *Acadiensis* 34, 2 (Spring 2005): 88–108, 89. My thanks to one of my anonymous reviewers for drawing my attention to this article.

65 Despite the growth of personal photography among the middle class in this period, I had fewer collections of tourists' own photographs available to illustrate this book (either because they have not survived, have become separated from the written texts, or did not exist in the first place). There are also surprisingly fewer references to taking photographs than I had expected. A few scrapbooks and collections of postcards are in the archives, and they attest to their creators' desire to capture their travels through visual media: see, for example, Postcard Collection, FHM, Fulford Family Papers; Pack, Scrapbook; Bilborough, Travel Diary 1896, which is a combination of diary and scrapbook.

1 'Porters, Guides, and the Middle-Class Tourist'

1 Fred C. Martin, Travel Diary 1881, 21 May, LAC, MG 29 D92.

2 Ibid.

3 Ibid.

4 Ibid., n.d. June.

5 See, e.g., Levenstein, *Seductive Journey*, esp. chapter 2, 'Getting There Was Not Half the Fun.'

6 Woollacott, *To Try Her Fortune in London*, 23.

7 Some travellers from British Columbia, such as Mary Bain, took the train through the United States and left for Europe from Boston or New York, ports also used by some Maritimers.

8 Simmonds, *Our Trip to Europe*, 5.

9 Pack, Travel Diary 1881, 30 May, and n.a., '*Franconia* Sunk,' *Victoria Colonist*, 6 Oct. 1916, PABC, MS 0729. The *Colonist* clipping is pasted into Pack's diary, as are various postcards and other Cunard promotional literature.

10 N.a., 'The Atlantic Passage,' *Canadian Magazine* (July 1906): 287.

11 James Hall, Travel Diary 1878, 18–23 June, AO, MU 3273 F285.

12 George Arthur Disbrowe, Travel Diary 1907, 20–9 Dec., UG-ASC, XAI MS A014, Disbrowe Papers 1907–1973.

13 Margaret Thomson, Travel Diaries 1897–9, 1910, 1914, AO, MU2965.

14 Murphy, *Impressions of Janey Canuck*, 2–3.

15 Lauder, *Evergreen Leaves*, 25.

16 Ibid., 27.

17 Ibid., 28.

18 For scholarly discussions of sentimental literature, see Shirley Samuels, ed., *The Culture of Sentiment: Race, Gender, and Sentimentality in Nineteenth-Century America* (Oxford: Oxford University Press, 1992); also Cecilia Morgan, '"Better than Diamonds": Sentimental Strategies and Middle-Class Culture in Canada West,' *Journal of Canadian Studies / revue d'études canadiennes* 32, no. 4 (1998): 125–48.

19 Pack, Travel Diary 1911, 2 June.

20 Murphy, *Impressions of Janey Canuck*, 4.

21 Edith Chown, Travel Diary 1910, Book 1, 14 May, QUA, Edith (Pierce) Chown Collection, 200/c, Box 15, 1909–49. As Chown completed the small journals that she used as her travel diary, she sent each one back to her family in Canada so that they might read about her trip.

22 Disbrowe, Travel Diary 1907, 22 Dec.

23 Ibid., 25 Dec.

24 Ibid., 22 Dec.

25 Thomas Langton, Travel Diary 1888, 8 Feb., LAC, MG 29 E87, Correspondence and Journals of Trips 1886–1907, File 3.

26 Chown, Travel Diary 1910, Book 1, 12 May.

27 Pack, Travel Diary 1911, 30 May.

28 J.E. [James Elgin] Wetherell, *Over the Sea*, 7–8.

29 Ibid., 10–11.

30 Murphy, *Impressions of Janey Canuck*, 5.

31 Greenshields, Travel Diary 1894, 14, 15 Dec.

32 Ibid., Travel Diary 1911, 16 Mar.

33 Ibid., Travel Diary 1913, 31 Jan., 4 Feb.

34 J.T.P.K., *Eastward Ho!*, 15. The 'late prisoner' refers to a mock trial that was held the previous evening (at 10–14).

35 Thomson, Travel Diary 1897, 25 May.

36 George Lindsey, *Cricket across the Sea*, 37–8. As Eleanor Watson Garrard and her companions rested after tea at the cottage they had rented in the Lakes District, they 'attempted, in spite of our fatigue, to sing "nigger songs"' (Travel Diary 1892, 3 Aug., PABC, MS 830, Garrard Family Papers, Box 1).

37 Woollacott has examined how white Australian women en route to England shaped racial identities through their observations of south Asian and Egyptian society. See, in particular, '"All This Is the Empire, I Told Myself."' For the 'black Atlantic,' see Paul Gilroy, *The Black Atlantic*. For work on the meaning and significance of minstrel shows, see David Roediger, *The Wages of Whiteness: Race and the Making of the American Working Class* (London: Verso, 1991); Eric Lott, *Love and Theft: Blackface Minstrelsy and the American Working Class* (London: Oxford University Press, 1993): William J. Mahar, *Behind the Burnt Cork Mask: Early Blackface Minstrelsy and the Antebellum American Popular Culture* (Chicago and Urbana: University of Illinois Press, 1999); Michael Pickering, 'White Skin, Black Masks: "Nigger" Minstrelsy in Victorian Britain,' in J.S. Bratton, ed., *Music Hall: Performance and Style* (Milton Keynes, UK: Open University Press, 1986), 70–91.

38 Aird Dundas Flavelle, Travel Diary 1900, 8 July, PABC, MS 875, Vol. 1/1, File 3.

39 Disbrowe, Travel Diary 1907, 29 Dec. See also Clara J. Bowslaugh, Travel Diary 1897, HPL-LC.

40 Martin, Travel Diary 1881, n.d.

41 Murphy, *Impressions of Janey Canuck*, 8.

42 Chown, Travel Diary 1910, Book 1, 17 May.

43 Gertrude Fleming, Travel Diary 1891, 25 Nov., LAC, MG 29 C96.

44 Martin, Travel Diary 1881, n.d.

45 Ada Pemberton, Travel Diary 1897, 7, 8 May, PABC, MS 2639, Pemberton Family papers.

46 The Vienna Exhibition of 1873 was probably responsible for the many editorials on overseas travel that appeared in the *Halifax Morning Chronicle* and *Saint John Telegraph* that year. For the *Chronicle*, see, e.g., n.a., 'Sea-Sickness,' 17 June 1873, and n.a., 'Customs House,' 8 July 1873; for the *Telegraph*, see: 'Courtesy in Travelling,' 7 Feb. 1873, and n.a., 'Pleasures of an Ocean Voyage,' 3 May 1873. For the *Ottawa Free Press*: see n.a., 'Tricks on Travellers,' 11 Feb. 1881; n.a., 'Railway Travelling,' 18 July 1885; and see also n.a., 'A Boon to Travellers from Canada to Europe,' *Montreal Daily Star*, 7 Mar. 1881.

47 N.a., 'The Traveller's Candle,' *Montreal Daily Star*, 9 Feb. 1884; n.a., 'International Exhibition in Vienna,' *Halifax Morning Chronicle*, 7 June 1873.

48 See, e.g., n.a. 'Jerusalem. Christianity's Capital, the Home of Filth, Disease, and Ignorance,' *Victoria Daily Times*, 27 Dec. 1884; C.D.E., 'A Trip Up the Mediterranean,' *Argosy* I, 1 (no year given), 25.

49 Albert R. Carman, 'Tipping – A Defence,' *Canadian Magazine* (Mar. 1905): 416–18; Servitor, 'The Philosophy of Tipping,' *Canadian Magazine* (Apr. 1911): 533–8.

50 Louise Hayter Birchall, 'How Much Shall I Tip?' *Canadian Magazine* (Oct. 1912): 552–6.

51 Chown, Travel Diary 1910, 22 June.
52 Hall, Travel Diary 1878, 22 July.
53 Simmonds, *Our Trip*, 71.
54 Priddis, Travel Diary 1906, 28.
55 Bain, Travel Diary 1910, 20 Dec.
56 Ibid., 21 Dec.
57 Greenshields, Travel Diary 1906, 9 May.
58 Ibid., 19 May. In this passage Greenshields does not tell us Lehuard's first
    name.
59 Ibid., Travel Diary 1911, 19 Mar., 19 Apr.
60 John Mackinnon, *Rambles in Britain, France, Prussia, Switzerland, Italy, Bel-
    gium, and Holland*, 138.
61 Thomson, Travel Diary 1898, 7 Nov.
62 Langton, Travel Diary 1888, 16 Feb.
63 Ibid., 28 Apr.
64 Ibid., 3 June. Langton also wrote scornfully of 'trying to follow that old
    jackass' Hare's vague directions for Venice's churches and 'objects of beauty
    and interest' (10 June).
65 Ibid., Travel Diary 1907, 22 Feb.
66 Osla Clouston, Travel Diary 1900, 19 Mar., in MM, Clouston Family Papers.
67 Langton, Travel Diary 1888, 28 Mar.
68 Bain, Travel Diary 1910, 26 Dec.
69 Denison, *A Happy Holiday*, 99. Denison told her readers that she was able to
    verify the boy's story with a picture exhibited at the Paris Exposition that
    depicted this custom (ibid.).
70 Langton, Travel Diary 1888, 28 Mar.
71 Martin, Travel Diary 1881, n.d.
72 Priddis, Travel Diary 1906, 26. Priddis's diaries were transcribed into type-
    written versions; for the most part no dates are given.
73 Ibid., 30.
74 Langton, Travel Diary 1907, 29 May.
75 Priddis, Travel Diary 1906, 114. See also her entry for Frankfurt (ibid., 108).
76 Ibid., 118.
77 Ibid., 122–3.
78 Ibid., 126.
79 Ibid., 143.
80 Pack, Travel Diary 1911, 22 July.
81 Hall, Travel Diary 1878, 17 July.
82 Langton, Travel Diary 1888, 22 Mar.
83 Greenshields, Travel Diary 1906, 6 May.

84 Pack, Travel Diary 1911, 15 July.
85 Ibid., 22 July; see also his observation made when first in Paris that 'the horses are poor ours looks hungry and abused' (ibid., 4 July). Denison also made a similar comment (in *A Happy Holiday*, 203). The plight of London's cabbies will be discussed in chapter 6.
86 Mackinnon, *Rambles in Britain*, 138. Simmonds also noticed the many women vendors of tourist goods in the Alps near Lucerne. One, she wrote, took Simmonds's party to her cottage to see her baby daughter: 'a little beauty,' Simmonds thought, with 'large brown eyes and curly brown hair, we all wanted to take her home with us' (*Our Trip to Europe*, 65). See chapter 4 for a discussion of Irish workers.
87 Langton, Travel Diary 1888, 28 Apr.
88 Murphy, *Impressions of Janey Canuck*, 143.
89 Simmonds, *Our Trip*, 78–9.
90 Pack, Travel Diary 1911, 8 July.
91 Bowslaugh, Travel Diary 1897, 23 July.
92 Hall, Travel Diary 1878, 21 July.
93 Pack, Travel Diary 1911, 13 July.
94 See, e.g., Clouston, Travel Diaries for 1894 and 1895.
95 Murphy, *Impressions of Janey Canuck*, 149.
96 Thomson, Travel Diary 1897, 28 July.
97 Ibid., Travel Diary 1898, 26 Oct.
98 Bain, Travel Diary 1910, 12 Dec.
99 Bowslaugh, Travel Diary 1897, 24 July.
100 Simmonds, *Our Trip*, 83–4.
101 Ibid., 82.
102 Tina Loo, *States of Nature: Conserving Canada's Wilderness in the Twentieth Century* (Vancouver: UBC Press, 2006), 54–5.

2 The Landscape of History and Empire, Part 1

1 N.a., 'The Advantages of Travel,' *Allisonia*, 10 Mar. 1910, 69.
2 Durie, *Scotland for the Holidays*, 2.
3 Gold and Gold, *Imagining Scotland*, 60–86.
4 Ibid., 90–1, 100–1.
5 Ibid., 93; Durie, *Scotland*, 132.
6 Gold and Gold, *Imagining Scotland*, 101–3; Durie, *Scotland*, 141–7.
7 On the declining popularity of scenery and history and the growing attractions of outdoor sports, see Durie (*Scotland*, 109), and Gold and Gold (*imagining Scotland*, 104–12). Both studies acknowledge that Scotland was

constructed for overseas tourists as the land of Burns, Scott, Ossian, and Barrie (Durie, 134; Gold and Gold, 112).

8   See, e.g., Jasen, *Wild Things: Nature, Culture, and Tourism in Ontario 1790–1914*, esp. chapter 6, 'Close Encounters.'

9   Greenshields, Travel Diary 1896, 9 Aug.

10 Ibid., 10 Aug.

11 Ibid., 19 Aug.

12 Ibid., Travel Diary 1911, 29 June.

13 W.C. Caldwell, Travel Diary 1874, 7 July, AO, MU 839.

14 Ibid., 29 Aug.

15 William F. Munro to Georgina Johnstone Munro, 5 Jan. 1881, AO, MU2180, W.F. Munro Papers, Correspondence 1862–83.

16 Wetherell, *Over the Sea*, 15–16.

17 Ibid.

18 Simmonds, *Our Trip to Europe*, 15.

19 Ibid., 14.

20 Martin, Travel Diary 1881, n.d.

21 This was the description used by 'A New Brunswicker Abroad,' *Saint John Daily Telegraph*, 30 Oct. 1878, and Wetherell, *Over the Sea*, 31.

22 Watson, Travel Diary 1892, 27, 28 July.

23 Ibid., 1 Aug. Like other English-Canadians, Watson assigned 'foreign' status to others even though her relationship to Britain was, like for many white colonials, less than straightforward. Her family was originally from Yorkshire but had lived for some time in Port Alberni; her father, A.M. Watson, had been one of the first European doctors in the area.

24 See, e.g., Lindsey, *Cricket across the Sea*, 75.

25 Bowslaugh, Travel Diary 1897, 24 Aug.

26 Martin, Travel Diary 1881, n.d.

27 See, e.g., Thomson Travel Diaries: 1897, 28, 29 May, 1 June, 13 Sept.; 1898, 4 Aug., 12 Dec. Caldwell also noted the city's fine buildings, shops, and cultural institutions (Travel Diary 1874, 13–15 July). Pack found Princes Street 'a grand street wide well kept' with 'fine stores' and 'splendid gardens' (Travel Diary 1911, 15 June).

28 Thomson, Travel Diary 1897, 5 June.

29 Ibid., 10 June.

30 Ibid., 9 June.

31 Ibid., 12 June.

32 For the challenges that women cyclists posed to middle-class norms, see Marjorie Gruber Garvey, *The Adman in the Parlor: Magazines and the Gendering of Consumer Culture, 1880s–1930s* (New York: Oxford University Press, 1996).

33 Thomson, Travel Diary 1897, 11 Aug.

34 Ibid., Travel Diary 1899, 14, 15 Jan.

35 Bowslaugh, Travel Diary 1897, 24 Aug.

36 Watson, Travel Diary 1892, 31 July.

37 See, e.g., Bowslaugh, Travel Diary 1897, 24 Aug.; Wetherell, *Over the Sea*, 38.

38 For visits to these Edinburgh sites, see Thomson, Travel Diary 1897, 31 May; Simmonds, *Our Trip to Europe*, 24; Bowslaugh, Travel Diary 1897, 24 Aug.; Martin, Travel Diary 1881, n.d.

39 For the role of 'Scottishness' in shaping Canadian identity, see Elizabeth Waterston, *Wrap't in Plaid*. In this context Canadians appear to have differed quite drastically from English tourists. Marjorie Morgan argues that, unlike their Scottish counterparts, English tourists were not only uninterested in Scottish history but were almost hostile to it, preferring the scenery of the Highlands to places such as Holyrood or Edinburgh Castle (*National Identities and Travel in Victorian Britain*, 193–4).

40 Simmonds, *Our Trip to Europe*, 18–28.

41 Ibid., 28.

42 Lindsey, *Cricket across the Sea*, 82.

43 Pack, Travel Diary 1911, 16 June.

44 See, for example, Simmonds, *Our Trip*, 25, 74.

45 N.A., 'A New Brunswicker Abroad.'

46 Ibid.

47 Martin, Travel Diary 1881, n.d.

48 Wetherell, *Over the Sea*, 34. See also Lauder, *Evergreen Leaves*, 109–10; Simmonds, *Our Trip*, 24–5; Thomson, Travel Diary 1897, 26 June; Caldwell, Travel Diary 1874, 15 July.

49 Greenshields, Travel Diary 1896, 1 Sept.

50 Bowslaugh, Travel Diary 1897, 24 Aug.

51 Wetherell, *Over the Sea*, 35.

52 Bowslaugh, Travel Diary 1897, 24 Aug.; see also Thomson, Travel Diary 1897, 10 Sept.

53 Pack, Travel Diary 1911, 16 June.

54 Newton MacTavish, 'Rat Holes of Edinburgh,' *Canadian Magazine* (Dec. 1910): 120–7. See also Greenshields, who complained that he made a mistake travelling to Edinburgh from Dunoon on a Saturday night: the Dunoon pier was full of drunken people, as was the train and the Edinburgh streets (Travel Diary 1896, 29 Aug.).

55 Canadian tourists do not appear to have differentiated between the central Highlands and the Northwest Highlands.

56 Wetherell, *Over the Sea*, 22–3.

57 Ethel Marion Davies, Travel Diary 1899, 6 Oct., LAC, MG 29 C109, Reel 1957.
58 Ibid.
59 Wetherell, *Over the Sea*, 26.
60 Simmonds, *Our Trip*, 22.
61 Penelope, 'For the Ladies: Our London Letter[2],' *Montreal Daily Star*,
    16 Sept. 1882.
62 Lindsey, *Cricket across the Sea*, 88. See also Fred T. Hodgson, 'Dunfermline
    Abbey,' for a discussion of its history and the civilization it represented, one
    brought by Queen Margaret (*Canadian Magazine* [Feb. 1894]: 337–44).
63 Mackinnon, *Rambles in Britain*, 70.
64 Waterson, *Wrap't in Plaid*, 46.
65 Wetherell, *Over the Sea*, 28–9. See also Greenshields, Travel Diary 1896, 20 Aug.
66 Pack, Travel Diary 1911, 15 June.
67 See Durie, *Scotland for the Holidays*, 139–40. As he points out, by 1913 more
    than 9,000 tourists viewed Abbotsford. The house was not advertised, and
    the influx appears to have been sparked by Scott's reputation alone; in 1913,
    375 visitors from Canada signed its guestbook.
68 Thompson, Travel Diary 1897, 9 July.
69 Ibid., Travel Diary 1898, 11 Aug.
70 Lauder, *Evergreen Leaves*, 101.
71 N.a., 'From Inverness to Glasgow via the Caledonian Canal,' *Saint John
    Daily Telegraph*, 15 Aug. 1879.
72 Waterston, *Wrap't in Plaid*, 46.
73 Emma Baker, 'Scotland and Scotchmen,' *Allisonia* (Nov. 1911): 48–53.
74 Ada McLeod, 'Skye: The Isle of Mist,' *Canadian Magazine* (Nov. 1911): 12–21.
75 Ibid., 'Beside the Peat Fire,' *Canadian Magazine* (Mar. 1913): 427–36.
76 Waterston, *Wrap't in Plaid*, 29–31; Gold and Gold, *Imagining Scotland*, 64.
77 Wetherell, *Over the Sea*, 19.
78 Ibid., 20.
79 Priddis, Travel Diary 1906, 202.
80 See Mackinnon, *Rambles in Britain*, 74–5; see also J. Campbell, 'The Nature
    of Robert Burns,' *Canadian Magazine* (Mar. 1896): 395–402.
81 Jean Blewett, 'Lanark: The Cradle of Scottish Liberty,' *Canadian Magazine*
    (May 1907): 65–8.
82 Lauder, *Evergreen Leaves*, 83–4.
83 Ibid., 102–3.
84 For a discussion of the uncanny, the 'not-yet-colonized' and the 'unsuccess-
    fully colonized' in tourist landscapes, see Judith Richardson, *Possessions*,
    esp. 23–4.

3 The Landscape of History and Empire, Part 2

1 N.a., 'Historic England,' *Canadian Magazine* (June 1905): 185.

2 Kate Stevens, in Ney, ed., *Britishers in Britain.*, 278; original emphasis.

3 Scholarship on nineteenth-century travel within England has explored issues that range from the impressions of literary figures from the United States, such as Harriet Beecher Stowe or Mark Twain to the impact of Thomas Cook's travel agency and the development of seaside resorts. See, e.g., Christopher Mulvey, *Anglo-American Landscapes*, and his *Transatlantic Manners*; Stowe, *Going Abroad*; Ian Ousby, *The Englishman's England*; Walton, *The English Seaside Resort*, and his 'British Tourism between Industrialization and Globalization'; Beckerson, 'Marketing British Tourism.' For a study of English tourists in Britain, see Morgan, *National Identities and Travel in Victorian Britain*.

4 Disbrowe, Travel Diary 1907, 29 Dec.

5 Lauder, *Evergreen Leaves*, 33.

6 Mackinnon, *Rambles in Britain*, , 3–4. In 'Liverpool To-Day,' Robert Machray stated that there is 'little or nothing of historical or antiquarian interest' in the city but that it had many modern sites to visit, such as its Town Hall and Corn Exchange and, in particular, its docks (*Canadian Magazine* [Sept. 1895]: 397–410, 397).

7 Murphy, *Impressions of Janey Canuck Abroad*, 10–11.

8 Machray, 'Liverpool To-Day.'

9 Priddis, Travel Diary 1906, 19–20.

10 Bain, Travel Diary 1911, 2 Feb.

11 Bowslaugh, Travel Diary 1897, 25 Aug.

12 Jane Lavender, 'The King's Highway,' *Canadian Magazine* (Jan. 1907): 212–17, 212.

13 Ibid., 217.

14 Ibid.

15 Mabel Cameron, Travel Diary 1911, 7 Mar., LAC, MG 30 C178.

16 Reverend Frederick Hastings, 'Rambles in the West of England [1],' *Saint John Daily Telegraph*, 7 Sept. 1874.

17 Rev. Frederick Hastings, 'Tramping in the West of England,' *Saint John Daily Telegraph*, 13 Oct. 1874.

18 Hastings, 'Rambles in the West of England [1].'

19 Hastings, 'Tramping.'

20 Hastings, 'Rambles [1]' and 'Tramping'.

21 Hastings, 'Rambles in the West of England [2],' *Saint John Daily Telegraph*, 27 Nov. 1874.

22 Mackinnon, *Rambles in Britain*, 6.
23 J. Rupert Elliott, *Rambles in Merrie, Merrie, England*, 42–3; also Mackinnon, *Rambles in Britain*, 7.
24 Hastings, 'Rambles [1]'.
25 Ibid.
26 Ibid., 'Tramping.'
27 Hastings, 'Rambles [2],'
28 See, e.g., McKay, *The Quest of the Folk*; also Donald A. Wright, 'W.D. Lighthall and David Ross McCord.'
29 G.L.B. Mackenzie, 'Walking in England,' *Canadian Magazine* (Aug. 1914): 416–22.
30 H.M. Clark, 'West Country Wanderings,' *Canadian Magazine* (June 1912): 149–57.
31 Goldwin Smith, *A Trip to England*, n.p. For a discussion of Smith's life and beliefs, see Ramsay Cook, ed., 'Goldwin Smith,' *Dictionary of Canadian Biography*, vol. 13 (Toronto: University of Toronto Press, 2000), 968–74.
32 Smith, *A Trip to England*.
33 Ibid.
34 Ibid.
35 For a discussion of masculinity within Canadian antimodernist discourses, see McKay, *Quest of the Folk*, 252–60.
36 Davies, Travel Diary 1899, 18 Nov. 'L' appears to have been a female relative, possibly a cousin.
37 Amy Redpath Roddick, Travel Diary 1902, 2 Aug., MU-RBR, MS 659, Sir Thomas Roddick Papers.
38 Peter H. Hansen, 'Albert Smith, the Alpine Club, and the Invention of Mountaineering in Mid-Victorian Britain.'
39 Priddis, Travel Diary 1911, 191, 185.
40 Ibid., 186.
41 Ibid., 190.
42 Ibid.
43 For a discussion of this concept and the tourist as pilgrim, see John Sears, *Sacred Places*.
44 Mackinnon, *Rambles in Britain*, 5–6.
45 Hugh Johnston, 'Letters. The Heart of the Lake District, Liverpool, and Its Surroundings,' *Christian Guardian*, 17 Aug. 1892. See also Hall, Travel Diary 1878, 25 June.
46 Chown, Travel Diary 1910, Book 1, 17 May.
47 Cameron, Travel Diary 1911, 1 Feb.
48 Ibid., 3 Feb.

49 Priddis, Travel Diary 1911, 179.
50 See, e.g., Greenshields, Travel Diary 1898, 17 Sept.
51 Marshall S. Snow, 'English History in Canterbury Cathedral,' *Canadian Magazine* (Jan. 1900): 252–71, 252–3.
52 Ibid., 254.
53 Ibid., 271.
54 Chown, Travel Diary 1910, Book 2, 20 June.
55 Priddis, Travel Diary 1911, 219.
56 Ibid., 222.
57 M.A. Black, 'Echoes from Our Trip,' *Allisonia* (Nov. 1907): 11–13, 12.
58 Chown, Travel Diary 1910, Book 2, 19 May.
59 Mackinnon, *Rambles in Britain*, 23. Others carefully listed the places they had been to in Oxford – the colleges, the Bodleian Library, Big Tom, and the Martyr's Memorial – but did not feel it necessary to describe them in detail. See Pack, Travel Diary 1911, 21 June; also Simmonds, *Our Trip to Europe*, 42.
60 Archibald MacMechan, 'Oxford for a Day,' *Canadian Magazine* (Aug. 1912): 345–54.
61 Ibid., 349.
62 Arnold Haultain, 'Oxford and the Oxford Man,' *Canadian Magazine* (May 1913): 32–6, 32.
63 Ibid., 33–4.
64 Ibid., 34.
65 Ibid., 35.
66 Ibid., 36.
67 See John Tosh, 'Manliness, Masculinities, and the New Imperialism, 1880–1900,' esp. 198–203.
68 Smith, *A Trip to England*, n.p.
69 Cameron, Travel Diaries 1910, 30 June to 15 Nov., 1911, 26 Oct. (for Cambridge), 6 Apr. to 20 June, 22 May (for Oxford). Most tourists seemed to prefer Oxford to Cambridge but see Ada Pemberton's discussion of her trip to the latter university where her brother Willie was studying (Travel Diary 1897, 15 June).
70 Ousby, *Englishman's England*, 51–3.
71 Pack, Travel Diary 1911, 20 June.
72 Chown, Travel Diary 1910, Book 1, 18 May.
73 Cameron, Travel Diary 1910, 12 Nov. See also Black, 'Echoes from Our Trip,' for a reference to the Avon and the 'immortal Shakespeare' (at 12).
74 Ney, ed., *Britishers in Britain*, 140.
75 Pemberton, Travel Diary 1897, 17–18 June.
76 Simmonds, *Our Trip to Europe*, 32.

77 See Ousby, *Englishman's England*, 168–9.
78 For a brief discussion of this phenomenon, see Walton, 'British Tourism between Industrialization and Globalization,' 119–121.
79 Dr Borden, 'European Educational Tour,' *Allisonia* (March 1907): 97–8.
80 Newton MacTavish, 'Manitoba Teachers Abroad,' *Canadian Magazine* (Nov. 1910): 25–33, 31.
81 Newton MacTavish, 'Windermere to Coniston,' *Canadian Magazine* (Nov. 1912): 3–9. 3.
82 Ibid., 4–5. He also recounted his argument with a woman on the coach about their direction, a dispute solved by the driver's intervention and explanation (at 6–8).
83 Ibid., 9.
84 Cameron, Travel Diary 1911, 10 May. She also recorded, in some length, her impressions of the wildflowers that grew alongside Coniston's shore (12 May). For other trips to the area, see Isabella Montgomery, Travel Diary 1895, 7–8 July, MTRL-BR, Vo8, and Greenshields, Travel Diary 1896, 3–5 Sept. Greenshields found the scenery of Lake Windermere 'softer and more domesticated, than the grander, and wilder Scotch lakes' (4 Sept.).
85 Cameron, Travel Diary 1911, 11, 12 May.
86 Ibid., 11 May.
87 Watson (Garrard), Travel Diary 1892, 2, 3, 9, 10, 16, 18, 23, 25 Aug.
88 Ibid., 1 Aug.
89 Ibid., 3, 19–20, 15 Aug.
90 Ibid., 15 Aug.
91 Ibid., 9 Aug.
92 Ibid., 2 Aug. This description comes after a photograph of Eleanor Watson and her companions, one of whom was her sister Winifred, pasted at that entry. Their brother joined them in the Lakes for five days (7–11 Aug.).
93 Smith, *A Trip to England*, n.p.; Priddis, Travel Diary 1911, 182.
94 Smith, *Trip to England*, n.p.
95 Ibid., n.p.
96 Priddis, Travel Diary 1911, 28–9.
97 Ibid., 30.
98 Ibid.
99 Ibid., 32.
100 Smith, *Trip to Britain*, n.p.
101 Black, 'Echoes of Our Trip.'
102 Mackinnon, *Rambles in Britain*, 19. Simmonds also toured the ruins but had little to say about them, sceptical or otherwise (*Our Trip to Europe*, 31).

103 Priddis, Travel Diary 1911, 241.
104 Murphy, *Impressions of Janey Canuck*, 88–9.
105 See, e.g., Hugh Johnston, 'The Homeland,' *Christian Guardian*, 3 Aug. 1892, 483; H.M. Clark, 'Canada's Cradle: the Bristol of Yesterday and To-day,' *Canadian Magazine* (Jan. 1913): 273–82; n.a., 'The Cabot Memorial at Bristol,' *Ottawa Free Press*, 31 May 1897, 9.
106 Johnson, 'Homeland'; Clark, 'Canada's Cradle,' 281–2.
107 Johnston, 'Homeland.'
108 Fred Hastings, 'A Pilgrimage to the Home of Bunyan,' *Saint John Daily Telegraph*, 12 Sept. 1873.
109 H.F. Bland, 'Jottings from England VII,' *Christian Guardian*, 8 Oct. 1890.
110 William Wakinshaw, 'The Wesleys in Bristol,' *Christian Guardian*, 20 June, 1912.
111 Greenshields, Travel Diary 1895, 4–5 July.
112 Ibid., 7 July.
113 Ibid. Greenshields returned to Wales the next year and spent a week touring its rural areas and admiring some of its 'magnificent' scenery (Travel Diary 1896, 2–7 Aug.)
114 Priddis, Travel Diary 1906, 167.
115 Ibid., 168.
116 Ibid., 170.
117 Ibid., 175.
118 Ibid., 179.
119 Ibid., 176.
120 Ibid., 180.
121 Frank Yeigh, 'The Welshman at Home,' *Canadian Magazine* (Mar. 1914): 477–86.
122 Ibid.
123 H. Linton Eccles, 'Nottingham through the Ages,' *Canadian Magazine* (Apr. 1913): 571–6; Priddis, Travel Diary 1911, 24–6.
124 Smith, *A Trip to England*, n.p.
125 Ibid. As chapter 7 will explore, he also could not resist making a dig at women's paid employment and its deleterious effects on English domestic life, discussing it in the same breath as the degradation of artisanal skills and the widening class division that large-scale urbanization and industrialization had brought.
126 Mackinnon, *Rambles in Britain*, 18.
127 Cameron, Travel Diary 1911, 2 Feb.
128 Ibid., 14 Mar.

392   Notes to pages 108–16

129 Thomson, Travel Diary 1898, 24 Aug.
130 Ney, *Britishers in Britain*, 4. For a discussion of Ney, the British-born but (by this time) Winnipeg-based high-school headmaster, and fervent imperialist, see James Sturgis and Margaret Bird, *Canada's Imperial Past: The Life of F.J. Ney, 1884–1973* (Edinburgh: Centre of Canadian Studies, 2000); see also Amy Tector and Sandy Ramos, '"Don't Let the Sun Go Down on Ney."' Ney developed teacher exchanges that would last for sixty years; he also went on to include high school and university students in these tours.
131 Ney, *Britishers in Britain*, 4.
132 Ibid., 5.
133 Ibid., 122, 132, 136, 140, 143.
134 Margaret Dickie, 'Continental Tour,' in Ney, *Britishers in Britain*, 238–9.
135 Thomas Laidlaw, 'Some Impressions of Our Visit,' ibid., 227.
136 Ibid., 228.
137 Ibid., 228–9.
138 See also, Mrs Humphrey, 'Canadian Ladies in London,' *Canada: An Illustrated Journal*, 4 May 1907, 131. This piece featured the charms and virtues of the wives and daughters of Canada's premiers who were in London to attend the Colonial Conference.
139 N.a., 'How Eleven of Ontario's Girls Have Won for Themselves a Free Trip to London Town,' *Toronto World*, 24 July 1907.
140 Ibid.
141 Ibid.
142 N.a., 'Our Girls Take a Hand at the Olympic Games,' *Hamilton Spectator*, 24 July 1908.
143 Adele Perry, *At the Edge of Empire* (University of Toronto Press, 2002); Katie Pickles, *Female Imperialism and National Identity*; see also Anne McClintock, 'No Longer in a Future Heaven: Nationalism, Gender and Race,' chapter 10 in McClintock, *Imperial Leather: Race, Gender and Sexuality in the Colonial Contest* (London: Routledge, 1995).
144 Ney, *Britishers in Britain*, 174.
145 N.a., 'First of Spectators Got Home Yesterday,' *Hamilton Spectator*, 27 July 1908.
146 N.a., 'How Eleven of Ontario's Girls Have Won … a Free Trip.'
147 N.a., 'Canada's "Maple Blossoms,"' *Daily Express*, 14 Aug. 1907.
148 See, e.g., Marta Danylewycz and Alison Prentice, 'Teachers' Work: Changing Patterns and Perceptions in the Emerging School Systems of 19th and Early 20th Century Central Canada,' *Labour / Le travail* 17 (spring 1986): 59–80; Sheehan, 'Philosophy, Pedagogy, and Practice.'

149 Ney, *Britishers in Britain*; n.a., 'How Eleven of Ontario's Girls Have Won'; n.a., 'First of Spectators Got Home Yesterday.'

150 Elliott, *Rambles in Merrie, Merrie England*, Part 1, 35.

151 Ibid., 36–7.

152 Ibid., 37–8.

153 Mackinnon, *Rambles in Britain*, 251–2. Smith also wrote of the military and navy's history and presence in England, although he noted that the number of troops that presently held India for the empire were quite small in proportion to the Indian population. This may have been possible because the empire now relied on a professional and scientific army and the navy's ships were much more threatening, albeit far less romantic, than the *Victory*. He was happy, though, that the volunteer army, 'the most wholesome movement' in England, could still be seen training at Aldershot (*A Trip to England*, n.p.).

154 Davies, Travel Diary 1899, 23 Oct.

155 Ibid., 27 Nov. Davies and her cousin were to be presented to the princess but the latter's travel plans were altered at the last minute 'so we did not have to make our curtsies.'

156 Ibid., Travel Diary 1900, 17 Jan.

157 Ibid., 1 Feb.

158 Ibid., 22 Feb., 1 Mar.

159 Ibid., 17 May.

160 Lindsey, *Cricket across the Sea*, 109.

161 MacMechan, 'Oxford for a Day,' 354.

162 Ibid. His after-dinner conversation with the male students included a discussion of Mary Kingsley and West Africa (ibid.).

163 Cameron, Travel Diary 1911, 4 Feb.

164 Priddis, e.g., stayed with relatives in England and Wales; Thomson visited her cousins in Scotland; and on her first trip to England as an adult, Roddick stayed with relatives outside London. Few seemed to have had the same critical and negative reaction to their relatives as did Mary Leslie.

165 A. Hawcridge, 'An Impression and a Plea,' in Ney, *Britishers in Britain*, 255.

166 Ibid., 260.

167 Ney, *Britishers*, 271–9. See also, n.a., 'Canada in England,' *Canada: An Illustrated Journal*, 15 June 1907, 307.

168 Thomson, Travel Diary 1910, 1 Dec.

169 Cameron, Travel Diary 1910, 10 Dec.

170 Bartlett, as quoted in Ney, *Britishers*, 290.

171 Ibid., 289.

172 Cameron, Travel Diary 1911, 4 Feb.

173 Priddis, Travel Diary 1911, 22.
174 Lindsey, *Cricket across the Sea*, 110.
175 Ibid., 117. For a discussion of the reception of Buffalo Bill's show, see Louis S. Warren, 'Buffalo Bill Meets Dracula.'
176 Cameron, Travel Diary 1910, 10 May; Chown, Travel Diary 1910, 17 June. For a discussion of how Australian women in London coped with English condescension, see Woollacott, *To Try Her Fortune in London*, esp. chapter 5, 'Metropolis as Crucible: Constructing Colonial, Imperial, and National Identities.'
177 See also articles in *Canada: An Illustrated Journal* which played with such themes and images: n.a., 'Canadian Apples in England,' 24 Feb. 1906, 257; n.a., 'Why British Women Should Emigrate: An Interesting Interview,' 17 Mar. 1906, 368; n.a., 'Two Vanishing Canadian Types,' 7 Apr. 1906, 500; Cy Warman, 'Lo and the Buffalo,' 14 Apr. 1906, 17–18; n.a., 'The Indian of Today – Progress and Prospects of the Red Man in Canada,' 11 May 1907, 155–7.
178 James Belich, *Paradise Reforged: A History of the New Zealanders. From the 1880s to the Year 2000* (Auckland: University of Auckland Press, 2001).
179 Woollacott's chapter entitled, 'Inhabiting the Metropolis: Gendered Space and Colonialism,' in her *To Try Her Fortune in London*, is a particularly insightful discussion of Australian women's hybrid status as 'white colonials.'
180 Woollacott makes the point that Australian women prided themselves on greater independence and resourcefulness than their British counterparts, partly as a means of countering British condescension to them as 'colonials' (ibid., 71–2).

4 'Paddy's Grief and Native Wit'

1 See, e.g. Michael de Nie, *The Eternal Paddy*; Roediger, *The Wages of Whiteness*; Noel Ignatiev, *How the Irish Became White* (London: Routledge, 1995). For recent work on the Irish in nineteenth-century Canada, see, e.g., Mark McGowan, *The Waning of the Green: Catholics, the Irish, and Identity in Toronto, 1887–1922* (Montreal and Kingston: McGill-Queen's University Press, 1999).
2 See, e.g., Barbara O'Connor and Michael Cronin, eds., *Tourism in Ireland*, and Martin Ryle, *Journeys in Ireland*. Much of the literature on travel in Ireland consists of analyses or reprints of travellers' accounts. See, e.g., Brian Ó Dálaigh, *The Stranger's Gaze: Travels in County Clare, 1534–1950* (Ennis, Ireland: Clasp Press, 1998); Glenn Hooper, *The Tourist's Gaze: Travellers to*

Ireland, 1800–2000 (Cork: Cork University Press, 2001); John P. Harrington, *The English Traveller in Ireland: Accounts of Ireland and the Irish through Five Centuries* (Dublin: Wolfhound Press, 1991).

3 N.a., 'Ireland,' *Montreal Daily Star,* 21 Jan. 1881, 2.

4 N.a, 'An Irish Fishing Village,' *Christian Guardian,* 31 Mar. 1880, 98. See also, n.a., 'Disease and Uncleanliness in Ireland,' *Saint John Daily Telegraph,* 15 Jan. 1874, 4.

5 Fred Hastings, 'A Peep at Ireland's Capital,' *Saint John Daily Telegraph,* 10 Oct. 1873. For discussions of conditions in Dublin during the late Victorian and Edwardian years, see Jacinta Prunty, 'Improving the Urban Environment,' 166–220, and Joseph Brady, 'Dublin at the Turn of the Century,' in Joseph Brady and Angret Simms, eds., *Dublin through Space and Time.*

6 E. Dowsley, 'A Plea for Ireland [1],' *Canadian Magazine* (Jan. 1894): 232–40, 234–6.

7 Mortimer L. Shea, *Across Two Continents and through the Emerald Isle,* 139.

8 Ibid., 140.

9 It is a relatively rare travelogue in the Canadian context: an account of tourism written in English by a Catholic for a Catholic audience (although it is possible that Shea also wished to convince Protestant readers of the many edifying and enjoyable sights of the Mediterranean, Palestine, Italy, Germany, France, and Britain).

10 Shea, *Across Two Continents,* 185–6.

11 Ibid., 186.

12 Ibid., 192–5.

13 Simmonds, *Our Trip to Europe,* 13.

14 Ibid.

15 Ney, *Britishers in Britain,* 152–3.

16 Pack, Travel Diary 1911, 7, 12 June; Martin, Travel Diary 1881, 9 Aug.; Pemberton, Travel Diary 1897, 11, 17 Sept.

17 Pemberton, Travel Diary 1897, 17 Sept.

18 Alf. S. Moore, 'Belfast: Ireland's Commercial Capital,' *Canadian Magazine* (Jan. 1911): 231–9, 232.

19 Ibid., 239.

20 Martin, Travel Diary 1881, 9 Aug. 1909.

21 See, e.g., Valverde, *The Age of Light, Soap, and Water.*

22 Pack, Travel Diary 1911, 11 June.

23 Richard Duke, 'Notes of a Trip II,' *Christian Guardian,* 18 Feb. 1891, 99.

24 Shea, *Across Two Continents,* 199–200.

25 See J.R. Miller, 'Anti-Catholicism in Canada: From the British Conquest to the Great War,' in Terence Murphy and Gerald Stortz, eds., *Creed and*

Culture: The Place of English-Speaking Catholics in Canadian Society, 1750–1930 (Montreal and Kingston: McGill-Queen's University Press, 1993), 25–48.

26 Occasional Correspondent, 'Dublin,' *Saint John Daily Telegraph*, 17 Sept. 1875, 1.

27 Hastings, 'A Peep at Ireland's Capital.' It may well be that both writers, contributing to a paper in a province that thirty years ago had seen its fair share of anti-Catholic riots, might have been touchy about such matters. For a discussion of those riots, see Scott See, 'The Orange Order and Social Violence in Mid-Nineteenth Century Saint John,' in Franca Iacovetta, ed., with Paula Draper and Robert Ventresca, *A Nation of Immigrants: Women, Workers, and Communities in Canadian History, 1840s–1960s* (Toronto: University of Toronto Press, 1999), 5–34. See also Michael Cottrell, 'St Patrick's Day Parades in Nineteenth-Century Toronto: A Study of Immigrant Adjustment and Elite Control,' in Iacovetta, *A Nation of Immigrants*, 35–54; Rosalyn Trigger, 'Irish Politics on Parade: The Clergy, National Societies, and St Patrick's Day Processions in Nineteenth-century Montreal and Toronto,' *Histoire sociale / Social History* 37, 74 (2004): 159–200.

28 Lindsey, *Cricket across the Sea*, 45.

29 Dowsley, 'A Plea for Ireland [1],' 234, 236. See also de Nie, *Eternal Paddy*, for the British press's reactions to the Phoenix Park murders, ones that ranged from blaming Irish-Americans to the belief that the situation in Ireland was hopeless (at 248–51).

30 Mackinnon, *Rambles in Britain*, 27.

31 Ibid., 29–30.

32 See de Nie, *Eternal Paddy*, for a discussion of Matthew Arnold's concepts of the Celtic character (of which Arnold was an admirer), at 24.

33 Mr P., 'Ancient Ireland,' *Saint John Daily Telegraph*, 18 Oct. 1875. See also n.a., 'An Adventure in Ireland,' ibid., 25 Sept. 1875, 4, which is a 'tale' of the author's (a 'loyal Irishman') involvement in a practical joke during the Fenian 'troubles' of 1867.

34 Fred T. Hodgson, 'The Round Towers and Irish Art,' *Canadian Magazine* (Nov. 1894): 38–46, 38.

35 Ibid.

36 Ibid., 39–41.

37 Ibid., 46.

38 Mackinnon, *Rambles in Britain*, 28; Pack, Travel Diary 1911, 9 June.

39 See, e.g., Simmonds, *Our Trip to Europe*, 12; Martin, Travel Diary 1881, 9 Aug.

40 Duke, 'Notes of a Trip III,' *Christian Guardian*, 1 Apr. 1891, 195.

41 Pack, Travel Diary 1911, 7 June.

42 Pemberton to ?, 6 May 1910, PABC, MS 2639, Pemberton Family Papers, File 4.

43 Pemberton, Travel Diary 1897, 14 and 17 Sept.

44 Simmonds, *Our Trip*, 12–13; Martin, Travel Diary 1881; 9 Aug.; Pack, Travel Diary 1911, 11 June; Dowsley, 'A Plea for Ireland [1],' 236.

45 Shea, *Across Two Continents*, 155.

46 Ibid., 185.

47 Ibid., 198. Shea's account was a little more dispassionate than that of Fred Martin, who noted in his diary that he had visited 'Drogheda on Boyne, with its celebrated siege by Cromwell and the Battle of the Boyne' (Travel Diary 1881, 9 Aug.).

48 See, e.g., David Glassberg, *American Historical Pageantry: The Uses of Tradition in the Early Twentieth Century* (Chapel Hill: University of North Carolina Press, 1990).

49 Duke, 'Notes of a Trip III.'

50 See, e.g., Thomson, Travel Diary 1898, 25 Oct.

51 Ryle, *Journeys in Ireland*, 27.

52 Ibid., 35–6. Although, as Ryle points out (at 36), these negative images of the island did not prevent British tourists from visiting it.

53 Dowsley, 'A Plea for Ireland [1],' 236–40, and 'A Plea for Ireland [2],' *Canadian Magazine* (Apr. 1894): 567–73.

54 See, e.g., Mackinnon, *Rambles in Britain*, 28; Simmonds, *Our Trip*, 8–9; Smith, *A Trip to England*, 82; Pack, Travel Diary 1911, 8–9 June; Greenshields, Travel Diary 1895, 15–18 May.

55 Shea, *Across Two Continents*, 161.

56 Ibid., 147–9, 161–3, 168, 169.

57 Ibid., 178, 187.

58 Duke, 'Notes of a Trip II.'

59 J.H. Bell, 'Trip to Paris and Back: Sketches by an Ottawa Visitor,' *Ottawa Daily Free Press*, 21 Nov. 1878. Simmonds (*Our Trip*, 14–15) also visited the Causeway, as did Shea; (*Across Two Continents*, 189).

60 Pemberton, Travel Diary 1897, 5 Sept.; Simmonds, *Our Trip*, 10.

61 Shea, *Across Two Continents*, 173–4.

62 Dowsley, 'Plea for Ireland [2],' 566–8.

63 Pack, Travel Diary 1911, 7 June.

64 Dowsley, 'Plea for Ireland [2],' 568.

65 Ibid.

66 Ibid., 571–2.

67 Duke, 'Notes of a Trip II.'

68 Bell, 'Trip to Paris and Back.'

69 Pemberton to ?, 6 May 1910.

70 Pemberton, Travel Diary 1897, 25 Aug., 2, 3, 4 Sept. Although, as Ryle points out, by the 1830s British travelogues made it clear that a variety of accommodations, both private homes and hotels, existed in places such as

398   Notes to pages 141–3

Connemara and transportation infrastructure (the sea crossing to Kingstown, better horse carriages, and improved roads) was much improved
(*Journeys in Ireland*, 34–5).

71 Pemberton, Travel Diary 1897, 7, 12, 13 Sept.
72 Pack, Travel Diary 1911, 6, 7 June.
73 Simmonds, *Our Trip*, 10.
74 Ibid., 11.
75 Shea, *Across Two Continents*, 159–60.
76 For discussions of guides in other tourist destinations, see Jasen, *Wild
Things*, esp. 133–49; Dubinsky, *The Second Greatest Disappointment*, esp.
chapter 3, 'Local Colour in the "Contact Zone": the Spectacle of Race.' See
also Loo, *States of Nature*, and her 'Of Moose and Men: Hunting for Masculinities in British Columbia, 1880–1939,' *Western Historical Quarterly* 32, no. 3
(2001): 296–320.
    Without further research into this aspect of Irish tourism, it is difficult to
know whether or not most guides were men. However, the tourists' writings display a widespread assumption that they would seek out men, not
women, to take them around. Dowsley reported that 'men and women'
alike at Glendalough clamoured for employment as guides but, like his
fellow-Canadians, he seemed to have automatically hired a male guide
('Plea for Ireland [1]' 236).
77 See Jasen, *Wild Things*, 137–40.
78 de Nie argues that this figure, a commonly found stereotype in seventeenth-
and eighteenth-century theatre, was replaced in the British press with the
image of the Irishman as a 'violent and alien Irish Other' (*Eternal Paddy*, 6). It
may well be that the conventions of tourist writing and the structures of tourism helped produce the figure of the amusing and harmless Paddy and not
the simian, Calibanistic figure depicted by de Nie.
79 Cronin, 'Contemporary Travel Writing in Ireland,' in O'Connor and Cronin,
eds., *Tourism in Ireland*, 56–58. Cronin also sees this process as feminizing
the Irish, although such a characterization is not as obvious in the case of
Canadian tourist writings.
80 Dowsley, 'Plea for Ireland [1],' 235. And it was not just guides who provided easy amusement for tourists. On docking in Derry, Lindsey's cricket
team 'received the thanks of many old Irish women from the steerage for
the assistance given in passing their trunks through the customs as the luggage of the Canadian Cricket Team.' The 'genial official' appeared satisfied:
'perhaps this is an instance of Irish credulity, perhaps of Irish hospitality, at
any rate the official knew that we were the "byes as was going to bate"
Dublin tomorrow.' In passing a costermonger's donkey with a loaded cart

in a back street, the 'moke set up a terrific he-hawing,' which gave Lindsey and his companions much 'merriment and called from our "kyar" driver the remark: "Begorra, gentlemen, but he's givin' yes a royal accipshin' (*Cricket across the Sea*, 43–7).

81 Ibid., 238.
82 Ibid., 238–9.
83 Simmonds, *Our Trip*, 10.
84 Ney, *Britishers in Britain*, 150–3.
85 Dowsley, 'Plea for Ireland [2],' 572.
86 See Loo, 'Of Moose and Men.'
87 Shea, *Across Two Continents*, 170.
88 Dowsley, 'Plea for Ireland [2],' 572.
89 These encounters between tourists and 'locals' bear some resemblance to the 'playful and expressive, ludic qualities of much tourist performance' which Tim Edensor argues should be considered as part of tourists' practice. Edensor, 'Staging Tourism, 324. Of course, my example suggests that playfulness was not the province or practice of only tourists.
90 Dowsley, 'Plea for Ireland [1],' 233–4.
91 Ibid., 234. See also Occasional Correspondent, 'Dublin,' for a similar portrait of parts of the city.
92 Pack, Travel Diary 1911, 9 June. Shea's account is full of attractive, modern sites where tourists would find comfortable hotels and activities such as bathing, fishing, and country drives at places such as Letterfrack, Westport, and Portrush (*Across Two Continents*, 183, 185, 188).
93 Pack, Travel Diary 1911, 7 June.
94 Ney, *Britishers in Britain*, 149. Along with northeast Wicklow, Killarney had been a tourist destination since the eighteenth century. By the early twentieth century, the area was visited by tourists from across Ireland but also Europe, the United States, and New Zealand. See K.M. Davies, 'For health and Pleasure in the British Fashion: Bray, Co. Wicklow, as a Tourist Resort, 1750–1914,' 29–50, and John Heuston, 'Kilkee – the Origins and Development of a West Coast Resort,' in O'Connor and Cronin, eds., *Tourism in Ireland*, 13–28.
95 Dowsley, 'Plea for Ireland [1],' 238.
96 Ibid., 47.
97 Pack, Travel Diary 1911, 7, 8, 9 June.
98 Ibid., 10 June.
99 Ibid.
100 Ibid., 11, 12 June.
101 Ibid., 12 June.

102 McDougall was born Margaret Dixon Carey in Belfast, 25 December 1828, and emigrated with her family to Canada, where she married Alexander McDougall and lived in Pembroke, Ontario. As well as her work as a teacher and journalist, she had six children and published a novel based on her Irish experiences, *Days of a Life* (1883). McDougall died 23 October 1899, while on a trip to Seattle. Bibliographic information on McDougall may be found in the database *Canada's Early Women Writers* (www.sfu.ca).
103 de Nie, *Eternal Paddy*, 190.
104 See Fintan Cullen, 'Marketing National Sentiment: Lantern Slides of Evictions in Late Nineteenth-Century Ireland,' *History Workshop Journal* 54 (2002): 162–79.
105 de Nie points out that the *Times* owner, John Walter, became convinced that land reform was inevitable after reading his correspondent's report (*Eternal Paddy*, 190).
106 Lawrence's photographs are reprinted in Cullen, 'Marketing National Sentiment.'
107 Cullen, 'Marketing National Sentiment,' 170.
108 Margaret Dixon McDougall, *The Letters of 'Norah' on Her Tour through Ireland*, 27.
109 Ibid., 28–9.
110 Ibid., 36–46.
111 Ibid., 119.
112 Ibid., 126.
113 de Nie's brief discussion of conditions in the northwest and west of Ireland during this period confirms McDougall's impressions (*Eternal Paddy*, 204).
114 Ibid., 161–2.
115 Ibid., 172.
116 McDougall, *Letters from 'Norah,'* 85.
117 Ibid., 92.
118 Ibid., 106.
119 Ibid., 146–8.
120 Ibid., 298.
121 Ibid., 67.
122 Ibid., 114.
123 Ibid., 141.
124 Ibid., 152.
125 Ibid., 70–1.
126 Ibid., 176.
127 Ibid., 233.

128 Ibid., 175.
129 Ibid., 208. For her description of the departure of American-bound emi-
      grants at Castlebar rail station, see ibid., 165. McDougall also participated
      in many 'tourist' activities; in Sligo, for example, she toured an estate,
      went for a boat ride, and wandered around the ruins of Brefni Castle
      (ibid., 133–40).
130 Ibid., 98.
131 Ibid., 87.
132 Ibid., 266.
133 Ibid., 268.
134 Ibid.
135 Ibid., 15.
136 Ibid., 72.
137 Ibid., 227.
138 Ibid., 256–8.
139 Ibid., 197.
140 Ibid., 228.
141 Ibid., 13.
142 Ibid., 21.
143 Ibid., 130–1. McDougall later noted that she was happy to read a newspa-
      per article that stated that this house had been censured by the medical
      profession (ibid., 157).
144 Ibid., 167–8.
145 Ibid., 82–4.
146 de Nie, *Eternal Paddy,* 257.
147 McDougall, *Letters from 'Norah,'* 148–9.
148 Ibid., 243.
149 Ibid., 66.
150 Ibid., 67.
151 Ibid., 116.
152 Ibid., 154.
153 Ibid., 155.
154 Ibid., 160.
155 Ibid., 276.
156 Ibid., 120.
157 Ibid., 90–1.
158 Ibid., 90.
159 Ibid., 233, 300–2.
160 Ibid., 302.
161 Shea, *Across Two Continénts,* 198–201.

5 'The Hot Life of London Is upon Us'

1 Black, 'Echoes from Our Trip,' 12.
2 A.H. Morrison, 'Vignettes from St Pilgrim's Isle,' *Canadian Magazine* (Jan. 1894): 224–32, 228.
3 Burton, *At the Heart of the Empire*; Woollacott, *To Try Her Fortune in London*; Parsons, *King Khama, Emperor Joe, and the Great White Queen*.
4 As feminist historians have pointed out, middle-class women's use of London's public spaces was fraught with numerous complexities and tensions during these decades. See, e.g., Walkowitz, *City of Dreadful Delight*, also her 'Going Public'; Nord, *Walking the Victorian Streets*; Rappaport, *Shopping for Pleasure*; Copelman, 'The Gendered Metropolis'; and Woollacott, 'Inhabiting the Metropolis: Gendered Space and Colonialism,' chapter 2 in *To Try Her Fortune in London*.
5 Birchall, 'City of Dreams,' 316.
6 Shea, *Across Two Continents*, 134–5.
7 See, e.g., Morrison, 'Vignettes'; see also Newton MacTavish, 'Dear Old Piccadilly,' *Canadian Magazine* (Dec. 1911): 101–9.
8 Smith, *A Trip to England*, 100.
9 Birchall, 'City of Dreams.'
10 MacTavish, 'Dear Old Piccadilly,' 104. Woollacott also discusses Australian women's alienation and loneliness (*To Try Her Fortune*, 65–6).
11 For South Asians' experience of being made to feel conspicuous in London, see Antoinette Burton, 'Making a Spectacle of Empire: Indian Travellers in Fin-de-Siècle London,' *History Workshop Journal* 42 (1996): 96–117, 130.
12 Britton B. Cooke, 'Many Londons,' *Canadian Magazine* (Apr. 1913): 525–9, 525. Some wrote bout the 'mysteries' of London. See, e.g., n.a., 'Recent Impressions of London,' *St John Daily Telegraph*, 26 Nov. 1878.
13 Smith, *Trip to England*, 116–18.
14 Shea, *Across Two Continents*, 135.
15 Disbrowe, Travel Diary 1908, 17 Jan.
16 W.F. Munro to [Georgina] Munro, 18, 27 Apr. 1883, AO, MU 280, W.F. Munro Correspondence 1862–1883, File 1864–1880, F 708.
17 Caldwell, Travel Diary 1874, 20 Aug.
18 Ibid., 17 Aug.
19 Elliott, *Rambles in Merrie, Merrie England*, part 1, 2–5.
20 R.J. McLoughlin, 'Mentographs of London,' *Saint John Daily Telegraph*, 19 Dec. 1872, 4
21 Ibid.
22 Davies, Travel Diary 1899–1900, 64–5. See also Greenshields, Travel Diary 1895, 9 Jan.

23 Thomson, Travel Diary 1898, 6 Sept.
24 Davies, Travel Diary 1899–1900, 64–5. No dates given.
25 Chown, Travel Diary 1910, Book 3, 17 June.
26 Elliott, *Rambles in Merrie, Merrie England*, part 1, 10.
27 Cameron, Travel Diary 1910, 20 Aug.
28 Ibid., 29 Aug.
29 Montgomery, Travel Diary 1895, 29 Aug., 1 Sept.
30 Martin, Travel Diary 1881, 3 June; Chown, Travel Diary 1910, 28 May.
31 Bowslaugh, Travel Diary 1897, 3 July; Smith, *A Trip to England*, 131; Thomson, Travel Diary 1910, 3 Sept. While most were reminded of Charles I in Westminster Hall, Thomson also pointed out that it had seen the trials of William Wallace and Mary Stuart.
32 Smith, *A Trip to England*, 124.
33 Thomson, Travel Diary 1897, 23 July.
34 Hall, Travel Diary 1878, 28 June. George Lindsey went with his fellow team members to the Commons, where they heard a debate on the land bill and had the 'pleasure' of hearing many Irish members give their views on fixing the rents of Irish farms (*Cricket across the Sea*, 131).
35 Albert R. Carman, 'A Visit to Westminster,' *Canadian Magazine* (Sept. 1901): 122–6.
36 Priddis, Travel Diary 1911, 45; Thomson, Travel Diary 1897, 23 July.
37 Chown, Travel Diary 1910, Book 2, 28 May; Pack, Travel Diary 1911, 26 June. The Manitoba teachers also visited the Commons when its 'sacred precincts were . . . barred to the ladies.' However, a 'fortunate few' were taken into the Inner Lobby and could then see many 'prominent leaders' for both sides (Ney, *Britishers in Britain*, 74).
38 Murphy, *Impressions of Janey Canuck Abroad*, 47.
39 Montgomery, Travel Diary 1895, 3 Sept.
40 Simmonds, *Our Trip to Europe*, 34; Pack, Travel Diary 1911, 26 June.
41 Mackinnon, *Rambles in Britain*, 221.
42 Lauder, *Evergreen Leaves*, 337.
43 William Harrison, 'London's Tragic Tower,' *Canadian Magazine* (Mar. 1897): 443–6, 444. It is more than likely that many of these English-Canadian tourists had garnered impressions of the Tower from the British history taught in Canadian schools. For a discussion of the Tower's construction as a historical monument, see Raphael Samuel, 'The Tower of London,' in his *Island Stories, Unravelling Britain: Theatres of Memory*, vol. 2 (London: Verso, 1998), 101–24.
44 Murphy, *Impressions of Janey Canuck*, 46.
45 Lauder, *Evergreen Leaves*, 335–6.
46 Harrison, 'London's Tragic Tower,' 444.

47 Bowslaugh, Travel 1897, 30 June.
48 Thomson, Travel Diary 1898, 25 Aug.; Bain, Travel Diary 1911, 31 Jan.;
    Chown, Travel Diary 1910, 30 May; Simmonds, *Our Trip*, 34; Davies, Travel
    Diary 1899–1900, 83–7.
49 Pack, Travel Diary 1911, 26 June.
50 Greenshields, Travel Diary 1895, 18 Jan.
51 Murphy, *Impressions of Janey Canuck*, 49.
52 Ibid., 48.
53 Ibid., 47.
54 Harrison, 'London's Tragic Tower,' 443.
55 Ibid., 446.
56 Davies, Travel Diary 1899–1900, 83–7.
57 Simmonds, *Our Trip*, 36–7.
58 Davies, Travel Diary 1899–1900, 167.
59 Pack, Travel Diary 1911, 28 June. See also Thomson, Travel Diary 1897,
    16 July; Priddis, Travel Diary 1906, 151.
60 Cameron, Travel Diary 1910, 4 Aug.
61 Ibid., 25 Oct., and Travel Diary 1911, 23 Mar.
62 Martin, Travel Diary 1881, 6 June.
63 Ney, *Britishers in Britain*, 74; Bowslaugh, Travel Diary 1897, 30 June.
64 Pack, Travel Diary 1911, 28 June.
65 The literature on these displays and performance is quite extensive. See,
    e.g., Cannadine, 'The Context, Performance and Meaning of Ritual,' and
    Tori Smith, '"Almost Pathetic ... but Also Very Glorious."'
66 For a discussion of the spectacle of British royalty in Canada, see Phillip
    Buckner, 'Casting Daylight upon Magic: Deconstructing the Royal Tour of
    1901 to Canada,' in Carl Bridge and Kent Fedorowich, eds., *The British
    World: Diaspora, Culture, and Identity* (London: Frank Cass, 2003) 158–89.
67 See, in particular, Smith, 'Almost Pathetic.'
68 Miss Peake, 'How a Toronto Girl Saw the Queen,' paper presented to the
    Women's Canadian Historical Society of Toronto, 1901, 2, AO, WCHS
    Papers.
69 Ibid., 2–3.
70 Ibid., 6.
71 Davies, Travel Diary 1900, 13 Mar.
72 Murphy, *Impressions of Janey*, 128.
73 See J.M. Bumsted, 'Sir Louis Henry Davies,' in Ramsay Cook, ed., *Dictio-
    nary of Canadian Biography*, vol. 15 (University of Toronto Press, 2004),
    257–60. During Ethel's stay in England her father was involved in the
    negotiations of the Alaska boundary.
74 Ibid.

75 Simmonds, *Our Trip*, 40. See also ? Redpath's impression of seeing the Prince and Princess of Wales and their two sons, who had returned from London from the Isle of Wight: 'such noble looking lads in sailour dress with hats on back of head' (? Redpath, Travel Diary 1875, 13 Aug., MU-RBR, MS 659, Thomas Roddick Papers.

76 Elliott, *Rambles in Merrie, Merrie England*, part 1, 21.

77 Mackinnon, *Rambles in Britain*, 12. It is not clear which Jubilee Mackinnon attended.

78 Pack, Travel Diary 1911, 22 June. Cameron, though, who saw royalty on a number of occasions during her stay in England, wrote in her diary that during the procession the 'Queen smiled *broadly* (first time we have seen this),' although the King 'looked extremely interested and was well received' (Travel Diary 1911, 25 June).

79 Mary Spencer Warren, 'The Queen's Horses and Carriages,' *Canadian Magazine* (June 1897): 128–37.

80 Elliott, *Rambles*, 13.

81 Thomson, Travel Diary 1910, 23 Aug.

82 Lindsey, *Cricket across the Sea*, 132–3.

83 Ibid. For a discussion of the domestication of Victoria's image, see Smith, 'Almost Pathetic.'

84 Emily Weaver, 'Victoria's English Palaces,' *Canadian Magazine* (June 1910): 145–53.

85 Cameron, Travel Diary 1910, 25 Oct.

86 Martin, Travel Diary 1881, 7 June. He did see the Princess Eugenie at Windsor and had a 'very good view of her'; then, upon returning to London, she was in the next rail compartment, 'tall slight and is a beautiful woman but now looks very sad.'

87 Chown, Travel Diary 1910, Book 3, 16 June.

88 Cameron, Travel Diary 1911, 6 Apr. to 20 June.

89 Priddis, Travel Diary 1910, 36. For a discussion of the Memorial's conception, execution, and dedication, see Tori Smith, '"A Grand Work of Noble Conception": The Victoria Memorial and Imperial London,' in Felix Driver and David Gilbert, eds., *Imperial Cities*, 21–39.

90 Cameron, Travel Diary 1911, 16 May.

91 Ibid., Travel Diary 1910, 29 Aug.

92 Chown, Travel Diary 1910, 29 May.

93 Mackinnon, *Rambles*, 242.

94 Simmonds, *Our Trip*, 44; Mackinnon, *Rambles*, 12.

95 Norman Patterson, 'London: The Heart of the Empire,' *Canadian Magazine* (Nov. 1905): 2–11. Noting that 'colonials and foreigners' could be found in London was not an observation limited to Canadians; as Woollacott points

out, Australians also registered their presence. See 'Contesting (Colonial) Men's Imperial Power: Australian Women's Metropolitan Activism and Commonwealth Feminism,' chapter 4 in *To Try Her Fortune in London*.

96   Montgomery, Travel Diary 1895, 3 Sept.; Mackinnon, *Rambles*, 11.
97   Ibid.
98   Elliott, *Rambles*, Part 1, 18–19.
99   Ibid., 20.
100 Pack, Travel Diary 1911, 22 June.
101 Prissis, Travel Diary 1911, 67.
102 For an analysis of such discourses, see Burton, *Burdens of History*. Priddis was either an interested observer or a member of various imperial and transnational organizations, such as the Imperial Club, the Victoria League, and the YWCA, and she spent a great deal of her time in London attending their meetings (Travel Diary 1911, 60–1, 90, 106, 109–13).
103 See, e.g., Murphy, *Impressions of Janey Canuck*, 14–20, 40, 72–3.
104 N.a., 'Canada's Status in London,' *Montreal Daily Star*, 14 Oct. 1882; n.a., 'Colonial News in London,' *Canadian Magazine* (June 1897): 173.
105 Priddis, Travel Diary 1911, 115–16.
106 Ibid., Travel Diary 1906, 106.
107 See, e.g., William Ball, 'London,' *Halifax Morning Chronicle*, 12 Oct. 1877, 4. Ball catalogued the presence of not only Irish and Scots but also Chinese, Africans, Indians, and Europeans as part of the city's spectacle, along with East End poverty, West End luxury, and the many other sights and sites that were to be found in the city.
108 Randolph Carlyle, 'The Festival of Empire,' *Canadian Magazine* (May 1910): 25–30. For a discussion of the Pageant of London held during the Festival, see Deborah S. Ryan, 'Staging the Imperial City: The Pageant of London, 1911,' in Driver and Gilbert, eds., *Imperial Cities*, 117–35.
109 Priddis, Travel Diary 1911, 42.
110 Ibid., 135.
111 Ibid., 40. It is likely that 'Miss Merritt' was Catharine Nina Merritt, who was an amateur playwright and had staged an imperial pageant in 1909. See Cecilia Morgan, 'Staging Empire, Nation, and Gender: Catharine Nina Merritt and Imperial Pageantry, Southern Ontario, 1890s–1910,' paper presented to the Canadian Historical Association, 83rd Annual Meeting, University of Manitoba, Winnipeg, 3–5 June 2004.
112 Cameron, Travel Diary 1911, 5, 3 June.
113 Priddis, Travel Diary 1911, 42–4.
114 Upper- and middle-class British and English-Canadian women's efforts to claim national and imperial membership through voluntary organizations

have been discussed by Julia Bush, *Edwardian Ladies and Imperial Power* (London: Leicester University Press, 2000), and Pickles, *Female Imperialism and National Identity.*

115 This was a long-standing concern with Canada's displays at imperial exhibitions. See E.A. Heaman, *The Inglorious Arts of Peace*, 196.

116 Ibid., 64. It was not just Canada's representation that interested these tourists. Edith Chown was fascinated by the British-Japanese Exhibition: 'the next best thing to taking a trip to Japan itself,' with its 'wonderfully arranged' replicas of villages and its displays of Japanese industries, painting, sculpture, and embroidery over different centuries. She and her aunt Alice found that there was too much to see in one trip and vowed to return (Travel Diary 1910, Book 2, 1 June).

117 Heaman points to the tensions that surrounded displays of Aboriginal people and their work at the exhibitions (*Inglorious Arts of Peace*, 297–310). For public performances of Native identity in England, see Morgan, 'A Wigwam to Westminster.'

118 N.a., 'Canada's Status in London,' 3.

119 Chown, Travel Diary 1910, 26 May.

120 N.a., 'Colonial News in London.'

121 See, e.g., n.a. 'An English View of Sir John A. Macdonald's View of the Relations of Canada and England,' *Saint John Daily Telegraph*, 24 Aug. 1880, 4; see also n.a. 'Canadian Ministers in London,' ibid., 2 Aug. 1880. Bernard, 'The Ladies' Empire Club of London,' 195–9.

122 Cameron, Travel Diary 1910, 30 July.

123 Priddis, Travel Diary 1911, 40, 90, 60–1,108, 113, 117, 130. Cameron went to many such places with her aunt; so too did Chown, who, e.g., went to Dr Barnardo's homes (Travel Diary 1910, 16 June). This form of tourism will be discussed in more detail in chapter 6.

124 Ibid., 17 June 1910. For a discussion of those parades, see Lisa Tickner, *The Spectacle of Women.*

125 Priddis, Travel Diary 1911, 74.

126 Cameron, Travel Diary 1910, 7 Nov.

127 Ibid., 16 Oct., 21 Nov.

128 Chown, Travel Diary 1910, Book 2, 26 May.

129 Thomson, Travel Diary 1910, 21 Aug.

130 Ibid., 25 Nov.

131 Ibid., Travel Diary 1914, 30 Apr.

132 Ibid., 21 May.

133 Ibid., 21 Nov. To date we know rather little about the visual presentation of suffrage and representations of the woman's rights movement,

although certain Canadian suffragists, such as Nellie McClung, staged mock parliaments that reversed anti-suffrage discourse.

134 Priddis, Travel Diary 1911, 98.

135 Nor have I found much evidence that Canadian women who resided overseas participated in suffrage organizations and networks to the same degree as Australian women living in London. For Australian women's participation in London's suffrage groups, see Woollacott, 'Contesting (Colonial) Men's Power,' in *To Try Her Fortune*. There has been very little work on the Canadian suffrage movement's links to the international movement, although thanks to Catherine Cleverdon's pioneering research we know such links existed. See Cleverdon, *The Woman Suffrage Movement in Canada*, introduction by Ramsay Cook (Toronto: University of Toronto Press, 1978), 31–2.

136 For a discussion of the use of historical representations in suffrage processions, see Tickner, *Spectacle of Women*, 125–30.

137 Roddick, Travel Diary 1897, 20 Oct. Two years after Roddick's visit the South Kensington Museum would be moved into a new building and renamed the Victoria and Albert Museum.

138 Arthur H. Whitman, Travel Diary 1888–9, 1, 5 Jan. 1889, DU-SC, MS–2–487.

139 Mackinnon, *Rambles in Britain*, 224–32.

140 Davies, Travel Diary 1899–1900, 90.

141 Flavelle, Travel Diary 1900; Davies, Travel Diary 1899–1900; Hall, Travel Diary 1878.

142 Penelope, 'Our London Letter [1].' 17 June. See also Penelope, 'For the Ladies: Our London Letter [2],' *Montreal Daily Star*, 15 Sept. 1882, 5. Two decades later this type of journalism was still being practised. See Gwen, 'La Canadienne en Voyage,' *Canada: An Illustrated Journal*, 9, 17 Jan., 25 Apr., 11 Aug. 1906.

143 See, e.g., Greenshields, Travel Diaries: 1895, 7, 9, 10, 14, 24 Jan., 5 Feb., 5, 6, 11, 13, 18, 21 June; 1906, 26, 28, 29, May; 1911, 20, 22, 23 May; 1913, 10, 17, Apr. Greenshields's tours of European art galleries will be discussed in chapter 8.

144 Ibid., Travel Diary 1895, 5 Jan.

145 Ibid., Travel Diary 1906, 31 May. As the *Canadian Magazine* noted in its review of Greenshields's *Landscape Painting and Modern Dutch Artists*, it was this particular group of artists that he chose as exemplary of artistic greatness (n.a., 'A Canadian Art Study,' [Apr. 1906]: 399).

146 Roddick, Travel Diary 1897, 11 Oct.

147 Ibid., 25 Oct.

148 Thomson, Travel Diary 1910, 24 Aug.

149 Whitman, Travel Diary 1888, 5, 8 Dec.; Pack, Travel Diary 1911, 26 July. See also Greenshields, Travel Diaries 1884–5, 5 Jan. 1885; 1906, 7 June; 1911, 10 July.

150 See Rappaport, *Shopping for Pleasure*.

151 Penelope, 'For the Ladies: Our London Letter [3],' *Montreal Daily Star*, 26 Aug. 1882, 2.

152 Ibid., 'Our London Letter [4],' 5 Jan. 1883, 3.

153 Ibid.

154 The examples are too numerous to cite completely but see Whitman, Travel Diary 1888; Pemberton, Travel Diary 1897.

155 Davies, Travel Diary 1899–1900, 157. See also Clouston, Travel Diaries: 1894, 30 Apr., 3, 8, 15 May; 1895, 9–13, 17 Sept.; Roddick, Travel Diary 1897, 11, 18 , 23 Oct.; Eliza Greenshields, Travel Diary 1913, 9, 14, 24 Apr. MM, Greenshields Family Papers, File 582; Montgomgery, Travel Diary 1895, 26–8, 31 Aug.

156 Davies, Travel Diary 1899–1900, 132.

157 Thomson, Travel Diaries: 1897, 25 Aug.; 1898, 27, 30, 31 Aug., 1, 7 Sept., 19, 22 Nov.; 1910, 22, 26, 27, 29 Aug., 14, 19 Sept.; 1914, 21 Apr.

158 Ibid., Travel Diary 1910, 26 Aug.

159 Bain, Travel Diary 1910, 26 Jan.

160 N.a., 'Canadian Ladies in London,' *Canada: An Illustrated Journal*, 24 Aug. 1907.

161 For work on fashion in the Canadian context, see Elizabeth Sifton, 'Montreal's Fashion Mile: St Catherine Street, 1890–1930,' and Barbara M. Freeman, 'Laced In and Let Down: Women's Fashion Features in the Toronto Daily Press, 1890–1900,' in Alexandra Palmer, ed., *Fashion*, 203–28 and 291–314 respectively. Further research is needed to determine whether London trumped Paris as the city with the most appeal to the upper middle class of both English and French Canada. Kristin Hoganson argues that, for elite American women, Paris was the winner ('The Fashionable World: Imagined Communities of Dress,' in Burton, ed., *After the Imperial Turn*, 260–78).

162 Marguerite S. Shaffer has argued that, in the American context, the development of national tourism and an 'emerging consumer consciousness' were linked, both through the production of souvenirs and through leisure pursuits such as staying at elite hotels (*See America First*, 262–3, 276). Further research on consumption among the English-Canadian middle and upper middle class for this period would be needed to see if transatlantic tourism played a role.

163 Penelope, 'For the Ladies [4].'

164 Martin, Travel Diary 1881; Whitman, Travel Diary 1888; Gertrude Fleming, Travel Diary 1891.
165 Lynda Nead, 'Animating the Everyday: London on Camera circa 1900,' *Journal of British Studies* 43 (Jan. 2004): 65–90.
166 Greenshields, Travel Diary 1895, 15 Sept.
167 Cameron, Travel Diary 1911, 20 May.
168 Pack, Travel Diary 1911, 27 July.
169 See, e.g., Whitman, Travel Diary 1888, 15 Nov., 26, 28 Dec. 1888; 3, 11, 12 Jan. 1889; Pack, Travel Diary 1911, 28 June; Martin, Travel Diary 1881, 2, 5 June; Hall, Travel Diary 1878, 28, 29 June.
170 See, e.g., Greenshields, Travel Diaries: 1895, 4, 5, 9, 11, 25 Jan., 11, 16, 19 Sept.; 1906, 29 May, 2, 8, 14 June; 1911, 19, 20, 22, 25, 26, 27 May, 11, 14 July; 1913, 14, 15, 16, 26, 28 Apr.
171 The exception was Bowslaugh, whose diary does not record any trips to the theatre, opera, or ballet. This may have been because Bowslaugh was on a Methodist church-sponsored trip, which may have ruled out theatre-going; her own religious convictions also may have played a role. For a discussion of the domestication and commodification of London theatre during this period, see Rappaport, 'Acts of Consumption: Musical Comedy and the Desire of Exchange,' chapter 6 in *Shopping for Pleasure*.
172 Fleming, Travel Diary 1891, 30 Nov. For a discussion of erotic and exotic dance in London in the following decades, see Judith R. Walkowitz, 'The "Vision of Salome."'
173 Fleming, Travel Diary 1891, 28 Nov.
174 Ibid., 2 Dec.
175 Ibid., 7 Dec.
176 Montgomery, Travel Diary 1895, 11, 14 Sept. Clouston, though, saw the same production (and possibly the same performance) and thought it 'very good indeed' (Travel Diary 1895, 14 Sept.).
177 Pemberton, Travel Diary 1897, 27 May, 5 June.
178 Ibid., 28 June.
179 Ibid., 17 May.
180 Cameron, Travel Diary 1910, 13 Dec.
181 Ibid., 30 Dec. Chown also was greatly impressed by *Blue Bird*, which she described as a 'great symbolic play' with 'beautiful' scenic effects (Travel Diary 1910, Book 2, 24 May).
182 Cameron, Travel Diary 1911, 13 June.
183 Ibid., 10 June, and Travel Diary 1910, 26 Dec.
184 Chown, Travel Diary 1910, Book 2, 3 June. Although she did not say so, it was probably Dublin's Abbey Players.

185 See Richard Foulkes, *Performing Shakespeare in the Age of Empire*, esp. chapter 6, 'The Imperial Stage: Beerbohm Tree and Benson.' My thanks to Matthew Hendley for the reference to Foulkes's work.
186 Davies, Travel Diary 1899–1900, 77. Davies saw this production 31 Oct. 1899.
187 Bain, Travel Diary 1911, 27 Jan.
188 Priddis, Travel Diary 1911, 59. It is likely that Priddis was referring to the British actor-manager William Charles Macready (1793–1873), who staged elaborate, spectacular Shakespearian productions at Covent Garden and Drury lane in the 1840s and 1850s.
189 They discussed their interactions with porters, guides, clerks, and others employed in the 'tourist trade' outside of London, especially in Europe. It is possible that they saw those employed in public service functions in the West End as being similar to retail workers in Canadian cities and thus did not treat them as representatives of a 'quaint' or exotic culture.
190 Joel H. Kaplan and Sheila Stowell, *Theatre and Fashion*, 11. As these authors point out, such a process was noted and marked by a 'wider public of journalists, middle-class householders, clergymen, and laborers,' seated in the theatres' stalls and galleries. For London theatre's symbiotic relationship to fashion, see also Christopher Breward, 'The Actress: Covent Garden and The Strand 1880–1914,' in his *Fashioning London*.
191 Bain, Travel Diary 1911, 24 Jan.
192 Ibid., 28 Jan.
193 Priddis, Travel Diary 1911, 115–16. Priddis also remarked on the number of 'colonials' who were in the crowd, although as a member of various imperial leagues she was keenly aware of how many members of the Empire were in London for the Coronation.
194 See Loren Kruger, *The National Stage: Theatre and Cultural Legitimation in England, France, and America* (Chicago: University of Chicago Press, 1992).

6 The Street, the Regatta, and the Orphanage

1 Cameron, Travel Diary 1910, 18 Sept.
2 James Rupert Elliott, *Rambles in Merrie, Merrie England, Part 2, By the Thames* (Saint John: J. & A. McMillan, 1897), 46.
3 Seth Koven, *Slumming*, 1.
4 Fred Hastings, 'How Sunday Is Spent in Some Parts of London,' *Saint John Daily Telegraph*, 8 Jan. 1874.
5 Murphy, *The Impressions of Janey Canuck Abroad*, 72–3.
6 Ibid.

7 Ibid., 74–5.
8 Ibid., 75–6.
9 Goldwin Smith, *A Trip to England*, 105–6.
10 N.a., 'Is London Immoral?' *Victoria Daily Times*, 19 Sept. 1885, 1. This piece was reprinted from *Pictorial World*.
11 N.a., 'Recent Impressions of London.'
12 Patterson, 'London: The Heart of the Empire,' 2–11.
13 Pack, Travel Diary 1911, 24 June, 1 July.
14 Mackinnon, *Rambles in Britain*, 246–7.
15 Thomson, Travel Diary 1898, 2 Dec.
16 Cameron, Travel Diary 1910, 23 Dec.
17 Ibid., 24 Dec.
18 Ibid., Travel Diary 1911, 23 Apr.
19 Ibid., 1 May.
20 Ibid., Travel Diary 1910, 31 Dec.
21 Mackinnon, *Rambles in Britain*, 247.
22 See, e.g., Langton, Travel Diary 1907, 19 Feb. Bain, Travel Diary 1910, 5–7 Dec., For articles on travel in these locations, see the following in the *Canadian Magazine*: Allan Sullivan, 'With Two Canadians in Algeria' (May 1894): 29–40; Rev. W.S. Blackstock, 'An Arab Dinner' (Mar. 1895): 444–48; Oscar Frederick Taylor, 'A Glimpse of Constantinople' (Jan. 1900): 278–84; M.H. Braid, 'Cairo and Its Panorama' (Sept. 1901): 399–402; Jean Templer, 'Jerusalem and Its Environments' (Dec. 1906): 99–109; Albert Carman, 'The Beauties of the Nile' (June 1910): 99–107.
23 Canadian teacher Margaret Addison was caught in that demonstration. See Jean O'Grady, *Margaret Addison*, 71–2.
24 Elliott, *Rambles in Merrie, Merrie England, part 1*, 12.
25 Ibid., 16.
26 Ibid., 16–17.
27 Chown, Travel Diary 1910, Book 2, 20 May.
28 Cameron, Travel Diary 1911, 4 May.
29 See, e.g., Patterson, 'London: The Heart of the Empire'; Cooke, 'Many Londons,' 525–9.
30 Birchall, 'A City of Dreams.' Like Birchall, Montreal's 'Penelope' took it for granted that middle-class women tourists would enjoy freedom of movement in London, at least in its West End. See Penelope, 'For the ladies [1] and [2].'
31 These examples are taken from writings about London, as it was the British city both visited most frequently and written about at greatest length, and, for these tourists, it had the most complete and complex system of public

transportation to supplement their urban strolling. However, as we have seen in chapter 2, Canadian women made their way around Liverpool, Glasgow, and Edinburgh, on foot, bicycle, and public transport.

32 See, e.g., Walkowitz, 'Going Public' and Nord, *Walking the Victorian Streets.*
33 Woollacott, *To Try Her Fortune in London*, 55–71.
34 Fleming, Travel Diary 1891, 27 Nov.
35 Bain, Travel Diary 1911, 24 Jan.
36 Priddis, Travel Diary 1911, 33–4. Priddis was not a novice traveller and tourist; by the time of her two, quite extensive trips to Britain and Europe in the 1900s, she had already been to Philadelphia for the 1876 Centennial of the American Declaration of Independence. As well, as a member of the London and Middlesex Historical Society, Priddis travelled frequently around southern Ontario to meetings of the Ontario Historical Society. For her work as a historian, see Cecilia Morgan, 'History, Nation, and Empire: Gender and Southern Ontario Historical Societies, 1890–1920s,' *Canadian Historical Review* 82, 3 (Sept. 2001): 491–528.
37 Priddis, Travel Diary 1911, 20–1.
38 Davies 1889–1900, Travel Diary, 76.
39 Priddis, Travel Diary 1906, 146.
40 Davies, Travel Diary 1899–1900, 132.
41 Cameron, Travel Diary 1910, 15 Aug.
42 Murphy, *Impressions of Janey Canuck*, 19–20.
43 Ibid., 20.
44 Ibid.
45 Ibid., 21–2.
46 Ibid., 23.
47 Ibid.
48 Priddis, Travel Diary 1911, 26 June.
49 V. Leonore Gordon, 'On the Visit to Margate,' in Ney, ed., *Britishers in Britain*, 284–5.
50 Greenshields, Travel Diary 1906, 10 June.
51 For public gardens, see Rebecca Preston, '"The Scenery of the Torrid Zone": Imagined Travels and the Culture of Exotics in Nineteenth-Century British Gardens,' in Felix Driver and David Gilbert, eds., *Imperial Cities*, 194–211. For an exploration of the permeation of imperialist discourses into the Regent's Park Zoo, see Jonathan Schneer, *London 1900, The Imperial Metropolis*, 97–104. While these tourists did not discuss gardens such as Kew or the Zoo in the language of imperialist imagery, it may well have been that such imagery struck them as 'natural' and thus they did not comment explicitly on it.

52 Lauder, *Evergreen Leaves*, 356; Thomson, Travel Diary 1898, 29 Aug.
53 Montgomery, Travel Diary 1895, 17 Sept.
54 Murphy, *Impressions of Janey Canuck*, 41–2. See also Clouston, Travel Diary 1895, 7 July.
55 Elliott, *Rambles in Merrie, Merrie England, part 2*, 35–6.
56 Priddis, Travel Diary 1911, 50.
57 Ibid., 64.
58 Hall, Travel Diary 1878, 28 June.
59 Ibid., 29 June.
60 Martin, Travel Diary 1881, 7 June. Greenshields also enjoyed watching women cycling, riding, and walking in Battersea Park (Travel Diary 1895, 14 June).
61 Murphy, *Impressions of Janey Canuck*, 57.
62 Ibid., 57–8.
63 Chown, Travel Diary 1910, 29 May.
64 Cameron, Travel Diary 1911, 25 Dec.
65 Priddis, Travel Diary 1906, 146. Osla Clouston's Uncle Henry took her to Rotten Row (Travel Diary 1895, 28 Sept.).
66 George W. Orton, 'Henley!' *Canadian Magazine* (Jan. 1900): 223–31, 224.
67 Elliott, *Rambles*, part 2, 41–5.
68 Ibid., 46. Greenshields also took in a cricket match at Lord's (Travel Diary 1895, 3 June) and enjoyed rowing on the Thames, watching his fellow-boaters and taking in riverbank views (15, 23 June).
69 Cameron, Travel Diary 1911, 1 Apr.
70 Ibid., 22 Apr.
71 Ibid., 31 May. Goldwin Smith was far less amused than Cameron; for him the Derby was no better than a Spanish bullfight and the croupier little more than a devil. One could only wish, he declared, that the racecourse be ploughed up for honest agriculture (*A Trip to England*, 140).
72 Priddis, Travel Diary 1911, 69–70.
73 Greenshields, Travel Diary 18945, 1 Jan.
74 Sara Jeannette Duncan (Mrs Everard Cotes), *Cousin Cinderella*.
75 Henderson, 'The Marchioness of Donegal,' 308.
76 Ibid., 310.
77 Wood, 'Presentation at Court.'
78 Ibid., 306–8.
79 Ibid., 308.
80 For discussions of such masquerades, see Judith Walkowitz, 'The Indian Woman, the Flower Girl, and the Jew'; also Koven, 'The American Girl in London,' in *Slumming*.

81 Mary Leslie's chronicling of her relatives' annoying habits, as discussed in the 'Prologue,' was an anomaly.

82 For a discussion of British men's and women's fascination with these places, see Koven, *Slumming*.

83 Smith, *A Trip to England*, 139.

84 Murphy, *Impressions of Janey Canuck*, 56.

85 Cameron, Travel Diary 1910, 17 Aug.

86 Brian Bellasis in the *Canadian Magazine*: 'The Green Lawn Club: New Year's Morning in a London Cab Shelter' (Jan. 1912): 245–8; 'A Dead Man's License: The London "Bobby" through Green Lawn Club Spectacles,' (Mar. 1912): 462–4; 'The Triumph of the Taxi' (May 1912): 31–4; 'Church and Stage' (Aug. 1912): 378–81.

87 Thomson, Travel Diary 1898, 4 Sept. She paid another visit later that year when her family returned to London (27 Nov.). See also Bilborough, Travel Diaries 1899, 1900.' Bilborough went to Shepherd's Bush Foundling Church and to a temperance meeting at Queen's Hall.

88 Montgomery, Travel Diary 1895, 25 Aug.

89 Davies, Travel Diary 1899–1900, 110–11.

90 Chown, Travel Diary 1910, 17 June.

91 Mackinnon, *Rambles in Britain*, 248; Smith, *A Trip to England*, 141.

92 Murphy, *Impressions of Janey Canuck*, 168. Although in general she found the display of the children engaging, Cameron's second visit to the Foundling's Hospital took her to the playrooms, which she found 'rather cheerless,' and the dormitories, 'long narrow rooms with a row of cots on each side' (Travel Diary 1910, 30 Oct.).

93 Murphy, *Impressions of Janey Canuck*, 40.

94 See, e.g., Linda Gordon, *Heroes of Their Own Lives: The Politics and History of Family Violence 1880–1950* (New York: Viking, 1988) for a discussion of the use of photography by social reformers; also Koven, 'Dr Barnardo's Artistic Fictions,' in *Slumming*.

95 Ney, *Britishers in Britain*, 65, 76, 79.

96 Ibid., 79–80.

97 Cameron, Travel Diary 1911, 22 Jan.

98 Ibid., 28 Jan.

99 Ibid., 1 Mar. She also visited the horticultural college at Arlesley in Kent, where she and her aunt had breakfast with 'the girls' and then toured the gardens and greenhouses. 'The work here is on a smaller scale than at Swanley but it seems rather more practical' (10 Mar.).

100 Ibid., 7 Mar.

101 Ibid., 7, 13 Mar.

102 Ibid., 3 Apr. The Manitoba teachers were taken to see the Royal Caledonian Asylum, a home for Scottish children whose fathers had died
while serving in the navy or army. Here they too were treated to sights
and sounds of the school band (in this case a pipe band) and the spectacle
of the children wearing uniforms with the Stuart tartan; they also planted
two maple trees and were given the children's pictures as souvenirs (Ney,
Britishers in Britain, 137–9).
103 Murphy, *Impressions of Janey Canuck*, 163.
104 Think, e.g., of Egerton Ryerson's transatlantic tours of schools in Europe,
undertaken to help design Upper Canada's common schools.
105 Cameron, Travel Diary 1911, 8 Mar.
106 Ibid., 14 Mar.
107 Ney, *Britishers in Britain*, 104–9.
108 Clouston, Travel Diary 1895, 6 Oct.
109 William F. Munro to Georgina Johnstone Munro, 12 Feb. 1881, AO, MU
2180, W.F. Munro Papers 1862–83, Correspondence File 1881, F 708.
110 Murphy, *Impressions of Janey Canuck*, 134–5.
111 Ibid., 98.
112 Ibid., 100–1.
113 Ibid., 101.
114 Ibid.
115 Ibid., 102.
116 Smith, *A Trip to England*, 90.
117 Chown, Travel Diary 1910, Book 2, 18 May.
118 Pemberton, Travel Diary 1897, 30 June; Murphy, *Impressions of Janey
Canuck*, 107–11.
119 Priddis, Travel Dairy 1911, 60–1, 90, 106, 109–13.
120 Ibid., 113.
121 Cameron, Travel Diary 1910, 19 Nov.
122 Ibid., Travel Diary 1911, 12 June.
123 Murphy, *Impressions of Janey Canuck*, 64.
124 Ibid., 65.
125 Ibid. See also Hall, Travel Diary 1878, 27, 28 June, for visits to the Courts
of Exchequer, the Lord Mayor's Court, and the new Law Courts.
126 Cameron, Travel Diary 1911, 23 Jan.
127 Lindsey, *Cricket across the Sea*, 149.
128 Murphy, *Impressions of Janey Canuck*, 85.
129 Ibid., 86. Murphy also inspected the exterior of Dartmoor prison, which
was lightly guarded but had little need of heavy security, given the lack of
hiding places, the frequent heavy fogs, and the dangerous bogs (at 94).

130 Cameron, Travel Diary 1911, 23 Oct.
131 Smith, *A Trip to England*, n.p. See also Davies's trip to Aldershot, Travel Diary 1899–1900, 114.
132 Ibid., 91–2.
133 Ibid., 177–8.
134 Caldwell, Travel Diary 1874, 12 July.
135 Ibid., 19 July.
136 Ibid., 2 Aug.
137 See, e.g., Hall, Travel Diary 1878, 30 June; Thomson, Travel Diary 1910, 21 Aug.
138 Greenshields, Travel Diary 1913, 21 May.
139 See Thomson, Travel Diary 1898, 4 Sept.; Cameron, Travel Diary 1911, 8 Jan.; Hall, Travel Diary 1878, 30 June; Thomson, Travel Diary 1910, 28 Aug.
140 Chown, Travel Diary 1910, Book 2, 22 May; Munro to Georgina Johnstone Munro, 9 Apr. 1883, Correspondence File Apr.–Dec. 1883, W.F. Munro Papers.
141 Munro to Georgina Johnstone Munro, 16 Jan. 1881, Correspondence File 1881, W.F. Munro Papers.
142 Thomson, Travel Diary 1898, 4 Sept.
143 Cameron, Travel Diary 1911, 8 Jan.
144 Ibid.
145 Murphy, *Impressions of Janey Canuck*, 13–14.
146 Ibid., 15–16.
147 Ibid., 16.
148 See also her discussions of: the 'ritualistic' church in Southend; London's St Clement's Ash Wednesday service; and the reasons for the Evangelical vs High division (ibid., 31–2, 102–5, 136–40). She approved of the Archbishop of Canterbury and of the Rev. W. Hay Aitken (ibid., 82–3).
149 Ibid., 80–1. Greenshields also had stringent criticisms of the Anglican church's 'High' wing; he believed its history was one of persecution of true Protestants and that the Church had not properly atoned for such behaviour (Travel Diary 1895, 20 Jan., 28 May).
150 Marguerite S. Shaffer points to the desire of elite American tourists to claim such exclusive spaces, ones where they socialized with their own kind and thus extended 'the upper-middle-class spaces that proliferated in modern cities and suburbs' (*See America First*, 276).

7 'This Sight-Seeing Is a Strenuous Business'

1 Bain, Travel Diary 1910, 19 Dec.

2 Fleming, Travel Diary 1892, 10 Jan.
3 See, e.g., Levenstein, *Seductive Journey*; Stowe, *Going Abroad*; Hansen, 'Albert Smith, the Alpine Club, and the Invention of Mountaineering in Mid-Victorian Britain'; John Pemble, *The Mediterranean Passion*; Endy, 'Travel and World Power.'
4 As well as the press, Canadian novelists also took as their subject matter Canadians abroad in Europe. See, e.g., Maria Amelia Fytche, *Kerchiefs to Hunt Souls*; also Alice Jones, *A Privateer's Fortune*. In *A Literary History of Canada*, Klinck discusses the number of Canadians who wrote novels about Europe (at 308–10).
5 For a few that did, see Denison, *A Happy Holiday*; see also the following from the *Canadian Magazine*: Winnifred Wilton: 'Glimpses of Norway, Part I' (July 1897): 208–12, 'Glimpses of Norway, Part II' (Aug. 1897): 289–95; 'Glimpses of Norway, Part III' (Sept. 1897): 483–5; Agnes Riddell, 'Letter from Scandinavia' (May 1912): 90–1; John Edgcumbe Staley, 'Finland and the Finns' (Nov. 1912): 65–72. See also Clouston, Travel Diary 1895, 15 July to 22Aug., for descriptions of her family's trip around the fjords, to a Lapp camp, and to Stockholm and Copenhagen.
6 For articles on Spain, see, e.g., n.a., 'A Spanish Passion Play,' *Saint John Daily Telegraph*, 7 May 1875; as well as the following from the *Canadian Magazine*: W.A.R. Kerr, 'Spain, as a Canadian Sees It' (Jan. 1903): 219–28; H.S. Scott-Harden, 'A Vision of Old Spain' (Apr. 1908): 494–6; Albert R. Carman, 'Foot-Prints of the Moor in Spain' (Apr. 1910): 409–506. Edward Greenshields and Osla Clouston also visited Spain. See Greenshields, Travel Diary 1911, 18 Mar. to 7 Apr.; see also Clouston, Account Book of Her Trip from Gibraltar through Spain and to Paris, 1905, MM, P007–A/4, Osla Clouston Diaries.
7 See, e.g., John Home Cameron, 'Glimpses of the Latin Quarter,' *Canadian Magazine* (Mar. 1893): 53–63; also J.S. Gordon, 'A Backward Glance at Paris,' *Canadian Magazine* (Dec. 1899): 108–21.
8 Bowslaugh, Travel Diary 1897, 7 July.
9 Roddick, Travel Diary 1902, 8 Aug. Thomson, Travel Diary 1897, 29 July.
10 Gordon, 'Backward Glance at Paris,' 111.
11 Martin, Travel Diary 1881, 21 July.
12 Mackinnon, *Rambles in Britain*, 185–7.
13 Ibid., 191–2.
14 Levenstein, *Seductive Journey*, 141.
15 Bowslaugh, Travel Diary 1897, 6 July.
16 Davies, Travel Diary 1899–1900, 171–2.
17 Hall, Travel Diary 1878, 7 July.

18 Priddis, Travel Diary 1906, 127.

19 Simmonds, *Our Trip to Europe*, 50; Bowslaugh, Travel Diary 1897, 8 July.

20 Thomson, Travel Diary 1897, 26, 28 July.

21 Hugh Johnston, 'Paris and the World's Fair,' *Christian Guardian*, 19 Sept. 1900.

22 Bowslaugh, Travel Diary 1897, 8 July.

23 Priddis, Travel Diary 1906, 123.

24 Ibid., 130.

25 Greenshields, Travel Diary 1911, 9 May. See W.D. King, *Henry Irving's Waterloo* (Berkeley: University of California Press, 1993), for a discussion of the British cult of Napoleon (at 112–13).

26 See, e.g., Martin, Travel Diary 1881, n.d.; Bowslaugh, Travel Diary 1897, 16 Aug.; Thomson, Travel Diary 1898, 26 Sept.

27 Mackinnon, *Rambles in Britain*, 91–3.

28 Hall, Travel Diary 1878, 21 July.

29 Ibid.

30 Estelle Kerr, 'Here and There in Belgium,' *Canadian Magazine* (Dec. 1914): 93–104.

31 Bowslaugh, Travel Diary 1897, 17 Aug.; see also Mackinnon for a long discussion of the Dutch liberation from Spain (*Rambles*, 75–95).

32 Thomson, Travel Diary 1898, 21 Sept.

33 Ibid., 22 Sept.

34 Simmonds, *Our Trip*, 54.

35 See, e.g., Murphy, *Impressions of Janey Canuck*, 145; Martin, Travel Diary 1881, n.d.

36 Pemberton, 1897, 12, 19 Aug.

37 See, e.g., Thomson, Travel Diaries 1897, 14 –17 Aug.; 1898, 27 Sept. to 20 Oct.; Mackinnon, *Rambles*, 95–127; Martin, Travel Diary 1881, n.d.; Priddis, Travel Diary 1906, 103–13; Bowslaugh, Travel Diary 1897, 12 Aug. See also n.a., 'The City of Hamburg,' *Ottawa Free Press*, 18 July 1885, 5. Mortimer Shea's trip through Germany involved its history (*Across Two Continents*, 98–117).

38 Priddis, Travel Diary 1906, 111.

39 Bowslaugh, Travel Diary 1897, 12 Aug. See also Priddis, Travel Diary 1906, 109–11; Mackinnon, *Rambles*, 95–7; Thomson, Travel Diary 1897, 18–19 Aug.

40 Martin, Travel Diary 1881, n.d.

41 Bowslaugh Travel Diary 1897, 13 Aug.

42 Priddis, Travel Diary 1906, 110.

43 Hall, Travel Diary 1878, 20 July.

44 Ibid.

45 See, e.g., E. Fannie Jones, 'Swiss Life and Scenery,' *Canadian Magazine* (June 1898): 117–23.

46 See, e.g., Priddis, Travel Diary 1906, 85–95.

47 Thomson, Travel Diary 1897, 30 July; Martin, Travel Diary 1881, 11 July.

48 Bowslaugh, Travel Diary 1897, 12 July.

49 Martin, Travel Diary 1881, 11 July.

50 Thomson, Travel Diaries: 1897, 7 Aug.; 1898, 21 Oct.

51 Ibid., Travel Diary 1898, 10 Nov.

52 See, e.g., Thomson, Travel Diary 1897, 4 Aug.; n.a., 'An Italian Tour,' *Allisonia* (Nov. 1907): 7; n.a, 'The Progress of Italy' n.a., 'Garibaldi's Projects for the Sanitary Improvements of Rome,' *Saint John Daily Telegraph*, 28 Oct. 1875.

53 C.R.W. Biggar, 'Rome Revisited,' *Canadian Magazine* (Apr. 1895): 572–85. 572–3.

54 For a discussion of those changes, see David Atkinson, Denis Cosgrove, and Anna Nelson, 'Empire in Modern Rome: Shaping and Remembering an Imperial City, 1870–1911,' in Felix Driver and David Gilbert, eds., *Imperial Cities*, 40–63.

55 See, e.g., Martin, Travel Diaries: 1881, n.d.; 1898, 25 Oct.; Simmonds, *Our Trip to Europe*, 68; Pack, Travel Diary 1910, 17 July.

56 Priddis, Travel Diary 1906, 48.

57 Bain, Travel Diary 1910, 24 Dec.

58 Bowslaugh, Travel Diary 1897, 27 July; see also Thomson, Travel Diary 1898, 29 Oct.

59 Fleming, Travel Diary 1892, 7 Jan.

60 Thomson, Travel Diary 1898, 8 Nov.; n.a., 'An Italian Tour'; Bowslaugh, Travel Diary 1897, 15 July; Priddis, Travel Diary 1906, 68.

61 Priddis, Travel Diary 1906, 41; Bain, Travel Diary 1910, 20 Dec.

62 Davies, Travel Diary 1899–1900, 182.

63 Simmonds, *Our Trip*, 77.

64 Bowslaugh, Travel Diary 1897, 19 July; Pack, Travel Diary 1911, 13 July.

65 Pack, Travel Diary 1911, 13 July.

66 Pemberton, Travel Diary 1897, 6 Dec.

67 Davies, Travel Diary 1899–1900, 183.

68 Pack, Travel Diary 1911, 12 July.

69 Bowslaugh, Travel Diary 1897, 20 July. See also Langton's description of seeing the spot where, he was told, St Paul's head was cut off and bounced three times before resting on the grounds (Travel Diary 1888, 28 Mar.).

70 Priddis, Travel Diary 1906, 20.

71 Bowslaugh, Travel Diary 1897, 21 July.

72 Priddis, Travel Diary 1906, 26–7. Ada Pemberton registered the saint's life and death while visiting her church, where she saw her bathroom and 'place of death' (Travel Diary 1897, 13 Dec.). She also was one of the few to mention Caligula (12 Dec.).

73 Priddis, Travel Diary 1906, 26–7. Bowslaugh understood the Forum as a place where civil and commercial business had been transacted, a site of religious duties: 'reached its highest pitch of splendour and remained the heart of the city until its fall' (Travel Diary 1897, 20 July).

74 Bowslaugh, Travel Diary 1897, 20 July. For another discussion of imperial Rome as evoked by the Forum and Coliseum, see the description of the talk about his European tour given by Mr Hammond, Mount Allison Ladies' College art teacher. *Allisonia* (Nov. 1906): 26–8. See also, 'An Italian Tour.'

75 Unlike Sigmund Freud, who Carl Schorske has argued, saw Rome as both masculine (the 'citadel of Catholic power') and feminine ('the holy Mother Church') English-Canadian tourists do not seem to have used gender as a means of assigning Rome's historical identity (*Thinking with History: Explorations in the Passage to Modernism* [Princeton: Princeton University Press, 1988], 202).

76 Boulton, 'A Canadian Bicycle through Europe, Chapter IV'.

77 Miss Graham, 'Letter from Italy,' *Allisonia* (May 1910): 92–3, 93.

78 Davies, Travel Diary 1899–1900, 185; Pemberton, Travel Diary 1897, 24, 25 Nov.

79 Bowslaugh, Travel Diary 1897, 23 July.

80 Bain, Travel Diary 1910, 12 Dec.

81 Simmonds, *Our Trip*, 80–3; Priddis, Travel Diary 1906, 17.

82 Langton, Travel Diary 1888, 13 Mar.

83 Ibid., 6 Apr.

84 Ibid., 14 Mar. Langton was speaking of his wife Edith but the observation also applied to Langton himself at that point in their travels.

85 Clouston, Travel Diary 1899, 6 Jan.

86 Ibid., 21 Jan.

87 Ibid., 18 Mar.

88 Bain, Travel Diary 1910, 28 Dec.

89 Ibid., 20 Dec.

90 Clouston, Travel Diary 1899, 20 Jun.

91 Ibid., 25 June.

92 Ibid., 21 June.

93 Greenshields, Travel Diary 1895, 21 Feb. 1895.

94 Greenshields, Travel Diary 1911, 8 May. See also Eliza Greenshields, Travel Diary 1913, File 582, where she mentions seeing *The Marriage of Figaro* and

Lohengrin in Paris (22, 26 Mar.). For descriptions of operas she attended, see ibid., 19, 22, 23, 26 Mar. See also Pemberton, Travel Diary 1897, 9 Aug., for a trip to Bayreuth to hear Wagner.

95 Edward Greenshields, Travel Diary 1913, 23 Mar.
96 Ibid., Travel Diary 1906, 5 May.
97 Ibid., Travel Diary 1913, 20 Mar.
98 Ibid., 25 Mar.
99 Fleming, Travel Diary 1891, 23 Dec.
100 Priddis, Travel Diary 1906, 62.
101 Gordon, 'Backward Glance at Paris.'
102 Levenstein, *Seductive Journey,* 201.
103 Hall, Travel Diary 1878, 3 July.
104 Ibid., 4 July. The next evening's entertainment, chariot races at the Hippo-drome, was much better and far more exciting (5 July).
105 Greenshields, Travel Diary 1911, 4 May.
106 Ibid., 5 May.
107 Bain, Travel Diary 1911, 14 Jan.
108 Fleming, Travel Diary 1891, 20 Dec.
109 See Kröller, *Canadian Travellers in Europe,* for a discussion of both English-and French-Canadians' desire for European culture, particularly art.
110 While in Florence in 1906, Greenshields had tea with 'Mrs Berenson, a charming American lady,' although he did not mention whether or not she was directly related to Bernard Berenson, the art critic whose judgments he admired (Travel Diary 1906, 4, 6 May). Greenshields published *Landscape Painting and Modern Dutch Artists* in 1906; for a brief review, see n.a., 'A Canadian Art Study.'
111 Thomson, Travel Diary 1897, 27, 29 July.
112 Ibid., Travel Diary 1898, 15 Nov.
113 Martin, Travel Diary 1881, 15 July; see also Pemberton, Travel Diary 1897, 21, 23 Oct.
114 Fleming, Travel Diary 1891, 21 Dec.
115 Priddis, Travel Diary 1906, 125.
116 Hall, Travel Diary 1878, 6 July.
117 Ibid., 9 July.
118 Thomson, Travel Diaries: 1897, 28 July; 1898; 17 Nov. See also Martin, Travel Diary 1881, 19 July.
119 Newton MacTavish, 'A Day in the Luxembourg,' *Canadian Magazine* (Dec. 1912): 121–7.
120 Priddis, Travel Diary 1906, 122–3.
121 Clouston, Travel Diary 1898, 4 Mar. She also took art lessons in Dresden (Dresden Travel Diary 1898, 23 Jan).

122 Sophie Pemberton to Ada Pemberton, n.d., PBAC, Pemberton Family Papers, Correspondence.

123 Ibid., 21 Jan. 189?. The *Canadian Magazine* ran a number of articles about Canadians, men and women, who were studying art in Paris during this period (the periodical also covered the careers of Canadian musicians and writers, particularly women, who trained and were enjoying success overseas). For coverage of women's careers, see, e.g., n.a., 'Literary Notes' (Feb. 1901): 388 (coverage of writer Joanna E. Wood); n.a., 'About New Books: Our Women Writers'; Allison, 'A New Canadian Poet [Helena Coleman]'; MacTavish, 'Laura Muntz and Her Art'; Deacon, 'The Art of Mary Riter Hamilton.'

124 Hall, Travel Diary 1878, 7 July. See also Pemberton, Travel Diary 1897, 20 Oct.

125 Martin, Travel Diary 1881, 19 July.

126 Ibid., 19? June. He also toured Antwerp's museums, including the Museum of Antiquities, and saw Rubens's house – 'a fine mansion now occupied having being rebuilt a few years ago' (ibid.).

127 Thomson, Travel Diaries; 1897, 20 Aug.; 1898, 22 Sept. For other visits to galleries in Rotterdam and Amsterdam, see Mackinnon, *Rambles in Britain*, 78, and Simmonds, *Our Trip*, 56–7.

128 Thomson, Travel Diary 1898, 22 Sept.

129 See, e.g., Langton, Travel Diaries: 1888, 13, 20 May; 1907, 13 Apr. to 8 May; Bain, Travel Diary 1911, 10, 11 May.

130 Bowslaugh, Travel Diary 1897, 27 July.

131 Bain, Travel Diary 1910, 20 Dec. Bain also saw Fra Bartolomeo, Guido Renis, Fra Angelico, and Botticelli's work while in Florence (21, 22 Dec.). Travelogues also stressed the centrality of art to seeing and experiencing Italy. See, e.g., Graham, 'Letter from Italy'; n.a., 'The Italian Tour', 7; Erie Waters, 'The Home of the Gondolier,' *Canadian Magazine* (Sept. 1906): 387–91.

132 Priddis, Travel Diary 1906, 43.

133 Martin, Travel Diary 1881, 15 July.

134 See, e.g., Bain, Travel Diary 1910, 24, 26, 28 Dec.; Davies, Travel Diary 1899–1900, 178–81; Thomson, Travel Diary 1898, 23–6 Oct.; Pack, Travel Diary 1911, 17 July; Langton, Travel Diary 1888, 27 May, 10 June; see also Katherine Hale, 'The Sistine Chapel,' *Canadian Magazine* (Apr. 1905): 491–9.

135 Greenshields, Travel Diary 1895, 22 Mar.

136 Bain, Travel Diary 1910, 16 Dec..

137 With one exception, Raphael's frescoes also lived up to his expectations (Langton, Travel Diary 1888, 24 Mar.). Pemberton made at least three trips

to the Vatican to view the galleries and the Sistine Chapel (Travel Diary 1897, 4, 13, 14 Dec.); Pack toured them with a guide and then visited an art school to watch an artist at work (Travel Diary 1911, 12 July).

138 Priddis, Travel Diary 1906, 24.

139 Langton, Travel Diary 1888, 24 Mar., 13 May.

140 Ibid., 13 May, 10 June.

141 Mackinnon, *Rambles in Britain*, 160–1.

142 Albert R. Carman, 'Church Art in Rome,' *Canadian Magazine* (Apr. 1904): 507–13.

143 See, e.g., Mackinnon, *Rambles*, 86–7, 94–5, 97–8, 102–5, 149–50, 153–61; Murphy, *Impressions of Janey Canuck*, 145; Denison, *A Happy Holiday*, 93; Shea, *Across Two Continents*, 66–70, 76–7, 82–3, 85–6, 99–102, 113–16; Bowslaugh, Travel Diary 1897, 16, 19, 21 July; Bain, Travel Diary 1910, 16, 20, 28 Dec.

144 Thomson, Travel Diary 1898, 7 Nov.; Langton, Travel Diary 1888, 19 May.

145 Thomson, Travel Diary 1898, 28 Sept. She thought, though, that Antwerp's cathedral was 'too gaudy' and that while Florence's was large, 'I don't like it' (23 Sept., 27 Oct.). See also Hall, Travel Diary 1878, 20 July.

146 Priddis, Travel Diary 1906, 40.

147 Ibid., 112.

148 Simmonds, *Our Tour of Europe*, 58–9.

149 Ibid., 76–7.

150 Murphy, *Impressions of Janey Canuck*, 145.

151 Pack, Travel Diary 1911, 13 July.

152 Priddis, Travel Diary 1906, 30; Bowslaugh, Travel Diary 1897, 21 July.

153 Bowslaugh, Travel Diary 1897, 14 July.

154 Priddis, Travel Diary 1906, 36–9.

155 Bowslaugh, Travel Diary 1897, 19 July. Having recovered from the sight of the Capuchin's gruesome bones, Simmonds enjoyed sneaking onto the papal throne in the Vatican, despite the chain draped across it; at the church of San Giovanni she received the guide's permission to do so (*Our Trip*, 74–5).

156 Pack, Travel Diary 1911, 7, 13 July. However, Martin's tour to Frankfurt's St Batholomew's Cathedral had to be rescheduled since a service was under way (Travel Diary 1881, n.d.). I have found only a few references to trips to Oberammergau's Passion Play for this period; the experiences of those who went in the interwar years will be explored in chapter 9. See, though, Dr Borden, 'The Ober Ammergau Passion Play,' *Allisonia* (Mar. 1911): 85–9; n.a., 'Europe and the Passion Play,' *Allisonia* (Nov. 1909), 2; n.a., 'The Summer Tour in Europe,' *Allisonia* (Mar. 1910), 69.

157 Thomson, Travel Diary 1898, 23, 30 Sept.
158 Simmonds, *Our Trip*, 52.
159 After touring the church of Mary of Maggiora and being told how the Pope raised money to build it, Pack commented disapprovingly 'not much respect here in Rome for the Pope' (Travel Diary 1911, 13 July).
160 Pemble, *Mediterranean Passion*, 212.
161 Simmonds, *Our Trip*, 71–3.
162 Thomson, Travel Diary 1898, 3 Nov.
163 Langton, Travel Diary 1888, 13, 22 May.
164 Levenstein, *Seductive Journey*, 209.

8 Natural Wonders and National Cultures

1 Langton, Travel Diary 1888, 25 May.
2 For a discussion of these concepts in nineteenth-century Ontario tourism, see Jasen, *Wild Things*.
3 Shaffer, *See America First*, 279.
4 Jones, 'Swiss Life and Scenery'.
5 E. Hedley Somner, 'The Witchery of the Alps,' *Canadian Magazine* (Aug. 1909): 352–9, 352.
6 Hall, Travel Diary 1878, 13 July.
7 Ibid., 14 July.
8 Montgomery, Travel Diary 1895, 28 July.
9 Shaffer, *See America First*, 278.
10 Bowslaugh, Travel Diary 1897, 4 Aug. See also Hall, Travel Diary, 1878, 17 July. Hall also had the experience of watching the sunrise but was not impressed: he did not enjoy getting up at 3:30 a.m., he found the Swiss horn that summoned them 'unmusical' and its player demanding centimes, and his fellow tourists 'a needier or stupider or more miserable crowd I never saw' (18 July). For other descriptions of the Alps, albeit ones not quite as effusive as Bowslaugh's, see Flavelle, Travel Diary 1900, 23 July; Amy Roddick, Travel Diary 1902, 7, 28 July; Thomson, Travel Diaries: 1897, 3, 5, 10 Aug., 1898, 20 Oct.; Simmonds, *Our Trip to Europe*, 60.
11 Greenshields, Travel Diary 1906, 13 May.
12 S. Howard, 'A Day in the Alps,' *Argosy*, 30, 4, 108–16; no years available.
13 George D. Abraham, 'Climbing the Chamonix Aiguilles,' *Canadian Magazine* (July 1906): 195–203. For a discussion of the formation of middle-class masculinity in Britain through the pursuit of mountaineering, including the links between danger and manly identity, see Hansen, 'Albert Smith, the Alpine Club, and the Invention of Mountaineering in Mid-Victorian Britain.'

14 Simmonds, *Our trip to Europe*, 62–3.
15 Mackinnon, *Rambles in Britain*, 145.
16 Greenshields, Diary 1906, 14 May.
17 Hall, Travel Diary 1878, 13 July.
18 Ibid., 14 May.
19 Flavelle, Travel Diary 1900, 25 July.
20 Bowslaugh, Travel Diary 1897, 5 Aug. At Berne she examined the surrounding mountains through a large telescope in her hotel garden (8 Aug.). As well as the luxurious resorts and hotels that sat alongside Alpine lakes, as noted in chapter 1, tourists also ran into souvenir vendors very similar to those at Killarney or the Giant's Causeway.
21 Hall, Travel Diary 1878, 21 July.
22 Pack, Travel Diary 1911, 6 July.
23 Thomson, Travel Diary 1898, 21 Sept. See also E.M. Yeoman, 'In the Land of Windmills,' *Canadian Magazine* (Aug. 1909): 339–47.
24 Greenshields, Travel Diary 1911, 17–28 Apr.
25 See Pemble, *Mediterranean Passion*, 114.
26 Bain, Travel Diary 1911, 11 Jan.
27 Davies, Travel Diary 1899–1900, 176.
28 Fleming, Travel Diary 1891, 22 Dec.
29 Ibid., 23 Dec.
30 Greenshields, Travel Diary 1895, 10 Apr.
31 Ibid., Travel Diary 1913, 27 Feb.
32 Ibid., 11 Mar.
33 Ibid., 12 Mar.
34 Priddis, Travel Diary 1906, 16. See also Clouston, Travel Diary 1900, 28 Feb.
35 Roddick, Travel Diary 1902, 8 Sept.
36 Langton, Travel Diary 1888, 13 Mar.
37 See, e.g., the discussion in chapter 7 of Simmonds's irritation with the litter-bearers (*Our Trip to Europe*, 82–3).
38 Priddis, Travel Diary 1906, 45.
39 Roddick, Travel Diary 1902, 22 Aug.; Waters, 'Home of the Gondolier'; Priddis, Travel Diary 1906, 46–7.
40 Langton, Travel Diary 1907, 12 June.
41 Martin, Travel Diary 1881, n.d.
42 Roddick, Travel Diary 1902, 22 Aug.
43 Ibid., 27 Aug.
44 Waters, 'Home of the Gondolier,' 390–1. See also n.a., 'An Italian Tour.'
45 Langton, Travel Diary 1907, 12 June.
46 In this they were not alone, as American tourists also were attracted to Paris's restaurants and cafés. They tended to write more extensively about

the food, though, than English-speaking Canadians (Levenstein, *Seductive Journey*, 152–4).

47 Denison, *A Happy Holiday*, 213.
48 Ibid.
49 Ibid., 119–20.
50 Priddis, Travel Diary 1906, 142.
51 Priddis may have read Henry James's *Daisy Miller*, the novel that Levenstein credits as probably being responsible for creating the notion that every summer 'Europe was being invaded by armies of pretty, young, empty-headed American "flirts"'' (*Seductive Journey*, 191).
52 Mackinnon, *Rambles in Britain*, 202.
53 Priddis, Travel Diary 1906, 105.
54 Hall, Travel Diary 1878, 21 July.
55 Ibid., 8 July.
56 Bain, Travel Diary 1911, 11 Jan.
57 Clouston, Travel Diary 1900, 21 Mar.
58 Martin, Travel Diary 1881, n.d.
59 Denison, *A Happy Holiday*, 106.
60 For a discussion of Canadians' preoccupations with such matters in their own country, see Mariana Valverde, *The Age of Light, Soap, and Water*.
61 For Gibraltar and Algiers, see Bain, Travel Diary 1910, 5–7 Dec.; also Greenshields, Travel Diary 1906, 19–21 Mar.
62 Pack, Travel Diary 1911, 11 July. He also noted them in Florence and 'no one seems to mind it at all' (16 July).
63 Greenshields, Travel Diary 1906, 30 Mar.
64 Ibid., 3 Apr. 1906. See Greenshields also on French hotel bathrooms, Travel Diary 1911, 22 Apr.
65 Bowslaugh, Travel Diary 1897, 22 July.
66 Pack, Travel Diary 1911, 14 July.
67 While crossing the Italian-Swiss border, for example, Pack was quizzed by health officials who wanted to know if he had been to Naples, as there had been a serious epidemic in that city (ibid., 19 July). He also was interrogated by French health officials on entering France: 'the bubonic plague seems to be following us up good at Marseilles Florence Venice it broke out right after we left' (21 July).
68 N.a., 'Dutch Impressions,' *Christian Guardian*, 4 Feb. 1880.
69 Thomson, Travel Diary 1898, 20 Sept. Mackinnon also took note of public hygiene, approving, e.g., of the Hague's 'wide and clean streets' (*Rambles in Britain*, 80).
70 Greenshields, Travel Diary 1906, 15 Apr. A few lines later he noted that one of the streets that ran beside his hotel was fairly clean but 'smelly in places'

and that his route to Naples's main piazza took him through a narrow little street 'which is decidedly unpleasant' (ibid.).

71 Langton, Travel Diary 1907, 22 Feb.
72 Ibid., Travel Diary 1906, 7 Apr.
73 Thomson, Travel Diary 1897, 29 July.
74 Mackinnon, *Rambles*, 185, 202.
75 Martin, Travel Diary 1881, 6 July.
76 Roddick, Travel Diary 1902, 21 Aug.
77 Langton, Travel Diary 1907, 14 Mar.
78 Bowslaugh, Travel Diary 1897, 22 July.
79 Fleming, Travel Diary 1891, 20 Dec.
80 Langton, Travel Diary 1888, 16 Feb.
81 Ibid., 3 June.
82 See ibid., Travel Diary 1907, 10 Mar. Langton also discussed photographs that he wanted to get, such as 'little girls going to and from school' (13 Apr.) and of missed photographic opportunities, such as a group of young women in Venice (Travel Diary 1888, 10 June). Langton filled his diaries with sketches and photographs of peasant men and women and of women in urban settings; the latter may have been taken by him (see his Feb. entries in Travel Diary 1907).
83 Thomson, Travel Diaries: 1897, 15, 17 Aug.; 1898, 17 Oct.
84 Martin, Travel Diary 1881, 14 July. See also Sophie Pemberton to Ada Pemberton, 14 July n.d., PABC, MS 2639, Pemberton Family Papers.
85 Langton, Travel Diary 1888, 22 Mar.
86 Thomson, Travel Diary 1898, 25 Oct.
87 Ibid., Travel Diary 1897, 17 Apr.
88 Fleming, Travel Diary 1891, 28 Dec.
89 Ibid., Travel Diary 1892, 11 Jan.
90 Bain, Travel Diary 1910, 18 Dec.
91 Pack, Travel Diary 1911, 14 July.
92 Greenshields, Travel Diary 1911, 24 Mar.
93 Ibid., 2 Apr.
94 Clouston, Travel Diary 1898, 23 Apr.
95 See Fytche, *Kerchiefs to Hunt Souls*. Pemble makes the same point about British tourists in the Mediterranean, arguing that their main contacts were with servants and shopkeepers (*Mediterranean Passion*, 260–3).
96 Clouston, Travel Diary 1900, 27 Mar.
97 See, e.g., Ned Clouston to Marjorie Clouston, 12 May 1906, MM, P0007–A/B-16a25, Marjorie Clouston Correspondence, 1903–1911.
98 Bain, Travel Diary 1911, 5 Jan.

99 Ibid., 8 July.

100 Pack, Travel Diary 1911, 9 July.

101 Fleming, Travel Diary 1891, 31 Dec.

102 Ibid., Travel Diary 1892, 1 Jan.

103 Langton, Travel Diary 1888, 18 Feb.

104 Greenshields, Travel Diary 1895, 19 Apr. American tourists also were drawn to casinos, where they thrilled themselves with the establishments' glamour and contemplated the gloomy fates of gamblers, being particularly taken by the myth of daily suicides (Levenstein, *Seductive Journey*, 174).

105 Greenshields, Travel Diary 1913, 10 Mar.

106 Pack, Travel Diary 1911, 9 July.

107 Clouston, Travel Diary 1894, 21, 31 July, 2, 12 Aug.

108 For a discussion of the complex attitudes towards gambling in twentieth-century Canada, see Suzanne Morton, *At Odds: Gambling and Canadians 1919–1969* (Toronto: University of Toronto Press, 2003).

109 Pack, Travel Diary 1911, 9 July.

110 Heaman, *The Inglorious Arts of Peace*, 215. For a discussion of Canadian exhibitions in Europe, see Heaman's chapter, 'Exhibitions in Europe after Confederation.'

111 Editorial, *Halifax Morning Chronicle*, 17 June 1873.

112 C.A.S., 'Paris Letter,' *Saint John Daily Telegraph*, 13 June 1878. See also n.a., 'The Vienna Exhibition,' *Ottawa Free Press*, 12 Nov. 1872; n.a., 'Vienna Exhibition,' *Halifax Morning Chronicle*, 17 June 1873; N.a., 'The Prince of Wales and Paris Exhibition,' *Ottawa Free Press*, 9 Mar. 1878; J.H.B., 'Paris Exhibition: Sketches by an Ottawa Visitor,' 17, 21 Sept.; 8, 26 Oct. 1878.

113 W.R. Stewart, 'Canada and the Paris Exposition,' *Canadian Magazine* (Sept. 1900): 387–403.

114 Hall, Travel Diary 1878, 4, 5 July.

115 Ibid., 3 July.

116 Ibid.

117 Ibid.

118 Martin, Travel Diary 1881, n.d.

119 Flavelle, Travel Diary 1900, 14, 15, 17, 21 July.

120 Ibid., 23 July. However, Davies was very impressed by the 'Great Exhibition,' even though it was unfinished when she visited. She was particularly delighted by the statues, fountains, and shrubberies, and the setting on the banks of the Seine (Travel Diary 1899–1900, 190).

121 Denison, *A Happy Holiday*, 197.

122 Ibid., 82–3.

123 Eleanor B. Moss, 'Life in a Typical German Boarding School,' *Allisonia* (Mar. 1911): 89–90.
124 Mackinnon, *Rambles in Europe*, 112. See Thomson, Travel Diaries: 1897, 14 Aug.; 1898, 13, 19 Oct.; see also Priddis, Travel Diary 1906, 106, for brief descriptions of Strasbourg and Heidelberg universities.
125 Bowslaugh, Travel Diary 1897, 8 Aug.
126 Denison, *A Happy Holiday*, 47–8. She was more impressed by the exterior of Prague's 'Home for poor ladies,' founded by Maria Theresa for women of 'good birth' who had fallen on hard times (ibid., 104).
127 Ibid., 207–9.
128 Ibid., 206.
129 Mackinnon, *Rambles in Europe*, 191–2.
130 The diaries of Bowslaugh, Pemberton, Hall, Martin, Pack, Thomson, Priddis, Fleming, Flavelle, Clouston, and Bain are full of references to such shopping expeditions.
131 Langton, Travel Diary 1888, 23 June.
132 Bain, Travel Diary 1910, 27 Dec.
133 Martin, Travel Diary 1881, n.d.
134 Denison, *A Happy Holiday*, 32.
135 Bain, Travel Diary 1911, 11 Jan.
136 Langton, Travel Diary 1888, 7 Mar.
137 See, e.g., Dona Brown, *Inventing New England*, and Michael Dawson, *Selling British Columbia*. It is possible that English-Canadian university students involved in the nascent fields of sociology and social work or in the settlement house movement may have gone on summer tours of model housing and city planning in Europe. New York University offered the chance to 'See Social Europe,' a tour led by Dr E.E. Pratt, with sailings to Chrstiana, Copenhagen, and Hamburg (n.a., 'See Social Europe,' *Survey* 30 [13 Apr. to 13 Sept. 1913], n.p.; also n.a., 'Social and Civic Tours of Europe', ibid.). My thanks to Suzanne Morton for this advertisement.
138 Alfred Andrews, 'Letter from Europe: Chamouni,' *Christian Guardian* 15 Aug. 1880. This interest in Swiss agriculture shaped a portrait of a country in which the majority were farmers, despite the fact that by 1900 only 31 per cent of the Swiss workforce was employed in agriculture (Oliver Zimmer, *A Contested Nation: History, Memory and Nationalism in Switzerland, 1761–1891* [Cambridge: Cambridge University Press, 2003], 166).
139 Langton, Travel Diary 1907, 25 June.
140 Bilborough, Travel Diary 1900, 14 Feb.
141 Mackinnon, *Rambles in Europe*, 144.
142 Ibid., 170. He went on to note that the clergy, though, appeared well fed on the local produce (ibid.).

143 Ibid., 165.
144 Ibid., 176.
145 Martin, Travel Diary 1881, n.d. See also Pack, Travel Diary 1911, 6 July; Priddis, Travel Diary 1906, 120; and Murphy, *Impressions of Janey Canuck*, 144.
146 See, e.g., Mackinnon, *Rambles in Europe*, 161; Pack, Travel Diary 1911, 6 July.
147 Langton, Travel Diary 1907, 10 Mar. They often remarked on, but appeared slightly less troubled by, the use of dogs in Holland and Belgium to pull loads. See Thomson, Travel Diary 1898, 20 Sept.; Martin, Travel Diary 1881, 18 June.
148 While English-speaking Canadians rarely made such explicit comparisons, it is not hard to imagine that these were part of the subtext of their discussions of Italian and Swiss peasants. Shaffer argues that white, middle-class American tourists used Chinese and other racial and ethnic groups as foils for their own class and racial identities (*See America First*, 281).
149 In 'In the Land of Windmills,' Yeoman wrote about the lack of change in the 'Dead Cities of the Zuyder-Zee' while on the same page he noted that children of these villages had learned enough English to demand money, that Volendam boasted a hotel well known as an artists' retreat, and that he and his party were the object of bitter looks from a party of elderly women whom, he thought, might have lost sons in the Boer War (at 246–7).
150 Hall, Travel Diary 1878, 2, 13, 14, 20 July.
151 Fleming, Travel Diary 1891, 25 Dec.
152 Bain, Travel Diary 1910, 25 Dec.
153 Ibid., 10 Dec.
154 The spice cake, garnished with candied fruit, was at first bite 'leathery and ancient' but improved as she ate it. Thomson, Travel Diary 1898, 24 Sept.
155 Thomson, Travel Diary 1897, 4 Aug.; Pack, Travel Diary 1910, 18 July.
156 Langton, Travel Diary 1907, 28 Mar.
157 Ibid., 6 Apr.
158 Ibid., 17 Apr. Food was a favourite subject for some Canadian tourists in the 1920s. Toronto's Ashbridge family had much to say about the enjoyable but too-abundant meals served in Holland. See, e.g., Mabel Ashbridge's comment: 'Holland seems to be a great place to feed people, for the dinner tonight had seven courses and no small portions at all' (Travel Diary 1927, 2 Aug.). For other, quite positive, discussions of food in Europe, see Effie Laurier Storer to Beth Henderson, 24 June 1923, PAS (Saskatoon), Effie Laurie Storer papers, S-A186 I. 2 and 3; also Violet McNaughton, Travel Diary 1929, 19 Aug., PAS (Saskatoon), Violet McNaughton Papers S-A1 E.74.

159 For literature on the relationship between dress and national identity, see, e.g., Kristin Hoganson, 'The Fashionable World: Imagined Communities of Dress,' in Burton, *After the Imperial Turn*, 260–78.

160 Frank George Carpenter, 'Glimpses of Holland,' *Ottawa Daily Free Press*, 5 Oct. 1886, 7.

161 Emily P. Weaver, 'Coiffe and Sabot in Brittany,' *Canadian Magazine* (Feb. 1911): 361–71.

162 E. Fannie Jones, 'Swiss Life and Scenery,' 288.

163 Hoganson, 'Fashionable World,' 272.

164 Clouston, Travel Diary 1895, 31 July.

165 Ibid., Travel Diary 1898, 30 July.

166 Simmonds, *Our Trip to Europe*, 56–7.

167 Thomson, Travel Diary 1898, 20 Sept.

168 Ibid., Travel Diary 1897, 20 Aug.

169 Thomson, Travel Diaries: 1898, 26 Oct.; 1897, 5 Aug.

170 Thomson, Travel Diary 1897, 28 July.

171 Ibid., 10 Aug.

172 Hall, Travel Diary 1878, 7 July.

173 Ibid., 21 July.

174 Greenshields, Travel Diaries: 1906, 2 Apr.; 1911, 24 Mar.; Fleming, Travel Diary 1891, 11 Jan.

175 Kerr, Estelle, 'In the Shadow of Etna,' *Canadian Magazine* (Dec. 1910): 185–92, 189–90.

176 Jones, 'Swiss Life and Scenery,' 285.

177 Langton, Travel Diary 1888, 23 June. For a discussion of the Swiss government's role in staging the nation through historical plays and pageants, see Zimmer, *A Contested Nation*, 189.

178 For a discussion of literature on tourist practices and sexuality, see Dubinsky, *The Second Greatest Disappointment*, 12–14. Ian McKay has pointed out the sexualization of Nova Scotia 'folk' by tourist promoters and folklorists (*The Quest of the Folk*, 11–15, 253–4).

179 See, e.g., n.a., 'A Montrealer in Europe,' *Montreal Daily Star*, 7 Oct. 1882; Cameron, 'Glimpses of the Latin Quarter'; Gordon, 'A Backward Glance at Paris.' Levenstein points out that France had been portrayed as the land of loose sexuality in the United States from the 1850s on (*Seductive Journey*, 198).

180 Pack, Travel Diary 1911, 5 July.

181 Ibid., 7 July.

182 Ibid., 8 July.

183 Greenshields, Travel Diary 1911, 6 May.

184 Ibid., Travel Diary 1906, 24 May.

185 Hall, Travel Diary 1878, 21 July.
186 Murphy, *Impressions of Janey Canuck*, 148.
187 Thomson, Travel Diary 1898, 8 Nov. Complaints about 'garlic-eaters' in France and Italy were, somewhat surprisingly, rare.
188 Denison, *A Happy Holiday*, 146–7, 152–4.
189 Ibid., 41.
190 Hall, Travel Diary 1878, 2 July. Many of Weaver's and Kerr's articles made such judgments and evaluations.
191 Langton, Travel Diary 1907, 18, 19 Apr.
192 Ibid., 5 Aug.
193 Thomson, Travel Diary 1897, 30 July.
194 Greenshields was one of the best connected to other members of the 'travelling classes' of Canada, the United States, and England, and ran into people he knew on a regular basis. See, e.g., Travel Diaries: 1895, 21, 24 Feb.; 1906, 2 Apr., 6 May; 1911, 11 Mar., 10, 13 Apr.; 1913, 13 Feb., 8 Mar. See also Eliza Greenshields, Travel Diary 1913, 3 May.
195 For an examination of Americans abroad, see Endy, 'Travel and World Power: Americans in Europe, 1890–1917.'
196 Albert R. Carman, 'Mamie in Venice,' *Canadian Magazine* (Mar. 1907): 436–40.
197 Denison, *A Happy Holiday*, 113, 164, 167–8.
198 Ibid., 179.
199 Ibid., 156.
200 Ibid., 219–20. Presumably this was Elizabeth Cady Stanton.
201 Chown, Travel Diary 1910, 25 June.
202 Greenshields, Travel Diary 1895, 10 Mar.
203 Priddis, Travel Diary 1906, 84, 111.
204 Ibid., 136–7.
205 Levenstein, *Seductive Journey*, 179–81.
206 Ibid., 182.
207 Ibid., 175, 184–91.
208 Martin, Travel Diary 1881, n.d.
209 Thomson, Travel Diary 1897, 24 July; Fleming, Travel Diary 1891, 7 Jan.
210 Ibid.
211 Albert R. Carman, 'My Bridal Trip,' *Canadian Magazine* (Nov. 1902): 10–21.
212 See, e.g., Denison, *A Happy Holiday*, 149; Priddis, Travel Diary 1906, 98, 33.
213 Langton, Travel Diary 1907, 14 Aug.
214 Ibid., Travel Diary 1888, 28 Apr.
215 Ibid., Travel Diary 1907, 20 Mar.
216 Ibid., 14 Mar.
217 Ibid., 19 Apr.

218 Ned Clouston to Marjorie Clouston, 4 May 1904, MM, P0007–A/B-16a26, Marjorie Clouston Correspondence 1903–11.
219 Bain, Travel Diary 1910, 26 Dec.
220 Langton, Travel Diary 1888, 28 Apr.
221 Ibid., Travel Diary 1907, 26 Feb.
222 Ibid., 23 Apr.
223 Priddis, Travel Diary 1906, 108. As chapter 6 discusses, on the road to Frankfurt Priddis was very happy to meet a group of Australians (ibid., 106).
224 Denison, *A Happy Holiday*, 109.
225 Bain, Travel Diary 1911, 17 Jan.
226 Langton, Travel Diary 1888, 25 May.
227 Ibid., 23 Jun. See also Priddis's comments about Cooks' tours (Travel Diary 1906, 114, 126).
228 Langton, Travel Diary 1907, 29 Mar.
229 Ibid., 6 Apr.
230 Sophie Pemberton to Ada Pemberton, 14 Mar. n.d., PABC, Pemberton Family Papers.
231 Fleming, Travel Diary 1891, 10 Jan.
232 Thomson, Travel Diary 1897, 10 Aug.
233 Langton, Travel Diary 1907, 24 Apr.
234 Thomson, Travel Diary 1897, 20 Aug.
235 For a discussion of Torontonians' patronizing attitudes towards rural Ontarians, see Keith Walden, 'Identity,' in his *Becoming Modern*.
236 Martin, Travel Diary 1881, 22 July; see also Davies, Travel Diary 1900, 17 May; Pack, Travel Diary 1911, 23 July.

9 'A Big Old Country Car'

1 See, e.g., John Herd Thompson and Alan Seager, *Canada 1922–1939: Decades of Discord* (Toronto: McClelland and Stewart, 1985), esp. chapter 8, 'The Conundrum of Culture'; see also Mary Vipond, 'Canadian Nationalism and the Plight of Canadian Magazines in the 1920s,' *Canadian Historical Review* 68 (Mar. 1977): 43–63.
2 Thompson and Seager, chapter 3, 'The Empire, America, and the League.' See also Vance, *Death So Noble*. But note also the arguments in Phillip Buckner, ed., *Canada and the End of Empire* (Toronto: University of Toronto Press, 2004), that see this process as more evident after the Second World War Two.
3 For a discussion of this phenomenon, see David W. Lloyd, *Battlefield Tourism*; also Vance, *Death So Noble*, 56–60, 77–9.

4 In *Canada: An Illustrated Journal (CIJ)*, see n.a., 'In Sunny Kent,' 23 Oct. 1915, n.p.; n.a., 'Welcome to Canadians!' 16 Sept. 1916, 354; the published lists of 'Canadians in London' – 23 Oct. 1915, 118; 29 Jan. 1916, v; 4 Jan. 1917, 30; 6 July 1918, 30; also n.a., 'Where Canadian Soldiers Can Visit Their Provinces,' 10 Feb. 1917, n.p,; Advertisement for Rex Ellis et al., 12 Feb. 1916, 354.

5 N.a., 'Canadians at the Front,' 'Officers Killed or Wounded,' and 'Back from Germany,' *CIJ*, 23 Oct. 1915, 93–5.

6 N.a., 'Notes of the Week: Canada's Wards,' *CIJ*, 27 July 1918, 95.

7 Frederick Loft, a Mohawk from Six Nations at the Grand River community in southern Ontario, served in the war as a lieutenant in the Canadian Forestry Corps. On his return, he attempted to organize the League of Indians of Canada. For a discussion of both Loft and Deskeheh, see E. Brian Titley, *A Narrow Vision: Duncan Campbell Scott and the Administration of Indian Affairs in Canada* (Vancouver: UBC Press, 1989), chapters 6 and 7, 'Indian Political Organizations' and 'The Six Nations' Status Case,' respectively. It is possible, though, that Deskeheh's travels overseas were covered, since a continuous run of issues from the 1920s is not available. Moreover, *Canada* covered the pre–First World War trips of Native peoples to Britain. See, e.g., n.a., 'Canadian Indians in London: A Day of Wonderful Sights,' *CIJ*, 11 Aug. 1906, 171.

8 N.a., *Canada*: 'Canadians in London,' *CIJ*, 22 Feb. 1919, 260; n.a., 'The Repatriation of British Wives,' and n.a., 'Repatriation Committee', *CIJ*, 1 Mar. 1919, 263, 276; n.a., 'Special Supplement: YWCA,' *CIJ*, 14 June 1919.

9 N.a., 'The Premier of Ontario,' *CIJ*, 4 July 1925, 4.

10 N.a., 'Winter Cruises,' *Canadian Magazine* (Dec. 1924): 503.

11 N.a., 'Cruises: Mediterranean–West Indies,' ibid. (Oct. 1924): 372.

12 N.a., 'Canadians and Newfoundlanders in London [1],' *CIJ*, 1 Oct. 1927, 364. Although these Canadian tourists did not mention it, it is possible that their desire to tour Britain might have been stirred by the 'Come to Britain Movement,' an organization formed by British hoteliers and that involved shipping lines, railways, London stores, and the Association of Health and Pleasure Resorts (see Beckerson, 'Marketing British Tourism,' 133–57, 140–1).

13 N.a., 'Purely Personal [1],' *CIJ*, 7 Oct. 1927, 371.

14 See, e.g., n.a. 'Canadians and Newfoundlanders in London[1]'; n.a., 'Canadians and Newfoundlanders Registered at the High Commissioner's Office in London [2],' *CIJ*, 18 Feb. 1928, 244; n.a., 'Canadians and Newfoundlanders in London [3],' ibid., 19 May 1928, 223.

15 For the debutantes, see n.a., 'Canadian Debutantes at Court,' *CIJ*, 1 July 1927, 8–10.

16 As well as Sophia Wilson's 1930 trip, which will be discussed in greater length, see n.a., 'Death of Lady Beaverbrook,' *CIJ*, 30 Nov. 1927, 563. According to her obituary, in 1926 Beaverbrook 'personally arranged and conducted a party of forty New Brunswick teachers on a tour of Great Britain.'

17 See, e.g., n.a. 'Purely Personal[2],' *CIJ*, 10 Dec. 1927, 587; n.a., 'Purely Personal[3],' ibid., 21 Jan. 1928, 71. See also n.a., 'Canadian Ladies at Court' which, among other presentations), lists those of mezzosoprano Isabel Burnada of Calgary, Haligonian portrait-painter Margaret Frame, and Montreal singer Ruth Shatford (*CIJ*, 19 May 1928, 207).

18 Frank Duggan, Travel Diary 1925, MM, P639/A/B/C, Duggan Family Papers.

19 W.G. Bligh, 'Across the Atlantic in a Horse Transport,' *Canadian Magazine* (Nov. 1922): 21–36.

20 For the impact of automobile tourism in the interwar North America, see Dawson, *Selling British Columbia*, 43; also Shaffer, 'A Nation on Wheels,' in *See America First*.

21 Frank Yeigh, 'Scotland Once Again,' *Presbyterian Witness*, 10 July 1925, 5, AO, MU 3153, Frank Yeigh Papers, Folder IV (a): Published Articles on Travel in Europe and General Travel Topics.

22 Ibid., 'St Malo and Its Brittany Background,' *Canadian Countryman*, 31 Jan. 1931, 11.

23 Ibid., 'Motoring in Ancient Brittany,' *Canadian Magazine* (Sept. 1924): 435–7.

24 Ibid., 'Motoring in the Motherland, Part II,' *Canadian Motorist* (Jan. 1924): 17–18.

25 Ibid., 'Motoring Experiences in Europe Today,' *Canadian Motorist* (May 1926): 183–5, 212.

26 Ibid., 'Motoring in Ancient Brittany.'

27 Mercy E. McCulloch, 'Seeing Great Britain by Motor, Part Two,' *Christian Guardian*, 22 June 1921.

28 Ibid., 2 Feb.

29 Ibid., 9 Feb.

30 See Shaffer, *See America First*, 250.

31 McCulloch, 'Seeing Great Britain,' 2 Mar. 1921.

32 See, e.g., Mabel Ashbridge, Travel Diary 1927, 29 Aug. Shaffer also makes this point (*See America First*, 132).

33 Mabel Ashbridge, Travel Diary 1927, 24 June.

34 For references to police speed traps, see ibid., 3 July and 23 Aug. 1927.

35 For a discussion of the advent of bus and car tourism in Scotland both prior to and after the First World War, see Gold and Gold, *Imagining Scotland*, 122–30.

36 Dorothy Ashbridge, Travel Diary 1927, 11 Sept.

37 Ibid., 15 Aug.; Betty Ashbridge, Travel Diary 1927, 15 Aug.

38 N. Tourneur, 'England's Medieval City, World Famous and Sleepy Old Chester,' *Christian Guardian*, 10 Sept. 1924.

39 McCulloch, 'Seeing Great Britain by Motor, Part Two.' See also Betty Ashbridge, Travel Diary 1927, 27 June, for a discussion of Lancaster Castle's panoply of judicial and penal history.

40 McCulloch, 'Seeing Great Britain by Motor Car,' 2 Feb. 1921.

41 Ibid., 16 Feb.

42 Ibid., 23 Mar.

43 Ibid., 25 Jan.

44 Ibid., 16 Feb.

45 Betty Ashbridge, Travel Diary 1927, 20 July.

46 Ada Dorothy Turville, *Travel Articles (with Illustrations) Written for the 'London Free Press'* (London, ON: Free Press, 1927), 6.

47 Effie Laurie Storer, Travel Diary 1923, 11 July, PAS (Saskatoon), Effie Laurie Storer Papers, S-A 186 I. 2 and 3. Storer's father, P.G. Laurie, founded the *Saskatchewan Herald*. She worked as a journalist in her father's office and then on Regina's *Leader-Post* and Moose Jaw's *Times-Herald*. Her husband, J.H. Storer, had been a corporal in the North West Mounted Police and was killed in the First World War.

48 Susie Almon to Rollie Almon, 9 Apr. 1923, PANS, MG1, Vol. 17A., Almon Family Papers, File 61.

49 Dorothy Hutchinson, Travel Diary 1927, 26? LAC, MG 55/30, No. 180.

50 Margaret Bell, 'Old Inns of London,' *Canadian Magazine* (Mar. 1922): 388–91.

51 Lyman B. Jackes, 'The Home of General Wolfe,' *Canadian Magazine* (Feb. 1924): 257–60.

52 Bell, 'Old Inns of London,' 388.

53 Grace Hunter, 'Canterbury,' *Canadian Magazine* (Feb. 1924): 285–8.

54 Ibid.

55 Lester B. Pearson, 'Oxford: Ancient, Yet Modern,' *Christian Guardian*, 16 Aug. 1922, 5.

56 For Yeigh's construction of the past in the Niagara area, see Colin M. Coates and Cecilia Morgan, *Heroines and History: Representations of Madeleine de Verchères and Laura Secord* (Toronto: University of Toronto Press, 2002), 238–40.

57 Dorothy Ashbridge, Travel Diary 1927, 29 Aug.

58 Ibid., 4 Sept.

59 Ibid., 9 Sept.

60 For a discussion of Walter Scott's decline in popularity, see Gold and Gold, *Imagining Scotland*, 119. The Ashbridges visited Burns's home (Betty Ashbridge, Travel Diary 1927, 10 July).

61 See, e.g., McCulloch, 'Seeing Great Britain by Motor,' 22 June 1921; Susie Almon to Rollie Almon, 30 May 1923; Hutchinson, Travel Diary 1927, 12 and 13?.
62 Mabel Ashbridge, Travel Diary 1927, 30 Jun.
63 Susie Almon to Rollie Almon, 30 May 1923.
64 Turville, *Travel Articles*, 4.
65 Mabel Ashbridge, Travel Diary 1927, 2 July.
66 Ibid., 3 July.
67 Ibid., 4 July.
68 Ibid., 6 July.
69 Storer to Henderson, 20 July 1923, Storer Papers.
70 Mabel Ashbridge, Travel Diary 1927, 1 July; Susie Almon to Rollie Almon, 3 June 1923; W.T. Chamberlin, 'The Beauties of Britain,' *Canadian Magazine* (Sept. 1924): 304–10. McCulloch, 'Seeing Great Britain,' 22 June 1921.
71 Morse, *Seeing Europe Backwards*, 51; Mabel Ashbridge, Travel Diary 1927, 1 July. Morse's Preface describes him as having come from Nova Scotia's Annapolis Valley and presently living in Cambridge, Boston.
72 Hutchinson, Travel Diary 1927, 17?.
73 Turville, *Travel Articles*, 8.
74 Ibid., 9.
75 Morse, *Seeing Europe Backwards*, 54; Chamberlin, 'Beauties of Britain,' 308.
76 Storer to Henderson, 20 July 1923.
77 Ibid., 26 July 1923.
78 Mabel Ashbridge, Travel Diary 1927, 1 July.
79 Ibid., 5, 8 July.
80 Hutchinson, Travel Diary 1927, 15?; Dorothy Ashbridge, Travel Diary 1927, 30 June, 11 July.
81 Mabel Ashbridge, Travel Diary 1927, 29 June; Wellington Ashbridge, Travel Diary 1927, 28 June. See also Dorothy Ashbridge, Travel Diary 1927, 28 June.
82 Morse, *Seeing Europe Backwards*, 47.
83 Ibid., 52.
84 Ibid., 46.
85 Ibid., 52.
86 Ibid., 55.
87 Mabel Ashbridge, Travel Diary 1927, 2 July.
88 Dorothy Ashbridge, Travel Diary 1927, 3 July; see also Mabel Ashbridge, Travel Diary 1927, 3 July.
89 Mabel Ashbridge, Travel Diary 1927, 13 July.
90 Ibid., 14 July.

91 Ibid., 13 July. The family was on its way to Glendalough for a day trip.
92 Betty Ashbridge, Travel Diary 1927, 13 July; Dorothy Ashbridge, Travel Diary 1927, 11 July.
93 Dorothy Ashbridge, Travel Diary 1927, 12 July; also Mabel Ashbridge, Travel Diary 1927, 12 July.
94 W.G. Worcester, Travel Diary 1925, 14 May, University of Saskatchewan Archives, MG 32S1, W.G. Worcester Papers, File IV.
95 Norman Tucker, 'Liquor and Old London,' *Christian Guardian*, 8 Nov. 1922, 11–12.
96 Morse, *Seeing Europe Backwards*, 40.
97 Ibid., 39.
98 Ibid., 41–2.
99 Mabel Ashbridge, Travel Diary 1927, 24, 26, 27 July.
100 Ibid., 25, 28 July.
101 Ibid., 3 Sept.
102 Hutchinson, Travel Diary 1927, 21 and 24?.
103 Mabel Ashbridge, Travel Diary 1927, 26, 28 July.
104 Betty Ashbridge, Travel Diary 1927, 26 July.
105 Hutchinson, Travel Diary 1927, 30?.
106 McCulloch, 'Seeing Great Britain by Motor Car,' 26 Jan. 1921.
107 Sophia Wilson, Trip to Europe [Travel Diary] 1930, 36, DU-SC, MS–2–359 E-19. Dates not consistently given.
108 Morse, *Seeing Europe Backwards*, 40.
109 Hutchinson, Travel Diary 1927, 31?.
110 Mabel Ashbridge, Travel Diary 1927, 2 Sept.
111 McCulloch, 'Seeing Great Britain,' 16 Feb. 1921.
112 Susie Almon to Rollie Almon, 12 Apr. 1923.
113 Ibid., 5 Apr.
114 Kathleen Coburn, Travel Diary 1930, 29 Dec., VU-SC Kathleen Coburn Papers, Box 68–2, Series 5.
115 Ibid., n.d.
116 Ibid.
117 Ibid., Travel Diary 1931, 13, 17 Dec. Barbara Bush has pointed to Robeson's warm reception by white, middle-class British liberals, men and women ('"Britain's Conscience on Africa": White Women, Race and Imperial Politics in Interwar Britain,' in Claire Midgley, ed., *Gender and Imperialism* [Manchester: Manchester University Press, 1998], 208.
118 Breward, *Fashioning London*, 107–11. As chapter 6 makes clear, going to see movies and newsreels had been part of tourists' experiences before the war; it does, however, seem to have been a much more popular activity.

119 Storer to Henderson, 22 June 1923.
120 Coburn, Travel Diary 1931, ? Feb. See also Duggan, Travel Diary 1929, 18, 19 Apr., and Hutchinson, Travel Diary 1927, 22?.
121 McCulloch, 'Seeing Great Britain,' 2 Mar. 1921.
122 Susie Almon to Rollie Almon, 13 Apr. 1923.
123 Ibid.
124 Ibid., 10 July 1923.
125 Susie Almon to Rollie Almon, 5 Apr. 1923; Dorothy Ashbridge, Travel Diary 1927, 23 July.
126 Morse, *Seeing Europe Backwards*, 9.
127 Ibid., 16.
128 Ibid., 23–6.
129 Ibid., 22. Morse may well have been influenced by Americans' writing on Paris in the 1920s which, as Harvey Levenstein has argued, became (in theory and practice) much more taken with a tourism of hedonism than of culture. See 'A Farewell to "Culture Vultures,"' chapter 17 in his *Seductive Journey*.
130 Ibid., 20–1.
131 Ibid., 26.
132 Violet McNaughton, Travel Diary 1929, 20 Aug.
133 Turville, *Travel Articles*, 17–20.
134 Ibid., 21–2.
135 Ibid., 23–4.
136 Ibid., 25–7.
137 Ibid., 28–9.
138 Ibid., 32. For similar views expressed by American commentators, see Hoganson, 'The Fashionable World,' 272.
139 Ibid., 34.
140 Mabel Ashbridge, Travel Diary 1927, 30 July.
141 Ibid., 31 July. See also Betty Ashbridge, Travel Diary 1927, 30, 31 July; Dorothy Ashbridge, Travel Diary 1927, 30, 31 July.
142 Betty Ashbridge, Travel Diary 1927, 30 July; Hutchinson, Travel Diary 1927, 23?.
143 Mabel Ashbridge, Travel Diary 1927, 4, 5, 6, 7 Aug.
144 Ibid.
145 Ibid., 5 Aug.
146 Ibid.
147 Ibid., 8 Aug.
148 Ibid., 10 Aug.
149 Ibid., 12, 13, 16 Aug.

150 Ibid., 15 Aug.

151 Ibid., 16 Aug.

152 Ibid., 17 Aug.

153 See Lloyd, *Battlefield Tourism*.

154 Storer to Henderson, 24 June 1923.

155 Ibid., 25, 26 June 1923.

156 Ibid., 25 June 1923.

157 Ibid.

158 Wilson, Travel Diary 1923, 3–4.

159 Ibid., 4.

160 Ibid., 6.

161 Ibid., 4.

162 Ibid., 8.

163 Ibid.

164 Ibid.

165 Ibid., 10.

166 Ibid.

167 Ibid., 14.

168 Ibid., 16–26.

169 Ibid., 26. The Ashbridges had a similar reaction when they arrived back in
England after their European tour. Mabel Cameron confided to her diary
that it was 'rather nice to be back in England and it seemed strange that
the taxi driver understood at once what was told to him, the English language looks good to me' (Travel Diary 1927, 18 Aug.).

170 Storer to Henderson, 24 June 1923.

171 Ibid., 25 June 1923.

172 Wilson, Travel Diary 1930, 5.

173 Ibid., 21.

174 Morse, *Seeing Europe Backwards*, 9.

175 Ibid., 61.

176 Coburn, Travel Diary 1931, ? Mar.

177 Ibid., 7 Nov. See also, e.g., her comment about the movement of 'old country people' into parts of Toronto that 'the Jews are moving out of' (Travel
Diary 1930, 13 Oct.).

178 Storer to Henderson, 20 June 1923.

179 Ibid., 19 July 1923.

180 Coburn, Travel Diary 1931, 4 Nov.

181 Ibid., 10 Jan.

182 Ibid., Travel Diary 1930, 14 Oct.

183 McNaughton, Travel Diary 1929, 19 Aug.

184 Duggan, Travel Diary 1929, 17, 18 Apr.
185 Ibid., 17 Apr.
186 Ibid., 11, 12, 14, 28, 29, 30 Apr.
187 Betty Ashbridge, Travel Diary 1927, 25 July.
188 Dorothy Ashbridge, Travel Diary 1927, 22 July.
189 Coburn, Travel Diary 1930, 9 Oct.
190 Ibid.,? Apr.
191 Ibid., Travel Diary 1931, 8 Jan.
192 Ibid., 11 Jan. Coburn subsequently sent him Romney's portrait of Joseph Brant.
193 See, e.g., ibid., 3 Nov. 1931, ? Feb. 1931, 7 Oct. 1931.
194 Ibid., 31 Jan. 1931.
195 Ibid., 4 Nov. 1931.
196 Storer to Henderson, 5 July 1923.
197 For a discussion of interwar travel and international work, see Mary Kinnear, *Woman of the World: Mary McGeachy and International Cooperation* (Toronto: University of Toronto Press, 2004). McGeachy, a former teacher who became an international peace activist and who also worked for the League of Nations, had her interest in international relations sparked by a trip overseas in 1927 as the Canadian Teachers' Federation representative to international education conferences (ibid., 42–3).
198 N.a., 'Canadians in London,' *CIJ*, 6 Apr. 1929.
199 Ibid., 28 May 1927; McCulloch, 'Seeing Great Britain,' 6 Apr. 1921.
200 N.a., 'To Prague,' *Saskatoon Star-Phoenix*, 31 May 1929, 8; see also McNaughton, Travel Diary 1929, Aug.-Sept.; also Marion Noel Sherman Papers, PABC, MS409, Box 1, File 1. Sherman's mother accompanied her husband to Geneva in the early 1920s, as he was the Canadian delegate to the League of Nations (Noel to Sherman, 11 July to 11 Nov. 192?).
201 Wilson, Travel Diary 1930, 18.
202 Ibid., 7.
203 Ibid., 22.
204 Ibid., 26.
205 Coburn stayed with the von Rupertises as part of a plan to improve her German while simultaneously improving the family's English. Max von Rupertis was the *Regierungs-Präsident* in East Prussia, a title Coburn describes as being 'a sort of Lieutenant-Governor.' See Kathleen Coburn, *In Pursuit of Coleridge* (London: Bodley Head, 1977), 33.
206 Coburn, Travel Diary 1931, 28 Aug., 8, 24, 25 Sept.
207 Ibid., 28 Aug.

208 Ibid.
209 Ibid.
210 Ibid., 7 Sept.
211 Ibid., 8 Sept.
212 Ibid., 16 Sept.
213 Simultaneously another Canadian, Helen Creighton, was beginning her career as a creator and promoter of this concept in Nova Scotia. See McKay, *Quest of the Folk*, esp. chapter 3, 'Helen Creighton and the Rise of Folklore.'
214 In her memoir, Coburn had much more to say about her discomfort with the rise of fascism and anti-Semitism, both in Britain and Europe (*In Pursuit of Coleridge*, 33). For a discussion of the memory of the war in Europe, see Modris Eksteins, *Rites of Spring: The Great War and the Birth of the Modern Age* (Toronto: Lester and Orpen Dennys, 1989), particularly chapter 9, 'Memory.'
215 Coburn, Travel Diary 1931, 24 Sept. Coburn continued to receive news of the deterioration of social and political conditions in the area, as funds for poor relief ran out and the local Communist Party clashed with the police (27 Dec.).

Epilogue

1 Martin, Travel Diary 1881, ? Sept.
2 Greenshields, Travel Diary 1906, 30 June. Greenshields had similar feelings as he sailed towards Quebec in 1911, telling his diary that 'there ended a very pleasant holiday. The motoring in France, England, and Scotland was delightful, and we have many happy recollections of days spent in Spain and these countries' (Travel Diary 1911, 22 July).
3 Davies, Travel Diary 1901, 12 June, 2 July.
4 Bain, Travel Diary 1911, 20 Feb. Mabel Ashbridge, Travel Diary 1927, 27 Sept.
5 Disbrowe, Travel Diary 1908, 2 Mar. Caldwell, Travel Diary 1874, 14 Sept.
6 This is the case, e.g., for Harriet Priddis, Clara Bowslaugh, Isabella Montgomery, and George Pack.
7 Walden, *Becoming Modern*, 338.
8 I would like to thank Karen Dubinsky for reminding me of this critically important dimension of transatlantic tourism.
9 See, e.g., Gail Bederman, *Manliness and Civilization*.
10 Six thousand Canadians went to Artois for the unveiling. See Vance, *Death So Noble*, 57, 68–70.

11 Frank Byron Fergusson, 'One "Old Soldier" Went Back! Or Eighteen Years Later,' 13, 1918–1936, 20, Dalhousie University Archives, MS–2–285.A.3. See also David Pierce Beatty, *The Vimy Pilgrimage July 1936: From the Diary of Florence Murdock Amherst Nova Scotia* (Amherst: Acadian Printing, 1987); Garrard (Watson), Travel Diary 1936.

12 Fergusson, 'One "Old Soldiers,"' 20.

13 John Risser, 'Scrapbook: Notes on Vimy Memorial Pilgrimage Tour, by a Member of the Party,' 30 July 1936, PANS, MS 1 791.

14 Ibid., 3 Sept. 1936.

15 Ibid.

16 Ibid., 4 Sept. Risser was not the first English-speaking Canadian to note the presence of fascists in Europe. Turville told her readers in 1927 'that it is not possible to be long within the Italian borders without noticing the Fascisit, for the sight of their black shirts and gray-green uniforms is most frequent in railway stations and patrolling every train' (*Travel Articles*, 25).

17 Risser, 'Scrapbook,' 28 July 1936. The hit song from the musical was 'I Won't Be Happy 'Till I Make You Happy Too.'

18 Ibid., 31 Aug. On in his last day in London, Risser also toured Broadcasting House, where he saw performers coming and going. Unlike the situation in Canada, he told his readers, broadcasting in Britain was controlled by the government (4 Sept. 1936).

19 Fergusson, 'One "Old Soldier,"' 22.

20 Risser, 4 Sept. 1936.

21 Ibid.

22 Fergusson, 'One "Old Soldier,"' 23.

23 See Vance, 'O Death Where Is Thy Sting,' chapter 3 in *Death So Noble*, for a discussion of First World War veterans' culture.

24 Fergusson, 'One "Old Soldier,"' 17, 12.

25 Ibid., 24.

26 Ibid.

27 Ibid., 26.

28 Ibid., 28.

29 Risser, 'Scrapbook,' 5 Sept. 1936.

30 Ibid., 18 July.

31 Ibid., 20 July.

32 Fergusson, 'One "Old Soldier,"' 13.

33 Ibid., 24.

34 Ibid., 26.

Bibliography

Primary Sources

Manuscript Collections
Ashbridges House Museum, Toronto
    Ashbridge Family Papers: Photograph album, 1927; Postcard album, 1927; Mabel Ashbridge, Travel Diary, 1927; Wellington Ashbridge, Travel Diary, 1927; Betty Ashbridge, Travel Diary, 1927; Dorothy Ashbridge, Travel Diary, 1927
Archives of Ontario
    William Clyde Caldwell, Travel Diary, 1874
    James Hall, Travel Diary, 1878
    Mary Leslie, Travel Diary, 1867–9
    George Lindsey, Travel Diary, 1887
    W.F. Munro, Papers, 1880–7
    Margaret Thomson, Travel Diaries, 1897–9, 1910, 1914
Dalhousie University, Special Collections
    Frank Fergusson, Travel Diary, 1936
    Frances Amelia Morse Tupper, Travel Diary, 1890
    Arthur H. Whitman, Travel Diary, 1888–9
    Sophia Wilson, Travel Diary, 1930
Fulford House Museum, Brockville
    Fulford Family Papers: Senator George Fulford, Letters, 1902–3; Martha Fulford, Letters, 1908; Postcard Collection
Hamilton Public Library, Local Collection
    Clara J. Bowslaugh, Travel Diary, 1897
Library and Archives Canada
    Ellen Bilborough, Travel Diaries, 1896, 1899–1900
    Mabel Cameron, Travel Diary, 1909–11

Ethel Marion Davies, Travel Diary, 1899–1901
Gertrude Fleming, Travel Diary, 1891–2
Dorothy Hutchinson, Travel Diary, 1927
Thomas Langton, Correspondence and Journals of Trips; Travel Diaries, 1886–1907
Fred C. Martin, Travel Diary, 1881
William Parker, Papers, 1855
McCord Museum
  Clouston Family Papers, 1884–1905
  Duggan Family Papers, 1925–9
  Greenshields Family Papers, 1890–1913
Metropolitan Toronto Reference Library, Baldwin Room
  Isabella Montgomery, Travel Diary, 1895
McGill University, Rare Book Room
  Roddick Family Papers, 1875–1947
Public Archives of British Colombia
  Mary Bain, Travel Diary, 1910–11
  Durrand Family Papers, 1927
  Aird Dundas Flavelle, Travel Diary, 1900
  Garrard Family Papers (for Eleonor Garrard Watson)
  Agnes Green, Travel Diary, 1892
  George Pack, Travel Diary, 1881, Travel Diary and Scrapbook, 1911
  Pemberton Family Papers, 1897–1920s
  William Phillips, Travel Diary, 1857
  Marion Noel Sherman Papers, 1922
  Frank C., Swannell, Travel Diary, 1933
Public Archives of Nova Scotia
  Almon Family Papers, 1923
  R.V. Harris, Travel Diary, 1933
  John Risser, Travel Diary, 1936
  R. Tibbs, Scrapbook and Letters of a Rotarian Trip to Vienna, 1931
Public Archives of Saskatchewan
  Annie Brown, Travel Diary, 1900
  Daniel Brown, Travel Diary, 1906
  Violet McNaughton, Papers, 1929
  Edmund Oliver, Travel Diary, 1908–09
  Effie Laurie Storer, Travel Diary, 1923
  W.G.H. Worcester, Travel Diary, 1925
Queen's University Archives
  Edith (Pierce) Chown, Collection 1909–49
  Agnes Douglas Craine, Travel Diary, 1897

University of Guelph, Archives and Special Collections
    George Arthur Disbrowe, Travel Diary, 1907–8
University of Western Ontario Archives
    Harriett Priddis, Journals and Travel Diaries, 1876–1911
Victoria University, Special Collection
    Kathleen Coburn, Travel Diary, 1930–1

Published Travel Accounts

Beatty, David Pierce, ed. *The Vimy Pilgrimage July 1936: From the Diary of Florence Murdock, Amherst, Nova Scotia*. Amherst, NS: Acadian Printing, 1987

B.E.E. *Wanderings in Distant Lands: A Brief Account of Our Ten Months' Tour. Dedicated, with much affection, to all my old friends*. England, 1884

Denison, Grace E. *A Happy Holiday*. Toronto, 1890

Elliott, James Rupert. 1897. *Rambles in Merrie, Merrie England: Glimpses of Its Castles, Its Cathedrals, Its Abbeys, Its Traditions and Its Rural Life*, parts 1 and 2. Saint John: J. & A. McMillan. 1897

J.T.P.K. *Eastward Ho! Being Some Account of a Voyage across the Atlantic, and a Few Notes for the Use of Colonial Visitors, When Pleasure Hunting in London*. N.p., 1878

Lauder, Maria Elise Turner. *Evergreen Leaves, Being Notes from My Travel Book, by 'Toofie.'* Toronto: Belford Bros. 1877

Lindsey, George. *Cricket across the Sea*. Toronto: James Murray and Co. 1887

Mackinnon John. *Rambles in Britain, France, Prussia, Switzerland, Italy, Belgium, and Holland*. Summerside, PEI: Schurmann and Taylor, 189?

McDougall, Margaret Dixon. *The letters of 'Norah' on Her Tour through Ireland: Being a Series of Letters to the Montreal 'Witness' as Special Correspondent in Ireland*. Montreal: Published by Public Subscription as a token of respect by the Irishmen of Canada, 1882

Morse, Wm. Inglis. *Seeing Europe Backwards*. Boston: Nathan Sawyer, 1922

Murphy, Emily. *The Impressions of Janey Canuck Abroad*. Toronto, 1902

Ney, Fred J., ed. *Britishers in Britain. Being the Record of the Official Visit of Teachers from Manitoba to the Old Country, Summer, 1910*. London: Times Book Club, 1911

Shea, Mortimer L. *Across Two Continents and through the Emerald Isle*. Montreal: Gazette Printing Co. 1907

Simmonds, Irene. *Our Trip to Europe*. Boston: Christopher Publishing House. 1917

Smith, Goldwin. *A Trip to England*. Toronto: Williamson and Co. 1891

Turville, Ada Dorothy. *Travel Articles (with Illustrations) Written for the 'London Free Press'*. London, Ont. 1927

Wetherell, J.E. *Over the Sea: A Summer Trip to Britain*. Strathroy: Evans Bros. 1892

Yeigh, Frank. 'Armageddon's Aftermath "Over There": An Automobile Trip through the Ypres Salient.' *Canadian Motorist* (Feb. 1924): 65–7

– 'From Arras to Vimy Today by Motor Car.' *Canadian Motorist* (Apr. 1924): 169–70

– 'Motoring in Ancient Brittany.' *Canadian Motorist* (Sept. 1924): 435–7

– 'Motoring Experiences in Europe Today.' *Canadian Motorist* (May 1926): 183–5, 212

– 'Motoring in the Motherland. Part II.' *Canadian Motorist* (Jan. 1924): 17–18

– 'The Passing Panorama of a Windshield.' *Canadian Motorist* (Apr. 1930): 123–5

– 'St Malo and Its Brittany Background.' *Canadian Countryman*, 31 Jan. 1931, 11

– 'Scotland Once Again.' *Presbyterian Witness*, 10 July 1924, 5

– 'Through the Land of the Midnight Sun by Car.' *Canadian Motorist* (Apr. 1925): 143–5

Novels

Duncan, Sara Jeannette (Mrs Everard Cotes). *Cousin Cinderella*. New York: Macmillan, 1908

Fytche, Amelia. *Kerchiefs to Hunt Souls*. Sackville, NB, 1895; reprint, Ralph Packard Bell Library, Mount Allison University, 1980

Jones, Alice. *A Privateer's Fortune*. Halifax, 1903; reprint, Halifax: Formac, 2002

Secondary Sources

Adler, Judith. 'Travel as Performed Art.' *American Journal of Sociology* 94, no. 6 (1989): 1366–91

Anderson, Benedict. *Imagined Communities: Reflections on the Origins and Spread of Nationalism*. London: Verso, 1991

Baranowski, Shelley, and Ellen Furlough, eds. *Being Elsewhere: Tourism, Consumer Culture, and Identity in Modern Europe and North America*. Ann Arbor: University of Michigan Press, 2001

Bayly, C.A. *The Birth of the Modern World, 1780–1914*. Oxford: Blackwell, 2004

Beckerson, John. 'Marketing British Tourism: Government Approaches to the Stimulation of a Service Sector, 1880–1950.' In Harmut Berghoff, Barbara Korte, Ralf Schneider, and Christopher Harvie, eds., *The Making of Modern Tourism: The Cultural History of the British Experience, 1600–2000*, Basingstoke, UK: Palgrave, 2002

Bederman, Gail. *Manliness and Civilization: A Cultural History of Gender and Race in the United States, 1880–1917*. Chicago: University of Chicago Press, 1995

Berger, Carl. *The Sense of Power: Studies in the Ideas of Canadian Imperialism 1867–1914*. Toronto: University of Toronto Press, 1970

Berghoff, Harmut, Barbara Korte, Ralf Schneider, and Christopher Harvie, eds. *The Making of Modern Tourism: The Cultural History of the British Experience, 1600–2000*. Basingstoke, UK: Palgrave, 2002

Black, Jeremy. *The British Abroad: The Grand Tour in the Eighteenth Century*. London: Sutton, 1992.

Brady, Joseph, and Anngret Simms, eds. *Dublin through Space and Time (c. 900–1900)*. Dublin: Four Courts Press, 2001

Breward, Christopher. *Fashioning London: Clothing in the Modern Metropolis*. Oxford and New York: Berg Press, 2004

Bridge, Carl, and Kent Fedorowich, 'Mapping the British World.' In Bridge and Federowich, eds., *The British World: Diaspora, Culture and Identity*, 1–15. London: Frank Cass, 2003

Brown, Dona. *Inventing New England: Regional Tourism in the Nineteenth Century*. Washington, DC, and London: Smithsonian Institution Press, 1995

Burton, Antoinette. *At the Heart of the Empire: Indians and the Colonial Encounter in Late Victorian Britain*. Berkeley: University of California Press, 1998

– ed., *After the Imperial Turn: thinking with and through the Nation*. Durham, Carolina: Duke University Press, 2003

– ed., *Gender, Sexuality and Colonial Modernities*. London and New York: Routledge, 1999

Buzard, James. *The Beaten Track: European Tourism, Literature, and the Ways to Culture, 1800–1918*. Oxford: Oxford University Press, 1993

Cannadine, David. 'The Context, Performance and Meaning of Ritual: The British Monarchy and the "Invention of Tradition," c. 1820–1877.' In Eric Hobsbawm and Terence Ranger, eds., *The Invention of Tradition*, 101–64. Cambridge: Cambridge University Press, 1983

Coates, Colin M., ed. *Imperial Canada, 1867–1917*. Edinburgh: Centre of Canadian Studies, University of Edinburgh, 1995

Codell, Julie, ed. *Imperial Co-histories: National Identities and the British and Colonial Press*. Madison, NJ: Fairleigh Dickinson University Press, 2003

Copelman, Dina. 'The Gendered Metropolis: Fin-de-Siècle London.' *Radical History Review* 60 (Fall 1994): 38–56

Cullen, Fintan. 'Marketing National Sentiment: Lantern Slides of Evictions in Late Nineteenth-Century Ireland.' *History Workshop Journal* 54 (2002): 162–79

Dawson, Michael. *Selling British Columbia: Tourism and Consumer Culture, 1890–1970*. Vancouver: UBC Press, 2004

de Nie, Michael. *The Eternal Paddy: Irish Identity and the British Press, 1798–1892*. Madison: University of Wisconsin Press, 2004

Driver, Felix, and David Gilbert, eds. *Imperial Cities: Landscape, Display and Identity.* Manchester: Manchester University Press, 1999

Dubinsky, Karen. *The Second Greatest Disappointment: Honeymooning and Tourism at Niagara Falls.* Toronto: Between the Lines, 1999

Durie, Alastair J. *Scotland for the Holidays: Tourism in Scotland c. 1780–1939.* Edinburgh: Tuckwell Press, 2003

Edensor, Tim. 'Staging Tourism: Tourists as Performers.' *Annals of Tourism Research* 27, no. 2 (2000): 322–44

Endy, Christopher. 'Travel and World Power: Americans in Europe, 1890–1917.' *Diplomatic History* 22, no. 2 (1998): 565–94

Foulkes, Richard. *Performing Shakespeare in the Age of Empire.* Cambridge: Cambridge University Press, 2002

Gilroy, Paul. *The Black Atlantic: Modernity and Double Consciousness.* Cambridge, MA: Harvard University Press, 1993

Gold, John R., and Margaret M. Gold. *Imagining Scotland: Tradition, Representation and Promotion in Scottish Tourism since 1750.* Alershot UK: Scolar Press, 1995

Grewal, Inderpal. *Home and Harem: Nation, Gender, Empire, and the Cultures of Travel.* Durham, NC: Duke University Press, 1996

Hansen, Peter H. 'Albert Smith, the Alpine Club, and the Invention of Mountaineering in Mid-Victorian Britain.' *Journal of British Studies* 34 (1995): 300–34

Heaman, E.A. *The Inglorious Arts of Peace: Exhibitions in Canadian Society during the Nineteenth Century.* Toronto: University of Toronto Press, 1999

Jasen, Patricia. *Wild Things: Nature, Culture, and Tourism in Ontario, 1790–1914.* Toronto: University of Toronto Press, 1995

Kaplan, Joel H., and Sheila Stowell. *Theatre and Fashion: Oscar Wilde to the Suffragettes.* Cambridge: Cambridge University Press, 1994

Klinck, Carl F., ed. *A Literary History of Canada: Canadian Literature in English.* Toronto: University of Toronto Press, 1967

Koven, Seth. *Slumming: Sexual and Social Politics in Victorian London.* Princeton, NJ: Princeton University Press, 2004

Kröller, Eva-Marie. *Canadian Travellers in Europe, 1851–1900.* Vancouver: UBC Press, 1987

Levenstein, Harvey. *Seductive Journey: American Tourists in France from Jefferson to the Jazz Age.* Chicago: University of Chicago Press, 1998

Lewis, Reina. *Gendering Orientalism: Race, Femininity, and Representation.* London: Routledge, 1996

Lloyd, David W. *Battlefield Tourism: Pilgrimage and the Commemoration of the Great War in Britain, Australia, and Canada, 1919–1930.* Oxford and New York: Berg Press. 1998

McKay, Ian. *The Quest of the Folk: Antimodernism and Cultural Selection in Twentieth-Century Nova Scotia.* Montreal and Kingston: McGill-Queen's University Press, 1994

Melman, Billie. *Women's Orients: English Women and the Middle East, 1718–1918: Sexuality, Religion, and Work.* Ann Arbor: University of Michigan Press. 1992

Mills, Sara. *Discourses of Difference: An Analysis of Women's Travel Writing and Colonialism.* London: Routledge, 1991

Morgan, Cecilia. '"A Wigwam to Westminster": Performing Mohawk Identity in Imperial Britain, 1890s-1900s.' *Gender and History* 15, no. 2 (2003): 319–41

Morgan, Marjorie. *National Identities and Travel in Victorian Britain.* Basingstoke, UK: Palgrave, 2001

Moss, Mark. *Manliness and Militarism.* Toronto: Oxford University Press, 2000

Moyles, R.G. and Douglas Owram. *Imperial Dreams and Colonial Realities: British Views of Canada, 1880–1914.* Toronto: University of Toronto Press, 1988

Mulvey, Christopher. *Anglo-American Landscapes: A Study of Nineteeth-Century Anglo-American Travel Literature.* Cambridge: Cambridge University Press, 1983

– *Transatlantic Manners: Social Patterns in Nineteenth-Century Anglo-American Travel Literature.* Cambridge: Cambridge University Press, 1990

Nead, Lynda. 'Animating the Everyday: London on Camera circa 1900' *Journal of British Studies* 43 (Jan. 2004): 65–90

Nelles, H.V. *The Art of Nation-Building.* Toronto: University of Toronto Press, 1998

Nord, Deborah Epstein. *Walking the Victorian Streets: Women, Representation, and the City.* Ithaca, NY: Cornell University Press, 1995

O'Connor, Barbara, and Michael Cronin, eds. *Tourism in Ireland: A Critical Analysis.* Cork: Cork University Press, 1993

O'Grady, Jean. *Margaret Addison: A Biography.* Montreal and Kingston: McGill-Queen's University Press, 2001

Ousby, Ian. *The Englishman's England: Taste, Travel, and the Rise of Tourism.* Cambridge: Cambridge University Press, 1990

Palmer, Alexandra, ed. *Fashion: a Canadian Perspective.* Toronto: University of Toronto Press, 2004

Parsons, Neil. *King Khama, Emperor Joe, and the Great White Queen: Victorian Britain through African Eyes.* Chicago: University of Chicago Press, 1998

Pemble, John. *The Mediterranean Passion: Victorians and Edwardians in the South.* Oxford: Clarendon Press, 1987.

Pickles, Katie. *Female Imperialism and National Identity: The Imperial Order Daughters of the Empire (IODE).* Manchester: Manchester University Press, 2002

Pollock, Della. 'Making History Go.' In Pollock, ed., *Exceptional Spaces: Essays in Performance and History*, 1–45. Chapel Hill: University of North Carolina Press, 1998

Rappaport, Erika Diane. *Shopping for Pleasure: Women in the Making of London's West End*. Princeton, NJ: Princeton University Press, 2000

Richardson, Judith. *Possessions: The History and Uses of Hauntings in the Hudson Valley*. Cambridge, MA: Harvard University Press, 2003

Ryle, Martin. *Journeys in Ireland: Literary Travellers, Rural Landscapes, Cultural Relations*. Aldershot, UK: Ashgate Press, 1999

Schneer, Jonathan. *London 1900: The Imperial Metropolis*. New Haven, CT: Yale University Press, 1999

Sears, John. *Sacred Places: American Tourists in the Nineteenth Century*. Oxford: Oxford University Press, 1989

Shaffer, Marguerite S. *See America First: Tourism and National Identity, 1880–1940*. Washington, DC: Smithsonian Institution Press, 2002

Sheehan, Nancy M. 'Philosophy, Pedagogy, and Practice: The IODE and the Schools in Canada, 1900–1945.' *Historical Studies in Education* 2, no. 2 (1990): 307–21

Smith, Tori. '"Almost Pathetic ... but Also Very Glorious": The Consumer Spectacle of the Diamond Jubilee.' *Histoire sociale / Social History* 29 (58): (1996): 333–56.

Story, Norah, ed. *The Oxford Companion to Canadian History and Literature*. Toronto: Oxford University Press, 1967

Stowe, William W. *Going Abroad: European Travel in Nineteenth-Century American Culture*. Princeton, NJ: Princeton University Press, 1994

Tickner, Lisa. *The Spectacle of Women: Imagery of the Suffrage Campaign, 1907–14*. Chicago: University of Chicago Press, 1988

Tosh, John. 'Manliness, Masculinities, and the New Imperialism, 1880–1900.' In Tosh, *Manliness and Masculinities in Nineteenth-Century Britain: Essays on Gender, Family, and Empire*, 192–213. Harlow, UK: Pearson, Longman, 2004

Valverde, Mariana. *The Age of Light, Soap, and Water: Moral Reform in English Canada, 1885–1925*. Toronto: McClelland and Stewart, 1991

Vance, Jonathan. *Death So Noble: Memory, Meaning, and the First World War*. Vancouver: UBC Press, 1997

Walden, Keith. *Becoming Modern in Toronto: The Industrial Exhibition and the Shaping of Late Victorian Culture*. University of Toronto Press, 1997

Walkowitz, Judith. *City of Dreadful Delight*. Chicago: University of Chicago Press, 1992

– 'Going Public: Shopping, Street Harassment, and Streetwalking in Late Victorian London.' *Representations* 62 (spring 1998): 1–30

- 'The Indian Woman, the Flower Girl, and the Jew: Photojournalism in Edwardian London.' *Victorian Studies* 42 (Fall 1999): 3–46
- 'The "Vision of Salome": Cosmopolitanism and Erotic Dancing in Central London, 1908–1918.' *American Historical Review* 108, no. 2 (2003): 337–76.
Walton, John K. 'British Tourism between Industrialization and Globalization: An Overview.' In Harmut Berghoff, Barbara Korte, Ralf Schneider, and Christopher Harvie, eds., *The Making of Modern Tourism: The Cultural History of the British Experience, 1600–2000*, 109–32. Basingstoke, UK: Palgrave, 2002
- *The English Seaside Resort: A Social History, 1750–1914*. Leicester: Leicester University Press, 1983
Warren, Louis. 'Buffalo Bill Meets Dracula: William F. Cody, Bram Stoker, and the Frontiers of Racial Decay.' *American Historical Review* 107, no. 4 (2002): 1124–56.
Waterston, Elizabeth. *Wrap't in Plaid: Canadian Literature and the Scottish Tradition*. Toronto: University of Toronto Press, 2001
Wilson, Kathleen. *The Island Race: Englishness, Empire and Gender in the Eighteenth Century.* London and New York: Routledge, 2003
Woollacott, Angela. '"All This Is the Empire, I Told Myself": Australian Women's Voyages "Home" and the Articulation of Colonial Whiteness.' *American Historical Review* 102 (Oct.1997): 1003–29
- *To Try Her Fortune in London: Australian Women, Colonialism, and Modernity.* Oxford: Oxford University Press, 2001
Wright, Donald A. 'W.D. Lighthall and David Ross McCord: Antimodernism and English-Canadian Imperialism, 1880s–1918,' *Journal of Canadian Studies / Revue d'études canadiennes* 32, no. 2 (1997): 134–53
Tector, Amy, and Sandy Ramos. '"Don't Let the Sun Go Down on Ney": Frederick James Ney's Battle to Save the Empire.' Paper presented to the 84th Annual Meeting of the Canadian Historical Association, University of Western Ontario, 31 May–1 Jun 2005

Index

ethnicity, 40–2, 55–7, 143–7, 368–9. *See also* civilization; Jews (perceptions of); imperialism; national identities/nationalism
exhibitions: British imperial, 181–4; in Europe, 288–91

Fergusson, Frank, 365
First World War (Great War): absence from this book, 21–2; effect on 1920s tourism, 318–19. *See also* battlefield tourism; Vimy pilgrimage
Flavelle, Aird Dundas, 44, 272, 289
Fleming, Gertrude, 45, 197–8, 210–11, 238, 246, 255, 257–8, 273, 284–5, 287, 298, 303, 311, 314
French Canada: absence from this book, 11–12; seeing en route to Britain, 32, 116; position within English-Canadian nationalism, 123
Fulford, George, 10
Fytche, Amelia, 15

gender: relations in shaping tourism, 12–13; women writers, 27–8; perceptions of Italian men, 55; Canadian women and English history, 75–7, 169–72, 369–70; perceptions of English rural society, 86–7; travel in English countryside, 87–8; Oxford and Cambridge, 94; presentations of Canadian womanhood in England, 106–18; displays of martial masculinity in England, 116–18; Irish women, 156–8; gendered appeal of British royalty, 174–6; representations of empire as masculine, 179–80; Canadian women's concerns over Canada's

representation, 183–4; Canadian women and suffrage movement, 185–9; Canadian women and London theatre, 197–201; masculinity and touring East End, 206; women's movement through London streets, 210–11; perceptions of European agricultural labourers, 295–6, 364; automobile tourism, 324–5; gendered perceptions of history, 327–8; masculinity in interwar tourism, 353, 369–70. *See also* woman's suffrage movement
Glasgow, 61–3; 333–4. *See also* class; historic sites; landscapes (industrial)
Gordon, J.S., 238, 256
Greenshields, Edward, 6, 13–14, 29, 43, 38, 53, 61, 67, 104, 169, 191, 196–7, 174–5, 213, 218, 232, 240, 252–5, 257, 261, 270, 272–4, 280–1, 285, 287, 303, 305–7, 301,361
guidebooks: Baedeker and Ruskin, 28, 32, 149, 136; for London, 203
guides, 7–8, 46–52, 140–5, 153–4, 272

Hall, James, 36, 47, 52, 54–5, 167, 215, 239, 240, 243–4, 256, 258–60, 269, 272–3, 278–9, 289, 298, 303
Harrison, W., 168–70
Hastings, Frederick, 82–4, 103, 125, 132, 203–4
Haultain, Arnold, 92, 94, 109, 121–2
Heaman, E.A., 288
Henderson, Margaret Eadie, 218
historic sites: Edinburgh, 65–8; Highlands, 69–71; Scottish Borders, 75–7; English countryside, 81–3, 99–104; English cathedrals, 88–90; in Wales, 104–6; in Ireland, 134–5; in